LOCAL BREADS

....

By Daniel Leader

Bread Alone: Bold Fresh Loaves from Your Own Hands (*with Judith Blahnik*)

LOCAL BREADS

SOURDOUGH AND WHOLE-GRAIN RECIPES
FROM EUROPE'S BEST ARTISAN BAKERS

DANIEL LEADER

with

Lauren Chattman

COLOR PHOTOGRAPHY BY JONATHAN LOVEKIN

LINE DRAWINGS BY ALAN WITSCHONKE

W. W. Norton & Company · New York London

CONTENTS

❋

Contents

✳

LIST OF ALL THE RECIPES IN THIS BOOK

ACKNOWLEDGMENTS

any of the recipes in this book come directly from a particular baker. The Alpine Baguette, for example, is from Clemens Walch, an Austrian baker who invited me into his bakery, gave me his recipe, and showed me how to make his bread. Other recipes are my interpretations of some of Europe's best bakers' signature loaves. In the case of the Buckwheat *Bâtard*, I visited legendary Parisian baker Eric Kayser at his shop on the Rue Monge, told him about my project, tasted his buckwheat loaf, and made my best attempt to re-create it in my own bakery. I am deeply indebted to the bakers who gladly shared the unique details of their baking lives. I am grateful beyond words to all of them for their generosity and the knowledge that they've given to me.

Here is a list, incomplete I am sure, of the people who contributed to this book in so many ways.

In France: Christian Danias; Bernard Ganachaud and his wonderful daughters, Valerie and Isabelle; Serge Barse; Basil Kamir; Eric Kayser; Bernard Lebon; Jean LeFleur; Andre Lefort; Leon Mader; Pierre Nury; Julian Oudard; Amandio Pimenta; Max Poilâne; Apollonia Poilâne; the late Lionel Poilâne; Michel Prothon; Patricia Wells; the entire staff of Fabiopain.

In Italy: Bernardino Bartolucci, Fabio Bartolucci, Sergio Bocchini, Aldo Cecchi, Silvia Dezane, Amos de Carlo, Giuseppe Colomonaco, Alberti Fausta, Stefano Galletti, Giacomazzi Giuseppe, Daniel Lattini, the Liciani brothers, Graziella Picchi, Michele Saponaro, Mimmo Scalera, Alberto Trentin, Carlo and Mateo Veggetti, Faith Willinger, the staff of Panificio Stella in Alto Adige, the staff of Marden in Verona, the staff of Metalvaneta in Verona, Eileen Holland and Lorenz DeMonaco and your company, Bike Riders.

In Austria and Germany: Phil Domenicucci, Gert Graf, Gabby Grimminger, Gert Kolbe, George Krachenfels, Theo Krekeler, Tobias Maurer, Josef

Schmidt, Juergen Schwald, Gerhard Seitz, Clemens Walch, Rudiger Weskamp.

In Poland and the Czech Republic: Eugene Forychi, Zbigniew Forychi, Eva Franka, Pawlow Mieczyslaw, the staff of the Czech Tourist Board in NYC.

In the U.S. and Canada: Robert Beauchemin, Rabbi Berger, Guy Boutet, Cindy Chananie, Noel Comess, Gerard and Nick Durand, Annie Farrel, Harry Jacoby, Rabbi Jay Kellman, Rabbi Jonathan Kligler, Jim Lahey, Tony Meade, Neil and Leanne Ratner, Matthew Reich, Joel Schoenfeld, Amy Scherber, Mark and Lisa Schwartz, Biaggio Settepani, Rick Steinberg, Jan Vargas and the Featherstone staff, Dr. Bruce Walker.

In South Africa: Jim and Lynette Riesenberger, thank you for being friends all these years and for opening the door to South Africa; Susan Ackerman; Peter Arnold; Annette Badenhorst; Costas Criticos; Louis De Beer; Helen Dufner; Dr. Helga Holst; Gail Johnson; Sister Marcos; Dr. Tony Moll; Piwe Ncoma; Dan Ntsala; Bisola Ojikutu; Linda Saacks; and a special thanks to Juanita Crous for arranging so many details for my travels. Thanks to the entire baking staff at the Pick n' Pay support bakery. It's been a life-changing experience.

Bread Alone bakery runs 24 hours a day, 7 days a week, 364 days a year. Without the commitment and hard work of my staff, Bread Alone couldn't exist. My travels over the years placed an added burden on you. I greatly appreciate the work of the entire Bread Alone team:

Julie Beesmer for making all those Woodstock customers happy;

Heather Berman-Waner, for always being there in all the cafés;

Connie Cowan for being the whiz kid in the office;

Daniel Crandall, thanks for keeping the money straight;

Charlie DeBellis for keeping all the machines, lights, sinks, pumps, heaters, mixers, and much more working;

Daniel Dumas for making sure all the bread gets delivered;

Ryan Fuller for keeping the Green Markets running;

Rosario Nava for being the cheerful face of Bread Alone Boiceville;

Linda Neu, for making all the thousands of pastries every week and I think being one of our first customers;

Tommy Oliveri, thanks for being there to build and maintain our ovens;

Carlos Robles for baking all the great bread;

Catalina Robles for making many, many cakes, pies, and more;

John Savory and Danny Deniz for being the all-night men I can count on;

Rosa Solis, for answering the phone all these years;

Adolpho Soliz, thanks for packing all the orders;

Tomas Swiapkowski, thanks for all the years of on-time deliveries;

David Temple for being the main man at Bread Alone, Kingston;

Douglas Leader, Tsewang Gonpo, Lopsang Dhonden: Thank you for working all these years at the Green Markets in NYC. The days are long and our customers are always thankful for your great work.

To my partner, Sharon Burns, who has tirelessly worked through the challenges of building and running a complicated and demanding business, thank you. I greatly appreciate your tremendous efforts.

To the entire staff of the Green Market in NYC, with special thanks to Kathy Chambers, Joe Cuniglie, Laurel Halter, and Tom Strumolo.

Linda Facci, thank you for your great graphic work for Bread Alone.

Strategic Coach, thanks for all your great ideas. They've really brought great changes to Bread Alone.

Thanks to Mary Miller and Andrea Micelli for your support and critical thinking.

Terry Funk-Antman, thanks for your insights and great wisdom.

A very special thank you to my longtime attorney and faithful Bread Alone supporter Paul Kellar. Bread Alone would not be where it is without you. Thank you, too, to Roselyn Daniell.

Acknowledgments

Thanks to the late Bob Green, you are still here every day, your memory is a blessing for all of us. I do miss your poetic way of describing problems here at the bakery.

Martha and Steve Heller for not telling me I was crazy when I walked into your store, Fabulous Furniture, 23 years ago and said I was opening a bakery.

Tim Ryan and Mark Erickson at the Culinary Institute of America, Rick Smilow at the Institute for Culinary Education, and the many students at ICE who tested these recipes while I was working on this book.

My family: Bennett and Fay Leader, Douglas Leader, Nancy Largay, Laurie Leader, Bruce Leader, Bill and Debbie Seidel, Teddy and Shirley Davis, Liv Leader, Nels Leader, Noah Leader, Octavia Fleck.

Lynne Sampson, thank you for helping develop the initial manuscript.

At W. W. Norton: Erik Johnson, Robin Muller, and Sarah Rothbard, thanks for taking care of all the thousands of details.

Thank you Angela Miller, my new agent, it's been a great beginning.

Thanks to Jonathan Lovekin, for his perfect photos.

I'll be forever indebted to Maria Guarnaschelli for her superhuman effort and infinite patience as we worked on this book. Thanks for all the years of support and for always believing in my abilities.

Thank you to Lauren Chattman for your tremendous hard work, your fine writing, your great ideas; I truly enjoyed creating this book with you. You and Jack, Rose, and Eve are just a joy.

Finally, thank you to the thousands of customers who support my bakery each day.

LOCAL BREADS

INTRODUCTION

✳

It's 10 P.M. on the Friday of Memorial Day weekend at Bread Alone, my bakery in the Catskill Mountains in upstate New York. This is the busiest night of one of the busiest weekends of the year, and the bakery is a beehive of activity. Nine bakers are mixing dough, shaping it, loading it in the ovens and pulling it out. Ranchera music blasts from a flour-dusted old tape deck. I always joke that salsa would make the bread taste better, but some of the bakers are from Pueblo, Mexico, and prefer the hometown sound. Hundreds of multigrain boules, Italian semolina loaves, and dark seeded German ryes are cooling on metal racks. By 1 A.M. thousands of different breads will be out of the oven, cooled to room temperature, and packed in paper bags that will keep their crusts crisp and their interiors moist, ready to be trucked to stores, farmers' markets, and restaurants within a 200-mile radius of Bread Alone. By 7:30 in the morning, my breads will

have made it up to Albany, throughout the entire Hudson Valley, down to Connecticut, into New York City and New Jersey, and all the way out to the east end of Long Island.

If I close my eyes, I can pick out each bread from the fragrance it exudes when it comes out of the oven. There is the dark, earthy, slightly sour aroma of rye, the clean wheat smell of the baguettes, the light and yeasty smell of the Italian white breads. A light haze from the toasted sunflower seeds and flour that spill onto the oven floor when the doughs are loaded clouds the air in the bakery throughout the night. All of these scents mingle in the warm air with the scent of wood smoke. I'm standing in front of my twin wood-burning ovens, built twenty years ago for me by the legendary mason André LeFort from bricks he hand-selected and shipped here from France. Since I baked my first French-style breads in them, the bakery has expanded out from and around these ovens. From my vantage point, I can see my flour storage room, one of the first additions to the bakery after the ovens were completed. Right now the room holds two thousand 40-kilo bags of certified organic white, whole wheat, rye, corn, multigrain, and spelt flour that is custom-milled to my specifications by my miller, Robert Beauchemin, whose mill is southeast of Montreal, from grain grown in Saskatchewan. We use about 100,000 pounds of flour a month, and after a fresh delivery the bags are stacked so high in the little room that the bakers need ladders to reach them.

In front of the flour room are our two huge mixers. Each one is 3 feet across and 4 feet deep. When local kindergarten classes tour the bakery, the kids have to stand on tiptoe to see inside the mixing bowls. The older one is a Mahot fork mixer, so called because of the two giant forks that spin and turn the dough as the bowl rotates. It is the mixer used in 90 percent of the bakeries in France, relied upon because it never breaks down. It's the same mixer the legendary French baker Max Poilâne was using when he taught me how to make sourdough *miches*. That was over fifteen years ago, and at the time his mixer was already twenty years old. I bet it's still churning dough in Max's basement bakery on the place du Marché Saint-Honoré. I ordered mine on the same trip to Paris when I met André LeFort. After André finished the ovens, I drove to the Mahot factory two hours west of Paris to watch my mixer being built.

The newer mixer was made by Pietroberto, a ninety-year-old company in Vicenza, in northern Italy. I bought it in the early days of my love affair with Italy, when I was discovering all the high-quality baking equipment Italy had to offer as well as a multitude of regional Italian breads. It too is a workhorse, like the Mahot mixer, and I use it for all my breads. The last 400-pound batch of baguette dough was mixed in it just an hour ago. I use the two mixers interchangeably, but they represent two periods in my baking life. The Mahot was the mixer I saw everyone use on my early trips to France. When I began to travel beyond France, I noticed that many younger European bakers were buying these newer-style Italian machines, so when I decided to buy a second mixer, I went with the new style too.

We use instant yeast in some of our breads, but breads raised with sourdoughs, natural wild yeast starters, are the heart of the business. They give the loaves complex flavor and a moist, open crumb characteristic of European artisan bread. At Bread Alone, four active sourdoughs are always ready and waiting to be used. Every time someone lifts the lid of one of the sourdough containers, the effervescent, earthy smell, like that of freshly turned soil in the springtime, bursts into the room. Next to the mixers is a special tank called a *fermento-levain*, designed to control the temperature, and thus the rate of fermentation, of the liquid sourdough I now use in my white French breads. It's another souvenir from Paris. I bought it at the urging of Eric Kayser, the iconoclastic Parisian baker who popularized the use of liquid sourdough in the 1980s. Eric's experimentation with liquid sourdough in breads made with unconventional flours such as buckwheat, barley, and amaranth continues to inspire me. Three other sourdoughs are in the walk-in refrigerator—the more traditional firm French *levain* (I use this one to bake French breads made with whole wheat flour), a German rye sourdough, and an Italian starter called *biga naturale*. They give my breads richness and complexity. I brought back recipes and techniques for each one from Europe over the years. Today I can't imagine how I ever baked bread without them.

Ten plastic tubs on wheels sit in a far corner of the 1,400-square-foot room. After we mix a dough, we dump it into one of these tubs. I walk over to them and touch the baguette dough to check on its development yet again. For the sake of consistency and quality, it's important for the dough to maintain a steady temperature of 77 degrees during its first rise. Ideally, I'd have a separate temperature-controlled fermentation room. But I haven't yet figured out where to build such a room, so I have thermometers hanging in every section of the bakery. The bakers look at these thermometers continually and move the tubs (which hold up to 400 pounds of dough) throughout the day and night to the spots where the temperature will encourage the wild yeast to multiply and the dough to expand.

When the doughs have fermented for several hours, it is time to divide them into loaf portions. Until a few years ago we had to heave tubs of dough onto a work table and cut and weigh the dough by hand. In Italy, it is common wisdom that a baker's career ends at the age of fifty, because that's when his back goes, after a lifetime of lifting and dumping tubs of dough. When I was forty-seven and visiting a bakery near Milan, I heard this nugget for the umpteenth time, and it finally sank in. On my return home, I ordered the same Japanese dough-dividing machine I had seen in Tobias Maurer's high-tech bakery in Stuttgart. (German bakers are known for utilizing cutting-edge technology in the service of tra-ditional bread-crafting.) The machine lifts the tubs onto a canvas conveyer belt and mechanically divides the dough.

Now we just stand at the conveyer belt and hand-shape the pieces, without having to break our backs. Tonight we will shape a dozen different breads, among them classic *pains au levain*, bubbly herbed focaccias, seven-grain rolls, German farm-house ryes with whole rye berries, *miches* flecked with bran. Right now I can watch three bakers shaping French country boules, transforming rough blobs of dough into tight spheres. When the bakers have shaped and scored all the dough, they transfer the loaves to 6-foot-long canvas trays, place the trays on rolling racks, and roll them into proofing boxes, which are actually little rooms concealed behind a series of doors built into one wall of the bakery. Each room has a thermostat that maintains the temperature and humidity at optimum levels for proofing dough. In the warmth of the proofing boxes, the loaves will double in size. When they look more like soft pillows than taut little balls, they will travel by conveyor belt to one of André's ovens

or one of two newer German-built gas deck ovens, superpowers of engineering outfitted with steam injection and stone hearths.

The bakers use wooden peels with 14-foot-long handles to unload the finished breads from the scorching ovens onto one of sixteen large cooling racks. They roll the racks into the packing room at the back of the bakery. The space is about the same size as the room with the ovens but even more con-gested. When I decided to add pastries to the Bread Alone menu, I installed separate ovens for them in here. It may not have been the most logical space, but it was the only space I had. On busy nights like this, the cooling breads create a bottleneck, and the pastry chefs have to push through it to make, shape, and bake a thousand croissants and hundreds of Danishes, muffins, scones, and cookies. Every loaf of bread, every croissant, every muffin has to be bagged or boxed and tagged for shipping. When the drivers pull up, they want to load the trucks and then get going in a matter of minutes.

This Friday night we will make eight thousand pounds of bread. My staff works with such economy that they will produce no more than twenty extra loaves, which are left on a single rack for whoever wants to take one home. At 4 A.M. the cleaning crew comes in to scrub the work tables, wipe down the mixers, and mop the floors. When they leave, the bakery is absolutely quiet and empty, but not for long. At 7 A.M. the first baker arrives to mix the longest-fermenting doughs, the peasant breads and *levains* that will sit in the tubs for three to five hours as the rest of the bakers come in to work. And the process begins all over again.

I smile to myself, comparing my fitfully expanding bakery to one I visited a while ago in eastern Germany. My friend Cindy Chananie, who sells ovens made by the German company Wachtel to U.S. bakeries, had invited me to the Ermer Bakery in Bernsdorf to check out a new high-tech oven that uses superheated ceramic plates to bake bread from the inside and out-side at the same time. The brand-new bakery that boasted the oven had been built with efficiency in mind. Production began in the back of the building, where the doughs were mixed and fermented in a temperature-controlled room. They were shaped and proofed on a manual conveyor in an adjacent space. They went from the conveyer to the oven. When the breads were fully baked, they were unloaded automatically out of the other side of the ovens and onto another conveyor, which carried them up to the rafters to cool. When they were cool, the conveyor slid them down into the packing room at the front of the building. At that bakery in Bernsdorf, I felt a stab of envy at the logical setup and the gleaming new equipment, all chosen and installed at the same time. Because Bread Alone has grown organically, from the center outward in every direction, my dough hardly follows a straight path as it is mixed, baked, and packed. It might crisscross the room several times in its journey from the mixer to the packing room. That my bakery operates so efficiently seems like a miracle. Still, when I look at what I've built here, I know that I wouldn't have it any other way.

My bakery has grown just as I have grown as a baker. Each new piece of equipment, each sack of stone-ground organic flour, each bucket of seeds or whole grain, represents something I've learned during an ongoing apprenticeship with artisan bakers of France, Italy, Germany, Austria, Poland, and the Czech Republic. When I stand before Andre's ovens and survey the scene, I see the story of my travels and my baker's education. I began my business with an unpredictable oven that I designed and built with a local mason and a repertoire of five breads that I learned how to make by reading books and through trial and error. Tonight at Bread Alone, looking at the twenty different kinds of breads in various stages of coming into being, I almost can't believe it. We still make hand-shaped, hearth-baked breads from organic ingredients, but the scale and scope of the operation are entirely different now. I admire the different shapes, sizes, and colors of the breads. I catalog the baking equipment from all over Europe and

beyond and think about the journey from one little oven and five kinds of bread to all this.

This book is a chronicle of my travels and the recipes I've collected from some of Europe's best bakers in the twenty years since I opened Bread Alone. In every chapter you will read about the talented and dedicated European bakers who shared their baking traditions and innovations and helped me become an artisan baker in their mold. What amazes me is that they all work with the same few ingredients—flour, water, and not much else—yet their breads are as different as their fingerprints. I learned how to make their breads, but I also learned from them the importance of putting my own mark on the loaves.

When I wrote my first book, *Bread Alone*, over ten years ago, my experience in Europe was limited to lessons with just a few gifted French bakers. I watched and listened and then experimented in my own bakery, trying to duplicate the breads I admired and come up with some personal adaptations. Those breads were good, but I like my loaves better now. Since then I've traveled extensively through Italy, Germany, Austria, and Eastern Europe to study with dozens of experts in local bread. I've gained a tremendous respect for traditional recipes and techniques. I've also learned a lot more about farming, milling, and the science of baking. I've worked hard, using not only the techniques I've discovered but all of my knowledge about the science of bread, to adapt the recipes I brought home so that I could produce batch after batch of authentic European breads in my Catskills bakery. At about the same time I was opening Bread Alone, others, like Steve Sullivan at the Acme Bread Company in Berkeley, were taking up the same challenge. Still more like-minded bakers would soon follow—among others, Nancy Silverton of La Brea Bakery in Los Angeles, Michael London of Rock Hill Bakery in upstate New York, and Jim Lahey of Sullivan Street Bakery, Noel Comess of Tom Cat Bakery, and Amy Scherber of Amy's Breads, all in New York City—until a thriving community of American artisan bakers had sprung up, all committed to exploring European bread traditions and innovations here in the United States. Over the years we've talked and visited, exchanging information about and opinions on different types of flour, sourdoughs, our trips to Europe, and how the industry has changed. Without their generous advice and support, I wouldn't have been able to imagine, much less build, the bakery that I have today.

Although my bakery has grown and I've purchased high-tech equipment like steam-injected deck ovens and the machine that lifts the mixing bowls, I am just as committed to monitoring my breads, from mixing to fermenting to baking to cooling, as I was when I worked alone, producing loaves by the dozens instead of the hundreds. My bakers and I know that we have to make adjustments for each new lot of flour, every change in air temperature, each shift in humidity, so that each batch of bread is as good as the last one. We never take any step in the process for granted, and this is what makes us and our colleagues across the United States artisans in the European mold.

For this book, I've adjusted the European recipes I perfected for my bakery further to ensure that home bakers will be able to produce loaves as close to the originals as possible with easily available equipment and ingredients. I'm confident that with practice and care, you will also be able to produce loaves that bear your own mark, because you've learned how to craft them step by step, as a true artisan does.

✳ THE FIVE KEYS TO MAKING LOAVES WITH INTEGRITY

The term "artisan" has become somewhat overused in recent years as bakers, food writers, and cookbook authors have attempted to cash in on the American consumer's desire for handmade, healthy foods. But for me, artisan bread isn't simply a loaf that's been touched at some point by human hands. In my mind, a loaf can be called artisan only if an experienced and sensitive baker has intimately overseen its baking every step of the way. My bakery may produce thousands of loaves a night, and we may use conveyor belts and computerized fermentation chambers, but this equipment is all in the service of better bread. If we no longer do the heavy lifting, this gives us more energy to hand-shape the loaves beautifully. Thermometers may monitor dough temperature, but the bakers still monitor fermentation, judging as only experienced bakers can when a dough has fermented for just the right amount of time before it needs to be shaped and baked.

When I see supermarket workers loading frozen baguettes into an oven behind a deli counter and later tagging those loaves as "artisan" because they were baked in an oven on the premises, I feel cheated on behalf of all the people who will take the breads home. These loaves were produced in an automated factory, parbaked, frozen, and shipped to supermarkets far and wide. A baker may have been consulted when the recipe was developed, but no skilled baker was overseeing the actual mixing, shaping, and baking of the breads. For all intents and purposes, they were machine-made. To equate them with European craft breads like the sourdough *miches* (page 118) from Poilâne in Paris and the *pane casareccio* (page 197) from the small bakeries in Genzano in Italy, or with American examples like Sullivan Street Bakery's Pugliese bread, Amy Scherber's semolina loaf, and Tom Cat's sourdough baguette, is like comparing large batches of characterless table wine fermented and bottled in huge plants and shipped to thousands of stores across the country to small-batch wine from a tiny vineyard where the grapes are grown and hand-picked and the fermentation process is monitored at every stage by a skilled and knowledgeable winemaker.

Just as handcrafted wines are unique from region to region and vineyard to vineyard, so the breads that I love best have a unique character found only in a particular region, town, or in some cases a single bakery. But these breads do have certain elements in common that help them achieve their singular greatness. These are also the keys to making authentic European artisan breads at home.

1. Seek out flour with integrity for the most delicious and healthful breads.

At the best European bakeries, flour is always of the highest quality and nutritional value. In different places, bread may be made with white flour, whole wheat flour, rye flour, or a number of other flours milled from specialty grains. But no matter what kinds of flour the best bakers use, they buy it from mills where excellent grain is minimally processed.

When it comes to flour, bakers in Europe have it easier than their brethren in the United States. In general, European mills, even the bigger ones, handle grain with more thought for good bread than American mills do. Here, bleaching and bromating flour have been standard practice for decades. In Europe there's no strong tradition of adding such chemicals to flour, so there's no need to seek out unbleached and unbromated flour. It's just there. Throughout Europe, even white flour retains some of the germ and bran because of gentle processing, so snowy white breads coming from artisan bakeries contain vitamins, healthy oils, and fiber that their American counterparts do not.

In Europe, milling techniques are in general gentler than they are in the States. Wheat berries are "tempered" (soaked) in water longer than they are here, so that whether the berries are stone-ground or put through modern roller mills, the crushing process doesn't take as long and is not as damaging. The result is just the right amount of starch damage to encourage enzymatic action for great fermentation but not enough to compromise the flour's ability to develop gluten. Even industrial-size mills often gear their milling practices toward good bread. In Paris there is a huge mill called Le Grand Moulin de Paris, which supplies countless bakeries throughout France. The company employs several test bakers who bake bread from each new lot of flour to assess the quality of the proteins. The bakers also travel to bakeries where the flour is used, to demonstrate recipes and techniques for getting the most out of the product, as it varies from lot to lot, year to year.

In some places farmers, millers, and bakers have forged close, quasi-familial relationships because of strong bread traditions. In the ancient town of Altamura in southern Italy, today's farmers, millers, and bakers come from long lines of farming, milling, and baking families that have done business together for centuries. They work together to produce the town's famous *pane di Altamura* (page 257), growing the local wheat, milling it into golden semolina flour, and baking it in the town's stone ovens, the oldest of which was built four hundred years ago. Europe's artisan bakers know that without superior flour, all the technique in the world will not help them make great bread. I'll never forget a conversation I followed between farmers and millers in the Auvergne region of France, where they discussed the local wheat and *terroir*, a term generally used by winemakers to discuss factors like soil quality, altitude, drainage, and position of the fields relative to the sun in influencing the growth of grapes.

There hasn't been enough of the same subtle thinking about wheat among farmers, millers, and bakers in this country, although that is changing. Commercial mills in America historically have paid farmers a premium for wheat with the highest protein, setting all other characteristics aside, because the higher the protein, the more extensible, or stretchy, the dough and the more easily it can pass through industrial dough-shaping machines. In other words, the wheat is selected and milled with the idea that dough made from it will never touch human hands. The tradition in Europe is to test not only for protein quantity but for overall quality. Some proteins, depending on the growing conditions during a particular season, can make bread tough and hard, while others give it just the right extensibility for a beautiful structure without toughening up the loaves.

Only by using top-quality, minimally processed flour can home bakers recreate the European breads I describe in this book. Thankfully, as the artisan baking movement in this country has grown, such flour is not as hard to find as it was when I wrote *Bread Alone*. Pioneers like Steve Sullivan of Acme Bread Company have worked with millers committed to producing European-style flours. Acme's desire to understand and optimize the functional and baking characteristics of the grain we use has led them to work with a variety of flour millers and brokers (including Cook's Flour, Giusto's, and Central Milling). In an effort to keep its bread local, Pearl Bakery in Portland, Oregon, uses flour milled from wheat grown in nearby Washington State. I would say that the most important business relationship I have is with my miller, Robert Beauchemin. We talk weekly about wheat, flour, and bread. He listens when I tell him what kind of flour I need for a particular recipe, and he will go out and search for the right grain and figure out how to mill it properly so I can bake the bread I have in mind. Countless times he has given me sage advice about new flours to try and how to get the most out of them.

There are hopeful signs that even the most commercial mills want to meet the growing demand for great flour and that they want to supply home bakers as well as professionals. Just recently, General Mills, in consultation with the Bread Bakers' Guild of America, has come out with a 100 percent hard winter wheat flour, specially milled to provide the kind of strength and tolerance needed during long fermentation that defines most artisan breads. Now sold exclusively to bakers, it will soon be available at supermarkets. If you can't yet find the flour you are looking for on a supermarket shelf, it is easily available online. You can now buy small bags of flour from mills like Giusto's in California, suppliers to some of the best artisan bakeries in the country. King Arthur, the specialty baking company based in Vermont, contracts with the best mills to package flour with the same characteristics as French "type 55" for knowledgeable consumers who know exactly what kind of European artisan breads

they want to bake. If you can't find stone-ground whole wheat flour from Bob's Red Mill or Arrowhead Mills, two widely distributed organic brands, at your supermarket or natural-foods store, you can buy them online.

Many of the breads in this book contain the healthful whole grains that Americans have just recently begun to recognize as part of a healthy diet. Whole-grain baking was commonplace throughout Europe, especially in the north, long before scientists and nutritionists agreed on its health benefits. Poilâne in Paris has been baking whole wheat loaves for three generations. In northern Germany, *volkornbrot* (page 292), a 100 percent rye bread, chewy and thick with whole rye berries, has been served at every meal for hundreds of years. European bakers, unlike some of their American counterparts, view whole-grain bread not as prescription medicine but as a natural part of healthy and pleasurable eating. The bread from Poilâne is often cited as one of the most delicious in the world, but it is also 80 percent whole wheat, a fact that Parisians take for granted. In bakeries in northern Germany, 100 percent whole wheat and 100 percent whole rye are the standard flours for bread baking. In the United States we have no such whole-grain traditions. American home bakers looking for healthful whole-grain breads can turn to authentic recipes for European whole-grain breads, many bursting with seeds and nuts containing additional nutrients. I've included my favorite recipes here, for breads that are first and foremost unique and delicious. It is a wonderful benefit that they are also packed with nutrients, vitamins, and fiber necessary for good health.

Farther south, especially in Italy, whole wheat and rye breads are less common. But the white breads made throughout Italy are free of saturated fats and rich in wheat germ from minimally processed flour. Just as important, they are a cornerstone of the Mediterranean diet, acknowledged by many scientists and nutritionists to be one of the healthiest in the world. Along with olive oil, lots of fresh vegetables, only small amounts of meat, and no processed foods,

Italian white bread contributes to good health and longevity. I first ate *pane casareccio di Genzano* (page 197), a unique white bread made in one small town outside of Rome, with a meal of sautéed olives, oven-dried tomatoes, pasta with porcini mushrooms, and some fresh fruit for dessert. Now when I eat this bread at home, it is with similarly healthful and delicious Italian food. If Americans enjoy Italian-style white breads made with minimally processed flour along with Italian-style meals, they will reap health benefits from both.

2. *Don't be afraid* to add water. All

bread contains water, but the very best artisan bread generally contains a higher percentage of water than commercial bread produced in the United States. Typical American commercial white bread is about 58 percent water. In comparison, Parisian Daily Bread (page 66) is nearly 70 percent water. Roman-Style White Pizza (page 214) is 85 percent water. The extra water in these doughs contributes to superior flavor and texture.

A well-hydrated dough will be softer and stickier than a dry one, and thus more extensible. This means that the gluten strands developed during kneading will be able to stretch further in the oven, creating a beautifully open and bubbly structure in the crumb. Extra water also improves the crust. The conversion of starches into sugars that are able to caramelize into a handsomely browned crust depends on water. A wet dough will result in rich caramelization of the crust. The crust of a dry dough will be pale and flavorless in comparison.

For home bakers, highly hydrated doughs present a few challenges. First of all, they may challenge your ideas about what dough should look and feel like. The first time you mix dough for Parisian Daily Bread, you may think you did something wrong, because it is so sticky. But the extra water you added keeps the bread moist, even without the benefit of a sourdough starter. Kneading times for wet doughs are longer than you may be used to, but

wet doughs require more kneading to give the flour a chance to absorb all that water. I learned at the side of bakers like Sergio Bocchini in Genzano, Italy, to trust that in time—a full twenty minutes—the almost liquid mixture of flour and water you start with will come together into a smooth, workable mass, which will eventually bake up into a majestic *pane di Genzano* (page 197). From Amandio Pimenta in the Auvergne I learned how to handle the extremely soft Auvergne rye dough, quickly shaping it into a loose boule with just a few motions so as not to deflate it. Throughout this book you'll find tips from bakers who handle only such wet doughs on successfully kneading, proofing, and shaping them and getting them into the oven in one good-looking piece.

3. *Use simple* sourdoughs to make the

best loaves. Some wonderful European breads are made with packaged yeast, and every chapter in this book includes at least one of these straight dough recipes for novice bakers or bakers in a hurry. But the majority of the great breads I have fallen in love with achieve incredible texture, flavor, and long shelf life from sourdough starters cultivated from scratch. Undoubtedly the most fascinating part of this whole experience for me has been comparing the similarities and differences between starter methods and ingredients from place to place. Parisian baker Basil Kamir raises his baguettes with *levain*, a hard, clay-like sourdough starter fermented at a cool temperature for sixteen to eighteen hours. His baguette dough is about 15 percent starter. In the Auvergne region, Amandio Pimenta makes a loose sourdough with the texture of pancake batter, ferments it at very warm room temperature for six hours, and then lets it cool down in a special fermenting chamber called a *fermento levain*. His bread dough is 30 percent or 40 percent starter. Not surprisingly, these bakers' breads are vastly different, even though their starters (and their bread doughs) are made from the same ingredients—wheat flour and water. Basil's neat baguettes have a mild flavor and a moist, regular crumb, while Amandio's *pain de Combraille* is explosively bubbly, with a tangy flavor verging on sour. I couldn't say which one is better. That would be like saying which is better, a great Bordeaux or a great Barolo.

I often thought about wine as I toured Europe's best artisan bakeries in search of recipes for this book, because no matter where I was, the subject of fermentation always came up. Nonbakers are used to thinking of bread as simply flour and water, but the best bread, like the best wine, is a fermented food, its yeast and lactobacilli cultivated to bring out the myriad flavor possibilities that lie dormant in the mixture. My favorite European artisan breads are unique. But most of them have in common a long fermentation period that lends them beautiful fragrance, a crust full of character, and above all the full flavor that can be achieved only when yeast and lactobacilli are allowed to develop over time.

One of my goals in this book is to persuade you that cultivating a sourdough culture is not at all difficult and that doing so will allow you to bake the most authentic and delicious breads possible. Early in my career, the Parisian baker Jean LeFleur showed me how he made the stiff dough *levain* (page 111) for his baguettes. Thinking that I was about to take a graduate course in sourdough, I was shocked when he mixed together some flour and water in seconds and placed the dough on a rack in the back of the cool basement. I watched him during the next few days as he kneaded in fresh flour and water and monitored the growth of the wild yeast captured in the culture. It took more patience than I was used to, but it required very little work. What a relief it was to discover that there was no big secret to creating sourdough, the foundation of every truly great European artisan bread. I returned to the Catskills confident that with his recipe I could do it myself at home. I've tinkered with his formula, as well as with the formulas for the other sourdoughs I encountered, so they'll be just as easy for you to create and maintain.

4. Learn about the little things that can make a big difference in the way your dough turns out. The great bakers I met all knew how to handle, and not overhandle, their particular doughs. When the Austrian baker Clemens Walch showed me how to make his Alpine baguette (page 279), he told me that the soft, sticky rye dough required a ten-minute rest between two periods of gentle kneading. This resting period, he explained, allowed the flour to absorb as much water as possible, making the dough much less sticky and much easier to work with when he finished the kneading. In the Auvergne, Pierre Nury had a special technique for stretching his baguette dough in just two quick motions, as opposed to the vigorous rolling common in Paris. He explained that because the local flour was softer than the flour used elsewhere in France, it was important to work quickly and gently so as not to destroy the structure of the dough. Because of the technique, his baguettes, tapered at the ends and bulging in the middle, were immediately recognizable as from the region.

The seemingly small things—letting a dough rest for ten minutes during kneading, rolling it in two motions instead of ten—contribute immeasurably to a bread's uniqueness. I was always on the lookout for the unusual ways that bakers handled their doughs, and in the recipes I give detailed descriptions of these techniques, essential for reproducing authentic loaves.

5. Simulate a European hearth oven at home. The best bread is always made on a stone hearth. There is no other way to achieve oven spring—that initial, incredible rise that dough achieves on contact with a superheated stone. That said, I saw so many variations on hearth baking, from a four-hundred-year-old wood-fired oven in Altamura to a brand-new computerized wonder with steam injection in Poland, that I realize there's no one authentic way to hearth-bake bread. Because breads baked in a wood-burning brick oven and a computerized deck oven both come into contact with a very hot stone base, they'll get equally good oven spring. To be true to particular recipes, I've devised ways to recreate the various oven conditions I've seen. Some breads, like *pane di Genzano* (page 197), are baked in an extremely hot oven with just a little steam, so in the recipe for this bread I tell you to pre-heat the oven for a full hour at the hottest setting and use 1/4 cup of ice cubes to create steam that will moisten the crust during the bread's initial rise. German rye breads, in contrast, require a longer baking time in a slightly cooler oven with a lot more steam, to bake the sticky interior fully without burning the crust. I instruct you on preheating your baking stone and adding adequate steam to duplicate the conditions in a German bakery oven.

It's been a joy to share breads from France, Italy, Germany, Austria, Poland, and the Czech Republic with my customers, seeing who buys the light Silesian rye (page 319) week after week or who has become a fanatic for the sunflower seed *levain* (page 128). I'm even more gratified, however, when some-one asks me where to buy the best mail-order flour or brings a copy of my first book to the bakery with a question about a recipe. Just after *Bread Alone* was published, I began to receive letters, accompanied by photographs, from a reader who wanted my advice about perfecting his baking technique. He'd describe his small dissatisfactions with the loaves—the rise wasn't as high as he had expected, the crumb wasn't as open as he had hoped it would be, the crust was a little soft, and so on. I'd write back, advising him to proof the dough a little longer, bake it for an extra ten minutes, be sure to add the right amount of ice cubes to the preheated pan at the bottom of the oven. Taking my advice, and trying over and over again, he eventually reached a point where he could tell when a bread was underproofed, underbaked, or under-steamed. And soon after, he was able to avoid these

mistakes altogether. Now he felt not only that he could duplicate my recipes but that he was an authority on his own bread. I wasn't at all surprised at his journey, because it was so similar to my own study of European artisan breads and my efforts through practice and experimentation to make them in my own bakery to my satisfaction. I'd like nothing more than for you to be able to experience the same joy of making an authentic European bread and put-ting your own mark on it.

I tell anyone who will listen that it is just not that difficult to make good bread at home. Gather a few simple ingredients, follow a good recipe, and see what happens. Your first, second, and even tenth try at the *flûte gana* on page 70 may not be as elegant as one of Bernard Ganachaud's signature loaves, but it will share some of the great flavor and textural quali-ties of the best Parisian breads. It might seem para-doxical, but my casual attitude is a direct result of my European training. When Clemens Walch showed me how to build a sparklingly acidic rye sourdough starter, he explained that his grandfather used to make the same one. Clemens is an extremely accom-plished baker with a diploma from the best baking school in Austria. But making sourdough is no big deal to him, because it's just something that the bak-ers in his family have always done, a basic kitchen routine.

This perspective is one of the most important things I brought home from Europe, and I'd like to pass it on to you with these stories and recipes. So many bread-baking books these days overwhelm readers with science and technical information. But making bread is not like building your own com-puter chip. It requires sensitivity, attention to detail, and practice, of course. But it is something that people have been doing at home without any spe-cial schooling, research, or technological assistance for literally thousands of years. Like growing toma-toes in the backyard, baking bread is something that anyone can do. Even novice weekend gardeners manage to coax a basketful of delicious tomatoes from their plants by the end of the summer. When spring rolls around, they are eager to try again. It's the same with the least experienced bakers—whatever comes out of the oven the first time around will be incredibly satisfying, and the next time around it will be even more so. Just recently, one of the students in my two-day workshop at the Institute of Culinary Education in New York City brought in a file of photos she had taken of all of the breads she had baked from *Bread Alone*. She told me that she had been baking from the book for years. Looking at the photos, I could immediately see how much time and effort she had devoted to learning how to bake—the breads were as beautiful and well-made as any I had ever seen. Her photos reinforced my belief that with enough practice, a home baker can produce heirloom-quality breads equal to those of Europe's best bakers, and also uniquely her own.

Enjoy!

CHAPTER I

✳

INGREDIENTS AND EQUIPMENT
FOR MAKING EUROPEAN ARTISAN BREADS
AT HOME

✳

Wherever I went in Europe, I carefully noted the local ingredients and unusual equipment that a particular baker was using to produce a unique bread. Whether it was the white rye flour made from Polish grain in the light Silesian rye bread at Pawlow Mieczyslaw's bakery in southwestern Poland or the black olives grown in nearby groves that went into the black olive rolls I ate in Lucca, Italy, I was quick to appreciate the character these ingredients imparted to the bread. My appreciation was sometimes bittersweet, because I knew I wouldn't be able to buy a particular Polish rye flour or local Tuscan olives in New York. Likewise, when I saw a new piece of equipment for making artisan bread, I wanted to learn everything about it. The *levain* breads I saw being made in France with a vintage Artofex mixer had

such perfect crumb structure that I immediately began to scheme to obtain a refurbished Artofex (they are no longer in production) for myself. Unfortunately, they come on the market rarely and are prohibitively expensive when they do.

There's no doubt that the bakers I met all use ingredients and equipment that they take for granted and simply couldn't do without. But it's also true that some of these items are difficult or impossible to find in the United States. Does that mean that it is impossible to make authentic European artisan bread here? Well, I hope not, since this is the premise on which this book, not to mention my business, is built. I don't mean to sound glib. This is an issue that I've agonized over since I began to bake professionally. Maybe it's because I'm a practicing baker rather than an anthropologist or a historian that I take a practical view of the subject. Pawlow gave me a couple of pounds of flour to take home, where I had a chance to compare it to the rye flours available here. Knowing that I couldn't bake his bread unless I made this compromise, I chose a white rye flour milled from grain grown in eastern Canada that was a close match. I made a similar compromise when developing my *pain au levain* recipes, inspired by the breads at Fabiopain in Alsace. If I couldn't buy an Artofex mixer, I'd figure out a way to knead my dough in the mixers I already had, using a very low speed to mimic the gentle massage that the Artofex gives the dough. My feeling is that if you choose the best ingredients that resemble those used in European bakeries and follow similar techniques, the result will be as authentic a European artisan bread as anyone can produce in an American home kitchen.

Maybe a better way to think about authenticity is in terms of making bread that's authentically your own. If you take the care to choose the best ingredients available to you and use some very basic home baking equipment to handle them with sensitivity, you will certainly wind up with bread that's very close to its European model but that also reflects your baking style and where you come from.

✳ GATHERING AND HANDLING INGREDIENTS

Here is a list of the ingredients you will need to make the recipes in this book. It's a rather short list, because bread baking just doesn't require a lot. The breads in this book can be made with very few items, so make sure that they're the best—the purest-tasting water, the most gently processed flour, the sea salt with the most flavor, the most active instant yeast. If your natural-foods store or supermarket doesn't stock stone-ground rye flour or sea salt from France, these ingredients are only a mouse-click away (see Resources, pages 333–34) and no more expensive than what you might purchase locally.

As important as gathering the best flour, salt, seeds, and nuts is knowing how to get the most out of them by handling them properly, so each of the entries below has advice on both shopping for and handling the ingredients that go into bread.

Water. Bottled or tap water is an extremely sensitive topic among bakers, and everyone has his or her own opinion about the best water for bread. I'm reluctant to endorse any particular kind of water, whether from a tap or bottled at a spring, since tap water's quality varies so greatly from municipality to municipality and many spring waters, when tested in laboratories, turn out to be no purer or more balanced than what flows from the tap.

I choose the kind of water I use according to what kind of dough I'm mixing and where I'm baking. At Bread Alone we use well water, filtered with ultraviolet rays to kill any bacteria, as mandated by the New York State Board of Health. We use this water to cultivate sourdough starters as well as to make bread dough. Because it comes from a well on our property and we test it frequently, I can be sure it doesn't contain a lot of chlorine or high mineral levels that could kill the yeast in a sourdough culture before the culture has time to become well established. When we mix it into bread dough, the dough rises reliably and the clean taste of wholesome grain predominates.

When I teach at various cooking schools across the country, I use bottled spring water to initiate a sourdough culture, because I can't be sure that the tap water in a new location hasn't been treated with a lot of chlorine or doesn't have high mineral levels that could inhibit the development of yeast. It's a precaution that's probably unnecessary, but I'd rather not take any chances. If you are cultivating a sourdough starter for the first time, I recommend that you do the same and use bottled spring water to activate it. Once a culture is thriving, you can refresh it with tap water without fear of inhibiting its growth. If you drink your tap water, then you should go ahead and use it for mixing bread dough.

I've met many bakers and food experts over the years who insist that water is the secret to the great taste of a certain region's bread. This may be true, although I've never seen any scientific study establishing what it is about, say, the water in Paris that contributes to the flavor of Parisian baguettes. I will say from my own experience that baking with terrible-tasting water does seem to affect the taste of bread adversely. When I gave a class in Las Vegas, a city known for its extremely hard, bad-tasting water, I used the same flour and yeast that I use at Bread Alone. My bread rose just fine and looked like my Catskills baguettes, but it had a flat taste that I suspect came from the minerals in the water. The lesson: if you drink bottled water at home because you don't like the taste of your tap water, then use the bottled water that you drink to make bread dough.

Just as important as choosing which water to use is paying attention to its temperature. With notable exceptions, my recipes call for tepid water. I mean that it should feel barely warm to the touch, like water in a swimming pool. It is cooler than your body temperature, about 70 to 78 degrees. Using water in this range rather than warm water—the 95 degrees that many bread recipes recommend—will make your dough rise slowly at first, allowing time for the flavors to develop.

Yeast. I call for **instant active dry yeast**, otherwise known as bread-machine yeast, because it is the most convenient to use and most commonly available to home bakers. Unlike traditional active dry yeast, instant active dry yeast does not need to be dissolved in water, so you can just add it to the flour when mixing the dough. It will become fully hydrated during kneading. I've tried every brand out there, and they all work, but I prefer SAF brand yeast for its consistency, liveliness, and flavor (see Resources, pages 333–34). You can buy instant active dry yeast in small envelopes and keep them in a cool, dry pantry, or you can buy it in a larger container, which is more economical and handier if you bake a lot. After you open the box or jar, transfer the yeast to an airtight container and refrigerate or freeze it.

If you like, you can substitute traditional **active dry yeast** in an equal amount. Just moisten it in the water (or, in a very few cases, milk) before adding the flour. Once the yeast particles are thoroughly wet, the dough can be mixed right away. It is a myth that dry yeast needs to sit in liquid until it bubbles, in order

for you to check that it is "working." Unless it has been contaminated by moisture, dry yeast will raise bread many months and even years beyond the sell-by date printed on the package.

More and more professional bakers are using instant active dry yeast for its convenience and long shelf life, but some still use **fresh compressed yeast**, which comes in little cakes and must be refrigerated. The disadvantage to using fresh yeast is that it must be used or discarded after three to five days. Fresh compressed yeast is no better than active dry yeast, but if you bake often and are comfortable using it, you can substitute twice as much (by weight) fresh yeast for the amount of dry yeast called for in the recipes. For example, if a recipe lists 0.5 ounce instant active dry yeast, substitute 1 ounce of fresh compressed yeast.

One kind of yeast that you should definitely avoid is called rapid-rise. This is dry yeast that has been packaged with a lot of yeast foods and enzymes to accelerate fermentation. Rapid-rise yeast was first developed for commercial bakers who wanted to save time and money. Using this yeast, they could skip the first rise and divide and shape the dough as soon as it was mixed. In contrast, the European bakers I met who were using packaged yeast prefer to add just a tiny amount and then give the dough a slow rise to develop its flavor. Pierre Nury, a master baker from the Auvergne, in central France, uses commercial yeast in his white baguettes, but instead of hurrying the process along, he mixes the dough at four in the afternoon and then lets it ferment until four in the morning. The long, slow rise is in part responsible for the bread's nutty flavor and moist crumb.

Wheat flour. Most of the breads in this book are made with at least a percentage of flour ground from wheat. Wheat berries consist of three parts: the starchy endosperm; the embryo, called the germ; and the indigestible outer husk, called the bran. Whole wheat flour is 100 percent of the grain, with all of the germ and the bran. White flour is sifted to remove the germ and the bran. Recipes in this book call for one or the other or particular combinations of the two to create breads of many different characters.

Beyond whole and white, the question is, which wheat flour is best for bread? I don't endorse any one brand, although I do strongly recommend using only unbleached, unbromated flours, preferably ones that have been stone-ground from organic wheat. In my experience, organic flours make better-tasting breads. Stone grinding, in contrast to commercial milling, removes less of the oily, vitamin-rich germ, which adds flavor to and encourages fermentation in bread. Bleaching is a way of chemically aging flour so that it will have more gluten-producing potential. Not only does this process remove natural beta-carotene pigments, which color and subtly flavor bread, but it can also inhibit fermentation in sourdoughs by killing the natural yeast. Unbleached flour is stored for three to eight weeks to allow it to oxidize naturally, giving it the same gluten-producing potential as bleached flour in the long run. Bromate (which is outlawed throughout Europe as a carcinogen) is also a gluten-maximizing additive. Large commercial bakeries often use bromated flour, because bromate makes bread dough very extensible and thus easy for machinery to handle. Home and artisan bakers are better off choosing unbromated flour with other gluten-friendly characteristics.

If you are not interested in flour science, seek out bread flour (or whole wheat flour or all-purpose flour if the recipe specifies them) that is labeled unbleached and unbromated and proceed with confidence. But it will help you to understand how your dough is developing if you know a little bit about the characteristics professional bakers look for when judging wheat flour. The first thing is protein level. Flour is classified in three categories: by growing season (winter or spring), bran color (red or white), and kernel hardness (hard or soft). Each of these classifications is an indication of protein content. Generally, hard red spring wheat has the highest amount of protein, as high as 15 percent, while soft white winter wheat has the least, 8 or 9 percent. Home bakers often assume that more protein makes better bread,

but the best hand-crafting bakers like a balanced flour, between 11.3 and 12.2 percent, with enough strength to hold the gases within the cell walls to give the bread a high rise but still soft enough to chew. Most national all-purpose and bread flour brands fall within this range. They will knead into smooth, elastic doughs that rise well in the oven. If you want to be absolutely certain that the flour you use contains the optimum amount of protein, buy it from a source like King Arthur or Giusto's (pages 333–34), where protein content is advertised in the catalog and on the label.

Artisan bakers prefer flours that absorb and hold water, for moist, long-keeping loaves. Highly hydrated dough produces bread with airy, irregular holes. High-protein flour can hold more water than flour with low protein. In her book *Cookwise*, Shirley Corriher, a biochemist, suggests this experiment to demonstrate the hydrating properties of bread and all-purpose flours: Put a cup of each kind of flour into a separate bowl and then stir 1/2 cup of water into each bowl. The higher-protein bread flour will make a drier dough than the all-purpose flour, because it will soak up more of the water. But protein level isn't the only thing that determines how much water a particular flour will absorb. Stone-ground flour absorbs more water than roller-milled flour, because stone milling produces more damaged starches, which soak up water like sponges. How much water a flour can hold will vary from brand to brand and from season to season. If you are certain you are measuring your bread ingredients accurately (on a digital scale) and your dough consistently comes out drier or wetter than described in a recipe, it means that your flour is more or less absorbent than the norm.

One last thing that professional bakers look for in wheat flour is a high ash content. This term indicates how many minerals the flour has retained after being milled. In stone grinding, wheat berries are crushed whole. Inevitably, some of the minerals from the bran and germ are left behind during sifting. In contrast, high-speed, high-heat roller milling strips out the endosperm before grinding, producing a pure white flour with fewer fermentation-friendly minerals and enzymes. A stone miller will be able to tell a professional baker what the ash content of his flour is, but ash content is not typically listed on flour bags sold to consumers. Your best bet for finding flour that has retained its minerals is to look for "stone-ground" on the label. Whole wheat stone-ground flours are relatively easy to find at online retailers like Giusto's and King Arthur. Stone-ground white flour, however, is becoming rare. Arrowhead Mills and Hodgson Mill are both good places to look for a wide selection of stone-ground flours and grains.

I highly recommend ordering flour by mail from one of the sources on pages 333–34. You can bake any of the wheat breads in this book with flour from the supermarket, but if you take just a little extra time and spend just a few extra pennies, you will be able to get flour of the quality that your favorite artisan bakers are using right now. It is incredibly exciting to me to see how easily available artisan-quality flour has become in the past few years. The same mills that supply artisan bakers have started to package flour for consumers, so you can now use the same flours that many of my colleagues use to make bread at home. It's wonderful that these sources let buyers know exactly what they're getting. At fifty cents a pound, you can afford to buy a 2-pound bag of King Arthur 100 percent certified organic flour produced from hard red winter and spring wheat with a protein level of 11.3 percent, perfect for making classic *pain au levain*, Parisian Daily Bread, or *pane di Genzano*. Or you can go to www.giustos.com and buy a 5-pound bag of stone-ground whole wheat flour with 13 to 13.5 percent protein, enough to bake two 2-kilo rounds.

If you find yourself ordering bulk quantities of flour, as many people do (artisan baking can be addictive), store it in airtight containers in the refrigerator or freezer. High-quality, minimally processed flour that still contains some germ oil will go rancid more quickly than commercial flour from which all oil has been removed. Remember to plan ahead and bring your flour to room temperature before you mix

your dough, so that it will rise in the time range suggested in the recipe.

Nonwheat flours. Flours ground from other grains and seeds are sometimes used alone or in combination with wheat flour in the recipes in this book. Here are brief descriptions of what to look for when shopping for these special flours. If you can't find them in your supermarket or local natural-foods store, you can easily order high-quality specialty flours by mail. If you don't bake with them frequently, store them in airtight containers or resealable plastic bags in the freezer to keep them fresh.

BUCKWHEAT FLOUR. Buckwheat flour is ground from the cereal-like seeds of buckwheat, which is actually not wheat at all but a relative of sorrel and rhubarb. It is ground into a fine flour with a distinctive blue-gray color and an earthy, slightly bitter taste. Because it has no gluten, which is essential for creating structure in bread dough, buckwheat must be used in combination with wheat flour to make bread.

FINE CORN FLOUR. Not to be confused with cornmeal, which is too coarse for bread baking, corn flour is a fine, pale yellow flour ground from whole corn kernels.

RYE FLOUR. Rye flour, like wheat flour, comes in whole and white varieties, but most rye flour sold in the United States is whole, with none of the germ and bran sifted out. To confuse matters, it is labeled not "whole" but "medium," to distinguish it from pumpernickel flour, which is a more coarsely ground whole rye flour. Finely ground whole rye flour is generally available only from mail-order sources. Unless otherwise noted, whole rye labeled "medium" or "fine" is called for in the recipes in this book. Both are medium gray and smooth. "Medium" flour has some grit from the bits of bran. "Fine" rye flour will be more powdery. You can use pumpernickel flour in the recipes that call for rye flour, but your breads will be a little darker than breads made with medium or fine rye flour. White rye flour, from which the bran and germ have been sifted, used in some of the lighter Polish and Czech rye breads, is paler than whole rye, grayish white rather than gray. It is rarely available in stores but easily ordered by mail.

FINE SEMOLINA FLOUR. Semolina is the flour ground from 100 percent whole durum wheat. It is easily recognizable by its bright yellow color. Fine semolina, sometimes sold as fine durum flour, is soft and powdery like bread flour. A coarser grind of semolina is sold for pasta making but is not suitable for mixing into bread dough.

Salt. I prefer the pure taste of sea salt in my breads. Table salt is flat-tasting in comparison with sea salt, which is multidimensional in flavor. In addition, fine sea salt dissolves most easily into dough. I like *fleur de sel*, sea salt imported from France, for its delicious flavor. Unfortunately, I haven't found a bulk source for it, so I use domestic refined sea salt at Bread Alone. But when I bake at home, I use *fleur de sel* (see Resources, pages 333–34) exclusively.

Grains and seeds. Buy whole, unprocessed grains and seeds, preferably organic, to give whole-grain and seeded breads the best texture and most flavor. I call for soaking grains and seeds for eight to twelve hours before mixing them into dough, to rehydrate them and plump them up. This way, they don't rob moisture from the dough as it bakes, and your bread will have a tender crumb without being dense and dry. Store unused grains and seeds in airtight containers or resealable plastic bags in the refrigerator or freezer, since they contain oils that go rancid quickly.

Dried fruits and nuts. Seek out unsulfured dried fruits and raw nuts, preferably organic. Soak dried fruits in water, for the same reason that you soak seeds: so they don't absorb water from the dough. In some cases I call for toasting nuts and cooling them before mixing them into bread dough, to bring out their full flavor.

✳ OUTFITTING YOUR KITCHEN TO BAKE ARTISAN BREAD

Artisan baking is a simple craft, and its practitioners often work in minimally outfitted kitchens to produce exceptional breads. When I first peeked into Daniel Lattanzi's bakery in Genzano, outside of Rome, I was shocked at the primitive setup. The room was furnished with a wooden work table, a large standing mixer, a blazing wood-fired oven, and a few iron racks. That's all Daniel needed to make his monumental bran-covered breads, which look like boulders. In fact, the very dearth of gadgets and modern baking machinery certainly contributed to the rustic, handmade goodness of the loaves. Even in a high-tech fantasy bakery like Amos de Carlo's Toscapan, near Florence, modern equipment was used in the service of Old World craftsmanship. Amos didn't invent his Ferris-wheel–like contraption for fermenting batches of *biga*, the Italian pre-ferment, to make bread more quickly or easily. He just wanted to figure out the most reliable way to make balanced *biga* consistently, so that he could produce traditional Tuscan breads perfectly and on schedule. Even though his bakery produced thousands of pounds of bread each day, to be shipped across northern Italy and into Austria and Germany, his loaves were identical to the handmade Tuscan breads produced by traditional one-room, one-oven *fornos* in ancient Florentine alleyways.

To make breads similar to Daniel's or Amos's, you will need just a few pieces of equipment. Here is a list of the essentials. Each recipe has its own equipment list, to help you get organized to bake.

Scale. All professional bakers weigh ingredients instead of measuring them by volume, because it is the surest way to wind up with uniform-quality breads, batch after batch. Depending on how much your flour has settled, 1 cup of it may weigh between 135 and 145 grams. The difference will result in breads with different qualities. If you only buy one new piece of equipment for bread baking, make it a digital scale that will show the weight of your ingredients in ounces and in grams. A tare function, so you can zero out the scale before adding a new ingredient, is very helpful. I use a Polder digital scale imported from Switzerland. It weighs up to 2,000 grams (4 pounds, 6 ounces), more than enough for the breads in this book. I prefer to weigh ingredients by grams rather than ounces, for the sake of precision. This is especially true when measuring small quantities. It's hard to weigh 1/2 teaspoon of salt but easy to measure out its metric equivalent, 3 grams, on a very sensitive scale.

Measuring cups and spoons. Use these if you must for measuring. Just be sure to use dry metal or plastic measuring cups for dry ingredients. Use the dip-and-sweep method: scoop your measuring cup into the bag of flour and fill it up, then level off the ingredients with a knife or spatula. Dry measures are also useful for scooping ingredients into bowls for weighing. Use glass liquid measuring cups for water and other liquids, although again, I prefer to weigh liquids rather than measure them. Gauge the accuracy of your measurement by looking at it at eye level as it sits on the counter. Small measuring spoons are fine for measuring salt and dry yeast, but again, be sure to level the ingredients with a knife before adding them to the dough.

Thermometers. When I wrote my first book, I was a fanatic for measuring the temperature of everything: the water, the flour, the dough, the oven. Although I am still a fanatic in my bakery, I've mellowed on this subject as it relates to home baking, and it shows in the recipes here.

When you have a batch of dough that weighs hundreds of pounds, it's important for it to be at a certain temperature when it is mixed, because if the dough is substantially colder or warmer than the room temperature of 77 degrees (the optimum temperature for fermentation), it will take a long time for such a large quantity to reach that temperature. At the bakery, I not only keep a careful eye on the temperature in various parts of our big room but take

the temperature of the flour and water before I mix the dough, and I make adjustments when necessary to ensure that each batch of dough ferments at the same rate every day. In the winter, when a new batch of flour has just been unloaded from a Canadian truck, it can take two days for the bags to reach 77 degrees, so I'll use warmer water to give the dough temperature a boost. In the summer, when the room temperature in the bakery reaches 80 degrees or higher, I'll use water as cool as 40 degrees to keep the batch relatively cool as it ferments.

At home it's a different story. If you are mixing a batch of dough that weighs just 2 pounds, it will reach optimum room temperature in twenty to thirty minutes, whether it is 67 or 87 degrees when mixed. I prefer to start with relatively cool dough, which takes longer to rise than a warm one. A longer rise allows the dough to develop more flavor. I strongly suggest that you mix your dough with tepid water (70 to 78 degrees) rather than warm water to encourage a slower fermentation. Use an **instant-read thermometer** to take the temperature of the water before you mix it with the other ingredients. After a while

Instant-Read Thermometer

you will be able to tell by touch, without using a thermometer, if it is in this range. If you store your flour in the refrigerator or freezer, weigh or measure it out and let it stand at room temperature for one hour before mixing it into dough. Of course, your kitchen may be warmer than 77 degrees in the summer. In this case, your dough will rise more quickly than the time given in the recipe, so the recipe also includes visual clues and time ranges to help you determine when your dough has fermented long enough. In the winter, if your kitchen is very cool, you can heat your oven for four minutes, turn it off, and then place the covered bowl of dough inside. The slightly warmed oven will cool off during fermentation but will provide a warmer environment for the dough than a chilly countertop.

When you are ready to bake, use an **oven thermometer** to make sure that your oven is actually at the temperature you've set it for. Some ovens run hot, and some run cold. If yours isn't accurate, it will affect the baking times in the recipes.

One way to test the doneness of bread is by taking its internal temperature with an instant-read thermometer. To do this, flip the bread over (so you don't mar the top with a hole) and insert the thermometer into the middle (for pan loaves, carefully lift the bread halfway out of the pan and insert the thermometer into the center). Softer, enriched breads like the Czech Christmas Braid (page 315) will be done at around 190 degrees. But the large majority of the breads in this book are better when cooked to a higher temperature, 200 to 205 degrees.

To be honest, I never judge a bread's doneness this way, and did not test the recipes in this book using an instant-read thermometer. Take your bread's temperature if your bread has baked for the recommended amount of time but you are worried that it isn't done yet. But don't use temperature alone as a guide when deciding to take a bread out of the oven. The visual clues provided in each recipe, along with your taste and eventually your experience with a particular bread and how long you've baked it in the past, are better gauges. Some people like their loaves with crusts on the pliant side. If that describes you, you might want to bake your bread a few minutes less than someone who likes extra-chewy, hard crusts. Sometimes a bread made from a particularly wet dough will register an internal temperature of 205 but may still need an additional five or ten minutes in the oven, not so much to get hotter as to dry out. It is difficult to get an accurate reading on breads that don't rise high, such as focaccia and Auvergne rye, because the center of the bread is not very far from the crust. For all these reasons, it's a good idea to develop your judgment of a bread's doneness apart from its internal temperature.

Small and large mixing bowls.

Use small bowls to mix sourdoughs and large ones to mix doughs before turning them onto the counter for hand-kneading. A set of inexpensive nesting stainless steel utility bowls will cover all your mixing needs.

Rubber spatula.
Use a rubber spatula for mixing dough ingredients together before kneading. Rubber spatulas also come in handy for scraping risen dough from an oiled bowl out onto a counter for dividing and bench proofing. Heatproof silicone spatulas are not necessary for bread baking, but if you are investing in new spatulas, these will be the most useful for other kitchen tasks as well.

Heavy-duty stand mixer with dough hook.
Several doughs in this book are so wet and sticky that they cannot be kneaded by hand. I tested these recipes with the smallest heavy-duty KitchenAid stand mixer (K45SS) with the dough hook attachment and was impressed with the results. Recipes that can be hand-kneaded can also be kneaded more quickly and with less mess by machine. If you use a machine, you also eliminate the temptation to add more flour to prevent the dough from sticking to your hands or to the counter.

Clear straight-sided 1- and 2-quart rising containers with lids.
Put your kneaded dough in a clear container and mark the container so that when the dough reaches the mark, you will know it

Straight-sided
rising container

has risen enough. The lid will keep the dough moist as it expands. King Arthur sells dough-rising buckets with quart markings on the sides to make these judgments simple.

Baker's peel or rimless baking sheet.
A peel is a thin, flat wooden or metal sheet with a long handle attached. Use it to slide loaves onto the baking stone. Alternatively, use a rimless baking sheet.

Baker's peel

Parchment paper.
I usually use parchment paper to cover the peel or baking sheet before placing loaves on top of it for the final rise. Then I slide the loaves, still on the parchment, onto the baking stone. This way, I don't have to worry that my risen doughs will stick to the peel and possibly deflate as I'm attempting to get them into the oven. I also use pleated parchment paper to simulate a *couche*, a traditional linen support for baguettes that helps them maintain their shape as they rise.

Bannetons or shallow bowls.
Bannetons are canvas-lined baskets that help dough rounds maintain their shape as they rise. Not simply utilitarian, they're beautiful handmade objects, a pleasure to look at and use. Even with regular home use, they'll last a lifetime. They don't require much maintenance. Just shake them after every use to remove excess flour and store in a dry place. I don't know anyone who's bought one who has regretted the expense. If you're just starting out and don't want to

make this investment right away, shallow bowls or colanders lined with floured kitchen towels work just as well.

Canvas-lined banneton

Oval banneton

Loaf pan.
A few of these breads are baked in 9-by-5-inch loaf pans. Use metal, not ceramic, for the most effective heat conduction and best-developed crust.

Loaf pan

Bench scraper or chef's knife. A bench scraper is a rectangular steel blade about 4 inches by 5 inches with a wooden handle on the long edge. I use it to lift soft or sticky doughs during kneading as

Bench scraper

well as to cut dough into pieces. It's also great for scraping up excess dough that sticks to the counter. If you don't have a bench scraper, use a sharp chef's knife to cut the dough.

Baking stone. An absolutely essential piece of equipment for making artisan breads at home, a baking stone made of fire-tempered brick will conduct heat instantly and efficiently right into the bottom of the loaves, mimicking the heat of a professional hearth oven. There is no other way to achieve optimum oven spring. Buy a large rectangular stone. Smaller round ones are meant for pizza and won't be able to accommodate the large breads in this book. Be sure to season a new baking stone by heating it once or twice at moderate temperature according to the manufacturer's instructions, to protect it from breaking in a very hot oven. Buy the biggest stone that will fit in your oven so that you'll be able to bake big breads—*miches* (page 118) and gigantic *pane di Genzano* (page 197)—and make sure it is at least 1/2-inch thick.

If you bake a lot of bread, you might consider buying a HearthKit (see Resources, pages 333–34), which is a three-sided ceramic insert that fits into your oven. In my opinion, it is the best way to simulate a hearth oven at home. It conducts heat more evenly and with greater intensity than a plain baking stone. I have tested one in my own home oven and have been impressed with the high rise and crisp, beautifully colored breads, indistinguishable from the

breads I bake in my brick ovens at Bread Alone. Leave your HearthKit in the oven permanently. It conducts heat beautifully at lower temperatures, producing excellent pastries as well as beautiful roast chicken and other meats.

Lame, single-edged razor blade, or serrated knife. Special bread-slashing knives called *lames* are sold through the Baker's Catalog. They cost less than $10. Their very sharp, curved blades easily cut through sticky dough. Using one will help you achieve the distinctive cuts of Bernard Ganachaud and other Parisian scoring masters. But a single-

Lame (scoring tool)

edged razor blade or a very sharp serrated knife will make effective and attractive cuts as well.

Cast-iron skillet. Slipping some ice cubes into a cast-iron skillet that's been heating in the oven along with the baking stone is the most effective way to bake breads with steam at home. When the ice hits the hot metal, it quickly turns to steam, keeping the crusts soft for those first crucial minutes so the bread can expand to its maximum potential. I don't recommend using a water spritzer bottle (you tend to lose a lot of heat from the oven when you keep the oven door open to spray the breads) or tossing ice cubes right onto the oven floor (carelessly aimed ice cubes have been known to shatter oven lightbulbs).

Wire racks. Transfer just-baked breads to heavy wire racks to cool. The racks, elevated from the counter, allow air to circulate all around the loaves so the bottoms don't get soggy. Buy the largest size you can find, to accommodate the larger breads in this book.

Pastry brushes. I use a pastry brush to moisten risen bread before applying seeds. This helps them stick. Dry pastry brushes are also useful for brushing excess flour from the surface of the dough. If you are in the market for new ones, I recommend the new silicone brushes, which don't shed any pesky hairs.

CHAPTER 2

✳

BREAD RECIPES, STEP BY STEP

✳

The recipes in this book produce breads that are as different from each other as the fingerprints of the bakers who make them. But the differences are not a result of vastly different ingredients and baking techniques. In fact, as I watched European artisans work, I was struck by how similar their routines were across borders and cultures. It was not wild variations but the little things—less or more water, gentle or vigorous machine kneading—that made the difference between *pain au levain* (page 124) and *pane di Genzano* (page 197).

In this section I will take you through the generic steps of a bread recipe. Once you understand the basic arc, from preparing your sourdough and measuring out ingredients to cooling and storing finished breads, you will be able to take on an individual recipe with all its quirks. Artisan bakers know from experience what to look for and what to expect from their dough at every step in the process, and are able to adjust their routines when necessary to allow the dough to develop properly. Armed with some basic information, you too will be able to react sensitively to the progress of a particular dough after just a few baking sessions at home.

Prepare the sourdough. Many, but not all, of the breads in this book are leavened with a sourdough starter. If you are making a sourdough bread, you will have to tend to your starter before you mix your dough. Cultivating a starter from scratch will take anywhere from three to ten days. If you already have an active sourdough culture in your refrigerator, you will need to refresh it with fresh water and flour eight to twelve hours before you want to bake. See Chapter 3 (page 41) for an in-depth discussion of sourdough cultivation, maintenance, and refreshment.

Mix the dough.
Weigh or measure out all the ingredients before mixing them together in a bowl with a rubber spatula to form a rough dough. Some recipes will instruct you to mix just the flour and water at this point and let the dough stand (see Rest the Dough, below). If the dough doesn't require a rest, the recipe will tell you in what order to add the remaining ingredients. For the sake of accuracy, I always weigh rather than measure. Volume measures are provided in each recipe, but there is more variability in this system of measurement, especially with dry ingredients such as flour. Measuring cups all differ slightly, and flour can settle, affecting how much will fit in a cup. If you must measure, use the dip-and-sweep method, dipping your dry measuring cup into the bag of flour and then leveling off the flour with a knife. Lightly pack other dry ingredients like nuts and herbs into measuring cups and make sure the tops are level. Use a glass measuring cup for water and other liquids and look at it at eye level to judge that you've measured precisely.

In addition to giving the weights and volume measurements of ingredients, I list the "baker's percentages"—that is, I list all the ingredients in terms of their percentage amount compared to the flour (or flours), which is always 100 percent. Bakers commonly share recipes with each other in these terms rather than listing ingredients in grams, ounces, or cups. No matter how large or small a batch of dough is, the baker's percentages never change. Home bakers don't need to know the baker's percentages in order to make a great loaf, but seeing the relationship between liquids and solids in a recipe is another good way to learn to think precisely about dough.

Rest the dough.
Some recipes will call for you to rest your dough for ten to twenty minutes after you have mixed together the flour and water. Called *autolyse* in France, this rest allows the starches and gluten to expand and fully absorb the water, shortening kneading time and making the dough easier to handle, especially when it is very soft. The longer the dough rests, the more water the flour is able to absorb without mechanical mixing. This full absorption results in a more extensible (stretchy) dough that will have a higher rise.

Knead the dough.
Kneading is a critical step, because it prepares the dough for the demands of becoming bread. Through kneading, dough is transformed from a rough, sticky mass into a smooth, strong, homogenous one able to rise high in the oven without collapsing. If you can recognize the stages that the dough passes through in the process, you'll be able to judge when it has been kneaded properly.

As soon as flour comes in contact with water, its proteins form clusters to trap the water. Damaged starches that were broken in the milling process absorb the water and swell. Undamaged starches become moistened. During the first couple of minutes of kneading, as water moistens flour and hydrates the starches, the dough is still lumpy and shaggy.

As kneading continues, the ingredients are distributed evenly throughout the dough. You can't see how yeast and salt are mixed in, but if you knead in larger pieces, such as nuts or seeds, you can witness the distribution process on a larger scale.

Kneading also introduces and evenly distributes another important ingredient, oxygen. The oxygen provides valuable food for the yeast.

Beyond these initial stages, kneading's primary function is to develop the gluten in the dough. Gluten is the primary protein aggregate in bread. It gives dough strength and structure so the loaves can rise and hold their shape during and after baking. Gluten is created when gliadin and glutenin, two proteins present in wheat flour, bond together on contact with water. (Rye and other flours have little or no gluten-forming potential. This is why all-rye breads don't rise much and have tight, closed crumb structures, and why most bread recipes include at least a little bit of wheat flour.) Gluten must be strengthened through the repeated action of stretching and folding the dough. During kneading, gluten becomes more extensible, so that it can stretch as air expands inside the dough during fermentation and baking. It becomes more elastic, so that the cells can hold their shape once they have expanded. These qualities combined are known as viscoelasticity. Most of the time and effort you spend in kneading dough is in the service of this gluten development. The more gluten a dough has, the longer it will take to develop it fully through kneading. This is why doughs made with higher-protein flours take longer to knead than doughs made with lower-protein flours, but it's also why higher-protein doughs can sustain a higher rise. As you knead, you can feel your dough getting smoother. This smoothness is the sign that your kneading is organizing the networks of gluten on a molecular level, creating the webbed cell structure so crucial to raising dough.

The dough continues to benefit from your kneading for hours after you have finished. The repeated action of kneading aerates the dough, which activates yeast and creates air cells. Once the dough is left to ferment, the cells fill with gas. The more thoroughly kneaded the dough is, the more cells there are to fill and the higher the rise and more open the crumb of the finished bread will be.

Unless otherwise noted in the recipe, dough can be kneaded either by hand or by machine. To knead comfortably and effectively by hand, work at a clean counter at least 2 feet square and low enough for you to extend your arms and use your body weight, rocking back and forth, to manipulate the dough. Lightly flour the counter and turn the dough out onto it. Flour your hands. Knead the dough by pushing it down and forward with the heels of both hands, then pulling back from the top and folding it over with the other. Resist the temptation to add flour to the dough. Instead, lightly flour your hands as necessary and stop occasionally and use a bench scraper to scrape the dough off the counter before you begin again. As the dough becomes smoother and more developed, it will be less sticky. The time guidelines for kneading by hand are based on a moderate pace of about sixty strokes per minute. But you can knead more slowly and take breaks when you are tired—the dough will wait for you. At a certain point, there will be a sudden shift when the dough becomes more workable and less sticky. From here on, shift your technique to make smoother and quicker strokes until the dough is very smooth and so extensible that when you pull a strand from the ball, it springs back like a rubber band.

Use your eyes and hands to judge when you have kneaded enough. Wheat doughs gradually become smooth and shiny. (Rye doughs, depending on how much or little wheat flour they contain, will be softer and more like batter. Follow the cues in individual rye recipes to determine whether you have kneaded sufficiently.) But smoothness alone isn't a confirmation that you're done. You also need to develop the elasticity of the gluten, which can take a bit longer. To judge whether you have kneaded adequately, give your dough the windowpane test: Pull off a golfball-sized piece and flatten it slightly. Put the fingers of

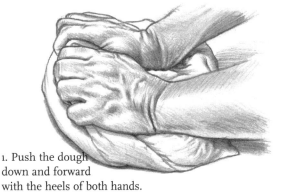

1. Push the dough down and forward with the heels of both hands.

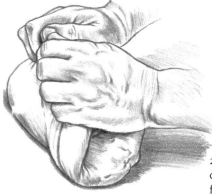

2. Pull the dough back from the top.

both hands underneath it and very gently stretch it. If you can pull the dough so that the center is so thin you can practically see through it, then it has developed enough elasticity. If it tears, continue to knead for a few more minutes and test again.

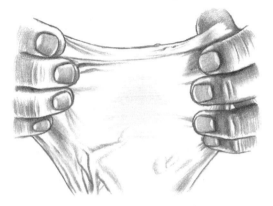

Put the fingers of both hands underneath the dough and very gently stretch it until the center is so thin you can practically see through it.

If you are up for the challenge, kneading a wet dough can be fun and gratifying. (Some doughs in this book, such as Roman-Style White Pizza, page 214, and Genzano Country Bread, page 197, are simply too wet to knead by hand and must be kneaded by machine. If this is the case, it is noted in the recipe.) Be prepared for the stickiness. Have a bowl of flour handy for flouring your hands, or oil both sides of your hands with vegetable or olive oil and reapply as necessary. Keep a bench scraper nearby and use it to scrape the dough from the counter as often as you need to. Don't worry about getting your hands and the countertop messy, and be patient. Use the heel of your hand to knead with a quick, light pulse. For the first few minutes, smear the dough, taking longer strokes that exaggerate the stretching. This develops the gluten more efficiently in the early stages. When the dough gets too spread out, scrape it back into a mound with the bench scraper and start again. Take frequent breaks, to rest your hands but also to give the dough some time to relax. I think of it like weight training: three sets of ten is more effective in developing muscle than

thirty repetitions in a row. Throughout the process, resist adding flour.

Kneading by machine is a simple matter of turning the mixer to the speed indicated and setting the timer, stopping occasionally to scrape down the dough hook and the sides of the bowl. Use only a heavy-duty stand mixer such as a KitchenAid or a home version of a professional mixer such as a Magic Mill (see Resources, pages 333–34). Lighter machines will not be up to the job of kneading these doughs, and their motors may burn out trying. Never leave the machine unattended. This is especially important when a recipe calls for mixing a dough on medium-high or high speed. In these cases the mixer may "walk," and you don't want it to walk off the counter when you've got your back turned. Look for the changes that will take place in the dough as it develops. Watch for it to become shiny and extensible, and when you think it might be ready, stop and give it the windowpane test, as described above.

Ferment the dough. After you knead your dough, transfer it to a clear container and let it rise at room temperature. "Fermenting" is the term bakers use for the first rise. During fermentation, yeast and bacteria feed off the sugars in the flour, producing carbon dioxide, alcohol, and acids. These byproducts make bread rise and give it flavor. If you've ever left a jug of apple cider in the refrigerator long enough for it to become bubbly and alcoholic, you've witnessed this complex biochemical process at home. Without fermentation, bread would be nothing more than a cooked lump of starch, like mashed potatoes or polenta. You don't need to know anything about fermentation for it to work, but if you understand the profound changes that occur in dough as it rises, you will gain confidence as a baker.

When yeast is mixed with flour and water, it digests the glucose and fructose in the flour and produces carbon dioxide and alcohol. The carbon dioxide molecules are trapped in the webbing of gluten that you developed through kneading, causing the pockets to expand and raise the dough. You can smell the alcohol in rising dough, but it cooks off in the oven, so your bread doesn't taste boozy. It doesn't matter what kind of yeast you use. Packaged yeast or the yeast in any sort of sourdough starter will ferment and have the same rising effect on bread dough. The big difference is that packaged yeast is a single strain that has been bred for speed and reliability. Wild yeast in sourdough is a a cocktail containing many different strains (scientists have identified 10,000 different types of yeast) and is less predictable. Therefore, in the recipes, rising times for sourdough breads range more widely.

Bacteria in bread dough also ferment, consuming maltose, a sugar that yeast can't digest. The byproducts, lactic and acetic acids, give sourdough breads their milky, tangy taste. (It takes eight to twelve hours for bacteria to ferment, so straight doughs made with packaged yeast and fermented for only a couple of hours won't receive the flavor benefits of bacterial fermentation.) In addition, when heated, these acids combine with the alcohol produced by yeast to form aromatic compounds called esters, which are responsible for the unforgettable aroma of baking bread.

Yeast and bacteria ferment well at the temperature range we're comfortable living in, between 68 and 81 degrees. Within this range, they will ferment more rapidly at the high end and more slowly at the low end. Professional bakers ferment their doughs in temperature-controlled chambers that can be programmed to a tenth of a degree, so the fermentation time will be the same for every batch. It's difficult to be so precise at home. The recipes assume a room temperature of 70 to 75 degrees. If your kitchen is within this range, your dough should ferment within the time frame given, but you'll have to watch it to determine exactly when it's ready. If your kitchen is colder or hotter than this, you'll need to adjust the rise time accordingly.

Check on your dough's progress when it has fermented for the low time given in the recipe. If it displays the characteristics described in the recipe, proceed to the next step. Different kinds of dough will exhibit different signs. A medium-soft to firm dough will expand into a dome like a mushroom cap.

Wheat doughs will rise to close to twice their original volume and sometimes more. Those with a large proportion of rye will be about one and one half times their original size. Poke the dough gently with a floured finger. It will feel airy but won't deflate. If your fingerprint springs back, that's another sign that the dough is ready. If you are unsure, don't be afraid to slice into the dough and take a peek. You will see a honeycomb of smaller and larger bubbles in a network of gluten strands throughout the dough, just like in a baked bread.

A wet dough will look pillowy and delicate. It will expand to twice its original size, unless it has a high proportion of rye flour, in which case it will have risen less. When you poke the dough gently with a floured finger, your fingerprint will spring back quickly and then deflate slightly. A wet dough that has fully fermented will be less sticky than it was when you finished kneading it. Look below the translucent surface and you will see a honeycomb of smaller and larger bubbles in a network of gluten strands throughout the dough.

The best way to tell if your dough is ready is through experience. After you've made a certain bread a number of times, you will be a better judge of the signs. If you are not sure whether your dough has fermented long enough, don't be afraid to give it an extra ten minutes, or let it stand for the full suggested fermentation time. Underfermenting is one of the most common mistakes that inexperienced home bakers make. The longer the dough ferments, the higher it will rise and the more flavorful it will become. But there is a time limit. If dough ferments too long, the yeast will exhaust its food supply and become weak. A loaf baked from overfermented dough will not rise well and will taste "off." It takes practice—and the occasional overproofed loaf—to learn when to interrupt the natural process of fermentation so the yeast's rising power and the flavors of the sugars and acids are at their peak.

Turn the dough. Some of the recipes call for turning the dough part of the way through the first rise. Flour your hands, then scoop up the dough

1. Scoop up the dough, and let it droop over your hands and then down.

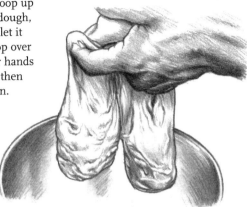

2. Place the dough back into the bowl.

3. Fold the drooping sides toward the center of the bowl.

from the sides. Let it droop down and then place the dough back into the bowl, allowing the drooping sides to flop toward the center. The folding action

invigorates the yeast and encourages the development of new cells for holding air. It also further develops the gluten, in a very gentle way. Don't punch down the dough. You don't want to deflate all the air cells that your dough has been working hard to pump up. Turning is especially good for wet doughs, since it helps develop gluten that will keep them from spreading instead of puffing up.

Divide the dough. When a recipe makes enough dough for two or more loaves, you must divide the dough after the first rise. Lightly dust the counter with flour. Use the flour that is predominant in your dough—bread flour, rye, semolina. Use a bench scraper or sharp chef's knife to cut the dough cleanly without sawing or tearing it. Overhandling the dough at this point will deflate it, affecting its rising ability in the oven.

Use a bench scraper or sharp chef's knife to cut the dough cleanly.

Rest the dough. If you will be shaping your dough into a baguette, *ficelle*, or *bâtard*, you will have to give it another brief rest (similar to *autolyse*) to relax the gluten and make it more cooperative. In about ten minutes, your dough will be easier to roll and stretch. If you live in a very dry climate, lightly drape your resting doughs with plastic wrap to prevent them from drying out. Otherwise, just leave them uncovered.

Shape the loaves. I was fascinated by the different shaping techniques I saw in bakeries across

Europe. Many unusual shapes, such as the folded Altamura loaf (page 257), are part of the unique bread-crafting traditions of a particular place. But even in Altamura, where the breads have been shaped the same way for hundreds of years, bakers create new shapes depending on need. Thus the semolina dough used for the bread is also pressed into pans to make pizza.

Shaping is a skill acquired through practice. If you are shaping your first or even your hundredth baguette, you may feel like a butterfingers while trying to coax your dough into the classic form. Try not to be dissatisfied with imperfect results. Experienced bakers make it look easy, but it's not. I remember very well the frustration I felt as I stood by Jean LeFleur's side at my friend Basil Kamir's bakery in Paris. As I struggled to shape just one homely baguette, he turned out six flawless ones without breaking a sweat. He smiled at my effort and reminded me that he had shaped thousands of baguettes—in the past couple of weeks! Who knows how many he had shaped during the course of his decades-long career?

Wet doughs are particularly hard to shape elegantly, because they tend to stick to and spread across the counter as they are manipulated. Resist the desire to keep trying until your loaf looks perfect. The most common mistake that home bakers make when shaping dough is to overhandle it. This may cause the air cells in the fermented dough to collapse, and it can also break down the gluten that you worked so hard to develop during kneading. If you are unable to shape your loaf to your satisfaction on the first try, leave it to proof in its imperfect shape. It might not look as beautiful as the breads coming out of a bakery, but its light texture and open crumb will more than compensate for its imperfect exterior. See pages 35–40 for detailed shaping instructions.

Proof the loaves. With a few notable exceptions, shaped loaves stand at room temperature (again, 70 to 75 degrees) for a final rise. "Proofing" is the term for this second rise. As with fermentation,

proofing time depends on several variables, including the exact temperature of your kitchen, the humidity level, and the liveliness of your yeast. Time ranges are given in the recipes, but it will be up to you to determine when your loaves are ready for the oven.

How do you know when your loaves are proofed? Loaves made from medium-soft to firm doughs will have a very smooth surface and look inflated. They will have expanded uniformly to one and a half to two times their original size. When you press a fingertip into the dough, your fingerprint will spring back slowly. Loaves made from softer, wetter doughs will look inflated and delicate, like balloons that you could pop with your fingertip. They will be very airy and soft but less sticky than when you shaped them. When you press a fingertip into the dough, your fingerprint will spring back slowly.

Retard the loaves. Sometimes instead of proofing your loaves in your room-temperature kitchen, you will cover them and place them in the refrigerator for up to twelve hours for a slower second rise. This technique for slowing fermentation is called "retarding." There are two reasons you might retard your loaves. First, it allows you some flexibility in your baking. In the refrigerator, your loaves will expand much more slowly, if at all, so you can bring them to room temperature and bake them when you want to, within the twelve-hour time frame. Second, retarding intensifies the flavor of the breads, because even though the yeast produces less gas at cooler temperatures, bacteria produce more lactic and acetic acids, giving slow-fermented breads their pleasantly sour flavor. (Beyond twelve hours, these acids will start to break down the gluten in the dough, inhibiting the bread's rise.) Retarding also results in darker, thicker, caramelized crusts with appealing brown bubbles, evidence of carbon monoxide escaping to the surface during baking.

I specifically recommend retarding certain doughs, like the Ganachaud *flûte* (page 70), because I want to coax the full wheat flavor from a bread without using sourdough. But you can retard any dough made with white flour and either packaged yeast or a sourdough starter, if you need to put off baking for the sake of convenience or if you want to develop a stronger sour flavor in your bread. Some professional bakers retard whole-grain and rye breads, but I wouldn't recommend this to home bakers. These doughs have a weaker gluten structure than white-flour doughs and are more sensitive to the acid buildup that occurs in the refrigerator. They may begin to break down as the acids build up and fail to rise adequately in the oven as a result.

Prepare the oven.

About one hour before you bake, place your baking stone on the middle rack and a cast-iron skillet on the lower rack and preheat the oven to get both nice and hot. A preheated baking stone will conduct heat right into the bottom of your dough. A hot skillet will be ready to turn ice cubes into steam, to keep the crust moist so your bread can expand optimally. If you are baking a bread without steam in a sheet or loaf pan rather than on top of a baking stone, just set the oven rack in the middle position and preheat the oven for fifteen minutes before baking.

Score the loaves.

Most French bakers make cuts in their loaves with a razor-sharp blade called a *lame* just before loading them into the oven. Scoring is decorative, but it is also a way to control the rise of the dough as it bakes. One way or another, bread dough that is teaming with yeast is going to

"Docking." Pierce the surface of the loaf in several places.

expand. Instead of letting it burst where it may, a baker can strategically slash a loaf to give it a place to expand in the first few minutes in the oven.

Not all breads are elegantly scored in the French style. German, Polish, and Czech bakers sometimes "dock" rye loaves (which don't expand as much as wheat breads do) by poking them all over with a skewer. Piercing the surface of the loaf in several places releases some of the steam created inside the dough as it expands in the oven, so the bread rises uniformly and doesn't crack.

Bake the loaves.

When the loaves are proofed, load them into the oven quickly so it doesn't lose too much heat. But don't hurry. The few extra seconds that it takes to be careful and deliberate will ensure that your loaves make it onto the baking stone in good shape and you come away without any burns. Breads that bake in sheet pans or loaf pans are easy. But breads that bake directly on top of the baking stone are a little bit trickier to get into the oven intact. I suggest covering your peel with parchment paper and letting the loaves proof on the parchment. Then loading them into the oven when they are ready is simply a matter of sliding the parchment onto the baking stone. This way you avoid the hazard of having your doughs stick to the peel and become misshapen as you jiggle the peel, attempting to release them.

When the cool dough hits the heat of the oven, the gluten-strengthened cells created during kneading inflate rapidly. Gases expand, carbon dioxide migrates, alcohol boils, yeast becomes more active, and steam is produced. The result is called "oven spring," the initial and dramatic increase of the loaf's volume during the first few minutes of baking. To maximize oven spring, be sure your loaf is well proofed and the oven and baking stone are hot.

In addition, many of the recipes call for baking the loaves with steam. Steaming them during the first minutes of baking keeps the crusts temporarily soft so that they can expand to their full potential while the yeast is still alive. Steaming will give your loaves a glossy, handsomely browned crust as they bake. There are several ways to add steam to the oven. Some bakers use a spray bottle filled with water to spritz the bottom and sides of the oven, avoiding the loaves and the oven light. I don't recommend this method. Not only does the oven lose heat every time you open the door to spritz, but the danger of shattering the oven light with misdirected water is high. Safer and better for maintaining temperature is the method I describe in the recipes: Place a cast-iron skillet on the lower rack of the oven and preheat it along with the baking stone. Just after you load the loaves onto the baking stone, slide some ice cubes into the skillet. When they hit the pan they will create a burst of steam and then continue to produce a longer, slower flow of steam as they evaporate.

Bread dough will reach its full volume after fifteen to twenty minutes of baking. As the interior of the loaf heats up, the starches gelatinize. At about 140 degrees, the chains of starches undergo molecular changes that cause them to uncoil and absorb water. At the same temperature, the proteins coagulate, like egg whites on a hot griddle, releasing the water trapped in their networks. The swollen starches and cooked gluten strands become firm and trap the gases within the air cells. When you slice into a loaf of bread, you are seeing this moment in time captured in the glossy bubbles of the crumb.

The crust of the bread dries out and firms up more quickly than the inside. At about 325 degrees, the sugars in the crust begin to caramelize, causing browning. Further browning is caused by a chemical reaction between amino acids and simple sugars in the crust, called the "Maillard reaction." The Maillard reaction is responsible for the alluring roasted aroma of baked bread.

The interior of the bread still needs to cook well after the crust has solidified and begun to brown. As the heat of the oven reaches the interior of the dough, the water in the dough migrates toward the crust. The redistribution of water molecules is called "starch retrogradation." When the inside of the loaf reaches 200 to 205 degrees, the trapped gases con-

tract and the dough starts to firm up. The recipes give suggested baking times, but you can't simply go by the clock to judge when your bread is done. The interior should be fully baked, moist but not doughy. If you insert an instant-read thermometer into the bread, it should read about 200 degrees. But I don't recommend judging a bread's doneness solely by internal temperature. A bread may be fully baked on the inside but still need an extra five or ten minutes in the oven to set its crust. Individual recipes will describe how the crust of a bread should look before you pull the loaf from the oven. Don't be afraid to bake it until it is as dark as I suggest. Many home bakers underbake their bread out of fear that they will burn it. Let me assure you that if you leave your bread in the oven for five minutes after you believe it to be done, it will not burn. Those extra minutes will ensure that any moisture left in the crust evaporates, and might just make the difference between a crisp, thick crust and one that gets soggy as it cools. Before you remove the loaf from the oven, give it one more test. Squeeze it—using a potholder or kitchen towel, of course. If it gives, let it bake another five minutes. If it resists on all sides, that's another indication that the interior is firm and the crust is set.

Cool and store the loaves. Slide

your loaves, still on the parchment, onto a wire rack as soon as you pull them from the oven. Air circulating underneath them will prevent them from getting soggy and help cool them down. The intoxicating aroma of your breads may drive you to slice them while they are still hot, but this is a mistake. Breads aren't fully cooked until they've cooled at least partially. As they cool, the process of starch retrogradation is completed and the water molecules move outward, evenly, toward the crust. This is why a crust that feels crisp just out of the oven will soften and why when you cut into a still-hot loaf, the crumb is still soft and the bread doesn't slice neatly. Breads aren't ready to eat until they have cooled to about body temperature and have firmed up enough on the inside to be sliced. This can take anywhere from fifteen minutes for rolls and flatbreads to two hours for a single large round. It's okay to slice baguettes while they're still warm; because baguettes have such a high crust-to-crumb ratio, not much interior cooking that needs to take place during cooling. But larger loaves should cool fully to allow the interior to finish cooking. Max Poilâne told me that he ate only day-old bread, to give it time to solidify its texture and develop its flavor. This makes sense when you are baking an extra-large sourdough round that will stay fresh and even improve with age.

A good serrated bread knife won't damage your breads as it slices through them. Choose a knife with a stainless steel blade that is stiff enough not to bend like a saw. It should be at least 8 inches long—long enough to cut the larger loaves in this book. The teeth should grab the crust to break through it in one stroke. Some people like a curved blade to cut through the thick bottom crust, but I usually just tip the loaf up on its side to cut through the crust cleanly. Cut with long, steady strokes, as if you were sawing a log. When you've cut about halfway through the loaf, tilt it away from you on its side to cut cleanly through the thick bottom crust.

Unsliced bread should be stored at room temperature. Sourdough loaves with crisp crusts should be kept in paper bags, so air can circulate around them. They will stay fresh for several days. Loaves made with packaged yeast will stay fresher longer (up to two days) in plastic bags. Their crusts will become soft but can be recrisped in a 350-degree oven for five minutes or so.

Bread stales because even after cooling, the redistribution of water molecules continues, until so much water migrates from the interior of the bread to the crust that it tastes dry. Any bread that is slightly stale can be improved enough to eat by reheating it. Reheating a dried-out loaf reverses the process and directs water back into the crumb, making it moist and flavorful again for a short time.

If you know that you won't be eating your freshly baked bread in the next couple of days, you can freeze it in a resealable plastic bag to preserve its freshness for several weeks. Thaw the bread at room temperature for two to four hours, depending on its size. Then reheat it in a 350-degree oven to crisp up the crust just before serving.

✳ GETTING IN SHAPE

Different places in Europe have different shaping traditions that distinguish their breads. The snub-nosed rye breads in Poland look completely different from the Czech rye rounds proofed in bannetons. In Germany, the rounds and logs I saw were invariably unscored and coated heavily with whole grains and seeds. There weren't many reasonable explanations for why the doughs were shaped a particular way. Most bakers I talked to said that they shaped their breads according to tradition. That's not to say that they were always bound by tradition. When the people in Genzano or Altamura decided that they wanted pizza, the bakers obliged by pressing bread dough into pizza shapes. When one of Max Poilâne's customers wanted rolls that tasted like the big *miches*, Max had his bakers cut some dough into little triangles. These are facts to keep in mind when shaping your own doughs. I give instructions for traditional shapes, but there are as many ways to shape breads as there are bakers. As you gain experience, your traditionally shaped loaves will begin to exhibit your personal shaping style. After you have gotten to know a particular dough very well, you might want to experiment with a new shape and see what happens.

Here are instructions for gently manipulating doughs into the classic bread shapes most commonly used by European bakers. After you divide the dough, place the pieces on a lightly floured counter and gently deflate the larger gas bubbles by putting even pressure on the pieces with your palms. Slightly deflated dough will be easier to shape than very bubbly, gassy dough. (Exceptions are noted in particular recipes. When shaping ciabatta, for example, you want to preserve the large bubbles in the fermented dough.) Use the heels of your hands rather than your fingertips to shape the dough pieces. This is especially important with wet doughs, which will trap your fingertips like quicksand. Regardless of the shape you are making, be sure to seal the seams carefully, or they will pop open during baking and your bread will take on an unexpected shape. When fermenting loaves on a baker's peel or baking sheet, place them seam side down. When fermenting them in a basket or bowl, put them in seam side up.

If shaping beyond these basic steps is necessary, you'll find additional instructions in the recipes. Individual recipes also note any modifications—to shape a piece of dough into a 12-inch baguette, for example, rather than a standard 14-inch baguette.

Round. Called a *boule* in France. On an unfloured counter, collect the dough into a rough ball. Cup your hands over the ball and then move them in tight circles as you pull it toward you with the heels of your hands. These simultaneous movements will pull any rough bits underneath the ball and create a taut "skin" around it. This takes some coordination. On the first try, it will seem like trying to pat your head and rub your stomach at the same time. It's better not to overwork the dough, even if you don't achieve a perfect round.

1. Cup your hands over the ball of dough.

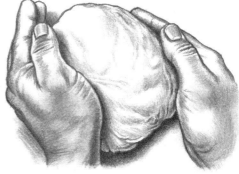

2. Move your hands in tight circles.

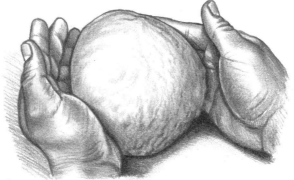

3. Continue moving your hands in tight circles as you pull the dough toward you.

Rolls. The technique for shaping small round rolls is similar to the technique for shaping a larger round. Place a small piece of dough on an unfloured work surface. Cup one hand slightly and cover the dough ball with it. Rotate your hand in small circles, applying a little pressure to the dough. As you rotate,

the dough will eventually form into a ball.

Rustic rolls may also be formed simply by flattening a larger piece of dough to a 2-inch thickness. Use a bench scraper or chef's knife to cut 2-inch-wide strips. Cut each strip into squares or rectangles.

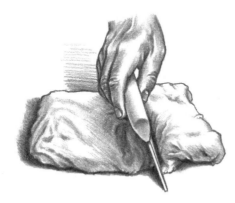

Flatten a larger piece of dough to a 2-inch thickness. Use a bench scraper or chef's knife to cut 2-inch-wide strips. Cut each strip into squares or rectangles.

Log or baguette. Breads across Europe are shaped into logs of varying lengths. The technique for creating the basic shape is the same, no matter the length or thickness of the bread. The classic French baguette is a particularly long log, distinguished by its elegant scoring and tapered ends. Classic French baguettes are 28 inches. I've adapted

the baguette recipes so that the breads measure 14 inches, to fit home ovens and baking stones.

On a lightly floured countertop, pat the dough into a rough rectangle measuring about 3 by 5 inches. With the longer side facing you, fold the top of the dough down about one third of the way toward the center. With the heel of your hand, press along

1. Pat the dough into a rough rectangle measuring about 3 by 5 inches.

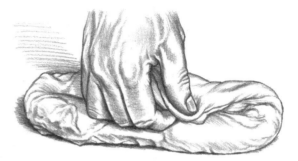

2. With the longer side facing you, fold the top of the dough down about one third of the way toward the center with the heel of your hand. Fold the bottom of the dough about one third of the way toward the center and seal the seam firmly.

the seam, using firm but gentle pressure. Fold the bottom of the dough about one third of the way toward the center and seal the seam firmly. Fold this skinny rectangle in half, bringing the top edge down to meet the bottom edge. Working from right to left, cup your hand over the log of dough and press the heel of your hand down firmly to seal the seam. Dust the counter with additional flour to prevent the

dough from sticking. To stretch the log, place your hands together, palms down, over the middle of the log. Using light, even pressure, roll the log back and forth as you spread your hands apart. Repeat three or four times, until the log is the desired length. Leave the ends rounded or taper them by applying gentle pressure to them as you roll. Avoid overhandling the loaves, which will burst their air cells.

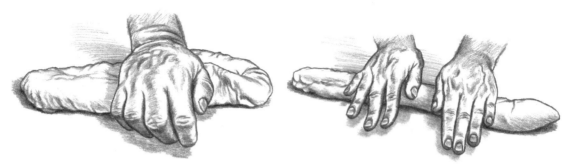

3. Fold this skinny rectangle in half, bringing the top edge down to meet the bottom edge. Working from right to left, cup your hand over the log of dough and press the heel of your hand down firmly to seal the seam.

4. To stretch the log, place your hands together, palms down, over the middle of the log. Using light, even pressure, roll the log back and forth as you spread your hands apart.

Bâtard. The *bâtard* is similar to the baguette, just shorter—about 12 inches long—and fatter. It is formed the same way. Pat the dough into a rough rectangle measuring about 3 by 5 inches. With the longer side facing you, fold the top of the dough down about one third of the way toward the center. With the heel of your hand, press along the seam, using firm but gentle pressure. Fold the bottom of the dough about one third of the way toward the center and seal the seam firmly. Fold this skinny rectangle in half, bringing the top edge down to meet the

bottom edge. Working from right to left, cup your hand over the log of dough and press the heel of your hand down firmly to seal the seam. Dust the counter with additional flour to prevent the dough from sticking. To stretch the log into a *bâtard*, place your hands together, palms down, over the middle of the log. Using light, even pressure, roll the log back and forth as you spread your hands apart. Repeat two to three times, until the log is the desired length, leaving the ends rounded or tapering them by increasing the downward pressure at the tips.

Torpedo. The torpedo looks like a slender football, fat in the middle with sharply tapered ends. To make a torpedo, form a round as directed above. Let the round rest on the counter for five minutes. Then cup your palms over the round and gently roll it back and forth, spreading your hands farther and farther apart to elongate it. As your hands reach the ends, increase the pressure on the dough to make tapered points.

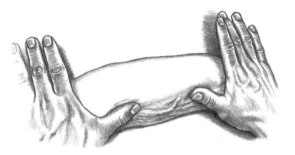

1. Cup your palms over the round and begin gently rolling the dough back and forth, spreading your hands farther and farther apart to elongate the dough.

2. As your hands reach the ends, increase the pressure on the dough to make tapered points.

3. Finished torpedo.

Pan loaf. To fit dough into a 9-by-5-inch loaf pan, form a round as directed above; let the round rest on the counter for five minutes. Then gently flatten it into a rectangle about an inch shorter than the length of the pan. Beginning at the long end, roll the dough into a tight cylinder. Gently roll the cylinder back and forth on the counter until it is the same length as the pan. Place the loaf, seam side down, into the pan and gently press on it so that it is touching the pan on all four sides.

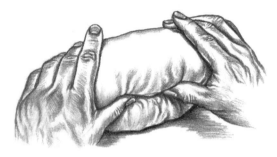

1. Beginning at the long end, roll the dough into a cylinder.

2. Continue rolling until the cylinder is tight.

3. Place the loaf into the pan, pressing on it gently so that the dough touches the pan on all sides.

CHAPTER 3

✳

MAKING AND USING
EUROPEAN STARTERS AND
SOURDOUGHS AT HOME

✳

Fermentation, the process during which yeast digests sugars, creating carbon dioxide and alcohol as byproducts, is responsible for the amazing transformation of grape juice into wine and milk into cheese. Although we often take bread for granted, it is also a product of fermentation. Without yeast, bread wouldn't be bread—it would be crackers. In the case of wine and cheese, fermentation takes months or even years. Fermenting bread dough takes time, but not that long. Depending on the technique you use and the kind of bread you want to wind up with, fermenting dough so that it will rise in the oven can take as little as a couple of hours or as long as two weeks. Until commercial yeast for bakers was invented at the end of the nineteenth century by an Austrian baron and distillery owner, Max von Springer, all bread was raised with yeast captured and cultivated in a simple mixture of flour and water.

For at least two thousand years, people routinely and exclusively used this mixture, commonly known as sourdough, to make bread.

Commercial yeast was developed to make professional bread baking quicker and more predictable. While one batch of sourdough can contain hundreds of strains of wild yeast, a package of commercial yeast contains a single strain, bred for its hardiness and fast action. Breads made with commercial yeast ferment quickly and reliably. When a baker uses the same brand of yeast, the same water, and the same flour every day, he or she can accurately gauge how long the fermentation time will be every time and speedily produce batch after identical batch. In contrast, breads made with sourdough are less predictable and ferment more slowly, so bakers have to judge each batch of dough individually and slow down to make sure that their dough ferments adequately. The payoff for such vigilance and patience is better bread. Only slow fermentation will coax the best from bread dough, resulting in full-flavored loaves with thick, burnished crusts and moist, light interiors.

If you've never used sourdough, you may be afraid to try it. You may have heard that it's difficult or nearly impossible to capture wild yeast; that the only worthwhile sourdough is a piece of a one-hundred-year-old culture from San Francisco or Paris; that you have to feed a sourdough every day or it will die. Once you cultivate your own sourdough, you will see that these tales are completely unfounded. Making sourdough at home and using it to bake bread is not difficult, and you don't have to live in California or France to cultivate a good one. Wherever you live, when you mix flour and water together in a clean bowl in a warm kitchen, fermentation is almost guaranteed. Wild yeast and bread-friendly bacteria live in the flour in your canister and the air in your kitchen. When water hydrates flour, it makes the flour's starches available to the yeast in and around the bowl. When the yeast feeds on the starches, it produces carbon dioxide, which makes the sourdough bubble. As the yeast multiplies, the sourdough becomes a powerful leavener. Give it food once a week, in the form of fresh flour and water, and you will be able to keep your sourdough in bread-raising shape indefinitely.

If I could convince you of just one thing about making bread, it would be how little effort it takes to cultivate a sourdough, even if you've never done it before. How hard can it be, if people were doing it thousands of years ago, without the benefit of modern baking equipment and no knowledge at all of the microorganisms that activate the culture? Consider this: under rabbinical law, unleavened bread, called matzoh, must go from the mixer to the oven in less than eighteen minutes. This regulation was established in the Middle Ages, because it was assumed that when flour and water were mixed, fermentation would naturally and spontaneously occur within minutes. I once visited a water-powered stone mill in Gardiner, New York, that milled flour for kosher bread. Rabbis were posted round the clock to make

sure that not even a drop of water touched the flour. The lesson: sourdough happens.

✳ THE FLAVOR OF SOURDOUGH

Sourdough gets its name from the acids that build up in the culture during fermentation. These acids are not produced by yeast. Although it is the yeast in sourdough that makes bread rise, it is the bacteria that you cultivate along with the yeast that give sourdough its flavor. Bacteria, like yeast, live in flour and air. They coexist harmoniously with the yeast, feeding from maltose sugars that yeast can't metabolize. Lactobacilli, the most common and important bacteria in bread dough, produce organic acids, including lactic and acetic acids, that flavor the bread. The acids are tangy, to be sure, but they also bond with other byproducts of fermentation to form more than fifty flavor compounds that give sourdough bread its unequaled complexity. As with yeast, there are thousands of known strains of lactobacilli and probably thousands more that have not been identified. Geography and climate determine which lactobacilli live and thrive in a particular place. San Francisco, with its damp air and moderate temperatures, is home to the most famous strain, *Lactobacillus Sanfrancisco*, which is at least partially responsible for the city's distinctly flavored bread. An agrohistorian in Umbria proudly told me about the two thousand identified strains of lactobacilli multiplying in local dough in the region, which ranges from the mountains to the ocean. These acids take between eight and twelve hours to produce, which is why straight doughs— breads made with commercial yeast in less than eight hours, start to finish—miss out on the flavor benefits of bacterial fermentation.

In the United States, if a bread is advertised as a sourdough, it does often have a pronounced sour quality, but this is only because the baker has purposely crafted the bread to bring the acidic flavors to the forefront, giving customers what they expect from the name. Sourdough bread isn't necessarily sour-tasting. In fact, across Europe bakers try hard to make balanced sourdough breads with a full spectrum of flavors: earthy, creamy, slightly sweet, malty. Slight tanginess is just one of these flavors, and not the most prominent one. In France and Italy, any detectable sourness in the bread is a sign of carelessness with the starter. Even in Germany and Austria, where the rye starters are deliberately left to ferment until they produce abundant acids, the goal isn't to bake bread that will make the mouth pucker. The starter may be highly acidic, but when it is mixed into bread dough, its flavor is tempered by the other flavors it brings out.

Most of the recipes in this book follow their European models and are only very mildly acidic or not acidic at all. If you prefer a more sour character in your breads, you can do a couple of things to bring out the acidic flavors inherent in the sourdough. For mild breads, the recipes direct you to refresh your sourdough and then let it stand at room temperature for eight to twelve hours before mixing it into bread dough. Instead of mixing it in at this point, you can let it ferment further, refrigerating it for fourteen to eighteen hours and then letting it stand for another six hours at room temperature before mixing it into the dough. The more "soured" sourdough will give your finished breads a distinct acidity. Even easier, you can retard your loaves (see page 32), refrigerating them for up to twelve hours and leaving them at room temperature for two to four hours before baking. Both methods use the cool environment of the refrigerator to encourage the development of acids that make bread taste more sour.

❋ A MENU OF EUROPEAN STARTERS AND SOURDOUGHS

Bakers in different countries, and even within countries, have different sourdough traditions. In Genzano, Daniel Lattanzi makes his *biga naturale* with white flour, while Mimmo Scalera in Altamura makes his *biga* with golden semolina. It was as important for me to learn how to make Eric Kayser's liquid *levain* as it was to bring back his recipe for buckwheat *bâtards*. I was just as interested in learning how Clemens Walch mixed and maintained his

rye sourdough as I was in his seeded rye bread recipes. For the sake of authenticity, I was determined to make European sourdough recipes available to American home bakers. Throughout this book you will find recipes for five different sourdoughs, so you can make these bakers' breads the way they do.

One kind of sourdough doesn't raise bread more effectively than another. But I do urge you to explore the differences between the sourdoughs. Their individual characteristics will be reflected in your finished breads, providing authentic flavors and textures. You could substitute an equal amount of liquid *levain* for German rye sourdough in the Soulful Farmhouse Rye (page 285), and it would raise your bread just as well. But if you made this substitution, you wouldn't wind up with an authentically earthy, dark, and distinctively acidic bread that's made in Germany with the traditional starter. It's simple and quick to use a sourdough that you already have to get another one going (see page 48), and that's what I suggest you do instead.

Liquid **levain.** This is a relatively new kind of sourdough, a batterlike culture made from wheat flour and water that is easy to mix and easy to measure out. It has gained in popularity in France because it ferments more easily and is easier to mix and measure out than stiff dough *levain*. Liquid *levain* has a fruity taste and a light, bubbly feel all over your tongue. It is mildly and immediately sour.

Stiff dough **levain.** This very firm sourdough is the traditional French bread starter. It ferments very slowly, a plus for French bakers who abhor overly sour bread and want to limit the production of acids in their sourdough. In contrast to liquid *levain*, stiff dough *levain* is mild but earthy and not as light on your tongue. Its flavor is richer and darker and develops slowly in your mouth.

Biga naturale. Although most Italian bakers use a *biga* (starter) made with commercial yeast, bakers from towns like Genzano with strong bread traditions cultivate a *biga* made with wild yeast, refreshing it every night before baking. Fermented more briefly than stiff dough *levain*, it is lighter in texture and flavor than the French starter.

Semolina sourdough.
Bread in Altamura, in Puglia, on the heel of Italy's boot, is made with semolina flour ground from local durum wheat, so naturally the bakers there use a sourdough made with the same flour. They stir some yeast-rich yogurt into the culture to stimulate fermentation. Semolina gives it a wonderfully sweet flavor, with a slight acidity to balance the sweetness.

German rye sourdough.
German rye sourdough is a thick mixture of spring water and stone-ground rye flour that resembles porridge. Rye makes the fastest-fermenting and sourest sourdough. It's strong and pungent, almost like vinegar. German bakers value the sourdough's acidity not just for its flavor but because the abundant acids in the sourdough slow the breakdown of starches that help prevent the finished bread from becoming sticky and heavy.

German spelt sourdough.
Spelt is an ancient variety of wheat, dating at least as far back as the pyramids. Many people who are gluten-intolerant can tolerate bread made with spelt (if you are concerned about wheat allergies, consult your doctor before baking), and it has become very popular in the United States during the last five years. I was excited to see sourdough cultures made with 100 percent spelt in Germany. Not surprisingly, the recipe for spelt sourdough is similar to the recipe for German rye sourdough, both of which I learned at Grimmingers in Munich. Like the bakers there, I used a little of my rye starter to begin my spelt starter, which I now use daily in 100 percent whole spelt bread.

✳ UNDERSTANDING SOURDOUGH RECIPES, STEP BY STEP

The myth that an old sourdough is better than a new one was debunked for me by master baker Jean LeFleur in Paris almost twenty years ago. He told me that he liked to create a new *levain* from scratch several times a year, to ensure that his was never too sour. Instead of asking him or another Parisian baker for a piece of sourdough to get my own culture going, I decided to create one from scratch, using Jean's recipe. The sourdough starters that I use today at Bread Alone all derive from this original culture, a simple mixture of flour, water, and nothing else.

When I was teaching at the American Institute of Baking, in Manhattan, Kansas, my students and I experimented with the many ways that different authorities recommend for getting a sourdough culture going: with raisins, grapes, cooked potatoes, yogurt. We activated cultures containing these ingredients along with a plain mixture of flour and water. After a week of regular refreshments, the starter made with stone-ground flour and spring water was as healthy as the more complicated starters—sometimes healthier, because no contaminants had piggybacked into it on top of an unwashed grape or potato skin. The test confirmed for me that simpler is always better: the fewer variables you have when growing a sourdough, the greater your chance for success. With the exception of semolina sourdough, which traditionally contains a little yogurt, the sourdoughs in these recipes are made with just flour and water. This way, in the unlikely event that your culture doesn't take, you can try again with confidence simply by buying a fresh bag of flour and opening a fresh bottle of spring water.

I know chemists who have devoted their careers to cataloging sourdough cultures, describing their flavor profiles, and calculating their pH (acidity) and TTA (total tritatable acidity). But even if you could send your sourdough to a lab to find out what kind of yeast is in it and how acidic it is, such testing would be beside the point. You can't pick and choose your wild yeast. Your culture will get its unique flavor characteristics from whatever yeast is present in your flour and your air. Say you obtain a sourdough culture from a baker in San Francisco. Once you bring it home and refresh it several times, it will adapt to its new environment. New yeast from your flour and air will begin to grow in the culture. A different mix of bacteria will emerge. To prove this to myself a few years ago, I asked Steve Sullivan, the owner of Acme Bread Company in Berkeley, California, for a small portion of his sourdough. Before I left, we sent it to a lab to see what kind of yeast it contained. I took the sourdough back to Poughkeepsie to use in some classes I was teaching at the Culinary Institute of America. Following Steve's recipe, I baked bread at the school. Within four days, my bread tasted delicious but nothing like Steve's. New lab tests confirmed that the yeast now growing in the culture was different from the yeast living in it on the West Coast. It's possible that particularly strong strains of yeast may survive a journey to a new location and continue to thrive in a culture fed with local flour and air and water. But it's been my experience that local yeast predominates, making every loaf of sourdough bread a local product.

Bakers will debate endlessly about whether or not sourdoughs from certain places are better than sourdoughs from other places. Ultimately it's a matter of taste. I *can* say unequivocally, however, that a hundred-year-old sourdough or one from an acclaimed baker like Steve will not raise bread more effectively than one you can make from scratch in your own kitchen. I can also guarantee that your culture will change over time, reacting to the weather, the year's crop of wheat, and other variables. Think about how grapes grown on the same vine make the same kind of wine year after year but how each vintage has slightly varying flavor characteristics. It's fascinating to observe the changes in your culture and how your changing culture affects your bread.

Home bakers who have already cultivated sourdough often complain of the tremendous amounts of flour that they use and the buckets of sourdough overflowing in their refrigerators. With this in mind, I developed my small-batch sourdough recipes to be as economical as possible. During the cultivation process, you will have to add fresh flour and water every day, and at the end of ten days you will have a rather large amount of sourdough. Once the culture is mature, you'll take just a small portion of it to use

and maintain and discard the rest. Try not to be distressed by the waste. It is the cost of building a culture. Rest assured that once your culture is active, you will not be tossing large quantities of it into the garbage. The recipes are designed so that you will use about half of your active culture for baking bread and refresh the other half for next time. A few tablespoons may be left over after you bake and refresh. Discard this small portion, or put it in a new container, refresh it, and give it to a friend.

Professional bakers use their sourdough every day. To keep it in shape, we also refresh it often. At Bread Alone we feed the sourdoughs at eight in the evening so they're ready to use in the morning, and then we feed them again at noon so we can use them at night. But home bakers may bake only once or twice a week, or even less frequently. So I have adapted the European sourdough recipes with the home baker's schedule in mind. To be sure that your starter has enough strength to raise bread and to keep its acidity to a pleasant minimum, you'll have to refresh it between eight and twelve hours before baking, depending on the particular kind of sourdough you're using. If you want to bake in the morning, refresh your sourdough the night before. If you want to bake in the evening, refresh it when you wake up in the morning. The exception is German rye sourdough, which requires refreshment twelve to twenty-four hours before baking, so it has time to develop the acids that make it more sour than the other starters. If you are using this starter, build a few extra hours into your schedule for fermentation.

The sourdough recipes vary slightly, but the basic method is the same. Just as I walked you through a generic bread recipe, here I'll take you through mixing, cultivating, and maintaining a sourdough. If you understand the basic techniques for creating a sourdough and know the signs for judging the health and activity of your culture, you will be able to make any of the sourdoughs in this book. You don't need any special equipment for making or storing your sourdough. Mix and briefly knead stiff sourdoughs right in a mixing bowl and cover the bowl with plastic. Liquid sourdoughs can be mixed right in a

1-quart container. If the container has a cover, use it. If not, cover the top with plastic wrap.

As for ingredients, use stone-ground organic flour, which contains more fermentation-friendly enzymes than commercially milled flour. Use bottled spring water to activate the culture and feed it. If your tap water has a lot of chlorine and minerals, they might inhibit the growth of the yeast and other microorganisms.

Activate the culture.

To activate the starter, simply pour the water into a bowl or clear plastic container and stir or knead the flour in. Cover it and let it stand at room temperature for twenty-four hours.

Feed the culture.

After twenty-four hours, uncover the culture and observe it. It may have risen very slightly, but it will probably look much the same as it did when you mixed it. Pour additional bottled water from the recipe into the container and stir it in, or use the back of a spoon to break up a stiffer dough. When you do this, the water will turn milky and bubble, signs that the yeast is already active. Stir in more flour. If you are making a stiff dough starter, you'll have to knead it briefly to incorporate the flour. If you are making a liquid starter, just use a spoon to stir until you have a slightly lumpy mixture. Cover your dough and let it stand for another twenty-four hours.

Repeat the feeding.

On the third day, uncover the culture and look at it. It should show some activity at this point. It may have risen anywhere from 50 percent to double its original volume. There may be bubbles on the surface. Inhale and see if you can detect an alcoholic effervescence. Feed it with fresh water and flour as you did the day before. Cover it and let it stand at room temperature for another twenty-four hours.

Test the culture.

On day four, examine the culture for signs that it is ready. Each sourdough recipe describes signs particular to that culture. But all sourdoughs exhibit certain characteristics when they are ready:

EXPANSION. Every sourdough starter will expand as the multiplying yeast produces more and more carbon dioxide. Some starters will double in volume and form a dome. Others won't rise as much but will show cracks on the top surface or froth with tiny air bubbles.

WEBBING. When you break the surface of an active culture with your finger or a paring knife, you will be able to see a network of elastic webbing that forms as the dough rises. With firm starters, there will be large and small bubbles. Liquid starters will have changed from a batter to a glistening, gelatinous mass that is very elastic when you stir it.

AROMA. When you break the surface, an aroma will rise from the starter to tell you that it is ready. It will be musty, fruity, and earthy but not unpleasantly overpowering.

TASTE. Tasting your sourdough is a simple way to gauge its progress. In addition to a mild tartness, you should be able to detect sweet and milky flavors. This complexity will carry over into your bread.

If your culture has these characteristics, it is ready to use. Refresh it according to the recipe instructions and let it stand at room temperature for eight to twelve hours before mixing it into bread dough. If you are not ready to bake, refresh it and let it stand for one hour at room temperature. Then refrigerate it for up to one week. (See Refresh and Store the Culture and Maintain the Sourdough, below, for particulars.) Fermentation will slow down drastically in the cold, preserving your sourdough's bread-raising abilities for when you are ready to bake.

Repeat the feedings if necessary.

Don't worry if your culture doesn't yet exhibit the signs of fermentation. It just needs a few more feedings. Repeat the feeding steps every twenty-four hours for up to six more days. Depending on the kind and quantity of yeast available to them, some cultures take longer to get going than others. Check the culture each day, and as soon as it shows signs that it is active, refresh and maintain it as described in the steps below.

If your culture remains inactive past this point, you will have to start again. Don't be discouraged. Whenever you are dealing with living organisms, whether you are trying to grow plants from seed or cultivating wild yeast and bacteria in a culture of water and flour, things can go wrong. It may have been that your bowl was dirty, your flour old, or your water overly hard, with too many minerals. Try again with fresh ingredients, and in a few days you will probably have a bubbling sourdough as your reward.

Refresh and store the culture.

Louis Pasteur, who first identified yeast fermentation, wrote, "What takes place in fermentation may be compared to what occurs in a plot of land that is not seeded. It soon becomes crowded with various plants and insects that are eventually harmful." If a starter is not refreshed regularly, the bacteria will produce an over-abundance of acids that are harmful to the yeast. To keep the acids in check and the yeast alive, you must add flour and water to your sourdough once it exhibits the signs of activity described above. Refreshment at this point will ensure that your culture is primed for baking, with just the right amount of active yeast and flavorful acids to raise and flavor your bread. Let it stand at room temperature for an hour, and then refrigerate it for up to a week, until you are ready to bake. Refrigeration will slow the rate of fermentation so your culture won't become overgrown.

Maintain the sourdough.

As the sourdough ages over several days in the refrigerator, it loses some of its leavening power and becomes too acidic. Weekly refreshment will keep it alive and healthy so that when you do bake, it will be capable of raising your dough. If your sourdough has been in the refrigerator for a week, it is time to refresh it again, whether or not you plan to bake. Just repeat the steps for refreshment and refrigerate it again for up to one week.

Ideally, you will follow this once-a-week routine, maintaining an optimally healthy starter and baking at your convenience. But if for some reason you don't—you go on vacation, you don't have time, you forget—your sourdough will not suddenly die. Like a houseplant, it will show signs of weakness and ill health. Excessive acid and alcohol buildup will give it a strong vinegary smell; it may release some grayish water; it may get crusty on top or even grow mold. I've left sourdough in the refrigerator for as long as three months without refreshing it, just to see what happens. I thought that some wild yeast would still be living in the old culture, and I was right. With just one refreshment, it became vibrant and ready to use again. If you discover an old sourdough in the back of your refrigerator and want to nurse it back to health, stir any liquid that has accumulated on top back into the dough and transfer it to a clean container. Refresh it twice a day for two to four days or until it shows the signs of activity described on page 46.

Once you have successfully grown a sourdough, it's difficult to run out of it. Even if you accidentally use all of your starter in a double batch of bread dough or throw your culture in the garbage, you can always scrape some culture from the empty container to start a fresh batch. A minute amount—a teaspoon or less—will transform into a bubbling sourdough in a day or two when you feed with the specified amounts of flour and water.

Prepare the sourdough for baking.

Whether or not you have refreshed your sourdough recently, you must refresh it eight to twelve hours before you want to bake to ensure that it is in optimum shape for raising and flavoring bread. Follow the refreshment steps as described. After the sourdough has fermented at room temperature for eight to twelve hours, measure out what you will need for your recipe. Then place a portion of what is left over in a clean container, refresh this portion, and refrigerate it for up to one week for use in the future.

SOURDOUGH SHORTCUT #1

Not all European artisan breads are made with sourdough. Some are made with pre-ferments, mixtures of flour and water activated by packaged yeast. Breads made with pre-ferments are mixed in two steps. First, a small amount of dough made with packaged yeast, water, and flour is mixed and allowed to ferment. Then, several hours later, the pre-ferment is mixed with more flour and water to make the bread dough. A bread made with a pre-ferment will have a more complex and wheatier taste than a bread made from a straight dough, which is a dough mixed with packaged yeast, kneaded, and left to rise in one step. Because of the longer fermentation, a bread made with a pre-ferment will also stay fresher longer than a straight dough bread. A pre-ferment is a convenient way to coax more flavor into the bread without committing to maintaining a sourdough starter.

Poolish is a French-style pre-ferment more commonly known as a sponge. It is a wet, batterlike dough made with packaged yeast and equal parts water and flour. Many modern bread recipes call for a quick sponge that is mixed one to two hours before the bread dough is made. In contrast, *poolish* is typically fermented for four to six hours, long enough for the dough to develop a nutty, slightly fermented flavor. It is used to make breads like the Ganachaud-style *flûte*, which is mild and light but not characterless because of the long-fermenting starter.

Pâte fermentée is a stiff dough made with packaged yeast that ferments for an hour at room temperature and then eight to twelve hours in the refrigerator before being mixed into bread dough. It's about 60 percent water, spongy and cream-colored, just like a stiff dough *levain*, and can be used in place of sourdough in any *pain au levain* recipe. It will raise dough twice as quickly as *levain*, so you'll need to adjust fermentation and proofing times accordingly.

Biga is a firm dough pre-ferment commonly used by Italian bakers. It is made with packaged yeast, two parts flour, and one part water and is left to ferment for one hour at room temperature and then refrigerated for twelve to sixteen hours to develop the flavorful acids.

SOURDOUGH SHORTCUT #2

Even if you want to bake every sourdough bread in this book, there is no need to cultivate and maintain all five traditional sourdough starters. Most European bakers maintain just one sourdough and use it to make a sometimes head-spinning variety of breads. At Tobias Maurer's Stuttgart bakery, two hundred different breads are produced from the same rye sourdough. It is true that the different sourdoughs contribute character to the different breads. It's important to use rye sourdough in traditional German and Austrian ryes, just as it's crucial to use semolina sourdough in Altamura bread. But if you had to cultivate a new starter from scratch every time you wanted to bake a new bread, you probably wouldn't bake as much as you wanted to. And keeping several starters healthy and active would get to be a chore after a while. If you have to keep a calendar to remind yourself to feed the liquid *levain* on Tuesday, then things are getting too complicated.

I recommend keeping just one sourdough going at a time. With a little bit of planning, you can use that culture to jump-start a new kind of sourdough and have the new one ready in forty-eight hours or less. Say you already have a liquid *levain* but you want to make a bread that calls for a rye sourdough. Mix 1/4 cup of the liquid *levain* into the culture on the first day, and the yeast in the *levain* will hasten the fermentation in the rye sourdough. Introducing active yeast this way will produce a mature culture in two days rather than the three to ten that it takes if you start from scratch.

SOURDOUGH SHORTCUT #3

Finally, you can buy packaged dehydrated wild yeast and bacteria from a baking supply company (see

Resources, pages 333–34) to give your sourdough culture a head start. Adding a teaspoon to any of the recipes will pick up the pace of fermentation and mature your sourdough days ahead of when it would be ready if mixed without the dehydrated sourdough supplement. Dehydrated sourdough has a long and venerable history. Archaeologists have discovered that Egyptian bakers raised bread with dehydrated sourdough thousands of years ago. They would roll out sheets of fermented dough and dry them in the sun, then crumble pieces of dried sourdough into their bread dough at their convenience. Today there are sourdough factories in France that cultivate liquid *levain* for the sole purpose of dehydrating it and selling it to professional and home bakers (see pages 333–34) for French dehydrated sourdough sources).

CHAPTER 4

✳

READ THIS FIRST:
FREQUENTLY ASKED QUESTIONS
ABOUT MAKING BREAD

✳

Whenever I visited a new European bakery, I reminded myself not to take anything for granted about making an unfamiliar bread. I'd ask questions about the starter, the flour, the fermentation and proofing times, shaping, baking, and even how long to cool and store the bread. I may not have had any idea how to make a *pane di Como* (page 222) before I visited a bakery on Lake Como to learn some secrets from a northern Italian baker, but I had enough baking experience to know that success is in the details. Although my Italian was rough, I made sure I understood the answers to my questions about how to make the *biga*, how to shape the dough into a round, and how to achieve the bread's signature "crown" before trying to make this bread at home.

One of the great joys of developing the recipes in this book has been sharing them with my students,

both professional and amateur, at the Institute of Culinary Education in New York City and at cooking schools across the country. Trying in turn to answer all *their* questions as we've made these breads together has improved the way I write recipes and has made me a better baker. At the end of each chapter, I've gathered the most common questions my students have asked about particular breads and techniques, along with my best explanations.

Many of the questions are anxious ones. Why isn't my sourdough rising? Why does my dough refuse to be shaped into a baguette? When I turned on the oven, I forgot to put the baking stone in, and now my loaves are ready to bake—what should I do? It has taken me years to develop enough confidence to bake without worry. But I've had enough bread disappointments and outright disasters to understand the feeling in the pit of your stomach when you put a loaf into the oven and peek in fifteen minutes later to see not a high-risen round but a flat pancake. I've watched as all the breads in a full oven at the bakery collapsed simultaneously. I've come into the bakery at night, ready to start shaping loaves, only to discover that my dough has leaped over the sides of overfilled buckets and spread across the floor. Once I accidentally threw out all my sourdough! Each time disaster struck, I'd do what I could to rescue the breads. If it was too late to save them, at least I could figure out what went wrong in each case and try not to make the same mistake the next time. I suggest you take the same practical approach. Do what you can while you are baking to prevent or solve problems, and learn from your mistakes.

Many worries that you will have as you bake are needless. If your dough is sticking to the sides of the bowl, that's fine. Wet doughs very often won't clear the sides, even toward the end of kneading. Some questions crop up as you are baking. If you forgot to mix in the salt with the rest of the ingredients and you've already kneaded the dough, do you have to start over? Once you know the answer—which is no—you can continue, worry-free. And then some questions come up only after you've tasted your bread. Why is it so dense? Perform a postmortem and you can avoid dense bread the next time around by making sure your sourdough is in good shape and by fermenting the dough a little longer.

The following questions and answers are organized to help you from the first steps of baking to the last. You can use them as a troubleshooting guide, consulting them as problems arise. But if you read through them before you begin, you won't worry so much every step of the way, and you may very well be able to avoid altogether the many common mistakes that can compromise your finished breads.

QUESTIONS ABOUT MIXING AND KNEADING BY HAND

. . . .

My dough looks dry. Can I add water?
Stir in 1 tablespoon of water at a time while mixing the dough or spoon it over the dough when knead-ing, and knead until the dough has the consistency described in the recipe. Let the dough stand for 1 minute after mixing in each tablespoon to absorb the water fully. If you weighed and measured everything accurately, you shouldn't need more than a table-spoon or two to achieve the right consistency.

My dough looks very wet and sticky. Is this normal?
Many of the recipes in this book have a higher pro-portion of water than you may be used to. When ade-quately kneaded, they will be soft and very elastic. But they won't be elastic until they have been kneaded for at least 80 percent of the suggested kneading time, so continue to knead until the dough becomes less sticky and more elastic. If you are con-vinced that the dough is unworkable, add 1 table-spoon of flour at a time until the dough is still soft and supple but not excessively sticky.

Is hand-kneading the best or most authen-tic way to knead artisan bread?
Most of the traditional breads in this book have been kneaded by machine since the advent of electricity, so feel free to use your heavy-duty mixer if you are after authenticity. Hand-kneading will help you develop a sense of how the dough should feel as its gluten develops, a sense that I value as an artisan and use on a daily basis when I test machine-kneaded dough for readiness, even though I rarely knead by hand anymore. Some doughs are so wet that they are difficult to knead by hand, in which case I say so in the recipe.

My dough is so wet that when I try to knead it, it sticks to the counter and my hands. Should I add more flour?
Adding flour should be the last resort. Kneading dough is a messy business. Try oiling your hands lightly and applying more oil as necessary. Use a bench scraper to scrape the dough off the counter periodically. If the dough is very difficult to work with, let it rest on the counter for five minutes to give it time to absorb more flour, and then continue.

I've hand-kneaded for the suggested amount of time and my dough still isn't smooth. Am I doing something wrong?

Kneading times will vary depending on your pace and how much pressure you are exerting on the dough. If your dough isn't smooth, continue kneading for three- to five- minute stretches, resting in between, until it is smooth. Don't worry about overkneading the dough.

Just as I finished kneading, I realized I forgot to add the salt. What should I do?

Just flatten the dough on the counter and sprinkle on the salt. Then knead for an additional few minutes to distribute the salt (or any other ingredient you may have forgotten, such as olives, nuts, or dried fruit).

QUESTIONS ABOUT
MACHINE MIXING AND KNEADING

. . . .

What should I do if my dough is so dry that it won't come together into a ball?

Stir in 1 tablespoon of water at a time until the dough comes together. Let the dough stand for one minute after you've kneaded in a tablespoon of water, to give the flour a chance to absorb it fully. An extra tablespoon or two should adequately hydrate the dough.

My dough is very wet, almost soupy-looking. Should I add more flour?

If the recipe describes the dough as "wet," don't worry and continue to knead until it becomes smooth and shiny. Otherwise, you can add flour 1 tablespoon at a time until the dough is still fairly soft but not as sticky.

My dough is so wet that it is sticking to the sides of the mixing bowl. Is this normal?

Turn off the mixer and scrape down the sides of the bowl once or twice to ensure even kneading. To encourage the dough to become a more cohesive mass, you can increase the mixing speed slightly. But not all bread doughs will clear the sides of the bowl, as the recipes indicate.

What should I do if the dough is climbing up the dough hook?

Just turn off the mixer periodically and scrape the dough back down into the bowl. The important thing is to make sure that none of the dough gets stuck at the top of the hook, or it might not be kneaded adequately.

Once my dough has come together, what should I do about any ingredients (extra flour, nuts, olive pieces) that remain unincorporated and at the bottom of the bowl?

To incorporate these ingredients, turn off the mixer and scrape them into the center of the dough. Or take the dough out of the bowl, scrape the ingredients on top, and knead by hand for a minute or two.

My machine-kneaded dough doesn't look smooth. Should I let it go in the machine a little longer?

Just continue to knead the dough in the machine until it reaches the described consistency. Or scrape the dough out of the bowl and knead it by hand for a minute or two until it is smooth.

I kneaded my dough by machine until it was smooth, then realized I had forgotten to add the salt. Can I just add it to the bowl and continue to knead?

Machine mixers are very effective at distributing ingredients quickly. Just add it the bowl and knead for an additional minute or two to incorporate.

QUESTIONS ABOUT
FERMENTATION

. . . .

Why hasn't my dough doubled in size during the prescribed fermentation time?

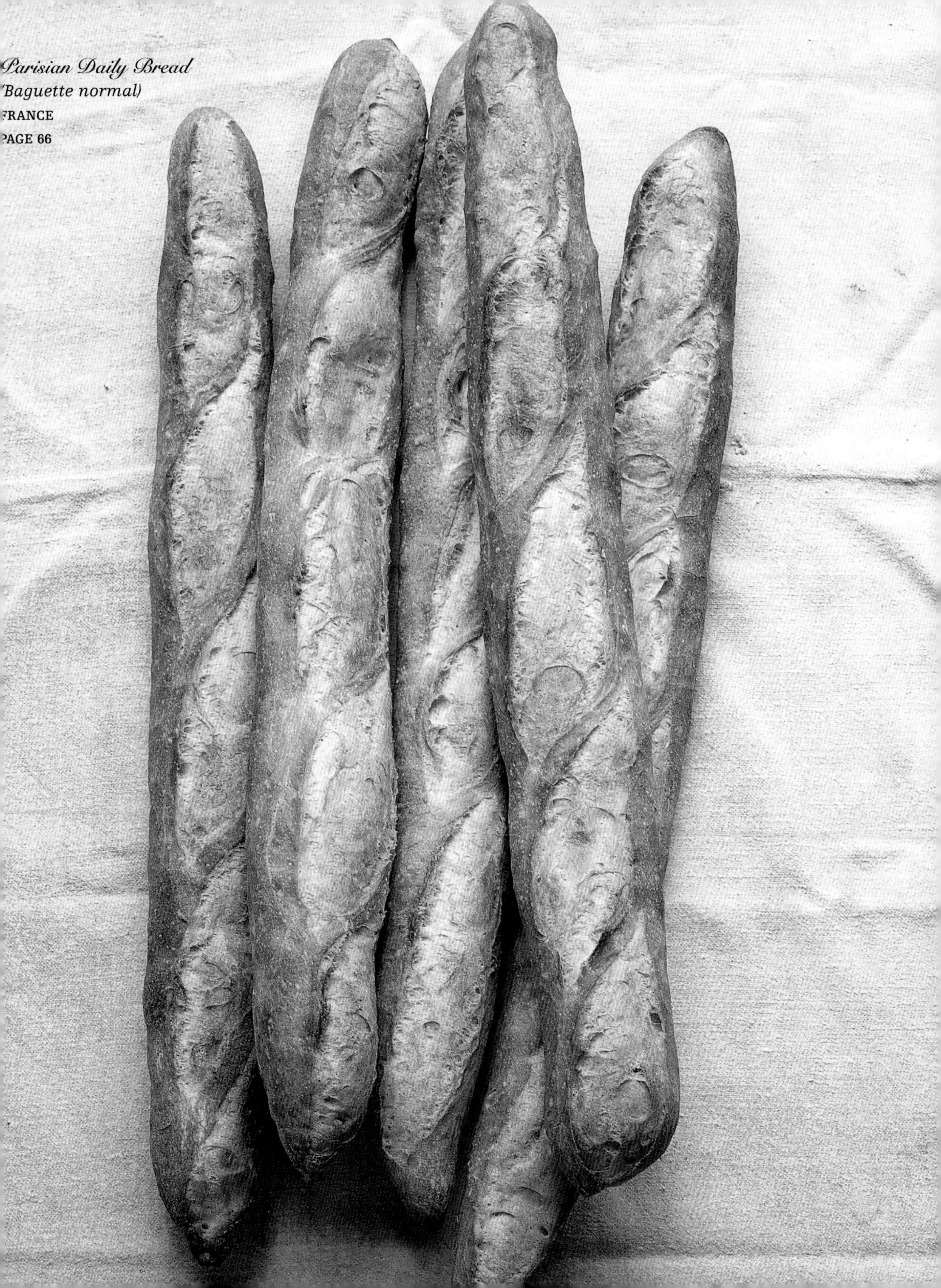

Parisian Daily Bread
(Baguette normal)
FRANCE
PAGE 66

Flaxseed Levain

(Pain au levain aux graines de lin)

FRANCE

PAGE 129

Buckwheat Bâtards
(Paline)
FRANCE
PAGE 81

Top: *Stiff Dough Levain,*
undeveloped, developed, page 111
Middle: *Rye Starter,*
undeveloped, developed, page 275
Bottom: *Liquid Levain,*
undeveloped, developed, page 76

*Chocolate Sourdough Croissants
(Croissants sur levain
liquide au chocolat)*
FRANCE
PAGE 99

Raisin-Nut Levain
(*Pain au levain aux noix et raisins*)
FRANCE
PAGE 132

French Walnut Bread
(Pain au levain complet aux noix)
FRANCE
PAGE 122

Unbaked scored breads

Baked scored breads

It may be a little cool in your kitchen, which will lead to a slower than normal fermentation period. Move the bowl to a warmer spot, 75 to 80 degrees if possible, and away from drafts. Give it a turn (see page 30) to invigorate the yeast. Check on it every half-hour or so until it has doubled.

My dough has doubled in size in less than the lower end of the recommended fermentation time. Should I just continue with the recipe?
If it's a very warm day, then yes, just continue with the recipe. But if it is average to cool in your kitchen, such quick doubling indicates a very active sourdough, not necessarily overfermentation. Give the dough a turn (see page 30) and continue to let it rise until the minimum amount of time indicated in the recipe has elapsed.

What should I do if my dough has risen to the top of the bowl and is sticking to the plastic wrap, with time still left to go according to the recipe?
Gently peel away the plastic wrap, leaving as much dough in the bowl as possible. Then use a rubber spatula to scrape the dough gently into a larger lightly oiled bowl, cover with fresh plastic wrap, and let it rise for the minimum amount of time in the recipe. Next time make sure to choose a bowl that's more than double the size of your dough.

My dough took much longer than I expected to ferment fully, and now I don't have time to shape it, let it proof, and bake it before I have to leave the house. What should I do?
Give the dough a turn, cover the bowl with plastic wrap, and refrigerate it for up to twelve hours (see page 32). When you are ready to proceed with the recipe, divide and shape the dough while it is cold and continue as directed. Proofing time will probably be longer than described in the recipe because the dough will take a while to come to room temperature: at least one hour, but no more than two.

QUESTIONS ABOUT DIVIDING AND SHAPING

. . . .

My dough is sticking to the counter and the bench scraper, making it difficult for me to divide it. Any suggestions?
Lightly flour the countertop and the top of the dough. Then dip the bench scraper into flour before cutting. Press the blade decisively into the dough and in one swift motion separate one piece from the other.

I'm not going to get as many rolls (or breadsticks or pretzels) out of my dough as the recipe indicates. Did I do something wrong?
If you are measuring by eye, you may be cutting your pieces a little larger than I recommend. That's fine—just be sure to adjust the baking time so that the rolls are baked through. Or use a scale to measure out the pieces so that they are all equal in weight. If you measured your ingredients instead of weighing them, or if you weighed inaccurately, you may come up with less (or more) dough than the recipe indicates.

How can I shape the dough if it keeps sticking to the counter?
A light dusting of flour on the counter should prevent the dough from sticking long enough for you to shape it. Avoid overhandling the dough, even if it means that your bread is imperfectly shaped.

My dough keeps slipping from my hands as I try to shape it. How can I get a better hold on it?
Too much flour on the counter will cause slipping. Brush away excess flour so that you can use friction to shape your loaves.

What should I do when the nuts, olives, or dried fruits fall out of the dough during shaping?
Just tuck them back in and continue. As the dough

proofs and bakes, it will surround these ingredients and trap them.

The seam on my baguette keeps popping open. How can I get it to stay closed?
Too much flour is probably keeping the two sides of the seam from sticking together. Use a pastry brush or your fingers to brush away excess flour from the seam and pinch it closed with the heel of your hand. Make sure you go down the full length of the baguette.

I'm not a perfectionist, but I'm terribly dissatisfied with the shape of my loaves. Can I try again?
It's better to let the loaves proof as is. As they rise, they will gain some uniformity. If you must, let the dough rest for ten minutes and then shape it again. But reshape only once, or you'll risk deflating the dough to the point that it won't rise well in the oven.

QUESTIONS ABOUT PROOFING

. . . .

Why haven't my loaves risen as described in the recipe, when they've been proofing for the designated amount of time?
The most likely reason is that your kitchen is cooler than recommended. Move them to a warmer spot (75 to 80 degrees) and continue to let them rise, checking them every half-hour.

My loaves have taken less time than indicated to rise. Should I let them stand for the minimum proofing time recommended?
It's sometimes hard to judge when loaves have risen to one and a half times their size. Since underproofing will compromise the crumb structure of your bread and negatively affect its ability to rise in the oven, be patient. Unless the loaves look so light that

they are in danger of collapsing, let them stand for the minimum proofing time suggested and then bake them.

Why have my loaves spread out instead of puffing up during proofing?
Either your dough was underkneaded (its structure was not developed enough to trap and hold rising gases) or your dough was proofed too long. For underdeveloped loaves, unfortunately, there is nothing you can do. This is a learning moment for you. Overproofed loaves can be reclaimed. Reshape them and proof them for half the recommended proofing time before baking, until they look pillowy but still have body.

My loaves have spread during proofing and are now stuck together. Should I just leave them this way?
No. Gently separate them with a sharp knife. Don't worry if they deflate slightly. Next time be sure to leave adequate space between the loaves.

My loaves are stuck to the banneton. What's the best way to get them out?
Gently pry them away from the linen with a spatula or the tips of your fingers. Next time use more flour in the banneton.

During proofing, my loaves stuck to the plastic wrap that was covering them. How should I take the plastic off? What's the best way to avoid this next time?
Gently peel the plastic from the loaves. They may deflate slightly. Next time sift some flour over the loaves and make sure the plastic wrap is loosely draped, not tightly wrapping the loaves.

I forgot to cover my loaves after I set them out to proof, and their surfaces are dried out. What should I do?
To rehydrate them before baking, lightly mist them with water, using a water spritzer. Otherwise, the

crusts of the baked breads may have a crackly look, like alligator skin. The rise and quality of the bread won't be affected.

My loaves are fully proofed, but I've been called out of the house on an emergency. What should I do?
Lightly cover them with plastic wrap and refrigerate them for up to twelve hours. Two to three hours before you are ready to bake, take them out of the refrigerator and let them come to room temperature. Then bake them as directed.

QUESTIONS ABOUT SCORING

. . . .

How can I slash my loaves cleanly, without getting my blade caught in the sticky dough?
Scoring takes practice. Make sure your knife or razor blade is very sharp, and use a swift, unhesitating motion. Stopping in the middle is a sure way to get stuck.

Why did my loaves deflate when I scored them? Was my scoring technique flawed?
It's more likely that your loaves were overproofed. When you ran the blade through the surface of the dough, it let out the air in the air cells, as if they were mini-balloons. Bake the loaves right away. They won't rise as high or look as beautiful as properly proofed loaves, but they'll taste fine.

QUESTIONS ABOUT BAKING

. . . .

How can I prevent my loaves from sticking to the peel?

This is one of the most annoying problems a home baker faces. After doing everything right, you ruin the shape and rise of your loaves trying to get them off the peel. You can sidestep this problem altogether by covering your peel with parchment paper and just sliding the paper, with the loaves on top, right from the peel into the oven. When they're done baking, slide them, still on the parchment, onto wire racks to cool slightly. They'll easily come off the parchment five minutes out of the oven.

Is there anything I can do if I realize after I put my loaves in the oven that I forgot to score them?
Not this time. The dough will very likely rupture in spots because of the pressure from the expanding gases inside. Use your mistake as an opportunity to observe uncontrolled oven spring. Enjoy the finished bread. It will taste fine, even if it has random fissures and burst bubbles.

Five minutes after I put the loaves in the oven, I noticed my measuring cup full of ice cubes on the counter. Is it too late to steam the loaves?
Go ahead and add the ice, if the breads have not yet been baking for fifteen minutes. After fifteen minutes, there's no point in trying to keep the crust soft by steaming. The bread has done all of its rising and the yeast has almost entirely died off in the heat of the oven.

My loaves are fully proofed, and I just realized that I forgot to turn on the oven. What should I do?
Suspend proofing by putting the loaves in the refrigerator while heating the oven for an hour. Don't forget to preheat the baking stone and cast-iron skillet too. If you are not using a baking stone, just leave the breads on the counter for an additional fifteen minutes while the oven heats up.

My bread is not finished baking but the

edges are scorching. Should I turn down the heat?

You can turn the oven down 25 degrees and rotate the loaves. There may be hot spots in your oven that are coloring parts of the bread more quickly than others. But remember, very dark browning and even blackening is desirable in some breads, especially very large rounds, and a mark of how well they are baked.

Should I take my loaf out of the oven before the time specified in the recipe if it looks very brown?

Resist taking your loaves out of the oven before the time given in the recipe. Remember that bread bakes from the outside in, and you can't judge the doneness of the interior by the appearance of the crust. Check the interior temperature with an instant-read thermometer. It should be 200 degrees. Then leave the bread in for an additional five minutes at the very least, to ensure that the interior has time to dry out and solidify.

As my loaves rose in the oven, they stuck together. Should I wait until they're out to tear them apart?

No. If they bake through stuck together, the parts of the loaves that are touching won't bake as quickly as the rest of the breads. For even baking, it's better to separate them just after they are set, twenty to thirty minutes depending on their size, and finish baking them apart.

My bread has been in the oven for as long as you suggest but it's still not as dark as you describe. Will the inside dry out if I continue to bake it until it's well browned?

My idea of dark may be your idea of golden. The interior of the bread can dry out, so if you've tested the temperature of your oven and know that it's accurate, take the bread out at the high end of the prescribed baking time.

QUESTIONS ABOUT FINISHED BREAD

. . . .

The worst has happened—my loaf didn't rise in the oven. It's flat. Why?

It may be that you underkneaded and didn't develop enough air cells to be filled during baking. It's also possible that your dough was too soft—did you use the right kind of flour, with an adequate amount of protein? Overproofing can also cause flatness.

Why are there seams in my baguette?

To shape a baguette, you have to fold the dough several times, creating a series of seams. If you don't seal up the seams tightly, they may be visible in the finished bread. Overly stiff doughs are more difficult to seal up, so if you added too much flour during kneading, that might be the cause of the visible seams. Too much flour on the counter during shaping will also dry out the edges of the dough and make the seams difficult to seal.

I scored my loaf, but it didn't blossom attractively in the oven. Why didn't it open up?

The most likely explanation is that you cut too deep, destroying the gluten structure. Make sure that your score is no more than 1/4 inch deep. Kneading the dough sufficiently will also ensure that there's enough structural integrity to open up your score in the oven.

Why did my dough split beyond the score? How can I gain control of the dough's oven spring next time?

If your loaves were underproofed, they didn't expand enough before going into the oven, so when they hit the heat of the oven they were more explosive, which accounts for the split. Make sure to proof the dough adequately next time, and its oven spring will be more controlled and the score marks more beautiful.

I was expecting light and bubbly bread, but mine turned out heavy and dense. What did I do wrong?

There are a couple of possibilities. If you used sourdough, it may not have been as active as it should have been. Did you refresh it eight to twelve hours before baking? Make sure to do so next time. Underfermenting and underproofing the dough can also result in heaviness, so next time let the dough ferment and proof for the full recommended times.

When I cut into my bread, I saw long troughs running through it. Each slice has a gaping hole. Why did this happen and what can I do to prevent it next time?

Ferment the dough fully and proof it completely before baking. Underproofed dough often has a lot of yeast activity in the center, which results in large holes. Loose shaping can also create air pockets that become troughs in the oven, so make sure that your shaping technique is nice and tight.

I was disappointed with the small, uniform holes in my loaf. How can I get larger, uneven holes in the crumb next time?

Wet doughs produce breads with light, bubbly crumbs. Perhaps you kneaded too much flour into the dough. Underfermenting and underproofing can also result in a tight, uniform crumb.

The crust of my bread was pale, even though I baked the bread longer than you suggested. Why couldn't I get it to brown?

Did you forget to add the salt to the dough? Saltless Tuscan Bread has a blond crust for this reason. Did you forget to add the ice cubes to the oven? Steam promotes a shiny brown crust. It may simply be that you didn't ferment and proof your dough long enough for it to develop the sugars needed for proper crust caramelization.

My sourdough bread is a little too sour for my taste. What can I do?

There are a few things you can do to make your bread less sour. Try letting your sourdough starter rise in the refrigerator and use it straight from the refrigerator when it has risen sufficiently. The colder rise will inhibit the development of too much acid. Or you could try using a little less (about 10 percent less) sourdough starter in the dough, which won't affect the rise but will make a mellower bread. Or ferment the sourdough for a shorter period of time. It doesn't have to smell and taste too sour to be ready to use. As long as it is active, it will raise your bread.

QUESTIONS ABOUT STARTERS AND SOURDOUGHS

. . . .

POOLISH AND *BIGA* QUESTIONS

Can I stir more water into my *poolish* or *biga* if it looks too dry?

Different brands and batches of flour can vary widely in their ability to absorb water. If your *poolish* or *biga* looks too dry, it may be that your flour can hold more water than the norm. Stir or knead in 1 teaspoon of water at a time until it has the consistency described in the recipe.

Can I stir in more flour if it looks too wet?

Stir or knead in 1 teaspoon of flour at a time until it has the consistency described in the recipe.

I've let my *poolish/biga* ferment for the time indicated in the recipe, and it hasn't risen at all.

Your yeast may be old or may have been compromised by moisture. Start again with a new package of yeast.

My *poolish/biga* rose just a little bit, but not as described in the recipe. Should I go ahead and use it?

Your culture may be sluggish because of the cool temperature in your kitchen or the coolness of your water and flour. Move the bowl to a warmer spot in your kitchen and let the *poolish* or *biga* continue to ferment until it looks the way the recipe describes.

My *poolish/biga* looks just right, but now I realize that I don't have time to bake the bread. Will it keep for a few hours while I run out of the house?
Suspend fermentation by refrigerating the *poolish/biga*. Use it within eight to twelve hours and it will be fine.

SOURDOUGH QUESTIONS

It's been three days since I prepared my sourdough culture, and it has not risen at all and shows no signs of activity. Should I throw it out and start over again?
Don't give up yet. Depending on your ingredients and the conditions in your kitchen, it can take as long as five days to see anything happening. That doesn't mean that there's no activity. Fermentation is undetectable in the early stages. Give it another day or two, modifying your feeding technique to give the culture a jump start. Transfer the mixture to a clean container. Increase the number of refreshments from once to twice a day. Use water that's warm (85 to 95 degrees) rather than room temperature. Use organic, stone-ground flour if you've been using a supermarket brand, or buy a fresh bag of flour if you've been using an old bag. Switch to bottled water if you're using tap water. If after three more days there's still no activity, throw out the mixture and start over again, following these guidelines.

My sourdough is doing something but doesn't look as active as it should.
To encourage more activity, move the container to a warmer spot in the kitchen (75 to 80 degrees). You can also feed it twice a day instead of once, using stone-ground organic flour, and switch to bottled spring water if you've been using tap water, since tap water may contain minerals and chlorine that are inhibiting yeast growth.

If my sourdough doesn't smell sour, should I worry?
As long as it's showing other signs of activity, it's fine. The characteristic sour smell develops only as the lactobacilli in the culture mature, so you may be able to observe the yeast at work, raising the bread, but have to wait several additional hours to smell the acids given off by the bacteria in the culture.

My sourdough smells *terrible.* Is this normal?
A mild aroma is normal, but if your sourdough smells unpleasantly sour or off, it may have produced an overabundance of acids. To correct this imbalance, discard half your culture and then refresh the remaining half according to the recipe directions.

My sourdough rose beautifully, but when I checked on it a half-hour later, it had deflated. Is it ruined?
No. As long as you've refreshed it in the last eight to twelve hours, it will raise your bread even if it looks deflated. If, however, you have left it on the counter for longer than twelve hours, you should give it another feeding and let it ferment before using it.

According to the recipe description, my sourdough is ready to use. But I have no time to bake. Will I have to refresh it again when I'm ready in a few hours?
If you keep your primed sourdough in the refrigerator for up to six hours, you can use it as is. Or refresh it according to the recipe instructions and refrigerate it for up to one week to maintain the culture. Then, eight to twelve hours before you are ready to bake, refresh it once more.

When I took my sourdough out of the refrigerator this morning, it had a layer of liquid on top. What is this, and does it mean there's something wrong with the culture?

Some sourdough cultures will separate as they stand. Just stir the liquid back into the sourdough and refresh as directed.

I was out of town for three weeks, and when I took my sourdough out of the refrig-erator to refresh it, I saw mold growing on it. Can I save it?

Simply scrape off the mold with a teaspoon and feed the culture twice a day for three days, and it will be fine.

CHAPTER 5

✳

FROM *BAGUETTE NORMAL* TO ERIC KAYSER'S CUTTING-EDGE *BÂTARDS*: REAL PARISIAN BREADS, OLD AND NEW

✳

It was in Paris more than twenty years ago, after a night spent observing the action in a typical basement bakery, that I decided to become a baker myself. When my bakery was in its infancy, I returned many times to Paris to learn old recipes and techniques from my mentors there, among them Basil Kamir and Bernard Ganachaud. Years later I was inspired anew by the iconoclastic Parisian baker Eric Kayser and his bold reworking of the recipe for *levain*, the traditional sourdough starter used by French bakers for hundreds of years. This chapter gathers together recipes for my favorite breads from these bakers. Their stories illustrate the commitment to craftsmanship that exists across the board in Paris, connecting someone like Basil, who is so devoted to tradition that he bakes his baguettes in a wood-fired oven built in 1850 by France's most venerable mason, to Eric, who invented a machine called the *fermento-levain* to bring sourdough baking into the twenty-first century. Each baker, in his own way, has made it his mission to manage the baking process so meticulously that the success of his loaves is guaranteed. You will be amazed that these artisans are able to conjure such different breads using the same or similar ingredients. I've learned from them—and you will too—the importance of consistency and care in baking both heirloom and boldly original loaves.

I gained most of my practical knowledge about the rhythms and routines of French baking at Le Moulin de la Vierge, the shop owned by my good friend Basil Kamir. Like me, Basil didn't set out to be a professional baker. He was a young music promoter with an office in an old Beaux Arts building that had once been a bakery. When the building was threatened by redevelopment, he found out that the only way to save it from the wrecking ball was to resurrect the antique wood-fired oven in its basement and reopen it as a *boulangerie*. Adapting to this extraordinary circumstance, he convinced a wonderful old-time baker, Jean LeFleur, to come out of retirement to teach him the trade. Over the course of just a few years, Basil left the music business behind and reinvented himself as a traditional *boulanger*. He was several steps ahead of me in terms of professional development, experienced enough to be my mentor but sharing my neophyte's fascination with traditional bread.

I must have made thirty trips to Basil's bakery over the years. After working a full day at Bread Alone, I would hop on the red-eye from Kennedy and Basil would pick me up at Charles de Gaulle airport at 5:15 A.M. He was always driving a van filled with freshly baked, unwrapped loaves, which we would then deliver on the way back into the city. After the deliveries and errands and a stop to sip espresso with Cognac in a smoky café, he would drop me off at the Hotel du Monaco in the student quarter near the place de la Sorbonne, where I would sleep until evening. At midnight I'd taxi over to Le Moulin de la Vierge and let myself in with the key hidden in a planter under the front window. From the depths of the bakery came the slow, pulsing sound of the electric mixer. I'd change in the storeroom and make my way down the dark, steep stairway and into the narrow bakery, as dimly lit as a Rembrandt painting. The tall brick face of the old hearth oven dominated the room, its cast-iron door closed and stone cold. Patrice, one of Basil's bakers, was alone, mixing 30-pound batches of dough. From his eyelashes to the hair on his bare calves, he was covered with the special stone-ground organic flour Basil insisted on using. Patrice held out his wrist for me to shake, the baker's standard gesture of greeting when his hands are sticky with dough.

I'd get to work flouring the insides of 160 bannetons, loading the oven's firebox with wood, and adjusting the *gueulard*, the movable cast-iron hood sitting on the oven's floor, to direct the heat into the cave-deep dome. Then I'd stand with Patrice at the workbench, laden with 160 mounds of dough. To the squawk of North African pop music coming from a flour-covered transistor radio (almost every Parisian bakery I've ever visited seems to have one, its antenna straining to pick up a signal from somewhere aboveground), we'd round one piece after another into a boule and place each one in a ban-

neton. By the time we were ready to shape the baguettes, Jean had usually arrived. I watched from the corner of my eye as he massaged and folded a piece of dough into a taut cylinder and rolled it back and forth under his palms, effortlessly stretching it into a baguette. No matter how fast I moved, I could manage to shape only one baguette in the time he shaped four. Even after all these years, I still don't think that I've shaped a single baguette as flawlessly as Jean shaped every one of his.

Patrice proclaimed the oven ready, and we flipped the boules out of their bannetons onto the 14-foot-long wooden peel, two at a time. We scored them with quick slashes of the *lame*, a razor blade clipped onto a thin metal handle. Then, with incredible nonchalance and finesse, Patrice slid them into the 16-foot-deep oven and slid out the peel in a split second. After they were all in the oven, he clamped the iron door shut and twisted the valve on the copper pipe to send water into a cast-iron tray inside the brick walls. The oven hissed and steam billowed out the door's seams. Each night we reheated the oven five times and baked a thousand loaves, two hundred at a time.

Basil arrived in the morning, as we were finishing up, and clambered down the stairs. He'd tease, "How's the American baker doing? Did he learn anything this time?" Here is a partial list: I learned how to look at the dough and judge whether or not it had been kneaded enough, how to take a piece of the stiff dough *levain* from the cooler and taste it to see if it had developed enough acidity, how to dust the bench with just the right amount of flour, how to shape a piece of dough into a perfect torpedo in two or three strokes and to form a boule with two turns of the wrist, how to touch the dough to tell when it was sufficiently proofed and ready to bake. Over the course of many nights, I internalized the rhythms that made Basil's bakery run so smoothly. I learned not to focus on a particular batch of dough but to make my routine so consistent that the loaves from one batch to the next were indistinguishable from each other. Learning to produce hundreds of consistently good loaves a night was one aspect of my informal Parisian apprenticeship.

Parisian Daily Bread (page 66), which I learned how to make at Le Moulin de la Vierge, takes just four hours from start to finish. Because of this bread, Basil and his daytime bakers live by a four-hour cycle, producing a fresh batch beginning in the early morning and then every four hours after that until the bakery closes at 8 P.M. It's a straight dough, meaning that it's raised with packaged yeast that's mixed right in with the flour and water rather than with a pre-ferment or *levain*. I'm pleased that it's the first bread recipe in this book, because not only is it one of the simplest and quickest to make, but it also highlights the simple, clean flavor of wheat without the added complexity of *poolish* or sourdough. Virtually every Parisian bakery offers a version of this bread, along with *pain au levain* and other sourdough breads, just as ice cream shops always stock plain vanilla along with rocky road and rum raisin.

Once I had learned how to make the bread baked daily by the mass of Parisian bakers (and in its ideal form by Basil), I wanted to learn how some bakers make bread so unique that it becomes their signature. I sought out Bernard Ganachaud, a living legend among bakers in France for developing a unique baguette called *la flûte gana* (page 70), a play on his name. Bernard was one of the first Parisian bakers to understand that the baguette was endangered by the compromises of industrialization. In the years immediately following World War II, traditional bread started to lose ground to low-quality bread produced at commercial bakeries. As a young baker in the 1960s, he maintained the old ways, even as old bakeries struggled. In the 1970s, when so many shops had gone out of business that artisan baking was truly endangered in Paris, he became an outspoken advocate for old-fashioned bread. He proudly baked with stone-ground flour and single-handedly renewed interest in the old technique of using *poolish*, a sponge starter, which gave his baguettes a clean, wheaty flavor and a longer shelf life than Parisian Daily Bread, but without any of the acidity of sourdough.

A gentlemanly fellow with a slight build and a silver mustache, Bernard was always immaculately dressed in a pressed white uniform with the red-white-and-blue-striped collar of a Meilleur Ouvrier de France (MOF), the honor earned by France's best bakers. His gleaming, tiled workroom looked more like a spotless bistro than a bakery. It was stylish and elegant, like his bread. When I interviewed him, he insisted that there was no secret to making his unique baguettes, "just discipline and care to do it right every day." His perfectly fermented *poolish*, the beneficiary of this care, is what made his loaves nutty and sweet, with a hint of fresh cream.

According to baking folklore, the technique was introduced in France by Polish bakers hundreds of years ago, hence the name. Compared with the stiff and fast-rising sponges familiar to American bakers, *poolish* contains more water and much less yeast. In contrast to regular sponges, which typically ferment for an hour or two, *poolish* needs to ferment for six to eight hours before it is ready to use. The longer fermentation coaxes as much flavor as possible from the wheat, giving the bread a fresh wheaty taste with subtly earthy undertones. The relatively large amount of *poolish* needed to raise the dough gives the bread its crackerlike crust and glossy crumb. Bernard and his bakers watched the *poolish* closely as it fermented. Indeed, his matter-of-factness about the starter concealed an obsessive concern. The *poolish* sat in a clear plastic tub on wheels. The tub was fitted with a thermometer so the bakers could be certain that the *poolish*'s temperature remained constant at 23 degrees Celsius. The tub was also fitted with a timer that went off after six hours. Bernard let the *poolish* ferment until it rose precisely to the same mark on the tub every time, no more and no less.

After shaping his dough into elegant thin baguettes, or *flûtes*, Bernard literally signed each one of them with a special score, a long slash rather than the three or four short cuts that mark conventional baguettes. His score isn't made just for show. When bread dough hits the hot oven, it is going to expand one way or another. Scoring is the baker's technique for directing that expansion, so it can rise to its full potential. Bernard's long score allows the loaf to expand uniformly and beautifully, and the score itself bakes up into a delicious walnut-brown ridge, my favorite part to eat. Many years after I first met Bernard, I stopped in the remote Auvergne region in central France. I was stunned to see this same score on baguettes hundreds of miles from 150 rue de Ménilmontant, where Bernard's bakery is located. I asked the baker, Amandio Pimenta, where he learned the score. "From a man who is my idol," he replied. "Bernard Ganachaud." Like Amandio's baguettes, my *flûte* recipe (page 70) is a tribute to Bernard. It utilizes a *poolish* and includes instructions for his signature slash. He spent many hours explaining to me the right and wrong ways to make a baguette, but he never divulged the special flour blend he uses to make his *flûtes*, and I would never ask. Some knowledge is proprietary, after all! So I've made my best guess about his formula (a touch of corn flour, I think). The result will get you pretty close to the real thing without having to travel to his namesake *boulangerie*.

The resurgence of traditional baking in Paris in the 1980s led some younger artisans to experiment with tradition. By far the most revolutionary of this breed was Eric Kayser, who pioneered the use of liquid *levain*, the first new leavening method to be introduced to French baking in over a hundred years. Until Eric came onto the scene, Parisian artisan bakers were making their sourdough baguettes with a mild, firm sourdough starter called *levain*. Bakers working without the benefit of modern heating and refrigeration had developed the technique for cultivating a stiff dough *levain*. After it is mixed, the starter is placed in the coolest part of the bakery, often a low shelf in the basement. Without much water, fermentation proceeds slowly, so there's little chance of the sourdough's becoming too sour and losing its leavening capability before the baker has a chance to refresh it. The results are spectacular—the mild sourdough raises and flavors dough to perfection, giving finished breads a glossy, even crumb with just a hint of acidity. But the method has its inconvenient aspects. Changes in temperature in the bakery will affect the rate of fermentation, so as the weather changes from day to day and season to season, the baker has to watch the starter as well as the

clock to gauge its readiness. Maintaining the starter requires some muscle. To keep it fresh, the baker has to knead new flour into the stiff *levain*.

Eric Kayser realized that bakers today could cultivate sourdough and control its fermentation more easily than their forebears if they used modern technology. He came up with a recipe for a sourdough starter made with a much higher proportion of water than was traditional. At the same time he helped develop and popularize the *fermento-levain*, a tank that enables bakers to mix fresh flour into a liquid sourdough and control its temperature with the turn of a dial. With the help of the machine, it's easy to prevent the fast-fermenting liquid from becoming too sour and losing its leavening capability. I first met Eric in the early 1990s at the EuroPain trade show, where he was demonstrating the *fermento-levain*. Bakers were immediately won over by this ingenious method for making foolproof sourdough and the breads it produced—loaves with porous crumbs and super-caramelized crusts. Young bakers bought the machine in droves and championed liquid sourdough as the wave of the future. I bought one myself so I could add liquid *levain* to my repertoire of sourdough starters at Bread Alone. I chose liquid *levain* as the first sourdough starter in this book precisely because it is so easy to mix and maintain—it's a perfect recipe for someone who has never cultivated a sourdough culture before.

Eric went on to develop a repertoire of brand-new breads inspired by traditional recipes, using liquid *levain*. He then opened a string of phenomenally successful bakeries to feature them. His recipes have a large percentage of liquid *levain*, about 500 grams for every kilo of flour. The *levain* gives the breads a sparklingly fresh taste and unique cell structure. Because doughs made with liquid *levain* have a higher percentage of water than doughs made with stiff dough *levain*, there is more starch gelatinization as the bread bakes, resulting in a gleaming, shiny crumb. It's a lighter style of bread than traditional *pain au levain*, not better but new and different, although still very much in the spirit of Parisian bread tradition.

Eric's influence on contemporary French baking

has been phenomenal. Today he is a food celebrity in France on a par with the star chef Alain Ducasse. The recipe for Buckwheat *Bâtard* (page 81) in this chapter is unique to Eric. It is rustic but elegantly shaped, with complex, unconventional flavors. The dough contains his trademark liquid sourdough starter and is itself very wet. Its crumb is open, its crust a deep, sweet brown. Many young artisan bakers have followed Eric's lead, embracing liquid *levain* as a quick and convenient alternative to the traditional stiff dough *levain* for producing excellent French bread. This chapter ends with recipes for two traditional Parisian breads, Old World Baguette Redux (page 85) and French Country Boule (page 90), updated because they are raised with a liquid *levain*. These breads are just like the breads you'll find in Paris today, made by young French artisans with one eye on the past and one on the future. Along with Basil's Parisian daily bread, Bernard's *flûte gana*, and Eric Kayser's buckwheat *bâtard*, they represent Parisian bread-crafting in its highest form and are among the loaves I couldn't live without.

☀ KITCHEN NOTES: BAKING PARISIAN BREAD AT HOME

In Paris, I learned how precise good bakers have to be to produce consistently excellent bread. Basil Kamir's clockwork routine for making baguettes, Bernard Ganachaud's meticulous handling of the *poolish*, and Eric Kayser's high-tech solution for foolproof *levain*—their constant care proves that great bread is in the details. Here are a few simple suggestions about techniques and ingredients, culled from my observations of Parisian artisan bakers. None of them may seem impressive on its own, but taken together they have helped me produce authentic Parisian-style bread at home.

A simple straight dough produces an authentic parisian baguette. Baguettes made with instant yeast are not only easy and quick to prepare, but they are authentically Parisian. All over the city, bakers turn out these legendary light, wheaty baguettes every four hours, and smart Parisians time their shopping so they can buy and then eat them fresh from the oven, when they taste best. What sets Parisian straight dough baguettes apart from baguettes made at an American supermarket? Stone-ground flour, for one thing. It is a mainstay in French bakeries and will give the bread you make at home that authentic Parisian flavor. French bakers also add only a small amount of yeast, and they let their breads rise at a relatively cool temperature, in the 70s, which further develops the flavor and texture. And they handle the dough with care, deflating it and shaping it with gentle hands, because overkneading and overshaping will destroy the texture of the bread. The ideal straight dough contains a higher proportion of water than is found in most American recipes for "French" baguettes. If the dough is too dry, the baguettes will bake up hard and dry.

A poolish creates a complex, longer-lasting baguette. This simple sponge starter, also made with flour, water, and instant yeast, helps to extend the shelf life of bread. While Parisian Daily Bread is best eaten within several hours of baking, a *flûte* made with a *poolish* will keep for two days or more.

A liquid levain is a stress-free sourdough. Parisian baker Eric Kayser simplified bakers' lives when he developed liquid *levain*. They were no longer at the mercy of a relentless schedule that required them to be at the bakery seven days a week. With the turn of a dial, they could cool down their culture, suspending its fermentation, close the bakery for a day, and set the timer to rewarm the starter automatically eight hours before the bakery's reopening, so it would be ready to use.

For the novice home baker, liquid *levain* is an exciting alternative to traditional stiff dough *levain*. Unlike stiff dough *levain*, which has to be kneaded into a smooth ball, liquid *levain* is just stirred together in a bowl or container. It is as simple to make as pancake batter. Likewise, refreshing the mixture is simply a matter of stirring in more flour and water, with no messy kneading. When you are working with a small quantity of the culture at home, you don't need an expensive machine to control its growth. A combination of room-temperature and refrigerator fermentation does the trick. Routine feedings maintain the flavor balance and rising capacity of your starter, enabling you to make great Parisian sourdough breads with a minimum of work. Best of all, liquid *levain* will enable you to make Eric Kayser's new style of sourdough breads and taste for yourself the sensational new loaves that he has become justly famous for.

Flour makes a difference, but don't obsess about it.

Flour has become something of a fetish in Paris. Every baker has a favorite, and bakeries now advertise baguettes made from high-quality brands like Banette, Retrodor, and Baguepi. These brands are unavailable to consumers in the United States, but there's no need to seek out a particular brand if you know the general characteristics of French bread flour, generically known as "type 55." Type 55 is unbleached, unbromated flour milled from white winter wheat with a protein content of 10.75 to 11.2 percent. It produces dough with a marvelous balance of elasticity and extensibility for trapping air pockets. Because of its high ash content, it imparts a lovely cream-colored crumb to the bread. King Arthur sells an American clone of type 55 called All-Purpose Artisan Organic Flour, and Giusto's version is called Baker's Choice Unbleached Organic Bread Flour (see Resources, pages 333–34). But unbleached all-purpose flour purchased at your supermarket or ordered from your favorite mill will also give you respectable results. The techniques you use will be of more consequence to your success than the brand of your flour. If you buy boutique, stone-ground, certified organic flour and then don't knead your dough enough or proof it long enough, your bread will suffer. If you buy supermarket flour and then use it to craft your bread carefully, you are bound to wind up with excellent loaves.

Learn the art of the score.

Parisian bakers like Bernard Ganachaud have turned scoring into an art. While unscored loaves are commonplace in Italy, Germany, and other parts of France, in Paris bread is always scored, often with intricate and beautiful cuts. There is a practical reason for cutting into bread dough just before baking. Scoring causes dough to expand in the oven more evenly and gives the finished bread a more uniform crumb. The Parisian ideal is a crumb that is consistently inconsistent, with a nice mix of small and medium-size bubbles and no giant, gaping holes. The texture of a bread affects its flavor, and since proper scoring enhances uniform crumb, it enhances the flavor of the finished bread. There is aesthetic value in scoring too. Unscored or improperly scored bread will distort the shape you've worked hard to create. Proper scoring will enhance the shape and overall beauty of the loaf. Artful slashing gives the bread of Paris its particularly elegant look.

Discover your signature bread.

All the breads in Paris are made from the same basic ingredients: flour, water, and yeast. That is why it is so incredible to me that each legendary Parisian baker I learned from was able to mark his loaves through practice, experimentation, and incorporation of personal quirks so they couldn't be mistaken for the loaves of another. Not every baker had developed *la flûte gana*, but each one had loyal customers who swore by his baguettes and traveled long distances to buy them. The lesson for home bakers is that it's possible to make a particular bread so many times with such care that the bread becomes an expression of your baking self. Your signature loaf might not be a Parisian baguette. It might be an Italian focaccia or a Czech rye. But in choosing it and baking it again and again until it becomes a staple on your table and a natural part of your daily or weekly routine, you will get an idea of what it is like to be a baker in the Parisian style.

PARISIAN DAILY BREAD
Baguette normal

. . . .

ALLOW 20 MINUTES TO MIX AND REST;

8 TO 12 MINUTES TO KNEAD;

1½ TO 1¾ HOURS TO FERMENT;

30 TO 40 MINUTES TO PROOF;

15 TO 20 MINUTES TO BAKE

. . . .

A version of this straight dough baguette is produced by bakers all over Paris. The first batch goes out when the bakery opens in the morning at around seven o'clock and a fresh batch is set out every 4 hours after that until closing time, at 8 P.M. I didn't include this baguette in my first book, *Bread Alone*, because it seemed too simple. But I see now that its accessibility accounts for its charm. There's nothing like tearing into a warm baguette, fresh from your oven, just a couple of hours after you decide to bake. There are just four ingredients, no pre-ferment or starter—just instant yeast, flour, water, and salt. Traditional baguettes are 30 inches long, too long for home ovens, so I've cut down the length to fit your oven. But the baguettes you bake at home will have the same wheaty flavor, holey crumb, and extra-crisp crust as Basil Kamir's *baguettes normales.*

✳ **MAKES 3 SLENDER LOAVES ABOUT 14 INCHES LONG
(9.4 OUNCES/260 GRAMS EACH)**

Equipment
BAKING STONE

CAST-IRON SKILLET

BENCH SCRAPER OR CHEF'S KNIFE

BAKER'S PEEL OR RIMLESS BAKING SHEET

PARCHMENT PAPER

2 KITCHEN TOWELS

LAME, SINGLE-EDGED RAZOR BLADE, OR SERRATED KNIFE

INGREDIENTS	VOLUME	U.S. WEIGHT	METRIC WEIGHT	BAKER'S PERCENTAGE
Water, tepid (70 to 78 degrees)	1½ cups	12 ounces	340 grams	68
Instant yeast	1 teaspoon	0.1 ounce	4 grams	1
Type 55–style flour from King Arthur or Giusto's or unbleached all-purpose flour	3¼ cups	17.6 ounces	500 grams	100
Sea salt	1½ teaspoons	0.4 ounce	10 grams	2

MIX THE DOUGH. Pour the water into a large mixing bowl or the bowl of a stand mixer. Add the yeast, flour, and salt and stir with a rubber spatula just until all the water is absorbed and a dry, clumpy dough forms. Cover the bowl with plastic wrap and let it stand for 20 minutes, to allow the flour to hydrate and the gluten to develop on its own.

KNEAD THE DOUGH. By hand: Lightly dust the counter with flour. Using the spatula, empty the dough and any stray flour out of the bowl and knead it with smooth, steady strokes for 10 to 12 minutes. After about 2 minutes, the dough will collect into a ball. It will feel tacky and you'll start to see it stretch. Continue to knead, dipping your hands in flour as necessary so they don't stick to the dough. Try to avoid kneading extra flour into the dough so your baguettes will be light. Relax into the rhythm of kneading. Take a 2-minute break if you become tired. Stop when the dough loses its stickiness, firms up, and feels silky smooth and resilient.

By machine: Use the dough hook of a stand mixer and mix the dough on low speed (2 on a KitchenAid mixer) for 8 to 10 minutes. It will clear the sides of the bowl, grabbing onto the dough hook, but look lumpy. Pull it off the dough hook and knead it by hand for a few strokes on an unfloured counter until it is very smooth and springy.

FERMENT THE DOUGH. Transfer the dough to a lightly oiled, clear, straight-sided 2-quart container with a lid. With masking tape, mark the spot on the container that the dough will reach when it has increased 1 1/2 times in volume. Cover and leave it to rise at room temperature (70 to 75 degrees) for 45 minutes. It won't double in volume but will increase by about 25 percent. If you slice into it, you will begin to get an idea of what your finished bread will look like, with a structure under the surface of bubbles, nooks, and crannies.

GIVE THE DOUGH A TURN. Lightly dust the counter with flour and, using a spatula, empty the risen dough out of the container. Pat it gently into a rectangle about 6 by 8 inches and fold it like a business letter: with the short side facing you, lift the top edge and fold it into the center of the rectangle; lift the near edge and fold it into the center so that it overlaps the top edge by about 1 inch (see illustrations, page 31). Quickly slide both hands under the dough and flip it over so the folds are underneath. Slip it back into the container, pushing it down to fit.

Cover the dough and let stand until it expands halfway to the masking-tape mark, 45 minutes to 1 hour.

PREPARE THE OVEN. About 1 hour before baking, place a baking stone on the middle rack of the oven and a cast-iron skillet on the lower rack. Heat the oven to 450 degrees.

DIVIDE AND PRESHAPE THE DOUGH. Lightly dust the counter with flour. Uncover the dough and turn it out onto the counter. With a bench scraper or chef's knife, cut the dough into 3 equal pieces (10 ounces/285 grams each). Gently pat each piece into a rough rectangle and fold it in half. Sprinkle the pieces of dough with flour and lightly drape them with plastic wrap. Let them relax on the counter for 10 minutes.

SHAPE THE BAGUETTES. Cover a baker's peel or rimless baking sheet with parchment paper. Shape each piece of dough into a baguette about 14 inches long and 2 1/2 inches wide (see Shaping Baguettes, pages 37–38). Leave the ends rounded. Avoid over-handling the loaves, which will burst their air cells.

FORM THE *COUCHE*. Lightly dust the parchment on the peel or rimless baking sheet with flour and place the baguettes on the parchment, seam sides down, about 2 inches apart. Lift the parchment paper between the loaves, making pleats and drawing the loaves together. Tightly roll up 2 kitchen towels and slip them under the parchment paper on the sides of the two outer loaves to support and cradle the baguettes (see illustration, page 74). Lightly dust the tops of the baguettes with flour and lightly drape them with plastic wrap.

PROOF THE BAGUETTES. Let the loaves stand at room temperature (70 to 75 degrees) for 30 to 40 minutes. They will increase about 1 1/2 times in size. When you press your fingertip into the dough, the indentation will spring back slowly.

SCORE THE BAGUETTES. Uncover the loaves, take away the towels, and stretch the parchment paper out so that it is flat and the loaves are separated on top of it. Score each baguette with a *lame*, a single-edged razor blade or a serrated knife. Starting from the tip, angle the blade 45 degrees to make 3 slashes, about 3 inches long and 1/2 inch deep. Slash quickly and confidently.

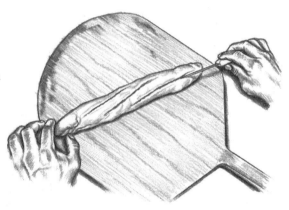

Starting from the tip, angle the blade 45 degrees and make 3 slashes, about 3 inches long and 1/2 inch deep.

BAKE THE LOAVES. Slide the loaves, still on the parchment, onto the baking stone. Place 1/2 cup of ice in the cast-iron skillet to produce steam. Bake the baguettes until they are caramel-colored, 15 to 20 minutes.

COOL AND STORE THE LOAVES. Slide the peel or the rimless baking sheet under the parchment paper to remove the loaves from the oven. Slide the loaves, still on the parchment, onto a wire rack. Cool for about 5 minutes and then peel them off the parchment paper. Parisian Daily Bread is best eaten within a few hours of baking. Toast day-old baguettes and spread with butter and jam for breakfast. For longer storage, freeze in resealable plastic bags for up to 1 month.

Variation: Four-Hour Dinner Rolls *Petits pains*

Making rolls from Parisian Daily Bread dough couldn't be simpler, since the dough just has to be cut into equal pieces but not shaped. To make rolls instead of baguettes, follow the recipe for Parisian Daily Bread through dividing and preshaping the dough. Turn the dough out onto a lightly floured counter. With your palms, gently press it into a square about 12 inches wide and 3/4 inch thick. Use a bench scraper or a chef's knife dipped in flour to cut the dough into 16 equal pieces (1.9 ounces/53 grams each). Place the rolls on a parchment-covered peel or rimless baking sheet, about 2 inches apart. Lightly dust them with flour and lightly drape them with plastic wrap until they have spread by about 20 percent, 30 to 40 minutes. Bake until lightly browned, 15 to 20 minutes, and serve immediately. Cool leftover rolls and freeze in resealable plastic bags for up to 1 month.

THE GANACHAUD *FLÛTE*
La flûte gana

. . . .

ALLOW 8 TO 10 HOURS TO MAKE THE *POOLISH*;
20 MINUTES TO MIX AND REST THE DOUGH;
8 TO 12 MINUTES TO KNEAD;
1½ TO 2 HOURS TO FERMENT;
12 TO 24 HOURS TO RETARD;
15 TO 20 MINUTES TO BAKE

. . . .

This is my tribute to Bernard Ganachaud and his famous *flûte*, which he started baking in the 1970s in protest against the pale, fluffy baguettes that were becoming more common as industrial baking gained a toehold in Paris. His *flûte*, in contrast, is caramel-colored and bubbly. He has guarded the exact recipe but generously shared the techniques that make this bread special.

Bernard begins with *poolish*, a pre-ferment of water, flour, and packaged yeast stirred into a thick batter. He lets his *poolish* ferment for 5 or 6 hours to develop the nutty, sweet wheat flavors that characterize the finished bread. (I've expanded the fermentation time to 8 to 10 hours, so you can go to work or sleep while the *poolish* rises.)

In addition to unbleached bread flour, this *flûte* dough contains a small amount of corn flour (not to be confused with cornmeal; see Resources, pages 333–34). I like the creamy texture, beautiful color, and slightly sweet flavor that it gives the bread, all qualities I enjoy in Bernard's bread.

Chilling the loaves in the refrigerator before baking ("retarding," in baker's parlance) serves a twofold purpose. The slower fermentation coaxes more flavor from the wheat and encourages all the best qualities of the bread to appear, from the glossy crumb to the crisp crust, to appear. Retarded dough will bake up with appealing brown bubbles on the surface, evidence of carbon dioxide escaping through the crust. Chilling the dough as it proofs also allows the home baker to bake when it's most convenient. The loaves will be proofed after 12 hours but can sit an additional 12 hours in the refrigerator without the risk of overproofing. You on hand to bake the breads in this chapter and use it as the "seed" to make the other sourdough cultures in this book: Stiff Dough *Levain* (page 111), *Biga semolina* (page 254), and Rye *Saurteig* (page 275).

Equipment
CLEAN, CLEAR, STRAIGHT-SIDED 2-QUART CONTAINER

DAY 1

INGREDIENTS	VOLUME	U.S. WEIGHT	METRIC WEIGHT	BAKER'S PERCENTAGE
Bottled spring water, tepid (70 to 78 degrees)	⅔ cup	5.6 ounces	160 grams	60
Type 55–style flour from King Arthur or Giusto's or unbleached all-purpose flour	3 tablespoons	0.9 ounce	25 grams	50
Fine or medium rye flour	3 tablespoons	0.9 ounce	25 grams	50

ACTIVATE THE CULTURE. Pour the water into the container and stir in the bread flour and rye flour with a rubber spatula until smooth. Scrape down the sides of the container and cover it loosely with plastic wrap. Let stand at room temperature (70 to 75 degrees) for 24 hours. Although you won't be able to see any signs yet, rest assured that the wild yeast and bacteria living in the culture you have just created have begun to ferment by feasting on the sugars in the starch.

After 8 hours and then again after another 8 hours during the 24-hour period, stir the culture with a rubber spatula for 30 seconds and recover with the plastic wrap. A shot of fresh oxygen will stimulate the wild yeast and bacteria and encourage fermentation. If you notice air bubbles the size of pinpricks on the surface of the culture, this is a good sign. But don't worry if you don't see any yet.

REFRESH THE CULTURE. Measure 1/4 cup (1.8 ounces/50 grams) of your culture into a clean 1-quart container and discard the rest. Pour in the water and stir with a rubber spatula until smooth. The mixture will be frothy and have the consistency of a milkshake. Stir in the flour until fairly smooth. It's okay if there are a few lumps. The culture may bubble up immediately, like a simmering pot of soup. Scrape down the sides of the container and cover loosely with plastic wrap. Let stand at room temperature (70 to 75 degrees) for 8 to 12 hours, until it has ripened.

These are the signs of a ripe *levain*: the culture will have expanded by about one third and its surface will be bursting with bubbles; it will smell wheaty and fresh with a very mild tanginess, but it will taste very sour; when you dip a rubber spatula into the mixture, you will pull up strands with amazing elasticity. Use the *levain* right away, or store it in the refrigerator for up to 1 week, covered.

MAINTAIN THE *LEVAIN*. If your *levain* has been in the refrigerator for a week, it is time to refresh it again, whether or not you plan on baking bread with it. Weekly refreshment will keep your liquid *levain* culture alive and healthy, so that when you do bake, it will be capable of raising your dough. Just repeat the steps for refreshment and refrigerate it again for up to 1 week.

PREPARE THE *LEVAIN* FOR BAKING. Whether or not you have refreshed your *levain* in the last week, you must refresh it 8 to 12 hours before you want to bake to ensure that it possesses the optimum vitality for raising and flavoring bread. Follow the refreshment steps as described. After the *levain* has fermented at room temperature for 8 to 12 hours, measure out what you will need for your recipe. Then place 1/4 cup (1.8 ounces/50 grams) of what is left over in a clean container, refresh this portion, again following the steps above, and refrigerate for up to 1 week for use in the future.

BUCKWHEAT *BÂTARD*
Paline

. . . .

ALLOW 8 TO 12 HOURS TO PREPARE THE BUCKWHEAT *LEVAIN*;

20 MINUTES TO MIX AND REST THE DOUGH;

8 TO 12 MINUTES TO KNEAD;

3 TO 4 HOURS TO FERMENT;

1 TO 1½ HOURS TO PROOF;

20 TO 25 MINUTES TO BAKE

. . . .

Two sorts of customers patronize Boulangerie Eric Kayser on the rue Monge in Paris's Latin Quarter. Some stand in the long line to buy Eric's traditional French breads, revivified by his liquid *levain*. Others wait patiently to purchase his all-organic contemporary loaves, breads that toy with traditional formulas by substituting unusual flours in new combinations. His buckwheat loaf, which he named *Paline*, is one of his most popular, and a favorite of mine. Shaped into a *bâtard*, a small, torpedo-shaped baguette, this bread is at once original, because of the unusual flour, and authentically Parisian, because of its classic shape.

Buckwheat has a distinctive gray-blue color and earthy flavor with hints of clay. If you like buckwheat blini, crepes, or soba noodles, you'll love this bread. Buckwheat is a low-gluten flour, so it can't raise bread on its own, but there is enough bread flour in the recipe to give the loaves a lift. I've also customized the liquid *levain*, adding some buckwheat to ensure that its particular sweetness can be detected in the finished bread. If you'd like to take a cue from master innovater Eric Kayser, play with this formula by substituting another low-gluten flour that you like, such as amaranth, garbanzo, or barley, in the *levain* and dough recipes, to create a signature bread of your own.

MAKES 4 TORPEDO-SHAPED LOAVES ABOUT 8 INCHES LONG (8 OUNCES/234 GRAMS EACH)

Equipment

BENCH SCRAPER OR CHEF'S KNIFE

BAKER'S PEEL OR RIMLESS BAKING SHEET

PARCHMENT PAPER

2 KITCHEN TOWELS

BAKING STONE

CAST-IRON SKILLET

LAME, SINGLE-EDGED RAZOR BLADE, OR SERRATED KNIFE

Note: If you don't have a liquid *levain* already prepared, you will have to make one from scratch (page 76) or substitute a commercial sourdough starter (see pages 333–34 for sources).

BUCKWHEAT *LEVAIN*

INGREDIENTS	VOLUME	U.S. WEIGHT	METRIC WEIGHT	BAKER'S PERCENTAGE
Liquid *levain* (page 76)	1½ cups	10.6 ounces	300 grams	60
Water, tepid (70 to 78 degrees)	2 tablespoons	1.2 ounces	35 grams	28
Buckwheat flour	¾ cup	4.4 ounces	125 grams	100

PREPARE THE BUCKWHEAT *LEVAIN*. Pour 1/4 cup of your liquid *levain* into a small bowl. (Refresh the remaining liquid *levain* following the directions on pages 79–80.) Pour in the water and buckwheat flour and stir with a rubber spatula to make a smooth, pasty dough. Cover with plastic wrap and let stand at room temperature for 8 to 12 hours. When ready, it will have nearly doubled in volume, turned a darker gray-blue color than when you mixed it, and give off a pungent, musty aroma.

BREAD DOUGH				
INGREDIENTS	VOLUME	U.S. WEIGHT	METRIC WEIGHT	BAKER'S PERCENTAGE
Water, tepid (70 to 78 degrees)	1⅓ cups	10.6 ounces	300 grams	60
Unbleached bread flour, preferably high-gluten	2¾ cups	15.9 ounces	450 grams	90
Buckwheat flour	½ cup	1.8 ounces	50 grams	10
Buckwheat *levain*	About ⅔ cup	4.4 ounces	125 grams	25
Sea salt	1⅓ teaspoons	0.4 ounce	10 grams	3

MIX THE DOUGH. Pour the water into a large mixing bowl or the bowl of a stand mixer. Add the bread flour and buckwheat flour and stir with a rubber spatula just until it absorbs all the water and a dry, crumbly dough forms. Cover with plastic wrap and let stand at room temperature for 20 minutes to hydrate the flour and give the gluten a chance to develop on its own.

ADD THE BUCKWHEAT *LEVAIN* AND SALT. Stir the buckwheat *levain* with the spatula to invigorate and deflate it. Measure out 2/3 cup (4.4 ounces/125 grams) of the buckwheat *levain* and discard the rest. Scrape it into the bowl of dough. Sprinkle the salt over the dough. Use the spatula to blend the *levain* and salt into the dough just long enough to combine.

KNEAD THE DOUGH. By hand: Dust the countertop with flour and scrape out the dough. Lightly oil your hands with vegetable oil. (I use olive oil because I

love the smell, which does not affect the flavor of the bread.) Knead the dough with long, smooth strokes for 10 to 12 minutes. Resist the temptation to add more flour. The stickier the dough is now, the airier and crisper your *bâtards* will be after baking. Every so often, use a bench scraper to collect the dough from the counter and oil your hands again. Take a 2-minute break if you need to. Halfway through the kneading time, the dough will become more cohesive and resilient. It will still be sticky but will become very smooth and elastic.

Give the dough a windowpane test to judge its readiness: Pinch off a golfball-sized piece and flatten it into a mini-pancake. Gently stretch it until the dough is thin enough to see through. If it tears, press the small piece back into the larger mass, knead it for 1 to 2 minutes more, and test again.

By machine: Use the dough hook and mix the dough on medium speed (4 on a KitchenAid mixer) until it is smooth and very stretchable, 8 to 9 minutes. It will not clean the sides of the bowl. Turn off the machine once or twice during kneading to scrape down the sides of the bowl and clean off the hook.

Give the dough a windowpane test to judge its readiness: Pinch off a golfball-sized piece and flatten it into a mini-pancake. Gently stretch it until the dough is thin enough to see through. If it tears, press the small piece back into the larger mass, knead it for 1 to 2 minutes more, and test again.

FERMENT THE DOUGH. Transfer the dough to a lightly oiled, clear 2-quart container with a lid. With masking tape, mark the spot on the container that the dough will reach when it has doubled in volume. Cover and leave it to rise at room temperature (70 to 75 degrees) until it doubles in size, reaching the masking-tape mark, 3 to 4 hours. It will be very spongy.

DIVIDE THE DOUGH. Lightly dust the counter with flour. Uncover the dough and scrape it out onto the counter. With a bench scraper or chef's knife, cut the dough into 4 equal pieces (8 ounces/234 grams each). Gently pat each piece into a rough rectangle and fold each rectangle in half. Sprinkle the pieces of dough with flour and lightly drape them with plastic wrap. Let the dough relax on the counter for 10 minutes.

SHAPE THE *BÂTARDS*. Cover a baker's peel or rimless baking sheet with parchment paper. Shape each piece of dough into a *bâtard* about 8 inches long and 2 1/2 inches wide (see Shaping Baguettes, pages 37–38). As you roll the log, taper the ends by increasing the downward pressure at the tips. Gentle handling works best with this wet, limp dough. Don't worry about shaping the pieces perfectly. They will bake into attractively knobby, rustic loaves.

FORM THE *COUCHE*. Dust the parchment-covered peel or baking sheet with flour and place the *bâtards* on the parchment, seam sides down, about 1 1/2 inches apart. Lift the parchment paper between the loaves, making pleats and drawing the loaves close

together. Tightly roll up 2 kitchen towels and slip them under the parchment paper on the sides of the two outer loaves to support and cradle the *bâtards* (see illustration, page 74). Lightly dust the tops of the *bâtards* with flour and lightly drape them with plastic wrap.

PROOF THE *BÂTARDS*. Let the loaves stand at room temperature (70 to 75 degrees) until they plump and bubbles form below the surface and your fingerprint springs back slowly, 1 to 1 1/2 hours.

PREPARE THE OVEN. About 1 hour before baking, place a baking stone on the middle rack of the oven and a cast-iron skillet on the lower rack. Heat the oven to 425 degrees.

SCORE THE *BÂTARDS*. Uncover the loaves and stretch the parchment paper out so that it is flat and the loaves are separated on top of it. Score each *bâtard* with a *lame*, a single-edged razor blade, or a serrated knife. Starting from the tip, angle the blade 45 degrees to make 3 slashes, about 3 inches long and 1/2 inch deep (see illustration, page 68). Dip the blade in water and use a fluid motion so that it doesn't snag and drag the dough.

BAKE THE *BÂTARDS*. Slide the loaves, still on the parchment, onto the baking stone. Place 1/2 cup of ice cubes in the skillet to produce steam. Bake for 20 to 25 minutes. The *bâtards* won't turn golden brown but will darken like fired pottery, and the crust will resist when you press it.

COOL AND STORE THE *BÂTARDS*. Slide the peel or the rimless baking sheet under the parchment paper to remove the loaves from the oven. Slide the loaves, still on the parchment, onto a wire rack. Cool for about 5 minutes and then peel them off the parchment paper. Enjoy them warm, torn or sliced. The *bâtards* will keep at room temperature for 2 to 3 days, stored in a resealable plastic bag and refreshed in a 350-degree oven for 5 minutes.

Perfectly scored Quintessential French Sourdough (Pain au levain)

FRANCE

PAGE 124

Multigrain Levain Boule
(Pain au levain aux quatre céréales)
FRANCE
PAGE 129

Auvergne Rye Baguettes with Bacon

(Baguettes aux lardons)

FRANCE

PAGE 146

Little Blue Cheese Rye Loaves
(Méteils au bleu)
FRANCE
PAGE 154

Classic Auvergne Dark Rye

(Seigle d'Auvergne)

FRANCE

PAGE 158

Rye-Fennel Crackerbread
(Schüttelbrot)
ITALY
PAGE 243

Auvergne Crown
(Couronne)
FRANCE
PAGE 142

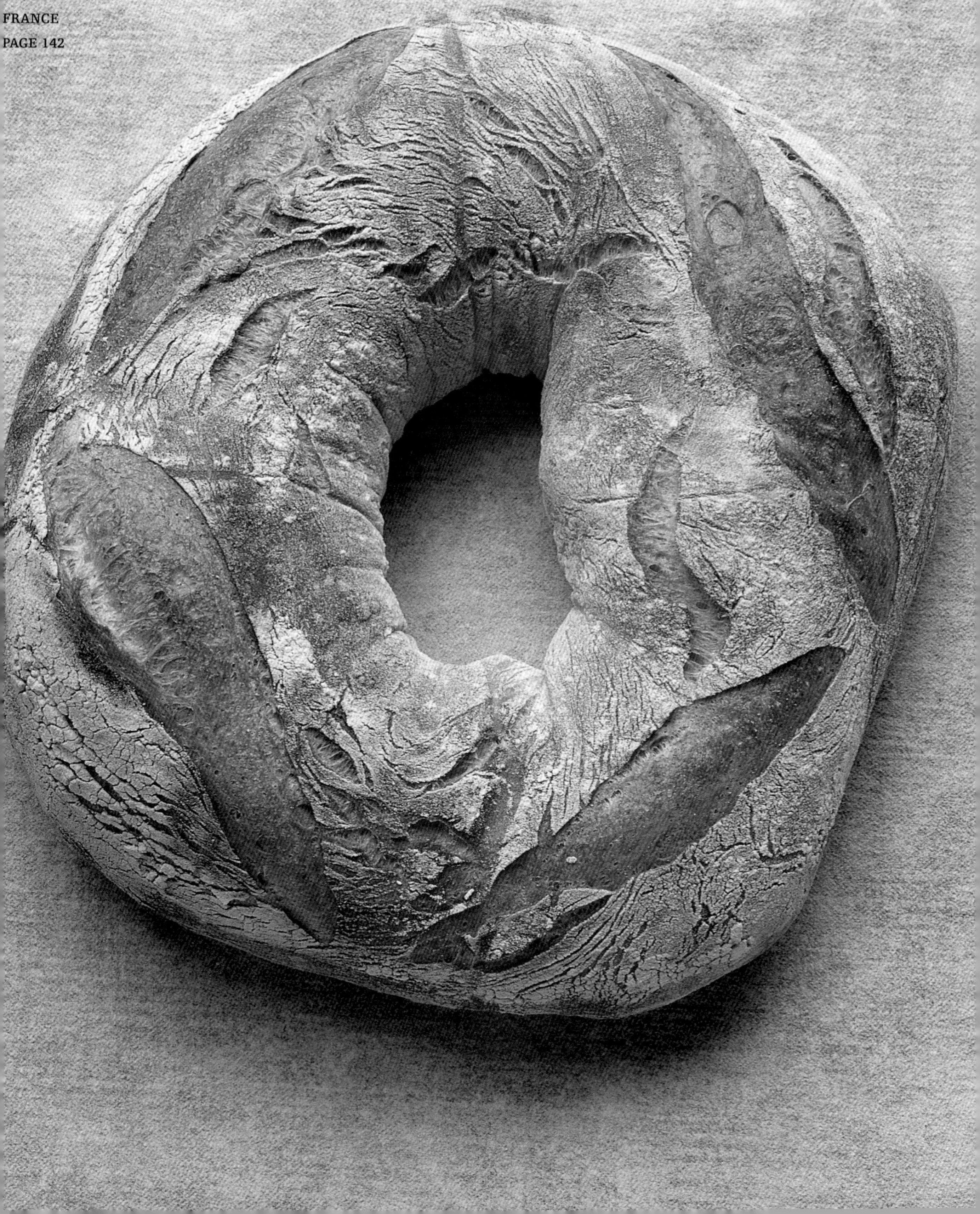

Biga,
undeveloped
and developed

OLD WORLD BAGUETTE REDUX
Baguette à l'ancienne

....

ALLOW 8 TO 12 HOURS TO PREPARE THE *LEVAIN*;
20 MINUTES TO MIX AND REST THE DOUGH;
8 TO 15 MINUTES TO KNEAD;
2 TO 3 HOURS TO FERMENT;
12 TO 24 HOURS TO RETARD;
20 TO 25 MINUTES TO BAKE

....

The name of this bread is deceiving, since it was developed relatively recently as part of the revival of Old World techniques by a handful of Parisian bakers in the 1980s. These bakers, Basil Kamir, Gerard Mulot, and Eric Kayser among them, wanted to decelerate the process of baguette making to produce a baguette with character. They accomplished this by mixing the dough with *levain* and allowing the dough to rise very slowly, by hand-shaping it, and by fermenting the shaped loaves in a retarder (a baker's refrigerator) for 12 to 24 hours before baking. The result is a tangy but never sour bread, rustic-looking, with a terra-cotta crust and tips as elegant as stilettos. No two baguettes look exactly alike, and that is the whole idea.

The high proportion of water to flour in this recipe produces a wet dough, which bakers love for the bubbly crumb and crackling crust that it delivers. If you have never worked with a wet dough, your first time may be a bit of a challenge. It's simplest to knead this and other extremely sticky doughs by machine. But if you are willing to wrangle with it by hand, you'll be able to feel the dough transform from an amorphous glob into slinky, elastic dough. Either way, you'll have to knead this dough longer than you would a dry dough to exercise the gluten. Soft and rather flabby, it can't be strong-armed into a baguette shape but must be coaxed with a light but confident hand.

**MAKES 3 SLENDER LOAVES ABOUT 12 INCHES LONG
(9.4 OUNCES/260 GRAMS EACH)**

Equipment

BENCH SCRAPER OR CHEF'S KNIFE

BAKER'S PEEL OR RIMLESS BAKING SHEET

PARCHMENT PAPER

2 KITCHEN TOWELS

BAKING STONE

CAST-IRON SKILLET

LAME, SINGLE-EDGED RAZOR BLADE, OR SERRATED KNIFE

Note: If you don't have a liquid *levain* already prepared, you will have to make one from scratch (page 76) or substitute a commercial sourdough starter (see pages 333–34 for sources).

LIQUID *LEVAIN* STARTER				
INGREDIENTS	VOLUME	U.S. WEIGHT	METRIC WEIGHT	BAKER'S PERCENTAGE
Liquid *levain* (page 76)	About ¼ cup	1.8 ounces	50 grams	37
Water, tepid (70 to 78 degrees)	¾ cup	6.2 ounces	175 grams	130
Type 55–style flour from King Arthur or Giusto's or unbleached all-purpose flour	¾ cup	4.8 ounces	135 grams	100

PREPARE THE *LEVAIN*. Pour the liquid *levain* into a small bowl. (Refresh the remaining liquid *levain* following the directions on pages 79–80.) Pour in the water and stir with a rubber spatula. The *levain* will froth. Mix in the flour until the mixture is fairly smooth (some lumps are okay), scraping down the sides of the bowl. Cover with plastic wrap and let stand at room temperature for 8 to 12 hours. When ready, it will have expanded by about one third and the surface will be bubbly, like a large pancake ready to be flipped. It will have a wheaty, fruity, mildly tangy aroma.

BREAD DOUGH				
INGREDIENTS	VOLUME	U.S. WEIGHT	METRIC WEIGHT	BAKER'S PERCENTAGE
Water, tepid (70 to 78 degrees)	½ cup plus 2 tablespoons	5.3 ounces	150 grams	55
Type 55–style flour from King Arthur or Giusto's or unbleached all-purpose flour	2 cups	10.6 ounces	300 grams	100
Liquid *levain* starter	About 1¾ cups	10.9 ounces	310 grams	103
Sea salt	1½ teaspoons	0.4 ounce	10 grams	3

MIX THE DOUGH. Pour the water into a large mixing bowl or the bowl of a stand mixer. Add the flour and stir with a rubber spatula just until it absorbs all of the water and a rough dough forms. Cover with plastic wrap and let stand at room temperature (70 to 75 degrees) for 20 minutes to hydrate the flour and give the gluten a chance to develop on its own.

ADD THE *LEVAIN* AND SALT. Stir the *levain* with the spatula to invigorate and deflate it. Scrape it into the bowl of dough. Sprinkle the salt over the dough. Use the spatula to blend the *levain* and salt into the dough. The dough will be very sticky, but resist adding extra flour.

KNEAD THE DOUGH. By hand: Begin by kneading the dough right in the bowl with the spatula. Use firm strokes and stir until it becomes smoother and more elastic, about 3 minutes. Scrape the dough onto an unfloured countertop. Expect it to stick, no matter what. Stickiness is a natural part of the process of making this bread. Lightly oil your hands with vegetable oil. Knead the dough with steady, relaxed strokes for 10 to 15 minutes. At first the dough will

stick all over the counter and your hands. Knead through this stage, using a bench scraper to collect the dough every now and then from the counter and oiling your hands again occasionally. Take a 2-minute break if you need to. Resist the temptation to add more flour. Believe it our not, the dough will evolve from a seemingly uncooperative, sticky mass into a resilient dough as soft as marshmallow and almost as sticky.

Give the dough a windowpane test to judge its readiness: Pinch off a golfball-sized piece and flatten it into a mini-pancake. Gently stretch it until the dough is thin enough to see through. If it tears, press the small piece back into the larger mass, knead it for 1 to 2 minutes more, and test again.

By machine: Use the dough hook and mix the dough on medium-low speed (3 on a KitchenAid mixer) until it is glossy, smooth, and very stretchable, 8 to 9 minutes. It will not clean the sides of the bowl. Turn off the machine once or twice during kneading to scrape down the sides of the bowl and clean off the hook. To check for readiness, give it a windowpane test, as described above.

FERMENT THE DOUGH. Transfer the dough to a lightly oiled, clear, straight-sided 2-quart container with a lid. With masking tape, mark the spot on the container that the dough will reach when it has doubled in volume. Cover and leave it to rise at room temperature (70 to 75 degrees) for 1 hour.

TURN THE DOUGH. Scrape the dough out onto a lightly floured counter. Flour your hands and fold the top third of the dough toward you, plopping it into the center of the mass. Lift the bottom edge, pull it away from you, and plop it into the center. Quickly slide both hands under the dough and flip it over so the folds are underneath. Slip it back into the container, pushing it down to fit if you need to. Cover the dough and let stand until it expands, rising into a dome twice its original size and reaching the masking-tape mark, 1 to 2 hours. It will feel a little less sticky but will still be slack and soft.

DIVIDE AND PRESHAPE THE DOUGH. Lightly dust the counter with flour. Uncover the dough and turn it out onto the counter. With a bench scraper or chef's knife, cut the dough into 3 equal pieces (9.4 ounces/260 grams each). Gently pat each piece into a rough rectangle and fold each rectangle in half. Sprinkle the pieces of dough with flour and lightly drape them with plastic wrap. Let the dough relax on the counter for 10 minutes.

SHAPE THE BAGUETTES. Cover a baker's peel or rimless baking sheet with parchment paper. Shape each piece of dough into a baguette about 12 inches long and 3 inches wide (see Shaping Baguettes, pages 37–38). As you roll the log, taper the ends by increasing the downward pressure at the tips. Gentle handling works best with this wet, limp dough. Don't worry if you are not completely satisfied with your first attempts to shape it into a baguette. Irregular sizes and knobby shapes are part of the bread's handmade appeal and the process of becoming an artisan baker.

FORM THE *COUCHE*. Dust the parchment-covered peel or baking sheet with flour and place the baguettes on the parchment, seam sides down, about 2 inches apart. Lift the parchment paper between the loaves, making pleats and drawing the loaves close together. Tightly roll up 2 kitchen towels and slip them under the parchment paper on the sides of the two outer loaves to support and cradle the baguettes (see illustration, page 74). Lightly dust the tops of the baguettes with flour and lightly drape them with plastic wrap.

RETARD THE BAGUETTES. Place the baking sheet in the refrigerator for at least 12 and up to 24 hours. About 2 hours before you want to bake, remove the baking sheet from the refrigerator. The loaves will feel dense and cool and will not rise noticeably. Keep them covered.

PREPARE THE OVEN. About 1 hour before baking, place a baking stone on the middle rack of the oven and a cast-iron skillet on the lower rack. Heat the oven to 450 degrees.

SCORE THE BAGUETTES. Uncover the loaves, take away the kitchen towels, and stretch the parchment paper out so that it is flat and the loaves are separated on top of it. Score each baguette with a *lame*, a single-edged razor blade, or a serrated knife. Starting from the tip, angle the blade 45 degrees to make 3 slashes, about 3 inches long and 1/2 inch deep (see illustration, page 68). Dip the blade in water and use a swift motion so that it doesn't snag and drag the dough.

BAKE THE BAGUETTES. Slide the loaves, still on the parchment, onto the baking stone. Place 1/2 cup of ice cubes in the skillet to produce steam. Bake until the baguettes are deep red-brown with a mottled crust, 20 to 25 minutes.

COOL AND STORE THE BAGUETTES. Slide the peel or the rimless baking sheet under the parchment paper to remove the loaves from the oven. Slide the loaves, still on the parchment, onto a wire rack. Cool for about 5 minutes and then peel them off the parchment paper. Enjoy them warm. Store cooled baguettes in a brown paper bag. The sourdough will help keep them fresh for about 3 days. Reheat in a 350-degree oven for 7 minutes to recrisp the crust. For longer storage, freeze in resealable plastic bags for up to 1 month.

Variation: Old World Mini-Baguettes Redux with Four Seeds
Petits pains à l'ancienne

Making mini-baguettes is a great way to practice shaping and scoring. The dough is easier to handle in small pieces, and you get sixteen chances instead of three to get it right. Or skip the shaping altogether and just cut the dough into squares with a sharp knife. Both kinds of roll, covered with a mixture of poppy, sunflower, and sesame seeds, freeze well for holidays, dinner parties, and any other time when you are too busy to fuss with baking bread right before dinner.

Mix, knead, ferment, and turn the dough as directed on pages 30–31. Then:

GATHER THE SEEDS AND PREHEAT THE OVEN. About 1 hour before baking, place a baking stone on the middle rack of the oven and a cast-iron skillet on the lower rack. Preheat the oven to 450 degrees. Place 1/4 cup each of poppy, sunflower, and sesame seeds in 3 separate small bowls. Fill another small bowl with water and set aside with a pastry brush.

SHAPE THE MINI-BAGUETTES. Line a baker's peel or rimless baking sheet with parchment paper. Lightly dust the counter with flour. Scrape the dough onto the counter and cut it into 16 equal pieces (1.8 ounces/50 grams each). Dust your hands with flour and shape each piece into a miniature baguette about 4 inches long by cupping one hand over a piece of dough and moving it in a circular motion to form a ball. The dough should grab the counter. If it slips, brush away excess flour. With one hand on top of the other, gently roll the ball to lengthen it into an oval about 4 inches long. Increase the pressure at the ends to taper them into points. Be patient with yourself and the soft dough. Place the mini-baguettes on the parchment-lined baking sheet about 2 inches apart.

OR MAKE RUSTIC ROLLS. Line a baker's peel or rimless baking sheet with parchment paper. Lightly dust the counter with flour. Flour your hands and gently pat the dough into a square about 12 inches wide and 3/4 inch thick. Dip a bench scraper or chef's knife in flour and cut the dough into 16 squares (1.8 ounces/50 grams each). The rolls are charming in irregular shapes, but try to make them close to the same size or weight so they rise and bake evenly.

COAT WITH SEEDS AND BAKE. Use the pastry brush to lightly moisten the top of each mini-baguette or roll with water. Pick up each roll from the bottom and dip the top into one of the bowls of seeds to coat. (There will be leftover seeds, which you can store and reuse.) Place the rolls on the parchment-lined baking sheet 2 inches apart. Lightly cover with plastic and let stand at room temperature until they have spread and you can see bubbles forming just below the surface. For baguettes, use a *lame*, a single-edged razor blade, or a serrated knife to make a single cut down the center of each roll from tip to tip, about 1/4 inch deep. Slide the rolls, still on the parchment, onto the baking stone. Place 1/2 cup of ice cubes in the skillet to produce steam. Bake until the rolls are lightly mottled brown, 15 to 20 minutes.

FRENCH COUNTRY BOULE
Pain de campagne

. . . .

ALLOW 8 TO 12 HOURS TO PREPARE THE *LEVAIN*;
20 MINUTES TO MIX AND REST THE DOUGH;
8 TO 12 MINUTES TO KNEAD;
2½ TO 3½ HOURS TO FERMENT;
1 TO 1½ HOURS TO PROOF;
35 TO 40 MINUTES TO BAKE

. . . .

You see *pain de campagne*, rustic, dark, thick-crusted rounds called *boules*, all over France. They vary wildly in quality, depending on the care with which they are made. The best bakers take the extra step of fermenting them with sourdough to develop a full-bodied crust and adding some rye flour for a deep flavor. I often eat this humble and satisfying bread as part of a quick lunch with a cup of soup at Bread Alone. Like any well-made sourdough loaf, it stays fresh for several days and can be toasted for breakfast for days after that.

This recipe uses liquid *levain* and adds a little whole wheat flour along with the rye to match the germ-rich, bran-flecked flour typically used by French bakers. Even small amounts of these darker flours tend to weigh the dough down, so it's important to knead the dough thoroughly, to make the gluten extensible and the dough springy. Use the windowpane test (see pages 28–29) to determine whether or not you have kneaded the dough long enough for it to rise to its full potential, and create a light, not leaden, texture.

✳ MAKES TWO 8-INCH ROUNDS
(20 OUNCES/560 GRAMS EACH)

Equipment

2 BANNETONS OR SHALLOW BOWLS (6 INCHES WIDE AND 4 INCHES DEEP)
  LINED WITH 2 KITCHEN TOWELS
BENCH SCRAPER OR CHEF'S KNIFE
BAKING STONE
CAST-IRON SKILLET
BAKER'S PEEL OR RIMLESS BAKING SHEET
PARCHMENT PAPER
LAME, SINGLE-EDGED RAZOR BLADE, OR SHARP SERRATED KNIFE

Note: If you don't have a liquid *levain* already prepared, you will have to make one from scratch (page 76) or substitute a commercial sourdough starter (see pages 333–34 for sources).

LIQUID *LEVAIN* STARTER

INGREDIENTS	VOLUME	U.S. WEIGHT	METRIC WEIGHT	BAKER'S PERCENTAGE
Liquid *levain* (page 76)	About ¼ cup	1.8 ounces	50 grams	37
Water, tepid (70 to 78 degrees)	¾ cup	6.2 ounces	175 grams	130
Type 55–style flour from King Arthur or Giusto's or unbleached all-purpose flour	¾ cup	4.8 ounces	135 grams	100

PREPARE THE *LEVAIN*. Pour 1/4 cup of liquid *levain* into a small bowl. (Refresh the remaining liquid *levain* following the directions on pages 79–80.) Pour in the water and stir with a rubber spatula. The *levain* will froth. Mix in the flour until the mixture is fairly smooth (some lumps are okay), scraping down the sides of the bowl. Cover with plastic wrap and let stand at room temperature (70 to 75 degrees) for 8 to 12 hours. When ready, it will have expanded by about one third and the surface will be bubbly, like a large pancake ready to be flipped. It will have a wheaty, fruity, mildly tangy aroma.

BREAD DOUGH

INGREDIENTS	VOLUME	U.S. WEIGHT	METRIC WEIGHT	BAKER'S PERCENTAGE
Water, tepid (70 to 78 degrees)	1 cup plus 1 tablespoon	8.8 ounces	250 grams	50
Type 55–style flour from King Arthur or Giusto's or unbleached all-purpose flour	2¾ cups	15.5 ounces	440 grams	88
Stone-ground whole wheat flour	¼ cup	1.1 ounces	30 grams	6
Fine or medium rye flour	¼ cup	1.1 ounces	30 grams	6
Liquid *levain* starter	About 1¾ cups	10.9 ounces	310 grams	62
Sea salt	1½ teaspoons	0.4 ounce	10 grams	2

MIX THE DOUGH. Pour the water into a large mixing bowl or the bowl of a stand mixer. Add the bread flour, whole wheat flour, and rye flour and stir with a rubber spatula just until it absorbs all the water and a rough dough forms. Cover with plastic wrap and let stand at room temperature for 20 minutes to hydrate the flour and give the gluten a chance to develop on its own.

ADD THE *LEVAIN* AND SALT. Stir the *levain* with the spatula to invigorate and deflate it. Scrape it into the bowl of dough. Sprinkle the salt over the dough. Use the spatula to blend the *levain* and salt into the dough.

KNEAD THE DOUGH. By hand: Lightly dust the counter with flour. Scrape the dough onto the counter and knead with steady, relaxed strokes for 10 to 12 minutes. Flour your hands as often as necessary but resist adding more flour to the dough. As you continue to knead, the dough will gradually become smooth, resilient, and tacky. Give the dough a windowpane test to judge its readiness: Pinch off a golfball-sized piece and flatten it into a mini-pancake. Gently stretch it until the dough is thin enough to see through. If it tears, press the small piece back into the larger mass, knead it for 1 to 2 minutes more, and test again.

machine: Use the dough hook and mix the dough on medium speed (4 on a KitchenAid mixer) until it is smooth, 8 to 9 minutes. It will be soft and tacky but will clean the sides of the bowl. Give the dough a windowpane test to judge its readiness, as described above. If it tears, press the small piece back into the larger mass, knead it for 1 to 2 minutes more, and test again.

FERMENT THE DOUGH. Transfer the dough to a lightly oiled, clear, straight-sided 2-quart container with a lid. With masking tape, mark the spot on the container that the dough will reach when it has doubled in volume. Cover and leave it to rise at room temperature (70 to 75 degrees) until it inflates into a dome and reaches the masking tape, 2 1/2 to 3 1/2 hours. It will feel springy and less sticky.

DIVIDE AND SHAPE THE BOULES. Heavily dust the bannetons or the two bowls lined with kitchen towels with flour. Lightly dust the counter with flour. Scrape the dough onto the counter. With a bench scraper or chef's knife, cut the dough into 2 equal pieces (20 ounces/560 grams each). Shape each piece into a boule (see Shaping Rounds, page 36). If you don't achieve a perfect round, leave it. It's important not to overwork the dough. Place each round, smooth side down, in a prepared banneton or bowl. Lightly sprinkle with flour and cover loosely with plastic wrap.

PROOF THE BOULES. Let the boules stand at room temperature (70 to 75 degrees) until they become pillowy and nearly double in size, 1 to 1 1/2 hours. When you press your fingertip into the dough, the indentation will spring back slowly.

PREPARE THE OVEN. About 1 hour before baking, place a baking stone on the middle rack of the oven and a cast-iron skillet on the lower rack. Heat the oven to 450 degrees.

SCORE THE BOULES. Lightly flour a baker's peel or rimless baking sheet. Uncover the loaves and tip them out onto the peel or sheet, guiding them for a soft landing and arranging them at least 2 inches apart. With a *lame*, a single-edged razor blade, or a serrated knife, make 3 parallel slashes centered on each loaf, each about 1/2 inch deep.

BAKE THE BOULES. Slide the loaves, still on the parchment, onto the baking stone. Place 1/2 cup of ice cubes in the skillet to produce steam. Bake for 15 minutes. Reduce the heat to 400 degrees and

---

Variation: Raisin-Walnut Boule *Pain aux noix et raisins*

French bakers often add raisins and walnuts to country bread dough. Buy organic raisins and nuts at a natural-foods store with a rapid turnover if possible. They are often fresher and taste better than those you find in the supermarket.

PREPARE THE FRUIT AND NUTS. Just before mixing the dough, place 3/4 cup chopped walnuts on a baking sheet and toast in a 350-degree oven until fragrant, 5 to 8 minutes. Let cool completely. Soak 3/4 cup raisins in hot tap water until plump and soft, about 15 minutes. Drain thoroughly and blot dry with a paper towel.

ADD THE FRUIT AND NUTS TO THE DOUGH. During the last 2 minutes of kneading, either by hand or by machine, add the raisins and walnuts. In the machine, some of the fruit and/or nuts may collect at the bottom of the bowl. If this happens, turn the dough out onto the counter and knead by hand to incorporate. Proceed with shaping and baking as described above.

continue to bake until the boules are red-brown, 20 to 25 minutes more.

COOL AND STORE THE BOULES. Slide the peel or the rimless baking sheet under the parchment paper to remove the loaves from the oven. Slide the loaves, still on the parchment, onto a wire rack. Cool the loaves completely, about 1 hour, before slicing. Store the cooled loaves in a brown paper bag. They will stay fresh for about 4 days. For longer storage, freeze in resealable plastic bags for up to 1 month.

SOURDOUGH CROISSANTS
Croissants sur levain liquide

. . . .

ALLOW 8 TO 12 HOURS TO PREPARE THE *LEVAIN*;

4 TO 5 MINUTES TO MIX AND KNEAD;

1 HOUR TO RETARD;

2 TO 3 HOURS TO FOLD AND CHILL;

12 TO 24 HOURS TO INCORPORATE BUTTER AND CHILL AGAIN;

1 TO 1 1/2 HOURS TO PROOF;

15 TO 18 MINUTES TO BAKE

. . . .

While bread bakers in Paris rarely offer sweet pastries such as fruit tarts alongside their baguettes and boules, they do sell croissants, most made with commercial yeast. I first had croissants raised with sourdough at Eric Kayser's bakery in Paris, and was immediately struck by their superiority. Although his pastries weren't remotely sour, they had a deliciously complex flavor, due to the combination of the wild yeast and the sweet dairy and butter. Their texture was incredibly flaky, and they stayed fresh longer (up to 1 day) than conventional croissants, which begin to stale in a few hours.

If you have never made croissant dough or puff pastry, you may be unfamiliar with the technique of tucking a packet of butter inside the dough and then repeatedly rolling and folding the dough to create the multiple layers of pastry. When the dough bakes, the layers of butter melt, creating steam between the layers of dough and giving the croissants their flakiness. Parisian bakers give their dough triple turns, folding it like a letter, for optimum flakiness without toughening the dough.

These croissants are rich, so I make them on the small side, as they do in France.

✳ **MAKES 24 CROISSANTS**
 (2.25 OUNCES/50 GRAMS EACH)

Equipment
PARCHMENT PAPER
ROLLING PIN
CHEF'S KNIFE
RULER
PASTRY BRUSH

Note: If you don't have a liquid *levain* already prepared, you will have to make one from scratch (page 76) or substitute a commercial sourdough starter (see pages 333–34 for sources).

LIQUID *LEVAIN* STARTER				
INGREDIENTS	VOLUME	U.S. WEIGHT	METRIC WEIGHT	BAKER'S PERCENTAGE
Liquid *levain* (page 76)	About ½ cup	3.5 ounces	100 grams	37
Water, tepid (70 to 78 degrees)	1½ cups	12.3 ounces	350 grams	130
Type 55–style flour from King Arthur or Giusto's or unbleached all-purpose flour	1½ cups	9.5 ounces	270 grams	100

PREPARE THE *LEVAIN*. Pour 1/2 cup of liquid *levain* into a small bowl. (Refresh the remaining liquid *levain* following the directions on pages 79–80.) Pour in the water and stir with a rubber spatula. The *levain* will froth. Mix in the flour until the mixture is fairly smooth (some lumps are okay), scraping down the sides of the bowl. Cover with plastic wrap and let stand at room temperature for 8 to 12 hours. When ready, it will have expanded by about one third and the surface will be bubbly, like a large pancake ready to be flipped. It will have a wheaty, fruity, mildly tangy aroma.

CROISSANT DOUGH

INGREDIENTS	VOLUME	U.S. WEIGHT	METRIC WEIGHT	BAKER'S PERCENTAGE
Whole milk, lukewarm (105 to 110 degrees)	1¼ cups	10.6 ounces	300 grams	60
Liquid *levain* starter	About ½ cup	3.5 ounces	100 grams	20
Instant yeast	1 tablespoon	0.5 ounce	15 grams	3
Unbleached all-purpose flour	3¼ cups	17.6 ounces	500 grams	100
Unsalted butter, softened,	4 tablespoons	2.1 ounces	60 grams	12
Granulated sugar	1 tablespoon	0.5 ounce	15 grams	3
Sea salt	1½ teaspoons	0.4 ounce	10 grams	2
Unsalted butter, chilled	14 tablespoons	7.1 ounces	200 grams	40

EGG WASH

INGREDIENTS	VOLUME	U.S. WEIGHT	METRIC WEIGHT	BAKER'S PERCENTAGE
Eggs	1 large	2 ounces	57 grams	—
Heavy cream	1 tablespoon	0.5 ounce	15 grams	—
Granulated sugar	1 teaspoon	0.2 ounce	7 grams	—

MIX THE DOUGH. Pour the milk into a large mixing bowl or the bowl of a stand mixer. With a rubber spatula, stir down the *levain* to invigorate and deflate it. Scrape it into the milk. Stir in the yeast, flour, 4 tablespoons softened butter, sugar, and salt just until a dough forms.

KNEAD THE DOUGH. By hand: Lightly flour the countertop. Scrape the dough onto the counter and knead it just long enough to incorporate the ingredients, 3 to 4 minutes. The dough will be smooth.

By machine: With the dough hook, mix the dough on low speed (2 on a KitchenAid mixer) just until the ingredients are well blended, about 2 minutes.

RETARD THE DOUGH. Transfer the dough to a lightly oiled, clear, straight-sided 2-quart container with a lid. Refrigerate for 1 to 2 hours. It will expand only slightly in the cold.

FORM THE BUTTER BLOCK. While the dough is chilling, remove the 14 tablespoons chilled butter from the refrigerator and let stand on the counter until still cool but pliable. Flour a sheet of parchment paper. Place the butter on the parchment and use a lightly floured rolling pin to pound it into a single mass. Cover the butter with another piece of parchment paper and roll it into a 5-inch square, about 1/2 inch thick. Wrap the butter block in plastic and refrigerate along with the dough.

FOLD THE BUTTER BLOCK INTO THE DOUGH. Remove the dough and butter from the refrigerator. They should both be firm and cold. Dust a baking sheet with flour and set aside. Lightly dust the countertop with flour and turn the dough out onto it. Roll the dough into a 5-by-10-inch rectangle, about 3/4 inch thick. With the long side facing you, place the butter block on the right-hand side of the dough, about 1/2 inch from the edge. Fold the dough over the butter, as if closing a book. Pinch the edges together to completely enclose the butter inside the dough. Roll the packet into a 10-by-14-inch rectangle, about 1/2 inch thick, dusting the dough and the countertop with more flour as necessary. With the short side of the rectangle facing you, fold the dough in thirds, like a business letter: Pick up the bottom edge and fold it two thirds of the way toward the top; pick up the top edge and fold it one third of the way down, laying it on top of the bottom third. Lay the dough on the baking sheet, wrap with plastic, and refrigerate for at least 1 and up to 3 hours.

MAKE THE SECOND FOLD. Remove the dough from the refrigerator and unwrap. Dust the counter with flour and place the dough on the counter with the long edge facing you. Roll the dough out into a 10-by-14-inch rectangle, about 1/2 inch thick. Repeat the business-letter fold: With the short side facing you, fold the bottom edge two thirds of the way and toward the top; pick up the top edge and fold it one third of the way down, laying it on top of the bottom third.

MAKE THE THIRD FOLD. Rotate the dough a quarter turn clockwise, so that once again the short side is facing you. Again, roll the dough out into a 10-by-14-inch rectangle, about 1/2 inch thick, dusting the countertop and dough as necessary. Repeat the business-letter fold to make a neat stack of three layers. Transfer the dough to the baking sheet, cover with plastic, and refrigerate for at least 12 and up to 24 hours.

SHAPE THE CROISSANTS. Cover two baking sheets with parchment paper and set aside. Remove the dough from the refrigerator and unwrap it. Lightly dust the countertop with flour. Roll the dough out into a 14-by-24-inch rectangle, about 1/4 inch thick, dusting the counter and the dough as necessary.

Fold the dough in half lengthwise to mark the center line, then open it up again and lay it flat. With a chef's knife or pizza wheel, cut along this center line to make two long strips. Keep the pieces side by side. Use a ruler to measure every 4 inches down the length of each strip, ticking the dough with a knife to mark it. Cut at each mark perpendicular to the center line to make 12 rectangles. Cut each rectangle diagonally to make 2 triangles. You will now have 24 triangles.

Starting at the wide end of one of the triangles, roll toward the tip. Place the rolled croissant on the parchment-covered baking sheet, curving the ends inward to make a crescent shape and making sure that the point is tucked underneath (see illustrations on page 313). Repeat with the remaining dough triangles, placing them in rows on the baking sheets and making sure to leave 2 inches between croissants. (If the triangles become too soft to work with, place them in the freezer for a few minutes to firm up.)

PROOF THE CROISSANTS. Let the croissants stand, uncovered, at room temperature (70 to 75 degrees) until they are puffy and delicate to the touch, 1 to 1 1/2 hours. (Alternatively, freeze the shaped croissants and bake them later: Place the baking sheets in the freezer until the croissants are firm, at least 1 hour. Peel them off of the parchment paper and transfer to resealable plastic bags. Before baking, let them thaw out on parchment-lined baking sheets overnight or at room temperature for 2 to 3 hours and then let them rise until puffy, about 1 hour.)

PREPARE THE OVEN. About 15 minutes before baking, set the oven racks in the top third and the middle of the oven. Heat the oven to 350 degrees.

MAKE THE EGG WASH. Whisk together the eggs, cream, and sugar in a small bowl.

BAKE THE CROISSANTS. Brush the croissants with the egg wash, coating them completely. Slide both baking sheets into the oven and bake the croissants until they are a glistening caramel color, 15 to 18 minutes, switching the position of the baking sheets after 8 minutes for even baking.

COOL AND STORE THE CROISSANTS. Transfer the baking sheets to wire racks, let the croissants cool for 5 minutes, and enjoy them while they are warm. To store, cool completely and freeze in resealable plastic bags. Let them thaw overnight in the refrigerator, or on the counter for an hour, then reheat in a 350 degree oven for 5 to 7 minutes before serving.

Variation: Chocolate Sourdough Croissants
Croissants sur levain liquide au chocolat
Makes 18 croissants

Shaping chocolate croissants is simpler than shaping plain ones, a matter of folding the dough over chocolate. I like to be generous with the chocolate, folding two layers of it into the dough rather than the usual one. You'll need a total of 9 ounces (255 grams) of chocolate, broken into small pieces or skinny bars.

Roll your croissant dough into a 24-by-9-inch rectangle. Cut the rectangle lengthwise into three 24-by-3-inch strips. Cut each strip into six 4-by-3-inch rectangles. With the short side of a rectangle facing you, place a 1/4-ounce (7-gram) bar or bits of chocolate about 1/2 inch from the bottom edge of the dough. Fold the dough one third of the way up, enclosing the chocolate. Place another 1/4-ounce (7-gram) bar or bits of chocolate on the unfolded side of the dough, right next to the folded edge. Fold the folded side up so that it meets the top edge of the dough and you have three layers. Place on a parchment-covered baking sheet. Repeat with the remaining dough and chocolates, placing the croissants 2 inches apart. Proof, egg wash, bake, and store as directed above.

WHOLE SPELT LOAF
Pain à lepautre

. . . .

ALLOW 12 TO 24 HOURS TO PREPARE THE SOURDOUGH;

13 TO 18 MINUTES TO KNEAD;

10 MINUTES TO REST;

2 TO 2 1/2 HOURS TO FERMENT;

1 TO 1 1/2 HOURS TO PROOF;

30 TO 40 MINUTES TO BAKE

. . . .

As spelt has become popular in France and Germany, I have found examples of spelt bread in both countries. Rather than create a spelt sourdough, I am using a rye sourdough to ensure that the gluten content is as low as possible. Whole spelt flour produces a dough that is less fragile than rye dough, but less stretchy and resilient than dough made with whole or white wheat. It will take quite a while for the gluten to develop and for the dough to come together into a shiny ball, but be patient. It will happen. A little honey in the dough speeds fermentation and also gives this earthy bread a hint of sweetness.

MAKES ONE 9-INCH PAN LOAF
(17 OUNCES/483 GRAMS)

Equipment
SINGLE-EDGE RAZOR BLADE OR SERRATED KNIFE

INGREDIENTS	VOLUME	U.S. WEIGHT	METRIC WEIGHT	BAKER'S PERCENTAGE
German rye sourdough (page 278)	About ¼ cup	1.8 ounces	50 grams	10
Water, tepid (70 to 78 degrees)	1⅓ cups	9.7 ounces	275 grams	55
Honey	3 tablespoons	1.8 ounces	50 grams	10
Whole spelt flour	3¼ cups	17.6 ounces	500 grams	100
Sea salt	1½ teaspoons	0.4 ounce	10 grams	2

PREPARE THE SOURDOUGH. 12 to 24 hours before you plan to bake, refresh your spelt sourdough following the instructions on pages 277–78.

MIX THE DOUGH. Pour the water and honey into a large mixing bowl or the bowl of a stand mixer and stir to dissolve the honey. Stir in the spelt flour and salt with a rubber spatula. Stir down the spelt sourdough, which will have risen during fermentation, to invigorate and deflate it. Measure out 1/4 cup (1.8 ounces/50 grams) of the sourdough and stir it into the dough. (Refresh and store the remaining spelt sourdough following the instructions on pages 277–78.) With the spatula, work the sourdough in just enough to bind it to the dough.

KNEAD THE DOUGH. By hand: Lightly dust the counter with flour. Scrape the dough onto the counter and knead with long, smooth strokes, flouring your hands as necessary, for 10 to 18 minutes.

By machine: Use the dough hook and mix the dough on medium-low speed (3 on a KitchenAid mixer) for 7 minutes. Increase the speed to medium (5 on a KitchenAid mixer) and continue to knead until the dough gathers into a firm, smooth, somewhat elastic ball, another 6 to 7 minutes. Turn off the machine and scrape the hook and the sides of the bowl.

FERMENT THE DOUGH. Transfer the dough to a lightly oiled, clear, straight-sided 2-quart container with a lid. With masking tape, mark the spot on the container where the dough will be when it has doubled in volume. Cover and leave it to rise at room temperature (70 to 75 degrees) until it doubles, reaching the masking tape mark, 2 to 2 1/2 hours.

SHAPE THE LOAF. Lightly dust the counter with whole spelt flour. Uncover the dough and turn it out onto the counter. Form the dough into a pan loaf (see Shaping a Pan Loaf, page 40). Nestle the loaf into the pan, seam side down, pressing it gently to fit. Lightly dust the top of the loaf with whole spelt flour and cover with plastic wrap.

PROOF THE LOAF. Let the loaves rise at room temperature (70 to 75 degrees) until they have expanded to 1 1/2 times their original size, coming to the top of the pan, 1 to 1 1/2 hours.

PREPARE THE OVEN. About 15 minutes before baking, place the oven rack in the middle position. Preheat the oven to 400 degrees.

SCORE AND BAKE THE LOAF. Use a serrated knife to score the loaf diagonally four times. Bake until it has mushroomed a little on top and is a rich brown color, 30 to 35 minutes.

COOL AND STORE THE LOAF. Pull the loaf from the oven. Bang the edge of the pan on the counter to release the bread. Invert it onto a wire rack and then flip it right side up. Cool the bread completely before slicing, about 1 hour. Store the cut loaf in a resealable plastic bag at room temperature. It will stay fresh for about 3 days. For longer storage, freeze in a resealable plastic bag for up to 1 month.

FREQUENTLY ASKED QUESTIONS ABOUT PARISIAN-STYLE BREAD

· ·

Why are the baguettes so good in Paris? How do French bakers achieve that incredible crust?
Ingredients and technique contribute to the quality of Parisian baguettes. In France, baguettes are always baked with soft winter wheat flour and are slowly fermented. Many French bakeries also use sophisticated steam-injected deck ovens that guarantee a uniformly steamed crust. In contrast, the "baguettes" you see at American supermarkets usually contain flour made from spring wheat, which has a higher protein content and bakes up very dry. Commercial American baguettes are often rushed through the fermentation process, resulting in characterless bread. They are baked without steam, so the heat of the oven kills off the yeast before the bread can expand to its full potential.

When I attempted to slash my dough, my knife got stuck, and by the time I extracted it my dough looked a little deflated and pretty misshapen. What did I do wrong?
Move your blade through the dough with quick, simple strokes rather than dragging it. Wet your knife with water before every slash, because a wet blade will cut through the dough more easily.

Are there some French breads that shouldn't be scored?
Scoring is part of the style and elegance of Parisian bread. I can think of many German, Austrian, and Italian loaves that aren't scored, but the only French examples I can think of are the rustic rye breads made in the Auvergne region.

I've made walnut bread before and the dough turns pink. Why does this happen and what can I do to prevent it?
The skin of the walnuts contains a natural dye. If the nuts are mixed into the dough too vigorously, that dye will rub off into the dough and color it pink. To prevent this, mix the nuts gently into the dough, just long enough to distribute them evenly.

What do Parisians do with their leftover baguettes and boules?
Like Americans, Parisians revive bread by toasting it, which remoistens the crumb and refreshes the flavor. But perhaps inspired by the quality of their bread, Parisians have elevated toast to the level of cuisine. The late Lionel Poilâne created an entire café menu based on toast and opened Cuisine de Bar right next door to his famous bakery on the rue du Cherche-Midi. I shared a memorable meal with him there: a slice of *pain Poilâne*™ topped with prosciutto and swiss cheese and run under the broiling element of a toaster oven. Poilâne also wrote two little paperback cookbooks, *The Best Tartines of Lionel Poilâne* and *The Best Sweet Tartines of Lionel Poilâne*, which included recipes such as Tartine Popeye (steamed spinach with garlic, onion, and yogurt) and Tartine Ali-Baba (dates, butter, walnuts, and mint). When you acquire the habit of making Parisian-style bread, its inherent goodness will inspire you to make open-faced sandwiches with leftover baguettes and boules.

CHAPTER 6

✳

ORGANICS IN ALSACE: REDISCOVERING *PAIN AU LEVAIN* AT FABIOPAIN

✳

As recently as 1890, when yeast was first packaged commercially, all *boulangers* baked with *levain*. This stiff sourdough starter made from flour and water sat in every bakery in France. It may have looked ordinary, but each bucket of it teemed with its own unique blend of wild yeast and lactobacilli. When mixed into bread dough, the wild yeast in the *levain* fed on the sugars and starches in the flour and then released carbon dioxide, creating air pockets that raised the bread. Acids produced by the bacteria during the long, slow fermentation added rich flavor. As long as a baker fed the *levain* with flour and water periodically, providing an environment in which the yeast and bacteria could thrive, he would always have a ready leavener for his bread. In theory, he would never have to cultivate a *levain* from scratch if he just maintained the original mixture. He could even save his children some work by passing along the *levain* when he retired.

My friend and mentor Basil Kamir is part of this long line of French bakers who use stiff dough *levain*. He didn't inherit his sourdough culture from his father; he cultivated it from scratch. But he learned how to do so from a master baker, Jean LeFleur, who himself had been an apprentice to another master baker, and so on and so on. I have always been fascinated by *levain*'s pedigree as the oldest and most traditional method for raising French bread. When, in 1984, Basil offered to show me how he mixed his *levain*, I felt like I was being initiated into a brotherhood of artisan bakers stretching back through the centuries.

I had experimented with various sourdough recipes at home and come up with my own sourdough recipe to use at Bread Alone, so I thought I could make a good guess about how Parisian bakers make their *levain*. But I wasn't at all prepared for what I saw. I watched as Basil pinched off a piece of the previous day's *levain*. He combined it with some flour and water in his mixer, began to mix, and then continued to add flour until the dough was harder and drier than the hardest bagel dough. When he was finished, the culture looked nothing like the sourdoughs I had used at home. How on earth could such a firm starter result in *pain au levain*, a bread whose crumb is so delicately patterned with bubbles of every size? He smiled at my skepticism and told me to watch and wait.

Of course, it wasn't quite so simple. For Basil, watching and waiting meant checking his *levain* every couple of hours to monitor its fermentation, tasting it to see how sour it had gotten, cutting into it to see how bubbly it was under its surface. If he had to jump up and leave a restaurant in the middle of dinner to do this, that's what he would do. For Basil, and for every French artisan baker I have ever met, understanding *levain* isn't about taking it to a lab to find out what species of yeast it contains (as San Francisco bakers are wont to do) but about working with it day after day to learn what a good *levain* looks, smells, and tastes like, and striving every day thereafter to make and use only good *levain*.

Basil explained to me that old-time French bakers use stiff *levain* because it ferments slowly, with very little acid build-up. Stiff dough *levain* is generally made with some proportion of whole wheat flour, and traditional *levain* breads also contain whole wheat, sometimes a little and sometimes a lot, as did breads of old. Basil's *pain au levain*, baguettes with a cream-colored, bran-flecked crumb, has 85 percent whole wheat. In contrast, most of the younger bakers using liquid sourdough leavened in a *fermento-levain* are baking a delicious but decidedly more modern, lighter style of bread, with 100 percent white flour. The choice of stiff dough *levain* is a matter of temperament and habit as well as taste. Bakers like Basil have well-established routines and value the old ways. A liquid sourdough fermented in a *fermento-levain* will raise bread just as well, and its high-tech thermometers and timers allow the baker some flexibility and time away from the bakery. But

the lure of a vacation day would not be enough for Basil and his brothers in baking to abandon a sourdough technique that they and their forebears have relied on for so long.

One afternoon after mixing his *levain*, Basil took me to the Musée de Pain for a history lesson. (Regrettably, this quirky little museum has since closed.) The museum, in a 6,000-square-foot warehouse in a quiet neighborhood near the Seine, was founded and overseen by a former baker who had spent his life collecting baking artifacts. It contained hundreds of different bannetons and flour containers, historical photographs of French bakeries, histories of the different families of masons who had built the brick ovens. That day we were the only visitors, and the proud curator took us on a private tour, finally leading us into a replica of a nineteenth-century *boulangerie*, complete with a basement workroom and an old-fashioned *levain* storage system used before the invention of the refrigerator. I was amazed at the remarkable measures French bakers took to keep their *levain* cool. In the basement, which was already cooler than the rooms above, a reservoir was sunk into the floor and filled with cool water. A covered iron container, partially submerged in the water, held the *levain*. The basement location, the cool reservoir of water, and the chilly iron container all contributed to the slow growth of the sourdough. Now I understood why so many old-fashioned French bakeries had workrooms in the basement. Keeping the firm *levain* cool by working with it underground was another way to make sure it didn't get too sour, so it would produce *pain au levain* with all the flavors in balance.

Baking bread with stiff dough *levain* is similarly leisurely. The first rise can take up to four hours, and once the dough is divided and shaped, it needs to proof for another one to two hours. *Pain au levain*'s unique reddish brown crust is super-caramelized because of the sugars produced by the wild yeast during its extra-long fermentation. It has a beautiful honeycomb crumb with lots of nooks and crannies for catching melting butter. I like to call its crumb consistently inconsistent, because you'll get holes of all different sizes in each slice but the slices' overall appearance will be uniform. You can definitely taste the acids in the bread, but I wouldn't call it sour. The acid just balances the sweetness from the whole wheat. I learned how to bake classic *pain au levain* with Basil over twenty years ago. I have baked it day after day at my own bakery for nearly as long. My business was founded on this bread, and it is the centerpiece of my first book, *Bread Alone*.

No discussion of *levain* baking would be complete without a tribute to *pain Poilâne™*, the traditional whole wheat peasant loaf made famous by Pierre Poilâne in the 1930s and expanded into a brand by his sons, Max and Lionel. No question about it, *pain Poilâne™* is the most famous sourdough bread in France and throughout the world. What's amazing to me is that the Poilânes have created a signature and a trademark out of perhaps the simplest kind of *levain* bread there is.

Visiting their bakeries is like traveling back in time. In the more than twenty years that I've been going to Paris and the dozens of times that I've visited both Lionel's and Max's shops, I've been unable to detect a single change in the setup. I learned about sourdough *miche* from Max, whose bakery was just a few blocks from Le Moulin de la Vierge, on rue Brancion at the edge of the fourteenth arondissement. Some mornings after finishing up at Basil's bakery, I'd walk over to see Max, who would be taking care of business in his ground-level office, wearing a dress shirt, bow tie, and cardigan. When we descended the stairs and walked into the work area of his bakery, I felt like I was stepping back two centuries, so primitive was the arrangement. Maybe the transistor radio has been replaced with a newer model, but that's it. What doesn't change is the relentless baking schedule. Max's bakery is open twenty-four hours a day, seven days a week. Every two hours, ninety 2-kilo boules are loaded into the oven.

Because of Max's demanding baking schedule, his system for maintaining his *levain* starter differs from Basil's. Basil keeps a starter separate from his dough, maintaining it by feeding it in the evening and then letting it ferment slowly so that it is ready to raise

bread when he needs it the next day. Max, in contrast, doesn't cultivate and maintain a separate starter. After a batch of dough is mixed, all but 20 kilos is cut into pieces to be shaped into boules. The remaining 20 kilos of dough are transferred to a tub near the mixer, mixed with fresh flour and water, and allowed to ferment. After several hours, when the next batch of dough is ready to be mixed, this fermented dough, now teaming with yeast and ready to raise bread, is added to the mixing bowl and the bakers start again. Originally there must have been a *levain* starter at Poilâne, if only to raise the very first batch of dough. But now they bake at such a quick pace that there's no time or need to refresh and maintain a separate starter. Somewhere along the line, one of the Poilânes modified the traditional technique to accommodate the round-the-clock baking routine.

The only machine I saw among stacks of huge linen-lined bannetons, metal mixing bowls, and a wood-fired oven was a one-speed mixer dating from World War II. Not only was a high-speed mixer unnecessary for making sourdough *miche*, it was undesirable. Max explained how slow, steady kneading gently conditions the gluten to create an extensible and elastic dough. The modern practice of high-speed mixing, while hurrying along the process, oxygenates the dough too much and bleaches it out, causing the bread to lose flavor and character. It was at Max's bakery that I first touched and tasted type 85 flour, which gives sourdough *miche* its distinctive color and whole-grain flavor. The dough felt surprisingly soft to me. I learned that it was a relatively soft flour, containing only about 10.5 to 11 percent protein. At an old work table, two bakers in shorts and sandals shaped giant 5-kilo rounds of dough called *miches*. I often jumped in to assist them. Then I'd follow Max to a café next door, where we'd sip Côtes du Rhone from tumblers and he'd recite some of his poetry for me until it was time to bake the bread, in just under 2 hours. We'd return to the bakery and watch the bakers load the rounds into the oven. An hour later they'd pull out the bulky chocolate-brown *miches*. As soon as the breads were unloaded, the bakers began to shape the next batch.

Max's sourdough *miche* has a mythic aura, but I learned from him how incredibly simple the whole process of sourdough baking can be when you reduce it to its basic elements and bake routinely.

I brought back the technique for stiff dough *levain* and incorporated it into my routine at Bread Alone, using it to turn out traditional *pain au levain*. I also used my *levain* to make peasant loaves, keeping it separate from my dough so that I could close the bakery for a few hours every day. I shared Basil's and Max's attitude, taking good care of it but not really considering it with curiosity anymore. It was an essential ingredient of these two foundational breads, and that was that. Then a remarkable journey initiated by an Alsatian visitor to Bread Alone led me to a tiny bakery in the village of Buhl, where traditional *levain* was being used to create decidedly untraditional breads. This bakery, Fabiopain (the "bio" stands for *biologique*, meaning organic), made me reconsider the potential of my own *levain* and inspired me to create some brand-new *pains au levain* of my own.

In the spring of 2001, Leon Mader, a retired engineer from Mulhouse in Alsace, burst into my bakery with a video camera and an eccentric request. He was visiting his sister, who lived in the Catskills and regularly bought my French-style sourdough breads. She had directed him to Bread Alone, where she thought he might be able to indulge in his peculiar hobby—making professional-quality videos of artisanal bakers practicing their craft! Would I mind if he followed me around for a day, taping me as I baked? Although it was hardly convenient—try getting five hundred loaves in and out of the ovens while fulfilling someone's request to sample the bread yet again for the camera, but this time with more feeling!—I had to indulge him when I saw his passion for his project. At the end of the day we exchanged e-mail addresses, and for the next six months he sent me weekly messages repeating his offer to put me up in Mulhouse and introduce me to his favorite bakers. I just didn't have the time to take off from Bread Alone, but I did wonder what I was missing. I hadn't explored much of northeastern

France, and if anyone knew the best bakers in that area, it was surely Leon.

Just a few days after receiving a message in late fall of that year, I got a call from my friend Juergen Schwald, the owner of a company that manufactures special bags to keep bread fresh, inviting me on a spring ski trip to the Austrian Alps. We agreed to rendezvous in Zurich and drive to Lech, a ski resort where one of my favorite bakers, Clemens Walch, lives. When I checked my atlas and noticed the town of Mulhouse in bold letters only an inch to the left of Zurich, I couldn't resist e-mailing Leon to tell him I would soon be passing through.

From the moment he picked me up at the train station, Leon devoted himself to showing me the best of the area's bread, chauffeuring me from one shop to the next and hosting a lunch with the president of the Alsatian Baking Association. I guess I shouldn't have been surprised that his baker friends seemed to know me already. Most of them had seen Leon's videotape from his day at Bread Alone. I was soon treated to videotapes of the local talent, after sumptuous dinners of roast chicken and pot-au-feu and home-baked tarts prepared by his talented and gracious wife.

The first bakery we visited was a typical village operation, with a machine mixer, a long wooden work table, an oven, and a fifteen-year-old apprentice assisting the owner in his work. They were setting out wooden proofing boards on the workbench, some of them lined with boules as smooth as river stones, others covered with linen *couches* cradling baguettes. "His father was a baker," Leon said of the owner. "His grandfather was a baker. This is the real French bread." Finding a traditional bakery like this should be one of the joys of traveling and eating in France. But I was jaded. My high hopes for the trip diminished as I took in the same details I'd seen in dozens of *boulangeries* on previous trips. All six of the bakers we visited in and around Mulhouse were welcoming and friendly. They were all curious about how I had learned to make French bread. We sat and talked over coffee about our work, while Leon beamed with pleasure. But every time I saw the familiar setting and the same baguettes, *bâtards*, and boules faithfully reproduced as they had been for generations, my enthusiasm waned. Was there nothing new for me to see? I was tempted to cut the side trip short and head back to Switzerland for skiing.

A stop at a farmstead museum on the way home from the final bakery changed my mood. The museum featured a windmill as tall as a schooner. Inside, a rough-hewn shaft turned an immense granite wheel in slow circles atop its twin. We watched it grind wheat berries into coarse whole wheat flour. This primitive process is still the best way to grind flour rich with germ oil and full of vital nutrients. For years I've made it a priority to use only stone-ground flour in my bread, not just for its flavor and healthfulness but because it stimulates strong fermentation. I turned to Leon and asked him if he knew anyone locally who was using stone-ground organic flour. "Well, I've heard there is a health-food store in Buhl that sells very good bread," he replied. "I've never been there myself. Shall we go?"

We headed for the parking lot and drove to the tiny village nestled into a hillside—just a scattering of shops, a few farmhouses, and a post office. I went straight to the health-food store, a funky, cramped place that smelled like cheese, hay, and incense. I strode right to a tall wooden rack at the front of the store that was crammed with dozens of loaves, their red-brown crusts telling me that they had to be *pain au levain*. I took one in my hands and squeezed. The crust resisted at first, then fracture lines shot out from my grip. One of the loaves was cut in half and on display, showing the contrast between the thick crust and tender crumb. The bread smelled like warmed dark caramel, toasted nuts, and wheat. Classic *levain* in perfect balance, I thought. Taking a closer look at the labels and then the breads, I was astounded. Yes, they were *pains au levain*, but varieties I had never heard of: kamut *levain* (page 130), spelt *levain* (page 130), sesame seed *levain* (page 129). The ponytailed young clerk told us they came from a nearby organic bakery called Fabiopain. I had encountered *pain biologique* in Paris, but finding it in this tiny town on the far eastern edge of the country

signaled that organic bread was no longer a fringe item. Leon and I grabbed one loaf of each kind, took them back to his house, and ate them with dinner that night. He remained calm, but I couldn't contain myself. "We've got to find this bakery tomorrow!" He nodded solemnly and got out his video camera.

What we found the next day was a spot so picturesque it could have been a movie set. Fabiopain was located in a meticulously renovated eight-hundred-year-old barn by the side of a country road, just outside the village we had visited the day before. Fields of spring flowers bloomed all around the fairy-tale structure with its hand-hewed beams and tiled roof. Inside was a perfect little bakery with a domed brick oven and glistening tile floors. Hand-crafted wooden racks held immaculate willow bannetons. Classical music played in the background.

I've visited a few bakeries where making *levain* is an esteemed art, as serious an endeavor as making Bordeaux wine. Fabiopain is one of them. At this bakery there was a thermostatically controlled room where the culture was fermented. Timers alerted the bakers to taste the sourdough every two hours. After tasting it, they initialed a chart on the wall and then described the dough's condition. Through such careful observation and note-taking, the Fabiopain bakers were able to identify and consistently produce the highest-quality *levain*.

At the center of the work area was an Artofex mixer, coveted by artisan bakers all over the world for its extreme slow-motion kneading. This legendary machine is no longer manufactured and can only be purchased used and refurbished. Its two mechanical arms move up and down within the mixing bowl at 45-degree angles, the mechanical fingers squeezing and pulling the dough as the bowl rotates very slowly. In most bakeries, loud pop music is played over the din of the mixer; at Fabiopain it was actually possible to listen to classical music while kneading because the Artofex is so quiet. Kneading a batch of dough in the Artofex takes twenty to twenty-five minutes, twice the time it takes in the standard spiral mixer used in most bakeries. It is difficult to overknead, and thus over-oxygenate, dough in an

Artofex. Its presence in the bakery was another sign of the high craftsmanship at Fabiopain.

Most bakers working with *levain* make wheat and rye breads. Here I saw breads that contained nuts, seeds, and a variety of organic whole-grain flours, every single one of them made with absolute adherence to traditional *levain* techniques. I was impressed beyond description with the delicious combination of *levain* qualities and whole-grain goodness. The combination was unforced and utterly natural. The focus at this very special bakery was not simply on making bread that was good for you. It was on crafting traditional bread using the best organic ingredients available and coming up with classics for the new century in the process. The organic breads from Fabiopain were the furthest thing imaginable from the dense "health loaf" on sale next to the supplements at an American health-food store. These breads had satisfying, not heavy, structures and rich flavor from all the healthy nut and grain oils. The mission at Fabiopain was to please the senses above all else. This is why the breads are admired just as much by fanatics for tradition like Leon as they are by the environmentally aware young French people in the area who are committed to living "green."

I didn't know what I was looking for when I set out for Alsace, but I realized it when I saw Fabiopain. I was searching for ways to merge my love of heirloom breads with my commitment to organic whole grains, and here it was. (Bread Alone is now a certified organic bakery, a distinction I worked hard to earn and am so proud of that I imprint each of my breads with a *Certified Organic* stamp.) I was looking for new breads that I could enjoy just as much as the old ones, and here they were. Down to the elegant wrapping paper, everything about this harmonious place was crafted with beauty and pleasure in mind. Each step in making the breads was a treat for the senses— soaking and squeezing the beautifully variegated seeds and grains, kneading the wonderfully textured doughs, inhaling their unique fragrances as they fermented. I couldn't wait to go home and experience the pleasure of making whole-grain and seeded variations on *levain*.

The recipe for stiff dough *levain* on page 111 is the same one I use at Bread Alone, scaled down in quantity for the home baker. It is identical to the recipe used in Basil's bakery. The recipe for Whole Wheat Sourdough *Miche* inspired by *pain Poilâne*™ (page 118) calls for stiff dough *levain*, because unless you bake bread every two hours, as they do at Max's bakery, you will have to make a separate starter to raise your bread. The recipe for Quintessential French Sourdough (page 124), reworked and refined over the years, is the basis for every one of the recipes that follows. Because of my visit to Fabiopain, I am able to give you not only a traditional recipe for my best *pain au levain* but new recipes for French-style sourdough breads made with sunflower, sesame, or flax seeds or with spelt, kamut, or soy flour. I've also revisited *pains des fantaisie*, traditional French breads mixed with savory bits like chopped olives, bacon, and cheese. Taking my lead from Fabiopan, I've tried to incorporate these rich ingredients in moderation, to maintain the wonderful balance that defines great *pain au levain*.

✳ KITCHEN NOTES: STIFF DOUGH *LEVAIN* AT HOME

Nothing gives a home baker confidence like making the same bread over and over again, each time learning more about the dough and improving the technique. No one bakes more confidently than Max Poilâne, who followed his father in choosing to make only one *levain* bread, the peasant loaf, and make it perfectly. You can go that route at home, perfecting your *levain* technique by baking this wonderful bread on schedule just as Max does. Or you can try classic *pain au levain* and its variations. With the *pain au levain* recipes in this chapter, there is just one dough to master, but the range of finished breads will make the results of your practice pleasurable and interesting in the extreme.

Here is some advice to give you a head start.

Wait. Your *levain* will rise. So much fear surrounds the idea of cultivating a sourdough that it is difficult to convince American home bakers to try their hand at it. Packaged yeast is so reliable. You can actually see the little granules of it when you tear open the envelope and spill it into a bowl. It's much harder to believe in the invisible wild yeast that I'm telling you exists in your flour and in the air in your kitchen. But building a *levain* is a simple process of cultivation. You aren't surprised when a tomato plant sprouts from a seed you've planted in some potting soil and watered faithfully. Why worry that your *levain* culture, properly watered and fed, won't grow? French bakers certainly don't question the outcome. They just mix a certain proportion of flour and water together and wait. No big deal. They know that *levain* will raise dough, not because they're scientists but because they've seen it work over and over again. Try cultivating your own *levain* and baking *pain au levain* just once and you will begin to develop the same trust in the wild yeast in your culture.

Acquire patience. Sourdough baking has a slower pace than and different rhythm from baking with packaged yeast. It doesn't take a lot of work to cultivate a *levain*, but it takes patience. The process may take four days or it may take ten, depending on the composition of your flour, the climate, the season. You'll have to judge the culture's ripeness not by the clock but by how it looks, smells, and tastes. You will know it's ready when it looks like spiderwebs with curds of cottage cheese clinging to it. It will smell musty and earthy and have a little effervescence.

The wild, homegrown yeasts that leaven *pain au levain* aren't as fast-acting or predictable as packaged yeast, and the dough won't feel or behave exactly the same from one baking session to the next. I take you through the steps of mixing, fermenting, proofing, and baking this dough so you will know through observation, if not by the clock, when to wait and when to move on. In the recipe for Quintessential French Sourdough, the dough ferments almost twice as long as a straight dough. This slow fermentation unlocks the deepest flavors of the grain. Baked longer than you might expect, the loaves will have a

very porous crumb and hardy crust, just like the loaves from Fabiopain.

Get to know your *levain* as it ferments. You don't have to keep a chart and initial it every two hours the way they do at Fabiopain, but the only way to become a *levain* expert is to study your culture with the same purposefulness and intensity. Watch it grow. Taste it every hour and a half. At first the flavors will be subtle, and then they'll get stronger and more distinctive. Observe how the weather or a new brand of flour affects the fermentation. Approach the study of your *levain* with excitement and curiosity rather than fear. Over the days, you'll notice how its texture lightens and it gives off an earthy, effervescent smell, like freshly turned earth. When you pinch off a tiny piece and taste it, as the bakers at Fabiopain do periodically, you'll note how the flavor becomes more pronounced. When you slice into it, you'll see the changing pattern of webbing and bubbles.

Knead your peasant loaf or *pain au levain* by hand at least once. I remembered how Max Poilâne set his mixer at a slow speed and how I watched the slow rotation of the Artofex mixer at Fabiopain. The slower pace of *levain* baking is an invitation to take a little extra time to work with the dough and get to know it. When you knead by hand, you'll be able to see the gluten begin to develop and smooth strands of it lengthen. You'll see the dough change from a ragged bundle into a smooth, satiny round. This particular bread dough, because it is a little stiffer than many of the other doughs in the book, is a little bit easier to handle, perfect for novices. Don't worry about getting tired. Stop and rest for a few minutes. This will only improve the dough, giving the proteins in the flour a chance to absorb the liquid and making the dough easier to knead when you resume.

Hand-kneading has benefits beyond getting to know the dough. It is work, but it can also be pleasurable and relaxing. When I'm teaching, I compare hand-kneading to filling up a big bathtub and then taking a long soak. It takes you away from your regular day and refocuses your attention on physical sensation. When I traveled to Alsace, I left my hectic routine behind. Visiting Fabiopain, I was reminded that bread-crafting is pleasurable work. The bread at Fabiopain isn't hand-kneaded, of course, and the bakery is a business, not a spa. But the careful nurturing of the *levain*, the thoughtful use of whole grains and seeds, the slow kneading of the dough in the Artofex mixer, reminded me that making bread by hand can be a wonderful sensory experience.

Stone-ground flour produces the ideal *pain au levain*.

The *levain* starter and the breads in this chapter all contain at least a percentage of whole wheat flour. Since it's not difficult to find stone-ground whole wheat flour (see Resources, pages 333–34), I highly recommend seeking it out for these recipes. Stone-ground flour hydrates differently from flour milled by machine, absorbing more water and baking up into a moister bread. Because the process preserves all of the grain's germ oil and enzymes, the flour is able to sustain a long fermentation, essential for creating lofty and crusty loaves. As a bonus, most stone-ground flour is now milled from organically grown wheat, which benefits your health and the environment.

Play with the recipe.

There is no need to learn a cookbook full of recipes to produce a bake-shop variety of breads. The genius of the Fabiopain bakers is that they have found a way to use one dough and vary it slightly to create a menu of breads that are profoundly different from each other. Once you have mastered the recipe for stiff dough *levain* on page 111 and are comfortable with the variations I suggest, you may even want to try some of your own. Just remember to keep things in balance. Stuffing your *pain au levain* with too many nuts or adding olives, bacon, *and* cheese instead of just one will obscure the wonderful qualities of the bread.

Consider pâte fermentée as a stepping-stone.

The number-one fear of inexperienced bakers is that they'll wind up with a rock-hard, unrisen loaf after spending so much time cultivating a sourdough starter. It would be a shame if such a fear prevented you from exploring the diversity of whole-grain breads in this chapter. If you aren't ready to take the sourdough leap, you can use a shortcut method called *pâte fermentée*. *Pâte fermentée* (see page 116 for the recipe) is a type of pre-ferment, a stiff dough leavened with packaged yeast and mixed eight to twelve hours before preparing the bread dough. Use it in place of *levain* in any of the recipes in this chapter. My secret hope is that *pâte fermentée* will be your stepping-stone to baking with *levain*. It will introduce you to the two-step process of mixing a special dough *before* you make the bread dough. It will help you accept the strange idea that a piece of well-fermented dough is all you need to raise a loaf of bread.

STIFF DOUGH *LEVAIN*

. . . .

Allow 1 day to activate the culture;
2 to 9 days to feed the culture;
8 to 12 hours to refresh the culture

. . . .

Using this recipe, you can create a *levain* culture that is as genuine as any 200-year-old mix. It may sound preposterous that anything could spontaneously spring to life from a mixture of flour and water. In *Bread Alone* I went so far as to suggest using a pinch of packaged yeast for insurance. But after working with French bakers and interrogating them about their methods over the years, I've learned to trust in what I can't see. Following this recipe, you will create a culture and feed it once a day. I coach you day by day to see, smell, and taste your *levain* so you'll know it is growing.

Use spring water and organic, stone-ground flour to offer the yeast and bacteria the purest environment for healthy growth. Once you've established a healthy culture, you can maintain it with tap water and nonorganic flour. On day 1, add some rye flour, which has more minerals and enzymes than wheat flour, to kick-start the fermentation process. On subsequent days, you'll blend bread flour and whole wheat flour into your culture to mimic the wholesome germ-speckled type 55 flour French bakers feed their *levain*.

Equipment

MEDIUM MIXING BOWL
CLEAN, CLEAR 1-QUART CONTAINER

DAY 1

INGREDIENTS	VOLUME	U.S. WEIGHT	METRIC WEIGHT	BAKER'S PERCENTAGE
Spring water, tepid (70 to 78 degrees)	1/3 cup	2.6 ounces	75 grams	75
Type 55–style flour from King Arthur or Giusto's or unbleached all-purpose flour	1/3 cup	1.8 ounces	50 grams	50
Organic, stone-ground fine rye flour	1/3 cup	1.8 ounces	50 grams	50

ACTIVATE THE CULTURE. Pour the water into a medium mixing bowl and stir in the bread flour and rye flour with a wooden spoon until you have a stiff, tacky dough. It will not be smooth. Scrape down the sides of the bowl and cover it with plastic wrap. Let stand at room temperature (70 to 75 degrees) for 24 hours.

DAY 2

INGREDIENTS	VOLUME	U.S. WEIGHT	METRIC WEIGHT	BAKER'S PERCENTAGE
Spring water, tepid (70 to 78 degrees)	2 tablespoons	1.1 ounces	30 grams	55
Type 55–style flour from King Arthur or Giusto's or unbleached all-purpose flour	1/3 cup	1.8 ounces	50 grams	91
Organic, stone-ground whole wheat flour	1 tablespoon	0.2 ounce	5 grams	9

FEED THE CULTURE. Uncover the culture. It may have risen very slightly, but it will look much as it did on day 1.

Pour the water into the bowl. Use a wooden spoon to press the dough on the bottom and sides of the bowl to break it up and soften it. The water will turn milky and will bubble—a sign that the yeast is already active. Add the bread flour and whole wheat flour and stir until all the water is absorbed. You will have a stiff, dry dough. Use the spoon to press the dough against the sides of the bowl, collecting as much of the flour as you can. With one hand, tilt the bowl toward you. With your other hand, knead the dough right in the bowl until you have worked in all of the loose flour (don't worry about the flour that sticks to the sides of the bowl). The dough will not be smooth. Cover the bowl with plastic wrap and let stand at room temperature (70 to 75 degrees) for another 24 hours.

DAY 3				
INGREDIENTS	VOLUME	U.S. WEIGHT	METRIC WEIGHT	BAKER'S PERCENTAGE
Spring water, tepid (70 to 78 degrees)	2 tablespoons	1.1 ounces	30 grams	55
Type 55–style flour from King Arthur or Giusto's or unbleached all-purpose flour	⅓ cup	1.8 ounces	50 grams	91
Organic, stone-ground whole wheat flour	2 teaspoons	0.2 ounce	5 grams	9

FEED THE CULTURE. Uncover the culture and see how much it has expanded in 24 hours—anywhere from one and a half to two times its original volume. The surface of the culture will be dimpled from bubbles forming below it. Move your face close to the dough and inhale the wheaty, effervescent scent, like the foam on Belgian ale. Slice through the surface with a paring knife and you will see the network of gas bubbles separated by strands of gluten. Pinch off a tiny piece of the dough and taste it. Already you will be able to taste the sugars that have been released and to feel the gumminess of the gluten. The culture will taste pleasantly tangy but not sour.

Pour the water over the culture. Use a wooden spoon to press the dough against the bottom and sides of the bowl to break it up and soften it. Again the water will turn milky and will froth. Add the bread flour and whole wheat flour and stir until all the water is absorbed, forming a stiff, dry dough. Use the spoon to press the dough against the sides of the bowl, collecting as much of the flour as you can. With one hand, tilt the bowl toward you. With your other hand, knead the dough right in the bowl until you have worked in all of the loose flour (don't worry about the flour that sticks to the sides of the bowl). The dough will not be smooth. Cover the bowl with plastic wrap and let stand at room temperature (70 to 75 degrees) for another 24 hours.

DAYS 4–10

TEST THE CULTURE. Uncover the bowl and examine the culture to determine if it is ripe enough to become a *levain*. If ready, it will exhibit most, if not all, of the following signs: it will have risen into a dome that may already be deflating; its surface will look dimpled; it will smell like ripe fruit with a hint of sourness; when you draw a paring knife through it, you will see large and small air pockets trapped in a complex of gluten strands; it will taste as tangy as a lime. If your culture shows these signs, you are only one step away from establishing a *levain*. Skip to Day 10 and Beyond: Refreshing the *Levain*.

Don't worry if your culture doesn't yet exhibit these traits. It just needs a few more feedings. Repeat the steps in day 3 every 24 hours for up to 6 more days. Use warm (100 to 110 degrees) water in place of tepid water, and be sure to keep the bowl in a warm (75 to 80 degrees), draft-free place. Check it each day, and as soon as it resembles the active culture I have described, move on to refreshing your *levain*.

If your culture remains inactive past this point, you will have to start again. Don't be discouraged. Whenever you are dealing with living organisms, whether you are trying to grow plants from seed or cultivating wild yeast and bacteria in a culture of water and flour, things can go wrong.

DAY 10 AND BEYOND: REFRESHING THE *LEVAIN*

Every living thing needs food to survive, including the microorganisms you have cultivated in your *levain*. To keep them alive and healthy so that they will be able to raise your *pain au levain* reliably, you must add flour and water to your sourdough on a regular basis, at least once a week, whether or not you plan to bake.

INGREDIENTS	VOLUME	U.S. WEIGHT	METRIC WEIGHT	BAKER'S PERCENTAGE
Spring water, tepid (70 to 78 degrees)	¼ cup	1.8 ounces	50 grams	50
Type 55–style flour from King Arthur or Giusto's or unbleached all-purpose flour	⅔ cup	3.4 ounces	95 grams	95
Organic, stone-ground whole wheat flour	2 teaspoons	0.2 ounce	5 grams	5

REFRESH THE CULTURE. Pinch off about 1/4 cup of your *levain* culture, or a piece the size of an Italian plum (1.6 ounces/45 grams), and discard the rest. (It might seem like a waste to throw away the culture you've so carefully nurtured, but if you keep a large amount it will produce excess alcohol and acids that will eventually kill the yeast and give your bread an off taste.) Place the piece of *levain* in a wide, shallow mixing bowl and pour the water over it. Use a rubber spatula to mash the *levain* against the sides of the bowl to break it up and soften it. The water will turn milky and bubble, as it has on the previous days. Add the bread flour and whole wheat flour and stir until you have a very dry dough with loose flour scattered all around it. Using the spatula, press the dough against the sides of the bowl to collect as much of the stray flour as you can. Then tip the bowl with one hand while you knead with the other, chasing down the last bits of flour and working them into a very stiff dough, 1 to 2 minutes. The dough will not be smooth.

Place the dough in a clean 1-quart container and cover it. Place a piece of masking tape on the side of the container to mark the level the dough will reach when it has doubled in volume. Let the *levain* stand to ferment at room temperature for 8 to 12 hours, until it has ripened. You will know that your *levain* is potent enough to raise bread when it rises into a dome and has at least doubled in volume. It will be airy and fragile-looking and will be filled with air bubbles and a honeycomb of gluten strands. It may already have begun to deflate. It will smell mildly vinegary and have a tangy taste.

Use the *levain* right away, or store it in the refrigerator for up to 1 week.

MAINTAIN THE *LEVAIN*. If your *levain* has been in the refrigerator for a week, it is time to refresh it again, whether or not you plan on baking. Weekly refreshment will keep it alive and healthy so that when you do bake, it will be capable of raising your dough. Just repeat the steps for refreshment and refrigerate it again for up to 1 week.

PREPARE THE *LEVAIN* FOR BAKING. Whether or not you have refreshed your *levain* recently, you must refresh it 8 to 12 hours before you want to bake to ensure that it is in optimum shape for raising and flavoring bread. Follow the refreshment steps as described above. After the *levain* has fermented at room temperature (70 to 75 degrees) for 8 to 12 hours, measure out what you will need for your recipe. Then place 1/4 cup (1.6 ounces/45 grams) of what is left over into a clean container, refresh this portion, and refrigerate for up to 1 week for use in the future.

PÂTE FERMENTÉE

. . . .

ALLOW 1 HOUR TO FERMENT AT ROOM TEMPERATURE;
8 TO 12 HOURS TO FERMENT IN THE REFRIGERATOR

. . . .

If you are in a hurry to try some of the recipes in this chapter, or if you don't want to commit to cultivating *levain* at this point, you can substitute this traditional French pre-ferment made with packaged yeast for *levain*. The stiff dough ferments for an hour at room temperature and then 8 to 12 hours in the refrigerator (the cold controls the rate of fermentation), and then it's ready to mix into bread dough. Professional bakers often add additional yeast to the dough, but my recipes rely on the leavening power of the *pâte fermentée* alone.

Pâte fermentée is a spongy, cream-colored dough just like a *levain*. But it is not a sourdough and won't give your bread the full flavor or dark, thick crust of true *pain au levain*. Nor will bread made with *pâte fermentée* remain fresh as long as *pain au levain*. But using this pre-ferment will give you bread that is tastier, airier, and crisper than bread that doesn't use a pre-ferment.

Substituting *pâte fermentée* for *levain* accelerates the baking process in more ways than one. The dough will rise twice as fast as with *pain au levain*, so keep your eye on the dough and adjust rising times and proofing times accordingly.

Equipment
CLEAN, CLEAR 1-QUART CONTAINER

INGREDIENTS	VOLUME	U.S. WEIGHT	METRIC WEIGHT	BAKER'S PERCENTAGE
Water, tepid (70 to 78 degrees)	¼ cup	1.8 ounces	50 grams	65
Instant yeast	1 teaspoon	0.1 ounce	4 grams	5
Type 55–style flour from King Arthur or Giusto's or unbleached all-purpose flour	½ cup	2.6 ounces	70 grams	93
Organic, stone-ground whole wheat flour	2 teaspoons	0.2 ounce	5 grams	7

MIX THE *PÂTE FERMENTÉE*. Pour the water into a small mixing bowl. Add the yeast, the bread flour, and the whole wheat flour and stir with a rubber spatula until all of the water is absorbed. Then use the spatula or your hand to press the dough against the bottom and sides of the bowl to collect any stray flour. The dough will be stiff and slightly tacky. It doesn't need to be perfectly smooth.

FERMENT THE *PÂTE FERMENTÉE*. Place the dough in the 1-quart container and cover it with a lid or plastic wrap. Place a piece of masking tape on the side of the container to mark the level the dough will reach when it doubles in volume. Let the dough stand at room temperature (70 to 75 degrees) for 1 hour. It will inflate visibly, maybe 25 to 30 percent,

and become spongy and airy. Place the container in the refrigerator to ferment more slowly, for at least 8 and up to 12 hours. It will continue to rise in the refrigerator until it reaches the masking-tape mark and will develop a fresh, wheaty, sweet smell that will carry over into the bread dough.

SUBSTITUTE THE *PÂTE FERMENTÉE* FOR *LEVAIN*. Use all of the *pâte fermentée* you have prepared in place of the *levain* in the recipe for Quintessential French Sourdough (page 124) or any of the variations and mix as directed. Reduce the rising times to 1 1/2 to 2 hours for fermentation and 45 minutes to 1 hour for proofing. Bake as directed. Breads made with *pâte fermentée* will keep at room temperature in resealable plastic bags for 3 to 5 days.

WHOLE WHEAT SOURDOUGH *MICHE* INSPIRED BY *PAIN POILÂNE*™
Pain au levain complet

. . . .

ALLOW 8 TO 12 HOURS TO PREPARE THE WHOLE WHEAT *LEVAIN*;

20 MINUTES TO MIX AND REST THE DOUGH;

10 TO 14 MINUTES TO KNEAD;

3 TO 4 HOURS TO FERMENT;

2 TO 3 HOURS TO PROOF;

40 TO 50 MINUTES TO BAKE

. . . .

Once upon a time this peasant-style loaf (*miche* is slang for "butt cheek") was deemed suitable only for Paris's poor. Pierre Poilâne opened his bakery, founded on the recipe, in 1932. His sons, Max and Lionel, made it chic in the 1980s, and now it is a symbol of artisanal excellence in France and around the world.

Dark, elemental, and soul-satisfying, *pain Poilâne*™ has inspired and influenced every baker I know. In this recipe I strove to develop a bread that has the same whole-grain essence and dense but never heavy texture as *pain Poilâne*™ but that's easy for Americans to make at home. This version uses a *levain* made with whole wheat. Whole wheat flour in France is a little more refined than the whole wheat flour generally available to American home bakers. To approximate the type 85 flour they use in France, from which 15 percent of the coarsest bran is sifted, you can blend stone-ground whole wheat flour with a little bit of bread flour. Partway through the first rise, give the dough an additional quick kneading to invigorate the yeast with a fresh supply of oxygen. This encourages a livelier fermentation and creates bigger and more numerous holes in the crumb of the baked loaf. As for shaping the bread, I've cut down the loaf's size so that it is still big enough to be called a *miche* but is small enough to fit in a home oven. If you're lucky enough to have a home hearth oven, double the recipe so you can enjoy this bread in its monumental form.

Although I suggest that beginning bakers try *pâte fermentée* rather than the *levain* recipes in this chapter, I would never make that recommendation in the case of *pain Poilâne*™. Sourdough is part of this bread's essence, and to use a shortcut would be to cheat yourself of experiencing it in all its glory. The bread is perfect for stenciling because of its large, open surface. For a special occasion, you can stencil a name or even a design on the top of your bread. At Thanksgiving time, we stencil a turkey shape on top of ours, to the delight of our customers. To make your own stencil, see the directions on page 123.

Equipment

BENCH SCRAPER

1 LARGE BANNETON OR A COLANDER LINED WITH A KITCHEN TOWEL

BAKING STONE

CAST-IRON SKILLET

BAKER'S PEEL OR RIMLESS BAKING SHEET

PARCHMENT PAPER

SINGLE-EDGED RAZOR BLADE OR SERRATED KNIFE

Note: If you don't have a stiff dough *levain* already prepared, you will have to make one from scratch (page 111) or substitute a commercial sourdough starter (see pages 333–34 for sources).

WHOLE WHEAT *LEVAIN*				
INGREDIENTS	VOLUME	U.S. WEIGHT	METRIC WEIGHT	BAKER'S PERCENTAGE
Stiff dough *levain* (page 111)	About ¼ cup	1.8 ounces	50 grams	50
Water, tepid (70 to 78 degrees)	⅓ cup	2.6 ounces	75 grams	75
Stone-ground whole wheat flour	⅔ cup	3.5 ounces	100 grams	100

PREPARE THE *LEVAIN*. Take your *levain* out of the refrigerator. Pinch off about 1/4 cup, or a piece the size of an Italian plum (1.6 ounces/45 grams), and discard the rest. Place the piece of *levain* in a wide, shallow mixing bowl and pour the water over it. Use a rubber spatula to mash the *levain* against the sides of the bowl to break it up and soften it. The water will turn milky and bubble. Add the bread flour and whole wheat flour and stir until you have a very dry dough with loose flour scattered all around it. Using the spatula, press the dough against the sides of the bowl to collect as much of the stray flour as you can. Then tip the bowl with one hand while you knead with the other, chasing down the last bits of flour and working them into a very stiff dough, 1 to 2 minutes. The dough will not be smooth.

Place the dough in a clean 1-quart container and cover it. Place a piece of masking tape on the side of the container to mark the level the dough will reach when it has doubled in volume. Let the *levain* stand to ferment at room temperature (70 to 75 degrees) for 8 to 12 hours, until it has risen into a dome and doubled in volume. It may already have begun to deflate. It will be riddled with air pockets that will be visible through the sides and bottom of the container. It will smell as sweet as overripe fruit.

BREAD DOUGH

INGREDIENTS	VOLUME	U.S. WEIGHT	METRIC WEIGHT	BAKER'S PERCENTAGE
Water, tepid (70 to 78 degrees)	1½ cups plus 2 tablespoons	13.2 ounces	375 grams	75
Type 55–style flour from King Arthur or Giusto's or unbleached all-purpose flour	¾ cup	3.5 ounces	100 grams	20
Stone-ground whole wheat flour	2½ cups	14.1 ounces	400 grams	80
Whole wheat *levain*	About 1¼ cups	7.9 ounces	225 grams	45
Sea salt	1½ teaspoons	0.4 ounce	10 grams	2

MIX THE DOUGH. Pour the water into a large mixing bowl or the bowl of a stand mixer. Add the bread flour and whole wheat flour and stir with a rubber spatula just until it absorbs all of the water and a rough dough forms. Cover with plastic wrap and let stand at room temperature for 20 minutes to hydrate the flour and let the gluten develop on its own.

ADD THE *LEVAIN* AND SALT. Uncover the *levain* and pinch off about 1/2 cup, or a piece the size of a tennis ball (4.4 ounces/125 grams). Uncover the dough, add the *levain* piece, and sprinkle on the salt. Use the spatula to work the *levain* and salt into the dough with a few firm strokes. (Cover the remaining *levain* and store it in the refrigerator, refreshing it at least once a week following the instructions on pages 114–15.)

KNEAD THE DOUGH. By hand: Scrape the dough onto an unfloured countertop. (Expect it to stick, no matter what.) Lightly oil your hands with vegetable oil (I use olive oil because I love its smell; the oil you use will not affect the flavor of the bread). Knead the dough with steady, relaxed strokes for 12 to 14 minutes. Stop periodically to collect the dough with a bench scraper. Oil your hands again if necessary. Take a 2-minute break if you need to. The dough will only benefit from a short rest. You will begin to see strands of gluten stretching farther with each stroke. The dough will still look coarse because of the whole wheat flour but will become very smooth and elastic.

Give the dough a windowpane test to judge its readiness: Pinch off a golfball-sized piece and flatten it into a mini-pancake. Gently stretch it until the dough is thin enough to see through. If it tears, press the small piece back into the larger mass, knead it for 1 to 2 minutes more, and test again.

By machine: Use the dough hook and mix the dough on medium speed (4 on a KitchenAid mixer) until it is glossy, smooth, and very stretchable, 10 to 12 minutes. It will not clean the sides of the bowl. Turn off the machine once or twice during kneading to scrape down the sides of the bowl and clean off the hook. Give the dough a windowpane test to judge its readiness, as described above. If it tears, press the small piece back into the larger mass, knead it for 1 to 2 minutes more, and test again.

FERMENT THE DOUGH. Transfer the dough to a lightly oiled, clear, straight-sided 2-quart container with a lid. With masking tape, mark the spot on the container that the dough will reach when it has doubled in volume. Cover and leave it to rise at room temperature (70 to 75 degrees) for 1 hour.

KNEAD AGAIN. Turn the dough out onto a lightly floured counter and knead for 1 to 2 minutes to stimulate the yeast with a fresh supply of oxygen. Round the dough and return it to the container. Cover and let stand until it doubles in size, reaching the mark, 2 to 3 hours. It will be soft and less sticky.

SHAPE THE *MICHE*. Heavily dust the banneton or the colander lined with kitchen towel with whole wheat flour. Turn the dough onto a lightly floured countertop. Flour your hands and shape it into a *miche* by tucking the edges of the dough underneath the bulk, as if you are making a bed, to shape a rough round. Place your hands on either side of the round and move them in tight circles as you pull the dough toward you. If the dough sticks to the counter, lightly dust the counter with flour again. These simultaneous movements will pull any rough bits under the ball and create a taut "skin" around it. Don't worry about making it perfectly round, but be sure to pinch the bottom edges to seal. Place the *miche*, pinched side up, in the banneton or colander, dust it with whole wheat flour, and cover loosely with plastic wrap.

PROOF THE *MICHE*. Let the *miche* stand at room temperature (70 to 75 degrees) until it is pillowy and has doubled in size, 2 to 3 hours. When you press your fingertip into the dough, the indentation will spring back slowly.

PREPARE THE OVEN. About 1 hour before baking, place a baking stone on the middle rack of the oven and a cast-iron skillet on the lower rack. Preheat the oven to 470 degrees.

SCORE THE *MICHE*. Line a baker's peel or rimless baking sheet with parchment paper. Uncover the loaf and tip it out onto the peel or sheet, guiding it with one hand for a soft landing. With a single-edged razor blade, *lame*, or serrated knife, make 4 straight slashes about 1 inch from the edge to form a square-shaped frame. Do not connect the score marks or the crust will rupture where they intersect.

BAKE THE *MICHE*. Slide the loaf onto the baking stone. Place 1/2 cup of ice cubes in the skillet to produce steam. Bake until the crust is walnut brown, 40 to 50 minutes. A large loaf like this needs to be fully baked, especially if you want a good crust, so don't hesitate to add an extra few minutes of baking time if necessary.

COOL AND STORE THE *MICHE*. Slide the peel or the rimless baking sheet under the parchment paper to remove the loaf from the oven. Slide the loaf, still on the parchment, onto a wire rack. Cool the loaf completely, about 2 hours, before slicing. To serve, halve the *miche*, then cut slices from each half. Store it cut side down on a plate or cutting board. For longer storage, wrap in plastic and then aluminum foil and freeze for up to 1 month.

Variation: French Walnut Bread *Pain au levain complet aux noix*

Walnuts are a classic addition to the standard whole wheat *miche*. I like to shape this dough into four small boules. This way, it's easier to cut thin slices to spread goat cheese or brie on.

TOAST THE NUTS. Before mixing the dough, place 1 1/3 cups chopped walnuts on a baking sheet and toast in a preheated 350-degree oven until fragrant, 5 to 8 minutes. Let cool completely.

ADD THE NUTS TO THE DOUGH. During the last 2 minutes of kneading, either by hand or by machine, add the walnuts. In the machine, some of the nuts may collect at the bottom of the bowl. If this happens, press them into the dough with your index finger.

DIVIDE AND SHAPE THE BOULES. Line a baker's peel or baking sheet with parchment paper. Lightly dust the counter with whole wheat flour. Scrape the dough onto the counter. With a bench scraper or chef's knife, cut the dough into 4 equal pieces (12.2 ounces/346 grams each). Shape each piece into a boule (see Shaping Rounds, page 36). Place the rounds, smooth side up, on the parchment-covered peel or baking sheet, about 3 inches apart. Lightly sprinkle with whole wheat flour and cover loosely with plastic wrap.

PROOF THE BOULES. Let the boules stand at room temperature (70 to 75 degrees) until they become pillowy and nearly double in size, 1 to 1 1/2 hours. When you press your fingertip into the dough, the indentation will spring back slowly.

SCORE AND BAKE THE BOULES. With a single-edged razor blade or serrated knife, make an X centered on top of each loaf, about 1/2 inch deep. Slide the loaves, still on the parchment, onto the baking stone. Place 1/2 cup of ice cubes in the skillet to produce steam. Bake until the crust is walnut-brown, 30 to 40 minutes. Cool the loaves completely, about 1 hour, before slicing.

Creating a Stencil

To create a stencil, trace the letters or design on a piece of thick paper or oak tag and cut out with an Exacto knife. Use bold shapes for easiest cutting and cleanest results. When you flip your proofed loaf onto the peel, brush away the excess whole wheat flour with a pastry brush. Take a mister and very lightly spray the surface with water. Place the stencil on top of the bread and sift the surface lightly with white flour. Very carefully but quickly lift the stencil up and away from the dough. Immediately transfer the bread to the oven.

1. Trace the letters or design on a piece of thick paper or oak tag and cut out with an Exacto knife.

2. Place the stencil on top of the bread.

3. Sift the surface lightly with white flour.

4. Lift the stencil up and away from the dough.

QUINTESSENTIAL FRENCH SOURDOUGH
Pain au levain

. . . .

ALLOW 8 TO 12 HOURS TO PREPARE THE *LEVAIN*;

20 MINUTES TO MIX AND REST THE DOUGH;

8 TO 15 MINUTES TO KNEAD;

3 TO 4 HOURS TO FERMENT;

1 TO 1 1/2 HOURS TO PROOF;

35 TO 40 MINUTES TO BAKE

. . . .

I've refined this recipe over the years, tweaking the proportion of *levain* starter and the blend of white, whole wheat, and rye flour. It now comes as close as possible to the germ- and bran-flecked bread flour called type 70 that the bakers at Fabiopain in Alsace use to make their *pain au levain*. Type 70 flour is ground from white winter wheat. It is sweeter, contains more fermentation-inducing enzymes, and has a lower protein content than commercial bread flour ground from hard spring wheat.

This recipe introduces you to a common French bread shape, the *bâtard*. It looks like an overweight baguette and involves the same shaping technique but is easier because there's not as much stretching or rolling. It's the only hand-formed shape that offers uniform slices from beginning to end, perfect for sandwiches.

The Multigrain *Levain* variation for this bread (page 129) is pictured in the color photograph as a round loaf (boule). To make this bread as a round instead of a *bâtard*, see page 36 for shaping instructions.

Traditional *pain au levain* is not nearly as sour as people expect a sourdough bread to be. The French like it this way. If you'd like a little more acidity in the finished bread, chill the dough in the refrigerator to slow down the fermentation, giving the bacteria a chance to produce more acids. The longer the dough chills, or retards, the tangier it will taste. See page 32 for retarding instructions.

✳ MAKES **2** *BÂTARDS* ABOUT **12** INCHES LONG
(17.4 OUNCES/**493** GRAMS EACH)

Equipment

BENCH SCRAPER OR CHEF'S KNIFE

BAKER'S PEEL OR RIMLESS BAKING SHEET

PARCHMENT PAPER

2 KITCHEN TOWELS

BAKING STONE

CAST-IRON SKILLET

SINGLE-EDGED RAZOR BLADE OR SERRATED KNIFE

Note: If you don't have a stiff dough *levain* already prepared, you will have to make one from scratch (page 111) or substitute a commercial sourdough starter (see pages 333–34 for sources), or use the *pâte fermentée* method (page 116) instead.

LEVAIN STARTER				
INGREDIENTS	VOLUME	U.S. WEIGHT	METRIC WEIGHT	BAKER'S PERCENTAGE
Stiff dough *levain* (page 111)	¼ cup	1.6 ounces	45 grams	45
Water, tepid (70 to 78 degrees)	¼ cup	1.8 ounces	50 grams	50
Type 55–style flour from King Arthur or Giusto's or unbleached all-purpose flour	⅔ cup	3.4 ounces	95 grams	95
Stone-ground whole wheat flour	2 teaspoons	0.2 ounce	5 grams	5

PREPARE THE *LEVAIN*. Take your *levain* out of the refrigerator. Pinch off about 1/4 cup, or a piece the size of an Italian plum (1.6 ounces/45 grams), and discard the rest. Place the piece of *levain* in a wide, shallow mixing bowl and pour the water over it. Use a rubber spatula to mash the *levain* against the sides of the bowl to break it up and soften it. The water will turn milky and bubble. Add the bread flour and whole wheat flour and stir until you have a very dry dough with loose flour scattered all around it. Using the spatula, press the dough against the sides of the bowl to collect as much of the stray flour as you can. Then tip the bowl with one hand while you knead with the other, chasing down the last bits of flour and working them into a very stiff dough, 1 to 2 minutes. The dough will not be smooth.

Place the dough in a clean 1-quart container and cover it. Place a piece of masking tape on the side of the container to mark the level the dough will reach when it has doubled in volume. Let the *levain* stand to ferment at room temperature (70 to 75 degrees) for 8 to 12 hours, until it has risen into a dome and doubled in volume. It may already have begun to deflate. It will be riddled with air pockets that will be visible through the sides and bottom of the container. It will smell as sweet as overripe fruit.

BREAD DOUGH				
INGREDIENTS	VOLUME	U.S. WEIGHT	METRIC WEIGHT	BAKER'S PERCENTAGE
Water, tepid (70 to 78 degrees)	1½ cups	12.3 ounces	350 grams	70
Type 55–style flour from King Arthur or Giusto's or unbleached all-purpose flour	2¼ cups	12.3 ounces	350 grams	70
Stone-ground whole wheat flour	¾ cup	4.2 ounces	120 grams	24
Fine or medium rye flour	¼ cup	1.1 ounces	30 grams	6
Levain starter	About ½ cup packed	4.4 ounces	125 grams	25
Sea salt	1½ teaspoons	0.4 ounce	10 grams	2

MIX THE DOUGH. Pour the water into a large mixing bowl or the bowl of a stand mixer. Add the all-purpose flour, whole wheat flour, and rye flour and stir with a rubber spatula just until it absorbs all of the water and a ragged-looking dough forms. Cover with plastic wrap and let stand at room temperature for 20 minutes to hydrate the flour and give the gluten a chance to develop on its own.

ADD THE *LEVAIN* AND SALT. Uncover the *levain* and pinch off about 1/2 cup, or a piece the size of a tennis ball (4.4 ounces/125 grams). Uncover the dough, add the *levain* piece, and sprinkle on the salt. Use the spatula to work the *levain* and salt into the dough with a few firm strokes. (Cover the remaining *levain* and store it in the refrigerator, refreshing it at least once a week following the instructions on pages 114–15.)

KNEAD THE DOUGH. By hand: Turn the dough out onto a lightly floured counter. Flour your hands and knead the dough with confident strokes until it is very smooth and elastic, 12 to 15 minutes. During the first few minutes it will be very sticky and will smear on the counter, but this stage will not last long. Keep kneading, stopping every 8 to 10 strokes to scrape the dough off the counter with a bench scraper and flour your hands again. Soon the dough will firm up, become less sticky, and form a ball. When it reaches this point, stop kneading for a moment, place your hands above the ball of dough, and rub them together vigorously to clean off as much of the excess dough as you can. Flour your hands and start kneading again. Continue until the dough is beautifully smooth and barely tacky.

Give the dough a windowpane test to judge its readiness: Pinch off a golfball-sized piece and flatten it into a mini-pancake. Gently stretch it until the dough is thin enough to see through. If it tears, press the small piece back into the larger mass, knead it for 1 to 2 minutes more, and test again.

By machine: Use the dough hook and mix the dough on medium speed (4 on a KitchenAid mixer) for 8 to 9 minutes. It will clean the sides of the bowl and collect around the dough hook. Give the dough a windowpane test to judge its readiness, as described above. If it tears, press the small piece back into the larger mass, knead it for 1 to 2 minutes more, and test again.

FERMENT THE DOUGH. Transfer the dough to a lightly oiled, clear 2-quart container with a lid. Cover and leave it to rise at room temperature (70 to 75 degrees) for 1 hour. It will not rise noticeably.

TURN THE DOUGH. Scrape the dough out onto a lightly floured counter. Pat it into a rectangle about 6 by 8 inches and fold it like a business letter: Lift the far edge of the dough with both hands, pull it toward you, and place it on the center of the rectangle; lift the near edge with both hands, pull it toward you, and place it in the center, overlapping the top edge by about 1 inch (see illustrations, page 31). Quickly slide both hands under the dough and flip it over so the folds are underneath. Slip it back into the container, pushing it down to fit if you need to. Cover the

dough and let it ferment for 2 to 3 hours more. *Pain au levain* is much less gassy than dough leavened with packaged yeast and does not rise as dramatically. Look for an increase in volume of about 25 percent, and look at the bottom through the container to scout for air pockets. Press your fingertip into the dough. It will feel dense but with a spongy quality. The indentation of your fingertip will spring back slowly.

DIVIDE AND SHAPE THE *BÂTARDS*. Cover a baker's peel or rimless baking sheet with parchment paper. Cut the dough with a bench scraper or chef's knife into 2 equal pieces (17.4 ounces/493 grams each). Shape each piece of dough into a *bâtard* about 12 inches long (see Shaping *Bâtards*, page 38). As you roll the log, taper the ends by increasing the downward pressure at the tips. It will be plump in the center with gently tapered ends.

FORM THE *COUCHE*. Dust the parchment-covered peel or baking sheet with flour and place the *bâtards* on the parchment, seam side down, about 3 inches apart. Lift the parchment paper between the loaves, making a pleat and drawing the loaves close together. Tightly roll up 2 kitchen towels and slip them under the parchment paper on the sides of the two outer loaves to support the sides of each *bâtard* (see illustration, page 74). Lightly dust the tops of the *bâtards* with flour and lightly drape them with plastic wrap.

PROOF THE *BÂTARDS*. Let the loaves rise at room temperature (70 to 75 degrees) until they spread and inflate about one and a half times in size, 1 to 1 1/2 hours. The dough will look slack and relaxed. When you press your fingertip into the dough, the indentation will spring back slowly.

PREPARE THE OVEN. About 1 hour before baking, place a baking stone on the middle rack of the oven and a cast-iron skillet on the lower rack. Heat the oven to 450 degrees.

SCORE THE *BÂTARDS*. Uncover the loaves and stretch the parchment paper out so that it is flat and the loaves are separated on top of it. Score each *bâtard* with a single-edged razor blade or a serrated knife. Starting from the tip, angle the blade 45 degrees to make 4 slashes, about 3 inches long and 1/2 inch deep (see illustration, page 000). Dip the blade in water and use a quick, fluid motion so that it doesn't snag and drag the dough.

BAKE THE *BÂTARDS*. Slide the loaves, still on the parchment, onto the baking stone. Place 1/2 cup of ice cubes in the skillet to produce steam. Bake for 15 minutes, lower the heat to 400 degrees, and continue to bake until the *bâtards* are evenly browned with a deep mahogany tone along the edges of the score marks, 20 to 25 minutes more.

COOL AND STORE THE *BÂTARDS*. Slide the peel or the rimless baking sheet under the parchment paper to remove the loaves from the oven. Slide the loaves, still on the parchment, onto a wire rack. Cool for about 5 minutes and then peel them off the parchment paper. Let the loaves cool completely, about 1 hour, before slicing. They will stay fresh for about 5 days stored in a brown paper bag.

Variations: WHOLE SEED, WHOLE-GRAIN *LEVAINS*

After viewing and tasting Fabiopain's many seeded and whole-grain varieties of *pain au levain*, I began to view my own *levain* recipe as much more than just a traditional sourdough starter. I suddenly realized that it had the potential to raise an array of boldly flavored and textured breads beyond Quintessential French Sourdough. The following breads are simple variations on that recipe, with the addition of whole sunflower, sesame, or flax seeds or a mixture of whole seeds and grains. They share the French sourdough's burnished crust and open, even crumb. At the same time, they are entirely new—the seeds infuse the breads with distinct flavors, and their oils add incredible richness. While they are nutty and hearty, they don't have even a trace of the heaviness of your typical health-food store "energy loaf."

Soaking the seeds ahead of time plumps and softens them so that they don't rob water from the bread dough. (This is a trick I picked up from German bakers, but it transfers beautifully to seeded *pain au levain*.) Because the soaked seeds bring so much moisture, the variations call for less water in the dough.

Sometimes the addition of seeds will slow down the fermentation of the dough. If it doesn't seem to have risen sufficiently after 3 hours, let it go an additional 45 minutes to 1 hour.

Sunflower Seed *Levain* *Pain au levain au tournesol*

SOAK THE SEEDS WHILE YOUR *LEVAIN* IS FERMENTING. After you prepare your *levain*, pour 3/4 cup (3.5 ounces/100 grams) raw sunflower seeds into a small bowl. Pour 3/4 cup (6.2 ounces/175 grams) tap water over them and let them sit uncovered at room temperature for 8 to 12 hours (the same amount of time you let your *levain* sit). They will not absorb all the water but will plump and soften. Strain off the excess water, draining them well.

MIX THE DOUGH. Reduce the amount of water in the dough to 1 1/3 cups (10.6 ounces/300 grams) and add the soaked and drained sunflower seeds when you mix in the flour.

Sesame Seed *Levain* *Pain au levain au sesamé*
SOAK THE SEEDS WHILE YOUR *LEVAIN* IS FERMENTING. After you prepare your *levain*, pour 2/3 cup (3.5 ounces/100 grams) raw sesame seeds into a small bowl. Pour 3/4 cup (6.2 ounces/175 grams) tap water over them and let them sit uncovered at room temperature for 8 to 12 hours (the same amount of time you let your *levain* sit). They won't absorb much of the water, but will plump and soften. Strain off the excess water draining them well.

MIX THE DOUGH. Reduce the amount of water in the dough to 1 1/3 cups (10.6 ounces/300 grams) and add the soaked and drained sesame seeds when you mix in the flour.

Flaxseed *Levain* *Pain au levain aux graines de lin*
SOAK THE SEEDS WHILE YOUR *LEVAIN* IS FERMENTING. After you prepare your *levain*, pour 2/3 cup (3.5 ounces/100 grams) brown or golden flax seeds into a small bowl. Pour 1 cup (8 ounces/227 grams) tap water over them and let them sit uncovered at room temperature for 8 to 12 hours (the same amount of time you let your *levain* sit). They will absorb all the water and cling together in a slippery gel that resembles tapioca.

MIX THE DOUGH. Reduce the amount of water in the dough to 1 cup (8.3 ounces/235 grams) and add the hydrated flax seeds when you mix in the flour.

Multigrain *Levain* *Pain au levain aux quatre céréales*
SOAK THE SEEDS AND GRAINS WHILE YOUR LEVAIN IS FERMENTING. After you prepare your *levain*, combine 2 heaping tablespoons (0.9 ounce/25 grams) flax seeds, 1/4 cup (0.9 ounce/25 grams) millet, 1/3 cup (0.9 ounce/25 grams) rolled oats, and 2 tablespoons (0.9 ounce/25 grams) coarse cornmeal in a small bowl. Pour 3/4 cup (6.2 ounces/175 grams) tap water over the mixture and let sit uncovered at room temperature for 8 to 12 hours (the same amount of time you let your *levain* sit). The seeds and grains will absorb all the water.

MIX THE DOUGH. Reduce the amount of water in the dough to 1 cup (8.3 ounces/235 grams) and add the soaked seeds and grains when you mix in the flour.

Variations: NEW-WAVE FLOUR *LEVAINS*
By substituting nutrient- and protein-rich spelt, kamut, or soy flour (available at natural-foods stores or by mail; see Resources, pages 333–34) for some of the flour in Old World *pain au levain*, you can dramatically change the texture and flavor of the bread. These flours don't contain as much gluten (in the case of soy flour, no gluten at all) as wheat flour. Like the Fabiopain bakers, I've kept the proportion of bread flour in the recipes high to preserve the structure and lightness of classic *pain au levain*.

(continued on the following page)

(continued from the previous page)

To make any of these *levains*, simply follow the recipe for Quintessential French Sourdough (page 124), replacing the combination of bread flour, whole wheat flour, and rye flour in that recipe with the combination of "new-wave flour" and bread flour specified below. Everything else—the amounts of water and salt, the rising times, shaping, and baking—is the same. The loaves you pull from the oven, however, will be entirely different.

Spelt Sourdough *Pain au levain à lepautre*

Whole spelt flour looks like its close relation, whole wheat flour. It also mixes and bakes like whole wheat flour, but absorbs more water into the dough and tans the crumb and the crust. This recipe, with about half spelt flour and half bread flour, makes the darkest, heartiest loaf of the group.

INGREDIENTS	VOLUME	U.S. WEIGHT	METRIC WEIGHT	BAKER'S PERCENTAGE
Whole spelt flour	1½ cups	7.9 ounces	225 grams	45
Type 55–style flour from King Arthur or Giusto's or unbleached all-purpose flour	1¾ cups	9.7 ounces	275 grams	55

Kamut *Levain* *Pain au levain au camut*

Pale yellow kamut flour, ground from an ancient relative of durum wheat, is complete with germ, germ oil, and bran. When baked, it contributes a buttery flavor to the bread.

INGREDIENTS	VOLUME	U.S. WEIGHT	METRIC WEIGHT	BAKER'S PERCENTAGE
Kamut flour	1¼ cups	5.3 ounces	150 grams	30
Type 55–style flour from King Arthur or Giusto's or unbleached all-purpose flour	2 cups	11.5 ounces	325 grams	65
Stone-ground whole wheat flour	3 tablespoons	0.9 ounce	25 grams	5

Soy *Levain* *Pain au levain au soja*

Soy is a legume, not a grain. Because soy "flour" doesn't contain any water-absorbing gluten, it mixes into a sticky dough with a vegetal scent. But it bakes into a golden brown loaf with a butter-yellow crumb and a wonderfully nutty taste.

INGREDIENTS	VOLUME	U.S. WEIGHT	METRIC WEIGHT	BAKER'S PERCENTAGE
Soy flour	1¼ cups	5.3 ounces	150 grams	30
Type 55–style flour from King Arthur or Giusto's or unbleached all-purpose flour	2 cups	11.5 ounces	325 grams	65
Stone-ground whole wheat flour	3 tablespoons	0.9 ounce	25 grams	5

Variations: **FANTASY *LEVAINS***

French bakers call breads stuffed with tasty bits like olives, bacon, or cheese *pains des fantaisie*. I have used my recipe for Quintessential French Sourdough to develop a menu of such savory breads. Follow the directions below for incorporating particular ingredients into the dough and proceed with the sourdough recipe as directed. Serve the breads on their own as hors d'oeuvres or use them to upgrade a salad into a meal fit for company.

Olive *Levain* *Pain au levain aux olives*

I love oil-cured black Niçoise olives in this bread, but Italian green olives or Kalamatas make wonderful olive bread too. Be forewarned that black olives will stain the dough a purplish gray color.

CHOP THE OLIVES. Before mixing the dough, roughly chop 1 cup (4.9 ounces/140 grams) pitted olives.

KNEAD THE OLIVES INTO THE DOUGH. Add the olives to the dough when it is fairly smooth, about 10 minutes into hand-kneading. Press them into the dough and continue to knead until

(continued on the following page)

(continued from the previous page)

they are well distributed and the dough is very smooth and elastic. If kneading by machine, add the olives during the last 2 minutes of kneading. Once you've turned the machine off, press any stray olives into the dough by hand.

Bacon *Levain* *Pain au levain au lard*

I like thick-cut all-natural bacon. I like the chewiness of the bigger pieces. You can substitute ham or prosciutto here if you like. The fat from the bacon flavors the bread and also moistens the crumb.

COOK THE BACON. Before mixing the dough, chop 7 strips of thick-cut bacon (about 10 ounces/280 grams) into 1/2-inch-wide pieces. Cook in a skillet over medium heat, stirring once or twice, just until some of the fat renders and the pieces start to brown around the edges, about 5 minutes. Remove the skillet from the heat and use a slotted spoon to transfer the bacon to a paper towel–lined plate. Let the bacon cool completely.

MIX THE BACON INTO THE DOUGH. Add the bacon to the dough along with the salt and *levain*.

Cheese *Levain* *Pain au levain au fromage*

Boldly flavored cheese such as buttery Cantal, nutty Comte, or a farmstead cheddar best complements the complex flavors of *pain au levain*.

PREPARE THE CHEESE. After you've mixed the dough, while it's resting but before you've added the *levain* and salt, cut 5 ounces of hard cheese into 1/2-inch cubes.

KNEAD THE CHEESE INTO THE DOUGH. Add the cheese to the dough when it is fairly smooth, about 10 minutes into hand-kneading. Press the cubes into the dough and continue to knead until the pieces are well distributed and the dough is very smooth and elastic. If kneading by machine, add the cheese during the last 2 minutes of kneading. Once you've turned the machine off, press any stray pieces of cheese into the dough by hand.

Raisin-Nut *Levain* *Pain au levain aux noix et raisins*

This is one of the most popular *levain* breads at Bread Alone. Use walnuts or pecans, your choice.

TOAST THE NUTS. Before mixing the dough, place 1 cup of nuts on a baking sheet and toast in a preheated 350-degree oven until fragrant, 5 to 8 minutes. Let cool completely. Coarsely chop.

KNEAD THE NUTS AND RAISINS INTO THE DOUGH. Add the nuts and 1/2 cup raisins to the dough when it is fairly smooth, about 10 minutes into hand-kneading. Press them into the dough and continue to knead until they are well distributed and the dough is very smooth and elastic. If kneading by machine, add the nuts and raisins during the last 2 minutes of kneading. Once you've turned the machine off, press any stray nuts and raisins into the dough by hand.

FREQUENTLY ASKED QUESTIONS ABOUT *LEVAIN* AND *PAIN AU LEVAIN*

. . . .

Is old sourdough that I can get from another baker or by mail better than the brand-new *levain* that I could cultivate at home?

It is a myth that a sourdough with a pedigree will raise dough more effectively or give it better flavor than a sourdough cultivated from scratch. Any sourdough that you nurture in your kitchen, no matter when or where it was originally cultivated, very quickly takes on local characteristics, because you feed it with your own water and flour and it captures the yeast native to your air. Bakers all over Europe have given me pieces of their sourdoughs, but once I bring them home and refresh them for a couple of weeks, there isn't much left of the original culture. As for older doughs being better than new ones just because they're older, that's a myth too. Remember, the goal in maintaining a *levain* is to get consistent results day after day and month after month, not letting it change and sour over time. Jean LeFleur, the master baker who taught Basil Kamir the essentials of *levain*, used to throw away his sourdough and start anew several times a year. (He believed that the best time to do this was after a thunderstorm, but I'm not sure why!) He didn't like a starter that was too old, believing that it was too sour and not powerful enough to raise the kind of light, sweet bread he favored.

Did you discover the secret of *pain Poilâne*™? What accounts for its mystique?

Type 85 flour, a whole wheat flour from which 15 percent of the bran has been sifted, makes *pain Poilâne*™ hearty but not heavy. Beyond the flour, I believe that the secret to its greatness is in the simple and repetitive process perfected by Max and Lionel Poilâne, a five-hour cycle of mixing, proofing, and baking that ensures uniform quality. The Poilâne bakeries bake only one kind of bread, and they do it right. Their success is a good argument for choosing one bread recipe and making it over and over until you can call it your own.

When I've made whole wheat sourdough bread in the past, I have been disappointed with its dense, claylike structure. What makes French whole wheat bread so much lighter than the American-style breads I've baked? How can I get similar results at home?

American bakers tend to underhydrate their whole wheat doughs, and the result is a typical health-food-store bread—a dry, heavy loaf that tastes stale just hours out of the oven. French bakers know that good whole wheat flour has the capacity to hold a lot of water and are not afraid to work with highly hydrated doughs. Wet doughs require additional kneading to develop structure, so you'll notice that the recipe for Whole Wheat Sourdough *Miche* (page 118), in which there is a high percentage of water, calls for what may seem like a very long knead time. The wet, well-kneaded dough will bake up into a beautifully structured bread.

Are there health benefits to baking with the "new-wave" flours milled from spelt, kamut, soy, and other grains?

Just the fact that these flours are whole-meal and stone-ground, retaining so many nutrients that are removed when grain is overprocessed, is reason enough to try them. But you might want to use them for a number of other reasons. For people who are sensitive to gluten, spelt is a low-gluten alternative to wheat. Kamut, another ancient grain related to wheat, contains more protein than its modern counterpart and higher nutritional values. Soy flour has the highest protein level of these flours and contains healthy oils and nutrients thought by many nutritionists to prevent disease and prolong life.

I'm curious about "new-wave" *pain au levain*, but what on earth do I serve with these breads? How are they served and eaten in Alsace?

There is no need to prepare a special health-food stew to serve with these breads. They can be enjoyed the same way as traditional *pain au levain*—at every meal and as a snack in between meals. Their unique flavors will just add variety to the table.

I know that you are a proponent of wet doughs, and my *pain au levain* dough seemed dry in comparison to the doughs from other chapters in this book. Is there a reason this kind of bread needs less water?

The doughs made with stiff dough *levain* may seem firmer than French doughs made with liquid *levain* and Italian doughs, but by American baking standards they are still quite soft and wet. You'll detect all the great qualities of well-hydrated dough in the finished breads—a pronounced sourdough flavor, moist honeycomb crumb, and days-long freshness.

How does slow kneading and fermenting translate into long shelf life?

When you knead and ferment dough slowly, you don't oxygenate it too much. The more oxygen there is in the dough, the more quickly it will get stale.

Will storing these breads in a plastic bag give them an even longer shelf life?

Paper won't change the original characteristics of the bread, which is why I prefer it if I am keeping the bread for just a couple of days. But storing the bread in a plastic bag will indeed keep it fresh longer. The plastic will make the crust softer, however, so plan on crisping the bread in the oven for a few minutes to restore its crackling exterior.

CHAPTER 7

✳

THE AUVERGNE:
SURPRISING WHEATS AND RYES FROM
TWO OF FRANCE'S MEILLEURS OUVRIERS

✳

The Auvergne is a rugged region in the heart of France, insular and largely undiscovered by tourists. Its capital, Clermont-Ferrand, has a population of just 140,000. Vichy, the next largest city, known for its mineral water, has evolved since its infamous role as the capital of Nazi-controlled France into a quiet destination for retirees. Much smaller towns and tiny villages are scattered far from each other across a lunar landscape of huge craters and monumental outcroppings of rock. The area is France's breadbasket, producing most of the grain used by the country's bakers. But instead of the endless fields and open skies of America's midwestern breadbasket, the Auvergne has a rocky landscape of dormant volcanoes and hot springs, with wheat and rye planted in patches between the big hills. The farmers grow old varieties of grain that flourish at high altitudes. Although not strictly organic, the farms have no need for pesticides and herbicides, because the climate and geography are so friendly to the crops.

The farmers, millers, and bakers in the Auvergne not only have business relationships, they are often friends, neighbors, and close relatives. They are accountable to one another for the quality of their products, and it shows in the uniformly excellent bread. There's another reason that I found the breads of the region exciting. The free-form but aesthetically pleasing light rye, the blue cheese–studded pan loaf, the white bread called *couronne*, shaped like a large bagel, are unique to this self-sufficient and remote area, utterly different from the breads made in any other part of France. They complement the rustic local cuisine, which is built on potatoes, cabbage, salted ham, and cured sausages.

I probably wouldn't have ventured into the Auvergne if it hadn't been for the fact that my mentor in Paris, Basil Kamir, was a native of the region.

During our long dinners at the bistro around the corner from his bakery, he would speak reverently and sometimes even tearfully (after finishing a bottle of wine) about the humble dark ryes and giant *couronnes* he had known as a child. I had tasted and enjoyed rye breads in Paris, but Basil insisted that they were nothing like the breads he had known as a child. In Paris, the rye breads typically contain about 8 percent rye flour. In the Auvergne, they are made with much more rye, sometimes 100 percent, and have the deep, rich flavor and color to show for it. He lamented the fact that Parisians wanted only Parisian-style baguettes and boules. We drove from Paris to his family's country house several times so he could show me the native bread, but we were always sidetracked by the beauty of the countryside and spent all our time hiking and horseback riding through the quiet hills instead of stopping at the bakeries I'd heard so much about.

Two years ago I decided that with or without Basil, I had to meet the region's two most distinguished bakers. Pierre Nury and Amandio Pimenta are both natives of the Auvergne and are both Meilleurs Ouvriers de France, winners of France's highest award for craftsmanship. I had read about their regional breads, made with locally grown and milled grain. So I planned a trip from Lyon to the South of France, with bread-related stops on either side (the bakery outside Lyon that supplied Paul Bocuse's restaurants; the medieval town of Thiers, known for its cutlery museum and knife artisans). The Auvergne would be the midpoint of this journey.

I drove into the tiny mountain village of Loubeyrat, about three hours west of Lyon, on a rainy Sunday morning. The town consists of maybe thirty houses, a one-room schoolhouse, a post office, and Pierre Nury's bakery, all clinging to a steep hillside. Obviously Pierre hadn't chosen the location for its foot traffic! In fact, he had bought the building from a retired baker because it came with an old wood-fired oven and the low price enabled him to own his own business. From the long line of customers snaking out the door of his shop, I guessed that a lot of people came from out of town to buy his bread. I

squeezed inside to get a closer look at the massive ten-pound rye rounds and the two-foot-long, unscored bronzed loaves swirled with flour. I noticed Pierre right away. He had to be the big, strong, grown-up country boy behind the counter wearing the peasant shirt. And it didn't take long for Pierre to notice me admiring his breads. Soon, he was offering me a slice of his signature rustic light rye, a bread he sold only on Sunday, which accounted for the crowd outside. It had a crackling crust and moist, chewy crumb riddled with troughs. Its rich wheat flavor was enhanced by a touch of earthy rye.

Although Pierre lives a small-town life and is Auvergnat to the core, he has traveled the world as a baking ambassador, teaching culinary students as far away as Korea and Japan about his specialty breads. I was a little bit intimidated when his wife tied an apron around my waist as he invited me to spend the morning working with his bakers. We went to the back room, with its very old wood-fired brick oven, and he tossed a piece of white dough in front of me. "Let's see what you can do," he said in his thick Auvergnat accent. I awkwardly attempted to shape a baguette while he and his three bakers watched. The dough felt softer and stickier than the dough I work with at Bread Alone. Made from local flour with relatively little gluten, it was fragile and sensitive to my touch. When I tried to lengthen it into a baguette shape by placing my hands in the middle of the log and firmly rolling it as I moved my hands toward the ends, I could feel it slithering out of my control. Pierre then showed me how they roll baguettes in the Auvergne, pushing one end of the dough away from himself with his left hand while rolling the other end toward himself with the right hand, and then reversing the motions. He repeated this scissorlike routine several times, until the baguette was the standard eighteen inches, with perfectly tapered ends.

Not all of Pierre's breads are hand-shaped. The bread I had first seen through the window, his rustic light rye (page 150), is made with *levain*, white flour, a little rye flour, and so much water that it can't be shaped at all. Pierre showed me how, after giving the dough an unusual double rise to develop its rye flavor, he cuts it into pieces and simply stretches it into oblong loaf shapes. The dough pieces go right into the oven, where they spread out more than they spring up. Their squat exteriors conceal airy interiors filled with large, shiny air pockets.

While the rye bread baked, Pierre told me about his commitment to the area and its traditions. He had deliberately opened a small bakery in a quiet town. The low overhead and out-of-the-way location allowed him to bake just a few sorts of bread, the old Auvergnat recipes. As the reputation of the bakery grew, people well beyond Loubeyrat sought out Pierre's old-style breads. He was now running at full capacity, but with no plans to expand. When the day's bread was sold out, disappointed customers just had to wait until the next day (or the next Sunday) and be sure to get there earlier. I was delighted to learn that he used a stiff dough *levain* to raise all his breads. This meant that they were related to the French breads I already knew how to make. In addition to the light rye, he was selling *couronnes*, bacon baguettes made with deliciously smoky chunks of local bacon, small pan loaves studded with pungent local blue cheese, and creamy yellow baguettes (made from the dough I had such difficulty shaping) that were labeled *pain de Combraille*. I had never heard the name, so Pierre explained that it simply meant bread made with Combraille flour, milled from an old variety of wheat that a few local farmers had decided to cultivate again and market to bakers and consumers as a local product. The stars must have been in alignment for my visit to the Auvergne, because Pierre then pointed to a sign posted in his window, advertising a wheat festival taking place the next day in Saint Julien la Geneste, a tiny farming village a few miles away. If I went, I could meet some of the farmers who were growing this wheat.

The next day I followed more hand-lettered signs through rolling hills to a rutted field-turned-parking-lot in front of an old stone house and wooden barn and walked toward a group of people clustered under two white tents. Serge Barse, a wheat farmer, stepped into the rain to greet me. When I introduced myself, saying, "*Je suis un boulanger américain*," he was

elated, and offered to show me around the farm. We traipsed through the mud to a nearby field where the wheat was still green and tender. Serge told me of his cooperative effort with two other local farmers to grow a kind of wheat suitable to this high altitude and ideal for bread baking. He planned to keep his family's farm alive by growing this specialty wheat. Already the collective was selling the flour milled from Combraille to thirty local bakers. The bakers, including Pierre, were featuring the baguettes they made from the flour as a regional specialty, calling it *pain de Combraille*. Serge led me to the barn, where mounds of the previous year's wheat kernels glowed golden in the silo. I reached in for a handful and popped the kernels into my mouth, as the wheat farmers in Kansas had taught me to do. I chewed them hard, crushing the hulls until the starches began to release their sweet, nutty flavors. Very soon I could feel the gumminess of the gluten forming, a quality I've learned to recognize in the best bread flours—even before they're milled. Like small organic farm collectives in the United States, this group of French farmers had decided to grow an old variety of wheat and market it to artisan bakers. Older varieties appeal to these bakers because they have great flavor and texture characteristics that have been bred out of most wheat varieties in favor of characteristics that make the dough very machinable (meaning that it is very elastic and able to go through big baking machines easily). In an agreement with the local miller, the Combraille wheat is minimally processed, retaining the germ as well as vitamins and minerals.

When we returned to the tents, I noticed what looked like the undercarriage of a stagecoach. It was red and stood on wooden wheels. There was Pierre, pulling a baker's peel from its interior. On top of the peel was an impossibly long, gorgeously dark-crusted loaf. Pierre explained to me that the vehicle was a vintage World War I mobile wood-burning oven, one of only four remaining in France. "Even on the battlefield, the French wanted to have hot bread!" he explained. It was wonderful to see Pierre in his white chef's jacket with its Meilleur Ouvrier de France insignia, baking bread alongside the more casually dressed farmers and their families. Pierre introduced me to the small, neat man working at his side: Amandio Pimenta, the Auvergne's other Meilleur Ouvrier de France. I was charmed to see these two decorated bakers standing in the grass and mud, wearing chef's whites but still very much a part of the farming community.

Their bread was made with Combraille flour and was to be served at the farm dinner. That night bakers, farmers, and most of the residents of Saint Julien la Geneste returned to the fields to enjoy a banquet of spicy merguez sausage, grilled pork, regional red wine, heirloom apples, local cheese, and the bread, with its creamy golden crumb and sweet wheat flavors. The elderly mayor, aristocratic in a black suit, welcomed me and in British-accented English explained his job: "I am in charge of the one hundred and twenty-seven people of this town, and it is my responsibility to see that they are well fed and happy." I was very moved by the solidarity of this small community, the people's enjoyment of the fruits of their labor, and their hospitality in sharing this feast with me.

After this unexpected introduction to the grain of the Auvergne, I was more eager than ever to meet with Amandio and see how he was using the local wheat and rye in his breads. The next day I went to his bakery in the small but busy capital of the region, Clermont-Ferrand. While Pierre's shop is deliberately rustic with a small menu of breads, Amandio's sparkling modern bakery produces an array of fancy pastries as well as the entire repertoire of Auvergnat and Parisian-style breads. The son of Portuguese immigrants, Amandio has been baking since he was a teenager. His bakery now probably serves a thousand customers a day, but when he first opened it, the odds were stacked against him. He committed himself to making traditional breads even as many older bakeries were failing and closing their doors. Alongside the cakes and croissants, I recognized the 100 percent rye breads and the gargantuan 5-kilo wheat and rye rounds. I asked him to tell me about the white *couronnes* (page 142) that looked like giant

bagels. Every other customer seemed to walk out of the shop with one. It was an everyday bread, he said, but we agreed that there was something festive about its shape. I looked at the slashes on its surface, which were split wide apart, indicating an explosive crumb structure. He cut one open and I admired its interior, its crumb a honeycomb of small and larger holes like the best *pain au levain*.

Amandio's signature bread, the *seigle d'Auvergne* (page 158), is a rugged-looking free-form rye, unscored so that its surface bubbles up and cracks as it bakes. Its casual appearance belies the care that Amandio puts into crafting it. He loves rye flavor, and this bread is made with almost 100 percent rye flour to highlight the grain. *Seigle d'Auvergne* is the only one of his breads to employ a rye starter, necessary to build the intense rye flavor, rather than a stiff dough *levain*. But even so, Amandio uses a piece of *levain* to initiate the rye sponge. Like his Parisian counterparts, he detests sour-tasting bread. But he used a technique I had never seen in Paris to keep this very Auvergnat bread sweet-tasting. I was astounded when he mixed his dough with very hot rather than tepid water. He explained that hot water speeds up the process of fermentation, discouraging the development of acids, which usually takes place when a dough made with a high proportion of rye flour and a sourdough starter sits at room temperature. Since the dough contains so much rye and so little wheat, it will never develop much gluten.

Because it is almost completely rye, with just a little bit of wheat flour holding it together, it is gooey and entirely inelastic. Instead of kneading it, Amandio simply mixed it for an extended period in the electric mixer (the dough was far too sticky to mix by hand), in order to give the flour a chance to absorb the water. As sticky as it was, though, not only did Amandio manage to shape this messy dough and get it into the oven, he fashioned it into rustic loaves that were beautiful and very polished. He demonstrated his technique for accomplishing the impossible: He dusted the work surface with rye flour, plopped a piece of dough on top of the dusted surface, and then dusted the top with more rye flour. With deft, committed motions, he slid his hands underneath the dough, scooped it up, and slid it into the oven. Because the dough doesn't have any body, it must be handled with confidence. Hesitate, and it will collapse in a puddle before you have had a chance to arrange it on the oven floor.

The farming and baking traditions of the Auvergne have fostered the talent of Amandio and Pierre, and a loyal crowd of local customers has buoyed their businesses. But their success, along with the success of Serge Barse's cooperative wheat farm, needs to be put in global perspective to understand the significance of what they have achieved. Pierre, Amandio, and Serge and all the other farmers in the area are not engaged in a project of historic preservation. Each in his own way is figuring out how to make the old traditions viable in a new marketplace. At the farm dinner in Saint Julien la Geneste, talk turned to the day's headlines: the story of the militant sheep farmer José Bové, who had recently led members of the radical Farmers' Confederation in taking over and demolishing a McDonald's franchise in southern France, and the entrance of Poland into the European Union. Bové was a hero to the bakers and farmers, for protesting the loss of France's cultural heritage and the globalization of farming embodied by McDonald's. At that beautiful table under the stars, the villagers bitterly lamented the fact that many young French people are as familiar with American fast food as they are with native cuisine, and that French farms are threatened every day by cheap grain from eastern Europe. But ultimately the day and the dinner celebrated the superior quality and continuing viability of the region's traditional grain and bread.

Back home in Boiceville, I got on the phone immediately with my miller in Montreal, Robert Beauchemin. I couldn't wait to tell him all I had learned from Serge Barse about Combraille flour. His enthusiasm matched my own. He told me about some farmers he knew in Saskatchewan who were growing old varieties of wheat that sounded similar to Combraille, and he offered to mill some of this wheat for me so I could bake with it and compare it to the

bread I had had in the Auvergne. The resulting breads were not exactly like Pierre's *pain de Combraille* but were uniquely delicious because of this special flour. I now use it in many of my other breads. Robert also sent me some rye flour milled from grain grown at a farm about an hour and a half's drive southeast of Montreal, right near his mill in Milan, Quebec, to see if it would match the flour I had seen Amandio use. Since these successes, Robert has become my most important adviser. I talk to him at least three times a week about this season's crops, the current stock of flour, and unusual wheat that his farmers may be cultivating. I have made a conscious effort to model my relationship with him on the collaborative relationships I saw between Pierre, Amandio, and the farmers and millers who live nearby. He is part of my baker's community, although geographically we are hundreds of miles apart.

The recipes for the rustic, dark, crackly Auvergne ryes and wheat breads in this chapter come directly from two of France's master bakers and are among the most delicious breads I've ever tasted. I treasure them especially because they reflect not only the artistry of the bakers but also the rustic character, rugged landscape, and hearty climate of the place where the grain is grown.

❋ KITCHEN NOTES: MAKING AUVERGNAT WHEATS AND RYES AT HOME

I was impressed by the sense of community in the Auvergne. The bakers supported the farmers and millers; the townspeople stood by the local bread 100 percent. I guess I shouldn't have been so surprised that the bakers did things differently in such a self-sufficient place. Here are some notes about the techniques and ingredients unique to the area that will help you make Auvergnat breads.

Use levain creatively. Even though Amandio, Pierre, and every other Auvergnat baker I met made regional breads very different in style from the usual

French baguettes and boules, they were still starting with a classic *levain*. This really brought home to me how versatile the French sourdough starter is, and how simple it is to take *levain* in a new direction. Even for breads made with almost 100 percent rye flour, these bakers didn't keep a separate rye sourdough going. Instead, they'd make a rye sponge using a piece of *levain* for *seigle d'Auvergne* and other typical ryes.

When buying flour, look for the qualities that make Combraille an exemplary bread flour. Combraille flour, milled from wheat grown by only a few farmers in the Auvergne, is not available outside the area. But many mills in North America are now milling flour from white winter wheat (see Resources, pages 333–34). Any one of these flours, which have a similarly high ash content, a high level of beta-carotene, and a relatively low level of protein (compared with most commercial American flours), will give you a bread similar in wholesomeness and flavor to *pain de Combraille*.

Hot water can be good for bread dough. Conventional wisdom has it that bread dough should be mixed with tepid water. Warm water encourages fermentation but won't allow yeast and bacteria to multiply wildly and sour the bread. I was shocked, then, when I watched Amandio Pimenta stir very hot water into the sourdough before adding it to the dough. He explained that Auvergnat bakers share an aversion to sour bread with their colleagues in Paris. Their ryes are as mild as any Parisian *pain au levain*, and a world away from the very sour rye breads of Germany and Austria. But these bakers come at the problem of making mild-tasting sourdough bread from a very different direction from Parisian bakers. By mixing the dough with very hot water and letting it ferment for just a short time, Auvergnat bakers get a lot of growth with very little acidity. In contrast, Parisian bakers keep their *levain* cool, are meticulous about adding only tepid water to their dough, and let the dough ferment for hours before baking, all to slow down the production of acid in the dough. Different techniques, similar results.

Don't expect perfectly shaped breads made from rye doughs. The high percentage of rye flour in these doughs makes them very soft, with no elasticity. They are more like stiff cake batter than typical bread dough. Such soft, inelastic doughs are difficult to shape into traditional baguettes and boules, so it's not surprising that in the Auvergne, no one places a high value on perfect shapes. Award-winning breads from Pierre Nury and Amandio Pimenta are pleasingly rustic and free-form because they are made from traditional recipes, using a healthy amount of local rye flour. This is not to say that the breads are unattractive. Pierre and Amandio handle the dough quickly and deftly, allowing no time or opportunity for it to stick to itself in clumps or to tear, so that when the bread rises, it has an even but cracked surface, with decorative swirls of flour where it has expanded during baking.

Use local bacon and cheese. Pierre Nury and Amandio Pimenta use bacon made from local pigs and cheese made at local dairies in their breads. The quality and freshness of these ingredients add to the greatness of the breads. When I am making Pierre's blue cheese bread, I buy either cheese imported from the Auvergne at my local cheese shop, where I know it has been stored and handled properly, or blue cheese made by an artisan cheesemaker who lives in the nearby Berkshires. One thing I never do is buy factory-made, shrink-wrapped cheese at the supermarket. The saltiness and off flavors of this industrial product would ruin the bread. Similarly, I skip the factory-packaged bacon at the supermarket. The bacon from a German pork store near my house is much, much better. Bacon made from organically raised pigs, available at many specialty-foods stores and good butcher shops will give you the most authentically Auvergnat bread.

Don't be afraid to turn the oven up. Soft rye doughs don't have the webbed structure of all-wheat doughs to trap the gases produced by yeast, so they need to get a lot of oven spring during the first few minutes of baking to rise optimally. A hotter oven will get the most rise out of this kind of dough. Preheat your oven for a full hour, and don't worry if the recipe calls for a temperature of 500 degrees. After 10 minutes or so, when the yeast has done its leavening job and the heat has killed it, you can turn the oven down to finish the bread.

AUVERGNE CROWN
Couronne

. . . .

ALLOW 8 TO 12 HOURS TO PREPARE THE *LEVAIN*;

20 MINUTES TO MIX AND REST THE DOUGH;

9 TO 12 MINUTES TO KNEAD;

3 TO 4 HOURS TO FERMENT;

1 TO 1 1/2 HOURS TO PROOF;

35 TO 45 MINUTES TO BAKE

. . . .

Couronne, a white bread that looks like an enormous bagel, is known throughout France as the specialty of the Auvergne. Auvergnat bakers typically make their *couronnes* from white bread dough, but they don't all use the same technique. One of the master bakers of the region, Amandio Pimenta, makes his crown bread with *levain*, the traditional firm French sourdough. He then gives the dough a nice long time to rise, letting the flavors of the wheat develop. This is one of those rare pure white breads I know with great character and complexity. It is served at every restaurant in the region with rich Auvergnat stews and roasted meats, or with chunks of local sausage and cheese.

✳ **MAKES 1 GIANT BAGEL-SHAPED LOAF**
(33 OUNCES/935 GRAMS)

Equipment
BAKER'S PEEL OR RIMLESS BAKING SHEET
PARCHMENT PAPER
BAKING STONE
CAST-IRON SKILLET
SINGLE-EDGED RAZOR BLADE OR SERRATED KNIFE

Note: If you don't have a stiff dough *levain* already prepared, you will have to make one from scratch (page 111), substitute a commercial sourdough starter (see pages 333–34 for sources), or use the *pâte fermentée* method (page 116) instead.

LEVAIN STARTER				
INGREDIENTS	VOLUME	U.S. WEIGHT	METRIC WEIGHT	BAKER'S PERCENTAGE
Stiff dough *levain* (page 111)	¼ cup	1.6 ounces	45 grams	45
Water, tepid (70 to 78 degrees)	¼ cup	1.8 ounces	50 grams	50
Type 55–style flour from King Arthur or Giusto's or unbleached all-purpose flour	⅔ cup	3.4 ounces	95 grams	95
Stone-ground whole wheat flour	2 teaspoons	0.2 ounce	5 grams	5

PREPARE THE *LEVAIN*. Take your *levain* out of the refrigerator. Pinch off about 1/4 cup, or a piece the size of an Italian plum (1.6 ounces/45 grams), and discard the rest. Place the piece of *levain* in a wide, shallow mixing bowl and pour the water over it. Use a rubber spatula to mash the *levain* against the sides of the bowl to break it up and soften it. The water will turn milky and bubble. Add the bread flour and whole wheat flour and stir until you have a very dry dough with loose flour scattered all around it. Using the spatula, press the dough against the sides of the bowl to collect as much of the stray flour as you can. Then tip the bowl with one hand while you knead with the other, chasing down the last bits of flour and working them into a very stiff dough, 1 to 2 minutes. The dough will not be smooth.

Place the dough in a clean 1-quart container and cover it. Place a piece of masking tape on the side of the container to mark the level the dough will reach when it has doubled in volume. Let the *levain* stand to ferment at room temperature for 8 to 12 hours, until it has risen into a dome and doubled in volume. It may already have begun to deflate. It will be riddled with air pockets that will be visible through the sides and bottom of the container. It will smell as sweet as overripe fruit.

BREAD DOUGH				
INGREDIENTS	VOLUME	U.S. WEIGHT	METRIC WEIGHT	BAKER'S PERCENTAGE
Water, warm (85 to 95 degrees)	1½ cups	12 ounces	340 grams	68
Type 55–style flour from King Arthur or Giusto's or unbleached all-purpose flour	3¼ cups	17.6 ounces	500 grams	100
Levain starter	About ½ cup, packed	4.4 ounces	125 grams	25
Sea salt	1½ teaspoons	0.4 ounce	10 grams	2

MIX THE DOUGH. Pour the water into a large mixing bowl or the bowl of a stand mixer. Add the bread flour and stir with a rubber spatula just until it absorbs all of the water and a dough forms. Cover with plastic wrap and let stand at room temperature for 20 minutes to hydrate the flour and give the gluten a chance to develop on its own.

ADD THE *LEVAIN* AND SALT. Uncover the *levain* and pinch off about 1/2 cup, or a piece the size of a tennis ball (4.4 ounces/125 grams). Uncover the dough, add the *levain* piece, and sprinkle on the salt. Use the spatula or your hands to work the *levain* and salt into the dough with a few firm strokes. (Cover the remaining *levain* and store it in the refrigerator, refreshing it at least once a week following the instructions on pages 114–15.)

KNEAD THE DOUGH. By hand: Turn the dough out onto a very lightly floured counter. Knead the dough with long strokes, stretching it thoroughly with each stroke, 10 to 12 minutes. It will become smooth and muscular and feel slightly tacky. Set a kitchen timer

to guide you, but judge ultimately by the texture of the dough, not the time you have been kneading, whether or not it is fully kneaded.

By machine: Use the dough hook and mix the dough on low speed (2 on a KitchenAid mixer) for 1 minute to incorporate the sourdough. Increase the speed to medium (4 on a KitchenAid mixer) and knead until the dough is smooth and muscular, an additional 8 to 9 minutes.

FERMENT THE DOUGH. Transfer the dough to a lightly oiled, clear 2-quart container with a lid. With masking tape, mark the level the dough will reach when it has doubled in volume. Cover and leave it to rise at room temperature (70 to 75 degrees) until it doubles, 3 to 4 hours. It will feel light and springy.

SHAPE THE CROWN. Cover a baker's peel or rimless baking sheet with parchment paper. Lightly dust the counter with flour and scrape the dough onto the counter. Roll the dough into a long, fat rope about 18 inches long and 3 inches wide. Connect the ends of the rope, overlapping by about 4 inches. Press the ends together firmly to seal. Place the dough on the peel or sheet and shape it into an even circle. Sift a veil of flour over the dough and cover it with plastic.

PROOF THE CROWN. Let the crown rise at room temperature (70 to 75 degrees) until it looks pillowy, 1 to 1 1/2 hours. When you press your fingertip into the dough, the imprint will spring back slowly.

PREPARE THE OVEN. About 1 hour before baking, place a baking stone on the middle rack of the oven and a cast-iron skillet on the lower rack. Heat the oven to 400 degrees.

SCORE THE CROWN. Uncover the crown. With a single-edged razor blade or serrated knife, trace a circle around the outer edge of the top of the loaf, cutting about 1/2 inch deep. Dip the blade in water and use a fluid motion so that it doesn't snag and drag the dough.

BAKE THE CROWN. Slide the loaf, still on the parchment, onto the baking stone. Place 1/2 cup of ice cubes in the skillet to produce steam. Bake until the crown is deep golden, 35 to 45 minutes. It's normal for the sealed ends to peel away from each other a little during baking.

COOL AND STORE THE CROWN. Slide the peel or the rimless baking sheet under the parchment paper to remove the crown from the oven. Slide the loaf, still on the parchment, onto a wire rack. Cool for about 10 minutes and then peel it off the parchment paper. Let the loaf cool completely, about 1 hour, before tearing or slicing. The crown will stay fresh for about 3 days, stored in a paper bag but with the cut end wrapped in plastic.

AUVERGNE RYE BAGUETTE WITH BACON
Baguette aux lardons

. . . .

ALLOW 8 TO 12 HOURS TO PREPARE THE *LEVAIN*;

15 MINUTES TO COOK AND COOL THE BACON;

20 MINUTES TO MIX AND REST THE DOUGH;

9 TO 15 MINUTES TO KNEAD;

3 TO 4 HOURS TO FERMENT;

12 TO 24 HOURS TO RETARD *OR* 1½ TO 2 HOURS TO PROOF;

20 TO 25 MINUTES TO BAKE

. . . .

Pierre Nury uses delicious local bacon and local grain in his traditional Auvergne rye, making it doubly the product of its location. Use thick-cut bacon and finely ground rye flour to make a bread just like his. Pierre doesn't precook the lean bacon that he buys from local pig farmers. Because American bacon has more fat, I like to render some before kneading the bacon into the dough. Pierre always retards his baguettes before baking, to give the dough a chance to absorb the smoky flavor of the meat and improve the texture of the crumb and crust. If you want to skip this step and bake them on the same day you shape them, simply leave the baguettes to rise at room temperature until they almost double in size, 1 1/2 to 2 hours, instead of refrigerating them. Then bake as directed.

MAKES 4 BAGUETTES ABOUT 12 INCHES LONG
(11 OUNCES/316 GRAMS EACH)

Equipment
BENCH SCRAPER OR CHEF'S KNIFE

BAKER'S PEEL OR RIMLESS BAKING SHEET

PARCHMENT PAPER

BAKING STONE

CAST-IRON SKILLET

SINGLE-EDGED RAZOR BLADE OR SERRATED KNIFE

Note: If you don't have a stiff dough *levain* already prepared, you will have to make one from scratch (page 111), substitute a commercial sourdough starter (see pages 333–34 for sources), or use the *pâte fermentée* method (pages 116) instead.

LEVAIN STARTER				
INGREDIENTS	VOLUME	U.S. WEIGHT	METRIC WEIGHT	BAKER'S PERCENTAGE
Stiff dough *levain* (page 111)	¼ cup	1.6 ounces	45 grams	45
Water, tepid (70 to 78 degrees)	¼ cup	1.8 ounces	50 grams	50
Type 55–style flour from King Arthur or Giusto's or unbleached all-purpose flour	⅔ cup	3.4 ounces	95 grams	95
Stone-ground whole wheat flour	2 teaspoons	0.2 ounce	5 grams	5

PREPARE THE *LEVAIN*. Take your *levain* out of the refrigerator. Pinch off about 1/4 cup, or a piece the size of an Italian plum (1.6 ounces/45 grams), and discard the rest. Place the piece of *levain* in a wide, shallow mixing bowl and pour the water over it. Use a rubber spatula to mash the *levain* against the sides of the bowl to break it up and soften it. The water will turn milky and bubble. Add the bread flour and whole wheat flour and stir until you have a very dry dough with loose flour scattered all around it. Using the spatula, press the dough against the sides of the bowl to collect as much of the stray flour as you can. Then tip the bowl with one hand while you knead with the other, chasing down the last bits of flour and working them into a very stiff dough, 1 to 2 minutes. The dough will not be smooth.

Place the dough in a clean 1-quart container and cover it. Place a piece of masking tape on the side of the container to mark the level the dough will reach when it has doubled in volume. Let the *levain* stand to ferment at room temperature (70 to 75 degrees) for 8 to 12 hours, until it has risen into a dome and doubled in volume. It may already have begun to deflate. It will be riddled with air pockets that will be visible through the sides and bottom of the container. It will smell as sweet as overripe fruit.

BREAD DOUGH				
INGREDIENTS	VOLUME	U.S. WEIGHT	METRIC WEIGHT	BAKER'S PERCENTAGE
Thick-cut bacon	7 strips	10 ounces	280 grams	56
Water, tepid (70 to 78 degrees)	1½ cups	12.3 ounces	350 grams	70
Type 55–style flour from King Arthur or Giusto's or unbleached all-purpose flour	3 cups	15.9 ounces	450 grams	90
Fine or medium rye flour	⅓ cup	1.8 ounces	50 grams	10
Levain starter	About ½ cup, packed	4.4 ounces	125 grams	25
Sea salt	1½ teaspoons	0.4 ounce	10 grams	2

COOK THE BACON. Cut the bacon into 1/2-inch pieces. Heat a skillet over medium heat. Add the bacon pieces and cook just until the fat sizzles and the bacon begins to brown. Use a slotted spoon to transfer the bacon to a paper towel–lined plate and cool completely.

MIX THE DOUGH. Pour the water into a large mixing bowl or the bowl of a stand mixer. Add the bread flour and rye flour and stir with a rubber spatula just until it absorbs all of the water and a dough forms. Cover with plastic wrap and let stand at room temperature for 20 minutes to hydrate the flour and give the gluten a chance to develop on its own.

ADD THE *LEVAIN*, BACON, AND SALT. Uncover the *levain* and pinch off about 1/2 cup, or a piece the size of a tennis ball (4.4 ounces/125 grams). Uncover the dough, add the *levain* piece and the bacon, and sprinkle on the salt. Use the spatula to work the *levain*, bacon, and salt into the dough with a few firm strokes. (Cover the remaining *levain* and store it in the refrigerator, refreshing it at least once a week following the instructions on pages 114–15.)

KNEAD THE DOUGH. By hand: Turn the dough out onto a lightly floured counter. Knead the dough with firm, smooth strokes until it is very smooth and springy, 12 to 15 minutes. Set a kitchen timer to guide you, but judge ultimately by the texture of the dough, not the time you have been kneading, whether or not it is fully kneaded.

By machine: Use the dough hook and mix the dough on low speed (2 on a KitchenAid mixer) for 1 minute to incorporate the sourdough. Increase the speed to medium (4 on a KitchenAid mixer) and

Rosemary Filone
(Panmarino)
ITALY
PAGE 175

Genzano Potato Pizza
(Pizza alle patate di Genzano)
ITALY
PAGE 201

Roman Red Pizza
(Pizza rossa alla romana)
ITALY
PAGE 217

Individual Focaccias with Cherry Tomatoes
(Schiacciate al pomodori)
ITALY
PAGE 185

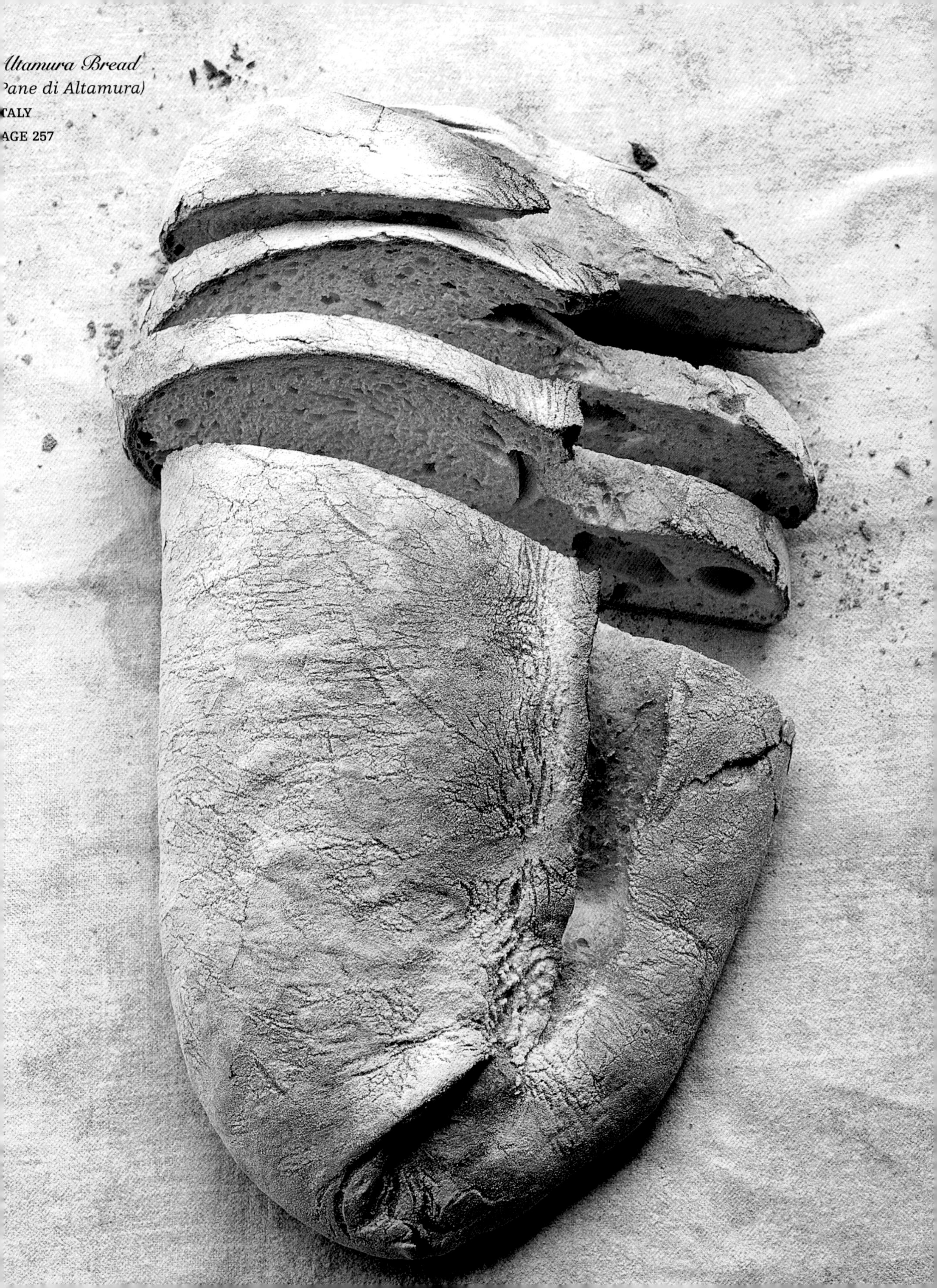

ltamura Bread
Pane di Altamura)
TALY
AGE 257

Genzano Country Bread

(Pane casareccio di Genzano)

ITALY

PAGE 197

Green Olive Sticks
(Pane di oliva verde)
ITALY
PAGE 230

Ciabatta Rolls
ITALY
PAGE 221

knead for 8 to 9 minutes longer, until the dough is smooth and springy.

FERMENT THE DOUGH. Transfer the dough to a lightly oiled, clear 2-quart container with a lid. With masking tape, mark the level the dough will reach when it has doubled in volume. Cover and leave it to rise at room temperature (70 to 75 degrees) for 1 hour. It will inflate only slightly.

TURN THE DOUGH. Scrape the dough out onto a lightly floured counter. With floured hands, lift the top edge of the dough and fold it so that it lands in the center of the mass. Lift the bottom edge and fold it so that it meets the top. In one fluid motion, slide both hands underneath the dough, turn it over so that the fold is now underneath, and slip it back into the container. Cover the dough and let it expand until it reaches the masking-tape mark, 2 to 3 hours more. It will feel smooth and firm.

DIVIDE AND PRESHAPE THE BAGUETTES. Cut the dough with a bench scraper or chef's knife into 4 equal pieces (11 ounces/316 grams each). Pat each piece into a rough rectangle and fold it in half. Drape the pieces with plastic wrap and let them rest on the counter for 10 minutes.

SHAPE THE BAGUETTES. Cover a baker's peel or rimless baking sheet with parchment paper. Shape each piece of dough into a baguette about 12 inches long (see Shaping Baguettes, pages 37–38). As you roll the log, taper the ends by increasing the downward pressure at the tips.

FORM THE *COUCHE*. Dust the parchment-covered peel or baking sheet with flour and place the baguettes on the parchment, seam side down, about 2 inches apart. Lift the parchment paper between the loaves, making pleats and drawing the loaves close together. Tightly roll up 2 kitchen towels and slip them under the parchment paper on the sides of the two outer loaves to support the sides of each baguette (see illustration, page 74). Lightly dust the tops of the

baguettes with flour and lightly drape them with plastic wrap.

RETARD THE BAGUETTES. Place the peel or baking sheet in the refrigerator for at least 12 and up to 24 hours. Two to 3 hours before you want to bake, remove it from the refrigerator and let the baguettes sit at room temperature. The dough will be firm and cool, relaxed but barely inflated.

PREPARE THE OVEN. About 1 hour before baking, place a baking stone on the middle rack of the oven and a cast-iron skillet on the lower rack. Heat the oven to 450 degrees.

SCORE THE BAGUETTES. Uncover the loaves and stretch the parchment paper out so that it is flat and the loaves are separated on top of it. Score each baguette with a single-edged razor blade or a serrated knife. Starting from the tip, angle the blade slightly and make 3 slashes, about 3 inches long and 1/2 inch deep (see illustration, page 68), so that they ascend like stairs, the second one in the middle of the bread and the third one ending at the other tip. Dip the blade in water and use a fluid motion so that it doesn't snag and drag the dough.

BAKE THE BAGUETTES. Slide the loaves, still on the parchment, onto the baking stone. Place 1/2 cup of ice cubes in the skillet to produce steam. Bake until the baguettes are a deep caramel color, 20 to 25 minutes.

COOL AND STORE THE BAGUETTES. Slide the peel or the rimless baking sheet under the parchment paper to remove the loaves from the oven. Slide the loaves, still on the parchment, onto a wire rack. Cool for about 5 minutes and then peel them off the parchment paper. Let the baguettes cool completely, about 30 minutes, before slicing. They will stay fresh for 2 to 3 days stored in a brown paper bag. Reheat in a 350-degree oven for 7 minutes to recrisp the crust. For longer storage, freeze in resealable plastic bags for up to 1 month.

PIERRE NURY'S RUSTIC LIGHT RYE
Bougnat

. . . .

ALLOW 8 TO 12 HOURS TO PREPARE THE *LEVAIN*;

20 MINUTES TO MIX AND REST THE DOUGH;

10 TO 12 MINUTES TO KNEAD;

3 TO 4 HOURS TO FERMENT;

12 TO 24 HOURS TO RETARD;

20 TO 30 MINUTES TO BAKE

. . . .

With my Parisian prejudices, I was surprised when Pierre Nury, recipient of the prestigious Meilleur Ouvrier de France award, presented this bread to me as his signature loaf. An oblong, free-form light rye, it has none of the defining characteristics of classic French bread: no finely tapered points, no artful scores, no elegant shape. With its bronze, flour-dusted crust and squat appearance, it looks like an Italian ciabatta. It didn't take me long to reconsider my first impression. Slicing through the crackling crust, I had to admire the open crumb, riddled with long, glossy tunnels. Pierre explained that he mixed *levain*, bread flour, and a touch of rye flour with a generous amount of water to create what bakers call a wet dough. Wet doughs don't hold their shape, but they bake into crusty, light, bubbly breads.

This bread is wonderful to make at home. It requires very little active work time and no shaping finesse. The high proportion of water in the dough makes it difficult to knead by hand, though, so I recommend using a heavy-duty stand mixer. It takes longer to develop the gluten in a wet dough, so you'll notice that the kneading time is longer and the mixer speed is faster in this recipe than in most others. To get the best rise, it's important to exercise the gluten gently, which is why you give the dough two turns, rather than just one.

Be aware going into the recipe that the timing is quite different from that of other French breads. Pierre ferments the dough during the first rise for a long time at room temperature and then gives it a second, slow rise in a low-temperature proofing chamber called a retarder (you'll use your refrigerator). The double rise is meant to develop the flavor of the rye. After he cuts the dough into pieces, he pulls it into long, slack loaves and bakes them right away.

✳ **MAKES 2 LONG FREE-FORM LOAVES**
(18 OUNCES/518 GRAMS EACH)

Equipment

HEAVY-DUTY STAND MIXER WITH DOUGH HOOK
BENCH SCRAPER OR CHEF'S KNIFE
BAKER'S PEEL OR RIMLESS BAKING SHEET
PARCHMENT PAPER
BAKING STONE
CAST-IRON SKILLET

Note: If you don't have a stiff dough *levain* already prepared, you will have to make one from scratch (page 111), substitute a commercial sourdough starter (see pages 333–34 for sources), or use the *pâte fermentée* method (page 116) instead.

LEVAIN STARTER				
INGREDIENTS	VOLUME	U.S. WEIGHT	METRIC WEIGHT	BAKER'S PERCENTAGE
Stiff dough *levain* (page 111)	¼ cup	1.6 ounces	45 grams	45
Water, tepid (70 to 78 degrees)	¼ cup	1.8 ounces	50 grams	50
Bread flour, preferably high-gluten	⅔ cup	3.4 ounces	95 grams	95
Stone-ground whole wheat flour	2 teaspoons	0.2 ounce	5 grams	5

PREPARE THE *LEVAIN*. Take your *levain* out of the refrigerator. Pinch off about 1/4 cup, or a piece the size of an Italian plum (1.6 ounces/45 grams), and discard the rest. Place the piece of *levain* in a wide, shallow mixing bowl and pour the water over it. Use a rubber spatula to mash the *levain* against the sides of the bowl to break it up and soften it. The water will turn milky and bubble. Add the bread flour and whole wheat flour and stir until you have a very dry dough with loose flour scattered all around it. Using the spatula, press the dough against the sides of the bowl to collect as much of the stray flour as you can.

Then tip the bowl with one hand while you knead with the other, chasing down the last bits of flour and working them into a very stiff dough, 1 to 2 minutes. The dough will not be smooth.

Place the dough in a clean 1-quart container and cover it. Place a piece of masking tape on the side of the container to mark the level the dough will reach when it has doubled in volume. Let the *levain* stand to ferment at room temperature (70 to 75 degrees) for 8 to 12 hours, until it has risen into a dome and doubled in volume. It may already have begun to deflate. It will be riddled with air pockets that will be visible through the sides and bottom of the container. It will smell as sweet as overripe fruit.

BREAD DOUGH				
INGREDIENTS	VOLUME	U.S. WEIGHT	METRIC WEIGHT	BAKER'S PERCENTAGE
Water, tepid (70 to 78 degrees)	1²/₃ cups	14.1 ounces	400 grams	80
Bread flour, preferably high-gluten	2³/₄ cups	15.9 ounces	450 grams	90
Fine or medium rye flour	¹/₃ cup	1.8 ounces	50 grams	10
Levain starter	About ¹/₂ cup, packed	4.4 ounces	125 grams	25
Sea salt	1¹/₂ teaspoons	0.4 ounce	10 grams	2

MIX THE DOUGH. Pour the water into a large mixing bowl or the bowl of a stand mixer. Add the bread flour and rye flour and stir with a rubber spatula just until it absorbs all of the water and a dough forms. Cover with plastic wrap and let stand at room temperature for 20 minutes to hydrate the flour and give the gluten a chance to develop on its own.

ADD THE *LEVAIN* AND SALT. Uncover the *levain* and pinch off about 1/2 cup, or a piece the size of a tennis ball (4.4 ounces/125 grams). Uncover the dough, add the *levain* piece, and sprinkle on the salt. Use the spatula to work the *levain* and salt into the dough with a few firm strokes. (Cover the remaining *levain* and store it in the refrigerator, refreshing it at least once a week following the instructions on pages 114–15.)

KNEAD THE DOUGH. By machine: Use the dough hook and mix the dough on medium speed (4 on a KitchenAid mixer) until it is glossy, smooth, and very stretchy, 12 to 14 minutes. This sticky dough will not clear the sides of the bowl. Turn off the machine at least once to scrape down the sides of the bowl and clean off the dough hook. Give the dough a windowpane test to judge its readiness: Gently stretch a golfball-sized piece until the dough is thin enough to see through. If it tears, press the small piece back into the larger mass, knead it for 1 to 2 minutes more, and test again. In order to get the maximum volume in the baked loaf, make sure not to under-knead.

FERMENT THE DOUGH. Transfer the dough to a lightly oiled, clear 2-quart container with a lid. With masking tape, mark the container at the level the dough will reach when it has doubled in volume. Cover and leave it to rise at room temperature (70 to 75 degrees) for 1 hour. It will inflate only slightly.

TURN THE DOUGH TWICE. Scrape the dough out onto a lightly floured counter. With floured hands, lift the top edge of the dough and fold it so that it lands in the center of the mass. Lift the bottom edge and fold it so that it meets the top. In one fluid motion, slide both hands underneath the dough, turn it over so the fold is underneath, and slip it back into the container. Cover the dough and let it rise for another hour. Repeat the turning and let the dough rise, covered, until it expands into a dome twice its original size, reaching the masking-tape mark, 1 to 2 hours more. It will feel supple, airy, and less sticky.

RETARD THE DOUGH. Place the container in the refrigerator and allow the dough to ferment slowly for 12 to 24 hours. It will develop flavor but not rise significantly. Two to 3 hours before you want to bake, remove it from the refrigerator and let it stand on the counter, covered. It will not rise and will feel cool.

PREPARE THE OVEN. About 1 hour before baking, place a baking stone on the middle rack of the oven and a cast-iron skillet on the lower rack. Heat the oven to 450 degrees.

SHAPE THE LOAVES. Just before baking, cover a baker's peel or rimless baking sheet with parchment paper. Generously dust the parchment with flour. Generously dust the counter with flour and scrape the dough onto the counter. Coat the top of the dough with flour. With your palms, press the mound of dough into a rough 10-inch square. With a bench scraper or chef's knife dipped in flour, cut the dough down the middle into 2 equal pieces (18 ounces/518 grams each). With floured hands, lift up one piece from the ends. In one smooth motion, gently stretch it to about 12 inches long and let it fall in whatever shape it may onto one half of the parchment paper. Repeat with the remaining dough, spacing the two pieces at least 2 inches apart.

BAKE THE LOAVES. Immediately after shaping, slide the loaves, still on the parchment, onto the baking stone. Place 1/2 cup of ice cubes in the skillet to produce steam. Bake until the crust underneath the swirls of flour is walnut-colored, 20 to 30 minutes.

COOL AND STORE THE LOAVES. Slide the peel or the rimless baking sheet under the parchment paper to remove the loaves from the oven. Slide the loaves, still on the parchment, onto a wire rack. Cool for about 5 minutes and then peel them off the parchment paper. Let the loaves cool completely, about 1 hour, before slicing. Don't be surprised by the long troughs running through the crumb. This is part of the bread's character. Store the loaves with the cut side covered in plastic at room temperature for 3 to 4 days. For longer storage, freeze in resealable plastic bags for up to 1 month.

LITTLE BLUE CHEESE RYE LOAVES
Méteils au bleu

. . . .

ALLOW 8 TO 12 HOURS TO PREPARE THE *LEVAIN*;

20 MINUTES TO MIX AND REST THE DOUGH;

9 TO 12 MINUTES TO KNEAD;

3 TO 4 HOURS TO FERMENT;

1 TO 1 1/2 HOURS TO PROOF;

25 TO 35 MINUTES TO BAKE

. . . .

Méteil is a classic French bread made from half bread flour and half rye flour. In the Auvergne it is often studded with large chunks of firm local blue cheese. Served warm, it's like eating bread with melted cheese. For authentic flavor, seek out *bleu d'Auvergne* at your local cheese shop. Roquefort or Stilton are good substitutes. This is Pierre Nury's recipe. He bakes the rich bread in little loaf pans, perfect for sharing.

**MAKES 4 SMALL PAN LOAVES
(10 OUNCES/284 GRAMS EACH)**

Equipment
4 MINI-LOAF PANS, 2 1/2 BY 5 BY 2 INCHES
BENCH SCRAPER OR CHEF'S KNIFE
SINGLE-EDGED RAZOR BLADE OR SERRATED CHEF'S KNIFE
CAST-IRON SKILLET

Note: If you don't have a stiff dough *levain* already prepared, you will have to make one from scratch (page 111), substitute a commercial sourdough starter (see pages 333–34 for sources), or use the *pâte fermentée* method (page 116) instead.

LEVAIN STARTER				
INGREDIENTS	VOLUME	U.S. WEIGHT	METRIC WEIGHT	BAKER'S PERCENTAGE
Stiff dough *levain* (page 111)	¼ cup	1.6 ounces	45 grams	45
Water, tepid (70 to 78 degrees)	¼ cup	1.8 ounces	50 grams	50
Unbleached bread flour, preferably high-gluten	⅔ cups	3.4 ounces	95 grams	95
Stone-ground whole wheat flour	2 teaspoons	0.2 ounce	5 grams	5

PREPARE THE *LEVAIN*. Take your *levain* out of the refrigerator. Pinch off about 1/4 cup, or a piece the size of an Italian plum (1.6 ounces/45 grams), and discard the rest. Place the piece of *levain* in a wide, shallow mixing bowl and pour the water over it. Use a rubber spatula to mash the *levain* against the sides of the bowl to break it up and soften it. The water will turn milky and bubble. Add the bread flour and whole wheat flour and stir until you have a very dry dough with loose flour scattered all around it. Using the spatula, press the dough against the sides of the bowl to collect as much of the stray flour as you can. Then tip the bowl with one hand while you knead with the other, chasing down the last bits of flour and working them into a very stiff dough, 1 to 2 minutes. The dough will not be smooth.

Place the dough in a clean 1-quart container and cover it. Place a piece of masking tape on the side of the container to mark the level the dough will reach when it has doubled in volume. Let the *levain* stand to ferment at room temperature (70 to 75 degrees) for 8 to 12 hours, until it has risen into a dome and doubled in volume. It may already have begun to deflate. It will be riddled with air pockets that will be visible through the sides and bottom of the container. It will smell as sweet as overripe fruit.

BREAD DOUGH				
INGREDIENTS	VOLUME	U.S. WEIGHT	METRIC WEIGHT	BAKER'S PERCENTAGE
Water, tepid (70 to 78 degrees)	1½ cups	12.3 ounces	350 grams	70
Unbleached bread flour, preferably high-gluten	1¾ cups	9.7 ounces	275 grams	55
Fine or medium rye flour	1½ cups	7.9 ounces	225 grams	45
Levain starter	About ½ cup, packed	4.4 ounces	125 grams	25
Sea salt	1½ teaspoons	0.4 ounce	10 grams	2
Blue cheese, cut into 1/4-inch pieces	—	5.3 ounces	150 grams	30

MIX THE DOUGH. Pour the water into a large mixing bowl or the bowl of a stand mixer. Add the bread flour and rye flour and stir with a rubber spatula just until they absorb all of the water and a dough forms. Cover with plastic wrap and let stand at room temperature for 20 minutes to hydrate the flour and give the gluten a chance to develop on its own.

ADD THE *LEVAIN* AND SALT. Uncover the *levain* and pinch off about 1/2 cup, or a piece the size of a tennis ball (4.4 ounces/125 grams). Uncover the dough, add the *levain* piece, and sprinkle on the salt. Use the spatula to work the *levain* and salt into the dough with a few firm strokes. (Cover the remaining *levain* and store it in the refrigerator, refreshing it at least once a week following the instructions on pages 114–15.)

KNEAD THE DOUGH. By hand: Turn the dough out onto a lightly floured counter. Knead for 10 to 12 minutes, until it becomes smooth and elastic. This is a soft and sticky dough, but resist adding extra flour as you knead.

By machine: Use the dough hook and mix the dough on low speed (2 on a KitchenAid mixer) for 1 minute to incorporate the *levain*. Increase the speed to medium (4 on a KitchenAid mixer) and knead for 8 to 9 minutes, until the dough is smooth and very elastic.

FERMENT THE DOUGH. Transfer the dough to a lightly oiled, clear 2-quart container with a lid. With masking tape, mark the container at the level the dough will reach when it has doubled in volume. Cover and leave it to rise at room temperature (70 to 75 degrees) for 1 hour. It will inflate only slightly.

TURN THE DOUGH. Scrape the dough out onto a lightly floured counter. With floured hands, lift the top edge of the dough and fold it so that it lands in the center of the mass. Lift the bottom edge and fold it so that it meets the top. In one fluid motion, slide both hands underneath the dough, turn it over so the fold is underneath, and slip it back into the container. Cover the dough and let it rise until it expands into a dome twice its original size, reaching the masking-tape mark, 2 to 3 hours. It will feel firm but springy and less sticky.

DIVIDE AND SHAPE THE LOAVES AND ADD THE CHEESE. Lightly oil 4 small loaf pans with vegetable oil. Turn the dough out onto a lightly floured counter. With a bench scraper or chef's knife, cut the dough into 4 equal pieces (10 ounces/284 grams each). Flour your hands and flatten each piece into about a 4-inch square. Arrange the chilled pieces of cheese over the dough, reserving 2 to 3 pieces for the top of each loaf. Roll up the dough tightly to avoid big gaps around the cheese. Nestle each loaf into a pan with the seam side down and press it gently into the edges (see Shaping Pan Loaves, page 40). With a single-edged razor blade or serrated knife, cut a slit down the length of each loaf, about 1/4 inch deep, and slip in the reserved cheese. Cover the loaves with plastic.

PROOF THE LOAVES. Let the loaves stand at room temperature (70 to 75 degrees) until they look slightly inflated and the fingerprint springs back slowly when you press your fingertip into one, 1 to 1 1/2 hours. These loaves do not rise dramatically.

PREPARE THE OVEN. About 15 minutes before baking, place one oven rack in the middle position and one in the lower position. Place a cast-iron skillet on the lower rack. Heat the oven to 400 degrees.

BAKE THE LOAVES. Slide the pans onto the middle rack. Place 1/2 cup of ice cubes in the skillet to produce steam. Bake the loaves until they are an even, ruddy brown on top and the cheese is melted and bubbling, 25 to 35 minutes. Weighted down by the cheese, these loaves will bake low in the pan.

COOL AND STORE THE LOAVES. Pull the pans from the oven. Bang the edge of each pan on the counter to release the bread and set the loaves on a wire rack. Cool completely, about 1 hour, then serve in thin slices. It's normal for little air pockets to surround the cheese. The loaves will stay fresh for 3 to 4 days in resealable plastic bags. For longer storage, freeze in resealable plastic bags for up to 1 month.

Variation: Pistachio and Golden Raisin Rye *Seigle aux raisins et pistache*
Substituting pistachios and golden raisins for the blue cheese creates an entirely different bread, sweet and crunchy and perfect with a cup of tea.

PREPARE THE NUTS AND RAISINS. At least 1 hour before mixing the dough, preheat the oven to 350 degrees. Spread 1 1/4 cups (5.3 ounces/150 grams) shelled pistachios in a single layer on a baking sheet. Bake them until they are fragrant and toasted, 5 to 8 minutes. Let cool completely. Meanwhile, place 1 cup (5.3 ounces/150 grams) golden raisins in a small bowl and soak in hot tap water until plump and soft, about 15 minutes. Drain thoroughly and blot dry with a paper towel.

ADD THE FRUIT AND NUTS TO THE DOUGH. During the last 2 minutes of kneading, either by hand or by machine, add the pistachios and raisins. In the machine, some of the fruit and/or nuts may collect at the bottom of the bowl. If this happens, turn the dough out onto the counter and press them into the dough by hand.

CLASSIC AUVERGNE DARK RYE
Seigle d'Auvergne

. . . .

ALLOW 8 TO 12 HOURS TO PREPARE THE RYE STARTER;

1 TO 1 1/4 HOURS TO MIX AND FERMENT THE DOUGH;

7 TO 8 MINUTES TO KNEAD;

1 TO 1 1/4 HOURS TO FERMENT AGAIN;

20 TO 30 MINUTES TO PROOF;

35 TO 45 MINUTES TO BAKE

. . . .

I first saw this earthy, dark rye in Amandio Pimenta's bustling bakery in Auvergne's capital, Clermont-Ferrand, and begged him to tell me how it was made. "You can't make this bread," he replied. It wasn't a state secret; he just believed that the *seigle d'Auvergne* was too challenging for anyone who hadn't spent years baking in the region. I wouldn't stop questioning him, and finally he relented. The recipe is astoundingly unconventional, so of course I fell in love with it on the spot. The soupy dough is mixed with very hot water. It is given three risings. Then it is baked in a fiery hot oven. The surface, unscored, becomes covered with cracks and bubbles as it bakes, so the finished bread resembles the volcanic landscape of the region. For bakers with a little experience and a sense of adventure, making this glorious French rye is well worth the effort.

**MAKES 1 LARGE SHOWPIECE ROUND
(42.2 OUNCES/1,195 GRAMS)**

Equipment
HEAVY-DUTY STAND MIXER WITH DOUGH HOOK

BAKING STONE

CAST-IRON SKILLET

BAKER'S PEEL OR RIMLESS BAKING SHEET

PARCHMENT PAPER

Note: If you don't have a stiff dough *levain* already prepared, you will have to make one from scratch (page 111), substitute a commercial sourdough starter (see pages 333–34 for sources), or use the *pâte fermentée* method (page 116) instead.

RYE STARTER				
INGREDIENTS	VOLUME	U.S. WEIGHT	METRIC WEIGHT	BAKER'S PERCENTAGE
Stiff dough *levain* (page 111)	¼ cup	1.6 ounces	45 grams	90
Water, tepid (70 to 78 degrees)	¼ cup	1.8 ounces	50 grams	100
Fine or medium rye flour	⅓ cup	1.8 ounces	50 grams	100

PREPARE THE RYE STARTER. Take your *levain* out of the refrigerator. Pinch off about 1/4 cup, or a piece the size of an Italian plum (1.6 ounces/45 grams) and discard the rest. Place the piece of *levain* in a wide, shallow mixing bowl and pour the water over it. Use a rubber spatula to mash the *levain* against the sides of the bowl to break it up and soften it. The water will turn milky and bubble. Add the rye flour and stir to make a rough, sticky dough.

Place the dough in a clean 1-quart container and cover it. Let the rye starter stand to ferment at room temperature (70 to 75 degrees) for 8 to 12 hours. It will look like bubbly, sticky buttermilk pancake batter.

BREAD DOUGH				
INGREDIENTS	VOLUME	U.S. WEIGHT	METRIC WEIGHT	BAKER'S PERCENTAGE
Rye starter	About ½ cup, packed	4.4 ounces	125 grams	18
Hot tap water (110 to 115 degrees)	1½ cups	12.3 ounces	350 grams	50
Fine or medium rye flour	3¼ cups	17.6 ounces	500 grams	71
Unbleached bread flour, preferably high-gluten	1½ cups	7.1 ounces	200 grams	29
Sea salt	1 tablespoon	0.7 ounce	20 grams	3

MIX THE DOUGH. Place the rye starter in the bowl of a stand mixer. Pour the hot water over it and stir with a rubber spatula to loosen it. Stir in the rye flour to make a thick, smooth batter. Cover with plastic wrap and let stand at room temperature (70 to 75 degrees) until it lightens in color and expands, 1 to 1 1/4 hours.

ADD THE BREAD FLOUR AND SALT AND KNEAD. Uncover the bowl and add the bread flour and salt. Mix the dough on low speed (2 on a KitchenAid mixer) until the dough develops body from the gluten in the wheat flour, 7 to 8 minutes. It will be a slack, sticky dough.

FERMENT THE DOUGH. Cover the bowl with plastic wrap and let stand at room temperature (70 to 75 degrees) until it is lightened and soft, 1 to 1 1/4 hours.

PREPARE THE OVEN. About 1 hour before baking, place a baking stone on the middle rack of the oven and a cast-iron skillet on the lower rack. Heat the oven to 500 degrees.

SHAPE THE LOAF. Cover a baker's peel or rimless baking sheet with parchment paper. Lightly dust the counter with rye flour. Uncover the bowl and scrape the dough onto the counter. It will easily deflate. Gently shape the dough into a loose boule (see Shaping Rounds, page 36) without overhandling it. Place the boule on the parchment, sift some rye flour over the top, and cover with plastic wrap.

PROOF THE LOAF. Let the loaf stand at room temperature (70 to 75 degrees) until it spreads and cracks appear on the surface, 20 to 30 minutes.

BAKE THE LOAF. Slide the loaf, still on the parchment, onto the baking stone. Place 1/2 cup of ice cubes in the skillet to produce steam. Bake until a caramelized brown, 35 to 45 minutes.

COOL AND STORE THE LOAF. Slide the peel or the rimless baking sheet under the parchment paper to remove the loaf from the oven. Slide the loaf, still on the parchment, onto a wire rack. Cool for about 5 minutes and then peel it off the parchment paper. Let the loaf cool completely, about 1 hour, before slicing. Store with the cut side covered with plastic wrap for 3 to 4 days.

FREQUENTLY ASKED QUESTIONS ABOUT AUVERGNE BREADS

. . . .

What is the effect of adding high-fat ingredients like cheese and bacon to bread dough?

The addition of high-fat ingredients has several benefits. The first, of course, is flavor. The fat in cheese or bacon, when it melts into the bread dough, flavors and perfumes the whole bread deliciously. Additionally, fat will make the bread very moist, with a finer, cleaner, shinier crumb than bread made without fat. Finally, because bread made with cheese or bacon is so moist, it will keep a day or two longer at room temperature than fat-free bread.

How can I tell if rye flour is coarsely or finely ground?

In the Auvergne, bakers use only finely ground whole rye flour. In Germany, more coarsely ground whole rye flour is the rule. Most rye flours on the market in the U.S.A. are finely ground whole rye. If the bag doesn't specify, it's a good bet that the flour is finely ground. If it is labeled "pumpernickel," that indicates a coarse grind. Better mills specify the grind and often offer selections in between fine and coarse. For these breads, choose the most finely ground whole rye flour that you can. Then you will wind up with a uniformly colored bread without the bran flakes of a coarser flour.

Why does only one of these recipes employ a rye starter while the rest use straightforward *levain*?

As remote and self-contained as the Auvergne is, it is

still a part of France and partakes of some of the bread-crafting traditions that you find across the country. Using *levain* is one of them. Although local rye flour is employed more frequently in baking in this region than it is in Paris, the rye breads are raised with *levain*. Even with the *seigle d'Auvergne*, where a rye starter is necessary to build the intense rye flavor of the bread, a piece of *levain* is used to initiate the rye sponge.

CHAPTER 8

✳

VERONA AND TUSCANY:
BIGA, *DOPPIO ZERO*, AND
REGIONAL ITALIAN BREADS

✳

About ten years ago, after a series of intense working visits to Parisian bakeries, I was bitten by the Italian bug. It began when I was invited to be the guest chef on a bike tour through the Italian wine country in Umbria. I really enjoyed cooking with the ingredients that we gathered during each day's tour. I picked fresh figs right from the trees at local orchards on our course and bought fresh porcini mushrooms at open-air markets. I was enchanted by the local food, like the tagliatelle with wild boar served in village trattorias. Every time we passed a wood-fired pizza place, I had to stop and compare the thin-crusted rounds to the pizzas we had eaten the day before. I ate countless cups of gelato, unable to settle on hazelnut, espresso, or Sicilian lemon as my favorite.

The breads I saw in Italian country bakeries were absolutely beautiful, and very different in style from the French breads I knew. The focaccias and grissini were a rustic contrast to the elegantly shaped and scored French breads. I would always love Basil's *baguette normal*, Poilâne's *miches*, and every variety of *pain au levain*, but I was exhilarated to be a beginner again, asking many questions and trying many breads for the very first time. When I came home, I made a conscious decision to learn all I could about Italian bread. I asked my baker friends here and in France about the best point of entry into Italian baking culture. That's how I wound up at the Salone Internazionale dell'Arte Bianca, or SIAB, an annual trade show for Italian bakers in Verona, the beautiful city in the Veneto best known as the setting of *Romeo and Juliet*.

SIAB takes place every year just outside the city, in a series of six exhibition halls, each the size of a football field. If you've never been to a baking trade show, this may sound enormous, but the Verona exhibition is an intimate affair compared with the huge baking shows mounted in France and Germany. At those shows, I would routinely run into twenty or thirty American bakers. The Verona show, in contrast, seemed like a well-kept secret, attended exclusively by Italian bakers, with a sprinkling of eastern Europeans. At that point, I didn't speak much Italian. I had asked two colleagues who had attended the show before, Jim Lahey of Sullivan Street Bakery in New York City and Biagio Settepani of Bruno Bakery, also in New York, if I could tag along as they spoke with equipment manufacturers, flour purveyors, and all the Italian bakers they knew from previous trips to SIAB. Jim, Biagio, and I were the only Americans in sight. I instantly felt immersed in Italian baking culture.

The bakers I met through Jim and Biagio came from all over the country. Most of them were owners of tiny storefront businesses, unnamed and simply designated by a FORNO sign above the door. It was in Verona, talking to these bakers, that I first understood Italian baking culture as a loose network of small bakeries spread out across the country. They all produce recognizably Italian breads, but the breads are also distinctly regional. Wandering around the exhibition halls, I sampled breads made by bakers from every part of Italy. Two elements defined Italian bread. Most of the loaves were leavened not with a French-style sourdough starter but with *biga*, a quick pre-ferment made with packaged yeast. Most of them were white breads made with bright white, finely milled *doppio zero* flour, quite different in look and feel from the bran-flecked type 55 and type 85 flours of France. I was astounded, then, at the diversity of the offerings, considering that virtually all the bakers at the show used the same starter and the same flour. First, there were the shapes. In place of baguettes and boules there were logs and loose round shapes entirely new to me. Little rosetta rolls and breadsticks coated with herbs and salt added to the picture. I could have written a book just on the vast selection of *pizze* and *foccacie* I sampled in the amazing pizza pavilion. Caputo, the Italian pizza flour company, was making individual pizzas to order, topped with zucchini blossoms, porcini, cured meats, and many other delicacies. A crowd twenty deep waited patiently as the bakers pulled them from the oven and handed them around. Judging from the offerings on show, Italy had many more regional breads than I had found in France, where *pain au levain* was the mainstay in bakeries throughout the country.

In broken Italian, I asked bakers and suppliers I met in Verona about Italian ingredients and techniques. I was impressed with the ovens, mixers, dough feeders, roll dividers, and ciabatta machines made in Italy specifically for Italian-style breads. Before I left the show, I asked Silvia Dezane, a representative of the venerable Italian baking equipment company Pietroberto, to take me on a tour of Tuscan bakeries where the company's ovens and other machinery were used. Not only would it be an opportunity to see how the Italian baking equipment worked in a variety of settings, it would give me a chance to learn more about *biga* and *doppio zero* flour. I'd gotten a taste of Tuscan bread at the show, but I hoped to learn more about the unique and interesting breads of the region, especially the most famous one, *pane Toscano*, a bread that lacks what is considered an essential ingredient in bread throughout Europe—salt.

At home again, I was determined to improve my Italian before my trip with Silvia. I subscribed to the weekly Italian baking newspaper, *L'Arte Bianca*. I hired an Italian tutor, and we used the paper as a textbook during our lessons. It also became my guide to the latest in Italian baking trends and technology and an address book of noteworthy bakeries. At Bread Alone, I began to experiment with some of the recipes I had gotten from an Italian flour company. I had never made focaccia before, and now we started making two kinds, one with herbs and one with onions and olives. They were immediate successes. When I visited Florence a few months later, I knew what questions I wanted to ask. Unlike most American tourists, who make a beeline for the Uffizi or Michelangelo's *David*, I headed straight for the bakeries. With Silvia as my guide, I visited five of them in and around the city.

Toscapan was a much larger bakery than the tiny artisanal *fornos* on my list, but I headed there first because of an intriguing article I had read in *L'Arte Bianca* describing the company's artisan origins and commitment to traditional Tuscan breads. Toscapan's owner, Amos de Carlo, had begun as a baker with a small, traditional shop and built his business into a huge commercial operation by mechanizing much of the baking process. Freshly baked breads from this bakery were loaded onto trucks several times a day and shipped by the ton all over northern Italy and into Germany. Each one had an edible decal baked into the crust claiming that the bread was authentically Tuscan. Most of the bread from Toscapan was baked in modern tunnel ovens, but I had read about Amos's bakery-within-a-bakery, complete with a brick oven that used shells from locally grown pignoli as fuel, where he baked smaller batches of traditional breads—white and whole wheat *pane Toscano* (page 168), Tuscan flatbreads made with corn flour, several types of focaccia—for local customers. He was described in *L'Arte Bianca* as a fanatic for perfectly fermented *biga*, and I hoped he would share with me his knowledge about using *biga* in Tuscan bread.

Toscapan is in a 40,000-square-foot building in an industrial park right off the *autostrada*, about 10 minutes' drive outside Florence. Its appearance does not suggest artisan tradition. Before entering the bakery proper, I had to sign in and tuck away my camera—no photos allowed. Wearing starched white lab coats and hygienic paper hats, Silvia and I passed a wall of shining steel tunnel ovens to get to a room with air purifiers and silent bakers in spotless uniforms working at individual stations. The familiar signs of artisan baking—the film of flour covering every surface, the bread rising on wooden boards—were missing. The atmosphere was guarded and standoffish. Was the passion for bread missing too?

Amos, a small, serious man in an immaculate white coat embroidered with the Toscapan logo, greeted us with a formal handshake and gave a brief and chilly description of his big business, consisting mostly of numbers: how many loaves were baked each day, the different varieties, the number of trucks they filled, the wholesale and retail prices of the different products. But when he led us into a temperature-controlled mixing room, he seemed to warm up. I wondered why. Attached to one wall was a steel contraption that looked like a miniature Ferris wheel. It was about 12 feet high. Where the seats on a Ferris wheel would have been, six white tubs, each filled with 10 kilos (about 22 pounds) of dough, hung. As we approached, the machine rotated forward, setting one of the tubs on the floor. After unclipping it, a baker dumped the contents into a huge mixing bowl. This, Amos proudly explained, was his invention for producing a consistent *biga* on the hour. The wheel turned every two hours, placing a perfectly fermented batch of *biga* on the floor. The bakers would clip a tub of freshly mixed *biga* in its place, and the cycle would continue. In twelve hours, this new batch would have traveled full circle, and would be ready to raise bread.

Although the temperature in the room was an even 77 degrees, I could see Amos's cheeks flush with animation as he described how the *biga* wheel was responsible for producing perfectly raised and flavored Tuscan bread, batch after batch. I asked him how he had thought up such an ingenious system. His reserve disappeared entirely as he confided, "I dreamed it one night!" *Ah*, I said to myself. Only a true artisan baker would dream about fantastic machines for making perfectly balanced *biga*.

Amos's invention is a logical step in the evolution of Italian bread baking. He designed it as a foolproof way to regulate the fermentation of the starter, something that Italian bakers have been trying to do since its invention over 120 years ago, when commercial yeast was first introduced. *Biga* is a firm dough made with yeast, flour, and water that is left to ferment in a cool place for no more than sixteen hours. The recipe is virtually the same in every bakery in Tuscany: 45 percent water to flour, with a half percent of yeast. Unlike *levain* and other sourdough starters, *biga* is made fresh before every batch of bread is baked. For generations, Italian bakers have prepared *biga* every day, because it is a practical and quick way to raise flavorful bread. Originally, it was important because it strengthened the gluten in Italian bread doughs, which were mixed with the relatively low-protein flour made from northern Italian wheat. *Biga* is a very stiff dough with a consistency of clay. It takes eight to sixteen hours to rise, and when it does, it has a lot of body and elasticity. Because it is added in large quantities to bread dough, it lends the dough some of its strength.

Italians value firm *biga* not only for its strengthening ability but because it gives their bread flavor. Before refrigeration, bakers preferred firm starters that fermented slowly and were less likely than liquid starters to become too sour and lose their leavening power before the baker was ready to mix the dough. Today, bakers like Amos de Carlo have higher-protein flour and refrigerated rooms, but they still use traditional *biga* to coax the full flavor of wheat from the dough. Fermented for less than a day, the *biga* is never in danger of developing too much acid, which would destroy the yeast and undermine the structure of the bread. This brief fermentation is just long enough to allow the yeast to multiply sufficiently and to develop the fresh, sweet flavors of the wheat. Not every baker has a high-tech method for controlling the acidity in the *biga*, but every single one does have a system for controlling its fermentation—a small refrigerator where it is kept and monitored, a series of shelves in a walk-in refrigerator where batches are rotated until they're ready, or a refrigerated room just for *biga* that's organized so the bakers know when a particular batch is ready to use.

What I found most interesting about the *biga*-based recipes at Toscapan and everywhere else in Italy was the amount of the starter that went into the doughs. Unlike French recipes, which use just a small percentage—typically 30 percent and no more than 50 percent—of a quick, freshly made starter like *pâte fermentée* or *poolish* in bread dough, Italian recipes generally contain a higher percentage of *biga*, sometimes as high as 90 percent. Having spent most of my professional life believing that sourdough was essential if you wanted to bake a complexly flavored bread with a long shelf life, I was amazed at the flavor of *biga*-based breads and their freshness several days after baking.

After my tour of Toscapan I had a better understanding of *biga* in Italian baking. But *doppio zero* was still something of a mystery. At the next four bakeries I visited, that mystery began to unravel. At each one I saw flour sacks marked "00" stacked in every storeroom. With no other kind of flour in sight, I was at first worried. How would I be able to duplicate Italian breads at home without this crucial ingredient? Because Italian breads are softer and more yielding than French breads, I assumed that *doppio zero* was a very soft white flour with less protein than the bread flour I was used to baking with in France and at home. But as I spent the rest of my trip actually working with the bakers, my Italian improved, and so did my understanding of what this term means.

Stefano Galletti, who is the head baker at Forno di via dei Cerchi, a delightful little bakery on a narrow cobblestone street in the middle of Florence, was especially helpful in demystifying "00." Stefano has been baking there since he was fifteen. Now thirty, he is a friendly and charming man with dark hair and a warm smile. In his Italian baking whites and baker's closed-toe sandals, he is exactly what you'd picture an Italian baker to be. And he knows so much about Italian ingredients and Tuscan breads. On my first visit, he took me into his storeroom and showed me two sacks of flour, one for pastry and one for bread. Both were marked "00." It turns out that 00 refers not to the strength of the flour but to its provenance and the way it's milled. *Doppio zero* flour is milled from winter wheat grown in Italy. It is unbleached and unbromated. Just like American flours, it comes in different strengths to accommodate different baking needs. So there's a lower-protein 00 for cake and a higher-protein 00 for bread. Studying farinograph readouts supplied by Stefano's miller (a farinograph is a machine millers use to measure the strength of gluten in flour and its ability to absorb water, among other characteristics), I saw that the *doppio zero* bread flour used to make *pane Toscano* was about 11 percent protein, the equivalent of our all-purpose flours. I realized that to make authentic Tuscan bread at home, it was more important to use a minimally processed American wheat flour with a protein content equivalent to the one Italian bakers use than to obsess about *doppio zero*, which is hard to find in the United States, even if you are a professional baker. I was less anxious about translating these recipes for Americans once I realized that the different 00 flours had counterparts available here.

I left Florence with a solid understanding of *biga* and *doppio zero* flour. On my next trip, I planned to see how they were put to use in Tuscan breads, and in saltless *pane Toscano* in particular, since it is probably the regional Italian bread best known outside Italy and it presents many interesting lessons for curious bakers. I asked the food writer and Tuscan food authority Faith Willinger to take me on a guided tour of Tuscan bakeries in search of answers to all my questions about this unusual bread.

Initially my interest was academic, but I began to understand the allure of *pane Toscano* at Forno a Legna in Empoli. When we arrived, Aldo Cecchi was baking immense 2-kilo loaves of *pane Toscano*. The imperfect rounds were cooled, cut into chunks, and sold by weight. He handed me a piece and asked me what I thought of its flavor. Being perfectly honest, I told him that the bread tasted strange to me, bland and flat. He nodded and told me to wait a second. From a small pot nearby, he scooped out a spoonful of white beans perfumed with olive oil, garlic, and rosemary and spread them on a fresh slice of the bread. "Taste it now, and tell me what you think." The bread wasn't fighting for attention with the food. Its pure wheatiness provided the bass note for a symphony of succulent flavors. During the course of that trip, I became accustomed to the bread and found myself craving it as the essential accompaniment to highly seasoned pastas, meats, and poultry.

For a lesson in making my ideal *pane Toscano*, I returned to Forno di via dei Cerchi and asked Stefano Galletti to teach me what I needed to know to bake this food-friendly bread. Making bread without salt presents several challenges. The most obvious is that without salt, the bread will be flavorless. Stefano explained that Tuscan bakers compensate for the lack of salt and enhance the flavor of their bread by mixing in a lot of flavorful *biga*. Another potential problem is that bread dough made without gluten-strengthening salt is fragile and can't be pummeled like a bouncier salted dough. I watched him as he mixed and kneaded the dough very gently to avoid breaking the short strands of gluten. Finally, there is the issue of fermentation. Salt slows fermentation in dough, so without it, this dough ferments very quickly. Within two hours of mixing, it is ready to bake. When I watched Stefano load his loaves into the oven, I realized why the crusts were so pale. It wasn't just a lack of salt but also the lack of steam, which enhances browning. Tuscan bakers want a thick, blond crust, so they turn off the oven and leave the bread inside for a few minutes after it's baked.

Although *pane Toscano* (page 168) is the best-known Tuscan bread, it is by no means the only regional specialty. This chapter includes recipes for other wonderful breads I learned to make in Tuscany, most of them *biga*-based. Italian baguettes made with salt, called *stirato* (page 172), are an alternative to saltless Tuscan bread. Lightly baked, sweet, and wheaty from the *biga*, they are also a good match for Tuscany's well-seasoned food. Tuscan bakers produce an array of breads that incorporate grapes, tomatoes, olives, and herbs and are delicious expressions of Tuscan culture and cuisine. Representing these breads is a recipe for olive rolls (page 179) I sampled in Lucca, one of Tuscany's legendary walled cities. The rolls I ate there were made with the same olives used to make the city's renowned olive oil.

The final recipe is for grape focaccia (page 183), the bread that first ignited my passion for Italian bread and that always reminds me of my incredible bike trip through Umbria. When I obtained these recipes, I felt like I was gathering precious fruit. I'm excited to pass along these tastes of Italy to you.

✳ KITCHEN NOTES: RELAXED BAKING, TUSCAN STYLE

Whenever I return from a baking trip to Tuscany, I loosen up in the kitchen. I'm less finicky about making perfect shapes, more content with simple white bread made from simple dough. When getting ready to bake, I imagine not only what the finished bread will taste like but what kinds of imaginative crostini and panini I'm going to make with it or the soups and sauces I'll mop up with it. Here are some ideas about techniques and ingredients that will help you enjoy Tuscan baking at home as much as I do.

Try biga as a quick and economical alternative to sourdough.

I have come to love *biga* not only for the sweet wheat flavor and extended shelf life it gives to Italian bread but for its ease and economy. What's great about this starter is that you mix it up in a bowl and let it sit in the refrigerator, and when you're ready to bake, you simply dump the rest of your ingredients into that bowl and mix. You don't have to cultivate a sourdough for days before baking. There's no fear about failure of fermentation, since you're using commercial yeast. You don't have to weigh or measure just a portion of it, as with other starters. You don't wind up throwing any of it away.

You can blend your own 00 flour.

When made in Italy, the doughs in this chapter would certainly be mixed with *doppio zero* flour. This flour is unavailable here, or at least very difficult to find, but that shouldn't stop you from trying the recipes. Different breads are made with particular strengths of oo. In experimenting with these recipes at home, I've come up with substitutions and blends of American bread, all-purpose, and cake flours with the same protein content as the flour used in Italy. In general, I use bread flour when I need an extensible (stretchy, in baker's language), chewy dough with a solid structure, to make a sturdy bread like Italian Baguettes, or *stirati* (page 172). When I'm baking a bread with a less substantial crust, like Grape Harvest Focaccia (page 183), I use all-purpose flour. For particularly tender breads, like Saltless Tuscan Bread (page 168), I mix all-purpose flour with a small percentage of cake flour.

Bake pane Toscano if you're on a special diet.

We get a lot of requests for salt-free bread at Bread Alone from customers who are on diets that restrict their salt intake. Recommending *pane Toscano* allows me to fulfill these requests and introduce people to an authentic artisan bread at the same time. If you or someone in your family can't eat salt, why not try this recipe instead of making a pallid, salt-free French baguette?

Try pane Toscano if you're in a hurry.

This dough expands rapidly because there is no salt to slow down fermentation. Yes, you'll need to keep an eye on the dough so you don't overferment or overproof it. But the up side to this fast fermentation is that this bread is incredibly quick to make from start to finish. I can think of no other classic European artisan bread with a total preparation time (excluding the fermenting of the starter) of under three and a half hours.

Use leftover pane Toscano to make bruschetta.

Home cooks in Italy use leftover saltless bread as a base for highly seasoned bruschetta toppings. They toast thick slices on Tuscan grills, special cooking racks that fit into the fireplace, and top the bread with chopped tomatoes, olive oil, and basil, or sautéed porcini and garlic, or thin slices of prosciutto and chopped artichokes. If you don't want to toast your bread in your fireplace, you can brush it with a little olive oil and grill or broil it before spooning on the topping of your choice.

Add the flavors of Italy to your dough.

Olive oil, olives, and herbs are everywhere in Italian cooking. Use the same ingredients in your bread as you do in your pasta sauces, braises, and roasts. For the most authentic breads, use locally grown and/or organic grapes and herbs, artisan olive oils from small producers, and unadulterated sea salt.

SALTLESS TUSCAN BREAD
Pane Toscano

. . . .

ALLOW 9 TO 17 HOURS TO MIX AND FERMENT THE *BIGA*;
10 TO 15 MINUTES TO KNEAD;
45 MINUTES TO 1 HOUR TO FERMENT;
45 MINUTES TO 1 HOUR TO PROOF;
45 TO 55 MINUTES TO BAKE

. . . .

Folklore has it that during the Middle Ages, Tuscan bakers decided to go without salt rather than pay a tax on the precious ingredient. *Pane Toscano* may at first have been baked in protest and because of economic necessity, but the simple, rustic loaves came to be revered for their food-friendliness. Saltless Tuscan bread has long been the only bread served at lunch and dinner, at home and in restaurants, throughout the region. This straightforward bread, with its thick blond crust and spongy crumb, never fights for attention with the local specialties. It is perfect for mopping up the gravy from a long-simmering stew or garlicky pasta sauce or for dipping into the extra-fruity olive oil produced in the area. For authentic Tuscan bread salad (*panzanella*), use stale saltless Tuscan bread torn into rough pieces. Cover the bread chunks with water to soak until they have softened, about 20 minutes. Then squeeze the bread to force out all the water and stir in chopped ripe tomatoes, chopped red onion, basil, tender lettuce, and maybe some diced cucumber and drained oil-packed tuna. Dress with extra-virgin olive oil and white wine vinegar and season with salt and pepper.

Tuscan *panettieri* are the only bakers I know of who traditionally leave salt out of their bread dough. Their recipes and techniques are designed to deal with the different way that saltless dough kneads, rises, and browns. Salt strengthens and lengthens the strands of gluten, so Tuscan bakers knead very gently in order not to break the shorter, more fragile strands of gluten in their dough. With no salt to slow down fermentation, the dough rises quickly, so bakers load the loaves into the oven within 2 hours of mixing. Saltless dough doesn't brown like salted dough, but this isn't viewed as a negative by Tuscan bakers. Unlike French bakers, who prefer dark, sometimes charred crusts, Tuscan bakers prize the pale color of the crust and bake without steam to discourage browning. To develop thick, chewy crusts without color, they turn the oven off and leave the bread inside for a few minutes to dry out without burning.

✳ MAKES 2 RUSTIC ROUNDS
(23.4 OUNCES/664 GRAMS EACH)

Equipment

BAKER'S PEEL OR RIMLESS BAKING SHEET
PARCHMENT PAPER
BENCH SCRAPER OR CHEF'S KNIFE
BAKING STONE

BIGA				
INGREDIENTS	VOLUME	U.S. WEIGHT	METRIC WEIGHT	BAKER'S PERCENTAGE
Water, tepid (70 to 78 degrees)	³/₄ cup	5.8 ounces	165 grams	60
Instant yeast	1 teaspoon	0.2 ounce	5 grams	2
Unbleached all-purpose flour	1³/₄ cups	7.9 ounces	225 grams	82
Cake flour	1/8 cup	1.8 ounces	50 grams	18

PREPARE THE BIGA. Nine to 17 hours before you want to bake, prepare the *biga*. Pour the water into a small mixing bowl. With a rubber spatula, stir in the yeast, the unbleached flour, and the cake flour just until a dough forms. It will be stiff like pie dough. Dust the counter with flour and scrape out the dough. Knead the dough for 1 to 2 minutes just to work in all the flour and get it fairly but not perfectly smooth. (This is a very small amount of dough, about the size of a plum.) Lightly oil the mixing bowl. Round the *biga* and place it back in the bowl. Cover the bowl with plastic wrap. Leave at room temperature (70 to 75 degrees) for 1 hour, then refrigerate it for at least 8 and up to 16 hours. The *biga* will double in volume (to about the size of an orange), becoming glossy and porous, and will smell mildly acidic.

BREAD DOUGH				
INGREDIENTS	VOLUME	U.S. WEIGHT	METRIC WEIGHT	BAKER'S PERCENTAGE
Biga	About 2½ cups	15.7 ounces	445 grams	89
Water, tepid (70 to 78 degrees)	1½ cups	13.2 ounces	375 grams	75
Instant yeast	1½ teaspoons	0.3 ounce	8 grams	2
Unbleached all-purpose flour	3¼ cups	17.6 ounces	500 grams	100

MIX THE DOUGH. Remove the *biga* from the refrigerator and uncover it. It will be soft, airy, and a bit sticky. Scrape it into a large bowl. Pour the water over the *biga* and stir it with a rubber spatula to soften it and break it into clumps. Stir in the yeast and flour until a dough forms.

KNEAD THE DOUGH. By hand: Scrape the rough mass of dough onto an unfloured countertop. Knead it with long, smooth strokes to collect all the bits and pieces into a firm dough. Knead the dough until it is shiny and smooth, 13 to 15 minutes. It will not be particularly elastic.

By machine: With the dough hook, mix the firm dough on medium speed (4 on a KitchenAid mixer) until it is shiny and smooth, 10 to 12 minutes. It will not be particularly elastic.

FERMENT THE DOUGH. Transfer the dough to a lightly oiled, clear 2-quart container with a lid. With masking tape, mark the container at the level the dough will reach when it has doubled in volume. Cover and leave it to rise at room temperature (70 to 75 degrees) until it doubles in volume, 45 minutes to 1 hour. When you press your finger into the dough, the fingerprint should spring back slowly.

DIVIDE AND SHAPE THE ROUNDS. Cover a baker's peel or rimless baking sheet with parchment paper and dust it with flour. Uncover the dough and turn it out onto the counter. With a bench scraper or chef's knife, cut the dough into 2 equal pieces (23.4 ounces/664 grams each). Shape each piece into a round (See Shaping Rounds, page 36). Place the loaves smooth side up on the parchment paper, 3 inches apart. Dust them with flour and drape them with plastic wrap.

PROOF THE ROUNDS. Let the rounds rise at room temperature (70 to 75 degrees) until they inflate and your finger leaves an impression, 45 minutes to 1 hour.

PREPARE THE OVEN. About 1 hour before baking, place a baking stone on the middle rack. Heat the oven to 425 degrees.

BAKE THE ROUNDS. Slide the rounds, still on the parchment, onto the baking stone. Bake until the rounds are honey-colored, 30 to 40 minutes. Turn off the oven and leave the loaves inside for 15 minutes to dry the crust.

COOL AND STORE THE ROUNDS. Slide the peel or the rimless baking sheet under the parchment paper to remove the rounds from the oven. Slide the rounds, still on the parchment, onto a wire rack. Cool the rounds briefly, then peel off the parchment paper. Let them cool completely on the rack, about 1 hour, before cutting into thick, 1-inch slices for serving with well-seasoned soups and stews, or 1/2-inch slices for crostini. Without the preserving effect of salt, this bread stales quickly. Freeze any uneaten bread in a resealable plastic bag for up to 1 month.

ITALIAN BAGUETTES
Stirato

. . . .

ALLOW 9 TO 17 HOURS TO MIX AND FERMENT THE *BIGA*;
10 TO 15 MINUTES TO KNEAD;
1 1/2 TO 2 HOURS TO FERMENT;
45 MINUTES TO 1 HOUR TO PROOF;
20 TO 30 MINUTES TO BAKE

. . . .

To make baguettes, Italian bakers use the same ingredients French bakers do, but the result is quite different. Where the Parisian baguette is sleek, the *stirato* (this means "stretched") is rustic. The unscored, flour-dusted loaves with knobby ends come out of the oven lightly baked, with golden rather than deep-red crusts. I love the way Italian bakers casually pile them on the counter like a bundle of logs.

If you have eaten only commercially baked Italian bread, you will be amazed at how the muted flavor of the wheat is amplified in the artisan version. Sweet and wheaty from the *biga*, the *stirato* has a delightful, lightly crisp crust and a moist interior. The long shape offers a high ratio of crust to crumb, making the bread perfect for tearing into chunks and enjoying with green salad, soup, and pasta.

✳ **MAKES 2 BAGUETTES**
(17.8 OUNCES/505 GRAMS EACH)

Equipment
BENCH SCRAPER OR CHEF'S KNIFE
BAKER'S PEEL OR RIMLESS BAKING SHEET
PARCHMENT PAPER
BAKING STONE
CAST-IRON SKILLET

BIGA				
INGREDIENTS	VOLUME	U.S. WEIGHT	METRIC WEIGHT	BAKER'S PERCENTAGE
Water, tepid (70 to 78 degrees)	⅓ cup	3.2 ounces	90 grams	60
Instant yeast	¾ teaspoon	0.1 ounce	3 grams	2
Unbleached all-purpose flour	1 cup	5.3 ounces	150 grams	100

PREPARE THE *BIGA*. Nine to 17 hours before you want to bake, prepare the *biga*. Pour the water into a small mixing bowl. With a rubber spatula, stir in the yeast and flour just until a dough forms. It will be stiff like pie dough. Dust the counter with flour and scrape out the dough. Knead the dough for 1 to 2 minutes just to work in all the flour and get it fairly but not perfectly smooth. (This is a very small amount of dough, about the size of a plum.) Lightly oil the mixing bowl. Round the *biga* and place it back in the bowl. Cover the bowl with plastic wrap. Leave at room temperature (70 to 75 degrees) for 1 hour, then refrigerate it for at least 8 and up to 16 hours. The *biga* will double in volume (to about the size of an orange), becoming glossy and porous, and will smell mildly acidic.

BREAD DOUGH				
INGREDIENTS	VOLUME	U.S. WEIGHT	METRIC WEIGHT	BAKER'S PERCENTAGE
Biga	About 1½ cups	8.6 ounces	243 grams	61
Water, lukewarm (85 to 95 degrees)	1¼ cups	9.9 ounces	280 grams	70
Instant yeast	1 teaspoon	0.2 ounce	5 grams	1
Unbleached all-purpose flour	2½ cups	14.1 ounces	400 grams	100
Sea salt	1½ teaspoons	0.4 ounce	10 grams	3

MIX THE DOUGH. Remove the *biga* from the refrigerator and uncover it. It will be soft, airy, and a bit sticky. Scrape it into a large bowl. Pour the water over the *biga* and stir it with a rubber spatula to soften it and break it into clumps. Stir in the yeast, flour, and salt until a dough forms.

KNEAD THE DOUGH. By hand: Lightly flour the countertop and scrape out the dough. Knead the dough with steady, confident strokes. At first it will be sticky, but resist adding more flour. Flour your hands as often as necessary and use a bench scraper to collect the dough from the counter. It will gradually become more cohesive but will still be tacky. Continue kneading until the dough is very smooth and elastic, 13 to 15 minutes. Check that the dough is well developed by pulling off a golfball-sized piece and stretching it into an opaque windowpane. If it tears, knead for an additional 2 to 3 minutes and test again.

   By machine: With the dough hook, mix the dough on medium speed (4 on a KitchenAid mixer) until it is smooth and elastic, 10 to 12 minutes. Check that the dough is well developed by doing a windowpane test, as described above. If the dough tears, knead for an additional 2 to 3 minutes and test again.

FERMENT THE DOUGH. Transfer the dough to a lightly oiled, clear 2-quart container with a lid. With masking tape, mark the container at the level the dough will reach when it has doubled in volume. Cover and leave it to rise at room temperature (70 to 75 degrees) until it doubles in volume, 1 1/2 to 2 hours. When you press your finger into the dough, the fingerprint should spring back slowly.

DIVIDE AND SHAPE THE BAGUETTES. Cover a baker's peel or rimless baking sheet with parchment paper and dust it with flour. Uncover the dough and turn it out onto an unfloured countertop. With a bench scraper or chef's knife, cut the dough into 2 equal pieces (17.8 ounces/505 grams each). Drape them with plastic wrap and let the dough rest on the counter for 10 minutes. Shape each piece into a fat baguette, about 12 inches long and 3 inches wide, keeping the ends rounded (see Shaping Baguettes, pages 37–38). Place the baguettes on the parchment, seam side down and 3 inches apart. Sift a wisp of flour over the baguettes and cover them with plastic wrap.

PROOF THE BAGUETTES. Let the loaves rise at room temperature (70 to 75 degrees) until they inflate and spread out, 45 minutes to 1 hour. Small bubbles will appear just below the surface, and when you press your finger into the dough, your fingerprint will spring back slowly.

PREPARE THE OVEN. About 1 hour before baking, place a baking stone on the middle rack and place a cast-iron skillet on the lower rack. Heat the oven to 450 degrees.

BAKE THE BAGUETTES. Slide the loaves, still on the parchment, onto the baking stone. Place 1/4 cup of ice cubes in the skillet to produce light steam. Bake the baguettes until they are honey gold, 20 to 30 minutes.

COOL AND STORE THE BAGUETTES. Slide the peel or the rimless baking sheet under the parchment paper to remove the loaves from the oven. Slide the loaves, still on the parchment, onto a wire rack. Cool the loaves completely, about 1 hour, before serving in 1-inch-thick slices. This bread is best eaten the day it is baked. For longer storage, freeze in resealable plastic bags for up to 1 month.

ROSEMARY *FILONE*
Panmarino

. . . .

ALLOW 9 TO 17 HOURS TO MIX AND FERMENT THE *BIGA*;
10 TO 15 MINUTES TO KNEAD;
1 1/2 TO 2 HOURS TO FERMENT;
45 MINUTES TO 1 HOUR TO PROOF;
30 TO 40 MINUTES TO BAKE

. . . .

Italian bakers typically make rosemary bread from dough flavored with *biga* and tenderized with olive oil. None do it with more gusto than Sandro Bernini, a baker in Donnini, one of Tuscany's beautiful hill towns. Evergreen shrubs of rosemary as tall as fence posts line the walkway to his bakery, pouring out their intoxicating aroma. A trained opera singer, Sandro sings romantic melodies while pulling flat, log-shaped loaves called *filone* from the oven. During baking, the bold scent and flavor of the rosemary permeate the dough, gradually mellowing so the herb is an alluring, not overpowering, element. Sandro's light, just-crusty bread is a flavorful match for grilled chicken, beef, or rabbit served with a squirt of lemon, Tuscan style.

✳ **MAKES 2 RECTANGULAR LOAVES ABOUT 12 INCHES LONG**
(19.7 OUNCES/560 GRAMS EACH)

Equipment
BAKER'S PEEL OR RIMLESS BAKING SHEET
PARCHMENT PAPER
BENCH SCRAPER OR CHEF'S KNIFE
BAKING STONE

BIGA				
INGREDIENTS	VOLUME	U.S. WEIGHT	METRIC WEIGHT	BAKER'S PERCENTAGE
Water, tepid (70 to 78 degrees)	⅓ cup	2.3 ounces	65 grams	65
Instant yeast	½ teaspoon	0.1 ounce	2 grams	2
Unbleached all-purpose flour	⅔ cup	3.5 ounces	100 grams	100

PREPARE THE *BIGA*. Nine to 17 hours before you want to bake, prepare the *biga*. Pour the water into a small mixing bowl. With a rubber spatula, stir in the yeast and flour just until a dough forms. It will be stiff like pie dough. Dust the counter with flour and scrape out the dough. Knead the dough for 1 to 2 minutes just to work in all the flour and get it fairly but not perfectly smooth. (This is a very small amount of dough, about the size of a plum.) Lightly oil the mixing bowl. Round the *biga* and place it back in the bowl. Cover the bowl with plastic wrap. Leave at room temperature (70 to 75 degrees) for 1 hour, then refrigerate it for at least 8 and up to 16 hours. The *biga* will double in volume (to about the size of an orange), becoming glossy and porous, and will smell mildly acidic.

BREAD DOUGH

INGREDIENTS	VOLUME	U.S. WEIGHT	METRIC WEIGHT	BAKER'S PERCENTAGE
Biga	About 1 cup	5.9 ounces	167 grams	33
Water, tepid (70 to 78 degrees)	1⅓ cups	10.6 ounces	300 grams	60
Instant yeast	1 teaspoon	0.2 ounce	5 grams	1
Unbleached all-purpose flour	3¼ cups	17.6 ounces	500 grams	100
Extra-virgin olive oil	⅓ cup	2.3 ounces	65 grams	13
Fresh rosemary, coarsely chopped	¼ cup	0.4 ounce	10 grams	2
Sea salt	2¼ teaspoons	0.5 ounce	15 grams	3

MIX THE DOUGH. Remove the *biga* from the refrigerator and uncover it. It will be soft, airy, and a bit sticky. Scrape it into a large bowl. Pour the water over the *biga* and stir it with a rubber spatula to soften it and break it into clumps. Stir in the flour, olive oil, rosemary, and salt until a dough forms.

KNEAD THE DOUGH. By hand: Lightly flour the counter and scrape the dough out onto it. Knead the dough with steady strokes until it is silky, smooth, and elastic, 13 to 15 minutes. Check that the dough is well developed by pulling off a golfball-sized piece and stretching it into an opaque windowpane. If the dough tears, knead for an additional 2 to 3 minutes and test again.

By machine: With the dough hook, mix the dough on medium speed (4 on a KitchenAid mixer) until it is silky, smooth, and elastic, 10 to 12 minutes. Check

that the dough is well developed by doing a windowpane test, as described above. If it tears, knead for an additional 2 to 3 minutes and test again.

FERMENT THE DOUGH. Transfer the dough to a lightly oiled, clear 2-quart container with a lid. With masking tape, mark the container at the level the dough will reach when it has doubled in volume. Cover and leave it to rise at room temperature (70 to 75 degrees) until it doubles in volume, 1 1/2 to 2 hours. When you press your finger into the dough, the fingerprint should spring back slowly.

DIVIDE AND SHAPE THE LOAVES. Cover a baker's peel or rimless baking sheet with parchment paper and dust it with flour. Lightly dust the counter with flour. Uncover the dough and turn it out onto the counter. With a bench scraper or chef's knife, cut the dough into 2 equal pieces (19.7 ounces/560 grams each). Shape each piece into a log about 12 inches long (see Shaping Baguettes, pages 37–38). Place the logs smooth side up on the parchment paper, at least 3 inches apart, and cover them with plastic wrap.

PROOF THE LOAVES. Let the logs rise at room temperature (70 to 75 degrees) until they spread and look puffy and light, nearly doubling in size, 45 minutes to 1 hour. Press your fingertip into the dough and your fingerprint will spring back slowly.

PREPARE THE OVEN. About 1 hour before baking, place a baking stone on the middle rack. Heat the oven to 400 degrees.

BAKE THE LOAVES. Slide the logs, still on the parchment, onto the baking stone. Bake until the logs are dark caramel in color, 30 to 40 minutes.

COOL AND STORE THE LOAVES. Slide the peel or the rimless baking sheet under the parchment paper to remove the loaves from the oven. Slide them, still on the parchment, onto a wire rack. Cool the loaves briefly, then peel off the parchment paper. Let them cool completely on the rack, about 1 hour, before slicing. The olive oil in the dough will help to keep them moist. Store uneaten bread in a resealable plastic bag at room temperature for 3 to 4 days.

Variation: **Rosemary Breadsticks** *Grissini rosmarino*

To bake Sandro's dough into breadsticks, mix and ferment the dough.

PREPARE THE BAKING SHEETS AND TOPPING. Lightly oil 2 baking sheets. Fill a small bowl with water and set it aside with a pastry brush. Pour 1 tablespoon coarse sea salt into another small bowl and set it aside.

PREPARE THE OVEN. About 15 minutes before baking, place one rack in the upper third of the oven and a second rack in the middle position and heat the oven to 350 degrees.

SHAPE THE BREADSTICKS. Lightly dust the counter with flour. Uncover the dough and turn it out onto the counter. With your palms, flatten the dough into a rough square about 1 inch thick. Drape with plastic wrap and let rest for 10 minutes. Uncover the dough and cut it into 16 strips (2.1 ounces/60 grams each), stretching each one to the length of the baking sheet as you cut it. Arrange the strips on the baking sheets about 1/2 inch apart. If you want them all to be exactly the same length, trim the ends even with the bench scraper or a pizza cutter. Lightly brush the breadsticks with water and sprinkle with the coarse salt.

BAKE THE BREADSTICKS. Place one baking sheet on each oven rack and bake the breadsticks until they are golden and crisp, 15 to 20 minutes. Halfway through baking, switch the baking sheets so they bake evenly.

COOL AND STORE THE BREADSTICKS. Cool the breadsticks briefly, about 5 minutes. Store in an airtight container or resealable plastic bags at room temperature for up to 2 weeks.

BLACK OLIVE CHEEKS
Puccia

....

ALLOW 9 TO 17 HOURS TO MIX AND FERMENT THE *BIGA*;
10 TO 15 MINUTES TO KNEAD;
1 1/2 TO 2 HOURS TO FERMENT;
45 MINUTES TO 1 HOUR TO PROOF;
20 TO 25 MINUTES TO BAKE

....

Plump with olives, smooth and round, these rolls look just like *puccia*, little cheeks. I first saw them in Lucca, a walled city in Tuscany famous for its superior olive oil. I arrived by train, and when I left the station in search of food, these rolls beckoned from the only bakery I found open during the midday lull. They were the perfect snack for a hungry traveler, moist and tender with the delectable crunch of cornmeal on the bottom crust. Dark, oil-cured olives give these rolls richness and great flavor. When you knead the olives into the dough, though, they can break down its structure, so I like to use bread flour for these rolls rather than the all-purpose flour that I usually use in Italian breads.

Serve the *puccia* as an antipasto, with some pecorino cheese and a glass of Chianti.

MAKES 20 ROLLS
(2.1 OUNCES/60 GRAMS EACH)

Equipment
2 BAKING SHEETS
BENCH SCRAPER OR CHEF'S KNIFE

BIGA

INGREDIENTS	VOLUME	U.S. WEIGHT	METRIC WEIGHT	BAKER'S PERCENTAGE
Water, tepid (70 to 78 degrees)	⅓ cup	2.3 ounces	65 grams	65
Instant yeast	½ teaspoon	0.1 ounce	2 grams	2
Unbleached bread flour	⅔ cup	3.5 ounces	100 grams	100

PREPARE THE *BIGA*. Nine to 17 hours before you want to bake, prepare the *biga*. Pour the water into a small mixing bowl. With a rubber spatula, stir in the yeast and flour just until a dough forms. It will be stiff like pie dough. Dust the counter with flour and scrape out the dough. Knead the dough for 1 to 2 minutes just to work in all the flour and get it fairly but not perfectly smooth. (This is a very small amount of dough, about the size of a plum.) Lightly oil the mixing bowl. Round the *biga* and place it back in the bowl. Cover the bowl with plastic wrap. Leave at room temperature (70 to 75 degrees) for 1 hour, then refrigerate it for at least 8 and up to 16 hours. The *biga* will double in volume (to about the size of an orange), becoming glossy and porous, and will smell mildly acidic.

BREAD DOUGH

INGREDIENTS	VOLUME	U.S. WEIGHT	METRIC WEIGHT	BAKER'S PERCENTAGE
Biga	About 1 cup	5.9 ounces	167 grams	33
Water, tepid (70 to 78 degrees)	1½ cups	13.2 ounces	375 grams	75
Instant yeast	1 teaspoon	0.2 ounce	5 grams	1
Unbleached bread flour	3¼ cups	17.6 ounces	500 grams	100
Sea salt	1½ teaspoons	0.4 ounce	10 grams	2
Oil-cured olives, pitted and coarsely chopped	1½ cups	5.3 ounces	150 grams	30
Coarse cornmeal for dusting	—	—	—	—

MIX THE DOUGH. Remove the *biga* from the refrigerator and uncover it. It will be soft, airy, and a bit sticky. Scrape it into a large bowl. Pour the water over the *biga* and stir it with a rubber spatula to soften it and break it into clumps. Stir in the yeast, flour, and salt until a dough forms.

KNEAD THE DOUGH. By hand: Lightly flour the counter and scrape the dough out onto it. Knead the dough until it is soft and almost smooth, about 10 minutes. With floured hands, press the dough into a rough rectangle and spread the olives over it. They will seem overabundant. Roll up the dough to contain as many of the olives as possible and continue kneading until the olives are evenly distributed and the dough is smooth and elastic, 3 to 5 minutes more. If olives pop out as you knead, push them

back into the dough. They will tint the dough a grayish color.

By machine: With the dough hook, mix the dough on medium speed (4 on a KitchenAid mixer) until it is fairly smooth, about 8 minutes. Stop the machine, scrape down the hook, and add the olives. Knead the dough on medium-low speed (3 on a KitchenAid mixer) until they are well distributed and the dough is smooth, 2 to 3 minutes. Or knead them in by hand as directed above. They will tint the dough a grayish color.

FERMENT THE DOUGH. Transfer the dough to a lightly oiled, clear 2-quart container with a lid. With masking tape, mark the container at the level the dough will reach when it has doubled in volume. Cover and leave it to rise at room temperature (70 to

75 degrees) until it doubles in volume, 1 1/2 to 2 hours. When you press your finger into the dough, the fingerprint should spring back slowly.

DIVIDE AND SHAPE THE ROLLS. Sprinkle a light coating of cornmeal over the surface of the baking sheets. Turn the dough out onto a lightly floured countertop and pat into a rough rectangle. With a bench scraper or chef's knife, cut the dough into 20 equal pieces (2.1 ounces/60 grams each). Shape each piece into a ball (see Shaping Rolls, page 37). Place them smooth side up on the baking sheets, about 1 1/2 inches apart. Sift a veil of flour over the tops of the rolls and drape them with plastic wrap.

PROOF THE ROLLS. Let the rolls rise at room temperature (70 to 75 degrees) until they expand to the size of a mandarin orange, 45 minutes to 1 hour. Press your fingertip into the dough and your fingerprint will spring back slowly.

PREPARE THE OVEN. About 15 minutes before baking, place one rack in the top third of the oven and another in the middle position. Heat the oven to 400 degrees.

BAKE THE ROLLS. Uncover the baking sheets and slide them onto the oven racks. Bake until the rolls are honey-colored, 20 to 25 minutes. Halfway through baking, switch the sheets so the rolls bake evenly.

COOL AND STORE THE ROLLS. Remove the baking sheets to a wire rack. Cool the rolls briefly, about 5 minutes, and enjoy them slightly warm. The oil from the olives will help to keep them moist. Store uneaten rolls in a resealable plastic bag at room temperature for 1 to 2 days.

GRAPE HARVEST FOCACCIA
Schiacciata all'uva

....

ALLOW 9 TO 15 MINUTES TO KNEAD;
1 TO 1 1/2 HOURS TO FERMENT;
30 TO 45 MINUTES TO PROOF;
20 TO 30 MINUTES TO BAKE

....

When a bicycle touring company asked me to be the traveling guest chef for a group of twelve bikers on a trip through the Umbrian countryside during the grape harvest in October, I immediately said yes, hoping to find some great bread during the adventure. The trip was a dream. We worked up enormous appetites while riding 50 to 70 miles a day through hilly vineyards where workers were picking plump clusters of Sangiovese grapes. Late one golden morning we parked our bikes at a roadside bakery near Todi and tramped into the small shop. The shelves were crowded with this beautiful harvest-time specialty. I still adore the combination of crisp bread and juicy grapes, their sweetness complemented by rosemary and coarse sea salt.

Red Flame grapes are a fine substitute for the local grapes Italian bakers use. But if you do live in a wine region, it's fun to seek out just-harvested grapes from a local vineyard.

This is a great bread for beginners and bakers in a hurry. There's no *biga* to mix the night before—the supple dough is easy to handle, and there is no tricky shaping—you just pat it into the pan. It proofs and bakes faster than any loaf. Depending on how big you cut the pieces, you can serve the focaccia as an appetizer, a snack, or a light dinner with a salad.

✳ MAKES 1 BAKING SHEET–SIZED FLATBREAD
(30.9 OUNCES/875 GRAMS)

Equipment
1 RIMMED BAKING SHEET

INGREDIENTS	VOLUME	U.S. WEIGHT	METRIC WEIGHT	BAKER'S PERCENTAGE
Water, tepid (70 to 78 degrees)	1¼ cups	10.6 ounces	300 grams	60
Instant yeast	1 teaspoon	0.2 ounce	5 grams	1
Unbleached all-purpose flour	3¼ cups	17.6 ounces	500 grams	100
Extra-virgin olive oil	⅓ cup	2.1 ounces	60 grams	12
Sea salt	1½ teaspoons	0.4 ounce	10 grams	2

TOPPINGS				
INGREDIENTS	VOLUME	U.S. WEIGHT	METRIC WEIGHT	BAKER'S PERCENTAGE
Red seedless grapes, washed and stemmed	1½ cups	7.1 ounces	200 grams	—
Fresh rosemary, coarsely chopped	2 tablespoons	0.2 ounce	6 grams	—
Coarse sea salt	1 teaspoon	0.2 ounce	5 grams	—

MIX THE DOUGH. Pour the water into a large mixing bowl or the bowl of a stand mixer. Add the yeast, flour, olive oil, and salt and stir just long enough to blend into a dough.

KNEAD THE DOUGH. By hand: Lightly flour the countertop and turn out the dough. Flour your hands and knead with smooth, steady strokes until it is supple, smooth, and very elastic, 12 to 15 minutes.

By machine: With the dough hook, mix the dough on medium speed (4 on a KitchenAid mixer) until it is supple, smooth, and very elastic, 9 to 10 minutes.

FERMENT THE DOUGH. Transfer the dough to a lightly oiled, clear 2-quart container with a lid. With masking tape, mark the container at the level the dough will reach when it has doubled in volume. Cover and leave it to rise at room temperature (70 to 75 degrees) until it doubles and inflates into a dome, 1 to 1 1/2 hours.

SHAPE THE FOCACCIA AND ADD THE TOPPINGS. Very lightly grease a rimmed baking sheet with olive oil. Uncover the dough and gently overturn it onto the baking sheet. Let it rest for 5 minutes. Oil your hands and press the dough with your fingers, gently stretching it toward the edges of the baking sheet without tearing it. If it springs back from the edges of the sheet, let it rest for 5 minutes, uncovered, and try again. Fully stretched, it will be about 1/2 inch thick. Use your hands to coat the dough with olive oil and dimple it all over with the pads of your fingers. Press the grapes into the dough, 1 to 1 1/2 inches apart, and sprinkle the chopped rosemary and coarse sea salt evenly over it. Cover the focaccia with plastic wrap.

PROOF THE FOCACCIA. Let the focaccia rise at room temperature (70 to 75 degrees) for 30 to 45 minutes, until the dough puffs up around the grapes and your fingerprint springs back slowly when you press a finger into the dough.

PREPARE THE OVEN. About 15 minutes before baking, place a rack in the middle position and heat the oven to 375 degrees.

BAKE THE FOCACCIA. Uncover the focaccia. Slide the baking sheet onto the oven rack. Bake the focaccia until the grapes have wrinkled, staining the dough with their juices, and the crust is honey gold, 20 to 30 minutes.

COOL AND STORE THE FOCACCIA. Remove the baking sheet to a wire rack. Cool the focaccia briefly, about 5 minutes. Slip a metal spatula under the edges all around the pan to release it and slide it onto a cutting board. Cut the focaccia into thin, finger-length rectangles for snacks or fat rectangles for a meal. It is best eaten the day it is baked but will stay moist stored at room temperature in a resealable plastic bag for 1 day.

Variation: Individual Focaccias with Cherry Tomatoes *Schiacciate al pomodori*
Makes 6 individual flatbreads (5.1 ounces/146 grams each)

In this variation, the prepared and fermented focaccia dough is cut into pieces and cherry tomatoes are substituted for the grapes and rosemary. The individual focaccias are like personal pizzas.

PREPARE THE TOMATOES. Wash and dry 1 1/2 cups whole cherry tomatoes and set aside with 1 tablespoon coarse sea salt.

SHAPE THE FOCACCIAS. Grease 2 baking sheets with olive oil. Lightly dust the counter with flour, uncover the dough, and turn it out. With a bench scraper or chef's knife, cut the dough into 6 equal pieces (5.1 ounces/146 grams each). Pat or use a rolling pin to roll each piece into a round, about 6 inches across and 1/2 inch thick. Arrange three on each baking sheet, at least 2 inches apart. Use your hands or a pastry brush to coat the dough lightly with olive oil. Dimple the dough all over with the pads of your fingers. Press the cherry tomatoes into the dough and sprinkle it with coarse sea salt. Cover the baking sheets with plastic wrap.

PROOF THE FOCACCIAS. Let the focaccia rise at room temperature (70 to 75 degrees) for 20 to 30 minutes, until the dough puffs up around the tomatoes and your fingerprint springs back slowly when you press a finger into the dough.

(continued on the following page)

(continued from the previous page)

PREPARE THE OVEN. About 15 minutes before baking, place one rack in the upper third of the oven and a second rack in the middle position and heat the oven to 375 degrees.

BAKE THE FOCACCIAS. Uncover the focaccia. Slide the baking sheets onto the oven racks. Bake the focaccia until the crust is honey gold, 12 to 15 minutes, switching the sheets after 8 minutes so the breads bake evenly.

COOL AND STORE THE FOCACCIAS. Remove the baking sheets to a wire rack. Cool the focaccia briefly, about 5 minutes, and eat warm. Focaccia with cherry tomatoes is best eaten the day it is baked.

RICOTTA BREAD
Pane alla ricotta

· · · · · · · · · · · · · · · · · · · ·

ALLOW 10 TO 15 MINUTES TO KNEAD;

30 MINUTES TO 1 HOUR TO FERMENT;

1 TO 1 1/2 HOURS TO PROOF;

20 TO 30 MINUTES TO BAKE

· · · · · · · · · · · · · · · · · · · ·

I saw this delicious bread, made with instant yeast added right to the dough rather than raised with *biga*, at countless bakeries throughout Tuscany. It's an example of the way Italian bakers incorporate wonderful foods into their breads to give them flavor. The ricotta cheese in this bread imparts a velvety soft crumb and subtle nuttiness. Stefano Galletti from Forni di via dei Cerchi in Florence generously shared this recipe with me, specifying full-fat ricotta, because butterfat gives the bread its richness and moist texture.

MAKES 2 ROUNDS
(17.8 OUNCES/505 GRAMS EACH)

Equipment

BENCH SCRAPER OR CHEF'S KNIFE

BAKER'S PEEL OR RIMLESS BAKING SHEET

PARCHMENT PAPER

BAKING STONE

CAST-IRON SKILLET

BREAD DOUGH

INGREDIENTS	VOLUME	U.S. WEIGHT	METRIC WEIGHT	BAKER'S PERCENTAGE
Water, tepid (70 to 78 degrees)	³/₄ cup	7.1 ounces	200 grams	40
Milk, tepid (70 to 78 degrees)	¹/₂ cup	3.5 ounces	100 grams	20
Instant yeast	1 tablespoon	0.7 ounce	20 grams	4
All-purpose flour	3¹/₄ cups	17.6 ounces	500 grams	100
Unsalted butter, cut into small pieces	2 tablespoons	1.1 ounces	30 grams	6
Whole-milk ricotta, room temperature	³/₄ cup	5.3 ounces	150 grams	30
Sea salt	1¹/₂ teaspoons	0.4 ounce	10 grams	2

MIX THE DOUGH. Pour the water and milk into a large mixing bowl or the bowl of a stand mixer. Add the yeast, flour, butter, ricotta, and salt and stir with a wooden spoon just long enough to blend into a dough.

KNEAD THE DOUGH. By hand: Lightly flour the countertop and turn out the dough. Flour your hands and knead with smooth, steady strokes. The dough will be sticky. Flour your hands as often as necessary and use a bench scraper to collect the dough from the counter. Continue kneading until it is supple, smooth, and very elastic, 13 to 15 minutes.

By machine: With the dough hook, mix the dough on medium speed (4 on a KitchenAid mixer) until it is supple, smooth, and very elastic, 10 to 12 minutes.

FERMENT THE DOUGH. Transfer the dough to a lightly oiled, clear 2-quart container with a lid. With masking tape, mark the container at the level the dough will reach when it has doubled in volume. Cover and leave it to rise at room temperature (70 to 75 degrees) until it doubles and inflates into a dome, 1 to 1 1/2 hours. It will deflate slightly when pressed.

DIVIDE AND SHAPE THE ROUNDS. Cover a baker's pe   or rimless baking sheet with parchment paper and dust the parchment with flour. Lightly dust the counter with flour. Uncover the dough and turn it out onto the counter. With a bench scraper or chef's knife, cut the dough into 2 equal pieces (17.8 ounces/505 grams each). Shape each piece into a round (see Shaping Rounds, page 36). Place the loaves smooth side up and 4 inches apart on the parchment paper and cover them with plastic wrap.

PROOF THE ROUNDS. Let the rounds rise at room temperature (70 to 75 degrees) until they look puffy and light and have nearly doubled in size, 1 to 1 1/2 hours. When you press a fingertip into the dough, your fingerprint will spring back slowly.

PREPARE THE OVEN. About 1 hour before baking, place a baking stone on the middle rack. Place the cast-iron skillet on the lower rack. Heat the oven to 400 degrees.

BAKE THE ROUNDS. Slide the parchment off the peel or baking sheet and onto the counter. Line the peel with a fresh sheet of parchment paper and dust the parchment with flour. Gently flip the rounds, one at a time, onto the parchment-lined peel or baking sheet. Slide the upside-down loaves on the parchment paper directly onto the baking stone. Slip 1/4 cup of ice cubes into the skillet to create light steam. Bake until the rounds are honey gold, 20 to 30 minutes.

COOL AND STORE THE ROUNDS. Slide the peel or the rimless baking sheet under the parchment paper to remove the rounds from the oven. Slide the rounds, still on the parchment, onto a wire rack. Cool the rounds briefly, then peel off the parchment paper. Let them cool completely on the rack, about 1 hour, before slicing. Store in a resealable plastic bag at room temperature. They'll stay moist for 2 to 3 days. For longer storage, freeze in a resealable plastic bag for up to 1 month.

FREQUENTLY ASKED QUESTIONS ABOUT TUSCAN BREADS

I notice that there are no sourdough recipes in this chapter. Are Italian breads all made with instant yeast?

The large majority of Italian breads, including the ones in this chapter, are raised with a pre-ferment made with instant yeast, commonly called *biga*. But there are areas where natural sourdough starter is used to bake breads, and in these places—Genzano, outside Rome, and Altamura, on the southeast coast, for example—the sourdough starter is called *biga naturale* but also just plain *biga* for short (see Chapters 9 and 10 for recipes). It can get confusing. For the sake of clarity, I use the term *biga* when referring to an Italian-style pre-ferment made with instant yeast and *biga naturale* when referring to Italian-style sourdough starter.

Is *biga* the Italian equivalent of French *poolish* or *pâte fermentée*?
Although *biga* serves the same basic purpose as *poolish* or *pâte fermentée*—to raise bread dough—it differs in a couple of important ways from the French-style starters. Historically, flour milled from wheat grown in northern Italy contained less protein and developed less gluten during kneading than French flour. To build doughs that would be able to rise into breads with structural integrity, Italian bakers had to use a very firm, dry starter, *biga*. Biga, which is the stiffest and driest pre-ferment I saw in Europe, ferments for a long time, allowing the protein in the flour to develop as much strength as possible. Italian bakers used to use a high proportion of *biga* (up to 90 percent) in their dough to give their breads strength and structure as well as to raise them. *Poolish* or *pâte fermentée* is typically no more than 45 percent of dough recipes.

Is there a reason that Italian bakers often bake without steam? Does unsteamed bread go better with Tuscan food than the more caramelized French-style bread?
There's no reason for the difference—it's just a difference in style. Just as you can say that Italian food is generally more casual than French food, I guess you can generalize about the bread too. Italian bakers don't care about creating the polished, shiny look and light, crisp texture that steam gives to bread

crust. They prefer the dense, hard crusts that are traditional in Italian bread.

Can dried rosemary be substituted for fresh in the rosemary dough? Can other herbs be substituted?

Italians use fresh rosemary in their breads, and I recommend that you do the same. It's easily obtainable year-round in most supermarkets. Italian bakers also add fresh (never dried) basil to their breads, sometimes with a little bit of fresh tomato.

CHAPTER 9

✳

THE PRIDE OF GENZANO:
ITALIAN COUNTRY BREAD WITH A
GOVERNMENT SEAL OF APPROVAL

✳

The name *pane casareccio di Genzano* doesn't immediately signal excellence, or even recognition, for that matter, to American bread lovers the way *pain Poilâne*™ or the mention of Neopolitan pizza does. But this rustic white loaf is famous throughout Italy, as I soon discovered when I began asking Italian bakers and well-traveled American friends where I might look for recipes and techniques unique to the country. Long before I actually tasted this bread, I heard stories about the little seaside town about thirty-five minutes by car from Rome where the bakers still used wood-fired ovens and the traditional Italian sourdough starter, *biga naturale*, traditions that practically disappeared in Italy with the invention of the electric oven and packaged yeast. People said that the giant rounds with a moist, open crumb and a quarter-inch-thick charred crust stayed fresh for a week. Depending on whom you talked to, it was the water, the flour, the wood burned in the ovens, or the ocean air that accounted for the unique and extraordinarily delicious flavor of the bread. I heard that hundreds of loaves were trucked to Rome every morning to satisfy the big city's connoisseurs and that this was the official bread of the Vatican.

Although *pane di Genzano* has long been a legend, it earned the Indicazione Geografica Protetta (IGP), a mark reserved for only the most prized foods and wines, just recently. In fact, it is the only bread to have gained this distinction (a circumstance that the organization of Tuscan wheat farmers, lobbying on behalf of Tuscan saltless bread, is hoping to change). By law, true *pane di Genzano* can be made only by bakers in Genzano, just as IGP-marked mortadella can be made only in Bologna and IGP-marked red radicchio must be grown in Treviso.

Rustic, earthy breads have always attracted me and have always pleased my customers. I reasoned that a trip to Genzano would be well worth my time if I could find an Italian bread as impressive in its simplicity as the Whole Wheat Sourdough *Miche* (page 118). One rainy Sunday night about two years ago, I drove from Rome to Genzano to see what everyone had been raving about.

I had a hint that I had arrived in bread nirvana as I cruised down Genzano's main street, which is maybe one mile long, and counted over a dozen signs reading FORNO (oven) or FORNO A LEGNA (wood-fired oven). That's one sign every hundred meters! In all my travels, I had never seen a town with such a density of bakeries (20,000 people live here). At the side door of each shop stood large bundles of long, skinny twigs, fuel for the ovens. I checked into my hotel, went down to the dining room for dinner, and told the waiter that I was an American baker and had come to Genzano to learn about the town specialty. He brought me a basket with a few slices of the bran-coated white bread. Its thick crust was charred, its crumb shiny and bubbly. Its flavor was mild but extremely tasty, and not the least bit sour. It was the quintessence of country bread, simple and satisfying. The waiter nodded approvingly at my pleasure. I told him that an American friend of mine, a food writer who had spent time in the town, said the water in Genzano was responsible for the bread's unique flavor. "It's not the water. It's the sea air that nourishes a special yeast," he said knowingly. Unlike bakers everywhere else, who used commercial yeast, he said proudly, the local talent used an ancient sourdough bubbling with the fresh-tasting local yeast and bacteria. I was impressed by his amateur's knowledge. In the next couple of days I would meet many nonbakers who evinced a similarly detailed knowledge of how the local bread was made. The waiter told me that if I wanted to learn about *pane di Genzano*, I had to go and see Sergio, the man who had made the bread I was eating. He was the best baker in town. All the others were *calzolai* (shoemakers), compared with Sergio!

After dinner I returned to my room, but knowing that so much baking was going on up and down the street, I couldn't fall asleep. At around midnight I

ventured outside and walked about halfway down the block before peeking through an unshuttered archway and into the closest *forno*, an unadorned room with a counter and some iron bread racks, manned by two bakers, one old and stout, the other young and skinny. A light fog of wood smoke hung in the air, from about eight feet off the ground all the way up to the top of the vaulted ceiling. Built into one wall was a big dome-shaped brick oven. Through its open door I saw an enormous, blazing fire. I could feel its intense heat, more like that of a blast furnace than a bread oven. I watched as the younger baker went to the side door, dragged in a bundle of wood, and threw it into the fire. The twigs erupted into flames and the two bakers turned away from the fire and toward a big bowl of dough. I stepped into the bakery and introduced myself. By any chance was either of them Sergio? The older baker, whose name was Daniel Lattanzi, gave a dismissive shake of his head. "Sergio is a shoemaker," he said (I gathered that this was a favorite expression in town). "Wait until you taste my bread."

During the next couple of hours I watched as Daniel and his apprentice made their bread. While the fire blazed in the oven, they turned their attention to a bubbly mass of dough at the bottom of a big mixer. This was the *biga naturale*, a piece of dough left over from the previous batch. After sitting in the mixing bowl for a short time to ferment, it would become the basis for the next batch. Daniel grabbed a bag of flour and poured the whole thing into the bowl. He dumped two buckets of water in. I was surprised at the casual way he added the ingredients without measuring, but I saw that after making countless batches of exactly the same bread, these bakers knew how much sourdough, flour, and water their bread required without having to weigh out their ingredients. This struck me as a great contrast with most bakeries in France. At Poilâne, for example, the bakers always carefully scale their ingredients every single time they mix a new batch of dough.

Daniel turned the mixer to high and sat back and told me to wait. I watched about 250 kilos of dough spin around. It was so gooey and loose that it looked more like pancake batter than bread dough. "But how will such a liquid mixture become bread?" I asked. "It takes time," Daniel assured me. Reading the skeptical look on my face, he admonished me to have patience. After about twenty-five minutes, the dough gathered together in a mass. Daniel let the mixer go another ten minutes. Then he let the dough rise in the bowl for another hour.

As Daniel mixed the dough and let it rise, we had plenty of time to talk. He told me that no place in Italy has bread like Genzano's. He dismissed the theories I had already heard about the Mediterranean air and the town's water. No, he said, it's the wood and our old, old ovens—he was sure of it. When it was time to shape the bread, he cut a hunk of dough away from the larger mass with a bench scraper, threw it onto a small work table, and quickly formed the soft mass into a big, loose round. Next to the table was an open box about 8 feet square with 4-inch-high sides, lined with a piece of canvas, a variation on a *couche*. The sides of the box were there to prevent the dough from spilling onto the floor. Daniel threw a handful of unprocessed bran across the canvas and placed the loaf in the box. He repeated the shaping seven more times, placing the rounds side by side and pleating the canvas in between the loaves to separate them. When he was done shaping, he threw another big handful of bran over the tops of the rounds. Then he repeated the process, filling up eight boxes with the giant rounds.

After just thirty minutes, the loaves were ready to go into the oven. If allowed to sit too long after shaping, the soft dough rounds would run into each other. At this point the fire in the oven had died down and the apprentice baker was using a metal hook to scrape the coals out and into a metal garbage can. He wiped the floor of the oven with a ragged, wet mop. Daniel and his assistant pushed the racks of bread boxes next to the oven. The young baker quickly flipped a round onto a long, narrow peel. The dough was so soft that it began to spread across the peel. He threw it into the oven in a split second and then loaded the next one. Within three minutes, all

sixty-four rounds were in. The bakers fitted the oven door into its arch and sealed the door with a dirty-looking wet rag that had obviously been used this way many times before. They waited an hour, never checking on the breads. Their lack of concern was unnerving to me. I was convinced that the dough would be incinerated, that when they finally opened the oven door there would be lumps of charcoal at the bottom of the oven instead of bread.

When Daniel unsealed the door and transferred the loaves from oven to cooling rack, I was astounded by the transformation. The breads had achieved incredible oven spring, morphing from flat, slack pieces of dough into towering boulders during the course of baking. Their charred, bran-covered surfaces were crackled all over like a mosaic, making them even more striking to look at. As soon as all the breads were out of the oven and cooling, these two bakers began again, throwing wood into the oven, mixing the dough with the leftover piece in the mixer, fermenting, shaping, and baking the *pane casareccio* (page 197), along with a whole wheat variation called *pane lariano* (page 205), into the morning.

I left them to their work, grabbed a few hours of sleep, and woke up on Monday wanting to see what the Genzano bakeries looked like during the daylight hours. Before I made it to the street, my waiter asked if I had found Sergio. "What are you wasting your time for?" he admonished. He gave me the address, and I promised I would go directly to Forno a Legna da Sergio. On my way there, I looked into the doorways of a handful of bakeries. Each one displayed large round loaves that looked identical to the ones Daniel had shown me the previous night. Each one prominently displayed the IGP mark in the window. None of the shops seemed to want for business. They were all crowded with customers who I assumed were regulars. In spite of my promise to the waiter, I had to stop and sample the bread at a couple of bakeries along the way. To my taste buds, each of the breads I tried was just as delicious as the slices from the hotel. If blindfolded, I don't think I could have told you the difference between any of these breads and the half-loaf I had taken back to my room after my night at Daniel's. *Pane di Genzano* was certainly different from other breads I had tasted in Italy, but the IGP-marked breads from any number of bakeries in town were remarkably similar to each other.

I kept this thought to myself as I strolled into Forno a Legna da Sergio. This bakery was a fancier version of Daniel's simple shop. The walls were tiled rather than plastered. There were skylights above the oven. The mixer was kept in a separate room off the main prep and baking area. But in all the important ways, the bakeries were identical. As in Daniel's bakery, Sergio's bread was made with the minimum amount of equipment, using the same techniques and ingredients and baked in a wood-fired brick oven.

Sergio Bocchini was a white-haired, refined, gentlemanly man of sixty who spoke with the authority of a mayor. He told me how he and another prominent baker in town had successfully lobbied for the IGP designation. It took many years, but the recognition for the town's bread was worth it. Now only bakers within the city limits could claim that they made real *pane di Genzano*, and as the bread's fame spread throughout the country, they had a monopoly on the product.

Because he was partly responsible for the IGP honor, I hoped he might be able to give me the official reasons that Genzano's bread was distinguished from bread made outside the town's confines. Sergio was surprisingly vague. Well, he said, when you see the IGP, you know that you are getting bread made in Genzano, that's all. I asked about the flour. Does it come from a special mill? No, he said nonchalantly. The bread is made from flour milled from local grain, but each baker chooses a miller he likes. He showed me the specifications provided by his miller for *farina di grano tenero tipo "O."* It was a strong, high-protein white flour he was using, which had similar qualities to the unbleached bread flour available in any American supermarket. I had already scratched water, air, and wood off my list of reasons that these bakers agreed made their bread unique. Now I removed flour.

There isn't a single ingredient or a specific technique that makes *pane di Genzano* worthy of its IGP distinction. This bread is unique because it has been made in a particular way in this particular place, with its water and air and flour and yeast, for so many years. The steps for fermenting the sourdough, for mixing and kneading the very wet bread dough, for shaping it, for baking it in a super-hot wood-burning oven without proofing it, have all been preserved as traditions and incorporated into the culture, so that the town's bakers make this bread as naturally as they breathe. Everyone in town will tell you that his or her favorite baker's bread is the best. But to an outsider, it's easier to admire the remarkably consistent quality of the breads from different shops. In the end, I left Genzano not with the "secret" to making this exceptional bread but with a renewed sense of the care and craftsmanship that goes into making any exceptional bread, and a respect for the local flavor that the same simple ingredients take on when handled by people in a particular place with particular bread-crafting traditions.

It was lunchtime when I left Forno a Legna da Sergio. The baker's wife handed me a piece of potato-topped pizza, fragrant with rosemary and dripping with olive oil. I wasn't at all surprised to hear that Sergio and all the other bakers in town made their pizza using exactly the same dough they use to make *pane di Genzano*, pressing it into a pan before baking rather than shaping it into rounds. I've included Sergio's pizza recipe here, along with his recipe for Genzano country bread and Daniel Lattanzi's recipe for whole wheat Genzano bread. These three recipes represent the entire repertoire of the town's bakers. I asked Sergio if any of his customers ever wanted baguettes or focaccia, and he looked at me as if I were crazy. Of course not. The limited selection not only satisfies the community but is the source of its tremendous civic pride.

✳ KITCHEN NOTES: MAKING ITALY'S MOST RUSTIC BREAD AT HOME

Pane di Genzano is such a product of its culture that it was at first difficult for me to imagine eating it, not to mention baking it, anywhere outside the Genzano city limits. But the bread is so wholesome and delicious, and the recipe is so simple and accessible, that I couldn't resist developing a version for American home bakers who would like to try it but can't get to Italy. You won't be disappointed. Everything about making this bread, from mixing the incredibly wet, almost soupy dough to shaping it into gargantuan loaves, is unique to the Genzano style. No other bread in Italy is made in quite this way, and no other bread has its unique flavor and texture characteristics. If you follow these recommendations, your bread will not qualify for the IGP mark, but it will have the essential qualities of great Genzano bread.

At Bread Alone, I make smaller rounds—just under three pounds, in contrast to Sergio's eight-pound monsters. Even so, these breads are large enough for my customers to keep around the house for several days, plenty of time to enjoy them with a rustic Italian dinner and then toasted for breakfast and sliced for sandwiches and bruschetta the next day.

You can approximate a *biga naturale* at home. Genzano is one of the rare places in Italy where bakers still work with a *biga* fermented with natural, or wild, yeast. *Biga naturale* contributes to irregular cell structure in the springy crumb and the deep caramelization in the crust. The bakers in Genzano use a piece of dough from the previous batch, a perpetual sourdough active with naturally occurring yeast and bacteria that raise and flavor the bread. For home bakers who are not constantly renewing their sourdough, I recommend building a *biga naturale* with an active sourdough that you already have on hand (or using a commercial sourdough starter).

Wet doughs make superior breads inside and out. When professional bakers evaluate a new recipe, one of the first things we look for is the hydration level of the dough. Hydration is the percentage of water (or sometimes another liquid) compared to the amount of flour used. Knowing the percentage of water in the dough allows us to predict how quickly the dough will ferment and how the

crumb and crust will develop during baking—in short, what kind of bread we'll end up with. As bakers' skills develop, we look for recipes for wet doughs, because more water in the dough means better bread. You may not have a piece of the *madre naturale* or a wood-burning brick oven at home, but to make your own version of *pane di Genzano* taste as authentic as possible, you can certainly make your dough just as wet as Daniel Lattanzi does.

Wet doughs make breads better inside and out. Hydration determines crumb structure. The more water you add to the dough, the softer and stickier it will be. A soft and sticky dough is more extensible, so the gluten strands you've developed during kneading will be able to expand more as the bread rises in the oven, creating a more open hole structure in the crumb. A dry, firm dough expands less, and the resulting bread will have a tighter, drier, more even crumb. A good amount of water will also encourage the large, irregularly spaced holes that artisan bakers value. Flour is mostly made up of starch (about 70 percent), which drinks up the water you mix into the dough. When the bread is baked, these hydrated starches gelatinize at 140 degrees, setting the gluten-lined, gas-filled pockets that form the holes in a slice of bread. In a wet and sticky dough, the starches hold more water, which turns to steam while baking and makes bigger holes. The bubbly, irregular crumb you see when you slice into a Genzano round is in large part due to the high percentage of water in the dough.

Hydration is also a key to the formation of a dark, chewy crust. The conversion of starches into sugars that are able to caramelize into a handsomely browned crust depends on water. A wet dough will result in rich caramelization of the crust. The crust of a dry dough will be pallid and tasteless in comparison.

Pull out the KitchenAid mixer and turn it to high. The bakeries in Genzano were probably the least professionally equipped of any of the bakeries I've seen in Europe. There were no proofing boxes and no dough-dividing machines. But every baker used an electric mixer, most often an Italian-made Pietroberto, to knead the extremely wet dough. With such a high proportion of water, this dough requires long and vigorous kneading to develop the gluten, make it manageable, and give the finished bread structure. A heavy-duty mixer like the KitchenAid is simply the easiest, best way to knead a highly hydrated dough adequately. If you've never made a bread in this style, your instincts and experience might tell you to turn off the mixer after seven to ten minutes. I know that I felt this way when I was in Daniel Lattanzi's bakery. But if you stop kneading too soon or knead at too low a speed, your dough will be a soupy mess rather than a silky mass, impossible to shape and unlikely to rise adequately in the oven.

It is possible to knead this dough by hand, but it takes courage, strength, and patience. Flour your hands, but resist adding extra flour to the dough. Use a bench scraper to scrape the sticky dough from the counter often. Expect to take frequent breaks, to give both your body and the dough a chance to rest. Know going into the project that it will probably take a good forty-five minutes.

Simulate a brick oven. The wood-burning ovens of Genzano radiate an intense heat that encourages the wet dough to rise impressively and char beautifully. Make sure to use a baking stone, which will collect heat and radiate it just the way bricks do. Preheat it in the oven for a full hour before baking. Your oven might be able to get to 450 degrees in fifteen minutes, but that's not enough time to heat the stone adequately. As your baking progresses, you might want to invest in a HearthKit.

Shape the dough quickly and get it right into the oven. I was trembling with anxiety as I watched Daniel Lattanzi's assistant prepare to load the dough rounds into the oven. They were so soft. How would they survive the transfer from the peel to the floor of the oven? Forming the dough into a round requires a quick touch. The longer you handle it, the more it will stretch and spread out of shape. Your best bet for maintaining the round shape is to slide your dough into the oven as quickly as you can and without any hesitation. If on the first few tries your rounds become somewhat misshapen, don't worry. They may not look as perfect as Daniel's or Sergio's rounds, but they will still have the incredible crumb and crust.

GENZANO COUNTRY BREAD
Pane casareccio di Genzano

. . . .

ALLOW 8 TO 12 HOURS TO PREPARE THE *BIGA NATURALE*;

18 TO 20 MINUTES TO KNEAD;

2 1/2 TO 3 HOURS TO FERMENT;

1 1/2 TO 2 HOURS TO PROOF;

50 MINUTES TO 1 HOUR TO BAKE

. . . .

Almost primeval-looking, Genzano Country Bread is a colossal, bran-coated round, its thick crust baked almost black. The rugged crust is balanced by a moist, full-flavored crumb. Baked with *biga naturale* (Italian sourdough), it is renowned for staying fresh for 7 days, a claim no other bread I know can make.

You'll need an active sourdough culture (or a commercial sourdough starter) for the *biga*. Use whichever starter you have on hand, or make the one that appeals to you most from scratch. I recommend mixing and kneading this dough with a heavy-duty stand mixer, because the recipe requires vigorous kneading for quite a long time. The dough is very soft and sticky even after such extensive kneading. The key to working with sticky dough is to handle it as little as possible, and that's exactly what Genzano bakers do. It takes several steps but little active work time to reproduce this truly exceptional bread.

Most home ovens can't accommodate a bread the size of an authentic *pane casareccio di Genzano*. This recipe makes a scaled-down but still substantial round loaf called a *pagnotta*. It fits easily on a baking stone in a home oven. Heat your stone for a full hour before baking, and bake the bread until it looks almost charred for the most authentic loaf.

※ **MAKES 1 SPECTACULAR ROUND**
(45.5 OUNCES/1,291 GRAMS)

Equipment

HEAVY-DUTY STAND MIXER WITH DOUGH HOOK

BANNETON OR COLANDER LINED WITH A KITCHEN TOWEL

BAKING STONE

CAST-IRON SKILLET

BAKER'S PEEL OR RIMLESS BAKING SHEET

PARCHMENT PAPER

Note: If you don't have a *levain* or German rye sourdough already prepared, you will have to make one from scratch (page 76, 111, or 275) or substitute a commercial sourdough starter (see pages 333–34 for sources).

BIGA NATURALE				
INGREDIENTS	VOLUME	U.S. WEIGHT	METRIC WEIGHT	BAKER'S PERCENTAGE
Liquid *levain* (page 76), stiff dough *levain* (page 111), or German rye sour-dough (page 275)	About 2 tablespoons	1 ounce	28 grams	14
Water, tepid (70 to 78 degrees)	²/₃ cup	4.9 ounces	140 grams	70
Unbleached bread flour, preferably high-gluten	1²/₃ cups	7.1 ounces	200 grams	100

PREPARE THE SOURDOUGH. If you have not refreshed your sourdough within the past 3 days, follow the recipe for refreshing it (pages 79–80 for liquid *levain*, pages 114–15 for stiff dough *levain*, pages 277–78 for German rye sourdough) so it will be in its prime.

CREATE THE *BIGA NATURALE*. Place the sourdough in the bowl of a stand mixer. Pour the water over it and stir with a rubber spatula to soften it slightly. Stir in the flour until a dough forms. Turn the dough out onto an unfloured countertop and knead just to blend all the ingredients, 1 to 2 minutes. It will not be perfectly smooth. Place the dough back in the bowl and cover with plastic wrap. Let stand at room temperature (70 to 75 degrees) for 8 to 12 hours. When ready, it will have doubled in size and become filled with bubbles, and it will have a fresh, tangy scent.

BREAD DOUGH

INGREDIENTS	VOLUME	U.S. WEIGHT	METRIC WEIGHT	BAKER'S PERCENTAGE
Biga naturale	About 1½ cups	13 ounces	368 grams	74
Water, tepid (70 to 78 degrees)	1¾ cups	14.1 ounces	400 grams	80
Unbleached bread flour, preferably high-gluten	3¼ cups	17.6 ounces	500 grams	100
Instant yeast	¾ teaspoon	0.2 ounce	4 grams	1
Sea salt	2 teaspoons	0.5 ounce	15 grams	3
Unprocessed bran for sprinkling	¼ cup	0.5 ounce	15 grams	—

MIX THE DOUGH. Uncover the *biga naturale* and pour the water over it. Stir with a rubber spatula to soften the *biga* and break it up. Blend in the flour, yeast, and salt just until a very wet dough forms.

KNEAD THE DOUGH. By machine: Use the dough hook and mix the dough on medium-high speed (5 or 6 on a KitchenAid mixer) for 10 minutes. At this speed the mixer will "walk," possibly off the counter, so do not leave it unattended. The dough will not clear the sides of the bowl and will climb up the dough hook. Periodically stop the machine and scrape down the hook and the sides of the bowl with a rubber spatula. Increase the speed to high (10 on a KitchenAid mixer) and knead for 8 to 10 minutes more. The dough will begin to pull away from the sides of the bowl, first in stringy strands, then in longer, thicker strands. Give the dough a window-pane test to judge its readiness: Pinch off a golfball-sized piece and flatten it into a mini-pancake. Gently stretch it until the dough is thin enough to see through. If it tears, press the small piece back into the larger mass, knead it for 1 to 2 minutes more, and test again.

FERMENT THE DOUGH. Transfer the dough to a lightly oiled, clear 2-quart container with a lid. With masking tape, mark the spot on the container that the dough will reach when it has doubled in volume. Cover and leave it to rise at room temperature (70 to 75 degrees) for 1 1/2 hours. Uncover the dough and gently deflate it by pushing it down in the center and pulling it up on the sides. Cover it again and continue to let it ferment until it doubles, reaching the masking-tape mark, 1 to 1 1/2 hours more. Tiny bubbles will break on the surface of the dough.

SHAPE THE ROUND. Generously coat a banneton or a colander lined with a kitchen towel with bran. Lightly dust the counter with bread flour. Uncover the dough and turn it out onto the counter. Gently shape the dough to approximate a round (see Shaping Rounds, page 36). It's best to handle dough this soft and sticky as little as possible. Place it into the banneton or bowl smooth side down. Coat the loaf with more bran and cover it with plastic wrap.

PROOF THE ROUND. Leave the round to rise at room temperature (70 to 75 degrees) until it is pillowy and nearly doubled in size, 1 1/2 to 2 hours. When you press your finger into the dough, your fingerprint will spring back slowly.

PREPARE THE OVEN. About 1 hour before baking, place a baking stone on the middle rack of the oven and a cast-iron skillet on the lower rack. Heat the oven to 450 degrees.

BAKE THE ROUND. Cover a baker's peel or a rimless baking sheet with parchment paper. Sprinkle the parchment with bran. Uncover the loaf and gently tip it out of the banneton or bowl, using one hand to guide it, onto the peel or baking sheet. Slide the loaf, still on the parchment, onto the baking stone. Place 1/4 cup of ice cubes in the skillet to produce light steam. Bake for 30 minutes, turn the temperature in the oven down to 400 degrees, and continue baking until the loaf is very dark, almost charred-looking, 20 to 30 minutes more. Do not worry about burning the loaf. It needs this much time in the oven for the interior to bake fully.

COOL AND STORE THE ROUND. Slide the peel or the rimless baking sheet under the parchment paper to remove the round from the oven. Slide the loaf, still on the parchment, onto a wire rack. Cool the round completely, about 2 hours, before slicing. This loaf will stay fresh for about 7 days stored at room temperature in a paper bag.

GENZANO POTATO PIZZA
Pizza alle patate di Genzano

. . . .

ALLOW 8 TO 12 HOURS TO PREPARE THE *BIGA NATURALE*;

18 TO 20 MINUTES TO KNEAD;

2 1/2 TO 3 HOURS TO FERMENT;

20 TO 30 MINUTES TO BAKE

. . . .

I first tasted this incredible pizza at Sergio Bocchini's bakery on via Italo Belardi in Genzano, Italy. The recipe for the dough is identical to the recipe for Genzano Country Bread (page 197). Why use a different recipe for pizza dough when you are already mixing a bread dough that can work just as well? Instead of shaping it into a round, Sergio simply presses it into a pan and tops it with potatoes, onions, rosemary, and salt. Like his original, this version is prepared with a *biga naturale*. The dough is not just a base for the toppings. It is the flavor foundation for the pizza and makes a perfect marriage with potatoes. Use a boldly flavored variety, such as Yellow Finn or Yukon Gold. Slice the potatoes very thin, as if you were making homemade potato chips, using a mandoline if possible.

MAKES 1 SHEET PAN PIZZA
(45.5 OUNCES/1,291 GRAMS)

Equipment
HEAVY-DUTY STAND MIXER WITH DOUGH HOOK

BAKING STONE

RIMMED BAKING SHEET

PASTRY BRUSH

Note: If you don't have a *levain* or German rye sourdough already prepared, you will have to make one from scratch (page 76, 111, or 275) or substitute a commercial sourdough starter (see pages 333–34 for sources).

BIGA NATURALE				
INGREDIENTS	VOLUME	U.S. WEIGHT	METRIC WEIGHT	BAKER'S PERCENTAGE
Liquid *levain* (page 76), stiff dough *levain* (page 111), or German rye sourdough (page 275)	About 2 tablespoons	1 ounce	28 grams	14
Water, tepid (70 to 78 degrees)	²/₃ cup	4.9 ounces	140 grams	70
Unbleached bread flour, preferably high-gluten	1²/₃ cups	7.1 ounces	200 grams	100

PREPARE THE SOURDOUGH. If you have not refreshed your sourdough within the past 3 days, follow the recipe for refreshing it (pages 79–80 for liquid *levain*, pages 114–15 for stiff dough *levain*, pages 277–78 for German rye sourdough) so it will be in its prime.

CREATE THE *BIGA NATURALE*. Place the sourdough into the bowl of a stand mixer. Pour the water over it and stir with a rubber spatula to soften it slightly. Stir in the flour until a dough forms. Turn the dough out onto an unfloured countertop and knead just to blend all the ingredients, 1 to 2 minutes. It will not be perfectly smooth. Place the dough back in the bowl and cover with plastic wrap. Let stand at room temperature (70 to 75 degrees) for 8 to 12 hours. When ready, it will have doubled in size and become filled with bubbles, and it will have a fresh, tangy scent.

PIZZA DOUGH

INGREDIENTS	VOLUME	U.S. WEIGHT	METRIC WEIGHT	BAKER'S PERCENTAGE
Biga naturale	About 1½ cups	13 ounces	368 grams	74
Water, tepid (70 to 78 degrees)	1¾ cups	14.1 ounces	400 grams	80
Unbleached bread flour, preferably high-gluten	3¼ cups	17.6 ounces	500 grams	100
Instant yeast	¾ teaspoon	0.2 ounce	4 grams	1
Sea salt	2 teaspoons	0.5 ounce	15 grams	3

TOPPINGS

INGREDIENTS	VOLUME	U.S. WEIGHT	METRIC WEIGHT	BAKER'S PERCENTAGE
Extra-virgin olive oil	2 tablespoons	1 ounce	28 grams	—
4 potatoes, peeled and sliced very thin	—	About 2 pounds	About 900 grams	—
1 medium onion, sliced 1/4-inch thick	About ½ cup	4.4 ounces	125 grams	—
Fresh rosemary, stemmed and roughly chopped	¼ cup	0.4 ounce	12 grams	—
Sea salt	½ teaspoon	0.1 ounce	4 grams	—

MIX THE DOUGH. Uncover the *biga naturale* and pour the water over it. Stir with a rubber spatula to soften the *biga* and break it up. Blend in the flour, yeast, and salt just until a very wet dough forms.

KNEAD THE DOUGH. By machine: Use the dough hook and mix the dough on medium-high speed (8 on a KitchenAid mixer) for 10 minutes. At this speed the mixer will "walk," possibly off the counter, so do not leave it unattended. The dough will not clear the sides of the bowl and will climb up the dough hook. Periodically stop the machine and scrape down the hook and the sides of the bowl with a rubber spatula. Increase the speed to high (10 on a KitchenAid mixer) for 8 to 10 minutes more. The dough will begin to pull away from the sides of the bowl, first in stringy strands, then in longer, thicker strands. Give the dough a windowpane test to judge its readiness: Pinch off a golfball-sized piece and flatten it into a mini-pancake. Gently stretch it until the dough is thin enough to see through. If it tears, press the small piece back into the larger mass, knead it for 1 to 2 minutes more, and test again.

FERMENT THE DOUGH. Transfer the dough to a lightly oiled, clear 2-quart container with a lid. With masking tape, mark the spot on the container that the dough will reach when it has doubled in volume. Cover and leave it to rise at room temperature (70 to 75 degrees) for 1 1/2 hours. Uncover the dough and gently deflate it by pushing it down in the center and pulling it up on the sides. Cover it again and continue to let it ferment until it doubles, reaching the masking-tape mark, 1 to 1 1/2 hours more. Tiny bubbles will break on the surface of the dough.

PREPARE THE OVEN. About 30 minutes before baking, place a baking stone on the middle rack of the oven. Heat the oven to 500 degrees.

SHAPE THE PIZZA AND ADD THE TOPPINGS. Oil the baking sheet with olive oil. Uncover the dough and scrape it into the pan. With oiled hands, press and gently stretch the dough without tearing it to fill the baking sheet. It will be about 1/2-inch thick. If it recoils from the edges of the sheet, let it rest for 10 minutes, uncovered, and try again. Spread a light coat of olive oil over the dough with the pastry brush. Layer the potato slices, overlapping them slightly, over the dough. Sprinkle the onions, rosemary, and salt evenly all over the pizza.

BAKE THE PIZZA. Place the baking sheet on the oven rack. Bake the pizza until the potatoes and onions are tinged brown and the crust is golden, 20 to 30 minutes.

COOL AND STORE THE PIZZA. Remove the baking sheet from the oven to a wire rack. Cool the pizza briefly before cutting it into generous rectangles. It is delicious hot or cold. Store leftover pizza in a resealable plastic bag at room temperature for 1 to 2 days.

WHOLE WHEAT GENZANO COUNTRY BREAD
Pane lariano

. . . .

ALLOW 8 TO 12 HOURS TO PREPARE THE *BIGA NATURALE*;

18 TO 20 MINUTES TO KNEAD;

2 1/2 TO 3 HOURS TO FERMENT;

1 TO 1 1/2 HOURS TO PROOF;

35 TO 40 MINUTES TO BAKE

. . . .

Whole wheat bread is unusual in Italy, so I was thrilled when Daniel Lattanzi introduced me to this version of Genzano Country Bread, made with a lighter style of wheat flour with less germ and bran than the whole wheat flour Americans use. I've adapted the recipe, using equal parts white bread flour and whole wheat flour to get the same result.

The Genzano bakers don't shape this slack dough into precise loaves but gently form it into squat rectangles called *filones*, handling them as little as possible to keep the breads airy. The crust bakes to a brown-black while the interior becomes light and filled with bubbles. Like white Genzano bread, this whole wheat version will stay fresh for a long time—up to 5 days.

✳ MAKES 2 SQUAT RECTANGULAR LOAVES
(22.9 OUNCES/651 GRAMS EACH)

Equipment
HEAVY-DUTY STAND MIXER WITH DOUGH HOOK

BAKER'S PEEL OR RIMLESS BAKING SHEET

PARCHMENT PAPER

BENCH SCRAPER OR CHEF'S KNIFE

BAKING STONE

CAST-IRON SKILLET

Note: If you don't have a *levain* or German rye sourdough already prepared, you will have to make one from scratch (page 76, 111, or 275) or substitute a commercial sourdough starter (see pages 333–34 for sources).

BIGA NATURALE

INGREDIENTS	VOLUME	U.S. WEIGHT	METRIC WEIGHT	BAKER'S PERCENTAGE
Liquid *levain* (page 76), stiff dough *levain* (page 111), or German rye sourdough (page 275)	About 2 tablespoons	1 ounce	28 grams	14
Water, tepid (70 to 78 degrees)	²/₃ cup	4.9 ounces	140 grams	70
Unbleached bread flour, preferably high-gluten	1²/₃ cups	7.1 ounces	200 grams	100

PREPARE THE SOURDOUGH. If you have not refreshed your sourdough within the past 3 days, follow the recipe for refreshing it (pages 79–80 for liquid *levain*, pages 114–15 for stiff dough *levain*, pages 277–78 for German rye sourdough) so that it will be in its prime.

CREATE THE *BIGA NATURALE*. Place the sourdough in the bowl of a stand mixer. Pour the water over it and stir with a rubber spatula to soften it

slightly. Stir in the flour until a dough forms. Turn the dough out onto an unfloured countertop and knead just to blend all the ingredients, 1 to 2 minutes. It will not be perfectly smooth. Place the dough back in the bowl and cover with plastic wrap. Let stand at room temperature (70 to 75 degrees) for 8 to 12 hours. When ready, it will have doubled in size and become filled with bubbles, and it will have a fresh, tangy scent.

BREAD DOUGH

INGREDIENTS	VOLUME	U.S. WEIGHT	METRIC WEIGHT	BAKER'S PERCENTAGE
Biga naturale	About 1½ cups	13 ounces	368 grams	74
Water, tepid (70 to 78 degrees)	1¾ cups	15 ounces	410 grams	82
Unbleached bread flour, preferably high-gluten	2 cups	8.8 ounces	250 grams	50
Stone-ground whole wheat flour	2 cups	8.8 ounces	250 grams	50
Instant yeast	1½ teaspoons	0.3 ounce	8 grams	2
Sea salt	2 teaspoons	0.5 ounce	15 grams	3
Unprocessed bran for sprinkling	3 tablespoons	1.8 ounces	50 grams	—

MIX THE DOUGH. Uncover the *biga naturale* and pour the water over it. Stir with a rubber spatula to soften the *biga* and break it up. Blend in the bread flour, whole wheat flour, yeast, and salt just until a very wet dough forms.

KNEAD THE DOUGH. By machine: Use the dough hook and mix the dough on medium-high speed (8 on a KitchenAid mixer) for 10 minutes. At this speed the mixer will "walk," possibly off the counter, so do not leave it unattended. The dough will not clear the sides of the bowl and will climb up the dough hook. Periodically stop the machine and scrape down the hook and the sides of the bowl with a rubber spatula. Increase the speed to high (10 on a KitchenAid mixer) for 8 to 10 minutes more. The dough will begin to pull away from the sides of the bowl, first in stringy strands, then in longer, thicker strands. Give the dough a windowpane test to judge its readiness: Pinch off a golfball-sized piece and flatten it into a mini-pancake. Gently stretch it until the bran-flecked dough is thin enough for light to shine through. If it tears, press the small piece back into the larger mass, knead it for 1 to 2 minutes more, and test again.

FERMENT THE DOUGH. Transfer the dough to a lightly oiled, clear 2-quart container with a lid. With masking tape, mark the spot on the container that the dough will reach when it has doubled in volume. Cover and leave it to rise at room temperature (70 to 75 degrees) for 1 1/2 hours. Uncover the dough and gently deflate it by pushing it down in the center and pulling it up on the sides. Cover it again and continue to let it ferment until it doubles, reaching the masking-tape mark, 1 to 1 1/2 hours more. Tiny bubbles will break on the surface of the dough.

SHAPE THE LOAVES. Cover a baker's peel or rimless baking sheet with parchment paper. Generously coat it with bran. Lightly dust the counter with flour. Uncover the dough and turn it out onto the counter. With a bench scraper or chef's knife dipped in flour, cut the dough into two equal pieces (22.9 ounces/651 grams each). With floured hands, shape 1 piece into a rough rectangle by flattening it slightly, but not deflating it. Fold the two long sides towards the center and flip the dough over onto one half of the parchment paper. Square off the sides and ends with your hands, but do not overhandle the dough. It will be a rough rectangle. Repeat with the remaining piece of dough, placing it at least 3 inches away from the first piece. Lightly coat each piece with bran and drape with plastic wrap.

PROOF THE LOAVES. Leave the loaves to rise at room temperature (70 to 75 degrees) until they are pillowy and have nearly doubled in size, 1 to 1 1/2 hours. When you press your finger into the dough, your fingerprint will spring back slowly.

PREPARE THE OVEN. About 1 hour before baking, place a baking stone on the middle rack of the oven and a cast-iron skillet on the lower rack. Heat the oven to 450 degrees.

BAKE THE LOAVES. Slide the loaves, still on the parchment, onto the baking stone. Place 1/4 cup of ice cubes in the skillet to produce light steam. Bake for 20 minutes, turn the temperature in the oven down to 400 degrees, and continue baking until the loaves are very dark, almost charred-looking, 15 to 20 minutes more.

COOL AND STORE THE LOAVES. Slide the peel or the rimless baking sheet under the parchment paper to remove the loaves from the oven. Slide the loaves, still on the parchment, onto a wire rack. Cool the loaves completely, about 2 hours, before slicing. They will stay fresh for about 7 days stored at room temperature in a paper bag.

FREQUENTLY ASKED QUESTIONS ABOUT *PANE DI GENZANO*

. . . .

I've never mixed dough for such a long time in my mixer. Is there any danger that it will overheat or the motor will burn out?
All of the recipes in this book, including those from Genzano, were tested with one KitchenAid Classic mixer (this is the smallest of KitchenAid's stand mixers; the Ultra Power is the next size up), and the machine is still going strong. If there is a danger in mixing bread for so long at such a high speed, it is that the machine will "walk," sometimes off the counter if you turn your back on it. So it's important to keep an eye on the machine to prevent this.

I have a baking stone, but is it worth investing in a HearthKit to bake breads like *pane di Genzano* at home? Will the results more closely resemble breads from a wood-fired brick oven?
A baking stone is an absolute necessity for all the breads from Genzano and for most of the breads in this book. The radiant heat coming from the stone gives the dough an immediate boost on contact. This terrific oven spring will not occur if you bake your bread on a metal baking sheet. The HearthKit is even better than a baking stone for simulating a Genzano hearth oven. This is a three-sided earthenware oven insert that is designed to form a chamber like a wood-burning brick oven, radiating heat into the bread from three sides instead of just one, which enables it to rise even higher and develop an even thicker crust than bread baked on a baking stone. For the most authentic rustic character, I highly recommend baking your *pane di Genzano* in a HearthKit. It is expensive—about $200—but the results are equal to the results I get from my wood-fired hearth ovens at Bread Alone.

What accounts for *pane di Genzano*'s long shelf life?

There are a couple of reasons that this bread stays fresh for so long. As in other sourdough breads, the natural starter locks moisture into the dough as it bakes. This dough has a very high water content, and all that moisture is sealed inside as the thick crust develops in the very hot oven. Genzano bread also has size on its side. It takes longer for a large bread to go stale than for a small bread, and *pane di Genzano* is massive, about 6 pounds, very large even when compared with Poilâne's 2-kilo (4.4 pound) loaves.

CHAPTER 10

IL FORNAIO AND ITALIAN INDEPENDENT BAKERS: BAKING LOCAL, FROM ROME TO THE DOLOMITES

The first time I visited a branch of Il Fornaio, the powerhouse Italian bakery chain, I was in Florence with Faith Willinger, the Italian food authority, sampling saltless Tuscan bread. The sparkling little shop in the center of the historic district, with its rustic wooden shelving and tiled floors, produced quintessential loaves with thick blond crusts. Just like other bakeries in town, it sold the bread in chunks, by weight. Judging from this bread and the other local specialties on display—*biscotti di Prato*, mini focaccia rolls, grissini (Tuscan breadsticks)—you would think Il Fornaio was an independently owned Florentine bakery, not one of hundreds of shops run by a large corporation. And you would be partly right. Although the Il Fornaio sign pops up everywhere in Italy, Spain, Greece, and eastern Europe, each branch is independently run, in cooperation with the Il Fornaio organization in Milan, by a baker who is free to make local breads as he or she sees fit.

As an independent baker who has resisted my share of corporate overtures in order to maintain the quality and character of my breads, I was intrigued by the way this business was run. On a trip to Milan a few years later, I met with its owners, the father-and-son team of Carlo and Matteo Veggetti. Through the Veggettis, I saw from a corporate perspective just how strong the tradition of regional Italian breads is. I also collected some superb regional bread recipes from Il Fornaio bakers in Lake Como. Because of the way Il Fornaio is operated, these breads are absolutely authentic, even though they are baked under the umbrella of a large parent company.

The history of Il Fornaio reflects the local character of Italy's artisan breads. Carlo Veggetti got into the bakery business by accident almost thirty years ago. Originally a manufacturer of shelving and other wooden furniture, he wound up as part owner of a bakery near Milan because one of his customers, a struggling baker, owed him money and couldn't pay him any other way. Instead of foreclosing, he kept the shop open, with the original baker still running things. He took control of the bakery's finances and helped it become profitable. Carlo had always been a bread lover, and when he looked around at how many small bakers were being pushed out of business by industrial bakeries, he saw an opportunity to combat the threat to small bakers and make some money at the same time by offering the Il Fornaio name, along with business advice and design services, to artisan bakers across Italy. He set up a baking school for his franchise-holders to learn the company's core recipes, but he encouraged them to produce local specialties as well. It was a key part of his business plan to foster Italian bread traditions, in opposition to the homogeneity of the breads coming from industrial bakeries. For a small licensing fee, bakers could open up a beautifully designed Il Fornaio shop, go to the Il Fornaio baking school to learn basic recipes and business skills, and be free to produce the breads that they had grown up with in their hometowns. Industry observers credit Carlo Veggetti with making small bakeries commercially viable again, spurring a renaissance of artisan baking since its low point in the 1970s.

Carlo's son Matteo now runs the company with him. Like his father, Matteo is a businessman, not a baker. But he has an impressive knowledge of Italian regional breads, because he oversees Il Fornaio shops from the Austrian border to the tip of Italy's boot. I met up with him in Milan and he offered to drive me to the Il Fornaio in Lake Como, just a few hours outside the city. It is one of the company's most picturesque shops, a real showcase of the Il Fornaio style. On the drive, he told me how the company grew very organically, without a strong corporate plan. It is a business built on inspiration and love, not spreadsheets and numbers. We pulled up to a beautiful little bakery overlooking the lake. At this shop, the head baker proudly showed me how he makes the region's specialty, *pane di Como* (page 222), from an extremely wet dough that is shaped into a round and then baked smooth side down so that each loaf unfurls in the oven into a rustic crown shape. The bread was beautiful, and completely unique to the area. I was shocked that it came out of a franchise bakery. To an American, it was like encountering delicious grits and shrimp at a McDonald's in Charleston.

Just as the Il Fornaio bakers are loosely associated with each other but free to bake the breads of their choice, Italian bakers in general are united by a strong network of baking associations and share some important baking techniques but produce very different breads depending on where they bake. White flour, typically 00, dominates their bread baking. *Biga*, the mild, stiff pre-ferment leavened with packaged yeast, gives the bread dough body and character without needing the time investment and care-taking of sourdough. The loaves are rustic in form because they are sold by weight, and their light crusts come from relatively short fermentation times and little or no steam in the oven. But because bread traditions are different from region to region and sometimes from town to town, it is impossible to generalize further about Italian bread. I've been to Italy dozens of times over the past fifteen years on reconnaissance trips, and every time I go I realize how much more bread there is to see and taste. To really know Italy's regional breads, you'd have to spend a lifetime sampling the hundreds of local specialties tied to the traditions of particular places. I very humbly offer the recipes in this chapter as a tiny sampling of breads made in Piedmont, Lombardy, the Veneto, and Alto Adige.

I've spent a lot of time in Italian bakeries, but I am far from an authority on the subject of Italian bread. I'm just an inquisitive traveler. The recipes here are my souvenirs. When I want to remember Rome, I make the absolutely all-time best Roman-style white pizza (page 214) I've ever tried, from the Antico Forno in the Campo de' Fiori. The rosetta rolls (page 226) help me recall the countless sandwiches I've eaten on the run but enjoyed immensely, exploring the streets of Rome, Turin, and Mantua. In the northern part of the country, I found breads with more variety of ingredients, shapes, and textures. When I make rye-fennel cracker bread (page 243), from the Alto Adige region in the far north, I break it up into pieces and eat it with speck, the local cured ham, just as I did with the bakers there.

Some of these recipes have become my favorites because they show how varied Italian bread is. As I traveled, I noticed how geography influenced the types of breads eaten in a particular place. The breads of the far north are a dramatic contrast to the all-white breads found in the rest of the country. The herbs and spices that flavor the herb twist I ate in Bolzano are commonly used in Austrian breads but not Italian ones. No surprise, since Bolzano is close to the Austrian border and has strong cultural links with that country. In the high-altitude climate of the Dolomites and Alto Adige, rye is easier to grow than wheat. In these areas, rye flour is blended with white flour, adding tremendous depth to prosciutto bread from Parma and corn-rye rounds from the Dolomites.

I've included some recipes that fascinated me because they flout common baking wisdom—with fabulous results. Ciabatta (page 218), like Roman-style pizza, is made with an improbably wet dough. The herb twist uses fresh rosemary, basil, and thyme instead of *biga* for flavor. Italian bakers have a way of shocking and surprising me. The recipes that follow represent some of the happiest surprises on the road from Rome to the Italian Alps.

❋ KITCHEN NOTES: MAKING REGIONAL ITALIAN BREADS IN AN AMERICAN KITCHEN

Because the breads in this chapter are so different from each other, tips for making them are included in the headnotes to the individual recipes. But I will offer this general advice:

Be adventurous and you will be rewarded with some of the most interesting and unusual breads in this book. I had to overcome my skepticism more than once when confronted with a strange technique or an improbable-sounding ingredient in a new Italian bread. Trust me, the way I learned to trust the Italian bakers I met, when you

see something that looks new, strange, or just plain wrong. It's not an error—it's the way things are done at a local bakery somewhere in Italy. Some examples follow.

Knead your pizza dough for twenty minutes. It sounds like a long time, and it is. But to achieve incredible crust development, you do have to mix this dough that long, and at a high speed. While the dough mixes, you need to keep an eye on your mixer. Don't leave the kitchen while it's on, because at this speed the mixer will "walk," possibly off the counter.

Yes, that's the correct amount of water. Pizza dough and ciabatta dough are both unbelievably wet. An abundance of water gives these breads their light, bubbly character. It also makes the doughs a little bit difficult to handle. Use an electric mixer and don't worry so much about perfect shaping. High hydration is more important than shaping in replicating the texture and flavor of these Italian classics.

Turn things upside down. In general, dough rounds are baked smooth side up. But Como bread gets its signature look from being baked smooth side down. If you ever wondered what would happen if you baked your bread upside down, you've got to try this recipe.

Just bake your *biga*. Rosetta rolls are made by mixing a large proportion of *biga* with just a little bit of flour. This unusual formula results in a very active dough, with the energy to spring up dramatically when it hits the oven. Because the dough has so much yeast, and because the special rosetta press forces the air pockets into one area, the rolls often come out of the oven with hollow centers, which makes them perfect for sandwiches.

Try an Italian rye. When most people think of rye bread, they imagine an Eastern European–style bread with caraway seeds. Rye is also grown in the

Auvergne region of France, as we have seen, and northern Italy, where the climate is as cool as it is in Austria and Poland. But rye breads from the north are distinctly Italian. Bake a Prosciutto Bread (page 233) or a Corn-Rye Round (page 240) to get a taste of northern Italian baking and also to understand the versatility of this grain.

ROMAN-STYLE WHITE PIZZA
Pizza bianca alla romana

....

ALLOW 17 TO 20 MINUTES TO KNEAD;
3 1/2 TO 4 HOURS TO FERMENT;
15 TO 20 MINUTES TO BAKE

....

I'll never forget the first time I went to the famous Roman market square called Campo de' Fiori. I watched, awestruck, as a baker pulled the longest pizza I had ever seen from a deep hearth oven. Paper-thin and dripping with olive oil, it was nearly 8 feet long. He draped it over his arms, holding it high to keep it off the ground, and set it on a wooden shelf to cool. Another baker ran over to drizzle it with more olive oil and sprinkle it with salt. A cluster of schoolchildren, office workers, and tourists stood by eagerly. Each was rewarded with a piping-hot piece of pizza folded in half and wrapped in waxed paper. As thin as pita bread and spotted with charred bubbles, this was Rome's famous *pizza bianca*.

Bernardino Bartocci and his cousin Fabio are the owners of Antico Forno, the legendary bakery opened by their fathers in the Campo de' Fiori decades ago. All day long they and their bakers make a variety of breads, but the patient crowds outside the shop are waiting to buy fresh slices of the unbelievably long and thin pizza, dripping with olive oil, which are sold by weight. When I introduced myself as a fan, Fabio offered to take me behind the scenes and show me how the pizza dough was made.

The recipe is unconventional, to say the least. The first time I saw this dough in the mixing bowl, I couldn't believe how soupy it was. It looked like vanilla cake batter. Fabio explained that the high proportion of water made the pizza incredibly bubbly. He was relaxed and assured, but I grew increasingly nervous as I stood next to the mixer, turned to the highest speed, for 10, 15, 20 minutes. *"Va bene?"* I would ask every few minutes. He just nodded approvingly and waited some more. The dough began to smooth out and became shiny from the gelatinized starch. Finally it collected around the dough hook and slapped against the sides of the bowl. *"Fini,"* Fabio said after 20 minutes. He pulled off a piece of the dough and stretched it so thin that you could see the light shining through it. It was perfectly smooth and elastic. Such a long, fast mixing is required to develop the gluten and give the wet dough some body. Fabio explained that he ferments his wet dough about three times longer than is typical for doughs made with packaged yeast. During this long fermentation, its only rise, the dough expands tremendously into a balloon-like dome and develops great flavor.

Using the techniques that Fabio demonstrated, you can make this pizza at home. An electric mixer is essential for adequately kneading the wet dough. Be sure to keep the mixer going for the specified time. Ferment it a nice long time to develop its flavor and get those big, beautiful bubbles. You won't be able to bake an 8-foot-long pizza in your home oven, but your Roman-style pizza will be astoundingly good. I've adapted Fabio's recipe to make two pizzas that fit one at a time onto a standard baking stone. Making two pizzas gives you two opportunities to practice dimpling the dough and stretching it out onto the baking stone, just the way they do in Rome.

MAKES 2 THIN RECTANGULAR PIZZAS (16.6 OUNCES/470 GRAMS EACH)

Equipment

HEAVY-DUTY STAND MIXER WITH DOUGH HOOK

BAKING STONE

PASTRY BRUSH

BENCH SCRAPER OR CHEF'S KNIFE

BAKER'S PEEL OR RIMLESS BAKING SHEET

PARCHMENT PAPER

PIZZA DOUGH				
INGREDIENTS	VOLUME	U.S. WEIGHT	METRIC WEIGHT	BAKER'S PERCENTAGE
Water, tepid (70 to 78 degrees)	1¾ cups	15 ounces	425 grams	85
Instant yeast	1 teaspoon	0.2 ounce	5 grams	1
Unbleached bread flour, preferably high-gluten	3¼ cups	17.6 ounces	500 grams	100
Sea salt	1½ teaspoons	0.4 ounce	10 grams	2

TOPPINGS				
INGREDIENTS	VOLUME	U.S. WEIGHT	METRIC WEIGHT	BAKER'S PERCENTAGE
Extra-virgin olive oil	⅓ cup	2.1 ounces	60 grams	—
Sea salt	1½ teaspoons	0.4 ounce	10 grams	—

MIX THE DOUGH. Pour the water into a large mixing bowl or the bowl of a stand mixer. Add the yeast, flour, and salt and stir just long enough to blend into a dough.

KNEAD THE DOUGH. By machine: With the dough hook, mix the dough on medium-high speed (8 on a KitchenAid mixer) for 15 to 17 minutes. At this speed the mixer will "walk," possibly off the counter, so do not leave it unattended. The dough will not clear the sides of the bowl and will climb up the dough hook. Periodically stop the machine and scrape down the hook and the sides of the bowl with a rubber spatula. Turn the machine to high speed (10 on a KitchenAid mixer) and knead until the dough becomes more coherent, clears the sides of the bowl, and collects around the hook, 2 to 3 minutes more. It will be glistening, creamy, and extremely elastic. Check that the dough is well developed by pulling off a golfball-sized piece. Stretch it into an opaque windowpane that does not tear. If it does tear, knead for an additional 1 to 2 minutes and test again.

FERMENT THE DOUGH. Transfer the dough to a lightly oiled, clear 3-quart container with a lid. With masking tape, mark the container at the level the dough will reach when it has tripled in volume. Cover and leave it to rise at room temperature (70 to 75 degrees) until it expands voluminously, reaching the masking-tape mark, 3 1/2 to 4 hours. It will feel somewhat less sticky.

PREPARE THE OVEN. About 1 hour before baking, place a baking stone on the middle rack. Heat the oven to 500 degrees.

DIVIDE AND SHAPE THE PIZZA AND ADD THE TOPPINGS. Coat a wide swath of the counter with flour. Uncover the dough and scrape it out onto the counter. It will collapse into a puddle. Lightly but thoroughly dust the top of the dough with flour. With a bench scraper or chef's knife, cut the dough into 2 equal pieces (16.6 ounces/470 grams each). Drape them with plastic wrap and let them rest on the counter for 10 minutes.

Coat a baker's peel or rimless baking sheet with flour. Uncover 1 piece of dough. Dust your hands with flour. Transfer the piece of dough to the peel, plopping it into the center. With the pads of your fingers, dimple the dough all over to press and gently shape it into a rough rectangle. Lift the two corners closest to you and stretch it in one fluid motion, as if you are shaking out a towel, dropping the end farthest from you at one end of the peel. Repeat with the opposite side, stretching the dough so that it is one inch shy of the depth of your baking stone. Dimple the dough all over with your fingers again to even it out as much as possible, but do not overhandle it. Use a pastry brush to coat the dough lightly with the olive oil. Sprinkle it with sea salt.

BAKE THE PIZZA. Slide the pizza onto the baking stone. Bake until the pizza is bubbled and golden brown, 15 to 20 minutes. A little charring is the sign of a well-baked *pizza romana*. Repeat shaping and baking with the second piece of dough.

COOL AND STORE THE PIZZA. Slide the peel or baking sheet underneath the pizza and place it on a wire rack. Brush the pizza with the remaining oil and serve immediately. Store any uneaten pizza in large pieces in a resealable plastic bag at room temperature, to snack on the next day.

Variation: **Roman Red Pizza** *Pizza rossa alla romana*

When customers reach the mobbed counter at Forno Campo de' Fiori, they quickly say just *bianca* or *rossa*, white or red, to place their order. In Rome, *pizza rossa* simply means dough dressed with fresh uncooked tomato sauce. The tomatoes are spread so thin that they cook and dry while baking, flavoring the dough but not weighing it down or making it soggy. The bakers drizzle the red pizza, crackling and crisp just like the white version, with olive oil, which pools and drips deliciously over the crust. To make the tomato sauce, you simply puree whole peeled canned tomatoes. It's thinner than American-style tomato sauce for pizza. But the Romans want the tomato flavor to enhance, not compete with, the dough, olive oil, and salt.

For this variation, just follow the mixing, kneading, fermenting, and shaping instructions for *pizza bianca*. Then spoon the tomato sauce onto the shaped dough just before baking.

TOMATO SAUCE				
INGREDIENTS	VOLUME	U.S. WEIGHT	METRIC WEIGHT	BAKER'S PERCENTAGE
Whole peeled tomatoes, drained	1 cup	One 14-ounce	400 grams	—

PREPARE THE TOMATOES. Drain the tomatoes and puree them in a food processor or food mill until smooth.

DIVIDE AND SHAPE THE PIZZA. Divide and shape the pizza as directed in the *pizza bianca* recipe. After shaping the pizza and brushing it with olive oil, use a rubber spatula to spread the sauce in a very thin layer to within 1 inch of the edges. Sprinkle it with sea salt. Bake, cool, and store as directed.

CIABATTA

. . . .

ALLOW 9 TO 17 HOURS TO MIX AND FERMENT THE *BIGA*;

15 TO 18 MINUTES TO KNEAD;

3 TO 4 HOURS TO FERMENT;

30 TO 40 MINUTES TO PROOF;

25 TO 35 MINUTES TO BAKE

. . . .

Ciabatta is a relatively new Italian bread (bakers I've talked to say it began to appear about 50 years ago) that has caught on in a big way. Legend has it that the bread is the result of a mixing accident. One day an absent-minded baker added too much water to his dough and didn't notice until he had already mixed it in. Thrifty and practical, as most bakers are, he shaped the soupy mixture into long, skinny rectangles and hoped for the best. He wasn't optimistic when he saw how the loose dough, unable to support itself, spread out as it proofed. But when he baked it, it became so bubbly and light that his customers immediately fell in love with the misshapen loaves. The bread became the mainstay of his business, and other bakers began imitating his funny-looking but exceptionally delicious loaves. Ciabatta, named for the old bedroom slipper it resembles, has only grown in popularity over the years and is now famous not only across Italy but in the rest of Europe and the United States.

I first saw this peculiar and charming bread being made by "Dr. Ciabatta" at the Italian baking show in Verona. An experienced artisan baker who had perfected the technique for making the airiest and chewiest bread, the "doctor" now demonstrated ciabatta baking, and sold his own brand of flour, at shows and master classes all over Europe. I watched with interest as he mixed stiff *biga* into a puddly dough. Once it had risen and fermented, he scooped it into long loaves, touching it as little as possible. Every half-hour a line would form in front of his booth as he pulled crisp, honey-colored breads from the oven with a long peel. Cut and tossed into baskets, they disappeared in seconds. I probably wasn't the only person timing my circuits through the displays to catch a slice before it was all gone.

Dr. Ciabatta used the same *doppio zero* flour and *biga* formula as most Italian bakers. Water, and lots of it, is the key ingredient in ciabatta. Water hydrates the starches that gelatinize and swell into glossy air pockets that distinguish this bread from other Italian loaves. Water also makes the dough extremely sticky and more challenging to handle than traditional bread dough, so use a mixer instead of kneading by hand. Wet dough takes longer to rise, which is why the fermentation time for this bread is longer than for any other bread in this chapter. It's during the slow rise that ciabatta develops its porous structure. Light steam gives the bread its characteristic soft crust, which makes ciabatta so perfect for sandwiches.

MAKES 2 SQUAT, DIMPLED LOAVES (19.6 OUNCES/556 GRAMS EACH)

Equipment

HEAVY-DUTY STAND MIXER WITH DOUGH HOOK
BAKER'S PEEL OR RIMLESS BAKING SHEET
PARCHMENT PAPER
BENCH SCRAPER OR CHEF'S KNIFE
BAKING STONE
CAST-IRON SKILLET

BIGA				
INGREDIENTS	VOLUME	U.S. WEIGHT	METRIC WEIGHT	BAKER'S PERCENTAGE
Water, tepid (70 to 78 degrees)	⅓ cup	2.3 ounces	65 grams	65
Instant yeast	½ teaspoon	0.1 ounce	2 grams	2
Unbleached bread flour, preferably high-gluten	⅔ cup	3.5 ounces	100 grams	100

PREPARE THE _BIGA_. Nine to 17 hours before you want to bake, prepare the _biga_. Pour the water into a small mixing bowl. With a rubber spatula, stir in the yeast and flour just until a dough forms. It will be stiff like pie dough. Dust the counter with flour and scrape out the dough. Knead the dough for 1 to 2 minutes just to work in all the flour and get it fairly but not perfectly smooth. (This is a very small amount of dough, about the size of a plum.) Lightly oil the mixing bowl. Round the _biga_ and place it back in the bowl. Cover the bowl with plastic wrap. Leave at room temperature (70 to 75 degrees) for 1 hour, then refrigerate it for at least 8 and up to 16 hours.

The *biga* will double in volume (to about the size of an orange), becoming glossy and porous, and will smell mildly acidic.

BREAD DOUGH

INGREDIENTS	VOLUME	U.S. WEIGHT	METRIC WEIGHT	BAKER'S PERCENTAGE
Biga	About 1 cup	5.9 ounces	167 grams	33
Water, tepid (70 to 78 degrees)	1³/₄ cups	15 ounces	425 grams	85
Instant yeast	2 teaspoons	0.4 ounce	10 grams	2
Unbleached bread flour, preferably high-gluten	3¹/₄ cups	17.6 ounces	500 grams	100
Sea salt	1¹/₂ teaspoons	0.4 ounce	10 grams	2

MIX THE DOUGH. Remove the *biga* from the refrigerator and uncover it. It will be soft, airy, and a bit sticky. Scrape it into a large bowl. Pour the water over the *biga* and stir it with a rubber spatula to soften it and break it into clumps. Stir in the yeast, flour, and salt until a dough forms.

KNEAD THE DOUGH. By machine: With the dough hook, mix the dough on medium-high speed (8 on a KitchenAid mixer) for 13 to 15 minutes. At this speed the mixer will "walk," possibly off the counter, so do not leave it unattended. The dough will not clear the sides of the bowl and will climb up the dough hook. Periodically stop the machine and scrape down the hook and the sides of the bowl with a rubber spatula. Turn the machine to high speed (10 on a KitchenAid mixer) and knead until the dough becomes more coherent, clears the sides of the bowl, and collects around the hook, 2 to 3 minutes more. It will be glistening, creamy, and extremely elastic. Check that the dough is well developed by pulling off a golfball-sized piece. Stretch it into an opaque windowpane that does not tear. If it does tear, knead for an additional 2 to 3 minutes and test again.

FERMENT THE DOUGH. Transfer the dough to a lightly oiled, clear 2-quart container with a lid. With masking tape, mark the container at the level the dough will reach when it has tripled in volume. Cover and leave it to rise at room temperature (70 to 75 degrees) until it inflates three times in size, 3 to 4 hours. When the dough reaches its peak, it will be bubbly and lively, and you'll be able to pull away long, stretchy strands.

DIVIDE AND SHAPE THE LOAVES. Cover a baker's peel or rimless baking sheet with parchment paper. Pleat the parchment down the center and dust it well with flour. Uncover the dough and turn it out onto a heavily floured countertop. With a bench scraper or chef's knife, cut the dough into 2 equal pieces (19.6 ounces/556 grams each). Pick up 1 piece of dough, holding one end in each hand. In one fluid motion, lift and stretch the dough and place it on one half of the parchment paper. Repeat with the other piece, laying it on the other half of the parchment paper,

with the pleat separating the pieces. Take your fingertips and, starting at the top, gently press into the surface of the dough, dimpling the surface as you go. Drape the loaves with plastic wrap.

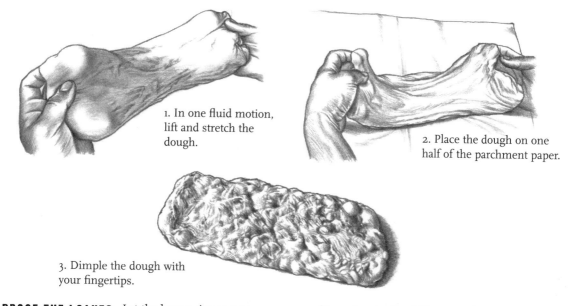

1. In one fluid motion, lift and stretch the dough.

2. Place the dough on one half of the parchment paper.

3. Dimple the dough with your fingertips.

PROOF THE LOAVES. Let the loaves rise at room temperature (70 to 75 degrees) until you see bubbles under the surface of the bread, 30 to 40 minutes.

PREPARE THE OVEN. About 1 hour before baking, place a baking stone on the middle rack and place a cast-iron skillet on the lower rack. Heat the oven to 475 degrees.

BAKE THE LOAVES. Uncover the loaves. Slide the loaves, still on the parchment, onto the baking stone and pull on the parchment so it lays flat. Place 1/2

cup of ice cubes in the skillet to produce steam. Bake until the loaves are light and golden-crusted, 25 to 35 minutes.

COOL AND STORE THE LOAVES. Slide the peel or the rimless baking sheet under the parchment paper to remove the loaves from the oven. Slide the loaves, still on the parchment, onto a wire rack. Cool completely, about 1 hour. Store uneaten loaves in resealable plastic bags for up to 2 days and reheat in a 350-degree oven for 5 minutes.

Variation: Ciabatta Rolls

To make ciabatta rolls, perfect for sandwiches, pour the fermented dough onto a flour-dusted countertop, and gently nudge it into a loose 10-by-12-inch rectangle. Dust the top of the dough with flour. Use a pizza wheel to cut the rectangle lengthwise into 2-inch-wide strips. Cut each strip into 3-inch pieces. You will have 20 pieces of dough. Transfer the dough pieces to a parchment-covered baking sheet, placing them 2 inches apart. Let stand until slightly pillowy, about 30 minutes. Bake at 475 degrees until light golden brown, about 20 minutes.

COMO BREAD
Pane di Como

. . . .

ALLOW 9 TO 17 HOURS TO MIX AND FERMENT THE *BIGA*;

10 TO 15 MINUTES TO KNEAD;

2 TO 2 1/2 HOURS TO FERMENT;

1 TO 1 1/2 HOURS TO PROOF;

20 TO 30 MINUTES TO BAKE

. . . .

This recipe, from the bakers at Il Fornaio in Lake Como, produces substantial white loaves with a mild, gentle flavor characteristic of the region. The high proportion of water in the recipe accounts for the bread's glistening, open crumb structure, but it makes the dough sticky and tricky to handle. Kneading in the mixer is best if you want to develop the gluten fully, but if you'd like to try hand-kneading, be sure to give yourself enough time to develop the gluten enough to lift the loaves to their full, airy potential. When baked, no two loaves look exactly alike. This is because they are baked seam side up. In the oven, the seam breaks open, forming a jagged ridge that browns deeply.

**MAKES 2 ROUNDS
(23.4 OUNCES/663 GRAMS EACH)**

Equipment
HEAVY-DUTY STAND MIXER WITH DOUGH HOOK (OPTIONAL BUT HIGHLY RECOMMENDED)

BENCH SCRAPER OR CHEF'S KNIFE

BAKER'S PEEL OR RIMLESS BAKING SHEET

PARCHMENT PAPER

BAKING STONE

CAST-IRON SKILLET

BIGA				
INGREDIENTS	VOLUME	U.S. WEIGHT	METRIC WEIGHT	BAKER'S PERCENTAGE
Water, tepid (70 to 78 degrees)	²/₃ cup	5.3 ounces	150 grams	60
Instant yeast	1 teaspoon	0.2 ounce	5 grams	2
Unbleached bread flour	1½ cups	8.8 ounces	250 grams	100

PREPARE THE *BIGA*. Nine to 17 hours before you want to bake, prepare the *biga*. Pour the water into a small mixing bowl. With a rubber spatula, stir in the yeast and flour just until a dough forms. It will be stiff like pie dough. Dust the counter with flour and scrape out the dough. Knead the dough for 1 to 2 minutes just to work in all the flour and get it fairly but not perfectly smooth. Lightly oil the mixing bowl. Round the *biga* and place it back in the bowl. Cover the bowl with plastic wrap. Leave at room temperature (70 to 75 degrees) for 1 hour, then refrigerate it for at least 8 and up to 16 hours. The *biga* will double in volume, becoming glossy and porous, and will smell mildly acidic.

BREAD DOUGH				
INGREDIENTS	VOLUME	U.S. WEIGHT	METRIC WEIGHT	BAKER'S PERCENTAGE
Biga	About 2 cups	14.3 ounces	405 grams	81
Water, tepid (70 to 78 degrees)	1¾ cups	14.1 ounces	400 grams	80
Instant yeast	1½ teaspoons	0.4 ounce	10 grams	2
Unbleached bread flour	3¼ cups	17.6 ounces	500 grams	100
Sea salt	2 teaspoons	0.6 ounce	12.5 grams	2

MIX THE DOUGH. Remove the *biga* from the refrigerator and uncover it. It will be soft, airy, and a bit sticky. Scrape it into a large bowl. Pour the water over the *biga* and stir it with a rubber spatula to soften it and break it into clumps. Stir in the yeast, flour, and salt until a dough forms.

KNEAD THE DOUGH. By hand: Scrape the dough out onto a lightly floured countertop. It will be very sticky, almost like batter, but resist adding extra flour. Knead the dough with long, steady strokes, flouring your hands and scraping the dough off the counter with a bench scraper as often as necessary. Continue kneading until the dough is very smooth and elastic, 13 to 15 minutes. Check that the dough is well developed by pulling off a golfball-sized piece. Stretch it into an opaque windowpane that does not tear. If it does tear, knead for an additional 2 to 3 minutes and test again.

By machine: With the dough hook, mix the dough on medium speed (4 on a KitchenAid mixer) until it is very smooth and elastic, 10 to 12 minutes. This sticky dough will not clear the sides of the bowl. At least once during the mixing time, stop the machine to scrape down the hook and the sides of the bowl

with a rubber spatula. Check that the dough is well developed by pulling off a golfball-sized piece. Stretch it into an opaque windowpane that does not tear. If it does tear, knead for an additional 2 to 3 minutes and test again.

FERMENT THE DOUGH. Transfer the dough to a lightly oiled, clear 2-quart container with a lid. With masking tape, mark the container at the level the dough will reach when it has doubled in volume. Cover and leave it to rise at room temperature (70 to 75 degrees) until it doubles, reaching the masking-tape mark, 2 to 2 1/2 hours. When you press a fingertip into the dough, your fingerprint will spring back slowly.

DIVIDE AND SHAPE THE ROUNDS. Cover a baker's peel or rimless baking sheet with parchment paper and dust with flour. Uncover the dough and turn it out onto a lightly floured countertop. With a bench scraper or chef's knife, cut the dough into 2 equal pieces (23.4 ounces/663 grams each). Shape each piece into a round (See Shaping Rounds, page 36) and place them smooth side down on the parchment paper, 3 inches apart. Drape the rounds with plastic wrap.

PROOF THE ROUNDS. Let the loaves rise at room temperature (70 to 75 degrees) until they spread, looking puffy and light and nearly doubling in size, 1 to 1 1/2 hours. When you press a fingertip into the dough, your fingerprint will spring back slowly.

PREPARE THE OVEN. About 1 hour before baking, place a baking stone on the middle rack and a cast-iron skillet on the lower rack. Heat the oven to 450 degrees.

BAKE THE ROUNDS. Uncover the rounds. Slide the rounds, still on the parchment, onto the baking stone. Place 1/4 cup of ice cubes in the skillet to produce light steam. Bake until the crust is glossy red-brown, 20 to 30 minutes.

COOL AND STORE THE LOAVES. Slide the peel or the rimless baking sheet under the parchment paper to remove the loaves from the oven. Slide the loaves, still on the parchment, onto a wire rack. Cool the loaves completely, about 1 hour, before cutting into 1-inch slices. Store unsliced loaves in a brown paper bag for up to 3 days. For longer storage, freeze whole loaves in resealable plastic bags for up to 1 month.

ROSETTA ROLLS
Rosetta soffiati

....

ALLOW 9 TO 17 HOURS TO MIX AND FERMENT THE *BIGA*;
10 TO 15 MINUTES TO KNEAD;
30 TO 45 MINUTES TO FERMENT;
3 TO 8 HOURS TO RETARD;
10 TO 15 MINUTES TO BAKE

....

The rosetta roll (called *michetta* in Piedmont and Lombardy) is Italy's answer to the Kaiser roll. Round, with a petal impression, it is chewy but not tough, with a lightly crisp crust. Its hollow interior is perfect for filling with salami or cheese. I developed such a love for this roll that I was determined to develop a recipe for making it at home. I had eaten rosetta rolls all over Italy, but it wasn't until I watched Bernardino and Fabio Bartocci make them at Antico Forno in Rome that I learned how to bake them. The very stiff, extremely active dough is made with a huge amount of *biga* and just a little bit of added flour. Diastatic malt, extracted from barley, is added. This ingredient breaks down the starch in the dough and makes more sugars available to the yeast, further stimulating the dough's fermentation and rising action. The *biga* and the malt give the rolls the structure and energy to spring up dramatically when they hit the hot oven. They also add flavor and enhance the crust color.

The dough rises just briefly before being shaped and stamped. After stamping, the rolls are turned stamped side down to preserve the impression and chilled in the refrigerator for anywhere from 3 to 8 hours. Chilling prevents the dough from becoming too acidic while allowing the sweet flavor of the wheat to develop. After a brief stint at room temperature, the cool rolls go into a very hot oven, where they blossom into shape. As with cream puffs, a combination of steam and heat inflates the small rounds of dough and creates an air pocket in the center. Italian bakers are judged on the size of the hollow (my best rolls have had air pockets the size of a golfball). But even if your rolls don't always have such hollow centers, they will still be delicious. Eat them warm from the oven, sliced and filled for panini, or spread with butter for breakfast or dinner.

✳ **MAKES 12 SANDWICH ROLLS**
(2.8 OUNCES/80 GRAMS EACH)

Equipment
BAKING SHEET
BENCH SCRAPER OR CHEF'S KNIFE
ROLL STAMP

BIGA				
INGREDIENTS	VOLUME	U.S. WEIGHT	METRIC WEIGHT	BAKER'S PERCENTAGE
Water, tepid (70 to 78 degrees)	1⅓ cups	11.1 ounces	315 grams	63
Instant yeast	2 teaspoons	0.4 ounce	10 grams	2
Unbleached bread flour preferably high-gluten	3¼ cups	17.6 ounces	500 grams	100

PREPARE THE *BIGA*. Nine to 17 hours before you want to bake, prepare the *biga*. Pour the water into a medium mixing bowl. With a rubber spatula, stir in the yeast and flour just until a dough forms. It will be stiff like pie dough. Dust the counter with flour and scrape out the dough. Knead the dough for 1 to 2 minutes just to work in all the flour and get it fairly but not perfectly smooth. Lightly oil the mixing bowl. Round the *biga* and place it back in the bowl. Cover the bowl with plastic wrap. Leave at room temperature for 1 hour, then refrigerate it for at least 8 and up to 16 hours. The *biga* will double in volume, becoming glossy and porous, and will smell mildly acidic.

BREAD DOUGH				
INGREDIENTS	VOLUME	U.S. WEIGHT	METRIC WEIGHT	BAKER'S PERCENTAGE
Biga	About 4½ cups	29.1 ounces	825 grams	1650
Water, tepid (70 to 78 degrees)	⅓ cup	2.5 ounces	70 grams	140
Unbleached bread flour, preferably high-gluten	⅓ cup	1.8 ounces	50 grams	100
Diastatic malt	1 teaspoon	0.2 ounce	5 grams	10
Sea salt	1½ teaspoons	0.4 ounce	10 grams	20

MIX THE DOUGH. Remove the *biga* from the refrigerator and uncover it. It will be soft, airy, and a bit sticky. Scrape it into a large bowl. Pour the water over the *biga* and stir it with a rubber spatula to soften it and break it into clumps. Stir in the flour, malt, and salt until a dough forms.

KNEAD THE DOUGH. By hand: Lightly flour the counter and scrape out the firm dough. Knead it with steady strokes until it is very smooth and elastic, 13 to 15 minutes.

By machine: With the dough hook, mix the dough on medium speed (4 on a KitchenAid mixer) until it is very smooth and elastic, 10 to 12 minutes.

FERMENT THE DOUGH. Transfer the dough to a lightly oiled, clear 2-quart container with a lid. Cover and leave it to rise at room temperature (70 to 75 degrees) for 35 to 40 minutes. It will inflate slightly and form bubbles just below the surface.

DIVIDE AND SHAPE THE ROLLS. Lightly dust a baking sheet with flour and set it aside. Uncover the dough and turn it out onto an unfloured countertop. Pat into a rough rectangle. With a bench scraper or chef's knife, cut the dough into 12 equal pieces (2.8 ounces/80 grams each). Round each piece into a tight ball (see Shaping Rolls, page 37). Stamp each piece with the roll stamp and place it on the baking sheet, stamped side down. This will help preserve the impression from the stamp. Arrange the rolls 2 inches apart and cover them with plastic wrap.

RETARD THE ROLLS. Place the baking sheet in the refrigerator for at least 3 hours and up to 8 hours. Twenty minutes before you want to bake, remove the baking sheet from the refrigerator, uncover the rolls, and turn them over so the stamped side is up. Redrape them with plastic wrap and let them sit at room temperature for about 20 minutes. They will soften and relax slightly but will not inflate or look proofed.

PREPARE THE OVEN. About 15 minutes before baking, place the oven rack in the middle position. Heat the oven to 500 degrees.

BAKE THE ROLLS. Uncover the rolls and slide the baking sheet onto the oven rack. Bake until the rolls are a pale sand color, 10 to 15 minutes. These rolls are best when they're lightly baked.

COOL AND STORE THE ROLLS. Remove the baking sheet to a wire rack. Cool the rolls briefly, about 15 minutes, before serving. Enjoy them on the day they are baked, and freeze any extra rolls in a resealable plastic bag for up to 1 month.

GREEN OLIVE STICKS
Pane di oliva verde

· · · · · · · · · · · · · · · · · · · ·

ALLOW 9 TO 17 HOURS TO MIX AND FERMENT THE *BIGA*;

10 TO 15 MINUTES TO KNEAD;

2 TO 2 1/2 HOURS TO FERMENT;

30 TO 45 MINUTES TO PROOF;

15 TO 20 MINUTES TO BAKE

· · · · · · · · · · · · · · · · · · · ·

I first tasted these breadsticks, jam-packed with moist green olive pieces, at a bakery just outside the train station in Milan. My customers have a passion for olives, so I knew that I'd have to make a version of these for Bread Alone. They always sell out before the end of the day. The dough is soft, easy to shape, and full of flavor from *biga*. Use water-packed green olives (I like Sicilian or Cerginola) and chop them small, but not too small, for best texture and flavor.

✳ **MAKES 20 BREADSTICKS**
(2.5 OUNCES/70 GRAMS EACH)

Equipment
BENCH SCRAPER OR CHEF'S KNIFE
12-BY-17-INCH BAKING SHEET

BIGA				
INGREDIENTS	VOLUME	U.S. WEIGHT	METRIC WEIGHT	BAKER'S PERCENTAGE
Water, tepid (70 to 78 degrees)	¹/₂ cup	4.1 ounces	115 grams	77
Instant yeast	³/₄ teaspoon	0.1 ounce	3 grams	2
Unbleached bread flour	1 cup	5.3 ounces	150 grams	100

PREPARE THE *BIGA*. Nine to 17 hours before you want to bake, prepare the *biga*. Pour the water into a small mixing bowl. With a rubber spatula, stir in the yeast and flour just until a dough forms. It will be stiff like pie dough. Dust the counter with flour and scrape out the dough. Knead the dough for 1 to 2 minutes just to work in all the flour and get it fairly but not perfectly smooth. Lightly oil the mixing bowl. Round the *biga* and place it back in the bowl. Cover the bowl with plastic wrap. Leave at room temperature (70 to 75 degrees) for 1 hour, then refrigerate it for at least 8 and up to 16 hours. The *biga* will double in volume (to about the size of an orange), becoming glossy and porous, and will smell mildly acidic.

BREAD DOUGH

INGREDIENTS	VOLUME	U.S. WEIGHT	METRIC WEIGHT	BAKER'S PERCENTAGE
Biga	About 1½ cups	9.5 ounces	270 grams	54
Water, warm (85 to 95 degrees)	1½ cups plus 2 tablespoons	13.2 ounces	375 grams	75
Instant yeast	1½ teaspoons	0.3 ounce	8 grams	2
Unbleached bread flour	3¼ cups	17.6 ounces	500 grams	100
Sea salt	1½ teaspoons	0.4 ounce	10 grams	2
Green olives, pitted and coarsely chopped	2 cups	7.1 ounces	200 grams	40

MIX THE DOUGH. Remove the *biga* from the refrigerator and uncover it. It will be soft, airy, and a bit sticky. Scrape it into a large bowl. Pour the water over the *biga* and stir it with a rubber spatula to soften it and break it into clumps. Stir in the yeast, flour, and salt until a rough, ragged dough forms.

KNEAD THE DOUGH. By hand: Scrape the dough out onto a lightly floured countertop. Knead the dough with smooth, confident strokes. It will be tacky at first. As often as necessary, flour your hands and use a bench scraper to collect the dough from the counter. Continue kneading until the dough is very smooth and elastic, 10 to 12 minutes. With your palms, press the dough into a rough rectangle and spread the chopped olives over it. Roll up the dough, cinnamon-roll style, and continue kneading until the olives are evenly distributed, 2 to 3 minutes more. Don't worry if there are some clumps of olives.

By machine: With the dough hook, mix the dough on medium speed (4 on a KitchenAid mixer) until it is smooth and elastic, 8 to 9 minutes. Stop the machine and scrape down the dough hook and the bowl with a rubber spatula. Add the chopped olives and mix the dough on low speed (2 on a KitchenAid mixer) until they are well distributed, 2 to 3 minutes more. Or knead the olives in by hand.

FERMENT THE DOUGH. Transfer the dough to a lightly oiled, clear 2-quart container with a lid. With masking tape, mark the container at the level the dough will reach when it has doubled in volume. Cover and leave it to rise at room temperature (70 to 75 degrees) until it doubles, reaching the masking-tape mark, 2 to 2 1/2 hours. When you press a fingertip into the dough, your fingerprint will spring back slowly.

DIVIDE AND SHAPE THE OLIVE STICKS. Lightly dust a baking sheet with flour. Uncover the dough and turn it out onto a very lightly floured counter. Pat it into a rough rectangle. With a bench scraper or chef's knife, cut the dough into 20 equal pieces (2.5 ounces/70 grams each). Cover them with plastic wrap and let them rest on the counter for 10 minutes. Keep the other pieces covered while you shape each one into a tiny baguette, about 6 inches long and 1 inch wide (see Shaping Baguettes, pages 37–38). Place the olive sticks seam side down on the baking sheet, at least 1 inch apart. Cover them with plastic wrap.

PROOF THE OLIVE STICKS. Let the olive sticks rise at room temperature (70 to 75 degrees) until they look puffy and light, nearly doubling in size, 30 to 45 minutes. When you press a fingertip into the dough, your fingerprint will spring back slowly.

PREPARE THE OVEN. About 1 hour before baking, place an oven rack in the middle position. Heat the oven to 450 degrees.

BAKE THE OLIVE STICKS. Place the baking sheet on the oven rack and bake the olive sticks until they are crisp and tanned, 15 to 20 minutes. If you prefer soft breadsticks, take them out just as they are beginning to color. If you want them with a little more snap, bake them until the crust is deep reddish brown.

COOL AND STORE THE OLIVE STICKS. Remove the baking sheet to a wire rack. Cool the olive sticks briefly, about 10 minutes, before serving. Store at room temperature in a resealable plastic bag for 1 to 2 days. For longer storage, freeze in a resealable plastic bag.

PROSCIUTTO BREAD
Pane con prosciutto

. . . .

ALLOW 9 TO 17 HOURS TO MIX AND FERMENT THE *BIGA*;

10 TO 15 MINUTES TO KNEAD;

1 1/2 TO 2 HOURS TO FERMENT;

1 TO 1 1/2 HOURS TO PROOF;

25 TO 30 MINUTES TO BAKE

. . . .

I've tried many variations on prosciutto bread, some with thin slices of prosciutto rolled up in the dough, others with tiny minced pieces added during kneading. But this is my favorite. Not surprisingly, it comes from a bakery north of Parma, the Italian city most closely associated with fine prosciutto. The baker, Giuseppe Giacomazi, from Forno a Legna in Fidenza, uses good-sized chunks. The fat from the ham melts during baking, permeating the bread with its flavor and tenderizing it. Giuseppe adds some rye flour to his dough. The earthiness of the rye mingles beautifully with the salty prosciutto. These special ingredients deepen the bread's flavor, already enhanced by the *biga*. The long torpedo shape ensures that the bread will have plenty of rich, dark crust encasing the soft interior.

Use top-quality imported prosciutto here, preferably prosciutto di Parma. Have it cut about 1/16-inch thick, so the chopped pieces are thin enough to chew but substantial enough not to get lost in the dough.

MAKES **2** TORPEDO-SHAPED LOAVES, ABOUT **12** INCHES LONG
(**20** OUNCES/**567** GRAMS EACH)

Equipment
BAKER'S PEEL OR RIMLESS BAKING SHEET
PARCHMENT PAPER
BENCH SCRAPER OR CHEF'S KNIFE
BAKING STONE

BIGA				
INGREDIENTS	VOLUME	U.S. WEIGHT	METRIC WEIGHT	BAKER'S PERCENTAGE
Water, tepid (70 to 78 degrees)	¹/₃ cup	2.3 ounces	65 grams	65
Instant yeast	¹/₂ teaspoon	0.1 ounce	2 grams	2
Unbleached bread flour	²/₃ cup	3.5 ounces	100 grams	100

PREPARE THE *BIGA*. Nine to 17 hours before you want to bake, prepare the *biga*. Pour the water into a small mixing bowl. With a rubber spatula, stir in the yeast and flour just until a dough forms. It will be stiff like pie dough. Dust the counter with flour and scrape out the dough. Knead the dough for 1 to 2 minutes just to work in all the flour and get it fairly but not perfectly smooth. Lightly oil the mixing bowl. Round the *biga* and place it back in the bowl. Cover the bowl with plastic wrap. Leave at room temperature (70 to 75 degrees) for 1 hour, then refrigerate it for at least 8 and up to 16 hours. The *biga* will double in volume (to about the size of an orange), becoming glossy and porous, and will smell mildly acidic.

BREAD DOUGH				
INGREDIENTS	VOLUME	U.S. WEIGHT	METRIC WEIGHT	BAKER'S PERCENTAGE
Biga	About 1 cup	5.9 ounces	167 grams	33
Water, warm (85 to 95 degrees)	1½ cups	12.3 ounces	350 grams	70
Instant yeast	2 teaspoons	0.4 ounce	10 grams	2
Unbleached bread flour	2 cups	10.6 ounces	300 grams	60
Rye flour	1⅔ cups	7.1 ounces	200 grams	40
Prosciutto, chopped into ½-inch pieces	—	3.5 ounces	100 grams	20
Sea salt	1½ teaspoons	0.4 ounce	10 grams	2

MIX THE DOUGH. Remove the *biga* from the refrigerator and uncover it. It will be soft, airy, and a bit sticky. Scrape it into a large bowl. Pour the water over the *biga* and stir it with a rubber spatula to soften it and break it into clumps. Stir in the yeast, bread flour, rye flour, prosciutto, and salt until a dough forms.

KNEAD THE DOUGH. By hand: Scrape the dough out onto a lightly floured countertop. Knead the dough with long, steady strokes. It will be somewhat sticky, firm, and less springy than white dough because of the rye flour. Continue kneading until the dough is very smooth and fairly elastic, 13 to 15 minutes.

By machine: With the dough hook, mix the dough on medium speed (4 on a KitchenAid mixer) until it is very smooth and fairly elastic, 10 to 12 minutes.

FERMENT THE DOUGH. Transfer the dough to a lightly oiled, clear 2-quart container with a lid. With masking tape, mark the container at the level the dough will reach when it has doubled in volume. Cover and leave it to rise at room temperature (70 to 75 degrees) until it doubles, reaching the masking-tape mark, 1 1/2 to 2 hours. When you press a fingertip into the dough, your fingerprint will spring back slowly.

DIVIDE AND SHAPE THE LOAVES. Cover a baker's peel or rimless baking sheet with parchment paper and dust the parchment with flour. Uncover the dough and turn it out onto a very lightly floured counter. With a bench scraper or chef's knife, cut the dough into 2 equal pieces (20 ounces/567 grams each). Shape each piece into a torpedo about 12 inches long and 3 inches wide (See Shaping Torpedos, page 39). Place the loaves seam side down on the parchment paper, about 3 inches apart from each other. Lightly drape them with plastic wrap.

PROOF THE LOAVES. Let the loaves stand at room temperature (70 to 75 degrees) until they look puffy and light and have nearly doubled in size, 1 to 1 1/2 hours. When you press a fingertip into the dough, your fingerprint will spring back slowly.

PREPARE THE OVEN. About 1 hour before baking, place a baking stone on the middle rack of the oven. Heat the oven to 425 degrees.

BAKE THE LOAVES. Slide the loaves on the parchment paper directly onto the baking stone. Bake until the crusts are deep red-brown, 25 to 30 minutes.

COOL AND STORE THE LOAVES. Slide the peel or baking sheet underneath the parchment paper and transfer the loaves, still on the parchment, to a wire rack. Let them cool for 5 minutes before peeling them off the parchment paper. Cool completely, about 1 hour, before slicing. Store the breads at room temperature in a resealable plastic bag. The fat from the prosciutto will keep the loaves moist for 1 to 2 days. For longer storage, freeze in a resealable plastic bag for up to 1 month.

FRESH HERB TWIST
Pane alle erbi

. . . .

ALLOW 10 TO 15 MINUTES TO KNEAD;
1 1/2 TO 2 HOURS TO FERMENT;
30 MINUTES TO 1 HOUR TO PROOF;
20 TO 30 MINUTES TO BAKE

. . . .

This is a large, handsome loaf flavored with fresh basil, rosemary, thyme, and coriander, from the Alto Adige region in northern Italy. These unusual flavors, an influence from nearby Germany, give the bread a provocative fragrance and bold character. Grind the coriander yourself for the best flavor. Preground coriander loses almost all of its spiciness. I ate this bread with finely sliced speck (cured ham) and mortadella, both pork products that are made in the region.

**MAKES 2 LARGE TWISTS
(17 OUNCES/482 GRAMS EACH)**

Equipment
BENCH SCRAPER OR CHEF'S KNIFE
BAKER'S PEEL OR RIMLESS BAKING SHEET
PARCHMENT PAPER
BAKING STONE
CAST-IRON SKILLET

INGREDIENTS	VOLUME	U.S. WEIGHT	METRIC WEIGHT	BAKER'S PERCENTAGE
Fresh basil, coarsely chopped	1 tablespoon	0.1 ounce	3 grams	—
Fresh rosemary, coarsely chopped	1 tablespoon	0.1 ounce	3 grams	—
Fresh thyme, coarsely chopped	1 tablespoon	0.1 ounce	3 grams	—
Water, tepid (70 to 78 degrees)	1½ cups	12.3 ounces	350 grams	70
Instant yeast	2 teaspoons	0.4 ounce	10 grams	2
Unbleached bread flour	2½ cups	14.1 ounces	400 grams	80
Rye flour	¾ cup	3.5 ounces	100 grams	20
Extra-virgin olive oil	¼ cup	1.8 ounces	50 grams	10
Toasted and ground coriander seeds	¼ teaspoon	—	—	—
Sea salt	1½ teaspoons	0.3 ounce	8 grams	2

MIX THE DOUGH. Combine the herbs in a small bowl and set them aside. Pour the water into a large mixing bowl or the bowl of a stand mixer. With a wooden spoon, stir in the yeast, bread flour, rye flour, olive oil, coriander, and salt just long enough to blend the ingredients into a dough.

KNEAD THE DOUGH. By hand: Turn the dough out onto a lightly floured countertop. Flour your hands and knead the dough with smooth, steady strokes. It will be sticky, but resist adding extra flour. Use a bench scraper to collect the dough from the counter periodically. Continue kneading until the dough is smooth and elastic but still a little tacky, 10 to 12 minutes. Flatten the dough out into a rough rectangle. Spread the herbs over it. Fold the dough over the herbs and continue kneading until the herbs are well distributed, 2 to 3 minutes more.

By machine: With the dough hook, mix the dough on medium speed (4 on a KitchenAid mixer) until it is supple, smooth, and very elastic, 8 to 9 minutes. Turn off the machine and scrape down the hook and sides of the bowl with a rubber spatula. The dough will be fairly sticky. Add the herbs and mix on medium speed until they are well distributed, 2 to 3 minutes more.

FERMENT THE DOUGH. Transfer the dough to a lightly oiled, clear 2-quart container with a lid. With masking tape, mark the container at the level the dough will reach when it has doubled in volume. Cover and leave it to rise at room temperature (70 to 75 degrees) until it inflates into a dome, reaching the masking-tape mark, 1 1/2 to 2 hours.

DIVIDE AND SHAPE THE TWISTS. Cover a baker's peel or rimless baking sheet with parchment paper and dust the parchment with flour. Uncover the dough and turn it out onto a lightly floured counter. With a bench scraper or chef's knife, cut the dough into 4 equal pieces. Shape each piece into a rope about 14 inches long. Lay two ropes side by side and pinch the ends together at one end. Twist the two ropes together and pinch the other ends to seal. Place the loaf on one half of the parchment paper. Repeat the shaping with the remaining 2 ropes and place the loaf on the other half of the parchment paper, 3 inches apart from the first one. Drape the loaves with plastic wrap.

PROOF THE TWISTS. Let the loaves stand at room temperature (70 to 75 degrees) until they look pillowy, 30 minutes to 1 hour. When you press a fingertip into the dough, your fingerprint will spring back slowly.

PREPARE THE OVEN. About 1 hour before baking, place a baking stone on the middle rack of the oven and a cast-iron skillet on the lower rack. Heat the oven to 425 degrees.

BAKE THE TWISTS. Slide the loaves on the parchment paper directly onto the baking stone. Place 1/4 cup of ice cubes in the skillet to produce light steam. Bake until the loaves are golden brown, 20 to 30 minutes.

COOL AND STORE THE LOAVES. Slide the peel or baking sheet underneath the parchment paper and transfer the loaves, still on the parchment, to a wire rack. Let them cool for 5 minutes before peeling them off the parchment paper. Cool the loaves for about 30 minutes and serve them warm. Store in a resealable plastic bag at room temperature for up to 3 days. For longer storage, freeze in a resealable plastic bag for up to 1 month.

CORN-RYE ROUNDS
Pane di mais

. . . .

Allow 10 to 15 minutes to knead;
1 1/2 to 2 hours to ferment;
1 to 1 1/2 hours to proof;
25 to 35 minutes to bake

. . . .

Corn flour and rye is an unusual combination, especially in Italy, where white flour dominates. But both grains grow well in the Dolomites, northwest of Venice as you get into the foothills of the Alps, where this bread is a specialty. Slightly crumbly and sunflower yellow on the inside, it has an interesting contrast of sweet and earthy flavors.

Corn flour is a very fine, pale yellow flour milled especially for bread. Don't confuse corn flour with cornmeal, which is too coarse for bread baking. This bread doesn't rise much because it contains a relatively small quantity of wheat flour and the dough can't develop much gluten. It will bake into a flattish round. It is excellent with butter and jam, honey, or cheese. Or eat it with cured meat— prosciutto and bresaola especially—as they do in the North.

❋ **MAKES 2 SQUAT ROUNDS**
(15.3 OUNCES/435 GRAMS EACH)

Equipment
BAKER'S PEEL OR RIMLESS BAKING SHEET
PARCHMENT PAPER
BENCH SCRAPER OR CHEF'S KNIFE
BAKING STONE
CAST-IRON SKILLET

INGREDIENTS	VOLUME	U.S. WEIGHT	METRIC WEIGHT	BAKER'S PERCENTAGE
Water, tepid (70 to 78 degrees)	1½ cups	12.3 ounces	350 grams	70
Instant yeast	1½ teaspoons	0.3 ounce	8 grams	2
Unbleached bread flour	1⅓ cups	7.1 ounces	200 grams	40
Corn flour	1⅔ cups	7.1 ounces	200 grams	40
Fine or medium rye flour	¾ cup	3.5 ounces	100 grams	20
Sea salt	1½ teaspoons	0.4 ounce	10 grams	2

MIX THE DOUGH. Pour the water into a large mixing bowl or the bowl of a stand mixer. With a wooden spoon, stir in the yeast, bread flour, corn flour, rye flour, and salt just long enough to blend the ingredients into a rough, ragged dough.

KNEAD THE DOUGH. By hand: Turn the dough out onto a lightly floured countertop. Flour your hands and knead the dough with smooth, steady strokes until it is fairly but not perfectly smooth, 13 to 15 minutes. This dough is not very elastic.

By machine: With the dough hook, mix the dough on medium speed (4 on a KitchenAid mixer) until it is fairly but not perfectly smooth, 10 to 12 minutes. This dough is not very elastic.

FERMENT THE DOUGH. Transfer the dough to a lightly oiled, clear 2-quart container with a lid. With masking tape, mark the container at the level the dough will reach when it has doubled in volume. Cover and leave it to rise at room temperature (70 to 75 degrees) until it doubles, reaching the masking-tape mark, 1 1/2 to 2 hours. When you press your fin-

gertip into the dough, your fingerprint will spring back slowly.

DIVIDE AND SHAPE THE ROUNDS. Cover a baker's peel or rimless baking sheet with parchment paper and dust the parchment with corn flour. Uncover the dough and turn it out onto a counter lightly floured with bread flour. With a bench scraper or chef's knife, cut the dough into 2 equal pieces (15.3 ounces/435 grams each). Shape each piece into a round (see Shaping Rounds, page 36). Place the loaves smooth side up on the parchment paper, 3 inches apart, and sprinkle them with corn flour. Drape the loaves with plastic wrap.

PROOF THE ROUNDS. Let the loaves stand at room temperature (70 to 75 degrees) until they look puffy and light, nearly doubling in size, 1 to 1 1/2 hours. When you press your fingertip into the dough, your fingerprint will spring back slowly.

PREPARE THE OVEN. About 1 hour before baking, place a baking stone on the middle rack of the oven and a cast-iron skillet on the lower rack. Heat the oven to 450 degrees.

BAKE THE ROUNDS. Slide the rounds on the parchment paper directly onto the baking stone. Place 1/4 cup of ice cubes in the skillet to produce light steam. These rounds will not spring up voluminously in the oven. Bake them until the crust is a rich brown, 25 to 35 minutes.

COOL AND STORE THE ROUNDS. Slide the peel or baking sheet underneath the parchment paper and transfer the rounds, still on the parchment, to a wire rack. Let them cool for 5 minutes before peeling them off the parchment paper. Cool them completely, about 1 hour, before slicing. Store in a resealable plastic bag at room temperature for up to 2 days. For longer storage, freeze in a resealable plastic bag for up to 1 month.

RYE-FENNEL CRACKERBREAD
Schüttelbrot

. . . .

ALLOW 4 TO 8 MINUTES TO MIX;

30 TO 45 MINUTES TO FERMENT;

30 TO 40 MINUTES TO BAKE

. . . .

This flatbread from Alto Adige in the far north of Italy is ultra-thin and crisp, with a firm texture and chew. The blend of rye flour, fennel, and anise gives it a distinct Austrian accent. *Schüttelbrot* is in the tradition of dried breads that never stale. Bakers told me how northern Italians relied on this bread during World War I, when other food was scarce, because it could be stored in bulk in an attic for up to a year. Today in Bolzano, the region's capital, the breads are displayed like china, separated by vertical wooden slats behind bakery counters.

Schüttelbrot dough is wet and loose like cake batter and requires no kneading. After a single quick ferment, the dough is rolled flat and immediately popped into a hot oven. Italians of German and Austrian heritage who live in Alto Adige typically break up the disks of *schüttelbrot* to eat with speck, a local cured ham similar to prosciutto, which is available at fine food stores in the United States. My recipe makes 6-inch rounds, but the bakers in Alto Adige make these breads in all sizes, as wide as a dinner plate (called *volser*) and as small as a water cracker (called *mini-schüttelbrot*). If you'd like to make larger or smaller breads, follow the same shaping instructions using larger or smaller pieces of dough and adjust the baking times accordingly.

**MAKES EIGHT 6-INCH DISKS
(4.3 OUNCES/121 GRAMS EACH)**

Equipment
2 BAKING SHEETS
ROLLING PIN
CAKE TESTER OR SKEWER

INGREDIENTS	VOLUME	U.S. WEIGHT	METRIC WEIGHT	BAKER'S PERCENTAGE
Water, tepid (70 to 78 degrees)	2 cups	15.9 ounces	450 grams	90
Instant yeast	1½ teaspoons	0.3 ounce	8 grams	2
Rye flour, preferably finely ground	1⅔ cups	8.8 ounces	250 grams	50
Unbleached bread flour	1⅔ cups	8.8 ounces	250 grams	50
Ground fennel	2 teaspoons	0.1 ounce	3 grams	—
Ground anise	1 teaspoon	.05 ounce	1.5 grams	—
Sea salt	1½ teaspoons	0.4 ounce	10 grams	2

PREPARE THE OVEN. About 15 minutes before baking, place one rack in the upper third of the oven and a second rack in the middle position. Heat the oven to 400 degrees.

MIX THE DOUGH. By hand: Pour the water into a large mixing bowl. With a rubber spatula, stir in the yeast, rye flour, bread flour, fennel, anise, and salt to make a stiff batter. Stir vigorously until you can see strands of gluten pulling away from the spoon, 7 to 8 minutes.

By machine: Pour the water into the bowl of a stand mixer. Add the yeast, rye flour, bread flour, fennel, anise, and salt. With the paddle attachment, stir the batter on low speed (2 on a KitchenAid mixer) until you can see strands of gluten pulling away from the paddle, 4 to 5 minutes.

FERMENT THE DOUGH. Cover the bowl with plastic wrap and let it stand at room temperature (70 to 75 degrees) until it puffs up slightly, 30 to 45 minutes.

SHAPE THE FLATBREADS. Dust 2 baking sheets with rye flour. Uncover the dough and scrape it onto a counter generously dusted with rye flour. With a bench scraper or chef's knife, cut the dough into 8 equal pieces. Use a heavily floured rolling pin to roll each piece into a 6-inch round about 1/8-inch thick. Place the flatbreads on the floured baking sheets, at least 2 inches apart. Poke them all over with a cake tester or skewer to keep them from rising too much.

BAKE THE FLATBREADS. Slide the baking sheets onto the oven racks. Bake until the breads have risen slightly and are nearly crisp, 20 to 25 minutes (switching the position of the baking sheets halfway through). They will not color significantly but will look barely toasted. Turn off the oven and leave the baking sheets inside for 10 to 15 minutes more to dry and crisp the breads.

COOL AND STORE THE FLATBREADS. Remove the baking sheets to wire racks. The flatbreads will cool quickly. Store completely cooled flatbreads in airtight containers at room temperature for up to 1 month.

FREQUENTLY ASKED QUESTIONS ABOUT REGIONAL ITALIAN BREADS

. . . .

What makes Roman pizza unique?
What I find interesting about Roman-style pizza is how similar it is to Italian country bread doughs like *pane di Genzano*. Although Roman pizza dough is raised with commercial yeast rather than a sourdough starter like Genzano bread, it is very wet like Genzano bread dough, so wet that it looks more like a liquid than a solid until it is adequately kneaded. Like Genzano bread dough, Roman pizza dough must be kneaded for an extended amount of time, to allow the flour to absorb the water. The high hydration level and extended kneading of both Roman pizza and *pane di Genzano* account for their family resemblance. Both the pizza and the bread have a beautifully bubbly, shiny crumb and wonderfully chewy texture.

Is the corn flour used in the Corn-Rye Rounds simply cornmeal that's been milled to a finer consistency? Or are there other differences between corn flour and cornmeal?
Corn flour is made from whole corn kernels. Cornmeal is made from just the outer husk of the kernels, which are ground after their starchy interiors have been removed. This is a crucial difference, so you can't substitute even very finely ground cornmeal for corn flour in bread recipes.

Is the roll stamper simply a device for decorating the Rosetta Rolls, or does it contribute something essential to the finished rolls' character?
In general, I avoid recipes that require special equipment. But a special roll stamper is essential for making authentic rosetta rolls, since it is the stamper that gives the rolls their characteristic hollow interiors. It's not a big investment, but if you want to make these rolls, you'll need to mail-order the device (see pages 333–34 for sources).

What would happen if I shaped the dough for the Green Olive Sticks into a regular-size baguette?
You can certainly make a regular-size olive baguette. Just increase the baking time to 20 to 25 minutes. But the smaller olive sticks will have a different character from a larger loaf. When you eat the smaller sticks, you get big chunks of olives just barely held together by a little bit of tasty dough. And there's a higher ratio of crispy crust to soft interior with the smaller sticks, something that I really enjoy.

✳

CHAPTER 11

UNTOUCHED BY TIME:
THE SINGULAR CASE OF
PANE DI ALTAMURA

✳

n my first few trips to Italy to study Italian baking, I stayed mostly in the northern and central regions, visiting the big baking shows in Verona and Milan, touring the headquarters of Pietroberto and other Italian baking equipment manufacturers in and around Vicenza, and checking out notable bakeries in Tuscany and Umbria. But even in the Italian Alps, I could hardly avoid hearing about the legendary bread of Altamura. Wherever I went, bakers would proudly share their local specialties with me and then urge me to travel south to the province of Puglia, Italy's heel. In the small town of Altamura, outside of Bari, they told me I would find the most delicious of Italian breads, a unique loaf made with 100 percent semolina flour and baked in very old wood-fired ovens. But Puglia was too far off the path I usually traveled. I never seemed to have the time to drive the eight hours from Rome across the Italian peninsula.

I finally saw and tasted *pane di Altamura* in Munich, of all places, in the Italian Pavilion of the International Baking Association trade show in 1994. Entering the exhibition hall, I stepped onto a Plexiglas floor under which bins of straw-colored wheat were illuminated. As I walked a little farther, I saw ocher wheat berries under my feet, and then, a little farther, bins of brilliant gold flour. At the end of this compelling trail was a table piled with the product—enormous, crudely shaped loaves the color of the sun, made with 100 percent semolina flour milled from wheat grown in the fields surrounding Altamura. I circled the table, viewing the imposing pile of rustic breads as I would an abstract sculpture in a museum. Giuseppe Colomonaco, the president of Durum Italia, the association of farmers, millers, and bakers who work together to market Altamura's crop, introduced himself to me and told me a little bit about this ultimate regional bread.

Semolina flour is the defining ingredient in Altamura bread. While about half of the locally grown durum wheat is milled to make high-protein flour for dried pasta, the other half is reserved for bread. To be used in bread, the very hard wheat has to be milled much more finely than it is for pasta. The wheat kernels are run through a series of steel cylinders over and over again to rub and break them, preserving the germ oil but making the resulting flour soft enough to bake with. Because semolina bread flour has a high protein content—12.5 to 14.5 percent—it makes dough with a lot of gluten. Dough made from this flour can absorb a lot of water and hold on to it during baking. The resulting bread is extremely moist, with a sweet, earthy flavor unique to semolina.

While many bakers were baking bread in ovens set up at the show, the association president had brought already-baked loaves from one of Altamura's bakeries to Munich. He wasn't worried about how the bread would travel. He knew that its unique sourdough would keep it fresh for at least five days. True *pane di Altamura*, he explained, is not simply bread made with semolina flour milled from durum wheat grown in the region. It can only be called *pane di Altamura* if it is raised with a 100 percent semolina sourdough fermented in the town and if it is baked in one of the town's very old wood-fired ovens. This wasn't simply a case of pride in a local product but a matter of law. Altamura bread had just recently been awarded the DOP (*denominazione di origine protetta*), a government designation reserved for agricultural and food products whose properties are essentially or exclusively derived from their geographical environment. It is the only bread in Italy so designated (Genzano country bread is similarly honored, but with the IGP, a slightly less prestigious mark). If a food product is labeled DOP, all phases of its production must be carried out within a delimited geographical area.

I was enchanted by the unusual coloring and rough, rustic shape of these gargantuan loaves. The reddish gold crust of each bread was split and cracked where the dough had risen explosively in a very hot oven, revealing a sunny yellow crumb. I had seen many beautiful breads with reddish brown tones, but the gold and yellow palette of the Alta-

mura loaves was new to me. The flavor of the bread did not disappoint me. The sweetness of the semolina was balanced by just a touch of mild acidity from the starter. The bread's fragrance, earthy but clean, was uniquely compelling. After I tasted this days-old *pane di Altamura* in Munich, I knew I had to travel to the source and taste it in the place where it was made.

It took me a while—almost ten years—to get there. Altamura was always in the back of my mind as I traveled through Europe collecting bread recipes and techniques, and I knew I couldn't complete this book without visiting the ancient town. So after a trip to Prague, a train ride to Poland, a stop in Paris, and then one in Milan, I flew to the seaport city of Bari one morning in late October 2003 and drove west to Altamura. Outside the city, olive groves in rocky hardpan soil gave way to terraced fields of wheat stubble, evidence of the recent harvest. Altamura is located on the high-altitude Murgia plain, sandwiched between the sea and the mountains. On a distant hill, I spotted the dark form of the town, an island in an ocean of wheat fields. I entered it at siesta time, early afternoon, and drove slowly through its almost deserted streets, passing medieval churches and one or two old men sitting and talking. I could easily picture the town bakers hundreds of years ago, calling out at dawn to announce that the bread was ready.

I had been invited to a lavish lunch with the secretary of Durum Italia to learn more about the wheat and the bread. We enjoyed a feast of fried olives, marinated eggplant and peppers, prosciutto and cured meats, semolina pasta with porcini mushrooms, and a delicious semolina focaccia layered with sun-ripened tomatoes, my first taste of semolina bread in Altamura. I will never forget it.

My hosts wanted me to understand and appreciate *pane di Altamura* as a product of the land, so they had arranged for Michele Soponaro, an agrohistorian from the local university, to take me on a tour of the wheat fields and mills after lunch. A clean-cut college professor in his mid-thirties with fashionable wire-rimmed glasses and a crop of curly hair, Michele had grown up in Altamura and was passionate about its agricultural history and eager to promote the region's wheat to the rest of the country and Europe. After lunch he drove me out of town, where stone walls made from gigantic boulders segmented endless wheat fields. Occasionally we would pass an ancient, abandoned shepherd's hut made of the same rocks, but the land was now uninhabited. We got out of the car at the edge of one of the stubbly fields. With no trees to shade us, the heat was intense and the air very dry, but a constant, cooling breeze made our walk comfortable and almost refreshing. Michele remarked that the wind and sun were a challenge to the growing wheat and forced the plants to develop strong, deep root structures. The farmers believed that wheat with such tenacious roots was harder and thus made superior flour for pasta and bread.

I scooped up the bone-dry, rocky red soil and asked him how long wheat had been grown here. Expecting the answer to be a few generations—a long time by any standard—I was taken aback when he responded that he couldn't say exactly, since there was no written record, but at least since Roman times. I was used to hearing French bakers talk about the good old days of the nineteenth century! I looked at the dirt on my palms as we walked back to the car, marveling at this unbroken connection that the farmers, millers, and bakers of Altamura have with ancient civilization.

Our next stop was a nearby mill, a five-story cement building with an attached silo just a short drive away over a hill. A tractor-trailer was emptying thousands of pounds of wheat berries into chutes in an opening in the middle of the structure as we drove up. We climbed a staircase to the top floor, where the whole berries were released from the silo and into the mill. The entire floor vibrated from the motion of the corrugated steel rollers as they ground the wheat. Michele reached into a bin and grabbed a handful of whole kernels, offering some to me to sample. I popped a few into my mouth. They were so hard I could barely chew them. I knew that durum was the hardest variety of wheat, with a protein con-

tent of 14 to 16 percent, but until now I hadn't experienced this quality in the unprocessed grain.

This very strong wheat undergoes a simple single milling before it is used to make pasta. But to be used in bread, it has to be milled over and over until it is a fine powder. In the gravity-driven bread flour mill, the whole kernels on the top floor were ground again every time they dropped to a lower level. As we descended the staircase, we reached into a hatch at each landing to feel the flour, which was increasingly fine. On the ground floor, where the pure yellow flour was bagged, it was as silky and fine as talcum powder. Michele remarked that mechanized milling is virtually the only nod to modernization in the making of Altamura bread. Documentary evidence suggests that durum wheat has been ground into fine flour and baked into bread for at least two thousand years. Before it was milled this way, Altamura grain was stone-ground over and over again. As we left the mill, he said, "Come, I'll show you the oldest oven in Altamura."

The last stop on the tour was Mimmo Scalera's bakery, Il Panettiere di Altamura. The primitive room had gray stone walls and stone floors polished from hundreds of years of foot traffic. At one end of the bakery was a wood-burning oven similar to those I had seen in Genzano. The oven's giant opening was ringed with black soot. Its heavy iron door stood ajar, and flames danced on the hearth. In Genzano the ovens are carefully constructed of small bricks. Occasionally a baker commissions a new oven from one of the town's masons, who has been trained by his father and grandfather to reproduce the old ovens. In Altamura there were no reproduction ovens. Mimmo's oven, like every other oven I saw in Altamura, was made with big stone blocks, and a new one hadn't been built in existing memory. Everyone in town agreed that this was the oldest working oven in town, but no one could say exactly how old it was. Michele guessed that it had been built at least three hundred and maybe four hundred years ago. Along one wall, golden lumps of dough were proofing on worn, canvas-covered wooden shelves. Baskets on the floor were filled with the enormous, almost mis-shapen breads.

As we spoke, an elderly woman walked into the bakery as casually as if she were entering her own house. In one hand she carried a silver tray with tiny porcelain cups—espresso for the bakers. In the other hand she had a small bundle wrapped in a linen towel, carefully knotted on top. "Antonia comes every week," Mimmo explained. "She continues the tradition of mixing her own dough and then bringing it to the communal oven to bake." For centuries, all the townspeople made their dough at home and brought it to the village baker, who marked it with a wooden stamp and baked it in exchange for a 300-gram piece of it. Mimmo put Antonia's loaf on the shelf alongside the two hundred bundles of his own *pane di Altamura*, but he didn't mark it. "I know her loaf because she kneads it by hand," he said. Her hand-kneaded dough wasn't quite as smooth as his. Mixing by machine is the only other accommodation to modernity (along with mechanized milling) that the bakers of Altamura make. Although they use electric mixers, the bakers mix and knead the dough at the lowest speed, generating the minimum amount of heat and friction. This gentle, slow mixing develops the dough gently, for bread with a very smooth crumb. I looked around for the mixer, and then Mimmo explained that this room was used only for proofing and baking the breads. The dough was mixed and shaped in a newer building a few blocks away. He invited me to visit that night to watch them knead and shape the dough.

I arrived at the new bakery at about 10 P.M. and saw a mixer turning some golden dough. "Is that tonight's bread?" I asked. "No, no, no!" said Mimmo. This was the *madre*, the semolina sourdough that was refreshed every night a few hours before the dough was made. Called *madre acida* or *madre naturale*, this "mother" sourdough is made with fine semolina flour according to traditions followed at least since the Middle Ages. The bakers I met explained that the strains of yeast have been perpetuated like family bloodlines.

At about 2 A.M. the starter was ready and Mimmo's bakers mixed the dough very slowly in antique-looking Artofex mixers that had probably been used here since electric power came to town. They let the dough ferment slowly in the bowl for about two hours and then cut the fermented dough into pieces. Each piece was rounded into a ball and wrapped in a muslin cloth to support it as it proofed, another custom from the old days, when villagers needed a convenient way to carry dough to the baker's oven. Now Mimmo's bakers carried the bundles from the new bakery to the old, where they sat for another couple of hours until ready to bake. At 4 A.M. the bakers gave the loaves their final shape: a series of rolls, folds, and sometimes cuts. When the loaves hit the oven they nearly burst, rising and expanding in unpredictable and dramatic ways. Out of the oven, they all looked a little different.

As I left town and headed for the airport in Bari with a long-keeping Altamura bread wrapped up for my trip back home, I marveled at the unique baking experience I had just had. Artisan bakers I had met in France, Germany, Austria, and Italy were part of a larger European movement to rescue old techniques and recipes that had been compromised or threatened by industrialization. In Altamura, there was no need to rediscover the past, since the past had never been lost in the first place.

As soon as I returned to Bread Alone, I introduced this wonderful bread to my family and staff. I wanted to put it into production immediately but was afraid that the unusual overlapped shape would scare customers away, so I shaped the dough into unscored torpedos and covered the loaves with sesame seeds. I had an instant hit on my hands. The semolina loaves were popular with my Italian customers, who were already familiar with semolina, but were also embraced by people who had never heard of the flour. My one regret is that I didn't have the courage to bake the bread in its traditional shape. As this book goes to press, I am making plans to introduce *pane accavallato* alongside the semolina torpedo. After baking this dough in its traditional shapes with my students and at home, I am certain now that customers who have enjoyed the semolina torpedo will be charmed by its ungainly ancestor.

❈ KITCHEN NOTES: LOW-TECH BAKING, ALTAMURA STYLE

As with Genzano bread, the challenge in making *pane di Altamura* at home is recreating a product that is defined by its place of origin. Of course bread that you make in your kitchen in New Jersey isn't going to have a DOP. But that's not the way to think about the project. Instead, keep in mind that baking in Altamura is decidedly low-tech, and if you have a mixer, a baking stone, and an oven, you are adequately equipped to make this bread. Gather the proper ingredients—fine semolina flour, water, and sea salt—and let yourself feel the same connection to the past that the Altamura bakers feel every day when they refresh their pedigreed starter, knead their dough, and bake these simple but extraordinary loaves.

Begin with the right flour. Semolina flour ground from durum wheat gives Altamura bread its rich, grainy sweetness. It is the only kind of flour used in both the sourdough and the bread dough. There is no substitute. Take care to buy semolina flour that's been *finely* ground. This is sometimes labeled "fancy" or "extra fancy" durum. It will feel as smooth as powder, without any trace of grit from bran or germ. Semolina flour that feels sandy and coarse can be used in combination with other flours in other breads but will not work in recipes that require 100 percent semolina flour. (For mail-order sources, see pages 333–34.)

Try a starter with yogurt. Think of the yogurt in traditional Altamura sourdough as a hedge against the failure of your culture to thrive. Yogurt, a fermented food itself, contains abundant quantities of the lactobacilli that you want to encourage in your sourdough. Mixing it in on day 1 will make you feel like you are a step ahead of the game.

Knead a little longer. Semolina has a lot of gliadin and glutenin, the proteins that form gluten when the flour is mixed with water. Gluten is responsible for structure and strength, so well-made semolina dough rises beautifully in the oven and the finished bread has a lovely even crumb. To develop the gluten fully, you'll have to knead this dough a little longer than you would knead dough made with a lower-protein bread flour, at least ten minutes by machine and up to eighteen minutes by hand. After this much kneading, your dough will be extremely elastic and extensible, able to rise dramatically in the very hot oven just as the loaves baked in Altamura's ancient ovens do.

Proof your loaf inside a towel. Altamura bread is preshaped and wrapped in a towel, where it is allowed to proof. This technique evolved because of the way the dough was originally mixed in village homes. Bakeries were small, with no room for proofing the entire village's dough, so the bakers would give the loaves a final shaping and get them into the oven quickly to save space. (This is one of the reasons Mimmo Scalera built his new bakery; the old bakery with its venerable oven could not accommodate all the dough he wanted to mix and ferment.) What's fascinating is that the bread's character is very much a product of this contingency. While other doughs are shaped and then stand at room temperature for a final proofing, during which they spread and rise, Altamura bread dough's final rise takes place entirely in the oven, resulting in its explosive oven spring. The abundant gluten from the semolina flour gives the dough enough elasticity to support this growth.

SEMOLINA SANDWICH LOAF
Pane in cassetta di Altamura

. . . .

ALLOW 8 TO 12 MINUTES TO KNEAD;

1 1/2 TO 2 HOURS TO FERMENT;

1 TO 1 1/2 HOURS TO PROOF;

35 TO 45 MINUTES TO BAKE

. . . .

The night before I left Altamura I received an urgent phone call from my expert guide, Michele Soponaro. There was a bread he had forgotten to show me, a straight dough semolina loaf made by Altamura bakers specifically for sandwiches (the larger sourdough loaves are difficult to slice this way). He delivered an example to my hotel room in a matter of minutes, and I was very glad that he did. The gorgeous red-gold loaf with a delicate crust and even golden crumb was unlike any sandwich bread I had tasted. I knew my customers would love its rich wheat flavor and olive oil perfume. A small amount of sugar gives the bread great tenderness.

This simple recipe will introduce you to the unique character of semolina flour. Once you try it, you may be inspired to make traditional Altamura bread.

MAKES 1 SANDWICH LOAF
(31.2 OUNCES/885 GRAMS)

Equipment
8 1/2-BY-4 1/2-INCH LOAF PAN
CAST-IRON SKILLET

INGREDIENTS	VOLUME	U.S. WEIGHT	METRIC WEIGHT	BAKER'S PERCENTAGE
Water, tepid (70 to 78 degrees)	1½ cups	10.6 ounces	300 grams	60
Instant yeast	1 teaspoon	0.2 ounce	5 grams	1
Fine semolina (durum) flour	3¼ cups	17.6 ounces	500 grams	100
Granulated sugar	1 tablespoon	0.5 ounce	15 grams	3
Extra-virgin olive oil	¼ cup	1.8 ounces	50 grams	10
Sea salt	1½ teaspoons	0.4 ounce	10 grams	2

MIX THE DOUGH. Pour the water into a large mixing bowl or the bowl of a stand mixer. Add the yeast, flour, sugar, olive oil, and salt and stir with a rubber spatula just until a rough dough forms.

KNEAD THE DOUGH. By hand: Lightly dust the counter with semolina flour. Scrape the dough out of the bowl and knead it with smooth, steady strokes until it is very smooth, shiny, and elastic, 10 to 12 minutes.

By machine: Use the dough hook and mix the dough on medium speed (4 on a KitchenAid mixer) until it is very smooth, shiny, and elastic, 8 to 9 minutes.

FERMENT THE DOUGH. Transfer the dough to a lightly oiled, clear 2-quart container with a lid. With masking tape, mark the spot on the container that the dough will reach when it has doubled in volume. Cover and leave it to rise at room temperature (70 to 75 degrees) until it inflates into a dome, reaching the masking-tape mark, 1 1/2 to 2 hours.

SHAPE THE LOAF. Grease a loaf pan with vegetable oil. Lightly dust the counter with semolina flour. Uncover the dough and turn it out onto the counter. Form the dough into a pan loaf (see Shaping a Pan Loaf, page 40). Nestle the loaf into the pan, seam side down, pressing it gently to fit. Lightly dust the top of the loaf with semolina flour and cover the pan with plastic wrap.

PROOF THE LOAF. Let the loaf rise at room temperature (70 to 75 degrees) until it crowns just above the rim of the pan, 1 to 1 1/2 hours.

PREPARE THE OVEN. About 15 minutes before baking, place one oven rack in the middle position and one in the lower position. Preheat the oven to 375 degrees.

BAKE THE LOAF. Place the loaf on the middle rack of the oven. Bake until the loaf pulls away from the sides of the pan and the crust is a deep golden brown, 35 to 45 minutes.

COOL AND STORE THE LOAF. Pull the loaf from the oven. Bang the edge of the pan on the counter to release the bread. Invert it onto a wire rack and then flip it right side up. Cool the bread completely before slicing, about 1 hour. Store the cut loaf in a resealable plastic bag at room temperature. It will stay fresh for about 3 days. For longer storage, freeze in a resealable plastic bag for up to 1 month.

ALTAMURA SEMOLINA SOURDOUGH
Biga semolina

. . . .

Here is a recipe for semolina sourdough, based on the culture that Mimmo Scalera uses at his old bakery in the village of Altamura, Italy. He called it his *madre acida*, as did all the bakers I met who used sourdough instead of packaged yeast to raise their breads. I use it for the sake of authenticity, and because it usually is ready a day or two earlier than sourdoughs made with just flour and water.

Equipment
CLEAN, CLEAR 2-QUART CONTAINER

DAY 1				
INGREDIENTS	VOLUME	U.S. WEIGHT	METRIC WEIGHT	BAKER'S PERCENTAGE
Spring water, tepid (70 to 78 degrees)	¼ cup	2 ounces	57 grams	81
Fine semolina (durum) flour	½ cup	2.5 ounces	70 grams	100
Plain yogurt, nonfat, low-fat, or full-fat, preferably organic	2 tablespoons	1 ounce	28 grams	40

ACTIVATE THE CULTURE. Pour the water into the container and stir in the semolina and yogurt until it is fairly smooth. Scrape down the sides and cover the container with plastic wrap. Let it stand at room temperature (70 to 75 degrees) for 24 hours.

DAY 2				
INGREDIENTS	VOLUME	U.S. WEIGHT	METRIC WEIGHT	BAKER'S PERCENTAGE
Spring water, tepid (70 to 78 degrees)	¼ cup	2 ounces	57 grams	81
Fine semolina (durum) flour	½ cup	2.5 ounces	70 grams	100

OBSERVE AND FEED THE CULTURE. Uncover the culture and observe any changes. It's still early, but the culture may have risen slightly. It will taste mildly tangy from the yogurt, with a little bit of sweetness from the semolina.

Pour the water into the container and stir with a rubber spatula to loosen the culture slightly. Add the semolina flour and stir vigorously to oxygenate the culture and blend until it is smooth. It will be a soft dough, not loose like a liquid sourdough. Scrape down the sides and cover with plastic wrap. Let it stand at room temperature (70 to 75 degrees) for 24 hours.

DAY 3				
INGREDIENTS	VOLUME	U.S. WEIGHT	METRIC WEIGHT	BAKER'S PERCENTAGE
Spring water, tepid (70 to 78 degrees)	¼ cup	2 ounces	57 grams	81
Fine semolina (durum) flour	½ cup	2.5 ounces	70 grams	100

OBSERVE AND FEED THE CULTURE. Today your culture will have risen up the sides of the container and may have a slight dome. The surface will be bubbly, and if you hold up the container, you'll see bubbles on the sides and bottom. It will smell slightly acidic and effervescent. It will taste tangy and lightly sour.

Pour the water into the container and stir to loosen the sourdough. You'll have to stir vigorously to work the water in, because of the strength of the dough. As you stir, you'll notice long strands of gluten. Add the semolina flour and stir vigorously to oxygenate the culture and blend the fresh flour into the sourdough.

Scrape down the sides and cover the container with plastic wrap. Let it stand at room temperature for 24 hours.

DAYS 4–10

TEST THE CULTURE. Uncover the container and examine the culture to determine whether it is ripe enough to become a semolina sourdough. By now it will have become a brilliant yellow-gold and expanded dramatically, maybe doubling. It will be spongy-looking and filled with big and small bubbles all the way through. It will smell lightly sour. If your culture doesn't show this much activity, don't worry.

Repeat the steps for day 3 every 24 hours for up to 6 more days. Use warm (100 to 110 degrees) water in place of tepid water, and be sure to keep the container in a warm (75 to 80 degrees), draft-free place. You may need to transfer it to a larger container. After these additional feedings, if your culture does not look active, the flour may have been old, the water may have been too chlorinated, or the container may not have been spotlessly clean. See page 46 for suggestions before starting again.

If your culture does look ready, repeat the recipe from day 3 but plan to check the culture after only 12 hours. Scrape down the sides and cover the container with plastic wrap. With masking tape, mark the spot on the container that the sourdough will reach when it has doubled in volume. Let it stand at room temperature (70 to 75 degrees) for 12 hours. You'll know you have a strong, healthy sourdough when it almost doubles and is spongy and filled with large and small bubbles after 6 hours. Refresh the sourdough (see below) before proceeding with the semolina bread recipe of your choice.

REFRESHING THE SEMOLINA SOURDOUGH				
INGREDIENTS	VOLUME	U.S. WEIGHT	METRIC WEIGHT	BAKER'S PERCENTAGE
Spring water, tepid (70 to 78 degrees)	¼ cup	2 ounces	57 grams	81
Fine semolina (durum) flour	½ cup	2.5 ounces	70 grams	100

Measure 1/4 cup (1.8 ounces/50 grams) of your culture into a clean 1-quart container and discard the rest. Pour in the water and break up the dough with a spatula. The water will turn milky and bubbly. Stir in the semolina flour until a wet dough forms. Cover loosely with plastic wrap. Let stand at room temperature (70 to 75 degrees) for 8 to 12 hours, until it has ripened.

These are the signs of a ripe semolina sourdough: It will have doubled in volume and its surface will be bursting with bubbles. It will smell fresh and sweet with a mild tanginess and will taste tart. When you pull at it, you will pull up very elastic, long strands of gluten. Use the sourdough right away or store it in the refrigerator for up to 1 week.

MAINTAIN THE SEMOLINA SOURDOUGH. If your sourdough has been in the refrigerator for a week, it is time to refresh it again, whether or not you plan on baking. Weekly refreshment will keep it alive and healthy so that when you do bake, it will be capable of raising your dough. Just repeat the steps for refreshment and refrigerate it again for up to 1 week.

PREPARE THE SOURDOUGH FOR BAKING.
Whether or not you have refreshed your sourdough recently, you must refresh it 8 to 12 hours before you want to bake to ensure that it is in optimum shape for raising and flavoring bread. Follow the refreshment steps described above. After the sourdough has fermented at room temperature (70 to 75 degrees) for 8 to 12 hours, measure out what you will need for your recipe. Then measure out 1/4 cup (1.8 ounces/50 grams) of what is left over in a clean container, refresh this portion, and refrigerate for up to 1 week for use in the future.

ALTAMURA BREAD
Pane di Altamura

. . . .

ALLOW 8 TO 12 HOURS TO PREPARE THE SEMOLINA *BIGA*;

10 TO 18 MINUTES TO KNEAD;

3 TO 4 HOURS TO FERMENT;

1 1/2 TO 2 HOURS TO PROOF;

40 TO 50 MINUTES TO BAKE

. . . .

Forget focaccia, pizza, and any other breads you've seen in Italy. *Pane di Altamura* is the only bread you'll find if you travel to this town near Bari on the Adriatic Sea. The giant, volcanic loaves with a yellow-gold crumb are instantly recognizable and unforgettable. There's no other bread like it anywhere in the country, which is why the Italian government has honored it with a DOP appellation.

The arc shape of this bread is a relic from the era when peasants took their kneaded dough to the village baker, who folded it and stamped it, charging a piece of dough as his fee. Called *pane accavallato*, or "overlapped bread," it is the shape Altamura bakers still favor. *Pane accavallato*, along with two other shapes made from the same dough, *pane del contadino* and *pane del capriccio*, form the family of breads called *pane di Altamura*. (See pages 260 and 261 for instructions on how to shape *pane del contadino* and *pane del capriccio*.)

✳ MAKES 1 ENORMOUS, UNPREDICTABLY SHAPED LOAF
(39.7 OUNCES/1,125 GRAMS)

Equipment
BAKING STONE
CAST-IRON SKILLET
BAKER'S PEEL OR RIMLESS BAKING SHEET

BREAD DOUGH				
INGREDIENTS	VOLUME	U.S. WEIGHT	METRIC WEIGHT	BAKER'S PERCENTAGE
Semolina sourdough (page 254)	About 1 cup	7.1 ounces	200 grams	40
Water, tepid (70 to 78 degrees)	1½ cups	12.3 ounces	350 grams	70
Fine semolina (durum) flour	3¼ cups	17.6 ounces	500 grams	100
Sea salt	2 teaspoons	0.5 ounce	15 grams	3

MIX THE DOUGH. Measure the sourdough into a large mixing bowl or the bowl of a stand mixer. Pour the water over it. Stir with a rubber spatula to soften it slightly. There will be globs of starter. Add the semolina flour and salt, stirring just long enough to blend them into a dough.

KNEAD THE DOUGH. By hand: Turn the dough out onto a lightly floured counter. Knead with smooth, confident strokes until it is very smooth and elastic, 15 to 18 minutes. It will still be slightly sticky.

By machine: Use the dough hook and mix the dough on medium speed (4 on a KitchenAid mixer) until the dough is smooth and very elastic, 10 to 12 minutes.

FERMENT THE DOUGH. Transfer the dough to a lightly oiled, clear 2-quart container with a lid. With masking tape, mark the spot on the container that the dough will reach when it has doubled in volume. Cover and leave it to rise at room temperature (70 to 75 degrees) until it rises into a dome, doubling in volume and reaching the masking-tape mark, 3 to 4 hours.

PRESHAPE THE LOAF. Uncover the dough and turn it out onto the counter. Shape it into a round

and dust it with semolina flour (see Shaping Rounds, page 36). Place the round in the center of a clean, dry kitchen towel and tie the opposite corners together to make a snug bundle.

PROOF THE LOAF. Leave the loaf to rise at room temperature (70 to 75 degrees) until it balloons inside the kitchen towel, 1 1/2 to 2 hours. When you press your finger into the dough, your fingerprint will spring back slowly.

PREPARE THE OVEN. About 1 hour before baking, place a baking stone on the middle rack of the oven and a cast-iron skillet on the lower rack. Heat the oven to 400 degrees.

SHAPE THE LOAF. Dust a baker's peel or rimless baking sheet with semolina flour and set it aside. Lightly dust the counter with semolina flour. Untie the loaf and place it on the counter. Pulling two sides of the loaf away from the center, stretch it into a long, thin rectangle, about 6 by 16 inches. Rotate the dough 90 degrees so that the short side is in front of you. Fold the bottom edge to meet the top and press to seal the dough. Bring the folded edge in front of you three quarters of the way to the top, so that it forms a lip. Seal the seam all the way around, flattening the protruding bottom edge of the dough. It will be shaped in an arc, like an orange section. Place the loaf on the peel or baking sheet and sprinkle it with semolina flour.

BAKE THE LOAF. Slide the loaf from the peel or baking sheet onto the baking stone. Place 1/4 cup of ice cubes in the skillet to produce light steam. Bake until the loaf is mahogany-colored all over and golden where it splits open, 40 to 50 minutes. Do

not be surprised at the way the loaf bursts open unpredictably.

COOL AND STORE THE LOAF. Slide the peel or the rimless baking sheet under the loaf to remove it from the oven. Transfer the loaf to a wire rack. Cool it completely, about 1 hour, before slicing. This loaf will stay fresh for about 5 days stored at room temperature in a paper bag, or freeze in resealable plastic bags for up to 1 month.

1. Pulling two sides of the loaf away from the center, stretch it into a long, thin rectangle, about 6 by 16 inches. Rotate the dough 90 degrees so that the short side is in front of you. Fold the bottom edge to meet the top.

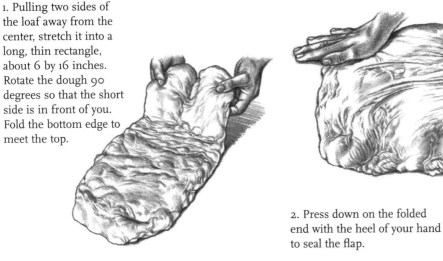

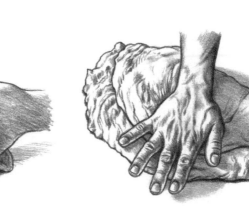

2. Press down on the folded end with the heel of your hand to seal the flap.

3. Bring the folded edge up three quarters of the way to the top.

4. Seal the outside seam by pressing with the heel of your hand all the way around, flattening the protruding bottom edge of the dough. It will be shaped in an arc, like an orange section.

Variation: **Altamura Peasant Loaf** *Pane del contadino*

This loaf was once made with a coarser grind of semolina flour, preferred by peasants and shepherds because one loaf stayed fresh for 2 weeks. Today the loaf is made with the same dough as the overlapped loaf and is sold throughout Puglia.

To make a Peasant Loaf instead of an overlapped loaf, follow the recipe for Altamura Bread until the shaping step. Then dust a baker's peel or rimless baking sheet with semolina flour. Lightly dust the counter with semolina flour. Untie the loaf and place it on the counter. Flatten one side of the round with a rolling pin so that it is about 1/2 inch thick and the dough looks like a baseball cap. Fold the flap up and all the way over the top of the loaf, pinching it at the center so that it doesn't unfold. Place the loaf on the peel or baking sheet and sprinkle with semolina flour. Bake, cool, and store as directed.

1. Gently shape the dough into a round.

2. Flatten one side of the round with a rolling pin so that it is about 1/2 inch thick.

3. The dough should look like a baseball cap.

4. Fold the flap up and all the way over the top of the loaf, pinching it at the center so that it doesn't unfold.

Variation: Altamura Tantrum Loaf *Pane del capriccio*

This shape got its name because it proofs and bakes more quickly than the other Altamura shapes and could be fed to children to keep them happy while the overlapped loaf was still in the oven.

To make a Tantrum Loaf instead of an overlapped loaf, follow the recipe for Altamura Bread until the proofing step, and let it proof only until it relaxes enough to shape, about 45 minutes.

To shape the loaf, dust a baker's peel or rimless baking sheet with semolina flour. Lightly dust the counter with semolina flour. Untie the loaf and place it on the counter. Flatten the round with a rolling pin. Make a cut in the center of the dough about 4 inches long. Stretch the round into an oval to elongate it and to open the center cut into a hole. Make 6 cuts evenly spaced around the outer edge, about 1 1/2 inches in toward the center hole. Pull the points out so they look like rays of the sun. Place the loaf on the peel or baking sheet and sprinkle it with semolina flour.

This flat shape bakes more quickly than the other two shapes, 20 to 30 minutes. Cool completely, about 1 hour, before breaking into pieces or slicing. Store as directed above.

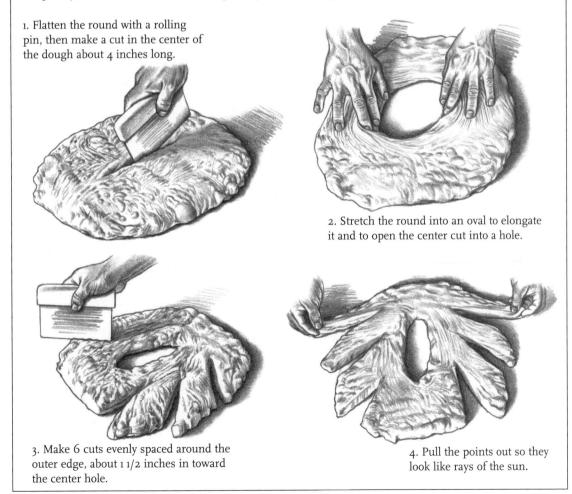

1. Flatten the round with a rolling pin, then make a cut in the center of the dough about 4 inches long.

2. Stretch the round into an oval to elongate it and to open the center cut into a hole.

3. Make 6 cuts evenly spaced around the outer edge, about 1 1/2 inches in toward the center hole.

4. Pull the points out so they look like rays of the sun.

ALTAMURA SEMOLINA FOCACCIA WITH SUN-RIPENED TOMATOES
Focaccia di Altamura

. . . .

ALLOW 8 TO 12 HOURS TO PREPARE THE SEMOLINA SOURDOUGH;

10 TO 18 MINUTES TO KNEAD;

3 TO 4 HOURS TO FERMENT;

30 TO 45 MINUTES TO PROOF;

25 TO 30 MINUTES TO BAKE

. . . .

As in Genzano, bakers in Altamura only make one kind of dough and then use it to make flatbreads like focaccia. I was lucky enough to visit Altamura at the end of tomato season, in late October, when bakers pat semolina dough into a pan and arrange rounds of ripe tomato on top, finishing with a drizzle of olive oil and a sprinkling of fresh rosemary. I enjoyed a memorable meal of this focaccia, accompanied by warm olives sautéed in garlic and olive oil, the day I arrived.

**✳ MAKES 1 SHEET PAN FOCACCIA
(39.7 OUNCES/1,125 GRAMS)**

Equipment
1 RIMMED HALF-SHEET PAN

PREPARE THE SOURDOUGH. If you have not refreshed your sourdough within the past 3 days, follow the recipe for refreshing it (page 256 for semolina sourdough, pages 79–80 for liquid *levain*, pages 114–15 for stiff dough *levain*) so that it will be in its prime. Let it stand for 8 to 12 hours at room temperature to ferment.

FOCACCIA DOUGH

INGREDIENTS	VOLUME	U.S. WEIGHT	METRIC WEIGHT	BAKER'S PERCENTAGE
Semolina sourdough (page 254)	About 1 cup	7.1 ounces	200 grams	40
Water, tepid (70 to 78 degrees)	1 ¾ cups	14.5 ounces	410 grams	82
Fine semolina (durum) flour	3¼ cups	17.6 ounces	500 grams	100
Sea salt	2 teaspoons	0.5 ounce	15 grams	3

TOPPINGS

INGREDIENTS	VOLUME	U.S. WEIGHT	METRIC WEIGHT	BAKER'S PERCENTAGE
Extra-virgin olive oil	2 tablespoons	1 ounce	28 grams	—
Ripe tomatoes, sliced into ¼-inch-thick rounds	3 medium	10.6 ounces	300 grams	—
Fresh rosemary, stemmed and roughly chopped	¼ cup	0.4 ounce	12 grams	—
Sea salt	½ teaspoon	0.1 ounce	4 grams	—

MIX THE DOUGH. Measure the sourdough into a large mixing bowl or the bowl of a stand mixer. Pour the water over it. Stir with a rubber spatula to soften it slightly. There will be globs of starter. Add the semolina flour and salt, stirring just long enough to blend them into a dough.

KNEAD THE DOUGH. By hand: Turn the dough out onto a lightly floured counter. Knead with smooth,

confident strokes until it is very smooth and elastic, 15 to 18 minutes. It will still be slightly sticky.

By machine: Use the dough hook and mix the dough on medium speed (4 on a KitchenAid mixer) until the dough is smooth and very elastic, 10 to 12 minutes.

FERMENT THE DOUGH. Transfer the dough to a lightly oiled, clear 2-quart container with a lid. With masking tape, mark the spot on the container that the dough will reach when it has doubled in volume. Cover and leave it to rise at room temperature (70 to 75 degrees) until it rises into a dome, doubling in volume and reaching the masking-tape mark, 3 to 4 hours.

SHAPE THE FOCACCIA AND ADD THE TOPPINGS. Oil a half-sheet pan. Uncover the dough and turn it out onto the pan. Use your hands to stretch the dough gently to fit the pan. It will be about 1/2-inch thick. Use your fingers or a pastry brush to coat the dough with the olive oil. Arrange the tomatoes on top of the dough without overlapping them. Sprinkle the rosemary and salt evenly all over the focaccia.

PROOF THE FOCACCIA. Leave the focaccia to rise uncovered at room temperature (70 to 75 degrees) until it puffs, 30 to 45 minutes.

PREPARE THE OVEN. About 15 minutes before baking, place the oven rack in the middle position and heat the oven to 425 degrees.

BAKE THE FOCACCIA. Place the baking sheet on the middle oven rack. Bake until the focaccia begins to brown around the edges, 25 to 30 minutes.

COOL AND STORE THE FOCACCIA. Remove the baking sheet to a wire rack and cool for 10 minutes. Slip a metal spatula underneath the edges of the focaccia all around to release it from the pan. Slide it onto a cutting board, cut into rectangles, and serve warm. Store cooled focaccia at room temperature in a resealable plastic bag for up to 3 days. Reheat in a 350-degree oven for 5 minutes before serving.

MUSHROOM FOCACCIA
Focaccia alle funghi

. . . .

ALLOW 8 TO 12 HOURS TO PREPARE THE SEMOLINA SOURDOUGH;

10 TO 18 MINUTES TO KNEAD;

3 TO 4 HOURS TO FERMENT;

30 TO 45 MINUTES TO PROOF;

25 TO 30 MINUTES TO BAKE

. . . .

Golden focaccia covered with a luxurious quantity of porcini mushrooms was one of my most memorable meals in Altamura. Fresh porcini can be difficult to find in the United States even when they are in season, so I've created a delicious topping using a combination of dried porcini and fresh cremini mushrooms. Cooked in a generous amount of olive oil and garlic, the small amount of porcini perfumes the whole mixture with an exotic, woodsy flavor. I love the way the porcini complement the sweet semolina crust.

**MAKES 1 SHEET PAN FOCACCIA
(39.7 OUNCES/1,125 GRAMS)**

Equipment
1 RIMMED HALF-SHEET PAN

PREPARE THE SOURDOUGH. If you have not refreshed your sourdough within the past 3 days, follow the recipe for refreshing it (page 256 for semolina sourdough, pages 79–80 for liquid *levain*, pages 114–15 for stiff dough *levain*) so that it will be in its prime. Let it stand for 8 to 12 hours at room temperature to ferment.

FOCACCIA DOUGH

INGREDIENTS	VOLUME	U.S. WEIGHT	METRIC WEIGHT	BAKER'S PERCENTAGE
Semolina sourdough (page 254)	About 1 cup	7.1 ounces	200 grams	40
Water, tepid (70 to 78 degrees)	1¾ cups	14.5 ounces	410 grams	82
Fine semolina (durum) flour	3¼ cups	17.6 ounces	500 grams	100
Sea salt	2 teaspoons	0.5 ounce	15 grams	3

TOPPING

INGREDIENTS	VOLUME	U.S. WEIGHT	METRIC WEIGHT	BAKER'S PERCENTAGE
Dried porcini mushrooms	About 1 cup	1 ounce	28 grams	—
Extra-virgin olive oil	½ cup	3.9 ounces	110 grams	—
Cremini mushrooms, thinly sliced	8 cups	1 pound	454 grams	—
8 garlic cloves, roughly chopped	¼ cup	0.9 ounce	25 grams	—
Fresh thyme, chopped	1 tablespoon	0.1 ounce	4 grams	—
Sea salt	½ teaspoon	0.1 ounce	3 grams	—
Freshly ground black pepper	⅛ teaspoon	—	—	—

MIX THE DOUGH. Measure the sourdough into a large mixing bowl or the bowl of a stand mixer. Pour the water over it. Stir with a rubber spatula to soften it slightly. There will be globs of starter. Add the semolina flour and salt, stirring just long enough to blend them into a dough.

KNEAD THE DOUGH. By hand: Turn the dough out onto a lightly floured counter. Knead with smooth, confident strokes until it is very smooth and elastic, 15 to 18 minutes. It will still be slightly sticky.

By machine: Use the dough hook and mix the dough on medium speed (4 on a KitchenAid mixer) until the dough is smooth and very elastic, 10 to 12 minutes.

FERMENT THE DOUGH. Transfer the dough to a lightly oiled, clear 2-quart container with a lid. With masking tape, mark the spot on the container that the dough will reach when it has doubled in volume. Cover and leave it to rise at room temperature (70 to 75 degrees) until it rises into a dome, doubling in volume and reaching the masking-tape mark, 3 to 4 hours.

PREPARE THE MUSHROOM TOPPING. About 1 1/2 hours before baking, place the dried porcini mushrooms in a small, heatproof bowl and cover them with boiling water. Let them soak until they have softened, about 20 minutes. While the focaccia is proofing, drain the porcini, reserving 1/2 cup of the soaking liquid. Rinse the soaked porcini to remove any grit. Roughly chop them. Pour the reserved soaking liquid through a fine strainer and into a measuring cup.

Heat 1 tablespoon olive oil in a wide, shallow pan over medium-high heat until it shimmers. Add the sliced cremini and the chopped porcini and the reserved soaking liquid. Cook the mushrooms until all of the liquid has evaporated and the mushrooms have softened and cooked down. Turn the heat down to medium and add the garlic and remaining olive oil. Cook until the garlic is softened, about 3 min-

utes. Stir in the thyme and add the salt and pepper. Scrape the mixture into a bowl and set aside to cool.

SHAPE THE FOCACCIA AND ADD THE TOPPING. Oil a half-sheet pan. Uncover the dough and turn it out onto the pan. Use your hands to stretch the dough gently to fit the pan. It will be about 1/2-inch thick. Spread the cooled mushroom mixture evenly on top of the dough.

PROOF THE FOCACCIA. Leave the focaccia to rise uncovered at room temperature (70 to 75 degrees) until it puffs around the mushrooms, 30 to 45 minutes.

PREPARE THE OVEN. About 15 minutes before baking, place the oven rack in the middle position and heat the oven to 425 degrees.

BAKE THE FOCACCIA. Place the baking sheet on the middle oven rack. Bake until the focaccia begins to brown around the edges, 25 to 30 minutes.

COOL AND STORE THE FOCACCIA. Remove the baking sheet to a wire rack and cool for 10 minutes. Slip a metal spatula underneath the edges of the focaccia all around to release it from the pan. Slide it onto a cutting board, cut into rectangles, and serve warm. Store cooled focaccia at room temperature in a resealable plastic bag for up to 3 days. Reheat in a 350-degree oven for 5 minutes before serving.

FREQUENTLY ASKED QUESTIONS ABOUT ALTAMURA BREADS

. . . .

Does Altamura bread share any flavor characteristics with pasta?
Altamura bread and dried pasta made from semolina don't share flavor characteristics, but both get their coloring from golden semolina. The high gluten

content that gives pasta its chew is also responsible for the strong structure of Altamura dough.

I'd like to try this bread, but its size is intimidating. What on earth am I going to do with such a big loaf of bread?
I get this question all the time from American students who are not in the habit of eating bread with every meal and making snacks of it too. All I can say is that once you have such a big, delicious loaf in your kitchen, I guarantee that you will find yourself eating slices of it throughout the day, just as the villagers in Altamura do. Remember, Altamura bread stays fresh for days and will probably be eaten up before it stales, even if your household is small. If you are afraid that you won't finish your bread in a week, wrap it tightly in plastic and freeze for later use.

CHAPTER 12

*

IN SEARCH OF AUTHENTIC GERMAN RYES: HIGH-TECH AND WHOLE-GRAIN BAKING ACROSS GERMANY AND AUSTRIA

*

ince I opened Bread Alone in 1983, I have had a steady stream of German American customers. Driving from New York City to their vacation homes in the Catskill Mountains, they make Bread Alone their weekend pit stop. They are always appreciative of Bread Alone's French-style ryes, but over the years quite a few of them have asked me why I didn't make the darker, seeded rye breads they remember from home. Once, two women from Bavaria brought me a moist, caramel-colored rye scented with cumin and coriander that they had lugged back from Germany, hoping that after I smelled and tasted the deliciously earthy bread, I would have no choice but to duplicate it at my bakery.

Naively, I thought it would be simple. I tasted their bread and vividly remembered other rich, stout loaves from my backpacking trips through Germany as a college student. But my attempts to recreate

these ryes at home were disasters. My breads were dense, pasty, and lifeless. Apparently all of my experience in baking French- and Italian-style breads was of no help. Those techniques were developed for doughs containing a high proportion of gluten-rich wheat. German-style rye doughs, in contrast, had much less gluten and refused to be shaped into baguettes or boules. Beyond that, my attempts were missing the complex aroma and taste of authentic dark ryes, and I suspected that my stiff rye sourdough starter, a French recipe I had adapted to make eastern European rye bread, wasn't lending enough character to the loaves.

After many such disappointments, I had to acknowledge that my memories alone could not conjure those breads. I would have to learn how to make an authentic German rye starter and how to mix and shape rye dough from bakers who had grown up with dark, sour ryes and for whom making them was second nature. Until this point, I had considered

Germany primarily as a source for fine baking equipment. I had been to Düsseldorf a couple of times to attend the big German baking show, where I had admired the state-of-the-art ovens and marveled at all the new gadgets for dividing, cutting, and shaping dough, so when I wanted to learn more about German bread, I turned to friends I knew from this world. Cindy Chananie owns the U.S. branch of Wachtel, maker of the finest German hearth ovens. She offered to introduce me to German bakers using ovens similar to the ones I had bought for Bread Alone years ago. My good friend Juergen Schwald, whose company, Brotkonig, manufactures special polyethylene-coated bread bags that keep rustic bread fresh without making its crust soggy, promised to take me to German artisan bakers who used his bags. With Cindy and Juergen as my guides, I made my first baking trip to Germany about eight years ago, in search of authentic rye breads.

During the course of several weeks I visited dozens of German bakeries and tasted hundreds of different rye breads. The bakeries I saw were a remarkable combination of new and old. Germany is known for its high-tech ovens, and most of the shops I visited had up-to-the-minute equipment and a modern feel. But the breads coming out of the state-of-the-art ovens were the same Old World ryes that German bakers were making a hundred years ago. Rye is the grain of choice in bakeries across northern Europe. It grows well in the colder climate. Rich, full-flavored rye breads, hearty but not heavy, complement the strong cheeses and cured meats, the bold soups and starchy stews that you find in the region. What surprised me most during this tour was the incredible number of shapes and styles of rye available in every bakery. In the United States, rye bread is either light or dark (although they usually taste the same) and is sometimes sprinkled with caraway seeds. But in Germany, rye isn't two or even ten kinds of bread. It is a whole spectrum of loaves, ranging from airy and light to coarse and dark. The lighter breads have more wheat flour than rye. The heartiest breads are made with all rye flour and a bounty of seeds and whole grains. Some are spiced

with cumin, fennel, and anise. I visited bakeries in Munich, Stuttgart, Hanover, and the Black Forest, and I almost never saw white bread. (Bavarian pretzels were the exception. Every baker made these with wheat flour, and I was often offered a pretzel, split, spread with mustard, topped with white sausage, and accompanied by a glass of beer, as a typical baker's breakfast.) In general, the breads in the south are made with a rye sourdough starter and a large proportion of wheat flour along with rye. Farther north there is more rye in the dough, sometimes 80 percent, often 100 percent, with whole rye berries as a bonus.

I learned about the rye spectrum from Tobias Maurer, a dynamic young German baker making traditional sourdough rye breads with the latest equipment. Tobias runs a business east of Stuttgart that's about twice the size of Bread Alone, making five to seven tons of bread a day. Typical of the modern German bakeries I saw, his operation is semiautomated, with machines mixing, preshaping, and even loading the dough into the ovens but with highly skilled bakers overseeing every step and hand-shaping the loaves when necessary. His menu lists two hundred different kinds of breads and rolls. (At Bread Alone we make about eighty bread products, an enormous selection by American standards.) The large number of breads is not at all out of the ordinary in a country where bread consumption is big and on the rise. He told me that the average German eats a kilo of bread a week—about 10 ounces of bread a day. That may sound like a lot to Americans who eat commercial white bread (two thirds of a loaf of Wonder Bread is about 10 ounces), but the whole-grain, seeded breads that Germans eat are more substantial. Before World War II, German bakers commonly made just a light and a dark rye. But German consumers now demand variety, and Tobias believes that if he doesn't provide choices, his customers will go to a baker who does. He and other German bakers I met joked about the Poilâne bread empire, incredulous and a little envious that anyone could have a successful business based on a single kind of bread. Tobias bakes breads and rolls with a myriad of grains and seeds and labels his loaves by the percentage of rye flour they contain, just as chocolate makers advertise the amount of cacao in particular bars: 50 percent, 65 percent, 80 percent, 100 percent.

In Germany, bakers must take a three-year professional course before opening a shop, and to earn the title of master baker they must study for an additional three years. This mandatory curriculum has resulted in a culture of bakers who understand and embrace every technological innovation and have learned a vast number of bread recipes from which they can pick and choose. Tobias showed me his bakery's ingenious system for storing and measuring the grains and seeds used in the breads. Computerized mini-silos stored golden flax; brown flax; sesame, poppy, pumpkin, and sunflower seeds; quinoa; cracked barley; whole rye berries; cracked rye berries; and rye flakes. The silos were programmed to release measured amounts of seeds or grain at just the right time into bowls filled with water. Attached timers alerted the bakers when the seeds and grains were thoroughly hydrated and ready to be mixed into one of the many rye bread doughs made daily. The mix-and-match possibilities were almost infinite. Seeing how technology was used in service to whole-grain bread baking warmed my heart and gave me hope for the future of the craft.

At Tobias's bakery and at every other bakery I visited in Germany, I saw that bread was raised with a brown-gray, bubbly liquid sourdough made by mixing fast-fermenting rye flour with water. Inhaling the pungent smell of overripe apples and experiencing its mouth-puckering acidity, I knew what my too-mild rye breads were missing. I observed the bakers and asked questions as they mixed and shaped the doughs, but it was difficult to get any hands-on training at these bakeries without disrupting the machinelike production process. As I was winding up my tour of bakeries in southern Germany, Juergen called and said he remembered another place that might interest me, a bakery owned by his good friend Clemens Walch. It was in Austria, just over the border and not too far out of the way. A smaller,

older place that made traditional rye breads, this was a bakery where I might be tutored in building a rye starter and making rye dough. Would I like the address? I jotted it down, along with directions, and the next day I was on my way.

Juergen had vaguely mentioned that the bakery was in the Alps but had not prepared me for its spectacular setting. As I followed his directions along increasingly twisting little mountain roads, higher and higher, I wondered exactly where this bakery was. I pulled into the town of Lech and saw that I had arrived in the Aspen of Austria, a ritzy ski resort with direct access from the village streets to the mountain via a gondola. I didn't have to search for the bakery. Driving up the main street, I saw a wood-fired oven sitting out in the snow and a baker standing in front of the oven loading it with bread dough. Skiers came directly off the mountain and into the bakery for the freshly baked loaves. Had Juergen steered me to some kind of hokey tourist attraction of a bakery? I got out of the car to find out.

This bakery in the clouds turned out to be the real thing. I walked inside and inhaled the dank smell of sourdough I had become familiar with during my tour of German bakeries. In contrast to the larger high-tech bakeries that I had seen in Germany, Clemens's Alpine shop was small and old-fashioned. Clemens, a broad-chested man with blondish red hair and pink cheeks, welcomed me heartily and told me a little about the business. His family had owned the hotel in which it was located for generations. His father was a baker who had run the small shop. Clemens went to baking school, and when he took over the business, he dedicated himself to maintaining his father's artisan traditions, baking traditional ryes using recipes he tweaked to meet his extremely high standards. Clemens now supplies all the hotels and restaurants in town with bread. No one in Lech ever has to worry about going hungry. Clemens has an extra flour silo that he keeps full, for those times when heavy snow makes flour delivery impossible. As we talked, I sampled some of his beautiful breads, bursting with seeds, aromatic from the rye, moist, light, and deeply satisfying. Clemens's breads are absolutely irresistible. Without a doubt he is one of the finest bakers I've ever met, a true artisan. He invited me to bake with him. That night, and for several nights after, Clemens taught me how to make the intense rye sourdough that I had seen throughout Germany and how to work with the soft, inelastic rye doughs, so different from the bouncy wheat doughs I had learned to make in France and Italy.

Even the strongest San Francisco sourdough is less assertive than the *saurteig* I smelled brewing here. Clemens stirred the muddy mixture, and I remarked that it was a liquid, not a stiff dough starter like the French *levain*. Liquid starters become sour more quickly, he replied. While French bakers do everything in their power to slow the fermentation process in the starter to get the mildest flavor possible, German and Austrian bakers go in the opposite direction, hurrying along fermentation by using fast-fermenting rye and a lot of water to create a hospitable environment for yeast and acids. Until I worked with Clemens, I didn't quite understand how such a sour mixture could possibly be good for bread. The rye flour caused such fast fermentation, I was sure that if I used this recipe, all the yeast would be killed by the abundant acids. With my French prejudice against acidic bread, I wondered how it was that such a sour starter didn't overpower the flavor of the grain. Clemens taught me to trust in the acidity of this starter. He explained that breads made with a lot of rye need a very acidic starter for structural reasons. Wheat breads get their structure from gluten. But rye doesn't have any gluten; it gets its structure from the sticky starches that would be broken down into sugars if not for the acids in the sourdough. This is why rye breads made with just commercial yeast are inevitably dense, with a tough, closed crumb. Their structure-building starches haven't been preserved, and the breads are unable to rise high as Clemens's breads do. German and Austrian bakers, Clemens included, often use a little commercial yeast along with the very sour starter to make sure that the bread gets a good rise. But they never skip the sourdough, because that is what rescues rye from heaviness. It might be hard to believe when you smell the pungent mixture, but the flavor that this sourdough lends to bread is only mildly sour and just deliciously earthy.

After baking with Clemens through the night, I borrowed his bright-red ski suit and spent the day on the slopes. I didn't realize at the time that this outfit, dotted with badges and emblems of Lech, was traditionally worn only by fifth-generation skiers like Clemens, and that was the reason I got so many looks and nods from old-timers as I went up and down the mountain. By lending me his ski suit, Clemens had warmly welcomed me into his community. For the next three days, as I skied during the day and baked through the night, he also welcomed me to the world of dark ryes, explaining what came naturally to him but was new to me about these breads.

Of course there was more to it than learning how to make and use rye sourdough. First he gave me a handful of the finely ground whole rye flour used in these breads. It was darker than most rye flour I had seen in the United States, because it retains all of the germ and bran. At the same time it felt powdery, not gritty, between my fingers. To make these breads, I realized, I'd have to use a finely ground whole rye flour with a similarly soft texture.

I also had a lesson in kneading rye dough. Clemens showed me how to mix and knead the sticky, inelastic dough slowly and gently. I was used to kneading wheat dough primarily to develop the gluten. With rye dough, kneading is all about blending the ingredients into a velvety smooth mass. The point isn't to wrestle the dough into submission but to let it relax. Clemens likes to give his dough a ten-minute rest in the middle of kneading. Resting the delicate dough gives it a chance to become smoother and more homogenous without any extra exertion for the baker.

He showed me how to judge when rye loaves have been sufficiently proofed. Unlike wheat dough, which will spring back when you poke it with your finger, rye dough that is ready for the oven won't spring back. Instead, it feels light and spongy to the touch.

Finally, Clemens explained why it is important to bake rye bread with heavy steam. Rye breads won't have dramatic oven spring, so you don't want to inhibit their small rise in any way. Keeping the crust moist for the first part of baking allows the breads to reach their maximum volume before the crust hardens, halting their rise.

When the breads had cooled, Clemens set some of them aside, pointing out a wonderful side benefit of baking with rye. Because rye flour is so absorbent, rye bread retains more moisture during baking than wheat bread does. This extends the bread's shelf life, keeping it fresh several days longer than sourdough bread made with wheat flour. So I wrapped up a few of these incredible breads in some of Juergen's bakery bags, packed them in my bag, and headed home, knowing that these authentic dark ryes would still be fresh when I returned from my surprise ski vacation to share them with family and friends.

❄ KITCHEN NOTES: GETTING COMFORTABLE WITH RYE

If you have baked wheat bread but are about to bake rye bread for the first time, the best advice I can give you is to park your expectations at the door. Don't expect rye dough to feel like wheat dough, don't expect it to ferment like wheat dough, and don't expect it to rise in the oven the same way wheat dough does. The German and Austrian bakers that I met did not use wheat dough as a reference point when baking their ryes. Rye was what they knew, and they worked with it on its own terms. Here is what you can expect when working with rye, so you too can bake as if you were born in the Alps.

Be prepared for rapid fermentation. Rye flour has a higher ash content (ash content is a measure of mineral content) than wheat, which fosters more rapid microbial growth and yeast activity. This is why I recommend rye sourdough to bakers who have never built a sourdough starter from scratch. It's reassuring to see how quickly rye sourdough begins to ferment. You may be able to see gases forming after just a few hours. In contrast, it

can take days for a sourdough made with mostly wheat to show visible signs of fermentation. Faster fermentation also applies to rye doughs, which rise more quickly than wheat doughs. To control fermentation, you'll want to keep your dough at room temperature (70 to 75 degrees). After you shape the loaves, watch the final proofing carefully, and if there's any question, err on the side of caution. Put them in the oven when they're slightly underproofed to get the maximum oven spring.

Use rye sourdough for structure. If you've ever baked a dense, heavy rye loaf, I can almost bet that you used packaged yeast instead of a rye sourdough starter. Rye sourdough certainly lends bread its earthy flavor, but just as important, it gives rye dough structure in the absence of structure-building gluten. Here is how it works: Amylase is an enzyme that breaks down starch, turning it into sugar. When starches in rye dough break down, the loaves collapse. If the dough contains rye sourdough, which is highly acidic, the acids will protect the starches (the pentosans), so that as the bread bakes, the starches can gelatinize, trapping the gases to give the loaf some shape. As long as you have a healthy, acidic rye sourdough and put some salt in the dough to slow fermentation, you won't have to worry about amylase breaking down your starch.

This isn't to say that you should stay away from commercial yeast when baking rye breads. German and Austrian bakers like their sourdoughs very sour, and the more acidic a sourdough gets, the less leavening power it has. They often use commercial yeast as a hedge against the possibly diminished leavening capability of the sourdough. The sourdough lends the bread flavor and structure while the commercial yeast gives it a lift.

Choose the right wheat flour. You'll notice in the recipes that contain both rye and wheat flours that the wheat flour specified is bread flour, preferably a high-gluten variety (see Resources, pages 333–34, for flour that meets this specification). The extra protein in this flour is a kind of insurance policy, guaranteeing that your bread will have a nice strong structure even though it is made with soft, gluten-free rye flour.

Embrace stickiness. You simply can't make a rye dough that isn't sticky. Rye flour doesn't contain gluten, the protein that gives wheat dough its resilient bounciness. Instead, it has sticky pentosans, starchlike chains of sugars which, when baked, trap gas and give the bread its structure. When you knead wheat dough, you are working to develop the gluten in the wheat, which makes the dough less sticky. When you knead rye dough, you are trying to hydrate the pentosans fully, which makes the dough stickier. So think of stickiness as a sign that you are kneading your way to success. Flour your hands well or oil them if you are kneading rye dough by hand. Then knead slowly and gently. If you are using a machine (definitely the easier route), use the lowest speed on the stand mixer. I recommend taking a ten-minute rest during kneading. The dough will still be sticky afterward, but it will be easier to handle because the flour will have absorbed some of the water. At any point, don't give in to the temptation to add more flour to the dough. Rye doughs with too much flour bake into coarse, grainy breads. Wet, sticky doughs become moist, tender, and light.

Bake rye bread long enough; enjoy its shelf life. Rye flour has twice as many pentosans as wheat. These starches absorb water like sponges, so rye absorbs more water. Because the dough is so moist, it will take longer to bake than a wheat loaf of the same size. The baking times in the following recipes might seem a little long; this is by design. To make sure your rye bread is not underdone, leave it in the oven for five minutes more than you would leave wheat bread. A fully baked rye loaf will register 180 degrees on an instant-read thermometer

The moisture-retaining properties of pentosans give rye a nice long shelf life, keeping it fresh and moist longer than white bread. The loaves in these chapters will be good for making sandwiches all week long.

GERMAN RYE SOURDOUGH
Sauerteig

. . . .

ALLOW 1 DAY TO ACTIVATE THE CULTURE;
2 TO 10 DAYS TO FEED THE CULTURE;
12 TO 24 HOURS TO REFRESH THE CULTURE

. . . .

German rye sourdough is a thick, porridgelike mixture of spring water and stone-ground rye flour that quickly becomes a hospitable environment for natural yeast. Of all the sourdoughs in this book, rye is the fastest to ferment and the sourest. German and Austrian bakers don't just use it for its sour flavor, however. Rye flour contains abundant amylases, enzymes that break down starches in the dough, which can result in bread with a dense, sticky crumb. The abundant acids in rye sourdough slow the breakdown of starches. Bread baked with rye sourdough is more elastic, rises higher, and has a more open, stable crumb. In short, if you use rye sourdough, you won't wind up with a rye bread doorstop.

This recipe walks you through the process of creating a rye sourdough from scratch. It takes between 4 and 10 days to activate the culture but requires just a few minutes of your time each day. It's impossible to say exactly how long the recipe will take, because the speed of fermentation depends on a host of variables, including the composition of your flour and the climate in your kitchen. The most important thing you can do is pay attention to your culture—and be patient. Stir it, smell it, taste it. This is what bakers do every day, and it is the only sure way to determine the ripeness of your culture. When you first mix the water and rye flour together, the culture will be very thick and sludgy. Over the next few days, as you mix in more water and flour—and oxygen—it will become spongy and airy, thinner and easy to stir. You'll see it come alive, growing bubbly and developing a pungent, tangy smell.

As with other sourdoughs, I recommend using spring water and organic stone-ground flour (see pages 333–34 for mail-order sources) to create the best environment for developing a culture. Tap water and highly processed flours may contain yeast- and bacteria-killing contaminants. Once you've established the rye sourdough, you can store it in the refrigerator and keep it indefinitely by feeding it once a week with fresh water and flour (see Day 11 and Beyond: Refreshing the Rye Sourdough, pages 277–78).

Equipment
CLEAN, CLEAR 2-QUART CONTAINER

DAY 1

INGREDIENTS	VOLUME	U.S. WEIGHT	METRIC WEIGHT	BAKER'S PERCENTAGE
Spring water, tepid (70 to 78 degrees)	¼ cup	2 ounces	57 grams	81
Organic, stone-ground rye flour, preferably finely ground	½ cup	2.5 ounces	70 grams	100

ACTIVATE THE CULTURE. Pour the water into the container and stir in the rye flour until it is fairly smooth. It will be quite thick. Scrape down the sides and cover the container with plastic wrap. Let it stand at room temperature (70 to 75 degrees) for 24 hours.

DAY 2

INGREDIENTS	VOLUME	U.S. WEIGHT	METRIC WEIGHT	BAKER'S PERCENTAGE
Spring water, tepid (70 to 78 degrees)	¼ cup	2 ounces	57 grams	81
Organic, stone-ground rye flour, preferably finely ground	½ cup	2.5 ounces	70 grams	100

OBSERVE AND FEED THE CULTURE. Uncover the culture and observe any changes. It's still early, but the culture may have risen slightly. It will have a sweet and musty smell and taste mildly tangy.

Pour the water into the container and stir with a rubber spatula to loosen it slightly. Add the rye flour and stir vigorously to oxygenate the culture and blend until it is smooth. It will be somewhat looser than on the previous day but still quite stiff, like oatmeal. Scrape down the sides and cover the container with plastic wrap. Let the culture stand at room temperature (70 to 75 degrees) for 24 hours.

Black Olive Cheeks
(Puccia)
ITALY
PAGE 179

Whole Spelt Loaf
(Pain à lepautre)
FRANCE
PAGE 100

Flax, Sesame, and Sunflower Ryes
(Dreikornbrot)
GERMANY
PAGE 282

Polish Cottage Rye
(Wiejski chleba)
POLAND
PAGE 327

Soulful German Farmhouse Rye
(Roggen-bauernbrot)
GERMANY
PAGE 285

Bavarian Pretzel Hamburger Buns
GERMANY
PAGE 299

Czech Christmas Braid
(Svátečni vánočka)
CZECH REPUBLIC
PAGE 315

DAY 3

INGREDIENTS	VOLUME	U.S. WEIGHT	METRIC WEIGHT	BAKER'S PERCENTAGE
Spring water, warm (85 to 95 degrees)	¼ cup	2 ounces	57 grams	81
Organic, stone-ground rye flour, preferably finely ground	½ cup	2.5 ounces	70 grams	100

OBSERVE AND FEED THE CULTURE. Today your culture will have risen up the sides of the container and may have already fallen. The surface will be bubbly, and if you hold up the container, you'll see bubbles on the sides and bottom. Smell its earthy, acidic aroma and taste the sour flavor.

Pour the water into the container and stir to loosen the sourdough. You'll notice short strands of gluten floating through the water. Add the rye flour and stir vigorously to oxygenate the culture and blend the fresh flour into the sourdough. Scrape down the sides and cover the container with plastic wrap. Let it stand at room temperature (70 to 75 degrees) for 24 hours.

DAYS 4–10

TEST THE CULTURE. Uncover the container and examine the culture to determine whether it is ripe enough to become a rye sourdough. By now it will have become a darker gray-brown and expanded dramatically, maybe doubling. It will be spongy-looking and filled with small bubbles all the way through. It will smell pungently sour and acidic, like a combination of overripe apples and moist fall leaves. When you taste it, the acid will sparkle on your tongue. If your culture doesn't show this much activity, don't worry. Repeat the steps for day 3 every 24 hours for up to 6 more days. Use warm (85 to 95 degrees) water in place of tepid water, and be sure to keep the container in a warm (75 to 80 degrees), draft-free place. You may need to transfer it to a larger container. After these additional feedings, if your culture

does not look active, the flour may have been old, the water may have been too chlorinated, or the container may not have been spotlessly clean. See page 46 for suggestions before starting again.

If your culture does look ready, repeat the recipe from day 3, but check the culture after only 12 hours. Scrape down the sides and cover the container with plastic wrap. With masking tape, mark the spot on the container that the sourdough will reach when it has doubled in volume. Let it stand at room temperature (70 to 75 degrees) for 12 hours. You'll know you have a strong, healthy sourdough when it almost doubles and is spongy and filled with large and small bubbles after 12 hours. It will smell pungent and taste tangy. Refresh the sourdough (see below) before proceeding with the rye bread recipe of your choice.

DAY 11 AND BEYOND

When you have successfully cultivated a rye sourdough, you must add water and rye flour to it on a regular basis to keep it in shape for bread baking. The yeast and bacteria that provide leavening power and great flavor need periodic nourishment. I recommend that you refresh your rye sourdough at least once a week and store it in the refrigerator when you're not baking. In the cold, it will slowly ferment. The 12- to 24-hour time range gives you flexibility to bake either in the morning or in the evening. Just be aware that the longer the sourdough ferments after refreshment, the more sour it and the bread you bake with it will be.

REFRESHING THE RYE SOURDOUGH

INGREDIENTS	VOLUME	U.S. WEIGHT	METRIC WEIGHT	BAKER'S PERCENTAGE
Spring water, warm (85 to 95 degrees)	½ cup	3.5 ounces	100 grams	133
Stone-ground rye flour, preferably finely ground	½ cup	2.6 ounces	75 grams	100

REFRESH THE SOURDOUGH. Measure 1/4 cup (1.8 ounces/50 grams) of your culture into a clean 1-quart container and discard the rest. (After you've been baking with your sourdough consistently, the exact amount is not critical; just make sure there is room in the container for the sourdough to expand.) Stir in the water and rye flour vigorously with a rubber spatula until the culture is fairly but not perfectly smooth. Scrape down the sides and cover the container with plastic wrap.

If you plan to bake, mark the container with masking tape to indicate the level the sourdough will reach when it doubles in volume. Let it stand at room temperature (70 to 75 degrees) for 12 to 24 hours. It is ready when it has expanded to twice its original size and tastes very tangy. It may already have deflated. If you do not plan to bake within 24 hours, leave the sourdough at room temperature for 1 hour and then refrigerate it.

MAINTAIN THE SOURDOUGH. If your sourdough has been in the refrigerator for a week, it is time to refresh it again, whether or not you plan on baking. Weekly refreshment will keep it alive and healthy, so that when you do bake, it will be capable of raising your dough. Just repeat the steps for refreshment and refrigerate it again for up to 1 week.

PREPARE THE SOURDOUGH FOR BAKING. Whether or not you have refreshed your sourdough recently, you must refresh it 12 to 24 hours before you want to bake to ensure that it is in optimum shape for raising and flavoring bread. Follow the refreshment steps described above. After the sourdough has fermented at room temperature (70 to 75 degrees) for 12 to 24 hours, measure out what you will need for your recipe. Then place 1/4 cup (1.8 ounces/50 grams) of what is left over in a clean container, refresh this portion, and refrigerate for up to 1 week for use in the future.

Variation: **Spelt Sourdough**

Spelt bread, made with an ancient variety of wheat, can be found in bakeries throughout Germany. Some German bakers simply use rye sourdough as the foundation for their spelt breads, but some, who want to produce 100 percent spelt loaves, use a similar starter made with spelt. To make a spelt sourdough, simply substitute whole spelt flour wherever rye flour is called for in the above recipe. The color will be different, more brownish than gray. It will rise more than a rye sour because spelt contains gluten to create pockets for trapping gases. But otherwise, spelt sourdough will work in exactly the same way as a rye starter to raise your bread.

ALPINE BAGUETTES
Alpler baguette

. . . .

ALLOW 12 TO 24 HOURS TO PREPARE THE SOURDOUGH AND SOAK THE SEEDS;

13 TO 18 MINUTES TO KNEAD;

10 MINUTES TO REST;

2 TO 2 1/2 HOURS TO FERMENT;

10 MINUTES TO REST AGAIN;

30 TO 40 MINUTES TO PROOF;

25 TO 30 MINUTES TO BAKE

. . . .

Clemens Walch inherited a memorable setting for his bakery—the base of a ski slope in the picture-perfect town of Lech in the Austrian Alps. But his bread would be unforgettable no matter where he sold it. The first time I tasted this colorful baguette, I had made my final run down the mountain and was starving. I took off my skis, walked into the shop, and tore into this incomparably flavored loaf.

Fatter and flatter than a classic French baguette, this loaf is crunchy, with a light, chewy crumb, tanned and aromatic from the rye sourdough. It is a good choice for those new to working with rye flour because the dough itself is mixed with bread flour, making it easy to handle from mixing to shaping. Clemens uses four kinds of seeds—sunflower, pumpkin, flax, and sesame—as well as rolled oats to give his bread texture and flavor. You can use any combination of seeds that you like, but I wouldn't want to make it without the pumpkin and sunflower seeds.

✳ MAKES **3** THICK BAGUETTES ABOUT **12** INCHES LONG
(**13** OUNCES/**368** GRAMS EACH)

Equipment
BAKER'S PEEL OR RIMLESS BAKING SHEET

PARCHMENT PAPER

BENCH SCRAPER OR CHEF'S KNIFE

BAKING STONE

CAST-IRON SKILLET

INGREDIENTS	VOLUME	U.S. WEIGHT	METRIC WEIGHT	BAKER'S PERCENTAGE
German rye sourdough (page 275)	About ½ cup	3.5 ounces	100 grams	20
Rolled oats	⅓ cup	1 ounce	28 grams	6
Sunflower seeds	⅓ cup	1 ounce	28 grams	6
Pumpkin seeds	⅓ cup	1 ounce	28 grams	6
Flax seeds	⅓ cup	1 ounce	28 grams	6
Sesame seeds	¼ cup	1 ounce	28 grams	6
Water, tepid (70 to 78 degrees)	2¼ cups	18.5 ounces	525 grams	105
Instant yeast	1 teaspoon	0.2 ounce	5 grams	1
Unbleached bread flour, preferably high-gluten	3¼ cups	17.6 ounces	500 grams	100
Sea salt	1½ teaspoons	0.4 ounce	10 grams	2

PREPARE THE SOURDOUGH AND SOAK THE SEEDS. Twelve to 24 hours before you plan to bake, refresh your rye sourdough following the instructions on pages 277–78. Pour the rolled oats and seeds into a small bowl and cover them with 3/4 cup (6.2 ounces/175 grams) water. Soak them overnight, uncovered, so they plump and soften.

MIX THE DOUGH. Pour the remaining 1 1/2 cups (12.3 ounces/350 grams) water into a large mixing bowl or the bowl of a stand mixer. Stir in the yeast, bread flour, soaked oats and seeds, and salt with a rubber spatula. Stir down the rye sourdough, which will have bubbled up during fermentation, to invigorate and deflate it. Measure out 1/2 cup (3.5 ounces/100 grams) of the sourdough and pour it over the dough, scraping the measuring cup clean. (Refresh and store the remaining rye sourdough following the instructions on pages 277–78.) With the spatula, work in the sourdough just enough to bind it to the dough.

KNEAD THE DOUGH. By hand: Lightly dust the counter with bread flour. Scrape the dough onto the counter and knead with smooth, steady strokes, flouring your hands as necessary, for 10 minutes. Cover the dough with plastic wrap and let it rest on the counter for 10 minutes. Uncover and continue to knead until it is smooth, silky, and elastic, 5 to 8 minutes more. The dough will be soft but not excessively sticky.

By machine: Use the dough hook and mix the dough on medium-low speed (3 on a KitchenAid mixer) for 8 minutes. Turn off the machine and scrape the hook and the sides of the bowl. Drape a piece of plastic wrap over the dough and let it rest in the bowl for 10 minutes. Turn the mixer back on to medium-low and knead until the dough is smooth, silky, and elastic, 5 to 7 minutes more.

FERMENT THE DOUGH. Transfer the dough to a lightly oiled, clear 2-quart container with a lid. With masking tape, mark the spot on the container that the dough will reach when it has doubled in volume. Cover and leave it to rise at room temperature (70 to 75 degrees) until it doubles, reaching the masking-tape mark, 2 to 2 1/2 hours. When you press your fingertip into the dough, your fingerprint will spring back slowly.

PREPARE THE OVEN. About 1 hour before baking, place a baking stone on the middle rack of the oven and a cast-iron skillet on the lower rack. Heat the oven to 450 degrees.

DIVIDE AND PRESHAPE THE BAGUETTES. Cover a baker's peel or rimless baking sheet with parchment paper. Lightly flour the counter. Uncover the dough and scrape it out. With a bench scraper or chef's knife, cut the dough into 3 equal pieces (13 ounces/368 grams each). Flatten 1 piece of the dough into a rough rectangle, fold it in thirds, like a business letter, and turn it smooth side up. Repeat with the remaining 2 pieces. Drape the pieces with plastic wrap and let rest on the counter for 10 minutes.

SHAPE THE BAGUETTES. Shape each piece of dough into a baguette about 12 inches long and 3 inches wide with rounded ends (see Shaping Baguettes, pages 37–38). Dust the parchment paper with flour and place the baguettes on it, seam side down, about 3 inches apart. Drape with plastic wrap.

PROOF THE BAGUETTES. Let the loaves rise at room temperature (70 to 75 degrees) until they look puffy and light, 30 to 40 minutes. When you press your fingertip into the dough, your fingerprint will spring back slowly.

BAKE THE BAGUETTES. Slide the loaves, still on the parchment, onto the baking stone. Place 3/4 cup of ice cubes in the skillet to produce heavy steam. Bake until the baguettes are reddish brown, 25 to 30 minutes.

COOL AND STORE THE BAGUETTES. Slide the peel or the rimless baking sheet under the parchment paper to remove the loaves from the oven. Slide the loaves, still on the parchment, onto a wire rack. Cool for about 5 minutes and then peel them off the parchment paper. Cool the loaves for about 30 minutes more and enjoy them warm. Store cooled baguettes in a brown paper bag. The sourdough will help keep them fresh for up to 2 days. Reheat in a 350-degree oven for 7 minutes to recrisp the crust. For longer storage, freeze in resealable plastic bags for up to 1 month.

FLAX, SESAME, AND SUNFLOWER RYE
Dreikornbrot

....

ALLOW 12 TO 24 HOURS TO PREPARE THE SOURDOUGH AND SOAK THE SEEDS;

13 TO 18 MINUTES TO KNEAD;

10 MINUTES TO REST;

2 TO 2 1/2 HOURS TO FERMENT;

1 TO 1 1/2 HOURS TO PROOF;

30 TO 40 MINUTES TO BAKE

....

This sunflower-crusted rye gets great chew from the flax, sesame, and sunflower seeds inside. Flax isn't familiar to most people, but it is one of my favorite bread-baking ingredients. The glossy, tiny golden brown seeds have a wonderful sweet nuttiness. Until I saw this bread at Tobias Maurer's bakery in Stuttgart, I wouldn't have believed it was possible to put so many seeds into one loaf. I had seen how an abundance of seeds can draw moisture from dough, drying out the bread as it bakes. Tobias showed me how an overnight soak softens the seeds, turning them into a gelatinous mass that does the opposite, moistening the dough as it bakes.

**MAKES 2 PAN LOAVES
(17 OUNCES/482 GRAMS EACH)**

Equipment
TWO 8 1/2-INCH-BY-4-INCH LOAF PANS
PASTRY BRUSH
BENCH SCRAPER OR CHEF'S KNIFE

INGREDIENTS	VOLUME	U.S. WEIGHT	METRIC WEIGHT	BAKER'S PERCENTAGE
German rye sourdough (page 275)	About ¼ cup	1.8 ounces	50 grams	10
Flax seeds	¼ cup	1 ounce	28 grams	6
Sesame seeds	¼ cup	1 ounce	28 grams	6
Sunflower seeds	¼ cup	1 ounce	28 grams	6
Water, tepid (70 to 78 degrees)	22 cups	10.6 ounces	300 grams	60
Instant yeast	1½ teaspoons	0.2 ounce	5 grams	1
Unbleached bread flour, preferably high-gluten	2 cups	10.6 ounces	300 grams	60
Fine or medium rye flour	1¼ cups	7.1 ounces	200 grams	40
Sea salt	1½ teaspoons	0.4 ounce	10 grams	2

TOPPING

INGREDIENTS	VOLUME	U.S. WEIGHT	METRIC WEIGHT	BAKER'S PERCENTAGE
Sunflower seeds	¼ cup	1 ounce	28 grams	—

PREPARE THE SOURDOUGH AND SOAK THE SEEDS. Twelve to 24 hours before you plan to bake, refresh your rye sourdough following the instructions on pages 277–78. Pour the flax, sesame, and 1/4 cup sunflower seeds into a small bowl and cover them with 1/2 cup (6.2 ounces/175 grams) water. Soak them overnight, uncovered, so that they plump and soften until they have absorbed all the water, becoming a gelatinous mass.

MIX THE DOUGH. Pour the remaining 1 1/2 cups (12.3 ounces/350 grams) water into a large mixing bowl or the bowl of a stand mixer. Stir in the yeast, soaked seeds, bread flour, rye flour, and salt with a rubber spatula. Stir down the rye sourdough, which will have bubbled up during fermentation, to invigorate and deflate it. Measure out 1/4 cup (1.8 ounces/50 grams) of the sourdough and pour it over the dough, scraping the measuring cup clean. (Refresh and store the remaining rye sourdough following the instructions on pages 277–78.) With the spatula, work in the sourdough just enough to bind it to the dough.

KNEAD THE DOUGH. By hand: Lightly dust the counter with bread flour. Scrape the dough onto the counter and knead with long, smooth strokes, flouring your hands as necessary, for 10 minutes. Drape the dough with plastic wrap and let it rest on the counter for 10 minutes. Uncover and continue to knead until it is firm, smooth, and slightly elastic, 5 to 8 minutes more.

By machine: Use the dough hook and mix the dough on medium-low speed (3 on a KitchenAid mixer) for 8 minutes. Turn off the machine and scrape the hook and the sides of the bowl. Drape a piece of plastic wrap over the dough and let it rest in the bowl for 10 minutes. Turn the mixer back on to medium-low and knead until the dough is firm, smooth, and slightly elastic, 5 to 7 minutes more.

FERMENT THE DOUGH. Transfer the dough to a lightly oiled, clear 2-quart container with a lid. With masking tape, mark the spot on the container that the dough will reach when it has doubled in volume. Cover and leave it to rise at room temperature (70 to 75 degrees) until it doubles, reaching the masking-tape mark, 2 to 2 1/2 hours.

DIVIDE AND SHAPE THE LOAVES. Pour the remaining 1/4 cup sunflower seeds onto a baking sheet. Have a spritzer on hand, or fill a ramekin or small bowl with water and set it aside with a pastry brush. Lightly flour the counter. Uncover the dough and scrape it out. With a bench scraper or chef's knife, cut the dough into 2 equal pieces (17 ounces/482 grams each). Shape each piece of dough into a loaf pan (see Shaping a Pan Loaf, page 40). Nestle each one into a pan, seam side down, pressing it gently to fit. Lightly spray or brush the loaf's surface with water and sprinkle with the sunflower seeds. Cover with plastic wrap.

PROOF THE LOAVES. Let the loaves rise at room temperature (70 to 75 degrees) until they have expanded to one and a half times their original size, spreading the sunflower seeds, 1 to 1 1/2 hours. When you press your finger into the dough, your fingerprint will spring back slowly.

PREPARE THE OVEN. About 20 minutes before baking, heat the oven to 400 degrees.

BAKE THE LOAVES. Place the loaves on the middle rack of the oven. Bake until they pull away from the sides of the pans and their crusts are deep brown and the sunflower seeds are well toasted, 35 to 45 minutes.

COOL AND STORE THE LOAVES. Pull the loaves from the oven. Bang the edge of the pans on the counter to release the bread. Invert them onto a wire rack and then flip right side up. Cool the bread completely before slicing, about 1 hour. Store cooled loaves in a brown paper bag at room temperature. They'll taste even better the day after you bake them.

SOULFUL GERMAN FARMHOUSE RYE
Roggen-bauernbrot

. . . .

ALLOW 12 TO 24 HOURS TO PREPARE THE SOURDOUGH;

8 TO 14 MINUTES TO KNEAD;

10 MINUTES TO REST;

2 TO 2 1/2 HOURS TO FERMENT;

1 TO 1 1/2 HOURS TO PROOF;

30 TO 40 MINUTES TO BAKE

. . . .

Rye breads this deep, dark, and sour can be found only in places like Oberseifers-dorf, Germany, where Gert Kolbe, a fifth-generation baker, has his shop. Canals still flow through the town, and a waterwheel works the mill where Gert gets his coarse whole rye flour. The grain is grown in the surrounding fields. The rolled rye flakes Gert uses as a topping make his loaves resemble the local thatched-roof houses. This hearty traditional bread in particular is why I made the trip to the bakery; I left not only with the recipe but with a long-keeping loaf that I snacked on with smoked sausages and spicy mustard on the five-hour drive back to Wiesbaden.

This dough contains so much rye that it is sticky and difficult to work with. Although it's possible to knead by hand, I recommend kneading it with a stand mixer. Because it doesn't have much wheat flour and therefore doesn't develop much gluten, the dough won't rise as high as bread dough made with wheat during fermentation or in the oven.

MAKES 2 ROUNDS
(15.6 OUNCES/443 GRAMS EACH)

Equipment

2 BANNETONS OR 2 SHALLOW BOWLS (6 INCHES WIDE AND 4 INCHES DEEP) LINED WITH 2 KITCHEN TOWELS

BENCH SCRAPER OR CHEF'S KNIFE

BAKER'S PEEL OR RIMLESS BAKING SHEET

PARCHMENT PAPER

SINGLE-EDGED RAZOR BLADE OR SERRATED KNIFE

INGREDIENTS	VOLUME	U.S. WEIGHT	METRIC WEIGHT	BAKER'S PERCENTAGE
German rye sour-dough (page 275)	About ½ cup	3.5 ounces	100 grams	20
Water, tepid (70 to 78 degrees)	1½ cups	12.3 ounces	350 grams	70
Instant yeast	1 teaspoon	0.2 ounce	5 grams	1
Rye flour	2¼ cups	12.3 ounces	350 grams	70
Unbleached bread flour, preferably high-gluten	¾ cup	4.6 ounces	130 grams	26
Wheat germ	1 tablespoon	0.7 ounce	20 grams	4
Toasted and ground coriander seeds	¼ teaspoon	—	—	—
Toasted and ground cumin seeds	¼ teaspoon	—	—	—
Toasted and ground fennel seeds	¼ teaspoon	—	—	—
Toasted and ground anise seeds	¼ teaspoon	—	—	—
Sea salt	1½ teaspoons	0.4 ounce	10 grams	2

TOPPING

INGREDIENTS	VOLUME	U.S. WEIGHT	METRIC WEIGHT	BAKER'S PERCENTAGE
Rolled rye flakes	1 cup	2.8 ounces	80 grams	—

PREPARE THE SOURDOUGH. Twelve to 24 hours before you plan to bake, refresh your rye sourdough following the instructions on pages 277–78.

MIX THE DOUGH. Pour the water into a large mixing bowl or the bowl of a stand mixer. Stir in the yeast, rye flour, bread flour, wheat germ, coriander, cumin, fennel, anise, and salt with a rubber spatula. Stir down the rye sourdough, which will have bubbled up during fermentation, to invigorate and deflate it. Measure out 1/2 cup (3.5 ounces/100 grams) of the sourdough and pour it over the dough, scraping the measuring cup clean. (Refresh and store the remaining rye sourdough following the instructions on pages 277–78.) With the spatula, work in the sourdough just enough to bind it to the dough.

KNEAD THE DOUGH. By hand: Lightly dust the counter with bread flour. Scrape the dough onto the counter and knead with smooth, consistent strokes, more to incorporate the ingredients thoroughly than to develop any elasticity, for 8 minutes. Flour your hands as necessary but resist adding extra flour to the dough. The dough will be soft but not excessively sticky. Cover the dough with plastic wrap and let it rest on the counter for 10 minutes. Uncover and continue to knead until it is soft, still somewhat ragged, and barely elastic, 4 to 6 minutes more.

By machine: Use the dough hook and mix the dough on low speed (2 on a KitchenAid mixer) for 5 minutes. Turn off the machine and scrape the hook and the sides of the bowl. Drape a piece of plastic wrap over the dough and let it rest in the bowl for 10 minutes. Turn the mixer back on to medium-low (3 on a KitchenAid mixer) and knead until the dough is soft, still somewhat ragged, and barely elastic, 3 to 5 minutes more.

FERMENT THE DOUGH. Transfer the dough to a lightly oiled, clear 2-quart container with a lid. With masking tape, mark the spot on the container that the dough will reach when it has risen one and a half times in volume. Cover and leave it to rise at room temperature (70 to 75 degrees) until it has increased one and a half times in size, reaching the masking-tape mark, 2 to 2 1/2 hours. It will look spongy and lighter in color.

DIVIDE AND SHAPE THE ROUNDS. Heavily dust 2 bannetons or shallow bowls lined with kitchen towels with the rye flakes. Lightly flour the counter. Uncover the dough and scrape it out. With a bench scraper or chef's knife, cut the dough into 2 equal pieces (15.6 ounces/443 grams each). Shape each piece into a round (see Shaping Rounds, page 36). Handle the fragile dough gently. The rounds will not look perfectly smooth. Place them smooth side down in the bannetons or bowls. Cover them with plastic wrap.

PROOF THE ROUNDS. Let the loaves rise at room temperature (70 to 75 degrees) until they inflate slightly and the surface looks smoother, 1 to 1 1/2 hours.

PREPARE THE OVEN. About 1 hour before baking, place a baking stone on the middle rack of the oven and a cast-iron skillet on the lower rack. Heat the oven to 450 degrees.

SCORE THE ROUNDS. Cover a baker's peel or rimless baking sheet with parchment paper and dust it with rye flour. Uncover the loaves and tip them out onto the peel or baking sheet, guiding each loaf with one hand for a soft landing. With a single-edged razor blade or serrated knife, make two sets of crisscrossing cuts, like a tick-tack-toe board.

BAKE THE ROUNDS. Slide the loaves, still on the parchment, onto the baking stone. Place 3/4 cup of ice cubes in the skillet to produce heavy steam. Bake until the rounds are dark walnut-brown, 30 to 40 minutes. They will not rise dramatically during baking.

COOL AND STORE THE ROUNDS. Slide the peel or the rimless baking sheet under the parchment paper to remove the loaves from the oven. Slide the loaves, still on the parchment, onto a wire rack. Cool for about 5 minutes and then peel them off the parchment paper. Cool the loaves completely, about 1 hour, before slicing very thin. The loaves are best eaten the day *after* baking. They will stay fresh for 4 to 5 days stored in a brown paper bag at room temperature. For longer storage, freeze in resealable plastic bags for up to 1 month.

SPICED RYE ROLLS
Vingchter

. . . .

ALLOW 12 TO 24 HOURS TO PREPARE THE SOURDOUGH;

15 TO 17 MINUTES TO KNEAD;

10 MINUTES TO REST;

2 TO 2 1/2 HOURS TO FERMENT;

30 TO 40 MINUTES TO PROOF;

20 TO 25 MINUTES TO BAKE

. . . .

When I visited Clemens Walch's bakery in the Austrian Alps very early one morning (it was about 3 A.M.), I was greeted by a strong, spicy smell. It drew me to a large bowl sitting at the back of the bakery, full of a pasty dough seasoned with an alluring combination of ground fennel and cumin. I watched as the bakers scooped the dough out by hand and let it fall into individual, irregular rolls. It was amazingly soft and puddly. I had seen dough this soft in Italy, but this dough was dark with rye flour, making it more fragile than Italian wheat doughs. Once the rolls were baked, I joined the bakers for breakfast, slicing a couple of rolls in half and making sandwiches with air-dried beef.

This is a very sticky, wet dough that's best mixed by machine. Be confident but gentle with it, and don't expect it to behave like wheat dough. It will feel more like batter than bread dough, and won't hold its shape.

**MAKES 9 SANDWICH ROLLS
(4 OUNCES/112 GRAMS EACH)**

Equipment
HEAVY-DUTY STAND MIXER WITH DOUGH HOOK
2 BAKING SHEETS
PARCHMENT PAPER
CAST-IRON SKILLET

INGREDIENTS	VOLUME	U.S. WEIGHT	METRIC WEIGHT	BAKER'S PERCENTAGE
German rye sourdough (page 275)	About 1/2 cup	3.5 ounces	100 grams	20
Water, warm (85 to 95 degrees)	1 2/3 cups	13.4 ounces	380 grams	76
Instant yeast	1 1/2 teaspoons	0.3 ounce	8 grams	2
Fine or medium rye flour	2 1/2 cups	13.4 ounces	380 grams	76
Unbleached bread flour, preferably high-gluten	3/4 cup	4.2 ounces	120 grams	24
Sea salt	1 1/2 teaspoons	0.4 ounce	10 grams	2
Toasted and ground fennel seeds	1/4 teaspoon	—	—	—
Toasted and ground cumin seeds	1/4 teaspoon	—	—	—

PREPARE THE SOURDOUGH. Twelve to 24 hours before you plan to bake, refresh your rye sourdough following the instructions on pages 277–78.

MIX THE DOUGH. Pour the water into a large mixing bowl or the bowl of a stand mixer. Stir in the yeast, rye flour, bread flour, salt, fennel, and cumin with a rubber spatula. Stir down the rye sourdough, which will have bubbled up during fermentation, to invigorate and deflate it. Measure out 1/2 cup (3.5 ounces/100 grams) of the sourdough and pour it over the dough, scraping the measuring cup clean. (Refresh and store the remaining rye sourdough following the instructions on pages 277–78.) With the spatula, work in the sourdough just enough to bind it to the dough.

KNEAD THE DOUGH. By machine: Use the dough hook and mix the dough on low speed (2 on a KitchenAid mixer) for 8 minutes. Turn off the machine and scrape the hook and the sides of the bowl. Drape a piece of plastic wrap over the dough and let it rest in the bowl for 10 minutes. Turn the mixer back on to medium-low (3 on a KitchenAid mixer) and knead until the dough is smooth and slightly elastic, 7 to 9 minutes. This sticky dough will not clear the sides of the bowl, but you will see strands of gluten pulling away from the hook.

FERMENT THE DOUGH. Transfer the dough to a lightly oiled, clear 2-quart container with a lid. With masking tape, mark the spot on the container that the dough will reach when it has doubled in volume. Cover and leave it to rise at room temperature (70 to 75 degrees) until it doubles, reaching the masking-tape mark, 2 to 2 1/2 hours. It will be noticeably less sticky.

SCOOP THE ROLLS INTO SHAPE. Cover two baking sheets with parchment paper and dust generously with rye flour. Oil your hands. Reach into the container and scoop out palm-sized portions of dough (about 4 ounces/112 grams each). Let them plop onto the parchment in free-form shapes, like drop biscuits. Space them at least 2 inches apart. Sift rye flour over the tops of the rolls and cover them with plastic wrap.

PROOF THE ROLLS. Let the rolls rise at room temperature (70 to 75 degrees) until they have spread and look pillowy, 30 to 40 minutes.

PREPARE THE OVEN. About 15 minutes before baking, place one oven rack in the top third of the oven and a second rack in the middle. Place a third rack as low as possible in the oven and place a cast-iron skillet on it. Heat the oven to 450 degrees.

BAKE THE ROLLS. Place the baking sheets on the top two oven racks. Place 3/4 cup of ice cubes in the skillet to produce heavy steam. After 10 minutes, switch the positions of the baking sheets for even baking. Continue to bake until the rolls are crisp, with a reddish brown crust, 20 to 25 minutes.

COOL AND STORE THE ROLLS. Transfer the baking sheets onto wire racks and cool the rolls for 5 minutes before serving warm. Store cooled rolls in a resealable plastic bag at room temperature for 3 to 4 days. For longer storage, freeze in resealable plastic bags for up to 1 month.

WHOLE RYE BERRY LOAF
Volkornbrot

· ·

ALLOW 12 TO 24 HOURS TO BUILD THE SOURDOUGH AND SOAK THE RYE BERRIES;
1 TO 1 1/2 HOURS TO FERMENT;
45 MINUTES TO 1 HOUR TO PROOF;
1 3/4 TO 2 HOURS TO BAKE

· ·

Volkornbrot ("whole kernel bread") is a 100 percent dark rye bread, chewy and thick with whole rye berries, the kernels of rye that are ground into flour. It is a staple throughout Germany and Austria, where it was served for breakfast in ultra-thin slices at every hotel, guesthouse, and inn I visited. I spoiled myself by enjoying this moist bread spread with good European butter every morning.

Because so much more—ten times more—rye sourdough is used than in most of the other recipes, I've included a refreshment step bakers call a "build" to make just the right amount. The dough itself is not a typical bread dough but more like a quick bread. It is a stirrable batter spooned into a loaf pan. Because it is wheat-free and has little gluten, there is no need to knead.

Traditionally, German bakers shape *volkornbrot* into a perfect rectangle by using a special pan with a lid, called a Pullman loaf pan (see Resources, pages 333–34). You can improvise one by putting a baking sheet on top of a loaf pan and weighing it down with a heavy ovenproof object like a cast-iron skillet. Or you can just bake the bread uncovered.

This bread is baked low and slow—325 degrees for about 2 hours—so the crumb becomes moist and sweet and a thin crust forms. It improves after baking because the moisture continues to redistribute throughout the loaf, and is best 12 hours or more after it comes out of the oven.

✳ **MAKES 1 SANDWICH LOAF**
(18 OUNCES/510 GRAMS)

Equipment

ONE 8 1/2-BY-4 1/2-BY-2 1/2-INCH LOAF PAN

BAKING SHEET

CAST-IRON SKILLET

SHEET PAN AND OVENPROOF WEIGHT SUCH AS A CAST-IRON SKILLET (OPTIONAL)

RYE SOURDOUGH

INGREDIENTS	VOLUME	U.S. WEIGHT	METRIC WEIGHT	BAKER'S PERCENTAGE
German rye sourdough (page 275)	About 1/4 cup	1.8 ounces	50 grams	33
Water, tepid (70 to 78 degrees)	1/2 cup	4 ounces	112 grams	75
Rye flour, preferably finely ground	1 cup	5.3 ounces	150 grams	100

RYE BERRIES

INGREDIENTS	VOLUME	U.S. WEIGHT	METRIC WEIGHT	BAKER'S PERCENTAGE
Whole or cracked rye berries	2/3 cup	4.4 ounces	125 grams	—
Water, boiling	3/4 cup	6.2 ounces	175 grams	—

PREPARE THE SOURDOUGH AND SOAK THE RYE BERRIES. Twelve to 24 hours before you plan to bake, refresh your rye sourdough and build enough for the bread. Measure out 1/4 cup (1.8 ounces/50 grams) of rye sourdough. (Refresh and store the remaining rye sourdough following the instructions on pages 277–78.) Scrape it into a large mixing bowl or the bowl of a stand mixer. With a rubber spatula, stir in the water and rye flour to make a smooth, thick paste. Cover the bowl with plastic wrap and leave it to ferment at room temperature.

Pour the rye berries into a small bowl. Pour the boiling water over the berries and leave them to soak, uncovered, at room temperature until they swell and soften, absorbing all the water.

BREAD DOUGH				
INGREDIENTS	VOLUME	U.S. WEIGHT	METRIC WEIGHT	BAKER'S PERCENTAGE
Rye sourdough	About 2 cups	14.1 ounces	400 grams	200
Water, tepid (70 to 78 degrees)	¼ cup	1.8 ounces	50 grams	25
Soaked rye berries	⅔ cup	4.4 ounces	125 grams	—
Rye flour, preferably finely ground	1⅓ cups	7.1 ounces	200 grams	100
Sea salt	1½ teaspoons	0.4 ounce	10 grams	5

MIX THE DOUGH. Uncover the bowl of rye sourdough. It will be darker in color than when you mixed it and will have doubled in volume. It will look spongy and smell tangy and effervescent.

By hand: Pour the water over the sourdough and stir with a rubber spatula to loosen it. Add the soaked rye berries, flour, and salt and stir with the spatula until the ingredients combine into a thick, batterlike dough.

By machine: Pour the water into the mixing bowl. Add the sourdough, soaked rye berries, flour, and salt. With the paddle, mix the dough on low speed (2 on a KitchenAid mixer) until the ingredients combine into a thick, batterlike dough, 1 to 2 minutes.

FERMENT THE DOUGH. Cover the bowl with plastic wrap and let it stand at room temperature (70 to 75 degrees) until it has risen slightly, by approximately one third its original volume, 1 to 1 1/2 hours. If you sweep through the dough with a rubber spatula or your fingers, you'll notice that it has developed a light, spongy quality.

PUT THE DOUGH IN THE PAN. Generously oil a loaf pan with vegetable oil and coat it with rye flour,

tapping out any excess. With a rubber spatula, scrape the dough into the pan, smoothing it into the corners. Cover the loaf with plastic wrap.

PROOF THE LOAF. Let the loaf rise at room temperature (70 to 75 degrees) for 45 minutes to 1 hour. It will rise only slightly but will form a dome.

PREPARE THE OVEN. About 15 minutes before baking, set an oven rack in the middle position and a cast-iron skillet on the lower rack. Heat the oven to 325 degrees.

BAKE THE LOAF. For a perfectly rectangular loaf, oil the bottom of a sheet pan and set it on top of the loaf pan. Weight it with a cast-iron pan or another heavy ovenproof object. Place the loaf pan on the oven rack. Place 3/4 cup of ice cubes in the skillet to produce heavy steam. Bake until the loaf shrinks from the sides and a cake tester or wooden skewer inserted in the center comes out clean, 1 3/4 to 2 hours. If you covered the loaf, remove the sheet pan to check it. If the loaf needs to bake longer, you can leave the cover off for the remaining time.

COOL AND STORE THE LOAF. Remove the loaf to a wire rack. Cool for 10 minutes in the pan before turning the pan over and releasing the bread. Let the loaf cool completely on the rack, at least 2 hours. It's best to wait at least 12 hours (and up to 24 hours) before slicing and eating. Cut into 1/4-inch-thick slices. Store the cooled loaf in a resealable plastic bag for 1 week or more.

BAVARIAN PRETZELS
Laugenbrezeln

....

ALLOW 9 TO 12 MINUTES TO KNEAD;
45 MINUTES TO 1 HOUR TO FERMENT;
2 TO 24 HOURS TO RETARD;
1 MINUTE TO 1 MINUTE AND 20 SECONDS TO BOIL;
30 TO 35 MINUTES TO BAKE

....

Every bakery in Germany makes pretzels, boiling them before baking them to gelatinize the starches on the surface, making the crust chewy like a good bagel's. They are the national snack food and a traditional baker's breakfast. This recipe was given to me by the bakers at Grimmingers, in Munich. Every morning, after finishing off the night's bread baking, they make these pretzels and then sit down to a breakfast of pretzels slathered with sweet mustard, sausages, and beer.

❋ **MAKES 8 LARGE PRETZELS
(3.8 OUNCES/108 GRAMS EACH)**

Equipment
1 BAKING SHEET
BENCH SCRAPER OR CHEF'S KNIFE
WIDE 6-QUART POT
SLOTTED SPOON

INGREDIENTS	VOLUME	U.S. WEIGHT	METRIC WEIGHT	BAKER'S PERCENTAGE
Unbleached bread flour	3¼ cups	17.6	500	100
Unsalted butter, chilled and cut into ½-inch pieces	3 tablespoons	1.4 ounces	40 grams	8
Water, tepid (70 to 78 degrees)	1¼ cups	10.6 ounces	300 grams	60
Instant yeast	1 teaspoon	0.2 ounce	5 grams	1
Sea salt	2¼ teaspoons	0.5 ounce	15 grams	3
Baking soda for boiling	⅓ cup	2.8 ounces	80 grams	—

TOPPINGS

INGREDIENTS	VOLUME	U.S. WEIGHT	METRIC WEIGHT	BAKER'S PERCENTAGE
Kosher salt	¼ cup	2 ounces	57 grams	—
Sesame seeds	⅓ cup	2 ounces	57 grams	—

MIX AND KNEAD THE DOUGH. By hand: Place the flour in a large mixing bowl. Crumble the butter into the flour by rubbing handfuls of flour and butter through your fingers, as if you are making pie dough. Lift and crumble rapidly until the mixture has the consistency of coarse cornmeal. Pour in the water and stir until it is absorbed. Sprinkle the yeast on one half of the dough and the salt on the other half. With a rubber spatula, work them both into the dough. Lightly flour the counter and turn out the dough. It will be very stiff. Knead with firm strokes until it is very smooth, muscular, and pliable, 10 to 12 minutes.

By machine: Place the flour in the bowl of a stand mixer. With the paddle attachment, stir in the butter on low speed (2 on a Kitchen Aid mixer) until it is distributed and the dough has the consistency of coarse cornmeal, 1 to 2 minutes. Pour in the water and sprinkle on the yeast and the salt. Switch to the dough hook and knead on medium (4 on a KitchenAid mixer) until it is very smooth, muscular, and pliable, 8 to 10 minutes.

FERMENT THE DOUGH. Shape the dough into a ball and place it in an oiled bowl. Cover with plastic wrap and let stand at room temperature (70 to 75 degrees) until it has slightly expanded and risen to a dome and feels light and springy, 45 minutes to 1 hour.

DIVIDE AND SHAPE THE PRETZELS. Lightly oil a baking sheet. Turn the dough out onto an unfloured countertop. Pat into a rough rectangle. With a bench scraper or chef's knife, cut the dough into 8 equal pieces (3.8 ounces/108 grams each). Round each piece and let them rest, covered with plastic wrap, for 5 minutes. On a bare countertop, roll each piece into a pencil shape about 18 inches long. Taper the ends slightly. Curve each pencil into a half circle. Shape each pencil into a pretzel by overlapping the ends inward to form a loop. Flip the bottom end over the top end to form a twist where they intersect. Lift the twisted ends and lay them on top of the loop to make the pretzel shape. Gently press the ends to seal. Arrange the pretzels on the baking sheet at least 1 inch apart. Cover with plastic wrap.

1. Roll each piece of dough into a pencil shape about 18 inches long. Taper ends slightly.

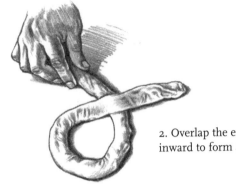

2. Overlap the ends inward to form a loop.

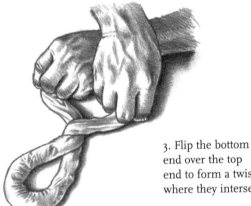

3. Flip the bottom end over the top end to form a twist where they intersect.

4. Lift the twisted ends.

5. Lay the ends on top of the pretzel and gently press them to seal.

RETARD THE PRETZELS. Place the baking sheet in the refrigerator for 2 to 24 hours. The pretzels will not rise significantly but will be chilled and will hold their shape while handling. Remove them from the refrigerator when you are ready to boil them.

PREPARE THE OVEN. About 15 minutes before baking, place an oven rack in the middle position. Heat the oven to 350 degrees.

BOIL THE PRETZELS. Bring 4 quarts of water to boil in a wide pot. Add the baking soda slowly, about 1 tablespoon at a time. (The baking soda will cause the water to bubble wildly.) Turn the heat down to a simmer. Uncover the pretzels and slip them into the pot one at a time. Allow each one to rise to the surface and float before adding another. Boil 3 or 4 at a time, being careful not to overcrowd the pot. Simmer on one side for 15 to 20 seconds and then flip them over with a slotted spoon and simmer on the other side for another 15 to 20 seconds. They will inflate. Remove the boiled pretzels from the water with the slotted spoon, draining them well, and place them back on the baking sheet at least 1 inch apart. Repeat with the remaining pretzels.

BAKE THE PRETZELS. Sprinkle the pretzels with kosher salt or sesame seeds, or both. Place the baking sheet in the oven and bake the pretzels until they are reddish brown, 30 to 35 minutes.

COOL AND STORE THE PRETZELS. Remove the baking sheet to a wire rack and let the pretzels cool on the baking sheet for 10 minutes (if you can wait that long!). Enjoy them still warm from the oven.

Store them in a plastic bag to keep them moist enough to slice for sandwiches, 1 to 2 days. In a paper bag they will become hard, like Pennsylvania Dutch pretzels, and make crunchy afternoon treats that are especially good dipped in coarse-grained mustard.

FREQUENTLY ASKED QUESTIONS ABOUT GERMAN AND AUSTRIAN RYE BREADS

. . . .

You say that rye sourdough is the fastest-fermenting sourdough. How can I tell if mine is too sour? If it does get too sour, what should I do?

It's true that if rye sourdough is left to ferment too long, it will lose its leavening capabilities. But it's difficult to tell by taste or smell whether or not the culture is too sour, because this kind of sourdough becomes very sour-tasting within 6 to 8 hours. To be safe, use it within 24 hours of refreshing it. If it's older than this, refresh it and let it stand for 8 to 12 hours before mixing it into bread dough.

What is the difference between rye flour and pumpernickel flour?

Usually flour that is called pumpernickel is a coarser grind of whole rye than the finely ground rye flour I like to use in these recipes. I go to a specialty mill for finely ground whole rye that is much like Clemens's powdery but dark flour. Supermarket rye labeled "medium" is whole, finely ground rye flour and will

---

Variation: Bavarian Pretzel Hamburger Buns

Instead of twisting the dough into pretzel shapes, you can simply divide it into 8 equal pieces, round each piece into a roll shape (see Shaping Rounds, page 36), and continue as directed, boiling and then baking the rolls for the same amount of time as you would the pretzels.

work in any of these recipes, but for the most authentic breads, it's worth seeking out organic, stone-ground flour, which has even more germ and bran than commercial whole rye. Rye flour can also be processed to remove its germ and bran, in which case it will be labeled "white rye." White rye flour is used in Polish- and Czech-style rye breads (see Chapter 13 for recipes).

What exactly are flax seeds? Is there a flavor difference between brown and golden? Why do they become so gelatinous when soaked, and what effect does that have on bread dough when it is baked?

The flax plant is an ancient crop that yields the fiber from which linen is woven as well as seeds and oil used in cooking. Flax seeds have received quite a bit of attention in the news lately for their supposed health benefits. The oil in the seeds is highly unsaturated and heart-healthy. They are full of antioxidants that may boost the immune system. The seeds are high in lignans, a kind of dietary fiber that has been studied for its cancer-preventing properties. Flax seeds are extremely high in both soluble and insoluble fiber, and when soaked in water, the hydrated fiber makes the seeds swell and gel. When soaked and then kneaded into bread dough, flax seeds lend moisture to the dough and help extend the shelf life of the bread. The oil from the seeds also lends moisture and flavor to the bread. There are no nutritional or flavor differences between brown and golden seeds, and they are used interchangeably.

I am very interested in high-altitude baking, since I live in the American Rockies. How does a baker like Clemens Walch tailor his recipes and techniques to the altitude of the Alps? Did you make any changes to his recipes that I should be aware of?

The air is drier at high altitude, which makes bread dough more fragile. Clemens adds less water to his doughs than I do in these recipes, so the dough is a little bit sturdier.

CHAPTER 13

❋

DISCOVERING NEW RYES IN THE CZECH REPUBLIC AND POLAND AND REMEMBERING MY GRANDPARENTS' LIGHT RYE

❋

I was born and raised in a section of Buffalo, New York, largely populated by Eastern European Jewish immigrants. All of my grandparents were from Russia or Poland, and the rye bread that they bought weekly at Mastman's deli in our mostly Polish neighborhood was the first bread I tasted and the bread I ate throughout my childhood. Because of that, even though I traveled extensively through France, Italy, Germany, and Austria to collect recipes for my business and this book, I still felt there was a gap in my coverage of European artisan bread as I was setting down these recipes on paper. I felt the lack of the Polish-style rye bread I remembered eating with corned beef, chopped chicken livers, and my maternal grandmother's beef and barley soup. This bread was nothing like the dark, sour, earthy rye breads I had eaten in Germany and Austria. It was dense and moist, with a cakelike light gray crumb and a beautiful perfume of rye and caraway. I wished that I could travel back in time, or

travel to Eastern Europe, to get a recipe for that bread.

The more I thought about it, the more I knew I had to make an attempt. At the time, in October 2002, Prague seemed like the most accessible place to search for the relative of my grandparents' rye. I called the Czech tourism board in New York, and they arranged for me to visit a half-dozen bakeries in and around Prague with a translator. It wasn't as personal as Poland, but I didn't have any contacts in Poland, so Prague looked like the closest I could get to the kind of bread I was looking for. Then, as had so often happened to me in the past, my wish to learn about a new bread was granted in an entirely unexpected way.

For several years I had noted the growing number of Eastern European customers at Bread Alone. I hear Polish, Russian, and Czech spoken all the time now in the bakery and cafés. In October 2002, just days after buying my ticket to Prague, I heard a man and a woman speaking Polish at the Bread Alone café in Boiceville. I recognized the man—about forty years old and blond, with broad, Slavic features—as a regular customer, so I walked over to introduce myself. His name was Eugene Forycki, and he told me that he was an antiques dealer in the city. He and his friend, the Polish-speaking woman next to him, had a weekend house nearby, and he had been buying my rye and peasant loaves for several years. Our ryes reminded him of those in his birthplace, Wroclaw, in southwestern Poland, he said, but weren't quite the same. I excitedly told him about my upcoming trip, described the bread at Mastman's, and confided that I really wanted to go to Poland but didn't know anyone there and wouldn't know where to start to look for the best bakeries making traditional rye breads. "Wroclaw is just a short train ride from Prague," he exclaimed. "I will help you find what you are seeking—Silesian rye bread." We exchanged e-mail addresses, and within two hours I received an invitation from his brother Zbigniew to come and tour the bakeries of Wroclaw, "It will be worth the trip," Zbigniew promised. In a few weeks I was on my way to Prague and Wroclaw. Eating rye bread in both places, I was reminded of my boyhood fascination with bread. I discovered remarkable breads during my journey, and I also rediscovered my origins as a baker.

I arrived in Prague eager to begin my search for breads that would satisfy my Eastern European customers as well as my memory. The search began inauspiciously. Leaving the Prague airport and driving toward the city center, I couldn't help but notice endless rows of Soviet-era block housing, referred to as "rabbit cages" by the cab driver. I hoped that handmade Czech bread had not been similarly replaced by a shoddy modern product. My translator, a tall, twenty-five-year-old linguistics student with a shiny brown ponytail, met me at my hotel. Her name was Eva Franka, and not only was her English perfect, but she was the daughter of a baker. I was disheartened, though, when she immediately took me not to a real Czech bakery but to the nearest supermarket. Expecting the worst, I was instead awed when, right inside the entrance to the store, we encountered the most massive mountain of bread I had ever seen, a towering display of at least five thousand gorgeous, sand-colored rounds with visible coil marks from being fermented in willow baskets. This was *chleba* (page 308), which simply means "bread" in both Czech and Polish but also signifies the basic wheat-and-rye loaf that Czechs and Poles eat with every meal. Customers crowded around the bread, grabbing loaves on their way into the store. As the breads quickly disappeared, they were just as quickly replenished. Eva told me that the display would shrink and grow many times throughout the day.

When I tasted this light rye sourdough sprinkled with caraway seeds, right at the checkout counter, I was immediately reminded of the rye bread I loved as a boy. This bread, fragrant with rye and caraway, had a milder flavor than German and Austrian all-rye breads, although it was a little more assertively sour than the bread I remembered from Buffalo. Its crumb was light gray, moist, and spongy. Its thick, chewy crust was reddish gold. We didn't make anything like it at Bread Alone, but I hoped we would soon. Eva and I visited a couple more supermarkets and the scene was similar. Impressed with the obvious love that consumers had for the bread, I asked her to take me to some of the bakeries where it was made.

We drove to a large Soviet-era bakery a couple of miles from the first supermarket. On the way there, Eva explained that during communism, bread baking had been taken over by the state. Small, privately owned bakeries closed. The city was carved up into territories, and large new bakeries supplied their territories with loaves. Amazingly, this industrialization of baking did not spell the end of the artisan tradition. Apparently the state bakeries were set up to control quality and keep prices down while producing traditional breads. When we arrived at our destination, the head baker graciously gave us a tour and explained how *chleba* was made. He had worked here since before the fall of the Berlin Wall, and explained to us that then, as now, no corners were cut to produce the same kind of rye bread that had been made in small shops before World War II. He showed us vats of liquid rye sourdough like the mixture I had seen in German bakeries. But this sourdough was allowed to ferment for only four hours before the bakers diluted the acids by stirring in fresh water and rye flour. Frequent refreshment resulted in the mildly sour bread I had tasted at the supermarket. How different this was from the way German bakers deliberately left their cultures to ferment for hours or even days to produce their distinctly acidic loaves!

We strode down assembly lines where dozens of bakers hand-shaped rounds and placed them in willow proofing baskets on automated conveyors. More bakers stood at stations at the other end of the conveyors, hand-scoring the proofed loaves before the conveyor loaded them into the oven. Unlike the bread from big factories in the United States, which are never touched by human hands, these breads were essentially handmade.

Later in the day, at a huge bakery in Pelhřimov, a small town just outside of Prague, I saw just how far Czechs would go to ensure quality in an industrial setting. The bakery was a plain, warehouselike structure made of shiny glazed bricks. On one end of the long, low building were a couple of silos. At the other end were loading docks for delivery trucks. Like the other bakeries I had already seen, this one had a special room solely for fermenting the rye sourdough, it had willow proofing baskets, it had bakers hand-scoring the loaves. But it also had something I had never seen in a bakery before: its very own mill. One silo, it turned out, held locally grown rye, which was milled right at the bakery, then stored in the other silo. The bakers were constantly assessing new crops of grain, monitoring the flour, and adjusting the milling specifications to suit the bread. It was easy, since the mill and the bakery were built to work together. I ran my fingers through some of the finely ground white rye flour. I could tell from the slightly gritty texture and pale golden color that even though this was white rye flour, it had been lightly processed, with some of the germ left behind.

Eva arranged a surprise for me on my final day in Prague. The Czech baking association was sponsoring a competition for cooking schools around the country, all of which had been established in the past couple of years. She had asked the president of the association if I could observe as fifteen teams baked traditional breads and pastries to see which school was the best. The competition's aims were to build pride in traditional techniques for making *chleba* and to showcase the expertise of the schools' students and bring prestige to the schools. Prizewinning team members would be recruited by big bakeries looking for fresh talent. Privatization had led to an intensely competitive environment among bakers. Since territories were no longer handed over to bakeries by the state, any bakery could try to sell bread to any market. The new owners of the bakeries were convinced that better bread would lead to bigger market share and bigger profits. Bread traditions in Prague had been preserved during communism. The proliferation of baking schools and the establishment of this competition were evidence that artisan baking was undergoing a renaissance. Now that the bakeries were privately held, the people would decide what they would buy and where they would buy it.

The Czech baking association had converted a former police station on the outskirts of the city into a temporary bakery, with ovens and exhaust systems carted in just for the competition. When we arrived, I was handed a pen and a notebook and informed that I would be one of the judges! The teams of student bakers wore white chef's aprons and different-colored neckerchiefs. Working at separate baking stations, the students prepared light and dark *chleba* (pages 319 and 323) along with richer white breads like the traditional *Sváteční vánočka* or Christmas braid (page 315) and tender *rohlik* (page 311). (Seeing the love that the bakers had for these last two, and tasting some of the best examples that the country had to offer, I asked the winning team's faculty representative for the school's recipes.) The teams brought their finished breads to the judges' table, where we gave points to each item for proper shaping, good crust caramelization, crumb structure, and flavor. The atmosphere was celebratory, and the breads were terrific. The head of the baking association told me, "You're looking at the future of the Czech baking business." I couldn't believe my luck.

Judging this contest, tasting the beautiful breads, and seeing the enthusiasm and skill of the students was not only a high point of the trip to Prague but one of the most enjoyable and interesting days I've had as an American baker in Europe. I departed Prague with warm remembrances and two recipes tucked in my bag. The winning team gladly handed over their Christmas braid and *rohlik* recipes.

As I settled into my seat on the train traveling northeast from Prague, I thought about how bread making in the Polish city of Wroclaw would compare. Eugene and Zbigniew had raised my hopes with their many e-mails describing neatly scored ovals of mild rye sprinkled with caraway seeds, which sounded very much like the breads I had admired at Mastman's years ago. Once I had bought my plane ticket, I contacted my friend Cindy Chananie, who sells German-made Wachtel ovens to U.S. bakers and who has traveled extensively throughout Eastern Europe, and asked her if she had any contacts in Wroclaw. As a matter of fact, she said, Poland was one of Wachtel's liveliest markets right then. Something of a baking renaissance was going on there too, and she arranged for me to meet some of the Wroclaw bakers who had recently purchased new ovens.

My spirits deflated somewhat during the next five hours. When the train crossed the border, it slowed to a speed of under 10 miles an hour, because the tracks in Poland were so old and dilapidated. As the train slowly chugged through the countryside, I got a good view of the desolate post-Soviet landscape, 100 miles of decaying factories and abandoned towns. It was hard to believe that I would find exciting bread at the end of the journey. But as the train pulled into Wroclaw, my mood improved. I could see that it was a place in transition, ringed with boarded-up or crumbling buildings but revealing in its center a thriving core of new construction, commercial activity, and increasing economic prosperity that was sending ripples to the edges of the city.

Zbigniew, who was a younger, blonder, stouter version of Eugene, picked me up at the train station in the early evening. He told me about his business, exporting Polish foods to other European countries.

Within thirty minutes I was shopping with him at the city's best pork store and touring its best food market. After a couple hours' rest, we met up with a representative from Wachtel for a midnight tour of some of Wroclaw's recently renovated bakeries. I was intrigued and excited to see these bakeries, equipped with new ovens like the one I had just installed at Bread Alone. The Mahot fork mixers, imported from Paris, were also just like mine. I wouldn't have to buy new equipment to make Polish-style ryes!

Unlike the large factories in Prague, each bakery that I visited was small, brand-new, and owned by a young, entrepreneurial baker who wanted to make traditional breads using modern equipment and technology. After the fall of communism, state-run bakeries had shut down and the government and private investors had released a flood of capital to bakers who wanted their own shops. The vigor of the bread business in this struggling city was embodied by the strapping young bakery workers I met that night, each one well over six feet tall and in bodybuilder condition. Every bakery made the same oblong loaves, just like the ones we used to buy every week in Buffalo. They were close cousins to the rye bread in Prague but with a character closer to the rye bread of my childhood. The flavor of the bread was perfectly balanced between sweet and sour. The crumb was less spongy and more cakey than that of the Prague ryes, perfect for soaking up gravy from slow-cooked, assertively seasoned Polish braises, just as the Buffalo rye mopped up gravy from one grandmother's pot roast and the other's stuffed cabbage.

These breads were wheatier than the breads in Prague. Each baker I asked gave me the same formula for Polish rye: 40 percent rye and 60 percent wheat. In Prague it had been the opposite, 40 percent wheat and 60 percent rye. The ryes in Wroclaw were oblong like the Prague ryes, but because they were proofed on boards instead of in baskets, they weren't as uniform or perfect. The biggest surprise was the sourdough. At every bakery in Wroclaw, the ryes were raised not with a liquid starter, as in Prague, but with a stiff rye sourdough more like a French *levain* in consistency and mild acidity. There was no particular reason for this, just tradition. This more slowly fermenting sourdough contributed to the breads' milder, less acidic flavor, a quality the Wroclaw bakers valued more highly than the bakers in Prague did.

Even though the breads were made with less rye than wheat, they were clearly rye breads. Most of the bakers I met in Wroclaw never considered making 100 percent wheat bread, so highly did they value the flavor of rye. There, pride in rye extends beyond the bread. One baker lectured me on the superiority of rye vodka, which he claimed had a richness and body that "everyday" potato vodka doesn't have (Chopin is the name of the Polish rye vodka most readily available in this country). The liquor has a syrupy thickness and deep, earthy punch from the grain. Both bread and vodka made with rye have dark undertones. They aren't light and clean like a 100 percent white wheat baguette or a vodka made with potatoes. They're more complex. Zbigniew and I ended our long night at a diner next door to the the last bakery we visited, where we ate bowls of Polish hunter's stew called *bigos*, made with pork sausage and sauerkraut, thick slices of Silesian light rye, and tumblers of rye vodka, to celebrate the preferred grain of the city's bakers.

Several of the young bakers I visited urged me to visit an old-style bakery a few miles outside the city to understand the evolution of Polish rye, so Zbigniew and I headed there the next afternoon to sample this old-fashioned style of rye. We pulled up to a nondescript brick building with a chimney in back, surrounded by fields of sugar beets. Pawlow Mieczyslaw, a vigorous man in his seventies, greeted us at the door and led us into a simple room where breads cooled on wooden boards laid across metal racks. Pawlow had worked at this bakery for fifty years and now owned the business. His handmade brick ovens were almost a century old and had been used continuously through both world wars and up to this day. The rye loaves he baked in them had a less polished look than their counterparts back in the city. The urban bakers made yeastier, lighter breads which they thought would appeal to contemporary

taste. Those loaves were more uniformly shaped than these rustic loaves. Pawlow said his were exactly the same as the loaves he had baked fifty years ago. Indeed, he claimed to be using the same sourdough that was there when he was hired as an apprentice, a sourdough that he had maintained through fifty years of communism. I have heard a lot of stories about old sourdoughs, but this was one of the most resonant. I thought about the possibility, remote but intriguing, that some of my ancestors had eaten rye bread made with the same starter that had been under Pawlow's guardianship for all those years.

This was the same stiff rye sourdough I had seen at the city bakeries the night before. Pawlow insisted that it was essential for making authentic Polish rye bread. "In order to understand how to make the bread, you have to stay here all night and watch how we build the rye sourdough," he said. So I stayed all night and watched him refresh the bowls of firm, pale gray sourdough with additional water and rye flour at four-hour intervals. The result was a smooth, stiff, stone-gray starter with very mellow acidity. The frequent feedings diluted the acids produced by the lactobacilli, preserving the starter's ability to leaven bread. Pawlow didn't use commercial yeast, a sign of the confidence he had in the leavening ability of his sourdough.

I asked Pawlow about his life as a baker in the time between the war and the day the Berlin Wall came down. His friendly, collegial tone turned bitter. "During this communist time," he told me, "we were betrayed by the United States. We fought alongside you against the Germans, and after the war, what happened? You left us to the Russians." With pride and more than a little anger, he said that bread had become even more important to Poles after the war than it had been before, because it was one of the few good things that everybody could afford. In this period of deprivation, traditional bread sustained people physically and emotionally.

I left Pawlow's old bakery with mixed feelings. I was excited by my discovery of his traditional bread, but his stories about postwar hardship made me sad. His perseverance in baking traditional Polish bread was remarkable. Could I have continued to bake under those circumstances? Because he was speaking as a baker as well as a Pole, he made me understand the desolation of postwar life in his country in a new way. I remembered the rye bread back in Buffalo that had led me here. It had helped to comfort and sustain my grandparents as they built American lives around old Eastern European recipes.

Thinking about my grandparents, I felt a strong urge to visit the single remaining temple in the city. On the Saturday morning before I left Wroclaw, I walked through the rain in search of the White Stork Synagogue, whose address I had found on the Internet before I left home. As I walked farther from my beautifully renovated nineteenth-century hotel, I noticed the neighborhood got shabbier and shabbier. About twenty blocks from where I had started, I found myself on a street of crumbling buildings, many of them abandoned. Here was the address, but looking at the tenement building covered with graffiti, I was sure I had the wrong place. Then I noticed a little archway adjacent to the tenement. I walked through it and saw construction fences around a grand but crumbling domed building. Designed in 1827 by Karol Friderick Langhans, the same architect who designed Berlin's Brandenburg Gate, it had been the center of Jewish life in the city (then a part of Germany and known as Breslau) until World War II. It took its name from an inn next door, the White Stork. Eastern European Jewish tradition forbade synagogues from taking names of their own; they were identified only by nearby landmarks.

I had read with horror the history of the building, once the headquarters of a thriving Jewish culture. During the war Jews were herded into the synagogue's courtyard before being deported to Nazi death camps. The synagogue was then desecrated and used as a stable. After the war it was used briefly as a university library and then sat empty, decaying, until the small Jewish community of a hundred families or so took possession of the building and began to plan its renovation.

I sneaked through the fence. No one was there and the project was clearly proceeding very slowly. I picked up a six-inch strip of fancy molding that sat at the perimeter of the worksite with other detritus from the construction. It had obviously once been part of the ornate decoration of the synagogue. I took it with me back to my hotel and packed it in my suitcase, wanting to preserve this small piece of Jewish life in Poland for myself and my family. I thought of the rye breads that my grandparents and other Polish Jews in Buffalo had eaten after the war and how those breads must have had an undertone of bitterness, reminding them of the family and friends that they had left behind and lost.

A couple of months after my return from Wroclaw, I was telling one of my Buffalo cousins about the trip and reminiscing about the rye bread from Mastman's. He told me that he knew where that bread had come from, a big bakery called Kaufman's that was owned by a friend of his, the grandson of the founder. Although Mastman's was no longer in business, I wondered if the bakery might still be making that bread. A few phone calls later, I learned from my cousin's friend that Kaufman's was indeed still baking Polish-style rye bread. He told me that when the bakery first opened, an elderly Polish baker had set up a rye sourdough system that sounded to me just like the one at Pawlow's bakery. Although now the bakers at Kaufman's mostly made commercial white breads, they still used the same stiff rye sourdough in the light rye bread, the only traditional bread from the old days still in their repertoire. I'd been right about the connection between my grandparents' rye and the ryes I ate in Poland! This confirmed for me the fact that an authentic sourdough is integral to making unforgettable bread. Polish-style ryes made by Kaufman's had left me with such vivid sense memories that I traveled back to Poland to understand the bread I had eaten. Thanks to Pawlow and the other Wroclaw bakers I met, I could now recreate it for myself, my family, and my customers.

❊ KITCHEN NOTES: AUTHENTIC EASTERN EUROPEAN BREADS AT HOME

Along with that discarded piece of synagogue molding, which I have put on my mantel as a reminder of my trip, I brought back essential information about making the rye breads I tasted in Prague and Wroclaw. Learning about the rye sourdoughs in both places, I became more convinced than ever that to make authentic European artisan breads, you have to start with an authentic starter. The mildly acidic rye sourdoughs used by the Eastern European bakers were the key to producing the bread that Eugene Forycki had been longing for and the bread I remembered from Mastman's. When I began to use a milder rye starter in my rye breads, I could close my eyes and imagine myself back in Buffalo. Polish customers have noticed the difference too. I have a wholesale account, a market called the Garden, in Greenpoint, Brooklyn, with a large Polish immigrant clientele. Even though it is right next door to a traditional Polish bakery, it still sells an impressive quantity of rye breads made with this starter. Quite a few of the Garden's customers have told its proprietors that our bread is more like the bread from home.

Think of France, not Germany. I was surprised at the similar tastes of French and eastern European bakers when it came to sourdough breads. Unlike German bakers, who value a strong acidic note in their breads, French and Eastern European bakers prefer mild sourdough breads. There were no dark, whole-grain pumpernickels in Prague or Wroclaw. The lightest of the rye breads, however, are very similar to French country loaves in style. If you are a fan of French bread but want to experiment with rye flour, you might try some of these breads before moving on to the more intense German ryes.

The bakers in Prague use a liquid sourdough, like the starter used in Germany and Austria, but don't let it ferment as long, so their finished breads are milder and less acidic. To make Czech Country Bread (page 308), refresh your German rye sourdough and let it stand at room temperature for eight to twelve hours instead of twelve to twenty-four. The culture won't be as strong or as bubbly and will lack the biting acidity of fully fermented German rye sourdough. The resulting loaves will taste gently sweet and sour at the same time, with an earthy undertone.

In Wroclaw, the rye breads are even milder than those in Prague, the result of a unique *levain*-like starter made with rye instead of wheat flour. The stiff dough starter produces a more slowly fermenting bread dough, and the breads tend to be less sour in character than German and even Czech doughs built from liquid rye starters with higher acid content. So you don't have to create a white rye *levain* from scratch, I show you how to use some German rye starter to quickly build a white rye sourdough similar to the one Pawlow Mieczyslaw maintains.

Use white rye flour. Rye flour, like wheat flour, can be processed to different degrees. German rye breads are made with whole rye flour, with germ and bran. In contrast, Czech and Polish ryes use white rye flour, which gives the bread a bubbly crumb and a delicate rye flavor. Polish flour is processed differently from the white rye flour available to American bakers and is not as refined. Although the bran is sifted, there is still a lot of germ in it. To get as close to this as possible, try to find organic white rye flour from a small mill (see Resources, pages 333–34). It will be processed but not overprocessed, like Polish flour.

Supplement sourdough with just a tiny bit of commercial yeast. German and Austrian bakers ferment their sourdoughs so much that the acids kill off some of the natural yeast, so bakers often add some commercial yeast to their doughs to give their rye breads a boost. Because Czech and Polish bakers employ more briefly fermented sourdoughs, they tend to add less commercial yeast. You can add some yeast to the doughs, but just a small amount. Your sourdough will be powerful enough to raise bread with this small bit. In the case of Dark Silesian Rye (page 323), skip the commercial yeast altogether, since you want it to ferment slowly to develop a rich sourdough flavor. You can omit the commercial yeast in any of the recipes in this chapter, for that matter, if you build in some extra time for fermenting and proofing the dough and you want your breads to have a slightly more pronounced sour flavor.

CZECH COUNTRY BREAD
Žitný chleba

· · · · · · · · · · · · · · · · · · · ·

ALLOW 8 TO 12 HOURS TO MAKE THE SOURDOUGH;

10 TO 15 MINUTES TO KNEAD;

10 MINUTES TO REST;

2 TO 2 1/2 HOURS TO FERMENT;

1 TO 1 1/2 HOURS TO PROOF;

30 TO 40 MINUTES TO BAKE

· · · · · · · · · · · · · · · · · · · ·

My Czech guide, Eva Franka, told me, "We eat this rye bread the way French eat baguettes." Indeed, I saw it at every meal I ate in Prague, with cheese for breakfast, with goulash-style braised veal or pork with paprika and onions at the main midday meal, and especially as the foundation for *chlebicky*, open-faced sandwiches topped with smoked fish, sausage, or ham and garnished with hard-boiled egg or tomato, which are eaten as snacks throughout the day and as light evening suppers.

The dough is raised with German rye sourdough that has been fermented only briefly (8 to 12 hours, as opposed to 12 to 24), so the finished bread has only a hint of acidity. It is moist, with an open, even crumb and a shiny, chewy crust. Czech bakers poke holes in the loaves just before baking, a technique known as docking, so the breads rise evenly and keep their shape in the oven. They use a wooden mallet studded with a nail, but a skewer will produce the same result.

✳ MAKES 2 ROUNDS
(17 OUNCES/482 GRAMS EACH)

Equipment
BAKER'S PEEL OR RIMLESS BAKING SHEET

PARCHMENT PAPER

BENCH SCRAPER OR CHEF'S KNIFE

BAKING STONE

CAST-IRON SKILLET

CAKE TESTER OR SKEWER

BREAD DOUGH				
INGREDIENTS	VOLUME	U.S. WEIGHT	METRIC WEIGHT	BAKER'S PERCENTAGE
German rye sourdough (page 275)	About ¾ cup	5.3 ounces	150 grams	30
Water, tepid (70 to 78 degrees)	1¼ cups	10.6 ounces	300 grams	60
Instant yeast	1 teaspoon	0.2 ounce	5 grams	1
Unbleached bread flour, preferably high-gluten	2½ cups	14.1 ounces	400 grams	80
White rye flour	¾ cup	3.5 ounces	100 grams	20
Sea salt	1½ teaspoons	0.4 ounce	10 grams	2

REFRESH THE RYE SOURDOUGH. Eight to 12 hours before you want to mix your dough, refresh the rye sourdough. Follow the directions for rye sourdough refreshment on pages 277–78, but let the sourdough stand at room temperature (70 to 75 degrees) for 8 to 12 hours rather than 12 to 24 hours.

MIX THE DOUGH. Pour the water into a large mixing bowl or the bowl of a stand mixer. Stir in the yeast, bread flour, rye flour, and salt with a rubber spatula just until a dough forms. Stir the rye sourdough to invigorate and deflate it. Measure out 3/4 cup (5.3 ounces/150 grams) of the sourdough and pour it over the dough, scraping the measuring cup clean. (Refresh and store the remaining rye sourdough again according to the directions on pages 277–78.) Use the spatula to work in the sourdough just enough to incorporate it into the dough.

KNEAD THE DOUGH. **By hand:** Lightly dust a clean counter with flour. Scrape the dough out of the bowl and knead it with smooth, steady strokes for 8 minutes. The rye flour will cause the dough to be fairly sticky. As you work, keep your hands floured but resist adding a lot of flour. Lightly drape the dough with plastic wrap and let it rest for 10 minutes. Remove the plastic and knead again until the dough is smooth and elastic, 5 to 7 minutes more.

By machine: Use the dough hook and mix the dough on medium-low speed (4 on a KitchenAid mixer) for 7 minutes. Turn off the machine and scrape down the hook and sides of the bowl with a rubber spatula. Lightly cover the dough with a piece of plastic wrap and let it rest for 10 minutes. Remove the plastic, turn the mixer back on to medium-low, and knead until the dough is smooth and elastic, 3 to 5 minutes more.

FERMENT THE DOUGH. Transfer the dough to a lightly oiled, clear 2-quart container with a lid. With masking tape, mark the spot on the container that the dough will reach when it has doubled in volume.

Cover and leave it to rise at room temperature (70 to 75 degrees) until it reaches the masking-tape mark, 2 to 2 1/2 hours. It won't feel as sticky.

DIVIDE AND SHAPE THE LOAVES. Cover a baker's peel or rimless baking sheet with parchment paper. Set aside. Lightly dust the counter with rye flour. Scrape the dough onto the counter and cut it into 2 equal pieces (17 ounces/482 grams each) with a bench scraper or a chef's knife. Shape each piece into a round (see Shaping Rounds, page 36).

PROOF THE LOAVES. Dust the parchment paper lightly with rye flour and place the loaves on the paper about 3 inches apart, smooth side up. Sift some more rye flour over the loaves, as if you were dusting them with confectioners' sugar. Lightly cover them with plastic wrap. Leave the loaves to rise at room temperature (70 to 75 degrees) until they have inflated and bubbles are visible just below the surface, 1 to 1 1/2 hours. At this point, when you press a fingertip into the dough it will spring back slowly.

PREPARE THE OVEN. About 1 hour before baking, place a baking stone on the middle rack of the oven and a cast-iron skillet on the lower rack. Heat the oven to 425 degrees.

DOCK THE LOAVES. Use a cake tester or skewer to poke about 20 holes, about 1/2 inch apart from each other, all over the tops of the loaves.

BAKE THE LOAVES. Slide the loaves, still on the parchment, onto the baking stone. Place 3/4 cup of ice cubes in the skillet to produce steam. Bake until the loaves are ruddy brown, 30 to 40 minutes.

COOL AND STORE THE LOAVES. Slide the peel or the rimless baking sheet under the parchment paper to remove the loaves from the oven. Slide the loaves, still on the parchment, onto a wire rack. Cool for about 5 minutes and then peel them off the parchment paper. Cool them completely on the wire rack, about 1 hour, before slicing. Store the loaves at room temperature in a brown paper bag for 3 to 4 days, or freeze in resealable plastic bags for up to 1 month.

CZECH CRESCENT ROLLS
Rohlik

. . . .

ALLOW 9 TO 15 MINUTES KNEADING TIME;

1 TO 1 1/2 HOURS TO FERMENT;

30 TO 45 MINUTES TO PROOF;

15 TO 20 MINUTES TO BAKE

. . . .

A Czech friend in New York told me to keep an eye out for these light yeast rolls in Prague. I didn't have to look for long. In fact, I bought one at the Prague airport within minutes of clearing immigration. They are sold everywhere—train stations, bars and cafés, delis, supermarkets—and eaten as snacks on the go, buttered on the flat side or sliced in half with some sausage or cheese tucked in. They are light, crisp, pretty, and fun. They are everywhere, like bagels in New York. And like New Yorkers and their bagels, the people of Prague have strong opinions about who makes the best ones. This recipe comes from the winning team at the Czech baking association competition, so you know it's one of the finest.

Because these rolls are raised with packaged yeast, they can be made, start to finish, in under 3 hours. If you parbake and then freeze them, you can have warm, fresh rolls anytime in just about an hour. *Rohlik* make great dinner rolls. Or bake some for a weekend brunch.

**MAKES 24 ROLLS
(1.3 OUNCES/37 GRAMS EACH)**

Equipment

2 BAKING SHEETS

ROLLING PIN

BENCH SCRAPER OR CHEF'S KNIFE

RULER

PASTRY BRUSH

INGREDIENTS	VOLUME	U.S. WEIGHT	METRIC WEIGHT	BAKER'S PERCENTAGE
Water, warm (85 to 95 degrees)	1¼ cups	10.6 ounces	300 grams	60
Instant yeast	1 tablespoon	0.5 ounce	15 grams	3
Unbleached all-purpose flour	3¼ cups	17.6 ounces	500 grams	100
Unsalted butter, softened	4 tablespoons	1.8 ounces	50 grams	10
Granulated sugar	1 teaspoon	0.5 ounce	15 grams	3
Sea salt	1½ teaspoons	0.4 ounce	10 grams	2

TOPPING

INGREDIENTS	VOLUME	U.S. WEIGHT	METRIC WEIGHT	BAKER'S PERCENTAGE
Poppy, sesame, or whole caraway seeds	½ cup	1.8 ounces	50 grams	—
Sea salt	½ tablespoon	0.4 ounce	10 grams	—

MIX THE DOUGH. Pour the water into a large mixing bowl or the bowl of a stand mixer. Add the yeast, flour, butter, sugar, and salt and stir with a wooden spoon just until a rough dough forms.

KNEAD THE DOUGH. By hand: Lightly dust the counter with flour. Scrape the dough out of the bowl and knead it with smooth, steady strokes. At first the dough will be gooey because of the warm butter, but it will soon become more coherent and less sticky. Keep your hands floured and continue to knead until the dough is very smooth and elastic, 12 to 15 minutes.

By machine: Use the dough hook and mix the dough on medium-low speed (4 on a KitchenAid mixer) until it is very smooth and elastic, 9 to 10 minutes.

FERMENT THE DOUGH. Transfer the dough to a lightly oiled, clear 2-quart container with a lid. With masking tape, mark the spot on the container that the dough will reach when it has doubled in volume. Cover and leave it to rise at room temperature (70 to 75 degrees) until it reaches the masking-tape mark, 1 to 1 1/2 hours. It will feel very springy.

ROLL OUT THE DOUGH. Lightly oil 2 baking sheets. Stir together the seeds and kosher salt in a small bowl. Fill another small bowl with water and set it aside. Lightly dust the counter with flour. Scrape the dough onto the counter. Using a rolling pin, roll the dough into a rectangle about 8 inches by 24 inches. Lightly dust the underside and the top of the dough once or twice as you roll so that it won't stick to the counter or the rolling pin. It will be soft and stretchy. Lightly cover it with plastic wrap and let it rest for 5 minutes.

SHAPE THE ROLLS. With the long side of the rectangle facing you, fold the dough in half lengthwise to mark the center line and then open it up again and lay it flat on the counter. With a bench scraper or chef's knife, cut along the center line. Keep the pieces side by side. With a ruler, measure out 4-inch-long portions on the long side of each strip of dough.

Cut the dough at each 4-inch mark. You should have twelve 4-inch-by-4-inch squares. Cut each square diagonally, so you have 24 triangles. Gently pull the two points of the longest side of one triangle to stretch it to about 6 inches. With one hand, roll the stretched side toward the opposite point while gently pulling on the point to elongate the triangle. Place the rolled dough on the baking sheet, curving the ends inward to make a crescent shape and making sure that the point is tucked underneath. Repeat with the remaining dough triangles, placing them in rows on the baking sheets, at least 2 inches apart. Lightly brush the rolls with water and sprinkle the tops with the seed mixture. Lightly drape them with plastic wrap.

1. Roll the stretched side toward the opposite point while gently pulling on the point to elongate the triangle.

2. Curve the ends inward to make a crescent shape, making sure that the point is tucked underneath.

PROOF THE ROLLS. Let the shaped and covered rolls rise at room temperature (70 to 75 degrees) until they are pillowy and expanded but the layers are still distinct, 30 to 45 minutes.

PREPARE THE OVEN. About 15 minutes before baking, place one oven rack in the top third of the oven and a second rack in the middle. Heat the oven to 350 degrees.

BAKE THE ROLLS. Remove the plastic wrap and place the baking sheets in the oven. Bake until the

tops are golden, 15 to 20 minutes, switching the rack position of the sheets halfway through baking.

COOL AND STORE THE ROLLS. Place the baking sheets on wire racks and let stand for 5 minutes. Serve the rolls warm or at room temperature. *Rohlik* are best eaten the day they are baked.

ALTERNATELY, PARBAKE THE ROLLS. Remove the rolls from the oven when they have risen and their crusts are set but they are still pale, 10 to 12 minutes. Set the baking sheets on wire racks and let them cool completely, about 30 minutes. Freeze the rolls in resealable plastic bags. To finish baking, place the frozen rolls on baking sheets, 2 inches apart, and let them defrost for 1 hour. Bake in a preheated 350-degree oven until lightly browned, 5 to 7 minutes. Serve warm.

Variation: Czech Crescent Rolls with Seeds

I saw multigrain *rohlik* in only one bakery in Prague, but because I am a fiend for multigrain breads and because these were particularly delicious, I had to include this version here. To make a multigrain variation, just decrease the amount of all-purpose flour to 400 grams (14.1 ounces, 2 3/4 cups) and add 28 grams (1 ounce, 2 tablespoons) each of sunflower seeds and pumpkin seeds and 14 grams (0.5 ounce, 1 tablespoon) of flax seeds when mixing the dough.

CZECH CHRISTMAS BRAID
Svátečni vánočka

. . . .

ALLOW 9 TO 15 MINUTES TO KNEAD;
1 1/2 TO 2 HOURS TO FERMENT;
1 TO 1 1/2 HOURS TO PROOF;
30 TO 40 MINUTES TO BAKE

. . . .

Golden, glossy Christmas braids caught my eye as I wandered through a supermarket in Prague. I learned from Eva Franka that although *Svátečni vánočka* used to be reserved for the holidays, it is so beloved that it is now baked daily and is in fact one of the three principal breads of the country. Every student at baking school has to learn to make this bread, and the teams at the Czech baking association were fiercely competitive about which of their Christmas braids was most evenly braided, who had the glossiest crust, and who boasted the lightest crumb.

While Czechs consider the Christmas braid rich because it contains milk, eggs, and butter, it is lighter than the muffins, croissants, and scones made in America. To American palates it tastes light, exceptionally tender, and not too sweet. It is a beautiful bread, with a radiant color and a light sprinkling of sliced almonds.

**MAKES 1 LARGE BRAID
(26 OUNCES/735 GRAMS)**

Equipment
1 BAKING SHEET
BENCH SCRAPER OR CHEF'S KNIFE
WHISK
PASTRY BRUSH

INGREDIENTS	VOLUME	U.S. WEIGHT	METRIC WEIGHT	BAKER'S PERCENTAGE
Whole milk, warm (75 to 85 degrees)	¾ cup	7.4 ounces	210 grams	70
Egg yolks	2	1.1 ounces	30 grams	10
Instant yeast	1¼ teaspoons	0.2 ounce	5 grams	2
Unbleached all-purpose flour	2 cups	10.6 ounces	300 grams	100
Unsalted butter, softened	4 tablespoons	1.8 ounces	50 grams	17
Granulated sugar	¼ cup	1.6 ounces	45 grams	15
Sea salt	1 teaspoon	0.2 ounce	5 grams	2
Raisins, preferably organic	2/3 cup	3.2 ounces	90 grams	30

EGG WASH

INGREDIENTS	VOLUME	U.S. WEIGHT	METRIC WEIGHT	BAKER'S PERCENTAGE
Egg	1 large	1.8 ounces	50 grams	—
Granulated sugar	½ teaspoon	0.2 ounce	5 grams	—

TOPPING

INGREDIENTS	VOLUME	U.S. WEIGHT	METRIC WEIGHT	BAKER'S PERCENTAGE
Sliced almonds	¼ cup	0.9 ounce	25 grams	—

MIX THE DOUGH. Pour the milk into a large mixing bowl or the bowl of a stand mixer. Whisk in the egg yolks until blended. Add the yeast, flour, butter, sugar, and salt and stir with a wooden spoon just until a rough dough forms.

KNEAD THE DOUGH. By hand: Lightly dust the counter with flour. Scrape the dough out of the bowl and knead it with smooth, steady strokes. At first the dough will be sticky. Keep your hands floured but resist adding more flour than you need to. Continue to knead until the dough is smooth, satiny, and very elastic, 10 to 12 minutes. Add the raisins and knead them until evenly distributed, 2 to 3 minutes more.

By machine: Use the dough hook and mix the dough on medium speed (4 on a KitchenAid mixer) until it is smooth, satiny, and very elastic, about 8 minutes. Turn off the machine and scrape the dough from the hook and the sides of the bowl. Add the raisins and knead them in until evenly distributed, 1 to 2 minutes more.

FERMENT THE DOUGH. Transfer the dough to a lightly oiled, clear 2-quart container with a lid. With masking tape, mark the spot on the container that the dough will reach when it has doubled in volume. Cover and leave it to rise at room temperature (70 to 75 degrees) until it almost but not quite reaches the

masking-tape mark, 1 1/2 to 2 hours. When you press your fingertip into the dough, your fingerprint will spring back.

SHAPE THE LOAF. Lightly oil the baking sheet. Lightly dust the counter with flour. Uncover the dough and turn it onto the counter. Use a bench scraper or chef's knife to cut the dough into 3 equal pieces (8.7 ounces/245 grams each). Using as little additional flour as possible, shape each piece into a 12-inch-long, 2-inch-wide rope. Place the 3 pieces side by side on the baking sheet. Join the ropes together at one end, pressing gently so they hold together. Weave them, following the illustrations below, to make a tight braid. Gently press the ends together and tuck them under the loaf.

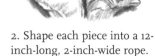

1. Use a bench scraper or chef's knife to cut the dough into 3 equal pieces.

2. Shape each piece into a 12-inch-long, 2-inch-wide rope.

3. Place the 3 pieces side by side on the baking sheet. Join the ropes together at one end, pressing gently so they hold together.

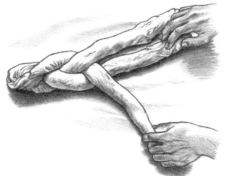

4. Weave them to make a tight braid.

5. Continue braiding down the length of the loaf until you reach the end.

6. Gently press the ends together and tuck them under the loaf.

PROOF THE BRAID. Lightly cover the braid with plastic wrap and leave it to rise at room temperature (70 to 75 degrees) until it looks very plump and feels springy, 1 to 1 1/2 hours.

PREPARE THE OVEN AND MAKE THE EGG WASH. About 15 minutes before baking, place an oven rack in the middle of the oven. Heat the oven to 350 degrees. Whisk together the egg and sugar in a small bowl. Set it aside with a pastry brush.

ADD THE TOPPING AND BAKE THE BRAID. Remove the plastic wrap and brush the braid thoroughly with the egg wash. Sprinkle the almonds over the loaf, gently pressing them into the top and sides so they adhere. Bake the braid in the middle of the oven until golden brown, 30 to 40 minutes.

COOL AND STORE THE BRAID. Place the baking sheet on a wire rack and let the bread cool completely on the sheet, about 1 hour. Christmas Braid is best eaten on the day it is baked, or freeze in a resealable plastic bag for up to 1 month.

LIGHT SILESIAN RYE
Chleba

. . . .

ALLOW 8 TO 12 HOURS TO MAKE THE SOURDOUGH;

7 TO 12 MINUTES TO KNEAD;

2 TO 2 1/2 HOURS TO FERMENT;

1 TO 1 1/2 HOURS TO PROOF;

30 TO 40 MINUTES TO BAKE

. . . .

These glossy golden loaves scattered with caraway seeds are the everyday bread of the southwest region of Poland. They have a delicate rye flavor, a spongy crumb, and a thin, chewy crust. On its native turf, *chleba* is toasted for breakfast, topped with cheese and sausage for snacks, and served alongside stews for dinner. Zbigniew Forycki told me that he and his family eat about a pound of light or dark *chleba* every day, and that's about average.

This particular recipe is based on baker Pawlow Mieczyslaw's rye bread. He uses an unusual white rye sourdough, creating a particularly mild bread. You can use an active German rye sourdough (or 1/4 cup of any active sourdough that you have in your refrigerator) to quickly build a white rye sourdough similar to Pawlow's. I've adapted his technique and recipe so that you can sleep while the rye sourdough ferments and still produce a well-balanced loaf.

For strong, pure caraway flavor, I sometimes add a teaspoon of freshly ground caraway seeds either to the rye starter or to the flour when I mix the dough. If you try this, you will immediately realize how lifeless and artificial-tasting most commercial rye breads made in America are. The caraway flavor in those breads is artificial, and the white flour is processed to within an inch of its life. There's simply no comparison. Whenever I pull this caraway-enhanced bread from the oven, I crave a reuben sandwich, stuffed with juicy corned beef and dripping with sauerkraut and Russian dressing, just like the ones I used to eat as a child.

MAKES 2 OVAL LOAVES
(17.9 OUNCES/508 GRAMS EACH)

Equipment

BENCH SCRAPER OR CHEF'S KNIFE

BAKER'S PEEL OR RIMLESS BAKING SHEET

PARCHMENT PAPER

BAKING STONE

CAST-IRON SKILLET

PASTRY BRUSH

SINGLE-EDGED RAZOR BLADE OR SERRATED KNIFE

WHITE RYE SOURDOUGH				
INGREDIENTS	VOLUME	U.S. WEIGHT	METRIC WEIGHT	BAKER'S PERCENTAGE
German rye sourdough (page 275)	About ¼ cup	1.8 ounces	50 grams	67
Water, tepid (70 to 78 degrees)	⅓ cup	2.6 ounces	75 grams	100
White rye flour	½ cup	2.6 ounces	75 grams	100

MAKE THE WHITE RYE SOURDOUGH. Scrape the German rye sourdough into a large mixing bowl or the bowl of a stand mixer. Stir in the water and white rye flour with a rubber spatula to make a smooth, thick, pale gray paste. Cover the bowl with plastic wrap and let stand to ferment at room temperature (70 to 75 degrees) for at least 8 to and up to 12 hours.

BREAD DOUGH				
INGREDIENTS	VOLUME	U.S. WEIGHT	METRIC WEIGHT	BAKER'S PERCENTAGE
White rye sourdough	About ¾ cup	7.1 ounces	200 grams	40
Water, tepid (70 to 78 degrees)	1¼ cups	10.6 ounces	300 grams	60
Instant yeast	1 teaspoon	0.2 ounce	5 grams	1
Unbleached bread flour, preferably high-gluten	3¾ cups	17.6 ounces	500 grams	100
Sea salt	1½ teaspoons	0.4 ounce	10 grams	2

TOPPING				
INGREDIENTS	VOLUME	U.S. WEIGHT	METRIC WEIGHT	BAKER'S PERCENTAGE
Caraway seeds (optional)	2 tablespoons	—	—	—

MIX THE DOUGH. Stir the white rye sourdough with a rubber spatula to break it up and soften it. Add the water, yeast, flour, and salt and stir just until a rough, ragged dough forms.

KNEAD THE DOUGH. By hand: Lightly dust the counter with white rye flour. Scrape the dough out of the bowl and knead it with long, smooth strokes until it becomes smooth, and springy, 10 to 12 minutes. The dough will be very sticky. Keep your hands floured but resist adding extra flour. Use a bench scraper to collect the dough every now and then.

By machine: Use the dough hook and mix the dough on medium-low speed (4 on a KitchenAid mixer) until it is smooth and springy, 7 to 8 minutes, stopping once or twice to scrape the dough from the hook and sides of the bowl. (The dough will be sticky and will not clear the sides of the bowl on its own.)

FERMENT THE DOUGH. Transfer the dough to a lightly oiled, clear 2-quart container with a lid. With masking tape, mark the spot on the container that the dough will reach when it rises one and a half times in volume. Cover and leave it to rise at room temperature (70 to 75 degrees) until it reaches the masking-tape mark, 2 to 2 1/2 hours. It won't feel as sticky, and lots of bubbles will be visible beneath the surface.

DIVIDE AND SHAPE THE LOAVES. Cover a baker's peel or rimless baking sheet with parchment paper. Lightly dust the counter with white rye flour. Scrape the dough onto the counter and cut it into 2 equal pieces (17.9 ounces/508 grams each) with a bench scraper or chef's knife. Shape each piece into a round (see Shaping Rounds, page 36). Elongate each round to about 6 inches by rolling it under your hands, using gentle pressure. Keep the center plump and the ends rounded.

PROOF THE LOAVES. Dust the parchment paper lightly with rye flour and place the loaves on the paper about 3 inches apart, smooth side up. Lightly cover them with plastic wrap. Leave the loaves to rise at room temperature (70 to 75 degrees) until they spread and are pillowy, 1 to 1 1/2 hours. When you press a fingertip into the dough, it will spring back slowly.

PREPARE THE OVEN. About 1 hour before baking, place a baking stone on the middle rack of the oven and a cast-iron skillet on the lower rack. Heat the oven to 400 degrees.

SPRINKLE THE LOAVES WITH SEEDS AND SCORE THEM. Brush the loaves lightly with water and sprinkle on the caraway seeds, if using. (Set aside the brush and water; you will need them when the loaves come out of the oven.) With a single-edged razor blade or serrated knife, score the loaves by making 4 parallel cuts straight across, about 1/2 inch deep.

BAKE THE LOAVES. Slide the loaves, still on the parchment, onto the baking stone. Place 3/4 cup of ice cubes in the skillet to produce steam. Bake until the crusts are an even, caramel brown at their centers and deeply browned on the ends, 30 to 40 minutes.

GLAZE, COOL, AND STORE THE LOAVES. Slide the peel or the rimless baking sheet under the parchment paper to remove the loaves from the oven. Slide the loaves, still on the parchment, onto a wire rack. Immediately brush them lightly with water to give them an extra-shiny crust. Cool for about 5 minutes and then peel them off the parchment paper. Cool them completely on the wire rack, about 1 hour, before slicing. Store the loaves at room temperature in a brown paper bag for up to 5 days, or freeze in resealable plastic bags for up to 1 month.

DARK SILESIAN RYE
Chleba

. . . .

ALLOW 8 TO 12 HOURS TO MAKE THE SOURDOUGH;

7 TO 12 MINUTES TO KNEAD;

2 TO 2 1/2 HOURS TO FERMENT;

1 1/2 TO 2 HOURS TO PROOF;

40 TO 50 MINUTES TO BAKE

. . . .

Everyone I met in Wroclaw had a passion for either dark or light rye and wouldn't think of switching for the sake of change. Dark rye is considered more old-fashioned and is made in the older, more traditional bakeries. It is shaped into giant rounds, which match its outsize, whole-grain, hearty character. This recipe employs artisan baker Pawlow Mieczyslaw's white rye sourdough but adds whole rye instead of white rye flour to the dough. No commercial yeast is added, so it takes a little longer for the dough to rise. Because this bread relies solely on the sourdough for lift, it tends to have an irregular, moist crumb, dense without being heavy. In Wroclaw, I ate this bread with potato and sausage soup, a slice of cheese, and a tall glass of Polish beer. To use pumpkin seeds in this rye, see the variation on page 326.

**MAKES 1 LARGE ROUND
(37.6 OUNCES/1,065 GRAMS)**

Equipment
BENCH SCRAPER

BANNETON OR COLANDER LINED WITH A KITCHEN TOWEL

BAKING STONE

CAST-IRON SKILLET

BAKER'S PEEL OR RIMLESS BAKING SHEET

PASTRY BRUSH

SINGLE-EDGED RAZOR BLADE OR SERRATED KNIFE

WHITE RYE SOURDOUGH

INGREDIENTS	VOLUME	U.S. WEIGHT	METRIC WEIGHT	BAKER'S PERCENTAGE
German rye sourdough (page 275)	About 1/4 cup	1.8 ounces	50 grams	67
Water, tepid (70 to 78 degrees)	1/3 cup	2.6 ounces	75 grams	100
White rye flour	1/2 cup	2.6 ounces	75 grams	100

MAKE THE WHITE RYE SOURDOUGH. Uncover your German rye sourdough and stir it with a rubber spatula. Scrape 1/4 cup (1.8 ounces/50 grams) of it into a large mixing bowl or the bowl of a stand mixer. (Refresh and store the remaining rye sour- dough as described on pages 277–78). Stir in the water and white rye flour with the spatula to make a smooth, thick, pale gray paste. Cover the bowl with plastic wrap and let stand to ferment at room tem- perature for 8 to 12 hours.

BREAD DOUGH

INGREDIENTS	VOLUME	U.S. WEIGHT	METRIC WEIGHT	BAKER'S PERCENTAGE
White rye sourdough	About 3/4 cup	7.1 ounces	200 grams	40
Water, tepid (70 to 78 degrees)	1 1/2 cups	12.3 ounces	350 grams	70
Unbleached bread flour, preferably high-gluten	2 1/4 cups	12.3 ounces	350 grams	70
Whole rye flour, preferably finely ground	1 cup	5.3 ounces	150 grams	30
Sea salt	1 1/2 teaspoons	0.4 ounce	10 grams	2

TOPPING				
INGREDIENTS	VOLUME	U.S. WEIGHT	METRIC WEIGHT	BAKER'S PERCENTAGE
Caraway seeds (optional)	2 tablespoons	—	—	—

MIX THE DOUGH. Stir the white rye sourdough with a rubber spatula to break it up and soften it. Add the water, bread flour, rye flour, and salt and stir just until a rough, ragged dough forms.

KNEAD THE DOUGH. By hand: Lightly dust the counter with white rye flour. Scrape the dough out of the bowl and knead it with long, smooth strokes until it becomes smooth and springy, 10 to 12 minutes. The dough will be very sticky. Keep your hands floured but resist adding extra flour. Use a bench scraper to collect the dough every now and then.

By machine: Use the dough hook and mix the dough on medium-low speed (4 on a KitchenAid mixer) until it is smooth and springy, 7 to 8 minutes, stopping once or twice to scrape the dough from the hook and sides of the bowl. The dough will be sticky and will not clear the sides of the bowl on its own.

FERMENT THE DOUGH. Transfer the dough to a lightly oiled, clear 2-quart container with a lid. With masking tape, mark the spot on the container that the dough will reach when it rises one and a half times in volume. Cover and leave it to rise at room temperature (70 to 75 degrees) until it reaches the masking-tape mark, 2 to 2 1/2 hours. It won't feel as sticky, and lots of bubbles will be visible beneath the surface.

SHAPE THE ROUND. Heavily dust a banneton or colander lined with a kitchen towel with rye flour. Lightly dust the counter with white rye flour. Scrape the dough onto the counter. Shape it into a round (see Shaping Rounds, page 36). Place the round, smooth side down, in the banneton or colander and cover with plastic wrap.

PROOF THE ROUND. Leave the loaf to rise at room temperature (70 to 75 degrees) until it increases one and a half times in size, 1 1/2 to 2 hours. At this point, when you press a fingertip into the dough it will spring back slowly.

PREPARE THE OVEN. About 1 hour before baking, place a baking stone on the middle rack of the oven and a cast-iron skillet on the lower rack. Heat the oven to 400 degrees.

SPRINKLE THE ROUND WITH SEEDS AND SCORE. Lightly flour a baker's peel or rimless baking sheet with whole rye flour. Uncover the loaf and tip it out onto the peel or sheet, guiding it to the center with one hand. Use a pastry brush to brush the round lightly with water. Sprinkle on the caraway seeds. With a single-edged razor blade or serrated knife, score the round by making 3 parallel cuts about 1/2 inch deep in the center.

BAKE THE ROUND. Slide the round onto the baking stone. Place 3/4 cup of ice cubes in the skillet to produce steam. Bake until the round is caramel-brown, 40 to 50 minutes.

GLAZE, COOL, AND STORE THE ROUNDS. Slide the peel or the rimless baking sheet under the round to remove it from the oven. Slide the round onto a wire rack. Immediately use the pastry brush to brush it with a light coating of water to give it an extra-shiny crust. Cool it completely on the wire rack, about 2 hours, before slicing. Store the round at room temperature in a brown paper bag for up to 5 days, or freeze in resealable plastic bags for up to 1 month.

Variation: **Dark Silesian Rye with Pumpkin Seeds**

I had a less traditional pumpkin seed version of this bread at one of Wroclaw's city bakeries. To make Dark Silesian Rye with Pumpkin Seeds, a variation rich in texture and flavor, omit the caraway seed topping and simply add 1 cup of unsalted pumpkin seeds to the dough toward the end of kneading, when the dough is already fairly smooth, and knead until the seeds are well distributed, about 2 minutes.

POLISH COTTAGE RYE
Wiejski chleba

. . . .

ALLOW 8 TO 12 HOURS TO MAKE THE SOURDOUGH;

12 TO 18 MINUTES TO KNEAD;

2 TO 2 1/2 HOURS TO FERMENT;

1 1/2 TO 2 HOURS TO PROOF;

40 TO 50 MINUTES TO BAKE

. . . .

This was the bread that my host, Zbigniew Forycki, and I were looking for when we made our pilgrimage to Pawlow Mieczyslaw's bakery. After the polished perfection of the golden city ryes, I was delighted by the boulder-sized, imperfect peasant rounds coming out of the hundred-year-old ovens. Not nearly as dark as pumpernickel, they were still quite a few shades darker than Dark Silesian Rye (page 323) and had an old-fashioned flavor that's impossible to find in the United States and more and more difficult to find even in modernizing Poland. The biggest surprise was how much sourdough Pawlow mixed into his very wet, dark dough, but in retrospect I understood that the large quantity of sourdough resulted in a distinctive, head-on rye flavor that wasn't present in the quieter *chleba*. Polish Cottage Rye is not exactly sour, but it has a definite tartness that I hadn't yet come across in Eastern Europe.

My recipe includes a step for increasing the amount of rye sourdough, what bakers call a "build," in order to boost flavor and ensure that the bread dough rises properly. This is especially important since no packaged yeast is added to the mix, just the wild yeast that thrives in the sourdough. The round that you will produce when you follow this recipe is not quite as large as Pawlow's, but it's still impressively hefty. Don't worry about waste. Because this bread is made with a large quantity of sourdough, it will stay fresh for at least 5 days, and its rye flavor will become more pronounced. This is the darkest, most rustic of the Polish ryes, "real bread," according to Zbigniew, who says that it is the best bread to stand up to the strong flavors of *bigos* (hunter's stew), Polish smoked sausages, and of course vodka.

✳ MAKES 1 LARGE ROUND
(42.9 OUNCES/1,215 GRAMS)

Equipment

BENCH SCRAPER

BANNETON OR COLANDER LINED WITH A KITCHEN TOWEL

BAKING STONE

CAST-IRON SKILLET

BAKER'S PEEL OR RIMLESS BAKING SHEET

RYE SOURDOUGH

INGREDIENTS	VOLUME	U.S. WEIGHT	METRIC WEIGHT	BAKER'S PERCENTAGE
German rye sourdough (page 275)	About 3 tablespoons	1.1 ounces	30 grams	17
Water, tepid (70 to 78 degrees)	³/₄ cup	6.2 ounces	175 grams	100
White rye flour, preferably finely ground	1 cup	6.2 ounces	175 grams	100

MAKE THE RYE SOURDOUGH. Scrape the German rye sourdough into a large mixing bowl or the bowl of a stand mixer with a rubber spatula. Stir in the water and white rye flour with the spatula to make a smooth, thick paste. Cover the bowl with plastic wrap and let stand to ferment at room temperature (70 to 75 degrees) for 8 to 12 hours. It will nearly double in volume, becoming dark and spongy, with a fruity smell and a tangy taste.

BREAD DOUGH				
INGREDIENTS	VOLUME	U.S. WEIGHT	METRIC WEIGHT	BAKER'S PERCENTAGE
Rye sourdough	About 2 cups	13.4 ounces	380 grams	76
Water, tepid (70 to 78 degrees)	1$\frac{1}{3}$ cups	11.5 ounces	325 grams	65
Unbleached bread flour, preferably high-gluten	3$\frac{1}{4}$ cups	17.6 ounces	500 grams	100
Sea salt	1$\frac{1}{2}$ teaspoons	0.4 ounce	10 grams	2

MIX THE DOUGH. Stir the rye sourdough with a rubber spatula to break it up and soften it. Add the water, flour, and salt and stir just until a rough, ragged dough forms.

KNEAD THE DOUGH. By hand: Lightly dust the counter with white rye flour. Scrape the dough out of the bowl and knead it with long, smooth strokes until it becomes smooth and springy, 15 to 18 minutes. The dough will be very sticky. Keep your hands floured but resist adding extra flour. Use a bench scraper to collect the dough every now and then.

By machine: Use the dough hook and mix the dough on medium speed (4 on a KitchenAid mixer) until it is smooth and springy, 12 to 13 minutes, stopping once or twice to scrape the dough from the hook and sides of the bowl. The dough will be sticky and will not clear the sides of the bowl on its own.

FERMENT THE DOUGH. Transfer the dough to a lightly oiled, clear 2-quart container with a lid. With masking tape, mark the spot on the container that the dough will reach when it rises one and a half times in volume. Cover and leave it to rise at room temperature until it reaches the masking-tape mark, 2 to 2 1/2 hours. It will feel spongy and less sticky.

SHAPE THE ROUND. Heavily dust a banneton or towel-lined colander with rye flour. Lightly dust the counter with white rye flour. Scrape the dough onto the counter. Shape it into a round (see Shaping Rounds, page 36). Place the round, smooth side down, in the banneton or colander and cover with plastic wrap.

PROOF THE ROUND. Leave the loaf to rise at room temperature (70 to 75 degrees) until it doubles in size, 1 1/2 to 2 hours. It will look airy and soft.

PREPARE THE OVEN. About 1 hour before baking, place a baking stone on the middle rack of the oven and a cast-iron skillet on the lower rack. Heat the oven to 450 degrees.

BAKE THE ROUND. Lightly flour a baker's peel or rimless baking sheet with rye flour. Uncover the loaf and tip it out onto the peel or sheet, guiding it to the center with one hand. Slide the round onto the baking stone. Place 3/4 cup of ice cubes in the skillet to produce steam. Bake until the round is dark reddish brown, 40 to 50 minutes.

COOL AND STORE THE ROUND. Slide the peel or the rimless baking sheet under the round to remove it from the oven. Slide the round onto a wire rack. Cool it completely on the wire rack, about 2 hours, before slicing. Store the round at room temperature in a brown paper bag for up to 5 days, or freeze in resealable plastic bags for up to 1 month.

FREQUENTLY ASKED QUESTIONS ABOUT CZECH AND POLISH RYES

. . . .

How are Polish and Czech artisanal rye breads different from the rye bread served at my kosher deli?

Today's deli rye has changed a lot, and not for the better, since my boyhood visits to Mastman's in Buffalo. The average deli rye bread is mass-produced in a factory. It's the rye equivalent of Wonder Bread. Commercial rye bread is mixed, proofed, and baked in an hour or two, allowing very little time for flavor and texture to develop. It is made with highly processed white rye flour, from which the bran, germ, oils, nutrients, vitamins, and minerals have been removed, so there's very little food value in what's left. Processing removes much of the flour's flavor as well. To compensate for this loss, manufacturers often add artificial caraway flavoring to the dough, and that's the predominant flavor of most deli loaves. Only if you make rye bread with stone-ground rye flour will you taste real rye flavor, which is taken for granted in Eastern Europe but difficult to experience in this country.

How do I know when my white rye sourdough starter is ready?

It's better to use rye sour when it's on the young side than to let it get too old. For one thing, if you let it sit too long, it will lose its leavening power. If it has already deflated, it has aged too much. (To refresh an old rye sourdough, see pages 277–78.) Another reason to use it young is for flavor. For the most authentic Eastern European rye flavor, you want a balance of sweet and sour in the starter. A rye sour will ferment

quickly, probably within four to six hours. The best way to judge its flavor readiness is to taste it. It should be musty, earthy, and tangy, with a mild, not explosive, acidity. Taste the sourdough after three hours and then taste it frequently thereafter, letting it rise and develop some acidity but using it before it becomes too sour and deflates.

Is it true that rye doughs are more difficult to handle than doughs made with 100 percent wheat flour?

These doughs aren't more difficult to handle, just different. If you are aware of the differences, then you'll know what to expect at each point in the process. One of the nice things about the rye breads from Prague and Wroclaw is that they all contain a good percentage of wheat flour, which gives them a more familiar feel for bakers experienced with wheat but new to rye. If this describes you, you might want to try one of them before progressing to breads made with 100 percent rye, like the Whole Rye Berry Loaf (page 292).

Even if your rye dough contains some wheat flour, it will behave differently from an all-wheat dough. Rye flour doesn't have gluten-producing proteins present in wheat flour, so doughs made with rye are stickier and softer than 100 percent wheat doughs. They won't have the elasticity and forgiving quality of doughs made with wheat flour, and they won't have the same satiny finish. A common mistake is to add extra flour to tighten up the dough, but resist this impulse or you will wind up with a tough, dry bread.

Be aware also that rye dough does not rise in quite the same way as wheat dough. While wheat dough expands from the outside in, as its surface warms up first, rye dough expands more uniformly, with the inside and outside growing at the same time and rate. Rye dough is more even-textured when it is rising. It doesn't have as much give as wheat dough, and has a spongy rather than elastic texture. When the sponginess feels softer and more delicate to the touch, you'll know it's ready. Don't expect the dough to puff up as it is proofing in the same way that wheat dough does. You are better off putting rye dough in the oven when it's on the young side, to avoid overproofing and to leave room for ample oven spring.

When I went to move the proofed rye dough, it deflated! Is it ruined?
I usually advise students baking wheat breads to err on the side of overproofing, but with rye breads I advise the opposite. Rye doughs, because they have less gluten, are more delicate than stronger wheat doughs. They can sustain only a certain amount of rising before they collapse. If you are at all worried that your dough is approaching its limit, get it in the oven. If you have overproofed your dough by no more than a few minutes and it collapses before you put it in the oven, you can still save it. Just reshape it, put it back in the basket, and proof it again, but not fully—try to take it three quarters of the way to full proofing. You have to be cautious, because over time acidity will build up and break down the dough. There is more of a risk of collapse the second time around than there was the first time, so you won't have as much wiggle room now. If your dough is slightly underproofed (and this is true whether it is underproofed for the first or the second time), don't try to compensate by overbaking it. The result will be an unpleasantly tough bread.

What's the trick to braiding bread dough with ease?
Warm dough is very sticky and will get even stickier as it expands in the short time that you are working with it. If your dough is destined for braiding, let it rise in the refrigerator. It will be much easier to work with when it is cool.

Sometimes I see a braided bakery loaf with a brilliant brownish red finish. How can I get that color and shine at home?
For that extra-dark and shiny finish, one coat of egg isn't enough. Egg wash twice, once after braiding and once after proofing, just before the loaf goes into the oven.

When I sprinkle caraway or poppy seeds on my proofed loaf, many of them roll off the bread either before or immediately after it is baked. How can I get an even coating of seeds and make sure that they will stick during baking?
If you like a thick coating of seeds rather than just a scattering, try applying the seeds before proofing, so they are gripped by the dough as it rises. Spread the seeds across the bottom of a rimmed sheet pan. Roll the dough in a dampened cloth after it is shaped, then roll the damp dough in the seeds. Let the dough proof with the seeds on.

I have leftover *rohlik* and no space in my freezer for them. What can I do with my day-old rolls, and in general with leftover breads made with packaged yeast that stale quickly?
Sourdough breads like Czech Country Bread (page 308) stay fresh for days, but *rohlik*, like any other white bread made with packaged yeast, quickly become stale. Amazingly resourceful, the Czech people have found so many uses for stale bread that you could almost describe their cooking as built on bread. Cubes of day-old bread are fried to make croutons and then added to soups, folded into scrambled eggs, and used to fill dumplings. Bread crumbs coat pork cutlets, thicken lentil soup, bind meatloaf, and dust cake pans for gingerbread. You can make croutons and bread crumbs from stale *rohlik* or any other stale bread, white or wheat.

✳

Each of these companies is a reliable source for high-quality baking ingredients and equipment.

The Baker's Catalogue, King Arthur Flour
58 Billings Farm Road
White River Junction, VT 05001
800-827-6836
www.bakerscatalogue.com
www.kingarthurflour.com

King Arthur offers one-stop shopping for the home baker. The choices of flour are impressive: unbleached bread flour with 12.7 percent protein, organic bread flour with 12.3 percent protein, organic whole wheat flour, both white and whole rye flours in a variety of grinds. To get closest to French type 55 flour for baguettes and other French breads, buy All-Purpose Artisan Organic Flour with 11.3 percent protein. For breads requiring high-gluten bread flour, either because the doughs are extremely wet or because they contain rye and other grains that lack gluten, use Sir Lancelot Unbleached High Gluten

Flour with 14.2 percent protein. King Arthur also sells fine semolina flour, which it calls durum flour, for *pane di Altamura*. While you are ordering flour, you can also stock up on excellent nuts and dried fruit. If SAF yeast isn't stocked at your local supermarket, get it here, along with dehydrated French sourdough to give your culture a jumpstart. You can order equipment here as well as ingredients: KitchenAid mixers, HearthKits, baking stones and peels, bannetons, Pullman loaf pans, parchment paper, bench scrapers, *lames*, pastry brushes, digital scales.

Giusto's Specialty Foods
344 Littlefield Avenue
South San Francisco, CA 94080
650-873-6566; 866-972-6879
www.worldpantry.com

Giusto's has been a pioneer in milling high-quality organic flour for over twenty years. The number-one choice of many West Coast artisan bakers, including

Steve Sullivan at Acme, Giusto's now sells small bags of its excellent organic flours and grains to consumers. To get closest to French type 55 flour for baguettes and other French breads, buy Baker's Choice unbleached organic bread flour with 11 to 11.5 percent protein. For breads requiring high-gluten bread flour, either because the doughs are extremely wet or because they contain rye and other grains that lack gluten, use High Gluten Bread Flour with 13.5 protein. Giusto's stone-ground whole wheat flour is also superb. Check out the reasonably priced selection of fine sea salts including fleur de sel, chosen for suitability in bread.

Bob's Red Mill
5209 SE International Way
Milwaukie, OR 97222
800-349-2173
www.bobsredmill.com

A good source for hard-to-find organic flours made from buckwheat, corn, kamut, and spelt.

Hodgson Mill
1100 Stevens Avenue
Effingham, IL 62401
800-347-0105
www.hodgsonmill.com

Hodgson Mill, a widely distributed brand found at supermarkets and natural foods stores, also sells certified organic and stone-ground flour and grain by mail and online.

Arrowhead Mills
The Hain Celestial Group
4600 Sleepytime Drive
Boulder, CO 80301
800-434-4246
www.arrowheadmills.com

Another widely distributed brand of organic and stone-ground flour and grains, Arrowhead Mills products are also available online.

War Eagle Mill
11045 War Eagle Road
Rogers, AR 72756
866-4-WarEagle; 479-789-5343
www.wareaglemill.com

Stone-ground whole wheat, rye, buckwheat, corn, and spelt flours from a historic water-powered mill in Arkansas.

Forno Bravo
8112 Chalk Hill Rd.
Healdsburg, CA 95448
707–836–0105
www.fornobravo.com

The American source for Caputo pizza flour, the Italian brand beloved by Neopolitan pizza makers. Order a five-pack of 1 kilo bags for $17.50.

Bread Alone
Route 28
Boiceville, NY 12412
800-769-3328; 845-657-3328
www.breadalone.com

Bread Alone sells fine organic flours, used at the bakery from Robert Beauchemin's mill. We also sell hard-to-find baking equipment such as rosetta roll stampers.

INDEX

Note: Page numbers in **boldface** refer to recipes themselves.

B

D

G

Q

S

T

tap water, 16
temperature
  cooling loaves and, 34–35
  interior, doneness and, 34
  monitoring, 7
  of oven, for rye breads, 140–41
  retarding loaves and, 32–33
  of water, 17, 140
tepid water, defined, 17
texture, problems with, 57
thermometers, 21–22
thyme
  Focaccia alle Funghi, 265–66
  Fresh Herb Twist, 237–39
  Mushroom Focaccia, 265–66
  Pane alle Erbi, 237–39
tomatoes
  Altamura Semolina Focaccia with Sun-Ripened
    Tomatoes, 262–64
  Focaccia di Altamura, 262–64
  Individual Focaccias with Cherry Tomatoes, 185–86
  Pizza Rossa alla Romana, 217
  Roman Red Pizza, 217
  Schiacciate al Pomodori, 185–86
Tom Cat Bakery, 6, 7
torpedoes, shaping, 39
Toscapan, 20, 163–65
turning dough, 30–31
Tuscan-style breads. *See* Veronese- and Tuscan-style
  breads
type 55 flour
  about, 65
  substitute for, 65, 334
type 85 flour, 133

U

unbleached flour, 18

V

Veggetti, Carlo, 210–11
Veggetti, Matteo, 210, 211
Veronese- and Tuscan-style breads, 162–90
  Black Olive Cheeks, 179–82
  frequently asked questions about, 189–90
  Grape Harvest Focaccia, 167, 183–86
  Grissini Rosmarino, 178
  Individual Focaccias with Cherry Tomatoes, 185–86
  Italian Baguettes, 167, 172–74
  Pane alla Ricotta, 187–89
  Pane Toscano, 57, 167, 168–71
  Panmarino, 175–78
  Puccia, 179–82
  Ricotta Bread, 187–89
  Rosemary Breadsticks, 178
  Rosemary Filone, 175–78
  Saltless Tuscan Bread, 57, 167, 168–71
  Schiacciata all'Uva, 167, 183–86
  Schiacciate al Pomodori, 185–86
  Stirato, 167, 172–74
  techniques and ingredients for making at home,
    166–67
Vingchter, 289–91
Volkornbrot, 9, 292–95, 330

W

Walch, Clemens, viii, 11, 12, 43, 106–8, 271, 279,
  289, 300
walnuts
  French Walnut Bread, 122
  Pain au Levain aux Noix et Raisins, 132
  Pain au Levain Complet aux Noix, 122
  Pain aux Noix et Raisins, 93
  Raisin-Nut *Levain*, 132
  Raisin-Walnut Boule, 93
  staining of dough by, 102
War Eagle Mill, 334

A NOTE ABOUT THE AUTHOR

Daniel Leader is the owner and baker of the Bread Alone bakeries in the Catskill mountains of upstate New York and the author of *Bread Alone: Bold Fresh Loaves from Your Own Hands,* which won an International Association of Culinary Professionals award. Leader studied philosophy at the University of Wisconsin and graduated from the Culinary Institute of America in Hyde Park, New York. He cooked in New York restaurants such as La Grenouille and the Water Club before opening Bread Alone in Boiceville, New York, outside of Woodstock, in 1983. He lives in the Catskills with his family.

SACRED PLACES, CIVIC PURPOSES

This book is a joint project of the Brookings Institution and the Pew Forum on Religion and Public Life.

THE PEW FORUM ON RELIGION & PUBLIC LIFE

The Pew Forum seeks to promote a deeper understanding of how religion shapes the ideas and institutions of American society. At a time of heightened interest in religion's public role and responsibilities, the Forum bridges the worlds of scholarship, public policy, and journalism by creating a platform for research and discussion of issues at the intersection of religion and public affairs. The Forum explores how religious institutions and individuals contribute to civic life while honoring America's traditions of religious liberty and pluralism.

Based in Washington, D.C., the Forum is co-chaired by E. J. Dionne Jr., senior fellow at the Brookings Institution, and Jean Bethke Elshtain, Laura Spelman Rockefeller Professor of Social and Political Ethics at the University of Chicago. Melissa Rogers serves as executive director. The Forum is supported by the Pew Charitable Trusts through a grant to Georgetown University.

SACRED PLACES, CIVIC PURPOSES

Should Government Help
Faith-Based Charity?

E. J. DIONNE JR.
MING HSU CHEN
editors

BROOKINGS INSTITUTION PRESS
Washington, D.C.

Copyright © 2001
THE BROOKINGS INSTITUTION
1775 Massachusetts Avenue, N.W., Washington, D.C. 20036
www.brookings.edu

Library of Congress Cataloging-in-Publication data

Sacred places, civic purposes : should government help faith-based
charity? / E.J. Dionne, Jr. and Ming Hsu Chen, editors.
   p. cm.
Includes bibliographical references and index.
  ISBN 0-8157-0259-0 (pbk. : alk. paper)
  1. Church charities—United States. 2. Church charities—Government
policy—United States. 3. Government aid—United States. 4. Church and
state—United States. I. Dionne, E. J. II. Chen, Ming Hsu.
  HV530 .S25 2001
  361.7'5'0973—dc21

                 2001006142

9 8 7 6 5 4 3 2 1

The paper used in this publication meets minimum requirements of the
American National Standard for Information Sciences—Permanence of Paper for
Printed Library Materials: ANSI Z39.48-1992.

Typeset in Adobe Caslon

Composition by Cynthia Stock
Silver Spring, Maryland

Printed by R. R. Donnelley and Sons
Harrisonburg, Virginia

For all who dedicate themselves to others, particularly those who gave so much to bring comfort and hope to those afflicted by the terrible events of September 11, 2001, and in memory of those who perished

Foreword

Long before there was a welfare state, religious congregations worked to alleviate poverty. They continued their efforts following the establishment of government programs to assist the poor, and now congregations commonly collaborate with government agencies to help feed, clothe, and care for the needy; run after-school programs; provide teen pregnancy counseling; and develop programs to prevent crime.

On some issues, such as that of school choice, adversaries have engaged in polarized battles involving both high principles and special interests. But much church-state cooperation has continued with limited challenge in the courts. Although to many among the poor the church and the government are both essential institutions, they rely on the church not only for assistance but also for a sense of community, power, and meaning.

In recent years a new dialogue has begun regarding the proper role of congregations in lifting up the poor and the proper nature of their relationship to government. The new debate has at times been deeply divisive, but it also has created an opening for new points of departure from the old debate and, at least occasionally, new opportunities to heal old breaches. The issue was addressed in the 2000 presidential campaign, when both Texas Governor George W. Bush and Vice President Al Gore proposed expanding cooperation between government and "faith-based organizations." After having been in office only a few weeks, President Bush created the White House Office of Faith-Based and Community Initiatives and proposed new legislation on government support for faith-based efforts.

The seeds of the new dialogue were sown in an earlier Brookings compilation, *What's God Got to Do with the American Experiment?* edited by E. J. Dionne Jr. and John J. DiIulio Jr., who served as the first director of the White House Office of Faith-Based and Community Initiatives through the fall of 2001. The possibility of a new debate became clear in a December 1997 conference, "Sacred

Places, Civic Purposes," funded by the Pew Charitable Trusts and sponsored by Brookings in cooperation with Partners for Sacred Places. The result was the beginning of a lively conversation that crisscrossed every party line and ideological divide.

Sacred Places, Civic Purposes: Should Government Help Faith-Based Charity? has evolved from that conversation. The volume focuses on five specific challenges: teen pregnancy, crime and substance abuse, community development, education, and child care. The objective is to explore what faith-based groups are doing, how government can help them without getting in the way, and when government involvement might be mistaken or counterproductive, from the standpoint of both the religious groups themselves and the constitutionality of the involvement.

The concerns of this book would have been well appreciated by Robert Brookings, the St. Louis businessman who founded the Brookings Institution. Although the Institution has become known mainly for its application of social sciences to public policy issues, the broader social concerns of its founder have been honored over the years. And, of course, there is a long and honorable tradition of the engagement of social science in the study of religious institutions. This book—which explores how sacred places have been empowered to serve civic needs and purposes—is very much at home in the broader tradition of Brookings scholarship. It presents the views of a politically and religiously diverse group of individuals—social scientists as well as clergy, government officials as well as neighborhood activists. Its goal is to describe, with an evenhanded treatment of the issues and an emphasis on problem solving, the tangible achievements of faith-based organizations.

The views expressed here are solely those of the authors and should not be attributed to the trustees, officers, or other staff members of the Brookings Institution.

Michael H. Armacost
President, Brookings Institution

Washington, D.C.
September 2001

Acknowledgments

This book is a tribute to the authors whose work it comprises. In every case, those authors took time out of extremely demanding schedules to consult on the project, to participate in conferences, and to write their essays and continually revise them to reflect the ever-changing context of faith in public life. We thank them for their contributions to this project—for the wide variety of opinions, broad range of expertise, and depth of insight that they have enabled us to present—and for their years of hard work on behalf of charity and justice. Our hope is that by presenting all of their voices—harmonious and discordant alike—we will foster a more open, rigorous, and rich national dialogue on the valuable contributions that faith-based organizations make and on what government's relationship to them should be.

In particular, we thank Avis Vidal and Joan Lombardi for serving as wise and able advisers and for helping to coordinate the voices in the areas of community development and child care, respectively—this on top of their duties as conference participants and authors. This book is far better because they shared their expertise and advice. We also thank Belle Sawhill, John DiIulio, Melissa Rogers, Bill Galston, Bruce Katz, Bill Dickens, Michael Cromartie, and Peter Steinfels for serving as informal consultants.

This book would not exist and this project would never have gotten off the ground without the extraordinary work of Staci Simmons. With intelligence and great ingenuity, she helped to conceive this project and then gracefully managed all aspects of the conferences on teen pregnancy, crime, and community development before leaving to take on another creative task in helping to establish the Pew Forum on Religion and Public Life. Ming Hsu Chen took responsibility for the last two conferences and for editing all of the papers.

Most of the voices here were enlisted through the conferences, which were held thanks to the support of the Pew Charitable Trusts. Special thanks go to

Luis Lugo of the Trusts, who also helped to conceive this project. He saw the importance of these issues long before they made the front pages of newspapers and the talk shows. Luis understands as well as anyone in the country the civic possibilities of America's diverse religious communities. We also are deeply grateful to the president of the Pew Trusts, Rebecca Rimel, and to Kimon Sargeant, Barbara Beck, Diane Winston, and Julie Bundt. The opinions expressed here are, of course, those of the authors and do not necessarily reflect the views of the Pew Charitable Trusts.

The conferences engaged some 500 people of diverse professional, political, and theological backgrounds in sometimes groundbreaking, often challenging, and always illuminating discussions. But anyone who has worked in event planning knows that it takes a team to do it right. The conferences ran more smoothly because of the very competent people at the Brookings Institution and the Pew Forum on Religion and Public Life. Susan Stewart and her staff provided valuable administrative and financial oversight. Andrea McDaniel, Melissa Rogers, Amy Sullivan, and Andrew Witmer volunteered boundless enthusiasm, support, and labor. Andrea in particular helped us through all troubles—and, more important, helped us avoid trouble in the first place. Stacey Rosenstein and Esperanza Valencia, along with their staffs in Conference and Catering Services, were true professionals, ensuring the smooth operation of all of the events.

At the conclusion of the conferences, we had more than 30 hours of discussion and several memorable presentations that nonetheless had to be transformed into a publishable form. Nothing would have come out right without Kayla Meltzer Drogosz. Kayla, whose knowledge of the subject is broad and deep—and whose commitment to social justice is lifelong and enduring—came on as the book was reaching its final stages. She acted as if it were her own, corralling final manuscripts from a far-flung group of authors, making sure that last-minute improvements saw the light of day (and print), and offering superb advice to all, including especially the editors.

Then the staff of the Brookings Press, along with Christina Counselman, Tommy Ross, and Ari Selman, performed magic. Tommy and Ari were critical in checking the final manuscripts. Eileen Hughes made large substantive and editorial improvements for which we are deeply grateful, and she did so with great sensitivity to the diverse views of our authors. Tanjam Jacobson provided invaluable assistance in revising the many chapter notes. Larry Converse creatively spun the pieces together into an attractive layout. Susan Woollen directed the design of a cover that we loved at first sight. Becky Clark made sure that the book would reach the hands of those who care about these issues. Robert Faherty lent leadership and vision to the project in innumerable ways.

And speaking of leadership, publication of this book could not have occurred without the leadership, vision, and encouragement of Michael Armacost, Paul Light, and Thomas Mann of the Brookings Institution. We feel blessed to have carried out this work in the exciting, collegial, and genuinely friendly environment they have created.

Most of these essays were completed before the events of September 11. But we are sure that all of the authors share the sentiments we express in our dedication.

Our thanks, above all, to Mary Boyle; to James, Julia, and Margot Dionne; to Stephen Chen; and to our parents, families, and many friends who lived through this with us. They help make faith, hope, and love believable propositions.

E. J. Dionne Jr.
Ming Hsu Chen

Contents

PART FOUR

The Role of Faith-Based Organizations in Education

FURTHER COMMENTS

PART FIVE

The Role of Faith-Based Organizations in Child Care

Sacred Places, Civic Purposes

CHAPTER ONE

When the Sacred Meets the Civic: An Introduction

E. J. DIONNE JR. and MING HSU CHEN

How can anyone oppose government help for religious congregations working so hard to shelter the homeless and battle crime in inner cities, to provide child care for poor children, and to bring investment to the neighborhoods they serve? Why shouldn't government do all it can to nurture these islands of hope?

How can anyone who believes in the First Amendment's promise of religious freedom support giving *any* government money to religious institutions that might use the funds to advance a particular faith? Why should government channel aid to the poor through congregations that might use a disadvantaged person's vulnerability as an opportunity for recruitment and conversion?

These are tendentious, but not necessarily unfair, questions. The fact that many Americans might see *both* sets of questions as reasonable helps explain why our great national debate over government help to faith-based organizations arouses such passion and engenders such division. It is not as simple as the country being split into hostile camps; Americans, as individuals, are often divided within *themselves*.

Large majorities like the idea of supporting the community work of religious congregations because they respect what they do and believe that religion can transform people's lives. They believe that greater choice in social programs will lead to better services and that faith-based providers are especially caring and compassionate.[1]

Yet majorities *also* worry that such programs might force recipients to take part in religious practices against their will. They are concerned that government might become too involved in religious organizations. And most Americans oppose allowing government-funded religious groups to make hiring decisions on the basis of an applicant's faith.[2]

In principle, Americans want the government to help faith-based organizations. In practice, they worry about what that help might mean.

As Peter Steinfels argues in his powerful closing chapter of this book, the current interest in the work of religious congregations reflects the confluence of many currents in American political thought going back some forty years. On this issue, the left's long-standing interest in granting power to grassroots organizations controlled by the poor meets the right's desire to find alternatives to government provision of social assistance. A general disaffection with government's performance meets a widespread belief that programs to uplift the needy must convey values and virtues as well as money. Our rendezvous with this issue, as Steinfels argues, now seems inevitable.

Those who sympathize with the work of religious congregations thus include people motivated by very different impulses and points of view. Some see social problems as the result of individual failures and disabilities. They see the poor as being poor primarily because they have made bad personal decisions. This view emerges at times in President Bush's rhetoric, which emphasizes the importance of individual conversion as a means of overcoming personal failures. He speaks quite honestly of the importance of conversion in his own life. Seen in this optic, supporting faith-based institutions means strengthening efforts to encourage the poor to make appropriate moral choices.

Others who sympathize with faith-based groups agree that the disadvantaged should be seen as morally responsible for themselves. But they insist that often the poor are poor because of unjust social structures, discrimination, government policies, and economic changes over which they have little control. Those who hold this view see religious congregations not only as a source of personal strength for individuals but also as "prophetic interrogators"—a phrase from Jim Wallis, another contributor to this book—who challenge social injustice. Those who believe this also want to strengthen the religious community, but they do not want government funding to still dissident voices in the congregations. Faith-based groups, after all, are often the most powerful advocates for those who are left out and among the only institutions over which the poor have control.

Related to this distinction is another, between those who see congregations primarily in individualistic terms and those who see them as builders of community. In one view, religion is fundamentally about saving people one soul at a time. Those who believe this and advocate government funding for faith-based services do so because they believe religion will strengthen *individuals*. In the other view, religious congregations are builders of *community* and civil society. As Mark R. Warren has put it, religion is seen as providing "an initial basis of cooperation by grounding such action in a set of common values, goals, and commitments to the public good. . . . At its best, religion has provided a moral basis to conceive of our place in a larger human society and inspired people to work for racial equality, social justice, and democracy."[3]

Some who support the work of religious congregations do so because they hope to win converts to their faith. Others believe that their faith requires them to serve those in need, whether the needy convert or not. Many believe both these propositions at the same time.

Finally, there are those who hope that religious congregations might take over important parts of the welfare state. Others see congregations' work as indispensable, but supplementary to the tasks of government. Those in the first camp are deeply skeptical of government and would like to reduce its role in American life. Those in the second camp believe profoundly in government's essential role in providing health care, education, supplementary income, and training to those who fall on hard times. But they believe that congregations can do things government cannot and reach people in a way no government employee, however well intentioned, ever could.

It must be added, of course, that many—including members of *all* of these groups—insist that congregations are not primarily about social work *or* community organization, but places of worship, instruction, and service to God.

And almost all of these distinctions may oversimplify the motivations of the competing camps. But to make them is to underscore one of the central purposes of this book: to suggest that seeing the work of religious congregations through a narrow ideological prism—conservative or liberal, "accommodationist" or "separationist," Republican or Democratic, religious or secular—is to miss the richness of their contribution to American life. It is also to miss the richness of the debate over what government should and should not do to encourage their work.

OPENING UP THE DEBATE

Our purpose here is not to impress upon readers a particular, dogmatic viewpoint or to give one and only one answer to the question posed in our subtitle. On the contrary, in an area where the lines are drawn sharply and harden quickly, this is very consciously *not* a party-line book. It is intended to open up the debate, not to narrow it.

We hope that even the staunchest critics of government funding for congregations might come away with a better understanding of why this idea appeals to many and with a better appreciation of the large contributions that congregations make. And we hope that even the strongest supporters of government assistance for these groups might better appreciate that serious questions about this idea are not simply the product of extreme secularist minds closed to religion altogether, but reflect genuine concerns about civil rights and religious freedom.

This book began taking shape well before President Bush took office and made the work of faith-based organizations a centerpiece of his administration. It grew out of a series of conferences held between 1999 and 2001 at the Brookings Institution with the support of the Pew Charitable Trusts. This volume is designed neither to praise nor to condemn the president's efforts; you will find both praise and criticism here. Most of the essays are concerned with problems that transcend the particulars of one administration's efforts, on the theory that we will be debating the role of religious institutions in our public life long after this administration ends.

The project reflects a certain frustration with the way the issue of government aid to faith-based organizations is usually confronted. In 1997, one of the editors and John DiIulio—who served as the first director of the White House Office of Faith-Based and Community Initiatives before his departure in August of 2001—put together a series of meetings to discuss what churches, synagogues, and mosques do to alleviate poverty and assist the marginalized. The meetings were highly productive and led to publication of the volume *What's God Got to Do with the American Experiment?*[4]

What became clear during those discussions is that, too often, advocates of competing viewpoints retreat too quickly to first principles. The word *retreat* is chosen intentionally. Of course, it is good to argue about first principles. But participants in this debate are so comfortable with disputes over what the First Amendment does or does not mean that they sometimes give short shrift to examining the actual contributions of religious congregations to social well-being.

Many insights are lost when this happens, among them the role of congregations as providers of service, as the creation and creators of community, and as organizers of efforts to push government and society to do more on behalf of social justice. The fact that much government money has long flowed in, through, and around religious institutions is ignored. And, as we have seen, important differences among those who admire the work of the congregations get lost, too.

The *Sacred Places, Civic Purposes* project was organized to put problem solving at the forefront and to deal with the broader constitutional and cultural issues in the context of the *specific* and important work that congregations do. You could say that we enter the discussion through a side door, beginning with the social problems and what can be done about them. Only then do we ask about the capacity of religious groups to alleviate them, and only after that do we look at government's role. This book is, first, about social problems, especially problems faced by the poor; second, about the contributions that religious groups make to meeting these social needs; and, third, about the ways in which government can help (and may hinder) the efforts of religious groups.

This focus is reflected in the organization of the book and the substance of the essays. The last section deals with the broad argument about government aid to faith-based organizations only *after* a series of essays that examine particular problems in which congregations are closely engaged. We focused on five: teen pregnancy, crime, community development, education, and child care. We know, of course, that the work of congregations extends beyond these areas, but they are particularly instructive and important.

Our goal was to gather together not only specialists on church-state issues but also social scientists, clergy, educators, government officials, social service providers, activists, and business leaders deeply engaged in these issues. We wanted to discuss what faith-based organizations do in the context of the efforts of others to deal with the problems at hand. The sessions, in which some 500 people participated, were notable not just for the work of the formal presenters but also for the quality of our audiences, which were made up of sober analysts, passionate practitioners, and impassioned critics. Some of the essays here grow out of comments from the audience and are not simply the work of those commissioned to write or respond to papers.

The first five sections of the book are organized in roughly the same way, containing two or three major papers from each session, followed by a series of shorter commentaries. This book is not a conference report. Transcripts of the meetings themselves can be found at the Brookings Institution website (www.brookings.edu). Instead, we asked authors to transform their comments into essays. We greatly appreciate their work. Many of the shorter essays are self-contained arguments and occasionally reply as much to each other as to the major papers. The essays by Keith Pavlischek and Julie Segal, for example, grew out of our session on crime, but they offer rich encapsulations of the views on opposing sides in the broader charitable choice controversy.

If we may be permitted a brief point of pride, we believe that the authors gathered in this book are among the best people in their particular fields. They offer a very wide range of viewpoints—religious and denominational as well as political and philosophical. Neither of the editors agrees with all of the essays gathered here, and we suspect that this will be true of virtually anyone who comes to this book. We hope this is one of its strengths. And many of the essays, designed to describe social problems and what is being done to alleviate them, may draw assent *across* ideological and philosophical barriers.

As the book makes clear, supporters of government aid for faith-based social service provision are not always themselves religiously active or even religious at all. Critics of these proposals include some who are now hard at work within the very congregations and faith-based organizations targeted for assistance. On many of these questions, those most involved in faith-based organizations are more interested in achieving a broader and more generous commitment by government to the poor than in receiving any particular help for their own institution.

FAITH-BASED PROBLEM SOLVING

Religious congregations play very different roles on different issues. On the matter of teen pregnancy, there is widespread concern about whether religious congregations are doing *enough*, and different denominations and religious traditions clearly have quite different views on what the content of sex education should be.

This often unnoticed fact should not be surprising. As Isabel Sawhill writes, those engaged in battling teen pregnancy tend to be divided into two broad camps. One camp, which she describes as *moralists*, is concerned primarily with the immorality of premarital sex and its dangers. Those she calls *consequentialists* are concerned primarily with the health consequences and the number of births to teens. She argues that strategies offered by *both* groups are essential to continuing the downward trend of teen pregnancy.

Debra Haffner, a consequentialist in Sawhill's terms, advocates an approach that emphasizes education (including education in contraception). Congregations, she says, should play an important part in supplementing the education that takes place in the home and in schools. Patrick Fagan, a moralist in Sawhill's schema, cautions that liberal approaches to sexuality have failed to produce results and that only a religiously based, abstinence approach can sustain the downward trend. Fagan argues that church attendance itself is powerfully associated with the avoidance of early sexual experience by teens and thus of pregnancy. We do not agree with all of Fagan's views—for what it is worth, our ideas run closer to those of Sawhill. But Fagan's essay underscores that the most important effects of religion often come from practice itself and not from any particular "faith-based program." One can believe this, of course, and still oppose government grants and contracts that directly support the practice of religion.

The control and prevention of crime entail some of the *least* and *most* controversial forms of faith-based engagement. It is impossible not to admire the work congregations have done to patrol neighborhoods, keep at-risk teens from falling into criminality, and help former prisoners rebuild their lives. John DiIulio, George Kelling, the Reverend Eugene Rivers, and Chris Winship, among others, discuss the success of Boston's Ten Point Coalition in grappling with these tasks.

Kelling, a noted criminologist, reflects broadly on the nature of "interorganizational collaborations" in fighting crime, drawing on his two decades of experience working on anticrime and community policing initiatives. As moral authorities that prod communities to take control of the "small things," Kelling argues, congregations play a crucial role in halting the deterioration of neighborhoods and reducing violence.

His criticisms of religious groups for their response to his own initiatives in reducing crime in the New York subway system also point to an aspect of religious engagement in social problems so often ignored in the current debate. As he shows, the interventions of churches, synagogues, and mosques are often on the *liberal* side of the public debate, to the frustration of the very conservatives who are usually so lavish in their praise of faith-based organizations. Whether or not one agrees with Kelling's overall view, he is surely correct in insisting that religious participants in the public debate have an obligation to "get the problem right." They must match their moral witness with an understanding of the practical trade-offs facing those trying to solve public problems. That is good advice to the left, the right, and the center.

One area in which faith-based organizations play a large role in the reduction of crime—the treatment of those addicted to drugs—is likely to be at the heart of the controversy over whether government funding for faith-based efforts is constitutional or not. Many of the most successful drug treatment programs may turn out to be those that place the greatest religious demands on participants. There are, as yet, not enough data to know that for sure, but assume for the moment that this claim is true. If religious conversion is a powerful tool for freeing individuals from drug dependency, and if cost-benefit analysis is to guide the spending of public money on drug programs, what is to be done? The *more* religiously demanding a program is, the *greater* is its potential to violate the First Amendment, a point alluded to by DiIulio.

Supporters of faith-based drug treatment would argue that government should put its money wherever it finds success, a point made forcefully by Pavlischek. But putting government money directly into such programs would almost certainly involve government support for religious conversion. Vouchers are a partial answer to the dilemma, but they do not make it go away.

In the work of community development, local religious institutions are often crucial as organizers who can stand up for the credibility of local organizations. They are the best link many of our poorest neighborhoods have to other institutions, especially those with the capacity to invest capital. "Congregations," writes Jeremy Nowak, "often serve as the most important place within low-income communities for building secular public relationships." Similarly, Avis

Vidal and Nowak both see religious congregations as aiding the typical community development corporation by serving as "incubators and organizers." Congregations provide a base of volunteers, create a direct link to financial resources, and promote public trust. Without necessarily receiving a dime in government funds themselves, congregations play a critical role in persuading investors, public and private, that a particular project is worthy and has authentic community support.

Father Joseph Hacala forcefully argues that community development is a special and especially enlightening case because faith-based institutions serve as far more than "service providers" or Samaritans trying to bind up individual wounds temporarily. In this work, the faith communities deal with the essential issues of social justice. They address the failures of economic structures even as they seek to develop the capacities of individuals. They seek not merely short-term spending to alleviate social problems but also long-term investments to reconstruct communities. Hacala, who headed the office on faith-based work at the Department of Housing and Urban Development during the Clinton administration and before that directed the Catholic Church's Campaign for Human Development, knows whereof he speaks. He underscores the existence of faith-based initiatives long before the current round of attention they've won.

In discussing the role of congregations in education, we consciously *avoid* focusing on the voucher issue. We do so in part because there has already been so much research and debate on this question. We also believe that the argument over vouchers shifts attention away from the many things that *even those religious congregations without schools of their own* already do to enhance the educational opportunities of children. As Ernie Cortes reports, the Industrial Areas Foundation (IAF) has used the churches as a base for organizing parents to demand improved public school curriculums, better teaching, and enhanced provision of child care. Dennis Shirley describes in detail the work of the IAF. "Congregations," he says, "can be powerful allies with schools in the struggle to create a safe environment for urban youth and to provide them with a high-quality education." Mavis Sanders offers a helpful catalogue of partnerships between public schools and faith-based institutions going on *right now.* They undertake their good work without raising constitutional problems or ideological controversy. David Hornbeck, the former school superintendent in Philadelphia, offers eloquent practical testimony about his work with faith-based institutions and his view that the churches, synagogues, and mosques are indispensable allies of *public* education.

All of these examples are important because they suggest one danger in the current debate: *so much attention is being paid to charitable choice programs, including the Bush proposals, that little notice is given to the vast array of activities un-*

dertaken by the religious institutions that are not constitutionally controversial. To some degree, both Bush *and* his critics might be faulted for suggesting that faith-based initiatives are much newer and bolder than they are. Bush himself seems to go back and forth on this matter, at times emphasizing the novelty of his program, at others suggesting—in the interest of reassuring critics but also accurately—that he is only building on past achievements.

In truth, Catholic Charities, Lutheran Services of America, and the Jewish Federations—representing religiously affiliated, but independently incorporated, nonprofit organizations—have long received public funds for the provision of secular services. It is worth noting, however, that charitable choice does not require houses of worship to form separate 501(c)(3) organizations to receive direct government grants or contracts. This is one of a number of charitable choice provisions that represents significant change in the relationship between the government and religious institutions, which is why it is controversial. But charitable choice does not represent some sudden entry by religiously affiliated groups into the social service field; such groups have always played a large role.

The case of education, like that of community development, underscores the danger of seeing religious congregations only as potential "service providers." This undervalues their role as community organizers and advocates. As the experience of the IAF and its Alliance schools shows, congregations often make their largest civic contributions as critics of the status quo who seek *not* government funding for themselves, but better and more responsive government for their members and their neighborhoods.

Government partnerships with faith-based organizations in the provision of child care is the subject of the fifth part of this book. This extremely important story is told well by Joan Lombardi, Mary Bogle, and the co-authors Fred Davie, Susan Le Menestrel, and Richard Murphy. The child care case should be playing a much bigger role in our current debate because it represents one of the oldest and most established forms of government partnership with faith-based groups. As Bogle notes, "Congregation-based early childhood programs have been supported by taxpayer dollars for at least thirty years." The Child Care and Development Block Grant, included in the Omnibus Budget Reconciliation Act signed by the first President Bush in November of 1990, provided for vouchers that parents could use in congregation-based facilities.

This is a government-subsidized faith-based program that seems to have worked and for that reason alone deserves study. But the entire area of child care is fraught with difficulty—in part because needs still outstrip available government resources. As Davie, Le Menestrel, and Murphy point out, these programs face enormous staff turnover. Teacher salaries are low. There is "a documented extreme need for after-school programming in schools, especially for low-income families."

One question that deserves further debate is whether the provision of child care piecemeal through vouchers, including vouchers that go to religious programs, may hinder the creation of broader networks of both preschool and after-school care within or attached to public school systems. Another is whether we are focusing so much of the debate on *whether* religious institutions should get public funds that we are evading the broader debate over whether *more* public funds, however spent, are needed for child care. Lombardi makes the trenchant point that faith-based institutions are popular among child-care providers because "religious institutions often have the only spaces available, especially for low-income families." The issue, she says, is often as much about a shortage of *space* as it is about *faith*. The religious congregations are, too frequently, the only nongovernmental institutions to which the very poor can turn, in part because they are often the only institutions over which they exercise a degree of control.

Still, Lisbeth Schorr notes that there may well be something special about faith-based child care because it is built on "the desire to instill the traits, norms, and beliefs of a particular culture or faith." Having faith as a "core value," she says, can allow programs and those who work in them "to persevere in the face of stress, uncertainty, and disappointment." Faith keeps hope alive.

WHAT'S TO BE DONE?

It is only after examining these particular problems that the book turns more squarely toward the contemporary debate over charitable choice and the Bush initiatives. Even here we have tried to introduce arguments that fall outside the usual confrontations over the First Amendment.

Mark Chaves of the University of Arizona has conducted what is perhaps the most extensive national survey of what congregations actually do in the sphere of social services and what they are likely to do with the dawn of charitable choice. His findings should inject a note of realism into the conversation:

> Although virtually all congregations engage in what might be considered social service activities and although a majority—57 percent—support provision of some type of more or less formal social service, community development, or neighborhood organizing projects, the intensity of congregational involvement varies widely.

Although supporters of charitable choice might hope that congregations engage in what he calls "holistic" services, Chaves finds that they stick with the basic and the immediate. On the whole, they do not have vast staffs dealing with social services. Only 6 percent of all congregations—and only 12 percent of congregations reporting some degree of social service involvement—have even one staff person "who devotes at least 25 percent of his or her time to social service projects."

"Congregations," he finds, "are much more likely to engage in activities that address the immediate needs of individuals for food, clothing, and shelter than to engage in projects or programs that require sustained involvement to meet longer-term goals." This is neither surprising nor in the least dishonorable. It does suggest the danger of placing excessive hopes in the transforming power of individual congregations, especially smaller ones, working all by themselves. As Chaves notes, many of the most effective congregational programs are carried out in partnerships with both religious and secular allies. Small may be beautiful, but Chaves finds that "the minority of large congregations provide the bulk of social services carried out by congregations."

African American churches "are more likely to be engaged in certain key types of social services, such as education, mentoring, substance abuse, and job training or employment assistance programs." Not only are African American congregations more engaged in social services now, but they also are more likely to apply for government funds under charitable choice programs in the future. Chaves finds that 36 percent of all congregations would be interested in applying for government money to support their human services programs. This, of course, also means that a substantial majority of congregations do *not* want to apply. But there is a huge difference by race: 64 percent of African American congregations express a willingness to apply for government funds, compared with only 28 percent of white congregations. (And, as John DiIulio has pointed out, inner-city Hispanic congregations are similar to African American congregations in their inclination toward social work and social activism.)

Chaves's findings mean that any realistic discussion of charitable choice and the Bush initiative must be candid about the centrality of African American congregations to this debate.

The Chaves study also finds that Catholic and liberal-to-moderate Protestant congregations are significantly more likely to apply for government social service funds than are conservative or evangelical congregations. This may help to explain why the Bush initiative does not excite the conservative evangelical base of the Republican Party to the degree many expected and has even drawn criticism from its ranks. The paradox of this initiative is that it most interests those congregations *least* likely to be conservative and Republican in their political orientation.

Chaves's conclusions are important. "The assumption that charitable choice initiatives are likely to involve *new* sorts of religious congregations in providing publicly funded social services—those that have not been involved before—is questionable." As we have seen, his findings suggest that religious social service providers are actually *more* likely to engage in holistic, long-term service if they collaborate with secular organizations, including the government.

For anyone who wants a preview of where this debate might go, *In Good Faith* is an excellent place to begin. This is a consensus statement worked out among critics and supporters of expanded government aid to faith-based organizations representing a variety of political perspectives and faith traditions—Protestant, Jewish, Muslim, Catholic, Buddhist, and Sikh. We include the document here. Over several years, some of the most distinguished and engaged parties in this debate hashed out their differences in a spirit of civility and questing. The consensus statement is important not only for where agreement was found, but also for where the points of disagreement were clarified and placed in relief. This group sought to narrow the differences, and its findings suggest that whatever the fate of the Bush initiative, there is broad room for cooperation between government and faith-based groups, even in the eyes of those most committed to church-state separation. Precisely because the participants searched so hard for consensus where they could find it, the points of disagreement they identify are likely to be the core sticking points as Congress and the country work through this issue. Melissa Rogers, one of the signers of *In Good Faith* and now the executive director of the Pew Forum on Religion and Public Life, offers a fascinating tour of areas where there is wide agreement, and places where there is deep dispute. She notes that divisions do not always fall neatly along the lines of left and right. On certain questions, even those who often find themselves allies discover that they have important and principled differences.

Other essays by John DiIulio, Rabbi David Saperstein, and Peter Steinfels provide powerful alternative—but also overlapping—perspectives on the current controversy. They disagree about the proper relationship of government to faith-based charity, but they share a desire to find constitutional and consensual ways of supporting the good works of religious people, their houses of worship, and their organizations.

It is striking, for example, that DiIulio, the Bush administration's point man on the faith-based initiative during its first months, is more concerned with enhancing the capacity of congregations to help the poor than he is with forwarding any particular conception of government's role in this effort. He would happily give way on legislation if he could count on vastly increased private sector support for the indispensable efforts of faith-based groups in improving the lives of the outcast among us. DiIulio has also included an important postscript, written after his departure from the Bush administration. He suggests that there are grounds for conciliation and compromise that might move legislation forward.

After the assaults of September 11, the administration and both parties in Congress were considering a stripped-down version of the president's proposal through which its least controversial provisions might be enacted into law. "What this means is that the time for any kind of complicated or contentious debate is not now," DiIulio told the *New York Times* in mid-October. "The pieces on which there is the broadest agreement should be moved now. There will be time aplenty to accomplish more later on. That is the spirit of the moment."

It is also striking that David Saperstein, a critic of the Bush initiative and a strong advocate of church-state separation, favors efforts to make it easier for congregations to create separate 501(c)(3) status, which could help these organizations to receive government funding. For all their disagreements, DiIulio and Saperstein want to strengthen the religious sector. Both would prefer this to happen in a way that brought the nation together behind efforts to lift up the disadvantaged.

Although we have not tilted this book toward our own conclusions, it is fair to ask what its editors believe about the fundamental questions raised here. We might both be described as cautiously optimistic about expanded government help to faith-based institutions. We are optimistic because, for all the reasons described in this book, it is clear that the faith-based institutions can work wonders—even, occasionally, miracles—and because they are so often the institutions most closely connected to those on society's margins. Without their houses of worship and the sense of personal and community obligation that they instill, many of our nation's neighborhoods would be lost. Faith-based institutions are, quite simply, essential to the achievement of social justice.

But we are cautious because we do not dismiss the constitutional difficulties these efforts raise. Lines have to be drawn somewhere, especially on the questions of whether the most needy might be proselytized against their will and how rules on employment practices can be written to protect both the integrity of religious institutions and the rights of individuals.

It must also be said that charitable choice programs raise different questions in large and religiously diverse metropolitan areas than they do in more religiously homogeneous communities. Charitable choice guarantees, in principle, that no one seeking social services should have to go to a program that he or she objects to on religious grounds. In metropolitan areas, seekers of services may have a wide range of choices among public, private secular, and religious providers. But those choices may not exist everywhere and certainly not in the same profusion. And, as Diana Jones Wilson argues in the case of child care, rural areas often face even larger shortages of resources and facilities than cities or suburbs. Much of the faith-based discussion has focused, for understandable reasons, on inner cities. As Wilson argues forcefully, attention must be paid to rural America as well.

We also are cautious because neither of us believes that enhancing the capacity of religious institutions is any substitute for increased government support to health care, child care, income supplements for the working poor, and education. It would be an injustice to faith-based groups if the controversy over government help for their good works became a distraction from a necessary debate over how our nation's social needs should be met. It is good that President Bush has said, "Government will never be replaced by charities and community groups." But there is more to be said and debated. Some who sympathize with the president's objectives—among them Senator Joe Lieberman—have questioned how much an initiative of this sort could do for the poor absent significant new spending.

This debate entails not just church-state questions. It is also about how government can strengthen civic and community institutions, whether they be secular or religious. After the House passed a version of the president's plan on a largely partisan vote in July of 2001, Lieberman, among others, suggested that the president's ideas would win more support if they were part of a broader effort to reinvigorate civil society and the nation's voluntary associations. And ultimately this is an argument about whether government should do more for—and how it could do better by—the very Americans, the poorest among us, for whom this initiative was created. Compassion is good, but justice is better.

The danger that greater dependence on government aid could still the prophetic voices of the churches in challenging government should therefore be taken seriously. A great debate is going on in the African American church over whether this initiative is designed in part for political reasons—to change the allegiances of the Democratic Party's most faithful allies. A different but parallel fear from some churches is that entanglement with government and government red tape could obstruct the preaching of the whole of their faith.

From the point of view of religious people, there is an additional danger. Will these programs so emphasize the *instrumental* character of religion—its capacity to create social service programs that "work"—that we will stop caring about the truth and validity of what a tradition teaches and preaches, the most important issue to any religious tradition that takes itself seriously? If government aid truly does dilute what makes religious programs special, this program could well turn out to be, as Melissa Rogers has said, "the wrong way to do right."

But these questions and doubts should not obscure the ways in which the new debate over the civic role of sacred institutions has been powerfully good for our nation. It has renewed our appreciation of what religious congregations contribute to the commonweal. It has reminded us of the dual roles of religious leaders as prophetic and critical voices, and as practical and loving service providers. It has led us to consider both religion's social impact and its effect on individuals—and how the two interact.

In his book *The Needs of Strangers*, Michael Ignatieff writes: "We need justice, we need liberty, and we need as much solidarity as can be reconciled with justice and liberty."[5] The current interest in the role of faith-based groups in public policy and the willingness of politicians—George W. Bush, Al Gore, and Joe Lieberman among them—to talk about their faith in public reflect a search for a new public moral language that tries to find a plausible route to Ignatieff's objectives. In that discussion, it is inevitable that the religious will encounter the secular, that the sacred will encounter the civic.

Sacred places serve civic purposes. That is the central theme of this book. But the sacred and the civic both need protection—sometimes from each other. Religion loses its integrity if its value is measured solely in civic terms. The civic life of a free and pluralistic nation can never be dominated by a particular faith, nor can it be stripped of faith. America's religious life has been strengthened, not weakened, by the Constitution's guarantees that the government cannot get in the way of the free exercise of religion, and cannot establish a public faith. Our government, in turn, has benefited from the challenges regularly put to it by people of faith who need not fear retribution for their demands that the state and the society reach for higher standards.

In its first phase, during the first half of 2001, the debate over the Bush initiative proved deeply divisive, and not only in partisan terms. It will be a great loss if the debate over faith-based charity and social action is locked into this frame in the coming years. If this book proves anything, it is that the work of our religious congregations engages the energy and commitment of Americans across all partisan and ideological divides. The challenge is to find ways in which government can foster this good work without so dividing Americans across religious and political lines that the work itself is jeopardized. This won't be easy. Good things often aren't.

Few events more powerfully underscore the relationship between the sacred and the civic than the public response to the terrorist assaults of September 11, 2001. Throughout the nation, citizens spontaneously flocked to their houses of worship in search of consolation, understanding, and solidarity. Prayer and meditation, along with the acts of generosity and mercy that so often followed, partook of both the sacred and civic realms. Americans discussed the urgency of religious toleration and the paradox that religious commitment, depending on how it is understood, can unite communities or divide them from each other. It can lead, we have learned, to love *or* hatred. The terrible events pushed the country toward a new spirit of seriousness and reflection—creating a moment that might allow us to begin anew our national conversation about faith-based initiatives and the meaning of faith in our public life.

NOTES

1. Pew Forum on Religion and Public Life and Pew Research Center for the People and the Press, *Faith-Based Funding Backed, but Church-State Doubts Abound: A Survey for the Pew Forum on Religion and Public Life* (Washington, D.C.: April 10, 2001). See section 1: "Funding for Faith-Based Organizations: Broader Support, Deeper Differences."

2. Ibid.

3. Mark R. Warren, *Dry Bones Rattling: Community Building to Revitalize American Democracy* (Princeton University Press, 2001), p. 27.

4. E. J. Dionne Jr. and John J. DiIulio Jr., *What's God Got to Do with the American Experiment?* (Brookings Institution Press, 2000).

5. Michael Ignatieff, *The Needs of Strangers: An Essay on the Philosophy of Human Needs* (New York: Viking, 1985), p. 141.

PART ONE

THE ROLE OF FAITH-BASED
ORGANIZATIONS IN PREVENTING
Teen Pregnancy

CHAPTER TWO

Framing the Debate: Faith-Based Approaches to Preventing Teen Pregnancy

ISABEL SAWHILL

The role of sacred places in addressing social problems has received heightened attention in recent years. The inclusion of a charitable choice provision in the welfare reform bill of 1996, together with President Bush's advocacy of faith-based approaches to social problems, has catalyzed new conversations about the wisdom and efficacy of these approaches. In my paper, I address five questions that I think we should be asking about faith-based approaches to preventing teenage pregnancy.[1] First, to what extent does our interest in preventing teen pregnancy turn on moral and ethical issues? Second, what is the role of faith-based institutions in resolving whatever moral dilemmas exist? Third, how should we think about the role of faith-based institutions in a specifically American context? Fourth, how should we deal with the conflict engendered by the fact that different faith communities have different views about the best way to reduce teen pregnancy? And, finally, what are the pros and cons of expanding government support for faith-based approaches?

To What Extent Do Our Views about Teen Pregnancy Turn on Moral Questions?

The basic fact is that four out of ten girls in the United States become pregnant before their twentieth birthday. Nearly everyone thinks that is a problem, but they do not necessarily agree about *why* it is a problem. If I had to simplify, I would say that there are two major camps: the moralists and the consequentialists. The moralists are people who, even if there were no adverse consequences, would still be concerned about the fact that sex is going on outside of marriage, particularly among those who are very young. The consequentialists are people who are worried about sexual activity among teens mostly because it leads to pregnancy or to disease.

I sometimes ask people to go through a thought experiment in which it is assumed that there is a perfect contraceptive, one that is in no way dependent on human motivation or human self-discipline. And, because there is a perfect contraceptive, there are no adverse consequences—there is no HIV or other sexually transmitted diseases, there is no AIDS, there is no pregnancy; there is just sex. Ask yourself how this set of assumptions might change your view of this issue. Would you be comfortable with your thirteen- or fourteen-year-old son or daughter being sexually active under those circumstances, or would you counsel them to abstain? How would you feel about sex outside of marriage? About sex between a twenty-three-year-old and a fifteen-year-old? About sex on a first date? Would you think sex could be an extracurricular activity like basketball in the schools? How would you view rape? Would you knock it down from a felony to a misdemeanor?

In the process of trying to answer such questions, one can begin to sort out the extent to which concerns about this problem stem from its consequences and the extent to which they relate to people's values and to the contexts in which they believe a sexual relationship between two people is more or less appropriate.

We do not yet have a perfect contraceptive. In fact, contraceptive failure rates are higher than most people realize. Teens who use contraceptives do not use them consistently. And even among consistent users of effective methods, 12 to 15 percent get pregnant in a year's time.[2] If you become sexually active on your fifteenth birthday and remain so for five years, your chances of becoming pregnant before age twenty are quite high (roughly 50 percent). Thus, even if you are a consequentialist, you can believe that abstinence for young people is a good thing. You do not have to moralize about it; you can simply say that it is the only sure way of preventing pregnancy and disease.

In fact, an earlier expectation that the widespread availability of modern methods of contraception would drastically reduce teenage pregnancy turned out to be wrong. The much greater use of contraceptives between 1970 and 1990 was not sufficient to reduce the teenage pregnancy rate. The reason the rate did not fall is because, although teens were increasingly likely to use contraceptives, many more of them were sexually active as well and thus at risk of getting pregnant. This increase in teenage sex was fueled by more permissive attitudes. According to the General Social Survey, in 1970, almost 47 percent of the American public agreed with the statement, "Sex before marriage is always or almost always wrong." By 1990, the share had fallen to 36 percent.[3] That is a huge change in attitude over a relatively short period. Over the same period, the proportion of girls ages fifteen to nineteen who reported ever having had sex increased from 29 percent to 55 percent. The net result was that the teen pregnancy rate rose 23 percent between 1972 and 1990.[4]

More recently, teen pregnancy and teen birth rates have been declining. This good news is the result of both more contraceptive use and less sex among teens. But why are teens, both boys and girls, having less sex? Numerous factors undoubtedly contribute to this trend, especially fear of AIDS and other sexually transmitted diseases, but one reason is a marked shift in attitudes or social norms. In contrast to the long-term trend of relaxing attitudes toward premarital sex, recent polls show that young people are becoming more conservative in their beliefs. For example, the percentage of college freshmen agreeing with the statement "It is all right to have sex if two people have known each other for a short time" decreased to 40 percent in 1999, down from 52 percent in 1987.[5]

My conclusion is that *values matter*. They matter both at the micro level—an individual's religious or moral values can influence that person's behavior, regardless of what others around them think or do—and they matter at the macro level—the social norms or practices of a particular era may reinforce or be in opposition to that individual's own values and behaviors. The two interact in subtle, but potentially powerful, ways. We know, for example, that the likelihood that a teenager will engage in sex is influenced by what that teenager believes his or her friends are doing.[6] These peer influences can cause small initial changes in attitudes and behavior to snowball into much bigger effects as the larger group adopts the attitudes and practices of a trend-setting or influential subgroup. Something like this seems to have happened between the 1950s and early 1990s. Premarital, including teen premarital, sex became increasingly acceptable, which is why, in the battle between sex and safe sex, sex won.

WHAT IS THE ROLE OF FAITH-BASED INSTITUTIONS?

If solutions to the problem of children having children are at least partly based on ethical and moral principles, which institutions should we look to for some answers? Basically there are three teaching institutions in our society: families, churches, and schools.

Public schools, because they are open to all, must teach "lowest common denominator curriculum." In fact, sex education in the schools, as desirable as it is, is often mostly about reproductive biology; it is much less about values and relationships.

Churches, because they consist of people who share certain moral values, can be more specific about such matters, especially about the appropriate context for sexual relationships. And families, because they dispense values on the most basic level of all, can be even more prescriptive. Most families, of course, do not exist in isolation; they tend to band together in congregations that are often defined by a shared set of religious or other beliefs.

So, faith-based approaches are appealing because they address some of the moral and ethical dimensions of teen pregnancy. They deal with the whole person; they do not deal just with the medical or reproductive aspects of the problem. And they do this in an environment—to use Bill Galston's words—of care, connection, and community.

Each faith community is going to do this in its own distinctive way. When the National Campaign produced its Nine Tips for Faith Leaders, we did not say, "Here is a particular curriculum or program that you should adopt in your church or synagogue or mosque." Instead we emphasized the need for different faiths to arm teenagers with a sense of belonging and a framework of values drawn from that faith's particular understanding of sex, love, and marriage and the relationships among them. The idea was to ask each faith community to tend its own garden, not to worry about what was planted in someone else's garden. The task for each faith community is to define when and under what circumstances sexual expression is appropriate and when and under what circumstances it is not.

Some churches have become much more proactive on this front in recent years. For example, consider a program called True Love Waits, sponsored by a loosely affiliated group of Christian ministries. The program encourages teens to take a pledge to remain abstinent until marriage. Several million teens have taken the pledge, and research by Peter Bearman and Hannah Brückner at Columbia University has shown that those who take the pledge are much more likely to remain abstinent than those who do not.[7] The program appears to work by creating a subculture within which virginity is considered "cool." However, the effectiveness of the program disappears once pledging becomes so prevalent that the teens involved no longer feel as if they belong to a special group. This suggests that faith is not just about values; it is also about a sense of belonging to a community that shares those values and about trying to live up to the expectations set by that community.

How Do We Think about This in a Specifically American Context?

Faith-based solutions are particularly appealing in the United States because of the very high level of religious engagement in this country. In 2001, almost two-thirds of Americans said religion was very important in their personal lives. The proportion is much higher among blacks (85 percent) than it is among whites (61 percent) and somewhat higher among women (71 percent) than among men (55 percent).[8] This high level of religiosity coexists with a tradition of religious tolerance. These are both distinctively American characteristics. A recent issue of *The Brookings Review*, edited by E. J. Dionne Jr. and John J. DiIulio Jr., called "What's God Got to Do with the American Experiment?" contains polling data that make this point well.[9]

On the one hand, the polls suggest that, relative to thirty years ago, the public is much more concerned about the moral failings of the population, particularly what they perceive to be the moral failings of the young. This finding holds even after adjusting for the fact that the older generation *always* tends to disapprove of the younger generation's behavior. What the data show is that the gap is wider now than in the past. In a survey conducted by the National Campaign to Prevent Teen Pregnancy, poor moral values were the most frequent reason given by adults for high rates of teen pregnancy.[10] On the other hand, the data suggest that tolerance is alive and well in the United States; that whatever moral failings people perceive around them, they are very tolerant of other individuals' right to live by their own lights. The challenge, then, is how to bring judgments to bear without doing so in a self-righteous, moralizing, or intolerant manner. How, for example, does one say that teen pregnancy is wrong without stigmatizing or denigrating those who are, or have been, teen mothers?

WHAT DO WE DO ABOUT CONFLICT?

Advocates of reducing teen pregnancy may agree about the importance of the goal but disagree about the best way of achieving it. Some want to focus on abstinence until marriage; others argue that the horse is already out of the barn and that it is far more urgent and realistic to provide teens with the information and contraceptive services that they need to protect themselves against pregnancy and disease.

Researchers have entered the fray with studies that support one view or the other. Some of these studies have been influential, but where the research conflicts with deeply held values it is likely to be rejected. For example, no matter how many times researchers tell those who advocate abstinence that providing contraceptives to teenagers has *not* been found to increase rates of sexual activity, these advocates believe that programs that teach about contraceptives—and especially those that advocate their use—send a very mixed message.

So, conflict is a problem, and it is not going to be resolved simply by looking at the facts. But we are beginning to understand that it is not necessary to convert others to our own view in order to reduce teen pregnancy in the aggregate.

Yes, it would be simpler if we could all agree on what to teach our children, and probably a little less confusing to them as well, but it is simply not true that only one approach will work. Abstinence until marriage clearly works to prevent teen pregnancy if you can convince people to adopt it. Contraceptives also clearly work to prevent teen pregnancy if they are used carefully and consistently. And many different combinations of these two approaches can work as well, including delaying sexual activity until one is through high school and practicing safe sex thereafter, just to take one of many examples. It does not have to be either/or; we should reject such a false dichotomy. Both abstinence and contraception are effective and appropriate in different circumstances.

In addition, a lot of confusion and unnecessary conflict emerges because of the tendency to label programs as either "abstinence-only" or as "comprehensive sexuality education." The reality is that most programs fall on a continuum, and this tendency to categorize and label them as falling into one camp or the other is not very useful. What happens in an actual classroom is much more complicated and nuanced than these labels suggest.

These conflicts are often barriers to collaboration. The National Campaign to Prevent Teen Pregnancy has worked with a number of local communities where disagreements about the best approach have paralyzed their efforts to do much of anything. In fact, the problem is so severe in some places that we have a favorite saying at the campaign: "While the adults are arguing, the teens are getting pregnant." The campaign has discovered that when we work through these disagreements at the local level by bringing everybody to the table and having a frank and open, but respectful, discussion—preferably one including teens themselves—the community can then move forward much more effectively.

The campaign's Task Force on Religion and Public Values, chaired by Bill Galston, has similarly had to work through its own disagreements. It is an enormously diverse group, and it spent two years trying to find common ground. By approaching its task in a positive and open-minded way, but without in any way trying to paper over the differences, it established a model for what needs to happen in the rest of the country.

The good news here is that much more common ground exists among the public at large than among the national political leaders and advocacy groups focusing on this issue. Although the organized groups have the loudest, and often the most strident, voices, polls show that the overwhelming majority of both adults and teenagers have a more middle-of-the-road, commonsense view. They are in favor of abstinence for school-age youth, but they also want contraceptives to be available for kids who need them. Specifically, in a survey released by the National Campaign to Prevent Teen Pregnancy in April 2001, 73 percent of adults and 56 percent of teens believed that teens should not be sexually active, but that those who are should have access to birth control.[11] More than 90 percent of both adults and teens want teens to receive a strong message that they should abstain from sex until they are at least out of high school.[12] The public is saying that we should embrace abstinence as the standard but recognize that not everyone will abide by the standard and that it is important to have a safety net. At the same time, by overwhelming majorities, they reject the view that it is okay for teens to be sexually active as long as they have access to birth control.[13]

WHAT ARE THE PROS AND CONS OF MORE GOVERNMENT SUPPORT FOR FAITH-BASED APPROACHES?

The values component of this issue and the fact that most religions have a point of view on it, together with the importance so many Americans attribute to religion, suggests that faith-based organizations have an important role to play in preventing teen pregnancy. President Bush has made faith-based approaches a centerpiece of his domestic agenda and has suggested that they might be especially effective in combating teen pregnancy. The public seems to agree. According to a Pew Research Center survey in cooperation with the Pew Forum on Religion and Public Life, 70 percent are in favor of government funding for faith-based programs. However, when asked what type of organization—religious, nonreligious, or government—is best equipped to address teen pregnancy, 39 percent thought religious organizations would do the best job, a slightly higher number (42 percent) favored other nonprofit organizations, and only 12 percent wanted the government directly involved.

Since more faith-based initiatives will arise because of the new White House office, a host of issues will need to be resolved. What is the capacity of this sector to deliver the services? Should the funding be provided directly to religious organizations or indirectly through vouchers that can be used to buy services from both sectarian and nonsectarian organizations, or through charitable tax credits for those who give to faith-based programs? Who will monitor the expenditure of funds and hold the recipients accountable for results? How does one maintain the kind of separation of church and state called for in the constitution? The charitable choice provision in the 1996 welfare bill provides one model. Under charitable choice, faith-based organizations can compete for funding on an equal basis with other organizations. Any faith-based program must be open to all, regardless of religious affiliation or belief; applicants for services must be provided with a choice of providers (including nonsectarian providers); and the funds cannot be used for purely sectarian purposes.

Assuming that such issues can be resolved, the question will still be: How much difference would more funding of faith-based programs make? Compared with secular programs, are faith-based programs a more effective means of reducing teen pregnancy? Is the "faith" component of faith-based programs a critical ingredient, or is allowing religious organizations to participate in running programs just one way of expanding program capacity? There is little hard evidence on these questions. A review of fifty research studies indicates that teens who are more religious (variously defined) are more likely to delay having sex, although they also may be less likely to use contraception once they do become sexually active.[14] However, the available research is not of high quality and cannot distinguish between two very different explanations. One is that teens with a commitment to delaying sex are, for a variety of reasons, also more likely to be religious. The other is that church attendance or religious beliefs actually produce this commitment. Because it would be difficult, if not impossible, to assign people randomly to programs with and without a faith component, we may never know with any certainty how important the faith ingredient in faith-based programs really is. In the meantime, many fear that expanding faith-based programs will infringe on people's civil liberties and pierce the wall between church and state or that they will teach about abstinence but leave young people with few defenses should they become sexually involved. Such concerns are not entirely unfounded. But my own view is that, on balance, we should expand the sector in ways that would enable more teenagers to find a faith-based "home" within their community. This contributes to the development of lifestyle values that lead to more responsible behavior by providing teens with the kind of social support and spiritual guidance that too often is missing in their lives.

NOTES

1. In answering these questions, I want to acknowledge my indebtedness to William Galston, Sister Mary Rose McGeady, Douglas Kirby, Pat Funderbunk Ware, Pat Fagan, E. J. Dionne Jr., and John J. DiIulio Jr.

2. Robert A. Hatcher and others, *Contraceptive Technology*, 17th rev. ed. (New York, Ardent Media, 1998).

3. Inter-University Consortium for Political and Social Research (ICPSR), *General Social Survey* (University of Michigan, 1998).

4. National Campaign to Prevent Teen Pregnancy, *Halfway There: A Prescription for Continued Progress in Preventing Teen Pregnancy* (Washington, D.C.: National Campaign to Prevent Teen Pregnancy, 2001), pp. 1, 9.

5. University of California, Los Angeles, "College Freshmen: Acceptance of Abortion, Casual Sex at All-Time Low," *Kaiser Daily Reproductive Health Report*, January 27, 1999, available on-line at report.KFF.org/archive/repro/1999/01/kr990127.6/html.

6. Bradford Brown and Wendy Theobald, "How Peers Matter: A Research Synthesis of Peer Influences in Adolescent Pregnancy," in *Peer Potential: Making the Most of How Teens Influence Each Other*, pp. 27–80 (Washington, D.C.: National Campaign to Prevent Teen Pregnancy, 1999). See also Peter S. Bearman and Hannah Brückner, "Peer Effects on Adolescent

Sexual Debut and Pregnancy: An Analysis of a National Survey of Adolescent Girls," in *Peer Potential*.

7. Peter S. Bearman and Hannah Brückner, "Promising the Future: Virginity Pledges and the Transition to First Intercourse," *American Journal of Sociology*, vol. 106, no. 4 (2001), pp. 859–912.

8. Pew Forum on Religion and Public Life and Pew Research Center for the People and the Press, *Faith-Based Funding Backed, but Church-State Doubts Abound: A Survey for the Pew Forum on Religion and Public Life* (Washington, D.C.: April 10, 2001), p. 31.

9. E. J. Dionne Jr. and John J. DiIulio Jr., eds., "What's God Got to Do with the American Experiment?" *Brookings Review*, vol. 17, no. 2 (1999).

10. National Campaign to Prevent Teen Pregnancy, *With One Voice: America's Adults and Teens Sound Off about Teen Pregnancy* (Washington, D.C.: National Campaign to Prevent Teen Pregnancy, 2001), p. 10.

11. Ibid., p. 5.

12. Ibid., p. 6.

13. Ibid., p. 5.

14. Brain Wilcox and others, *Adolescent Religiosity and Sexual Behavior: A Research Review* (Washington, D.C.: National Campaign to Prevent Teen Pregnancy, 2001).

CHAPTER THREE

Joseph's Promise:
Extending God's Grace
to Pregnant Teens

DEBRA W. HAFFNER

A young teenage woman is found to be pregnant. She has been denying it to herself for months. It is only now, as her belly swells, that someone else notices. Her boyfriend, to whom she is engaged, decides to leave her quietly. "Not mine," he thinks. She is afraid and alone. She is desperate. Thus opens the Gospel of Matthew, but it is a scene that occurs every day in inner-city America, in rural, small-town America, and in suburban, middle-class America. Her name could be Melissa Dressler, Amy Grossberg, Towanda Cunningham, or Linda Hall. In the Gospel of Matthew, her name is Mary.

Teen pregnancy is so pervasive—and its consequences so far-reaching—that it seems to me that the relevant question is not "Why should faith communities be involved?" but instead "How can they not be?" Faith communities must be involved with helping young people prevent pregnancies. When that fails, they must be involved in helping teen parents raise their children in a loving and supportive environment. More fundamentally, faith communities can give young people the skills and attitudes they need to lay a foundation for healthy adult intimate lives for themselves and their future families. We have known for more than two decades that teenagers need two things to avoid teen childbearing: capacity and motivation. Faith communities can help to provide both. They can promote capacity by helping teens remain abstinent and by helping sexually active young people use contraception. They can promote motivation by pro-

This paper is adapted from the author's publication, *A Time to Speak: Faith Communities and Sexuality Education* (New York: SIECUS, 1998).

viding important adult connections to young people who need guidance and support.

We need to deal with young people holistically. Teen pregnancy, HIV/AIDS, and adolescent sexually transmitted diseases are not separate problems for separate, young individuals; they are all related to adolescent sexuality. Faith communities need to address sexuality and their youth from preventative, pastoral, restorative, scientific, and spiritual views.

I learned in the seminary that the word "gospel" literally means the good news. I am going to focus on the good news about faith communities and teen pregnancy, but I want to offer two caveats. First, the fact that I am going to talk about the good news does not mean that I think that the faith communities are doing enough or that, in every faith community I discuss, all congregations are involved in teen pregnancy issues. The second caveat is that faith communities alone are not the answer to this problem—no more than schools alone, or parents alone, or government alone, or the media alone can be the answer. During the last quarter century, we have searched for the magic bullet. In 1976, we thought that just giving teens information would be enough. Then we thought that just opening school-based clinics would be enough. Youth development and education approaches, whether secular or faith-based, also will not be enough. Every church, every synagogue, and every mosque in this country could be involved in this issue, but we still would have a teenage pregnancy problem in this country.

RELIGIOUS INSTITUTIONS REACH YOUTH

Thirty years ago, the National Council of Churches, the Synagogue Council of America, and the United States Catholic Conference called on churches and synagogues to become actively involved in sexuality education within their own congregations and within their communities. On June 8, 1968, they released a statement that remains remarkable today for the tenor of its call for religious involvement in sexuality issues for young people. They wrote:

> We recognize that some parents desire supplementary assistance from church or synagogues and other agencies. Each community of faith should provide resources, leadership, and opportunities, as appropriate, for young people to learn about their development into manhood and womanhood and for adults to grow an understanding of their roles as men and women in family, society, and in the light of their religious heritage. In addition to parents and the religious community, the school and other community agencies can have a vital role in sex education in two particular ways: first,

they can integrate sound sexual information and attitudes with the total education which the child receives in social studies, literature, history, home economics, and the biological and behavioral sciences. Second, they can reach the large numbers of young people whose families have no religious identification but who need to understand their own sexuality and their role in society. . . .

The increased concern and interest in this vital area of human experience now manifested by parents, educators, and religious leaders are cause for gratitude. We urge all to take a more active role, each in its own area of responsibility and competence, in promoting sound leadership and programs in sex education. We believe it is possible to help our sons and daughters achieve a richer, fuller understanding of their sexuality so that their children will enter a world where men and women live and work together in understanding and cooperation and love.[1]

It would be exciting and much anticipated for those three bodies to reaffirm their commitment to this call, issued more than thirty years ago. Religious institutions have the ability to reach young people, and therefore they have a unique role to play in preventing teenage pregnancy. Indeed, after the schools, religious institutions commit themselves to serving teenagers in this country more than any other community agency. Moreover, they are specifically empowered to do so from a moral perspective. Almost 90 percent of teens report that they have a religion.[2] More than 60 percent of young people spend at least an hour a week in a church or synagogue-based activity.[3] And 75 percent of teenagers say that religion and church are "somewhat important" to them, including almost half who say they are "very important."[4]

Yet young people report that faith communities are ignoring their sexuality issues. Only four in ten young people say they receive support and care from adults in their religious community.[5] That is a remarkable statement: six in ten teens *do not* think that the adults in the faith community are there for them. Four in ten teenagers report that they have spent less than six hours in their lifetime addressing a sexuality issue in their church or synagogue.[6] Only half of young people say that their congregation is doing a "good" or "excellent" job at helping prepare them for life.[7] Only 4 percent of youth workers report that they address sexuality at least once a month with teens.[8]

Involvement in a religious community actually protects young people from risk-taking behaviors, including involvement with sexual intercourse at an early age. Teenagers who say that religion and prayer are important to them are more likely to delay sexual intercourse, less likely to use alcohol, less likely to use tobacco, and less likely to use drugs.[9] Almost half of teens say they have "made a conscious decision to wait to have sex." The more importance a teen boy or girl places on religion, the more likely he or she is to name this as the reason for delaying intercourse.[10] More than 21 percent of girls who consider religion important make a conscious decision to wait.[11] Boys who consider religion very important in their lives are half as likely to have had sexual intercourse, as compared to boys who do not consider religion important.[12]

Religious commitment is also correlated with whether a teen has engaged in sexual or intimate activities other than intercourse. The more importance a teen places on religion, the less likely he or she is to have engaged in activities such as French kissing and petting.[13]

Religious Institutions Support Involvement

Although teens see the congregations as caring too little about their struggles with sexuality, religious institutions increasingly *want* to be involved in these issues. Indeed, a majority of Christian and Jewish clergy support religious involvement in sexuality issues. According to a survey by the Religious Coalition for Reproductive Choice, 89 percent of clergy agree that sexuality needs to be part of a congregation's program, 95 percent agree that it is appropriate to speak about sexuality issues in religious programs, and 75 percent consider it a problem that religious programs do not address sexuality issues.[14] More than 2,000 clergy and theologians have endorsed the Religious Declaration on Sexual Morality, Justice, and Healing, which calls for comprehensive sexuality education in congregations, schools, and seminaries.[15]

Many denominations and faith institutions have issued statements strongly supporting sexuality and HIV education, both within their congregations and in their communities. For example, the American Baptist Church, the Central Conference of American Rabbis, the Disciples of Christ, the Episcopal Church, the Mennonite Church, the National Council of Churches of Christ, the Presbyterian Church USA, the Unitarian Universalist Association, the United Church of Christ, the United Methodist Church, and the United Synagogues of Conservative Judaism have passed resolutions supporting sexuality education within their faith community. For example, the Christian Church of Christ adopted this resolution in 1987:

> Whereas the number of teen pregnancies is increasing, and it is evident that there is a need for sexuality education for teenagers and their parents; and, whereas human sexuality is recognized as a gift from God and sexuality is therefore a concern of the Church; and, whereas the Church affirms the basic values of love, respect, and responsibility in all human relationships; therefore, be it resolved that Disciples' congregations will play

a central role in the education of their young people and parents by offering clear and responsible information on human sexuality.[16]

Some faith communities have called for sexuality education in the public schools. The American Jewish Congress, the Conference of American Rabbis, the Church of the Brethren, the Episcopal Church, the National Council of Churches of Christ, the Presbyterian Church, the United Church of Christ, the Unitarian Universalist Association, and the United Methodist Church all call on communities to take a role in this issue. For example, the policy of the Church of the Brethren says:

> Education for family life is appropriate within the public schools. It is needed to supplement instruction in the home and church. Public school instruction should include information about the body, sex organs, the reproductive system, but the emphasis should be on values and relationships. Teachers who are responsible for this task should be well trained themselves, and they themselves should be worthy models of mature and responsible sexuality. The Church supports responsible family life education in the public schools, as long as the religious commitment of all students and residents of the community is respected. Parents should keep themselves informed about the content of family-life education courses in which their children are influenced and use that educational experience to foster open discussion of the topic of sexuality with their children. Parents should also be acquainted with the content of such courses for the purposes of continuing dialog with school officials. In such dialog, parents should clarify their Christian principles to insure that their own ethical values are not undermined. Family-life education will not solve all sex, marriage, and family problems. The task requires the coordinated efforts of home, school, and church.[17]

Several denominations have called on congregations to actively support sexuality and HIV education programs in the community. For example, in 1996, the United Methodist Church passed the social principle:

> All children have the right to quality education, including full sexual education appropriate to their stage of development that utilizes the best educational techniques and insights. . . . We recognize the continuing need for full, positive, and factual sex education opportunities for children, youth, and adults. The church offers a unique opportunity to give quality guidance and education in this area.[18]

Another example is the 1994 Presbyterian Church of the USA resolution:

Whereas, the Presbyterian Church (USA) recognized at the 204th General Assembly (1992) that sexuality education is a positive factor in preventing unintended pregnancies and the need for abortion; and whereas, Christian sexuality education should first be done within the family; and whereas, the Church can support and train parents and other custodial adults, youth directors, and clergy in this important task; and whereas, the church recognizes that the public schools are also an appropriate setting for educating students about sexuality as an important part of human growth and development, especially when that education is not available in the home or church; and whereas, the Presbyterian Church (USA) feels strongly that the public education system should include quality sexuality education as a component of any human growth and development curriculum beginning in the elementary grades; therefore, the 206th General Assembly (1994) of the Presbyterian Church (USA): (1) Supports the United States Department of Health and Human Services and the U.S. Surgeon General in planning and implementing comprehensive school health education that includes age and developmentally appropriate sexuality education in all grades as a part of human growth and development curriculum for youth. (2) Calls upon state legislatures to require that all schools provide comprehensive kindergarten through twelfth grade human growth and development education that is complete, factual, accurate, free of bias, and does not discriminate on the basis of sex, race, national origin, ancestry, creed, pregnancy, marital or parental status, sexual orientation, or physical, mental, emotional, or learning disability. (3) Calls upon the congregations of the Presbyterian Church (USA) to provide additional sexuality education that reflects the values of the Reformed theological tradition.[19]

In summary, many denominations have developed their own curricula and guides for sexuality education in faith communities. A few denominations, including the Presbyterian Church USA, the United Church of Christ, and the Unitarian Universalist Association, have developed life span curriculums. Other denominations have programs for teenagers, including the Church of the Brethren, the Evangelical Lutheran Church in America, the Mennonite Church, the Salvation Army, the Southern Baptist Convention, and the United Methodist Church. The Catholic Church has adopted the Benziger Family Life Program for young people, kindergarten through eighth grades. The United Methodist Church has a curriculum for older elementary school children.

There is a need for life span sexuality programs in faith communities, beginning with parents of pre-schoolers and continuing through programs for the elderly. One of the frequent mistakes is to treat sexuality information as an immunization given to the early teens once, with an expectation that it will last them for life. The development of sound sexual values and attitudes begins in early childhood and continues through adolescence and adulthood. The type of information and support needed at each stage differs; for adults, the need for information on sexuality at age forty-five is very different than the need at age eighteen, and it will be very different again at age seventy-eight. And while programs such as those of the Presbyterian Church, the United Church of Christ, and the Unitarian Universalist Association take seriously the need for faith communities to address sexuality for people throughout their lives, most church-based and secular programs concentrate their sexuality education programs at the level of teenagers. Those programs should be broadened for greater effect.

CONGREGATIONAL ACTIVITIES

Faith communities can offer young people many types of support and programs that could contribute to the prevention of teenage pregnancy. For example, congregations offer young people opportunities for service, a positive peer group, and a faith-based foundation for decisionmaking. Congregations could support not only prevention programs but also pregnant teenagers as well. While researching this paper, I found that there have been many reports, going back to 1975, from states, communities, and the National Academy of Sciences on what congregations should do to *prevent* pregnancy. I could not find a single one that discussed the role that congregations should play with *already pregnant* teenagers.

Congregations can help to prevent teen pregnancy by encouraging youth groups to participate in community activities related to sexuality. For example, a young person might volunteer at an AIDS hospice, work at a hospital nursery, educate or minister to peers, or staff a community hotline. These activities would offer teens an opportunity for service, while directly adding to the resources that teens can draw on as they continue to learn about themselves, their sexuality, and the consequences of various sexual behaviors. Congregations also can hold after-school programs in the church or temple facility for pre-teens and teenagers. These programs may include sexuality topics as discussed above, or they may have a primarily recreational purpose. After all, even without sexuality-related programming, young people who are involved in after-school activities, particularly in religious institutions, are less likely to become involved in sexual behavior.

Congregations also can influence peer cultures by implementing a peer education program around sexuality issues. When trained high school youth groups provide education and information about sexuality to middle school students and pre-adolescents, both groups benefit. It is no secret that many congregations "lose" their adolescents after their coming-of-age ceremonies. Offering a sexuality education program for high school youth might help to keep them involved. It is important for youth ministers to address sexuality issues, to offer guidelines for youth retreats, sleepovers, and camping trips, and to be explicit about expectations for youth and leaders. In this way, congregations can help youth to learn skills, such as assertiveness, communication, negotiation, and decisionmaking, that will help them to avoid unplanned and premature sexual behavior. They also can provide them with opportunities to explore controversial issues.

Congregations can help young people to find adult mentors and positive role models. Young people need significant adults in their lives in addition to their parents. And congregations can provide important support for parents, who are the primary sexuality educators of their children. Most parents welcome the assistance of their faith community in helping to provide their children with morals and values. In addition to imparting knowledge, congregations can help adults to develop the skills they need to be good parents, and that includes helping them talk to their children about sexuality. Pastors can encourage parent/child communication on sexuality issues. It is important that religious education programs keep parents informed and up-to-date on efforts to educate their youth about sexuality. Parents need an opportunity to review the curricula and materials, meet with the adult leaders, and complete parent/child homework sessions to increase communication about sexuality issues. Life span religious education can hold retreats for middle school students and their parents.

Faith communities have a unique role to play in sexuality education and teen pregnancy prevention within the context of the religious values supported by that denomination. The Southern Baptists' True Love Waits program, which revolves around young people taking virginity pledges, and the United Church of Christ and the Unitarian Universalist Association's Our Whole Lives program differ dramatically. The programs differ vastly in their approach, and yet both are grounded in the faith principles of the denominations, and both reflect the wishes of the parents who attend them. Neither would be appropriate in the public school setting without major adaptation. But within their own faith context, they are appropriate and responsive to the needs of young people.

Congregations also can play a supportive role in helping pregnant teens and their families to cope with pregnancy. Pastors and congregations should reach out with love to families coping with a pregnant teen girl and her partner. Such support might include counseling on pregnancy options; adoption assistance; adoption, prenatal, and abortion referrals; premarital counseling; and support for the newborn and mother, consistent with the values of the religious community.

When we think about safe communities and teen pregnancy prevention, we need not think just about sexuality education and HIV education programs. The faith community is a place where young people can be connected, where they can become involved in volunteer activities, where they can interact with other significant adults in addition to their parents, where they can make friendships, where they can develop relationships, and where they can find mentors. Teenage pregnancy can be prevented when young people are offered hope for their future. Our faith communities do that, even when they do not explicitly address sexuality issues.

GOVERNMENT FUNDING TO FAITH COMMUNITIES FOR TEEN PREGNANCY PREVENTION

Congregations across the United States have been involved in a variety of programs to promote abstinence among teenagers under federal grant programs. Many congregations received funding under the Adolescent Family Life Act demonstration grants (a program known as AFLA) to prevent teenage pregnancy through teaching abstinence and promoting adoption as the appropriate choice for teenagers who become pregnant. In 1983, a group of clergy and other individuals filed suit against AFLA claiming it was administered in a way that violated the Establishment Clause of the First Amendment in the U.S. constitution. The plaintiffs in *Kendrick* v. *Sullivan* claimed that the program constituted a federal endorsement of a particular religious point of view.

Although the Supreme Court ruled that the statute was constitutional on its face, litigation continued over the manner in which the program was administered. In January 1993, an out-of-court settlement stipulated that AFLA-funded sexuality education not include religious references, be medically accurate, respect the principle of self-determination of teenagers regarding contraceptive referrals, and not allow grantees to use church sanctuaries for their programs or give presentations in parochial schools during school hours.[20] The settlement expired in 1998, at the same time that the new Abstinence Only Until Marriage program under Title V, Section 510(b), began. During the first year of implementation of the program, eighteen states made Section 510(b) grants directly to faith-based institutions, and twenty-four states reported that abstinence programs took place in faith-based institutions.[21]

CONCLUSIONS

Let us end where we started: at the opening section of the Gospel of Matthew. The text says that Joseph is going to dismiss Mary quietly. Then he goes to sleep, and he has a dream. In the dream, he is told that the child to be born will fulfill the prophecy of Emmanuel, which means "God is with us." Joseph decides that he will support Mary, marry her, and help her to raise the child.

Our faith communities have a role to play in helping our children understand that our sexuality is a sacred gift of creation and that its power needs to be exercised responsibly. We must extend God's grace to all of our children: to the virgins, but also to the young people who are engaged in sexual activity, to those who struggle with their sexual orientation, and to those who face unplanned pregnancies or sexually transmitted diseases. Our faith communities should provide our welcome, our love, and our support to all teens. "God is with us." Isn't that the promise of every child? Of every teenager, regardless of the circumstances of his or her birth? Are we called to do any less than Joseph?

NOTES

1. National Council of Churches Commission on Marriage and Family, the Synagogue Council of America Committee on Family, and the United States Catholic Conference Family Life Bureau, "Interfaith Statement on Sex Education" (National Council of Churches Commission on Marriage and Family, the Synagogue Council of America Committee on Family, and the United States Catholic Conference Family Life Bureau, 1968).

2. Michael D. Resnick and others, "Protecting Adolescents from Harm: Findings from the National Longitudinal Study on Adolescent Health," *Journal of the American Medical Association (JAMA)*, vol. 278, no. 10 (September 10, 1997), pp. 823–32.

3. P. L. Benson, P. C. Scales, and E. C. Roehlkepartain, *A Fragile Foundation: The State of Developmental Assets among American Youth* (Minneapolis, Minn.: Search Institute, forthcoming).

4. Kaiser Family Foundation and YM Magazine, "National Survey of Teens: Teens Talk about Dating, Intimacy, and Their Sexual Experiences" (Menlo Park, Calif.: Henry J. Kaiser Family Foundation, Spring 1998), pp. 6–7.

5. E. C. Roehlkepartain and P. L. Benson, *Youth in Protestant Churches* (Minneapolis, Minn.: Search Institute, 1993), p. 61.

6. Ibid., p. 108.

7. Ibid., p. 110.

8. E. C. Roehlkepartain and P. C. Scales, *Youth Development in Congregations: An Exploration of the Potential Barriers* (Minneapolis, Minn.: Search Institute, 1995).

9. Resnick and others, "Protecting Adolescents from Harm."

10. Kaiser Family Foundation and YM Magazine, "National Survey of Teens."

11. Ibid.

12. Ibid.

13. Ibid.

14. Rabbi Bonnie Margulis, "Clergy Attitudes towards Sexuality and Reproductive Choice" (Washington, D.C.: Religious Coalition for Reproductive Choice, March 1998).

15. See the website, www.religionproject.org: June 4, 2001.

16. Christian Church of Christ, "Resolution no. 8718: Resolution Concerning Sexuality Education" (Christian Church of Christ, 1987), p. 270.

17. Church of the Brethren, "Annual Conference Statement: Human Sexuality from a Christian Perspective" (Church of the Brethren, 1983).

18. United Methodist Church, "Social Principles" (United Methodist Church, 1996), p. 15.

19. Presbyterian Church USA, "Sexuality Education for Youth" (Presbyterian Church USA, July/August 1994).

20. Daniel Daley, "Exclusive Purpose: Abstinence-Only Proponents Create Federal Entitlement in Welfare Reform," *SIECUS Report,* vol. 25, no. 4 (April/May 1997), p. 4.

21. Daniel Daley, *Between the Lines: States' Implementation of the Federal Government's Section 510(b) Abstinence Education Program in Fiscal Year 1998* (New York: SIECUS, 1999).

CHAPTER FOUR

Conservative Triumph: Successes of Worship and Family in Preventing Teen Pregnancy

PATRICK F. FAGAN

The dust is clearing from the falling rubble of the sexual revolution, and social scientists are measuring the fallout. This paper argues that some of the major conservative tenets on sexual issues are increasingly solid or, at minimum, defensible in social science terms. Conservative, religious approaches to sexual morality have a firmer grasp on what is good for teenagers (as well as adults and society as a whole) than do liberal, secular ideas—and they have a clearer, though not necessarily easier, path to that good. The time is ripe for conservative beliefs on sexual morality to claim their place in the public discussion on sex education because conservatives now have the data to illustrate, even in mere utilitarian terms, the reasonableness of their principles.

I also intend to introduce to participants in the debate on sex education a variable in teenage sexual behaviors that is both powerful and neglected: regular worship of God (with the sociological proxy of "frequency of attendance at religious worship" as the measure of this practice). The weekly practice of worship is not just a major part of comprehensive sex education. It is likely the *most* powerful of all influences in attaining the goals of *liberal* sex education, especially when combined with the influence of parental involvement. This conclusion is different from the new development among liberals (with which I agree) that religious institutions have a significant role to play in the delivery of sex education. But independent of sex education, the practice of religious belief—and especially religious worship itself—is perhaps the most powerful variable for good in the formation of sexual attitudes and habits among young people.

In contrast to the effects of liberal sex education programs, the practice of religious beliefs has strong effects in bringing about desired conduct. When adolescents, their peers, or their parents worship God regularly in congregations, adolescent sexual activity is reduced. When parents and their adolescent children *all* worship together, the effect is even greater.

THE POSITIVE EFFECTS ON SEXUAL BEHAVIOR OF THE WORSHIP OF GOD BY ADOLESCENTS

Personal worship of God by adolescents sharply reduces the incidence of premarital intercourse.[1] The more regularly adolescents worship God, the less they engage in sexual activity outside of marriage. Those who do not worship at all engage in high levels of sexual activity. For example, the association between the frequency of worship by all adolescents ages twelve to seventeen and their rate of virginity is striking, based on data from the National Longitudinal Survey of Adolescent Health (often called Add Health); see figure 4-1. Those who worship weekly are more than twice as likely to be virgins as those who do not.

Figure 4-1. *Sexual Experience and Frequency of Worship, Teenagers 12–17*

Percent virgin/nonvirgin

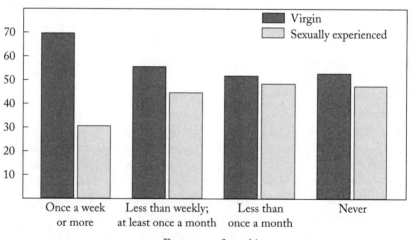

Frequency of worship

Source: Heritage Foundation domestic policy chart based on data collected 1994–1996 from J. Richard Udry, *The National Longitudinal Study of Adolescent Health* (University of North Carolina at Chapel Hill, Carolina Population Center).

Personal religious practice has a significant and positive impact on the choices that adolescents make regarding their initiation of sexual intercourse. Researchers have found, for example, that the more importance adolescents give to religion and prayer, the longer they retain their virginity.[2] Significantly, this connection between personal religious worship and virginity is noticeable for all adolescent males regardless of their testosterone levels, despite the fact that levels of testosterone normally affect the onset of sexual intercourse among males.[3]

The link between adolescent virginity and personal religious practice is further supported by the findings of Emogene Fox and Michael Young, health educators in Arkansas. In a 1989 survey of 200 freshmen, they find that virgins are significantly more likely than nonvirgins to participate in worship, prayer, and Bible reading and to view the maintenance of virginity as part of God's will for them.[4]

Not only is personal religious practice strongly associated with adolescent sexual abstinence, but the absence of religious practice also is associated with increased premarital sexual involvement. These relationships hold into early adulthood for women (figure 4-2) and for men.

Figure 4-2. *Sexual Experience of Young Adult Females in 1983 and Church Attendance in 1982*

Percent virgin/nonvirgin

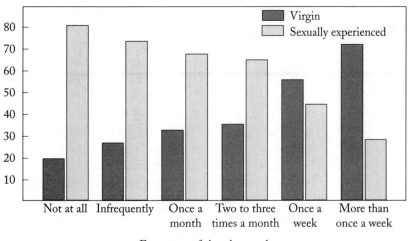

Frequency of church attendance

Source: Heritage Foundation domestic policy chart based on data from *National Longitudinal Study of Youth* (U.S. Department of Labor, Bureau of Labor Statistics). Original analysis by Center for Data Analysis, Heritage Foundation.

Data on the association between the absence of personal religious worship and early adolescent sexual behavior have been available for some time, including a 1991 analysis of the National Survey of Family Growth and a 1989 study by Arland Thornton of the University of Michigan.[5]

Research on adults further confirms the connection between lack of religious practice and high-risk sexual behavior. For example, never-married and divorced adults who have no religious *affiliation* (a much weaker link than regular religious *practice*) are two and three times, respectively, more likely to have multiple sex partners than those who *have* a religious affiliation.[6] These differences play out in higher rates of sexually transmitted diseases.[7]

Similarly, young women who do not worship regularly and who lose their virginity early are more likely to have multiple sex partners.[8] Researchers also have found that the earlier a young woman loses her virginity, the more likely she is to become pregnant. Moreover, among adolescent girls who do lose their virginity, one in five becomes pregnant as an adolescent.[9]

THE POSITIVE EFFECTS OF PEERS WHO PRACTICE THEIR RELIGIOUS BELIEFS

Personal practice is only one religious variable affecting adolescent sexual activity. The religious practice of peers also significantly affects rates of adolescent sexual activity. In the same way that personal religious practice provides a moral compass for adolescents, religious peers act as a community that reinforces religious norms regarding sexual activity. This positive community reinforcement by religious peers has a tremendous impact on the sexual behavior of adolescents.

Both for better and for worse, peer attitudes affect the rates of sexual activity among adolescents. For example, a Utah State University team has found that the combined influence of peer sexual activity and frequency of religious worship is dramatically correlated with subjects' rate of virginity, as shown in figure 4-3.[10] (Figure 4-3 does not, however, separate the effects of frequency of worship and of peer sexual activity.) For example, Best Friends is a peer-based program that teaches abstinence. In the period studied, only 1 percent of program participants became pregnant, and 90 percent remained sexually abstinent throughout adolescence. This is a testament to the power that peer attitudes can have on rates of adolescent sexual activity.

A research team in Philadelphia confirms these findings: the attitudes of peers strongly influence the choices that adolescents make regarding sexual activity. Early sexual intercourse does not happen spontaneously; rather, peers' patterns of dating, premarital sex, and church attendance accurately predict the loss of virginity among young women.[11] Similar results emerge from a 1985 study

Figure 4-3. *Sexual Experience, Peers' Sexual Experience, and Frequency of Worship*

Percent nonvirgin

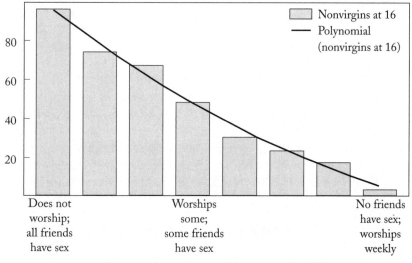

Peer sexual experience and frequency of worship

Source: E. Jeffrey Hill and others, "Religiosity and Adolescent Sexual Intercourse: Reciprocal Effects," unpublished manuscript (Utah State University, 1999).

of black teenagers. The study finds a strong connection between adolescents' frequency of church attendance and their attitudes toward sexual permissiveness. The study also finds a connection between adolescents' judgment of their friends' sexual behavior and their own.[12]

True Love Waits, a faith-based program run by the Southern Baptist Convention, also illustrates the positive influence of religious peers: between 1994 and 2000, more than 2.4 million adolescents between fifteen and nineteen pledged to remain sexually abstinent until marriage.[13] The effects of such programs are appearing in national surveys. According to the National Longitudinal Survey of Adolescent Health, nearly 16 percent of adolescent girls and 10 percent of adolescent boys have made such pledges.[14] When adolescents pledge abstinence until marriage, they are much more likely to delay intercourse.[15] Elayne Bennett, president of Best Friends, reports that of all the girls in the Best Friends program who pledge to delay first sexual initiation, 90 percent intend to abstain until marriage.[16]

The Positive Effects of Family Religious Practice on Adolescent Sexual Behavior

Family religious practice is another potent factor in discouraging adolescent sexual activity. Parents have great influence on their children's sexual decisionmaking.[17] They influence their adolescents' sexual behavior in many ways: through their level of religious worship, through the family life they construct for their children, and by their commitment to their marriage.

Family religious practice deters sexual activity among adolescents. As figure 4-4 illustrates, the religious worship of parents is powerfully linked to the sexual behavior of their children. There is a very high connection between a father's religious practice and his children's virginity—even greater than the strong connection between a mother's religious practice and her children's virginity. When both parents worship, the relationship is magnified: there is a powerful, positive relationship with their children's sexual activity.[18] Thus it is not surprising that

Figure 4-4. *Teenagers' Sexual Experience and Frequency of Worship of Mother and Father*

Percent virgin/nonvirgin

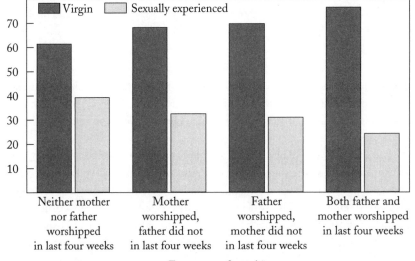

Frequency of worship

Source: Heritage Foundation domestic policy chart based on data collected 1994–96 from J. Richard Udry, *The National Longitudinal Study of Adolescent Health* (Carolina Population Center, University of North Carolina at Chapel Hill).

a faith-based sex education program involving mostly black teenage girls and their mothers in poor Southern communities almost totally eliminated out-of-wedlock births among the high-risk, single-parent population.[19]

Religious families are more likely to encourage sexual abstinence, and this has an effect on the sexual behavior of adolescents. When parents hold strong opinions on sexual abstinence and make sure their children know their views and wishes, adolescents are more likely to maintain their virginity and refrain from becoming pregnant.[20] Conversely, in their 1981 study "Adamant Virgins, Potential Non-Virgins, and Non-Virgins," E. S. Herold and M. S. Goodwin find that "parental acceptance of pre-marital intercourse was more common among the non-virgins [21 percent] than the potential non-virgins [9 percent] or adamant virgins [3 percent] [$p < 1.001$]."[21] After reviewing the recent National Longitudinal Study of Adolescent Health data, Michael Resnick and his colleagues conclude that, for American adolescents in the 1990s, "significant family factors associated with delaying sexual debut include . . . parental disapproval of their adolescent's using contraception."[22]

MARITAL STABILITY AND TEEN SEXUAL ACTIVITY

The literature shows a strong relationship between marital stability and teenage virginity, neatly summed up in Utah State University Brent Miller's rule of a 33 percent increase in sexual initiation for every change in parents' marital status.[23] However, this stability is, in turn, related to the parents' own practice of the worship of God.

The literature repeatedly shows that parents' levels of religious belief and practice clearly influence their own marital stability, happiness, and satisfaction.[24] Researchers back in the 1950s found that couples with long-lasting marriages frequently explained that the practice of religion was the reason for their marital happiness.[25] In the early 1980s Nick Stinnet of the University of Alabama and John DeFrain of the University of Nebraska come to the same conclusion: 84 percent of strong families identify religion as an important contributor to the strength of their family life.[26] More recent systematic reviews of the research literature also confirm that church attendance is the best predictor of marital stability.[27]

Regular worship attendance, rather than the doctrinal teaching on marriage, seems to be the critical factor in marital stability across denominations. For instance, in the 1960s, black Protestants in the South and white Catholics in Massachusetts had similarly low rates of divorce and similarly high rates of church attendance, although they held to very different doctrines on the indissolubility of marriage.[28] When marital separation occurs, the level of worship by each spouse influences reconciliation rates. Rates are higher among regular church attendees, and they are highest when both separated spouses have similarly high levels of church attendance.[29] Furthermore, couples who have some religious belief are less likely to file for divorce. In a study at California State University, sociologists Jerry S. Moneker and Robert P. Ranken analyze records for couples who filed for divorce in California between 1966 and 1971. They find that "couples who report no religious affiliation appear to be at greatest risk of early filing for divorce."[30]

The link between stable home life and family practice of religion has been demonstrated repeatedly. "Middletown," one of the classic sociological research projects of the twentieth century, studied the lives of inhabitants of a typical American town, first in the 1920s and later in the 1980s. Howard Bahr and Bruce Chadwick, professors of sociology at Brigham Young University, conclude on the basis of these studies that "there is a relationship between family solidarity—family health, if you will—and church affiliation and activity. Middletown [church] members were more likely to be married, remain married, and to be highly satisfied with their marriages and to have more children.... The great divide between marriage status, marriage satisfaction, and family size is ... between those who identify with a church or denomination and those who do not."[31]

Arland Thornton, a family sociologist at the University of Michigan, finds the same strong intergenerational transmission of religious belief and practice among Detroit families. He concludes, "These data indicate a strong intergenerational transmission of religious involvement. Attendance at religious services is also very stable within generations across time."[32] Scott Myers published similar findings in the *American Sociological Review* in 1996.[33] There is a connection between religious practice and stable marriage and adolescent virginity.

In 1993, the University of Wisconsin reported on a nationally representative sample survey of 2,441 white women and 1,275 black women. The research team found strong evidence linking the birth of out-of-wedlock children to a "change in family structure" while growing up, controlling for the usual variables of income and education.[34] Adolescents in "high-crime areas" who lost their virginity early had experienced an average of two transitions in their parents' family life (that is, separation/divorce and a "re-partnering" by their parents).[35] By contrast, most virgins had no such family transitions in their lives. Only 18 percent of all adolescents who lost their virginity early were from intact families.[36]

Complementing this finding, Brent Miller and his colleagues find that the rate of adolescent pregnancy increases 33 percent for each change in parents' marital status while the child is growing up.[37]

CONCLUSIONS

Church attendance is correlated with other factors that reduce teen pregnancy: many teens who attend religious services regularly are raised in intact and attentive families. Nonetheless, there is no doubt that high levels of religious worship are very much in the public good. George Washington's advice in his "Farewell Speech to the Nation" is now bolstered by the findings of the social sciences:

> Of all the dispositions and habits which lead to political prosperity, religion and morality are indispensable supports . . . A volume could not trace all their connections with private and public felicity . . . And let us with caution indulge the supposition that morality can be maintained without religion. Whatever may be conceded to the influence of refined education on minds of peculiar structure, reason and experience both forbid us to expect that National morality can prevail in exclusion of religious principle.

The founding traditions of our nation, the common experience of people, and now the findings of the social sciences all point in a clear direction: the regular worship of God in community gives parents and their offspring many strengths, advantages, and benefits, especially in the challenge of directing teenage sexuality. Any honest national strategy of reducing teenage out-of-wedlock births, sexually transmitted diseases, and abortions will place the worship of God squarely within its parameters because of the power of its effects. Such would be a more truly "comprehensive" sex education strategy.

NOTES

1. Bernard Spilka, Ralph W. Hood, and Richard L. Gorsuch, *The Psychology of Religion: An Empirical Approach* (Englewood Cliffs, N.J.: Prentice Hall, 1985). See also Cheryl D. Hayes, ed., *Risking the Future: Adolescent Sexuality, Pregnancy, and Childbearing*, vol. 1 (Washington, D.C.: National Academy Press, 1987); Michael J. Donahue, "Aggregate Religiousness and Teenage Fertility Revisited: Reanalyses of Data from the Guttmacher Institute," paper presented at the Society for the Scientific Study of Religion (Chicago, October 1988); Catherine S. Chilman, "Adolescent Sexuality in a Changing American Society: Social and Psychological Perspectives," NIH Publication 80-1426 (Washington, D.C.: U.S. Government Publications, 1980); L. E. Hendricks, D. P. Robinson, and L. E. Gary, "Religiosity and Unmarried Black Adolescent Fatherhood," *Adolescence*, vol. 19, no. 74 (1984), pp. 417–24; David Larson and others, "The Faith Factor: An Annotated Bibliography of Clinical Research on Spiritual Subjects," Occasional Series Publication, vol. 3, no. 3840 (Rockville, Md.: National Institute For Healthcare Research, 1995), pp. 65–66.

2. Michael D. Resnick and others, "Protecting Adolescents from Harm: Findings from the National Longitudinal Study on Adolescent Health," *Journal of the American Medical Association (JAMA)*, vol. 278, no. 10 (September 10, 1997), pp. 823–32.

3. Carolyn Tucker Halpern, J. Richard Udry, Benjamin Campbell, Chirayath Suchindran, and George A. Mason, "Testosterone and Religiosity as Predictors of Sexual Attitudes and Activity among Adolescent Males: A Biosocial Model," *Journal of Biosocial Science*, vol. 26, no. 2 (1994), pp. 217–34.

4. Alan Carlson, editor of Family in America, Digital Archive, the Howard Center, Rockford, Ill., commenting on Emogene Fox and Michael Young, "Religiosity, Sex Guilt, and Sexual Behavior among College Students," *Health Values*, vol. 13, no. 2 (1989), pp. 32–37.

5. Arland Thornton and Donald Camburn, "Religious Participation and Adolescent Sexual Behavior and Attitudes," *Journal of Marriage and the Family*, vol. 51 (August 1989), pp. 641–53.

6. S. N. Seidman, W. D. Mosher, and S. O. Aral, "Women with Multiple Sexual Partners: United States," *American Journal of Public Health*, vol. 82, no. 10 (1988), pp. 1388–94. Larson and others, "The Faith Factor," pp. 133–34.

7. Thomas P. Eng and William T. Butler, "The Hidden Epidemic: Confronting Sexually Transmitted Diseases" (Washington, D.C.: Institute of Medicine, National Academy Press, 1997).

8. J. K. Cochran and Leonard Beeghley, "The Influence of Religion on Attitudes towards Non-Marital Sexuality: A Preliminary Assessment of Reference Group Theory," *Journal for the Scientific Study of Religion*, vol. 30, no. 1 (1991), pp. 45–62; Larson and others, "The Faith Factor."

9. Resnick and others, "Protecting Adolescents from Harm."

10. E. Jeffrey Hill and others, "Religiosity and Adolescent Sexual Intercourse: Reciprocal Effects," unpublished manuscript (Utah State University, 1999).

11. Sara B. Kinsman, Daniel Romer, Frank F. Furstenberg, and Donald F. Schwarz, "Early Sexual Initiation: The Role of Peer Norms," *Pediatrics*, vol. 102, no. 5 (November 1998), pp. 1185–92.

12. S. V. Brown, "Premarital Sexual Permissiveness among Black Adolescent Females," *Social Psychology Quarterly*, vol. 48, no. 4 (1985), pp. 381–87.

13. "1998 True Love Waits Report on Sexual Abstinence," available from True Love Waits, 127 Ninth Avenue North, Nashville, Tenn. 37234-0152.

14. Resnick and others, "Protecting Adolescents from Harm."

15. Ibid.

16. Personal communication.

17. Brent C. Miller, "Families Matter: A Research Synthesis of Family Influences on Adolescent Pregnancy Research" (Washington, D.C.: National Campaign to Prevent Teen Pregnancy, 1998).

18. In the National Longitudinal Study of Adolescent Health, the only question for father's worship is whether he had worshipped in the last four weeks. Given the pattern already discernible between the level of parental worship and other outcomes, it seems safe to predict that the father who worships weekly will have a still greater protective impact on the virginity of his children.

19. This study, "Fertility Appreciation for Families," involved a matched control design. It is an unpublished, but peer-reviewed, paper available from Family of the Americas, P.O. Box 1170, Dunkirk, MD 20754.

20. Resnick and others, "Protecting Adolescents from Harm," p. 830.

21. E. S. Herold and M. S. Goodwin, "Adamant Virgins, Potential Non-Virgins, and Non-Virgins," *Journal of Sex Research*, vol. 17, no.1 (1981), pp. 97–113. Reported in Larson and others, "The Faith Factor." p. 68.

22. Resnick and others, "Protecting Adolescents from Harm."

23. Brent C. Miller and others, "The Timing of Sexual Intercourse among Adolescents: Family, Peer, and Other Antecedents," *Youth and Society*, vol. 29, no. 1 (1997), pp. 54–83.

24. R. A. Hunt and M. B. King, "Religiosity and Marriage," *Journal for the Scientific Study of Religion*, vol. 17, no. 4 (1978), pp. 399–406; Larson and others, "The Faith Factor," pp. 49–50.

25. Lee G. Burchinal, "Marital Satisfaction and Religious Behavior," *American Sociological Review*, vol. 22, vol. 2 (January 1957), pp. 306–10; M. J. Sporakowski and G. A. Hughston, "Prescriptions for Happy Marriage: Adjustments and Satisfaction of Couples Married for Fifty Years or More," *Family Coordinator*, vol. 27, no. 3 (1978), pp. 321–28; Larson and others, "The Faith Factor," pp. 73–74.

26. Nick Stinnet, Greg Saunders, John DeFrain, and Anne Parkhurst, "A Nationwide Study of Families Who Perceive Themselves as Strong," *Family Perspective*, vol. 16, no.1 (1982), pp. 15–22.

27. David B. Larson, Susan S. Larson, and John Gartner, "Families, Relationships, and Health," in *Behavior and Medicine,* edited by Danny Wedding (Baltimore, Md.: Mosby Year Book, 1990).

28. Wesley Shrum, "Religion and Marital Instability: Change in the 1970s?" *Review of Religious Research*, vol. 21, no. 2 (1980), pp. 135–47.

29. David B. Larson: "Religious Involvement," in *Family Building*, edited by G. E. Rekers (Ventura, Calif.: Regal, 1985), pp. 121–47.

30. J. S. Moneker and R. P. Rankin, "Religious Homogamy and Marital Duration among Those Who File for Divorce in California 1966–1971," *Journal of Divorce and Remarriage*, vol. 19, no. 2/3, pp. 233–46.

31. Howard M. Bahr and Bruce A. Chadwick, "Religion and Family in Middletown, USA," *Journal of Marriage and Family*, vol. 47, no. 2 (May 1985), pp. 407–14.

32. Arland Thornton, and Donald Camburn, "Religious Participation and Adolescent Sexual Behavior and Attitudes," *Journal of Marriage and the Family*, vol. 51, no. 3 (August 1989), pp. 641–53.

33. Scott M. Myers, "An Interactive Model of Religiosity Inheritance: The Importance of Family Context," *American Sociological Review*, vol. 61, no. 5 (1996), pp. 858–66.

34. Lawerence L. Wu, "Effects of Family Instability, Income, and Income Instability on the Risk of a Premarital Birth," *American Sociological Review*, vol. 61, no. 3 (1996), pp. 386–406.

35. Close to 25 percent now lose their virginity before age fifteen.

36. Deborah M. Capaldi, Lynn Crosby, and Mike Stoolmiller, "Predicting the Timing of First Sexual Intercourse for At-Risk Adolescent Males," *Child Development*, vol. 67, no. 2 (1996), 344–59.

37. Miller and others, "The Timing of Sexual Intercourse among Adolescents."

> ◆ ◆ ◆ <

Teen Pregnancy, Faith, and Social Science

WILLIAM A. GALSTON

Despite a welcome and unexpected decline during recent years, the teen pregnancy rate remains far higher in the United States than in any other advanced industrial country. Roughly four in ten young women will become pregnant before their twentieth birthday, the vast majority out of wedlock. The costs for the children, for the young women and their partners, for communities, and for society as a whole are very high. In this context, it makes sense to mobilize all the forces in our society that can help to keep the recent progress going. I am not alone in believing that faith communities represent a vital, and thus far underused, element of this social movement.

FAITH COMMUNITIES IN U.S. CIVIL SOCIETY

The potential and actual role of faith communities in reducing teen pregnancy is absolutely critical because faith communities are at the heart of America's civil society—not of every country's, but certainly of ours. If you examine international statistical comparisons and ask what keeps us in the lead as a "nation of joiners," the answer is our distinctive propensity to band together in faith-based communities. Some European nations have more secular communities and organizations per capita than we do. What gives America the edge overall is the extraordinary diversity pervading our faith-based communities.

To the extent that America's leaders and citizens are now focusing on civil society as a vital complement to public sector activity and individual self-help, therefore, we must focus on religion. In some neighborhoods, especially in our cities, faith communities are the dominant institutions, the true center of community-based action. Not to look at this carefully would be to ignore the greatest reservoir of energy and commitment and hope in many parts of America today.

WHY FAITH COMMUNITIES CAN HELP

If we ask why faith communities are potentially important in helping us to reduce teen pregnancy, some answers (or at least suggestions) emerge not only from common sense but also from the social science literature.

In the first place, faith communities are an important part of the process of cultural change in the United States, and cultural change is an important part of social change. Since the early 1990s, there has been a significant (some would say providential) reduction in early teen sexual activity and in teen pregnancy, startling the pessimists of the late 1980s and early 1990s. I do not think we can say that all the successful pregnancy reduction programs put together could account for more than a small percentage of the total change. Something larger is happening—a perceptible shift in public opinion—and faith communities, historically and up to the present day, have played a very important role in changing the climate of opinion.

Faith communities are also very important as centers of care, connection, and community. A lot of the social science literature suggests that young people who are connected to something outside themselves are more likely to grow up positively. Similarly, a growing body of social science evidence suggests that there is a connection between serving others and caring for one's self. Faith-based communities are in a distinctive (although not entirely unique) position to forge and strengthen that connection. I also would argue that faith-based communities are in a distinctively strong position to engage the whole person in the process of growth and renewal, rather than treating young persons as clients and addressing a single dimension of their lives in isolation from the rest. A study recently published by the National Campaign to Prevent Teen Pregnancy includes essays by Barbara Whitehead and a research team headed by Brian Wilcox and Sharon Scales Rostosky summarizing the historical, qualitative, and quantitative knowledge of these issues.[1]

As we consider the role of faith-based communities in reducing teen pregnancy, we must distinguish between faith-based programs, on the one hand, and religious belief and observance, on the other. The correlation between deep, family-reinforced belief, regular worship, and sexual restraint and self-control is strong and well established. There is good reason to believe that if more teens were "churched," teen sexual intercourse, pregnancy, and out-of-wedlock births all would decline significantly, even if faith communities did nothing to enhance their programs directed explicitly toward these ends.

Having said this, there is also reason to believe that faith-based programs to reduce teen pregnancy are also helpful and that faith communities could be far more energetic in promoting them. While many religious denominations have issued impressive statements on teen sexuality and some have devised specific curricula and programs of action, these steps at the national level have trickled down only sporadically to local practice. Some congregations are held back by the scarcity of resources and multiple responsibilities, others by the delicacy of the topic and the inherent difficulty of engaging it. Not surprisingly, a recent survey conducted by the National Campaign to Prevent Teen Pregnancy has found that only 5 percent of teens say that they learned the most about preventing teen pregnancy from religious organizations and only 9 percent cite religious organizations as "most influential" in shaping their sexual decisions. If we are to sustain the progress of recent years in reducing teen pregnancy, these numbers must rise substantially. That will not happen unless local faith communities become much more engaged in the fight.

One thing is clear: if faith communities do become more engaged, the American public will be supportive. A recent survey of American views on religion, politics, and public policy conducted by the Pew Research Center for the People and the Press and the Pew Forum on Religion and Public Life shows that 39 percent of Americans believe that religious organizations could do the "best job" of addressing teen pregnancy.

FAITH AND SOCIAL SCIENCE

In my judgment, we need to think through carefully the complex relationship between faith communities and social science. Social scientists in general (and program evaluators in particular) tend to think in ways that philosophers call "consequentialist," and they tend to focus on the results of particular interventions rather than on the nature of those interventions themselves. But from the standpoint of faith communities, the issue is only in part the effectiveness of particular programs. They also are concerned about the consistency of programs with their specific faith traditions. It is entirely possible that, from the perspective of a particular faith community, a program will be effective as measured by the canons of social science, but nonetheless inappropriate when examined in light of the specific commitments of their faith. One would expect that the extraordinary religious diversity in the United States would be—and I would argue from the faith perspective should be—mirrored in the variety of approaches to teen pregnancy reduction that they adopt. Accordingly, the National Campaign to Prevent Teen Pregnancy has used the slogan "Unity of Ends, Diversity of Means" to characterize the contribution of faith communities in this area.

By the very definition and meaning of faith, faith-based social action will (and ought to) get out in front of social science. Some traditions teach us that faith is the evidence of things unseen. That is a distinctive kind of evidence. It may be that, over time, this distinctive kind of evidence will influence the kinds of evidence that social scientists typically measure.

Can this sequence of events be justified from a secular point of view as well? I think it can be, because our demonstrable knowledge of program effectiveness frequently lags behind the actual effectiveness of individual programs. A faith community may be doing something that works, even though from a social science perspective we cannot tell the rest of the social science community that we know it is working.

For this reason, among others, I believe that society at large should invest (in constitutionally appropriate ways) in expanded efforts by faith communities to address teen pregnancy. It would be unreasonable to demand rigorous social scientific demonstrations of effectiveness as a prior condition of public support. It would be entirely reasonable, however, for the public to require evidence of effectiveness after programs have been up and running for a few years. And it would be reasonable for responsible public entities to spell out the basic features that make such evidence credible.

NOTE

1. National Campaign to Prevent Teen Pregnancy, *Keeping the Faith: The Role of Religion and Faith Communities in Preventing Teen Pregnancy* (Washington: 2001).

The Why's behind Reducing Teen Pregnancy

MARY ROSE McGEADY

Despite wide agreement that efforts should be made to reduce teenage pregnancy in the United States, the response to the question of *why* such efforts are needed differs according to who is offering it. Some replies concentrate on social considerations of such pregnancies and usually are accompanied by research emphasizing the negative impact of adolescent childbearing on both child and mother, including poor prognoses for the social future of the child. Other responses emphasize medical considerations. Many moms are physically immature and not ready for childbearing. Many teenage pregnancies end in miscarriages, and many more lead to babies with low birth weights. Still other responses emphasize economic reasons, noting the high impact on our culture and the public responsibility for funding and caring for these teenage mothers. They cite the high costs of delivery, of prenatal and postnatal care, of caring for premature or handicapped babies, or of day care for mothers who are forced to work.

Lastly, answers to the question of why we should work to prevent teenage pregnancy frequently deal with moral or religious considerations. This is the most complicated area, with responses coming from both positive and negative positions. While some view teen pregnancy as a violation of morality or judge such pregnancies as behaviors contrary to religious teachings about sex, marriage, and family, others concentrate on the child and its future rather than on the sex act itself. Traditional attitudes and cultural considerations differ on the issue of out-of-wedlock births. In some cultures, out-of-wedlock pregnancy is not as stigmatized as it is in the United States. Although these cultures host various religious traditions that still may consider such pregnancies as sinful or undesirable, their acceptance of the child creates a much more welcoming atmosphere.

All of these considerations are part of the dialogue that we must engage in if our efforts to reduce teen pregnancy are to succeed. A member of the Religion and Values Task Force of the National Campaign to Prevent Teen Pregnancy said at one meeting, "You know, we have to be very careful not to throw the baby out with the bath water. We have to be very careful as a society that we don't begin to look upon the baby as a bad result of a bad action by a teenager. Instead, we have to continue as a culture to love and care for those babies and love and care for the mothers of those babies."

Because I deal directly with troubled children, I would like to talk a little about the why from the viewpoint of the teenagers themselves. First of all, we now have fifteen Covenant Houses in the United States, two in Canada, and four in Mexico and Central America. In every one of those cultures, teenage pregnancy and birth are a growing reality. Unfortunately, the number of pregnant teens and teen mothers is growing. I was recently at our Covenant House in New Orleans. I met a nineteen-year-old girl who was on the verge of delivering her fourth baby. To give this teen mother hope and to help her to plan a healthy future for herself and her four children are tremendous challenges for us.

These kids have very few satisfactions in their lives. I think that this is one of the reasons that some of them turn to sex. Sex is one area where they can find satisfaction. Several papers have examined the characteristics of teenagers who get pregnant. I see in the lives of these kids very few experiences that build self-esteem. Often they come from families characterized by internal conflict and breakdown. A lot of them have been passed around all their lives.

For these reasons, it is very important for churches to become a significant presence in the lives of these kids. They need more than religious education, more than worship, more than a religious identity. They need a relationship with God. They need to hear that there is a God who loves them, who created them, to whom they can pray, who really cares about them.

We need to care for youth in a holistic way, not by addressing a single dimension of their lives in isolation from the rest. We need to make them happy when they are with us and to help them to plan for a future of happiness. These kids are starving for relationships. So many of the significant others in their lives have let them down. Often they have had conflictual or temporary relationships with their parents. Many have a history of relationships filled with disaster. So, we need to model positive relationships and then begin to say, "You can develop a relationship with God." They are not used to having relationships with people that are positive and caring. Attempts to deal effectively with the sexuality issues must come in the context of total caring.

It is very rare that we have a second pregnancy among those girls. We attribute that to the fact that we embrace the whole of their lives in a caring atmosphere. We teach them the morality of sexuality—that it is very much part of their relationship with God—and we teach them that they need to care for themselves because God expects that from them, too. But morality and hard realities have to be part of a whole, integrated package.

More than the questions about *why* we should prevent teen pregnancy is the question of *how*. The best answer to that question is "with great love and care for the individual young woman and her baby!"

Faith-Based Sexuality Education
Breaks the Silence in Black Churches

CARLTON W. VEAZEY

In 1996 the Religious Coalition for Reproductive Choice began the Black Church Initiative to identify and address sexuality issues with African American clergy and laity. The black community was ravaged by teen pregnancy, dangerously strained family relations, domestic violence, homicide, and HIV/AIDS. We faced a crisis of staggering proportions: more than 60 percent of black children were born into single-parent homes, and 22 percent were born to teenagers. An unmarried teenager who becomes pregnant and has not finished high school has an 80 percent likelihood of being poor, and her child is more likely to be hungry and lack health care. Yet the Black Church—the sanctuary of freedom and progress—was silent. Some even claimed the silence of the church had contributed to these tragedies.

Clearly, the government has the main role in reducing poverty, but the government cannot provide the religious teachings and spiritual guidance that instill the values and build the moral fiber so critical in bettering our lives.

As a pastor for more than thirty years, I felt that black clergy, myself included, did not know how to talk about sexuality prayerfully and realistically. If sex was mentioned at all, it was in a shaming, negative way. It seemed that talking about teen pregnancy and AIDS meant we were doing something morally wrong.

I set about bringing together black religious leaders from across the country to the Howard University School of Divinity for what we called the Black Religious Summit on Sexuality. As Kelly Brown Douglas wrote in *Sexuality and the Black Church*, this conference represented a monumental stride toward breaking the silence about sexuality.[1] When we began to talk about the most serious problem we faced—the health and lives of our young people—we had to admit that most were already sexually active and that we could not help them, or others, with abstinence education. We faced another problem, reaching young people who had left the church. We realized that we could not win them back simply by saying "Jesus saves."

We developed a faith-based sexuality education curriculum called "Keeping It Real!", which is one of the first organized efforts in African American faith communities to address sex and sexuality in both a biblical and secular context. The typical response of teens to moral platitudes and scare tactics about sex is "Get real!" "Keeping It Real!" speaks to youth with respect and honesty. Teens meet in small groups of twelve to fifteen to talk about their feelings and experiences with the support and guidance of trained facilitators from their church. For many teens, this is the first time they have spoken openly, positively, and comfortably about sexuality with a caring, nonjudgmental adult and with members of the opposite sex. We teach young people to be responsible stewards of all God's gifts and prepare them to make healthy, responsible decisions as spiritual and sexual beings. This teaching takes sexuality out of the "do and don't" school, which we know is not effective, and makes it a spiritual principle.

To those who charge that we are promoting sexual activity by teaching about it, we respond that we place abstinence first but recognize that churches have a responsibility, consistent with Christian values, to assist those who are sexually active by providing information that can make the difference between life and death in this age of HIV/AIDS. In the same spirit of living our Christian values, we provide information on family planning and contraception because many young people already have children and need this knowledge to improve their future. And we live our faith by developing serious dialogue about sexual orientation—an issue that has torn apart too many African American families that deny a son's or daughter's sexual preference.

As the Black Church Initiative has found, religious institutions can effectively provide sexuality education because they offer accurate, comprehensive information (including abstinence) in a community that truly cares about the individual. In my own work with African American churches, I have learned that young people are more likely to postpone sexual activity if they can discuss sexuality openly, without fear and judgment, in a setting that reinforces their faith and self-worth.

The Bush administration's promotion of abstinence-only education through charitable choice and welfare reform must be carefully considered. We cannot allow government to dictate how we teach our children to be responsible spiritual and sexual beings. This is clearly the work of the church, not of the government.

NOTE

1. Kelly Brown Douglas, *Sexuality and the Black Church* (Orbis Books, 1999).

Religious Sins: Churches Dealing (Or Not Dealing) with Human Sexuality

JOHN BUEHRENS

I write as a religious leader who must make moral calls about the personal and public issues that social scientists in this volume get to study. I also write as a parent, having raised two daughters with my wife, Gwen (an Episcopal priest), while serving parishes in Knoxville, Tennessee; Dallas, Texas; and New York City. When I was in Knoxville, at the Clergy Consultation Service for Problem Pregnancy, my wife and I had a steady series of young women in our living room, with our two daughters in their cribs upstairs. Gwen preached the gospel and served the poor as a caseworker for young women placing their children up for adoption.

I think both of my daughters would agree with me that the field of religion and sexual justice is replete with sin, but not of the sort popularly associated with sex. Rather it is sin of the spiritual sort, steeped in self-righteousness: temptations to point fingers, project anger, and misconstrue the ideal and the real. Few escape this, and I have no doubt had my own share of faults in this regard.

Religion was dominant in the culture of East Tennessee, and I became angry with the failure of most churches to deal openly with issues of human sexuality. Thirty years later, I am less angry, but I remain afraid of the polarization that is possible in this field. I am glad that many of the more conservative churches are beginning to offer programs of sexuality education that arise out of their own values. Yet I worry that they focus on the single goal of abstinence before marriage instead of dealing with a multiplicity of potential goals, including reducing the early onset of sexual activity and the number of partners, but also increasing the use of available contraceptives and reducing the fear and hatred concerning homosexuality. When religious leaders shy away from such matters, they threaten to let fear prevail over love, which is another form of spiritual sin.

It would be a mistake to expect the church to provide a complete solution in this highly secularized society where media penetrates every aspect of our young people's lives. The sex education and HIV education programs that the Unitarian Universalist Association (UUA) has championed for the last thirty years have made a positive difference, but they have not reached much beyond our own churches. The conservatively oriented abstinence-only programs now so in vogue will not solve the problem either. Nor will leaving the matter to parents and churches.

My feelings on these matters arise on both the pastoral and the prophetic sides of my ministry. Over the years, I have conducted at least twenty funerals for people with AIDS. I have done almost a dozen funerals for young people who took their own lives, a distressing number of them because they were confused about their sexuality and feeling rejected. Nearly all of these funerals were not for my own church members, but for people who were rejected by their own faith communities and families.

What I bring to the table as a progressive religious leader is a concern for the spirit in which we have our discussions and hope for the possibility of the churches making an impact. Over the past five years the UUA has worked with the United Church of Christ (UCC) to develop a new comprehensive sexuality education program called Our Whole Lives. The UUA and UCC have tried to design this comprehensive sexuality education curriculum so that it can be used not only in the voluntary setting of the church, where we can get fairly explicit and talk about *all* of the sexual feelings and relational issues and dilemmas that people have, but also in more public settings.

More parents want comprehensive sexuality education for their children than is currently recognized in today's polarized debate. Our experience suggests that religious communities can help: we can develop good materials to help fill the gap, we can promote the discussion of values, and we can help identify common ground—or at least middle ground—on which more comprehensive, realistic public policies can be built.

PART TWO

THE ROLE OF FAITH-BASED ORGANIZATIONS IN FIGHTING

Crime and Substance Abuse

CHAPTER FIVE

Defining the Terms of Collaboration: Faith-Based Organizations and Government in Criminal Justice

GEORGE L. KELLING

There was a time when the role of the Christian church in the community was of particular interest to me. After graduating from St. Olaf College—a Lutheran college—I spent two years in a Lutheran seminary. That was a long time ago, during the 1950s. Crime was not yet a widespread issue. World War II was still vivid in our memories, as was the role of the church in pre-war Germany and during the war itself. Clearly, my fellow students and I had not achieved professional maturity, yet we debated the moral and ethical issues associated with church involvement in civic life vehemently. For Lutherans who were fastidious about doctrinal and theological issues, the debate had special meaning. Martin Luther's theology of vocation fed the debate: "A cobbler, a smith, a farmer, each has the work and office of his trade, and yet they are all alike consecrated priests and bishops, and everyone by means of his own work or office must benefit and serve every other, that in this way many kinds of work may be done for the bodily and spiritual welfare of the community, even as all the members of the body serve one another."[1] Nonetheless, one professor loved to taunt us with being advocates of the "social gospel," "more concerned about sewer systems," as he disparaged it, "than the Word of God." But for us, many of German descent, the evils of the holocaust and war kept our attention on the church in the world. (Besides, sewer systems were not to be dismissed.)

That was long ago, and while whatever insights I may or may not have had certainly have shaped my world view, they are long lost to recollection. But two aspects of my training remain with me: homiletics (preaching) and hermeneutics (managing texts). I am not merely a detached academic; I am also an advocate, trying to improve public policy. So, alas, I still preach at times.

What every practical preacher knows is that despite the variety of Gospel and Epistle lessons that are read each Sunday, it is tough to get up every week with a fresh and stirring homily based on the day's lesson. Hence, since one cannot keep up with scholarship on all the lessons and since at times one wants to preach about a topic that is neither explicit nor implicit in the lessons, one "twists the text" to meet his or her message for the day. If readers are attentive they will find both in what follows—preaching and twisting the text to meet my message.

Let me first put forward several assumptions. I have written extensively about each, so I will be brief.[2] The first is that crime control is achieved primarily by what Jane Jacobs, in her classic book *The Death and Life of Great American Cities*, calls "the small change" of life.[3] By that, she is referring to the expression of all those intricate but routine obligations, controls, sanctions, and expectations that shape daily life in communities: the glances, gestures, body positions, actions, and facial casts that communicate approval, wariness, concern, or condemnation. Probably the key concept here is civility: citizens behaving, and expecting others to behave, in ways that are culturally understood to be predictable, reassuring, and respectful. The view that the small change is basic to crime control does not mean that police and criminal justice agencies are unimportant; it means that they are secondary, or ancillary, to the routine controls of communities. That is why the ideas of *community* policing and, more recently, community justice are so important.

The second assumption is that the extraordinary crime wave that occurred from 1970 to 1990 was the result of the erosion of the authority of the institutions that develop and maintain the small change: the family, schools, religious institutions, neighborhoods, and communities. Certainly major social, economic, and cultural changes attended the weakening of these institutions; however, public policies and judicial decisions played a major role as well. Think, for example, of what has been done to neighborhoods and communities by urban renewal programs, expressway construction, conceiving of public housing as housing of last resort, building tower block public housing, instituting school busing, withdrawing police from neighborhoods and communities and isolating them in cars, deinstitutionalizing the emotionally ill, and decriminalizing (or virtually decriminalizing) minor offenses. The list could go on. The intent of such programs and policies was benevolent, but they have eviscerated many urban areas, especially in inner cities. Police and criminal justice agencies, locked into a reactive law enforcement mode, simply were overwhelmed by the breakdown in public order that resulted from such policies.

My third assumption is that the current major reductions in crime are the result of communities organizing themselves to regain the control of public spaces and young people that they had in the past. Neighborhood organizations, religious institutions, developers, business associations, schools, transportation systems, housing authorities, and others, including police and criminal justice agencies, not only are striving to regain control of public spaces and youth on their own, they also have formed, and are forming, powerful working relationships that increase their impact. Those working relationships, the central theme of this chapter, are surprisingly vigorous and enduring.

Note that these three assertions—that crime is controlled by "the small change" of life, that the recent crime wave was the result of the weakening of social institutions, and that the current reduction in crime is the result of communities organizing to regain control of public spaces and youth—are *assumptions*. Evidence for them is anecdotal, inferential, and historical, not empirical. Nor can they be proven empirically in the near future. Hence, the criminological debate—often rancorous and sometimes silly, both about why crime increased during past decades and why it is declining now—is likely to go on for a long time.[4]

It also is important to note that these assumptions are at odds with the view of crime control that has reigned since the 1960s. Since the publication of the report of President Lyndon B. Johnson's crime commission in 1967, "root cause" theories of crime have dominated criminological and criminal justice thinking and practice. In that model, police and criminal justice agencies are primarily "case processors," police being the front end of a criminal justice "system" that focuses almost exclusively on responding to serious crimes once they occur. Such "crime fighting" is a professional responsibility, best left to police and prosecutors, with the role of citizens limited to reporting crime to professionals and serving as good witnesses. Crime *prevention* can be achieved only through broad social change; "minor" problems like drunkenness, prostitution, and other "victimless" crimes are the responsibility of social agencies. While both the political left and right have their variations on this theme, most criminologists and practitioners have subscribed to the left's version. Their thinking went so far that many of them "de-policed" the crime problem—that is, they put forward the idea that police and criminal justice agencies could have only minimal, if any, impact on serious crime. After all, those agencies had nothing to do with crime's root causes, ergo, they could do little about it.

Finally, these assumptions make clear that I believe that the faith institutions can contribute enormously to community order and safety. Having personally accepted that as a given, I will make two basic points in this chapter. The first

is that we must come to a clearer understanding of the interorganizational relationships that develop under the rubric of "partnership," "collaboration," and
other such terms if the relationships are to thrive. The second is that if faith institutions are to be true to themselves and their values, if they are to live up to
their potential to contribute to the quality of civic and community life, they must
be prepared to enter into rigorous problem-solving exercises that have as their
starting point the awareness that most often the real problems are not what they
appear to be. In other words, "doing good" is both hard and thoughtful work.
My comments will be based on the evaluation of two federal programs, research
into community prosecution (a shift in prosecutorial strategy that is akin to the
shift toward community policing), and my current work in Newark, New Jersey,
where I have become the "neutral convener" of an interorganizational anticrime
collaboration that includes representatives of the faith community. Also, I will
give special attention to work that I did for the New York State Metropolitan
Transportation Authority, which is important because it illustrates both the
points I want to emphasize.

In early 1989, I was asked by Robert Kiley, chairman of New York's Metropolitan Transportation Authority, to confer on problems in the New York City
subway. It was out of control. Despite the recent investment of $8 billion in in-
frastructure, ridership was in steep decline.

Kiley consulted me because of my article with James Q. Wilson, "Broken
Windows," which was published in the *Atlantic Monthly* in 1982. The article argued that small things, incivilities, matter a lot in urban life, and that disorderly
behavior, fear of crime, serious crime, and urban decay are sequentially linked.
Moreover, it implied that taking care of minor offenses could help reduce fear
of crime, serious crime, and urban decay.

Those arguments flew in the face of the predominating sociological, criminological, and criminal justice theories. More or less explicitly, they re-raised the
issues of the decriminalization of minor offenses and the deinstitutionalization
of the mentally ill, and they challenged the idea that the proper use of criminal
justice institutions was almost solely for reactive case processing. Finally, the article suggested that crime could be prevented without massive social change.

The main problem that I faced in New York was that virtually everyone "understood" the city's subway problem: the media, the transit police, civil libertar-
ians, advocates, the faith community, and the New York City Transit Authority
itself. For virtually everyone, the problem was "homelessness." And, of course,
everybody knew how to deal with homelessness: provide emergency care, jobs,
apartments, and welfare. That is where the faith community came in. Homeless
people obviously need food and clothing; thus a role for churches, many of them
suburban, in confronting the problem was to provide food and clothing. And

where better than in the subway? Lots of "homeless" people congregated there, especially in stations. So suburban Christians came into subway stations on a regular basis to hand out food and clothing with the promise that next week—same time, same place—they would return with more.

Framing the problem as one of homelessness was not only wrong, at least in my reasoning, it also made whatever the problem was virtually unsolvable. Clearly, the New York Transportation Authority could make minimal contributions to solving the city's homeless problem. But 250,000 people a day going over, under, and around the turnstiles to avoid paying fares was not a *homeless* problem. Certainly, some farebeaters were homeless, but only a small percentage of the total. The problem was *unlawful behavior*. To be sure, most of the farebeaters were harmless: some really did not have money but needed to travel; others were so irritated by the quality of service that they felt justified in not paying; others wanted to catch an incoming train and did not want to wait in a line for a token; and others had simply gotten into a bad habit, rationalizing it by demanding, "Why should I have to pay when nobody else does?" But farebeating, when combined with graffiti, predatory panhandling, youths loitering around the toll booths obviously casing them *and* the passengers, public urination and defecation, open sexual activity, and fare scams (including blocking the turnstiles, holding gates open, and extorting fares from passengers)—with the police, all along, *doing absolutely nothing*—sent a powerful message. To ordinary citizens it said "Enter the subway at your own risk"; to predators, "This is a good place to operate."

Moreover, even the tag "homelessness" was a misnomer that masked a tragic amalgam of personal and social problems and their interaction: alcohol and drug abuse, mental illness, criminality, and social policies ranging from decriminalization to deinstitutionalization that virtually ensured a permanent street population. The idea that such a population should receive even the slightest encouragement to camp or hang out in the subway was a terrible one, indeed an immoral one. It not only jeopardized the viability of the subway, it exposed the "homeless" population to very real dangers. We knew, for example, that up to twelve people a month who did not have identifiable addresses lost their lives in the subway, where they were found murdered by other "homeless" people, accidentally electrocuted or killed by trains, or dead from hypothermia, exposure, and other "natural" causes.

We redefined the problem. New leadership energized the police department, which began to curtail unlawful disorderly behavior. The transit authority expanded efforts to link the genuinely needy with social and emergency services. We successfully defended our policies in court. Within months, order was restored. Crime began to decline immediately; currently it is down about 80 percent.

It is not too strong to say that fear and crime are no longer problems in New York City's subways.

My interest here, however, is in the role of the church in all of this. For those of us trying to restore order, churches were an integral part of the problem. Their involvement complicated the problem in several ways: first, their physical presence contributed to the chaos in the subway; second, their treatment of the problem, bringing food and clothing into the subway, put them into a practical alliance with "homeless" advocates who had a clear political agenda; and, finally, they claimed the high moral ground and, in their practical alliance with advocates, gave the advocates high moral credence as well. We faced the dilemma of having to confront the moral authority of the faith community. (We even had to figure out how to deal with a panhandling "nun." To this day we do not know whether she was legitimate or not.)

The transportation authority was able to capitalize on public indignation about conditions in the subway, and the argument was turned. We uncoupled "homelessness" and disorder, and instead linked disorder to serious crime. Moreover, we countered the moral and legal argument that restoring order was a "war on the homeless" that protected the interests of the rich at the cost of the poor with evidence that the "homeless" were dying in the dangerous environment of the subway and that subway users were not rich—they were primarily workers and students who deserved decent, hassle-free transportation.

The relationship of some churches to the state transportation authority clearly could be described best as one of defiance. Despite the transportation authority's request that they not conduct charitable work in the subways, those churches did as they saw fit. I am certain that they believed that they were fulfilling their moral obligation to feed the hungry and clothe the poor, seeing themselves as their defenders. Despite my belief that the actions of the churches were shortsighted and misguided, they highlight the complex nature of the relationship between the faith community and other organizations, especially government organizations. This example extends the range of possibilities of how, for simplicity's sake, two organizations—say, a faith institution and a police department—relate. As we shall see, properly understanding the terms of a relationship is critical to establishing and maintaining a long-term relationship. I have had the opportunity to observe attempts to develop and sustain such relationships more systematically in my research.

UNDERSTANDING THE TERMS OF THE RELATIONSHIP

In the past two decades I evaluated two federal programs that provided funding for attempts to coordinate crime control activities among organizations under the assumption that the synergy that results from a coordinated effort produces a greater impact than that produced when each organization acts independently and continues with business as usual. The first was the Urban Initiatives Anti-Crime Program of the early 1980s, which was funded by a variety of federal agencies but operated through the U.S. Department of Housing and Urban Development. The second, the Comprehensive Communities Program (CCP), was funded during the mid- and late 1990s by the Bureau of Justice Administration. The first initiative was an unmitigated disaster, primarily because nothing happened. Relationships never were formed; money went unspent; and virtually all programs turned into cash transfer mechanisms, giving people jobs whether they performed work or not. Furthermore, almost every site had bitter feelings toward the "feds" who administered the program.

CCP was another story. At virtually all of the sites, strong relationships had developed among citizen groups, service agencies (including faith institutions), public and private sector organizations, and police and criminal justice agencies, although the mix of participants was particular to each site.[5] In at least three sites—Baltimore, Boston, and Columbia, South Carolina—faith institutions were major players. At a fourth site, in Salt Lake City, the enormous impact of the Mormon Church on the city's culture and values always was felt, although the church was not formally at the table.

Observing the sixteen sites and studying community prosecution in four sites with my wife and colleague, Catherine M. Coles, forced me to try to think about how to characterize relationships among groups, organizations, individuals, and entities.[6] At each site an extensive set of relationships developed. Terms like "coalition-building," "collaboration," "coordination," and "partnership" were used to describe those relationships, and in my own writings about them I have used those terms rather indiscriminately. But the range of relationships that I observed was characterized by considerable variety, and the differences were of consequence. The consequences were evident in a conversation that I had with the head of a chamber of commerce that had formed a business improvement district (BID) in a southern city.

A business improvement district is formed by an organization of businesses that arrange to tax themselves to provide ancillary services within the district. They often start with holiday and other street decorations, move on to street maintenance, and ultimately move into providing security and other services. The chamber representative indicated that he had just concluded a rather nasty political fight with the newly appointed chief of police. Some years ago, the chamber, the city, and the police department had negotiated an understanding. The chamber would provide certain kinds of downtown maintenance services and employ guides who would patrol the district, providing information to the public but, most important, intervening if aggressive panhandlers hassled shoppers or other people on the street. They had no arrest powers, but they did have direct radio contact with the police department. The police department, for its part, agreed to permanent deployment of a foot patrol in the district. The new chief, exercising what he believed to be his sole prerogative, decided in the name of efficiency to end the foot beats. He was stunned by the ensuing brouhaha. After all, who but the chief of police should have final say about the allocation of patrol officers and the use of particular police tactics? Yet the city was confronted with a major political crisis: the BID, of course, challenged the chief before both the mayor and city council.

The *collaboration* that the department had entered into had administrative and tactical consequences; it limited the *internal* discretionary authority of the police chief. While the conflict ultimately was resolved, a partnership had turned sour and contentious because at least one party had not really thought through the implications of being a partner.

Just as some churches had established a relationship of defiance with subway officials, so the BID had established a relationship of collaboration with a police department. But there are many other forms of relationships as well. Figure 5-1 organizes different types of relationships on a continuum from collaboration, the closest and most complex type of relationship, to active opposition, the most remote and conflictual.

While these categories and definitions are arbitrary, they help to demonstrate the range of possibilities, and consequences, of interorganizational activity. Some examples will, perhaps, elucidate in more detail the differences among categories. The anecdote about the business improvement district and the police department is an example of a *collaboration*—clearly one that went awry, but a collaboration nonetheless: boundaries were permeated, and each organization departed from its traditional ways of conducting business. Conflict resulted because the police chief did not understand that the department essentially had agreed to limit its discretion in deciding how to police a particular neighborhood. Ongoing church activity in the subway is an example of *defiance*. Churches, feeling a moral imperative, defied public policy. In many communities, school systems have shown relative *indifference* to attempts to establish some form of working relationship with other parties. Court litigation—for example, by the New York Civil Liberties Union to stop efforts to maintain order in the subway—is a type of *active opposition*. In New Jersey, despite their *passive protest* against racial profiling by the New Jersey State Police, African American church leaders appeared at a press conference giving *consent* to a collaboration of Essex County, the city of Newark, and state and federal criminal justice agencies that planned aggressive action to prevent violence.

Figure 5-1. *Continuum of Interorganizational Relationships*

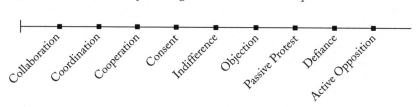

Definitions

Collaboration: an implicit or explicit contract between two entities in which each agrees to implement, conduct, or refrain from certain activities in ways that depart from each entity's traditional business and that permeate traditional boundaries.

Coordination: two entities identify a common problem, adjusting and aligning their activities in light of it and each other; traditional organizational boundaries, however, remain intact.

Cooperation: two entities conduct their respective traditional activities while agreeing to support each other and ensure that their programs do not overlap, conflict, or cross jurisdictional or professional boundaries.

Consent: an ongoing public declaration that one entity approves of the activities of another.

Indifference: Two entities that, if they are aware of each other's activities, do not believe them to be significant to each other.

Objection: an ongoing public declaration that one entity disapproves of the activities of another.

Passive Protest: one entity attempts to stop the activities of another through public declarations and dissemination of information.

Defiance: one entity attempts to block implementation or maintenance of another's program by advocating, implementing, and maintaining conflicting programs.

Active Opposition: active hostility between two entities enacted through political, legal, or violent attempts to stop each other's activities.

Source: Developed by the author in collaboration with Catherine M. Coles.

Moreover, such relationships need not be static; they may change over time. Winship and Berrien, for example, have offered us a fascinating account of the interaction of the Boston Police Department and the Ten Point Coalition, an association of African American clergy.[7] In it, they describe the evolution of the relationship from one of objection to one of consent—describing consent metaphorically as the "umbrella of legitimacy." They also provide an interesting account of one of the forms that consent can take: the Police Youth Leadership Award, a public award to "good cops." Clearly, even since Winship and Berrien wrote their article, the relationship between police and the Ten Point Coalition has moved beyond being one that merely offers an "umbrella of legitimacy" to police. Clergy and police are patrolling and making home visits together.[8]

Developing such categories is more than an academic exercise. The terms of the relationship, as demonstrated by the BID example, influence the quality of the relationship of agencies and contribute to their success or failure. They also have enormous consequences for participating organizations and staff. Let me give an example.

In both of my current areas of research, CCP (still ongoing at most sites) and community prosecution, I have observed staff burnout in innovative partnerships. The common interpretation of burnout is that it occurs when highly motivated and talented people succumb to the pressures of hard work, intensity, great demand, and long hours and leave the project, often frustrated and bitter. My own impression is that this interpretation is wrong. With rare exceptions, most participants love the hard work and intensity that go with interorganizational problem solving. Burnout usually occurs when an individual becomes caught between conflicting demands. On one hand, staff are "captured" by their projects: working with citizens and new colleagues and doing the research associated with problem solving turn into exciting, satisfying activities. I have seen police officers, for example, "cheat" and violate union rules by working more overtime than they can claim for reimbursement. The problem comes when staff find themselves caught between the routine ways that their parent organization does things and the need for innovative problem solving that is associated with interorganizational activities. In other words, such staff come to the table with others from a variety of organizations, come to understand the problem at hand in new ways, see the need for new approaches, but then find themselves unable to "play" because their parent organization wants them to continue to respond to problems in traditional ways. Caught in the middle as they are, they find that they lose both ways: they cannot deliver to their new colleagues and their organizational peers, and superiors view them as disloyal and untrustworthy.

Managing the terms of the relationship can be exceedingly difficult. Most collaborations have support at the top level—no collaboration would last long without it. And it is not hard to buy in at the operating level, at least for those individuals at the table; most recognize that the collaboration enriches their job and affords them new and interesting experiences. It is not the top executive who makes life hell for the involved staff person; it is the immediate supervisor or mid-manager. Attempts to manage difficulties by making end runs around supervisors or mid-managers to top managers often exacerbate, rather than alleviate, problems. Consequently, those who sponsor or coordinate interorganizational activities must help top managers to understand that they have to invest significant time and energy in preparing their organization for collaborative efforts—although doing so often is a difficult sell to executives who are under constant pressure to achieve quick results.

For some staffs and organizations, that is an exciting challenge. The Boston Police Department (BPD), both in ways described by Winship and Berrien and in a variety of other ways, is an example of a department that finds opportunities in such challenges. Indeed, it is so committed to the collaborative approach that it simultaneously maintains multiple relationships with the same organization. For example, as intense and genuine as is the collaboration between the BPD and Reverend Eugene Rivers's Ten Point Coalition in their attempts to prevent gang violence, the Ten Point Coalition can still publicly object to other practices of the BPD without jeopardizing the collaboration.

It is impossible to exaggerate the importance of getting the terms of the relationship right. The political, social, and organizational world in which institutions, organizations, and individuals operate is so complex—and often their business overlaps enough, as with police and prosecutors—that some conflict is unavoidable. In my own experience as the neutral convener of police and criminal justice agencies, service providers, and the faith community in a collaborative effort to reduce violence in Newark, New Jersey, the group often has found itself in a situation in which participants are fighting at one level while skillfully collaborating on another. While a variety of factors keep players at the table, the group's intense awareness of the severity of the problem probably is the most important in compelling the participating agencies to surmount their conflicts. The reality that young people are killing each other and that terror reigns in many neighborhoods, combined with the increasing certainty that only through collaboration can the killing be stopped, makes it hard to back away from or to interfere with what goes on at the table, even for those participants who are the most resistant to change or protective of their agency's domain.

Getting the terms of the relationship right is one matter; getting the *problem* right is another. That is the first step in developing and maintaining any partnership.

GETTING THE PROBLEM RIGHT

The defiant relationship that suburban churches established with the New York Transportation Authority was based on their understanding of both the problem and the means by which the problem should be approached. In a sense, the church members were right. There were desperate homeless people in the subway. Feeding and clothing the homeless is a merciful act.

At least two questions can be raised, however, about the churches' behavior. First, did they consider the possibility that their behavior could have negative consequences for the very people they were trying to help? Second, did they consider the impact of their activities on other subway users? I do not know the answers to those questions. The churches might well have considered them and decided to proceed; I suspect, however, that they did not. I suspect that they had only the most superficial understanding of the nature of the problem—that they were responding to a pop, media-driven understanding of the problem rather than a careful analysis to ensure, first, that they understood the nature of the problem; second, that the means they used to solve the problem were appropriate; and third, that they were in a position to lend their moral authority to any particular side in the ideological, legal, and policy conflicts that were being acted out.

Getting the problem right is a research issue, more or less formal.[9] For anyone thinking outside the box of conventional wisdom about the subway and New York City, only the most cursory "research" was required to understand that labeling the subway's problem as one of homelessness was at best a gross trivialization of a complex issue; at worst, a deliberate misrepresentation of the problems for ideological and partisan reasons. If one defined the major problem as homelessness, the solution was obvious: provide housing and jobs. If one defined the problem as lawlessness, the solution also was obvious: enforce the law. Yet one had only to go into the subway and look to see what the problem was. To be sure, more formal research was required for several reasons. First, we had to be sure that we had gotten the problem right. Second, we had to convince others—the media, the courts, and significant leaders—many of whom were confident that they fully understood the problem already. Finally, we had to make sure that we understood the nature of any sub-problems. To give an example from another site: in studying Boston's violent gang problem, police and researchers discovered the disturbing fact that "good kids"—youths without a history of violence—were starting to carry guns and join gangs in order to protect themselves.[10] That finding was important because the best way to deal with such youths is very different from the best way to deal with hard-core, violent repeat offenders. Indeed, mishandling the youths probably would have worsened the problem. Likewise, to return to the subway example, we knew that on occasion homeless families, including children, sought shelter in the subway. They had fallen through community and family safety nets and, for one reason or another, had drifted into New York City and its subways. They needed help and they needed it quickly; they were extraordinarily vulnerable and often were targeted by predators. Such genuinely homeless people needed to be located, contacted, gotten out of the subway, and linked to social services as quickly as possible.

Also, we identified another population of people, "couchies," who, almost literally, had gone into the subway to die. Couchies were burned out drug dealers/users who had no place to go; they were so desperate that they had stolen from their families to such an extent that their families had kicked them out. They wound up on friends' couches, from which they got their name, but soon, because they stole from their friends as well, they were kicked out again. They ended up in small colonies in the depths of the subways. Many died of hypothermia; others were murdered, electrocuted, or, in one case, burned to death while trying to keep warm near an electric hotplate. Identifying and contacting these people in the warren-like subway tunnels was grim and dangerous work. Every attempt was made to talk them out of the subway and to get them social and medical services. On several occasions when police had convinced one or more couchies to come out of the tunnels and accept a sandwich while being transported to a shelter or service agency, homeless advocates would attempt to dissuade them from entering the buses or talk them off the buses after they had boarded. Keeping the "homeless" in the subway, regardless of the personal cost to homeless individuals, furthered the political agenda of many advocates by keeping the homeless "under the noses" of citizens. Where better to do that than in the subway, with its captive audience of passengers? But, again, the main point is that research is required to fully understand the nature of the problem.

Remembering that problems often are not what they seem and that they have many dimensions is especially important in the context of this discussion, because the framing of the problem ought to determine the terms of the relationship of collaborating organizations. The fact that in Boston good kids as well as hard-core, violent repeat offenders were carrying weapons was more than just a warning sign about how *not* to treat them, it also suggested specific roles for the police, service providers, and the faith community.

For a faith institution, with its special mandate and role in society—often that of moral arbiter—getting the problem right ought to be the sine qua non of any effort to decide how to position itself on any problem. That suggests to me that first, faith institutions must come to the table early on as players in any community problem-solving effort if they are going to be active in dealing with the problem. They must be convinced—in a rigorous sense—that their understanding of the problem is correct.

Second, once the problem is understood, the means or tactics proposed to solve it must stand up to moral, legal, and constitutional scrutiny. Faith institutions are very good at scrutinizing, or, at least, they ought to be. They are trained in considering values and morality. While disagreements will arise about the moral legitimacy of specific tactics, at least faith institutions will (or should) make certain that the *right questions* are asked about any proposed solution to a community problem.

Moreover, the morality of the proposed solution as well as the nature of the problem should determine how a faith institution positions itself on the continuum of relationships. The methods ultimately used to solve a problem may not be acceptable to a faith institution, and therefore it will oppose the program.

And depending how deeply those methods conflict with its core values, the faith institution might position itself farther out on the continuum, toward active opposition.

For example, in Newark, the faith community has become an active part of an ongoing effort to prevent violence. As in Boston's Operation Cease Fire, young violent repeat offenders who are on probation or parole are required to attend a "notification session," a group meeting in which representatives of both the criminal justice and service/faith communities speak to the youths. The faith/service members assure the youth of a wide range of services, from jobs to mentoring to drug treatment. The criminal justice agencies make it clear that any further violence will result in a swift and severe reaction. While the faith community understood that that policy could result in prolonged incarceration for some offenders and did not object to that fact, members insisted, with the backing of the service community, that no arrests be made during the notification session, even if probationers or parolees with a warrant out for their arrest came to the session. (The faith/service representatives understood that if someone who was wanted for a serious violent offense came to the session that he or she would have to be arrested, but they believed that that was very unlikely. As far as they knew, the only warrants outstanding for the population in question were for minor offenses.)

The rationale of the faith community was that the central message should be optimistic and hopeful—delivered with a strong "or else" message if youth do not respond—but positive nonetheless. Representatives made it clear that they would object and withdraw if any arrests were made at the notification sessions. The criminal justice agencies agreed. The clergy understood, however, that some youths might be arrested at subsequent "accountability sessions"— post–notification session meetings of groups of youths with the chief judge or head of the parole board to discuss how they were doing—if they had committed offenses or were not meeting the conditions of their probation or parole.

While a faith institution may share a common understanding of a problem and agree that the tactics proposed to handle it are acceptable, it may lack the capacity to do more than offer consent. Or, like any organization, a faith institution may decide to increase its capacity. That approach was most graphically described to me by an African American minister in Columbia, South Carolina: "We have lost touch with our male youths. I don't want to be in the recreation business, but my new church will have a gymnasium—a good one. I've got to get at these youths."

Finally, as the faith community becomes more involved in partnerships, it has to become keenly aware of the consequences of its ministry to communities, as well as to individuals. The suburban churches that fed and clothed "homeless" people in the New York subway gave little thought to the impact of their activities on the subway environment and other riders—the litter and discarded food and clothes, not to mention the concentration of troubled individuals in a small area of the subway and how their presence affected a station and passengers. Likewise, faith institutions that attract troubled or troublesome persons to their facilities have to understand that their responsibility goes beyond what happens inside their buildings. Many programs are run in communities that already are unstable and overwhelmed with troubles; attracting more troubled individuals to such neighborhoods can further destabilize them. Many community groups, for example, have complained about the concentration of food programs in some neighborhoods, especially when those running the program do not ensure that their clients not litter the neighborhood or create other difficulties. And I am not referring to middle-class or suburban neighborhoods; I am referring to struggling inner-city areas. That by no means should discourage faith institutions from providing services, but their obligations go beyond their own doors. They have to ensure that they and their clients are good neighbors, strengthening their neighborhoods rather than creating additional difficulties. Again, this is the type of issue that ought to be considered in a thorough problem-solving exercise.

CONCLUSION

We are in an exciting era. Communities are reasserting control of public spaces and the behavior of young people. In most communities, streets are safer, and citizens know it and appreciate it. The community policing movement is spreading throughout law enforcement agencies, and relationships have been formed among groups and agencies that are surprisingly strong and enduring. I am optimistic about their ability to continue to reduce crime.

But I am not a Pollyanna. We have much to worry about: the generation of African American youths that have been or are imprisoned; the militarism that persists in law enforcement agencies; the fear that police feel in many neighborhoods; the persistence of domestic violence—the list could go on. But we have made progress, and there is reason to hope that success will build on success.

Many observers have offered what I consider to be oversimplified explanations of why people are committing fewer crimes. They attribute the decrease to police tactics, to demographics, to the economy. Aside from taking credit from those in neighborhoods and communities, including police and criminal justice professionals, who have worked so hard to regain control of public spaces and young people, such explanations reduce our ability to learn from history. Bad public policy and practice got us into the crime mess, and improved public policy and practice is getting us out of it. Economic and demographic determinism allows us to avoid our personal, social, professional, and political responsibility for what happened. That is just too easy.

NOTES

1. Martin Luther, "An Open Letter to the Christian Nobility on the German Nation," in *Three Treatises* (Philadelphia: Muhlenberg Press, 1943), p. 17. This treatise was originally published in 1520 (a record for my professional citations).

2. George L. Kelling and Catherine M. Coles, *Fixing Broken Windows: Restoring Order and Reducing Crime in Our Communities* (New York: Free Press, 1996).

3. Jane Jacobs, *The Death and Life of Great American Cities* (New York: Vintage Books, 1961).

4. For a discussion of these issues, see George L. Kelling and William J. Bratton, "Declining Crime Rates: Insiders' Views of the New York City Story," *Journal of Criminal Law and Criminology*, vol. 88, no. 4 (Summer 1998), pp. 1217–31.

5. Although it is not central to this chapter, the differences between the early 1980s' Urban Initiative program and CCP seemed to include the maturing of citizen groups, a belief that no organization could go it alone, a sense of despair about youth violence in the late 1980s and early 1990s, and a willingness on the part of the "feds" to "let good things happen." Regarding the latter, CCP essentially bought into ongoing agendas and relationships in each site. The major contributions of the Bureau of Justice Administration seemed to be three: the provision of some funds, which in turn made some outside expertise available, and an insistence on careful but time-bound planning.

6. Dr. Coles studied community prosecution in Austin, Texas; Boston; Indianapolis; and Kansas City, Kansas. All of those sites emphasized the importance of working closely with other organizations and neighborhood groups.

7. Christopher Winship and Jenny Berrien, "Boston Cops and Black Churches," *Public Interest*, no. 136 (Summer 1999), pp. 52–68.

8. Personal conversation with Commissioner Paul Evans, April 27, 2001.

9. University of Wisconsin professor emeritus Herman Goldstein introduced the idea of problem-oriented policing to criminal justice and described the method. See Herman Goldstein, *Problem-Oriented Policing* (Philadelphia: Temple University Press, 1990).

10. Personal conversations with David Kennedy, research fellow, Kennedy School of Government, Harvard University.

CHAPTER SIX

Not by Faith Alone:
Religion, Crime, and Substance Abuse

JOHN J. DiIULIO JR.

Under what, if any, conditions can the communities and life prospects of America's most disadvantaged children, youth, and families be improved? How, if at all, can religion in general or faith-based organizations in particular foster those conditions? How should the rest of us, whether as tax-paying citizens or concerned neighbors or in other civic and social capacities, support fellow citizens who, partly or totally out of religious conviction, help "the least of these" among us and "promote the welfare of the city"? To the extent that we deploy government authority or dollars to support community-serving religious individuals and institutions, how can we do so in a way that bears witness to common sense, social compassion, and respect for our constitutional laws and civic traditions? Regardless of how much public or private support faith-based organizations receive, how much should we reasonably expect them to achieve in solving tough social problems such as violent crime and drug abuse?

Those are not academic or abstract legal questions, nor will the usual answers now suffice. The sacred and the secular already are quite mixed, not only in literally scores of organizations like Catholic Charities and the Salvation Army, but also throughout entire social service "industries" in the civic sector.

For example, University of Pennsylvania social work professor Ram A. Cnaan has found that fully one-third of all daycare services in America today are provided through churches and other religious nonprofit or faith-based organizations. Through systematic surveys in six cities and a virtual census of religious social service organizations and community-serving ministries of all faiths (big

This piece is adapted from a paper written and presented at the Sacred Places, Civic Purposes Conference at the Brookings Institution in September 1999.

and small, old and new) in Philadelphia, Cnaan has documented beyond a reasonable empirical doubt that poor children, youth, and families in urban areas of the United States remain critically dependent on "the churches." Even by conservative estimates, in Philadelphia alone it would cost about 1 billion dollars a year to replace what faith-based organizations do for the city's needy, including many people who are receiving public assistance. The single biggest beneficiary of the city's faith-based organizations are poor children and young adults who are neither church members themselves nor from families that are "churched."[1]

Religious organizations that are not necessarily churches make many civic contributions. In just six months of research in the poorest neighborhoods of Washington, D.C., two young Princeton University graduates, Jeremy White and Mary de Marcellus, documented the existence of 129 small faith-based organizations that together served some 3,500 poor neighborhood children and young adults each week. Only a few of them received any public money—no surprise when only about 3 percent of all larger, more traditional religious congregations and ministries nationwide receive public money.[2]

To the civic contributions of grassroots faith-based organizations documented in both systematic surveys and ethnographic studies, add the tens of billions of dollars that traditional religious congregations raise and spend each year on charitable and community-serving good works. Who, we must begin to ask, is subsidizing whom?

That question is not any easier to answer empirically when it comes to specific corners of the civic square where faith-based organizations have long been a major and socially beneficial, if unheralded, presence. It is difficult, for example, to imagine the daily operation of the U.S. criminal justice system and its programs without the contributions of communities of faith.

As Public/Private Ventures vice president Harold Dean Trulear has documented through his work on how faith-based organizations serve high-risk youth in nine cities, throughout urban areas of the United States a large but hard-to-quantify fraction of all community-based crime prevention mentoring programs, including those funded in whole or in part by government, are, in fact, ministering programs. Likewise, many victim services agencies, like many aftercare programs for ex-prisoners and their families, depend almost exclusively on volunteers drawn directly from religious organizations and operate rent free out of "sacred places."

Father Andrew Greely, a sociologist, has aptly summarized the evidence on godly people in the civic square: "People who attend services once a week or more are approximately twice as likely to volunteer as those who attend rarely if ever," and even a third of persons who do not volunteer for specifically religious activities relate their civic service "to the influence of a relationship based in their religion."[3] Much of the data behind Greely's conclusion are derived from surveys of religion in American life by pollster George H. Gallup Jr.[4] Although one often hears journalists doubt that most Americans truly believe in God, the data make plain that they in fact do, and no Americans more than African Americans. Neither can there be the slightest rational doubt that, as Gallup has observed, "churches and other religious bodies are the major supporters of voluntary services for neighborhoods and communities."

So, how should we begin to understand and answer the policy-related and other questions about godly people in the civic square with which I began?

THE TEN POINT COALITION MODEL

One can begin with the community-serving ministry founded by Boston's Reverend Eugene F. Rivers III, a Pentecostal preacher and ordained minister of the Church of God in Christ, the country's single largest black church denomination.

The Rivers ministry began in the mid-1980s, distributing food and clothing from its quarters on the campus of Harvard University, then relocated to the poorest streets of Boston's Dorchester neighborhood. The tiny Dorchester row home of Reverend Rivers and his wife, Jacqueline, a Harvard *summa cum laude* graduate and education specialist, was sprayed with gunfire twice. Once the bullets barely missed their three-year-old son, asleep in his bed. But they stayed and built a prototypical small-budget, inner-city, preschool-to-prison ministry. Since 1990, their ministry has helped thousands of poor minority children, youth, and young adults to achieve literacy, obtain jobs, and avoid drugs.

The Rivers ministry is best known, however, for its role in assisting local police and probation officials in community-oriented crime-control efforts that arguably contributed to Boston's dramatic post-1993 drop in gun-related youth homicides and violence. Through its National Ten Point Leadership Foundation, the ministry has seeded kindred antiviolence "police-preacher" partnerships in Philadelphia, Indianapolis, and other cities since 1996.

Reverend Rivers, Jacqueline Rivers, and their dedicated Dorchester cadre of co-ministers and volunteers, many of them young black professionals with advanced degrees in the sciences from top colleges and universities, are unmistakably and unapologetically evangelical Christians. Or, as the Reverend puts it in his inimitable phrasing, "We're saved like the Bible says. Up on Jesus, love Jesus, walk among and serve the poor like Jesus. No winking or blinking on Christ. We're committed for real to these kids unto death. That's why we're willing to forsake the money thing, the nine-to-five thing, the big church thing . . . and even die ourselves in the name of Jesus. Die that they might live and make it."

Yet not one among the eclectic bunch of writers, analysts, and private funders who have witnessed what the Rivers ministry does on a daily basis has concluded either that it features no "God talk" or that it features nothing but such talk, except during Sunday morning services. Not one has reported either that Rivers and company are not interested in spiritual deliverance or that they are so obsessed with spiritual deliverance that it colors or conditions their every act of social service delivery.

Indeed, no one has found even a single beneficiary of the ministry who was either told explicitly or subtly made to feel or understand that the price of entering the ministry's buildings, receiving its services, eating its food, enjoying its gifts, participating in its programs, or otherwise getting its help was immediate or eventual profession of faith, attendance at Sunday services, or any type of expressly religious commitment: not a single child in the literacy program, in the summer recreation program, or at a Christmas party; not a single drug addict, gang member, accused killer, prisoner, or member of the fatherhood program; and not one welfare mother seeking help finding work.

How does a minister who has received so much local and national media attention gladly preach each Sunday to fewer than thirty people, most of them adults who have been with him for years? "The kids and the others get Christ by our example of prayerful daily service to them. They know I'm the minister, but they have no idea with what denomination or such. If more would go to some church, any church, great. If some become professing Christians, amen. But reaching and teaching is not only or even mainly about preaching. Their hearts and the 'hood will bear our Christian witness to them regardless," says the preacher.

The good news is that, like the Rivers ministry, few of America's thousands of preschool-to-prison ministries are simply or solely about spreading the Good News. There are, to be sure, community-serving ministries that focus on transforming troubled individual lives and that manifest the faith in "faith-based" in ways that rightly make them strictly ineligible for public funding. That would hold even if there were hard empirical data that the services of such ministries were far more cost-effective and rehabilitative than anything anyone had ever seen. But most community-serving ministries, including most inner-city preschool-to-prison ministries, do not do all or most of what they do exclusively in a religious fashion. Even the strictly faith-based programs that succeed often do so in partnership with other individuals and organizations, religious and secular, public and private.

Thus, whether we focus narrowly on what "sacred places" can contribute to specific "civic purposes" such as reducing rates of crime and substance abuse or whether we focus more broadly on all the many good, community-serving works that they indisputably do, *the key to making rational policy judgments will be to make rational, empirically grounded, socially compassionate, public-spirited distinctions.* We need to move beyond—and stay beyond—the strawman arguments, catch-all categorizations, exaggerated fears, and exaggerated hopes that still dominate much church-state discourse and policy debate.

On one extreme is anyone who is so reflexively hostile to religion in the public square—and so intellectually dishonest or devoid of true historical and legal knowledge—that he or she stands ready to act as an inquisitor in *any* effort to deploy government in support of fellow citizens who serve the poor if they do so in the vicinity of a religious symbol or say "God bless you" when nobody has sneezed.

On the other extreme is anyone who is so reflexively devoted to religion as faith alone—and so intellectually dishonest or devoid of true historical and legal knowledge—that he or she stands ready to damn *any* effort to deploy religion in support of fellow citizens who serve the poor if they accept even a nickel of Caesar's coin, partner with people of other faiths, or work with secular social services bureaucrats or other public employees who rarely say "God bless you" even when someone *has* sneezed.

Fortunately, there are very few such extremists on either side, and they deserve not our scorn but our fraternal correction: the former so that they stop viewing all faith-based organizations as social toxins, the latter so that they stop viewing only faith-alone organizations as social tonics.

So, how can we best keep faith with political leaders? How willing and able are we, whatever our religious and political leaning, to be compassionate yet dispassionate when it comes to the "how" of helping those who help the disadvantaged, their communities, their cities, and, by turns, our one nation—which is still, for most Americans, "one nation under God"?

CIVIC "VALUE INVESTING" IN FBOS

After five years of studying and assisting faith-based organizations in cities across the country, with a special eye on ministries that have special promise as agents for reducing crime and substance abuse, I would suggest that government, business, and the rest of the civic sector should approach the utility of the sacred places sector of the nonprofit "market" in achieving civic purposes much the way so-called value investors approach the stock market to achieve financial gains. Let me briefly elaborate upon the analogy.[5]

Basically, value investing is predicated on the view that a company does not need to be outstanding for its stock to outperform the market or to yield big profits; it only needs to be better than investors think it is. Any stock that is viewed with undue pessimism or rejected irrationally by investors is a likely bargain. Value investors buy stocks of sound, if not sensational, companies that research reveals to be undervalued because they represent an industry that has long been out of favor, because they once experienced management or other problems to which investors overreacted, because they have an erratic history of earnings, or for other reasons.

Value investors buy stocks that are priced low in relation to company assets, sales, earning power, and management ability; changes in commercial environments; and other factors that history proves matter economically. Value investors thus profit by paying close attention to economic fundamentals and trading against the economically unwarranted emotions of others. So, rather than picking or riding high-priced hot stocks, they make lots and lots of small bets on cheap stocks. Rather than courting sudden growth in hot sectors, they court steady growth in cheap sectors. Value investing beats its opposite number, so-called growth investing.

By analogy, faith-based organizations (FBOs) are the value stocks of the community-serving nonprofit sector. From the 1960s until quite recently, they were out of favor, not only because of the irrational exuberance that the policy elite expressed in strictly secular, government-centered solutions to social problems, but also because of widespread doubts about their future assets—since religion was supposedly on the wane in the United States—and their management fundamentals, given corruption scandals, charges of politicization, and an innocent yet debilitating lack of administrative competence.

The FBO sector's volatile hot stocks were big-church, big-name ministries that promised much but delivered little. Today's FBO "industry," however, has begun to regain public and "consumer" trust and confidence in a country that turns out to be stubbornly religious. Many of its new "CEOs" are quite willing to open themselves and their organizations to outside scrutiny by skeptical secular researchers and professional foundation auditors, and they are quite eager to engage in interdenominational and interfaith partnerships and program "mergers."

There are various kinds of community-serving FBOs, and only recently have we begun to identify the common characteristics and best practices of those FBOs that seem especially effective in achieving various civic purposes among disadvantaged residents of poor urban neighborhoods. Nevertheless, people of quite different faiths, traditions, partisan leanings, and ideological orientations have developed strikingly similar lists of those characteristics and practices.

One common characteristic is that the community-serving FBO is community-based, not just in rhetoric, but in reality: the ministers and religious volunteers have the same zip code as the people they serve, and they subject themselves to all or some of the same hardships that neighborhood residents suffer. They do not "live large" either within the neighborhood or outside of it. They walk the same crime- and drug-infested streets.

Another characteristic is that the FBO came into existence before anyone—government agencies, foundations, parent churches, or others—offered its leaders financial or other support. Once the FBO was established, its leaders might well respond to government or foundation requests for proposals (RFPs), *but only to strengthen some effort that already was part of their core mission or to expand some program that they already offered.* Said a veteran community-serving minister in Washington, D.C., "Anybody that's got time or staff enough to mess with all them government forms or fill out thirty, forty pages of what the foundation wants you to say, they ain't got no real heart for [these children] and they ain't about doing no real work [in this school or] on those ugly streets."

One FBO best practice that follows naturally from the two common characteristics mentioned above—and appears on absolutely everyone's list—might be labeled "keeping the 'faith' in faith-based, but not by faith alone." Think of the Rivers ministry.[6]

It is increasingly apparent that the biggest civic purposes bang for the sacred places buck is to be found among small religious congregations, para-church groups, and grassroots inner-city outreach ministries. To be worthwhile to government, business, and nonprofit "investors," civic value investing in FBOs does not need to produce daily miracles of individual or social transformation; it needs only to outperform its nonprofit market competition over time, even if only by producing the same civic results at a smaller human and financial cost. As we shall see below, given the record of big-budget, nonreligious, arid crime-reduction and substance abuse programs, that should not be terribly hard to achieve.

Some small grassroots FBOs are widely credited with yielding tremendous social "profits," seemingly overnight. That would appear to be the story of, for example, the Rivers ministry and of FBOs like Washington, D.C.'s Alliance of Concerned Men. Led by Tyrone Parker, the alliance's five principals brokered a truce among rival gangs in a D.C. neighborhood that had witnessed more than fifty murders in five square blocks within two years. The murders ceased, and the press noticed. But even though, as Tyrone Parker says, the alliance has unquestionably helped to "stop the noise" in its neighborhood, and even though its crime-reduction "stock" was "advertised" through stories in the local and national media, this tiny FBO remains radically undervalued. Funds to help monitor, mentor, and minister to ex-gangbangers and their younger brothers and sisters remain scarce, and no one has yet supplied any civic "venture capital" to determine whether the alliance could cut gang violence in other neighborhoods. "If we were McDonald's," says one of Parker's compatriots, "we'd already be franchised." "Amen to that!" chimes in Rivers.

Civic value investing in FBOs should be relatively easy for corporate, philanthropic, and other private institutions and individuals. After all, they can pick their favorite "sacred places" by religious affiliation, location, civic purpose focus, or just about any other organizational characteristics and performance criteria that they choose. They can provide selected FBOs money, technical assistance, or both. They can identify themselves closely with an FBO's religious mission and character or remain detached from all except the FBO's secular dealings and achievements. And they can rather flexibly fund, defund, or increase funding and other support to FBOs as their resources and preferences dictate.

Civic value investing in FBOs by government, however, is a much taller and trickier order. There are all of the usual church-state issues, and there is all of the resulting red tape. That probably is a good thing. As Yale and Brookings political scientist Herbert Kaufman once memorably reminded bureaucracy bashers, "one person's government red tape is another person's treasured procedural safeguard."

The extant survey data suggest that the leaders of the larger and least evangelical Protestant denominations, plus urban Roman Catholic and Jewish congregations, are most willing to seek public funds for their community programs. Even they, however, have been slow to explore, let alone to tap, the charitable choice program authorized by Congress in 1996. Most congregation leaders simply do not know it exists. Some who do and might want to take advantage of it fear having to contend with assorted legal threats to their religious autonomy, employment practices, and more. As a supporter of charitable choice and expanded efforts to bolster the faith-based sector, I am tempted to say, "Let the litigation begin!" But, then again, who really wants to witness any public law intended to assist worthy community-serving FBOs turn into a full-employment policy for analysts, activists, journalists, judges, lobbyists, and lawyers?

Besides, even if every religious congregation in the United States were willing to break bread with federal funding agencies, and even if nobody sued or countersued anybody, would the federal government be any better at civic value investing in FBOs than it would be at picking stocks?

The real church-state policy challenge is the moral, strategic, and spiritual challenge of civic value investing in FBOs, not as directed by Washington, but as led by state and local governments and their governors, mayors, agency chiefs, and other subnational leaders and public employees. How should we understand and meet that challenge? Let us examine two separate but related areas, FBOs and crime and FBOs and substance abuse,[7] through case studies of fellow citizens who, out of religious conviction and through FBOs, are struggling to promote public safety and enhance individual well-being in our poorest urban neighborhoods.

FBOs, Crime, and "Unchurched Youth"

Inspired in part by Boston's renowned police-preacher partnerships, Philadelphia's district attorney, probation officials, recreation department chiefs, and other city leaders joined together in May 1999 with then Mayor Edward G. Rendell to launch an innovative youth violence reduction initiative involving local FBOs. It came not a moment too soon.

Unlike Boston and many other cities, in the 1990s Philadelphia had little good news about youth violence. The number of young homicide victims dropped from 164 in 1995 to only 157 in 1998, and the number of young gunshot victims "fell" from 137 to 136 over the same period. Philadelphia has the highest rate of gun-related homicide in big-city America—more than 80 percent of total homicides. Philadelphia's youth violence reduction project targets the 100 juveniles in each police district who, based on data shared by city law enforcement and social services agencies, have an extreme probability of "killing or being killed." Each targeted youth is given access to a combination of community-oriented, community-anchored prevention, intervention, or enforcement resources deemed likely to prevent the youth from harming others or being harmed.

The project's leaders aspire to repeat the pilot in each of at least a dozen police districts. "It is a bit like painting a bridge," says John Delaney, the deputy district attorney who chairs the project, "in that once you do the first 100 in each of twelve districts, you start all over again with another coat of prevention, intervention, and enforcement services for another 1,200. God willing, before the youth bulge we're seeing in the elementary school reaches its teens, there won't be a single kid in the city who prosecutors, social welfare street workers or ministers, or others think is in real danger and needs real help fast but gets none."

In conjunction with the project, the city's police commissioner, John F. Timoney, revived a once-vibrant police-clergy training program. So far, about 200 local clergy of different denominations and faiths have joined. Eventually, they will be relied upon as quasi-official counselors, conciliators, and high-profile presences on the streets. Already, many clergy have participated in probation officer-preacher ride-alongs in police patrol cars.

Lest anyone should begin to entertain unfounded fears, or hopes, about the city's youth violence reduction project and police-clergy program, it should be understood that no youth is required to interact with any member of the clergy, religious volunteer, or FBO. And, as probably goes without saying, no youths are directly or indirectly pressured to go to church or to "get religion."

James Q. Wilson stated in "Two Nations," his December 1997 Francis Boyer lecture for the American Enterprise Institute, "Religion, independent of social class, reduces deviance," but added that there are "church programs that work and ones that do not." The only minor amendment I would make to Wilson's statement is that, church-anchored or not, there are FBOs that work and ones that do not in reducing crime and delinquency and that, as Wilson stated, we still "have no way of finding out which is which, save by intense personal inquiry."

I have committed myself to such intense inquiry in the cause of finding, funding, or partnering with the right sacred places for those civic purposes. I believe that faith works, at least under some conditions. But let us back up a bit.

Violent crime has dropped about 26 percent across the nation since 1993, while youth crime has fallen from its horrific 1994 peak. True, we are by no means out of the woods, despite decades of massive public spending on both prevention programs and prison building, massive private spending on security devices and systems, massive suburbanization, and the individual efforts we all reflexively make to avoid crime where we live, work, attend school, recreate, and shop.[8] Still, the happy post-1993 fact is that crime is down almost everywhere. Abortions, births to unwed teens, number of welfare recipients, and many other indexes of social distress are down, too.

But the empirical reality is that almost none of that can yet be systematically related to an undercurrent of national religious revival, the churching of formerly unchurched youth, or specific local faith-based anticrime programs.

But what about Boston? I am second to none in my admiration of and support for the Rivers ministry and cognate anticrime, community-serving ministries in Boston. I also am second to none in my respect for Operation Ceasefire and other law enforcement–led programs that partnered with clergy to help reduce the number of homicides—from 153 in 1990 to "only" seventeen in 1999. And I believe Christopher Winship when he credits Rivers and company with deracializing aggressive police-probation tactics.

But I also am second to none in my view that we live in a multivariate world in which things that happen at time T cannot logically be attributed to things that happen at T plus one year and in which there are many competing theories and conflicting data. No one, including Harvard University economist Anne Morrison Piehl, a researcher trained in econometrics who has written seriously about the "Boston miracle," claims that we can determine with certainty the degree to which those initiatives have been responsible for Boston's good news. It would have been nice if New York City, in the course of its dramatic, ostensibly police-driven, post-1993 reduction in crime, had pursued more community-clergy partnerships, but that was not the case. Nevertheless, the big drops in crime came during the same years in New York as they did in Boston, but without the deracializing, just as they did in other cities with varying degrees of racial tension.

We need to remind ourselves that, as Berkeley political scientist Raymond Wolfinger once quipped, "the plural of anecdote is not data." There are good, published empirical studies suggesting that—across the nation and independent of any changes in policing and of any efforts of religious denominations or FBOs—a sizable fraction of the post-1993 crime drop can be attributed to each of the following factors: abortion; incarceration; laws that restrict gun ownership; laws that relax gun ownership; demographic dips in the number of young males; improved economic conditions; and others. Without reference to policing or preaching, one could scientifically explain all of the post-1993 crime decline. Indeed, if all the crime analysts were somehow right, we would now be free of crime, living in a society of saints. As you may notice, however, we are not living in such a society, so they cannot all be right. Thus we reopen the door to common sense and to such systematic evidence as exists of the effects of the "faith factor" on crime and delinquency.

And we also open the door to criminologist Byron Johnson, who, on his own and with faith factor research pioneer David Larson of the National Institute of Healthcare Research, has catalogued some of the best empirically credible evidence on the relationship of religion and crime. The evidence, as Johnson has carefully scored it, is generally quite positive. In his December 1998 report with Larson for the Manhattan Institute's Jeremiah Project, for example, Johnson concludes that the most rigorous scientific studies to date are nearly unanimous in their finding (consistent with James Q. Wilson's verdict cited earlier) that "religiosity is inversely related to delinquency"—that is, religiosity has "an inverse, or beneficial, impact on delinquency."[9]

But the relevant scientific literature remains thin, and, in most studies, religion is a poorly measured or omitted variable—"the forgotten factor," as Johnson writes. And what counts as "religiosity"? In much of the more advanced research on religion's relationship to a variety of outcomes, religiosity normally has been measured by whether an individual does or does not go to church. There was a great deal of excitement surrounding Harvard University economist Richard Freeman's 1985 working paper that reported that churched low-income young black men were more resilient—for example, less likely to use drugs, commit crimes, or remain unemployed—than otherwise comparable young black men who were not churched. But, as a radio humorist said, "if you think going to church makes you religious, you must think sitting in your garage will make you a car." "Churched" or "not churched" is not only a crude measure of religiosity, it is a largely irrelevant one in community-serving FBO anticrime programs in which many high-risk youth and adults are unchurched.[10]

Research by Johnson and others indicates that prisoners who participate in Bible studies are considerably less likely to recidivate than otherwise comparable prisoners who do not. But, as Johnson himself would likely agree, even in the best study recidivism was measured by whether an individual had been re-arrested only one year out. Thus, the research design was sturdy, but not experimental; the measures of statistical significance were suggestive, but not robust. Johnson's ongoing study of a Bible-based low-security prison program will be rich in inmate survey and related ethnographic data, employ a sophisticated multidimensional measure of religiosity, and use a matched design to test for post-release effects of the program. Whatever the findings, few prisoners of any faith will ever experience anything like the "total immersion" program he is expertly analyzing.

So, what do we know about the influence of faith on prisoners? What might be the impact if Operation Starting Line, a new multimillion-dollar effort by a coalition of the nation's leading Christian para-church ministries, were successful in its mission to evangelize every prisoner in America before the year 2010? It would no doubt depend in part on what "evangelize" turned out to mean—a few extra visits from an outside minister, Bible studies, prisoner after-care programs? Meaningful estimates of impact are impossible at this stage of our knowledge.

But suppose reliable empirical knowledge were no obstacle. Suppose that getting unchurched youth churched, getting prisoners into Bible studies, or employing other expressly religious means of cutting crime and delinquency were invariably successful. What would that mean for public policy? Public officials must be supremely careful not to coerce individuals under any form of custodial supervision into accepting or participating in any expressly faith-alone religious activity, and they must ensure that whether those individuals participate has no bearing on the legal disposition of their case.

So, let's get back down to basics. Does anyone really *not* want Philadelphia to involve clergy and community-serving FBOs in its youth violence reduction initiatives? Does anyone really want the godly people of the city's sacred places to stop serving low-income children and youth, families of prisoners, ex-prisoners, and crime victims in partnership with the city's justice system and social welfare agencies? Does anybody really *not* want crucifix-bedangled religious volunteers manning job-placement programs for young offenders or contributing disproportionately to community-based government programs that divert first-time delinquents from possible jail terms?

Or, to go back to the case of Boston's Rivers ministry, would anyone actually prefer that the Dorchester clergy had *not* helped Boston's police and probation officers to deracialize or otherwise cut crime? Would anyone like the Rivers ministry *not* to serve as ombudsman for juveniles in the court system or to visit local jails? Would anyone really feel safer in Dorchester if the ministry's summer recreation and other "idle hands" faith-based, but not faith-alone, programs were not in session sunrise to sundown last July? Does anyone really need to seek comfort, constitutional or any other, in the fact that the ministry's single best veteran youth outreach worker is not a card-carrying Christian, but is instead Jewish?

Finally, would anyone really prefer it if local police had dialed 1-800-S-E-P-A-R-A-T-E when instead, on June 27, 1999, Reverend Rivers was called to talk—and, if necessary, to "God talk"—an armed juvenile murderer into surrendering peacefully, and succeeded? On exiting the boy's hideout, should he first have taken off his collar, put on a police hat, and pretended for the cameras that he was "Officer Rivers"?

Most Americans would answer no to most of those questions, thank God for how much sacred places contribute to public safety and all phases of crime prevention, and pray for more and better partnerships between well-supported community-serving FBOs and their government.

FBOS, SUBSTANCE ABUSE, AND TRANSFORMATION

In 1999, past presidents of the nation's two leading professional associations of probation executives and officers issued a powerful, if disturbing, report on the state of their field. Probation, they argued, was failing not only to protect the public, but to enforce court orders and help offenders. "The probation discipline," they noted, "has long argued that probationers need to obtain community-based substance abuse treatment."[11] In Massachusetts, at least 80 percent of all probationers have significant substance abuse problems. But only 37 percent of all probationers nationwide participate in any type of drug treatment program during their sentence, and only 32.5 percent are tested for drug use once they receive treatment.

On any given day, there are more than 3 million people on probation in the United States, 52 percent of them convicted of one or more felony crimes yet under "community supervision." The nation's top probation experts concur that most felony probationers have some substance abuse history and are not getting any substance abuse treatment, public or private, religious or secular.

Likewise, if you think that the social costs of substance abuse have been exaggerated, guess again—the costs are huge. For example, substance abuse consistently has been found to increase, or to have a multiplier effect on, an individual's marginal propensity to commit violent crimes. By "substance abuse," I mean not just use of certain presently illegal drugs, but also alcohol consumption.

In fact, I have argued that the alcohol-crime nexus is at least as potent, and undoubtedly more destructive, than the illegal drugs-crime nexus.[12]

James Q. Wilson has noted that religion "lies at the heart of programs such as Alcoholics Anonymous (A.A.), an extraordinary success that no government could have produced and no business could have sold." As usual, Wilson is right. But do most scientific studies of religion, spirituality, and faith-based substance abuse programs indicate that, others things being equal, "religion" varies inversely with substance abuse? I have been studying the drug treatment literature on and off for more than a decade, and my answer is a qualified yes.

"Qualified" because there is not yet expert consensus about what works best in the way of treatment. There are two basic approaches. One is the "medical model," the twenty-eight-day, short-term approach exemplified by A.A. and kindred "higher power" 12-step programs. The other is the long-term (usually six to twenty-four months), residential, "therapeutic community" approach. Both have their respective academic, practitioner, political, and other champions. Neither works consistently. Nevertheless, both tend to generate successful outcomes, whether with multiple-problem populations like older probationers or otherwise well populations like older professors, but only with individuals who have tried treatment before and failed.

One confounding factor in assessing the efficacy of any type of faith-based substance abuse treatment program—and there many different types—is that many troubled people tend to seek God only after they have tried everything else. Call this "spiritual selection bias," for it is not uncommon for faith-based programs to get clients who may be new to religion but are old to treatment. Someone on his or her fifth or sixth try might have a higher probability of succeeding at whatever the next mode of treatment is, whether secular or religious or both.

Good science sorts and controls for such data biases. David Larson has produced numerous good scientific studies that find that faith works in preventing, coping with, or kicking substance abuse. Aaron Todd Bicknese's June 1999 political science dissertation on the much-discussed Christian drug treatment program known as Teen Challenge presents similar findings. Teen Challenge is at least as successful in checking substance abuse as most secular antidrug programs. More generally, the exhortation to stay drug free embodied in Teen Challenge, Fellowship of Christian Athletes "campus huddles," and other faith-based programs is at least as efficacious as that of many government drug education programs like the much-maligned D.A.R.E.

Why do faith-based substance abuse programs seem to work at least as well as many or most of the secular or purely public alternatives? The answer is buried in a finding from a 1995 evaluation by Public/Private Ventures of the Big Brothers Big Sisters of America mentoring program. The strongly experimental study found that, in addition to generating a host of other social benefits, low-income minority youth who had a Big Brother or Big Sister were 52 percent less likely to initiate drug use than otherwise comparable youth who did not. The "Bigs," if only for a few hours a week, put a caring, responsible, nonparental adult presence directly in the lives of poor children who were in many cases without any other positive, one-on-one, up-close and personal adult presence, parental or nonparental. If, as some seem sure, faith-based antidrug programs on average outperform secular ones, I would speculate that is because *ministering is the original species of mentoring.* Like many others who study and assist preschool-to-prison ministries, I have witnessed ex-prisoners who had been addicted to drugs for years, both in prison and out, get and stay straight and sober in faith-based programs run by unassuming clergy and religious volunteers. Why? Because, in the words of a Jamaica, Queens, youth and former drug dealer I once interviewed, "I know the man loves me, and that God loved me even when I was doing all that evil to myself and others. He's always here for me. Even when he's not, I know God is."

Byron Johnson could fill volumes about how just one prison ministry program has changed the lives of prisoners who were previously untreated, drug-addicted, problem-drinking probationers. Maybe, as the eminent University of Pennsylvania psychologist Martin E.P. Seligman suggests, "religion" as manifest in such programs is a particularly powerful instance of the applied "psychology of the positive." Or, maybe, as Penn's Pastor William Gibson would suggest, it has something to do with God.

For whatever reason, it is an empirically documentable reality that programs that attempt not so much to "treat" as to "transform" the self-concept of substance-abusing individuals—that attempt to get drug-addicted youth to understand themselves not as problem children but as children of God or to get binge-drinking ex-convicts to forgive themselves as God has forgiven them—are often passably effective *and* do not cost lots to administer. Civic value investors, take heed.

Besides, would anyone truly prefer that hundreds of thousands of probationers go untreated when there are good faith-based, but not faith-alone, anti–substance abuse ministries that could help? Does anyone really want to prohibit a probation officer who has read a prisoner's file and noticed that he identified himself as a Christian from encouraging that prisoner to look up Victory Fellowship or a kindred program as he leaves the jail detox center? Does anyone really want to keep even a penny of government money from, in effect, providing vouchers for probationers who voluntarily seek faith-based treatment for drug or alcohol problems? I sure don't.

A GREAT COMPROMISE?

Those Americans who serve God with gladness by serving their needy and neglected neighbors deserve our praise. We should mobilize more support, both
public and private, for faith-based organizations that help to achieve civic purposes. But I would gladly forsake the push for federal funding if I could be assured that henceforth even strict separationists, whether secular or religious,
would join those of us who work and pray for private value investing in faith-
based, but not faith-alone, FBOs. To wit: James Wilson has suggested that what
we really need is not a generation of conflict over church-state issues, but in each
and every city "privately funded groups that would evaluate the fiscal soundness
and programmatic intensity of church efforts . . . and help raise money for ones
that pass this initial screening."

Amen. Any takers? Or must it be "See you in court"?

NOTES

1. Ram A. Cnaan and Stephanie Boddie, *Black Church Outreach*, CRRUCS Report 2001-
1 (Center for Research on Religion and Urban Civil Society, University of Pennsylvania, 2001).

2. Jeremy White and Mary de Marcellus, *Faith-Based Outreach to At-Risk Youth in Washington, D.C.*, Jeremiah Project Report 98-1 (New York: Manhattan Institute, 1998).

3. Andrew Greeley, "The Other Civic America: Religion and Social Capital," *American
Prospect* (May-June 1997), pp. 70, 72.

4. Gallup's bedrock studies on religiosity in America merit citation: George H. Gallup
Jr., *Religion in America* (Princeton, N.J.: Princeton Religious Research Center, 1996) and *The
Spiritual Life of Young Americans* (Princeton, N.J.: George H. Gallup International Institute,
1996).

5. The next four paragraphs are based largely on Sanford C. Bernstein & Co., Inc., *Global
Investment Strategies* (New York: September 1999).

6. And to get a sense of how such an approach to community-serving good works is mandated and justified theologically in the Judeo-Christian tradition, read, for example, the recently revised Catechism of the Roman Catholic Church (no kidding!), specifically the sections that deal with "human community" in God's plan. To get a sense of how it is now being
justified, even among "by faith alone" Protestant evangelicals, read two new books by steadfast Christians, one by the politically liberal Ronald J. Sider, *Just Generosity: A New Vision for
Overcoming Poverty in America* (Grand Rapids, Mich.: Baker Books, 1999), the other by politically conservative Charles W. Colson, *Now How Shall We Live?* (Wheaton, Ill.: Tyndale
House Publishers, September 1999). Even the most unmistakably and unfailingly Christ-
centered voices in the field of community-serving ministry today are exhorting their fellow
Christians to revitalize their faith commitment, not just through intercessory prayers for the
poor, not just by preaching and proselytizing, and not just by getting more people directly into
church pews, but by bearing religiously motivated "witness" on the model of Christ's everyday love for and "walk" among "the least of these."

7. Readers who wish to violate their own Eighth (if not anyone else's First) Amendment
rights (that is, "no cruel and unusual punishments") may follow up with my chapters in two
Brookings volumes: "Black Churches and the Inner-City Poor," in Christopher H. Foreman,

ed., *The African American Predicament,* and "Federal Crime Policy: Declare a Moratorium," in Henry J. Aaron and Robert D. Reischauer, eds., *Setting National Priorities.*

8. For more detailed party pooping on crime, see my "How Goes the Battle?" *The New Democrat* (July/August 1999).

9. David B. Larson and Byron R. Johnson, *Religion: The Forgotten Factor in Cutting Youth Crime and Saving At-Risk Youth* (Manhattan Institute, Center for Civic Innovation, 1998).

10. Richard B. Freeman, "Who Escapes? The Relation of Church-Going and Other Background Factors to the Socio-Economic Performance of Black Male Youths from Inner-City Poverty Tracts," Working Paper 1656 (Cambridge, Mass.: National Bureau of Economic Research, 1985), as cited in *What's God Got to Do with the American Experiment?* (Brookings, 2000).

11. Reinventing Probation Council, *Transforming Probation through Leadership: The "Broken-Windows" Model* (Center for Civic Innovation, Manhattan Institute and the Robert A. Fox Leadership Program, University of Pennsylvania, July 2000).

12. For a brief but sobering analysis, see my "Broken Bottles: Alcohol, Disorder, and Crime," *Brookings Review* (Spring 1996).

>──◯──<

Effectiveness over Ideology:
Church-Based Partnerships in Crime Prevention

EUGENE F. RIVERS III

I am glad that the faith community, policymakers, and academics are starting to come together to address important issues such as crime and substance abuse. Indeed, one of the things that has made the Ten Point Coalition in Boston unique—and many would say uniquely successful—is the interface between the clergy and academics and policymakers. My colleagues—Jeffrey Brown, Ray Hammond, and a group of other members of the clergy—and I were in regular communication with scholars like Christopher Winship as we developed our strategies and carried out our work in Boston. We invited and encouraged systematic evaluation of our work so that we would not be deluded into smoking our own press clips. We also invited the social science community in to help us analyze our efforts so that we could distinguish rhetoric from reality.

As a result, the "academic" issues of how we researched, tested, replicated, analyzed, and evaluated our work were more easily resolved and our work was more successful. But that kind of interface is still pretty unique to our experience; often academics and community members don't work together that well.

George Kelling's chapter is right on target and helpful in a number of ways. First, he talks about churches getting and doing things wrong. Up until 1988, there was a fairly traditional black church model in which cops were considered racists and the black community was considered a victimized community. What was significantly different in my work in Dorchester through the Azusa Christian Community and the Ten Point Coalition—and this relates to Kelling's broken-window thesis—is that we were forced to deal with what happened on the street, not just our preconceived ideas or theories. We learned that the discourse changes when you are confronted with reality: it is one thing to go to meetings and do the dog-and-pony show and talk about racism; it's another when you are forced to confront the criminal elements of your own community.

Being forced to confront the criminal activity in Boston through the first-person testimonials of young men who reported to us what they were doing complicated life. But for the better. George Kelling's and Christopher Winship's work suggests that once someone gets on the ground and really deals with what's going on, it is inevitable that the ideological nonsense will collapse. I've found that to be true in my own experience. I have been on the left side of most things for thirty years, and I could have used that position to come to quick and easy conclusions. However, once I was forced to deal with criminal activity at the street level, all of my left-leaning rhetoric and ideology collapsed. The same is true of proselytizing. In thirty years, never have I come across a person on the ground who was committed to saving lives who said to a kid that if he didn't accept the ideological party line or religious dogma, he'd go to hell. It has never happened.

The debate about church and state becomes stupid once you arrive on the scene and you deal with people where they actually live and come to understand their real problems. When it is a matter of life or death, certain debates quickly become irrelevant. But when you live safely removed from the problem, your priorities change, because you do not have to worry about who's on the other side of the door. In that case, you can be as philosophically elegant and interesting and abstract as you like.

Increasingly, the thinking of many of us across the country who come out of the black community is that at the end of the day we want to see sacred spaces empowered to serve secular needs and purposes. For us, at the end of the day, serving the needs of the poor is the priority. And that's not about religion, it's about results. It's not about proselytizing, it's about performance. And we want sacred institutions to be judged on the basis of their performance and results, not by the fact that they are religious.

Now, if it is a crime that our religion can produce a strong result, then we plead guilty. Our argument is that people should not be discriminated against on the basis of religion. If, in fact, the most effective model for reducing violence and shootings among black youths is a faith-based model, we don't think that we should be discriminated against by the Department of Justice just because we happen to follow Jesus. If people who happen to pray to Allah or Yahweh are the ones who are close to the problem, produce measurable results, and demonstrate disinterested concern, they also should be evaluated on the basis of their performance, not their religious beliefs. So the question is not about religion, but about results.

We are simply attempting to get those sacred institutions sufficiently strengthened to serve the secular needs of millions of very poor people whose needs must be met if society is to be fair or compassionate or rational. There needs to be philosophical debate, but we can't let that debate keep us from serving the needs of kids who are too frequently ignored by the elite, on both sides of the political aisle, for different ideological reasons.

Maintaining Legitimacy: Church-Based Criticism as a Force for Change

CHRISTOPHER WINSHIP

Churches are not always on the side of progress, a fact verified by George Kelling's chapter and my own experience. I lived for a period on the South Side of Chicago during the early 1970s, when many of the major African American churches were very closely allied with the Daley machine. During that time community activists made a concerted effort to desegregate Chicago's trade schools; it was a particularly important goal because it was necessary to attend a trade school in order to get into a trade union. The churches, however, supported the Daley machine indirectly by refusing to openly support the desegregation effort.

The dangers of church involvement in reform are not limited to Chicago. In the book *The Color of School Reform*, Jeffrey Henig and others discuss the role of black churches in school reform in four cities—Atlanta, Baltimore, Washington, D.C., and Detroit—from 1960 to 1980.[1] They point out that in earlier periods, when whites controlled the public school system in those cities and teachers were predominantly white, black churches were strong supporters of reform efforts. Over time, however, those school systems became increasingly important sources of jobs for blacks. As a result, large black middle-class churches, many of whose parishioners were teachers or, more generally, government employees, often sided with the teachers' unions in strongly opposing reform.

Even in Boston, the home of one of the most highly acclaimed examples of a successful partnership of religious and community leaders to reduce youth violence, the role of the church is not as unqualifiedly positive as one might initially think. Reverend Eugene Rivers's work with the Ten Point Coalition focuses on a small neighborhood with twenty-eight churches, many of which are storefront churches. The vast majority do not serve people who live there; the churches are there because the rent is cheap. As a result, disagreement has arisen among the churches and others in the community about the direction the community should take. Because the churches enjoy the low rents, they sometimes have opposed economic development initiatives that would bring new businesses into the neighborhood and thereby raise rents.[2]

Churches are complicated institutions with multiple goals and varied interests. At times their goals may conflict with the public good. I say that as a strong *proponent* of church and religious community involvement in society's problems. We need to expand the policy options available, and the story of the Ten Point Coalition and many others demonstrate that the churches, despite their necessarily complicated agendas, can act as a force for needed change.

We have not made a lot of progress in dealing with poverty over the last decade in this country. We have not made a lot of progress in dealing with single-parent households. We have not made a lot of progress in dealing with inner-city schools. Those are the factors that the political left typically has pointed to as the root causes of crime. Yet we *have* made enormous progress in reducing crime. The subway example offered by Kelling suggests how important it is to look outside the box and think about solutions that may not necessarily be associated with root causes.

At the moment everybody is aglow with the need to partner with everybody else, as if partnering alone can solve the world's problems or single-handedly reduce youth violence. The Ten Point Coalition's partnership with the police in Boston often has been held up a model. But there is very little discussion in the research literature about the nature of such partnerships, what their purpose is, and what their limits are.

What the Ten Point Coalition, along with others, has accomplished in Boston is to get the police to focus on the small number of youths who truly are a problem and to stop harassing the large numbers of inner-city minority young people who are not. When the police act in a way that is consistent with the community's interests, the coalition publicly supports them. When the police do not, the coalition is more than willing to expose them to a rain of public criticism.

So it is a peculiar partnership, one that has changed the way the police (and other elements of the criminal justice system) and the inner-city community relate to each other. In its role as intermediary between the two parties, the Ten Point Coalition strives for balance between the community's desire for safe streets and its reluctance to see its children put in jail, and it does so in a way that offers an "umbrella of legitimacy" to the police in exchange for the fair and just exercise of their power. They support the police when the police act appropriately. But the coalition's very effectiveness rests on its willingness to criticize any police behavior that falls outside the bounds. Indeed, members of Boston's religious community—led by Rivers, who always is willing to exercise a prophetic voice and to speak truth to power—have at times been among the most vocal and publicized critics of the police department, even after the two parties became strong and long-standing partners in the battle against youth violence.

For example, a Boston street minister of color was arrested in the middle of a fight that he was trying to break up. He was out of collar, and the police did not realize that he was a minister and ignored him when he said that he was. Rivers was vocal in the press about the importance of investigating the matter and holding the police accountable for the minister's unfounded arrest. His statements were essential to maintaining his credibility. Had he not openly criticized the police, many in his community would have assumed that he had been bought off, that his silence was repayment of a debt.

The lesson of the Boston experience, along with that of other cities, is this: in the struggle against crime, the police cannot go it alone; they need the cooperation of community leaders. Such partnerships help reduce youth violence and, equally important, delineate what constitutes legitimate police behavior. Police strategies can acquire legitimacy within inner-city communities only if the community harshly criticizes inappropriate police tactics while supporting appropriate tactics. Under those circumstances, ministers and police are ideal partners, because the clergy can maintain a prophetic voice even while actively partnering with the police. At the very least, the possibility that faith-based organizations in Boston have found an effective strategy for reducing youth violence, without severely and broadly compromising the civil liberties of inner-city residents, certainly is promising. But further research on and rigorous analysis of the complex nature of church-state partnerships in all cities is necessary if we are to truly understand the potential of faith-based organizations in reducing crime.

NOTES

1. Jeffrey R. Henig and others, *The Color of School Reform: Race, Politics, and the Challenge of Urban Education* (Princeton University Press, 2001).

2. Omar M. McRoberts, *Saving Four Corners: Religion and Revitalization in a Depressed Neighborhood,* Ph.D. dissertation, Department of Sociology, Harvard University, 2000.

>––◦––<

The Enforcer: The Role of Churches in Maintaining Social Control

JOYCE A. LADNER

George Kelling discusses the destruction of the social institutions and relationships that have maintained social control by meting out negative sanctions to punish misbehavior and positive sanctions to reinforce conforming behavior. My firsthand experience with the function of sanctions to reinforce conforming values and behavior occurred during my coming of age in a small community called Palmers Crossing, near the town of Hattiesburg, Mississippi. My mother, Annie Ruth, who was also known as Miss Annie, was one of the reinforcers of the social norms in our tiny community.

For example, two young adults in the community who dated each other appeared drunk in public on a regular basis. The woman's nickname was Slingshot, and her boyfriend's nickname was Sa Poe. I think his name was Sam Poe, but his neighbors gave him the nickname Sa Poe. Whenever they passed our house drunk, they walked hurriedly to avoid Mother's sermonizing. More often than not, Mother saw them. "Oh, you're not going to slip past me. I see how drunk you are. Come here." Mother invited them to sit at our kitchen table, where she had them drink loads of black coffee; no sugar was allowed. Then she gave her standard lecture about how they should change their deviant ways and how they needed to make something of themselves and how "your mama is very disappointed in you and you don't want to hurt her by continuing to misbehave this way. You know this is not the way you were raised."

However, the small tightly knit communities that existed then have declined across the nation and with them the informal relationships and mores that exert control. Moreover, there is less consensus among community residents on what constitutes appropriate norms and who should enforce them. Kelling understands that it is not the big events that define an era or that are the most important underlying phenomena. Instead, it is the cumulative impact of the little events—the day-to-day sanctions of "Miss Annies" who remind individuals and groups of the traditional boundaries that the community has established for them. The informal mediators and enforcers of societal norms are critical to maintaining social control.

How does society maintain informal social control in an era when the formal institutions have declined and there are fewer informal arbiters of behavior? Those changes have come with massive changes in the way we relate to each other: we are less likely to know our neighbors; we do not dare to discipline a neighbor's children; teachers are hesitant to discipline students for fear that parents will object or file formal complaints against them. There has been a rapid deterioration of community values and with it decreased interest in participating in the reciprocal relationships—with their implicit obligations—that reflect shared values and responsibilities. That, indeed, is what constitutes the most serious problem in our communities.

My view is that we no longer have a uniform set of norms and values, no agreed-upon definitions of appropriate informal conduct. Nor is there a common language, a common understanding of concepts such as that evident in the 1960s when Americans collectively said that to deny some Americans the right to vote constituted a national problem. That is how Martin Luther King Jr. was able to organize citizens across racial, religious, and ethnic boundaries—by using agreed-upon standards of what was morally, legally, and socially right and proper.

An underlying theme of this discussion is the decline of the patterned behavior that both reflects and imposes social order, or the weakening of civility and its disappearance in large part from American life. With the decline of civility has come the emergence of deviant behavior. Kelling's discussion made me ponder the reasons why we embrace community policing. Is it because it is a way to recreate a sense of community among people for whom the community no longer exists? When members of Boston's Ten Point Coalition, including Eugene Rivers, Jeffrey Brown, and other members of the clergy, walked the streets in territory controlled by gangs and talked to the young men, they were successful, in part, because the young men were responding to face-to-face interaction and the restoration of community.

There are countless examples of communities in which the tide is turning and community norms are being restored. A recent Public Broadcasting Service program featured the dismantling of warring drug gangs in Washington, D.C.'s Benning Terrace, where members of the Alliance of Concerned Black Men convinced gang members to stop the killing that helped Washington earn its notoriety as the "murder capital" of the nation a decade ago. All of the gang members put down their weapons, and there has not been a murder in Benning Terrace since then.

Another question raised by Kelling is that of how to practice a social gospel today, how to apply the rules and norms of the faith community to solve today's social problems. A model may be the community-based organizing efforts led by churches in the 1960s, when civil rights activists were welcomed by many church leaders and members and when a social gospel that fought for equal rights for all was an indispensable part of faith-based initiatives. Which of today's problems demand the application of a social gospel? How do we merge the secular and the sacred—or the sacred and the profane? How is it that so many religious institutions continue to exist in the middle of the most crime-riddled communities? How is it that they open on Sundays and Wednesday nights for prayer meeting and but feel no obligation to become a safe haven for the young and the elderly?

How can we provide more incentives for faith-based institutions to remain open? How can community be strengthened when church members move to suburban communities and return only for Sunday services? More important, as more churches follow their members to the suburbs, who and what will fill the void in urban neighborhoods?

John DiIulio states that only a small percentage of churches, synagogues, temples, and mosques apply for available government grants. How can technical expertise be provided to the smaller congregations that exist amid the worst kinds of social problems? What type of assistance can help them? Can crime be prevented without recapturing public space?

The issue of how to develop more effective partnerships already has been dealt with. But how do we approach the problem through the re-creation of community and uniform values? How can consensus be built around which values are most important? How do we socialize young people to become law-abiding and respectful of authority if those values are not taught in the home and if the traditional institutions have abdicated the responsibility for teaching them? How can we decide which are the most important problems to tackle?

I am concerned about how to diminish or eliminate those problems on the front end, at the prevention stage, so that we do not have to deal with them at the criminal justice level. How can churches get law enforcement agencies to parole some of the people who have committed lesser offenses to their congregation instead of continuing to lock them up? I do not reject the importance of dealing with root causes—and rejecting it lets the government off the hook. But how can we develop an approach to crime prevention that combines immediate measures to reduce crime with long-term measures to deal with root causes?

The most important question that has been raised is how faith-based organizations that are designed to solve problems can be made more effective. How can we empirically validate the effectiveness of the work that faith-based organizations carry out? Allow me to use the Nation of Islam as an example of a faith-based organization that has a proven track record of getting men off drugs and engaged in productive activities so that they can be assimilated back into the mainstream of society. What is the role of faith in the treatment of drug addicts? How is that Chuck Colson, a former White House staff member under President Richard Nixon, can take his ministry behind prison walls and help turn people's lives around? How do we design rational, empirical studies and make socially compassionate, public-spirited policy judgments based on that research?

I do not think that the successes we have observed in solving individual manifestations of social problems are due solely to the influence of faith-based organizations. I would like to see a form of multivariate analysis used to examine the effect of different factors, including that of faith-based organizations. We *must* also examine root causes; the role of government; and the role of the individual in his or her own rehabilitation.

I think it is time for us to become advocates for the replication or dissemination of models that have proven effectiveness, especially those that are cost effective. There are many, such as Sandtown, a faith-based, community program in Baltimore that has successfully provided a variety of services with little funding.

The final question I would like to raise is how relevant charitable choice can be when according to Dilulio only a small number of clergy are even aware of its existence. How can charitable choice become more widely used? How can those in the field make sure that all individuals who are eligible to take advantage of it in fact do so?

>–•–⊖–•–<

Fighting Crime: Overcoming the Arguments of Church-State Separationists

KEITH PAVLISCHEK

We should not be so naïve as to think that the heated opposition to the White House Office of Faith-Based and Community Initiatives or to public funding of faith-based organizations has all that much to do with empirical or social science data on the effectiveness of such funding. Whether faith-based organizations are in fact more effective than non–faith-based organizations in addressing the problems of the poor and disadvantaged is open to debate. But even if they are proven to be more effective, it would not matter to the church-state separationists. They oppose the funding of FBOs, or at least those "pervasively sectarian" ones that refuse to secularize, because they believe that it violates the First Amendment prohibition against the establishment of religion. They reason that just as government would not violate other First Amendment rights—freedom of speech or freedom of the press, for example—in the interest of "social effectiveness," so it should not violate the establishment clause.

But what if you reject the radical separationist views of Americans United for the Separation of Church and State, the American Civil Liberties Union (ACLU), and People for the American Way as historically and jurisprudentially preposterous? What if you were committed to a social policy that would help establish a healthier relationship between government and the institutions of civil society? Certainly a primary goal of such a policy would be to nourish and sustain the integrity and identity of a wide array of nongovernment institutions and organizations and to end discrimination against institutions that currently are discriminated against. That is the best way to view charitable choice. It should not be seen first as a funding mechanism for faith-based institutions. Rather, it is an important attempt to restore a healthy relationship between government and the institutions of civil society.

The ideology embraced by the separationists, however, can only produce an unhealthy and dysfunctional relationship between government and civil society because it is inherently discriminatory against one very important class of institutions of civil society. It inevitably excludes organizations and institutions from fair and equitable funding simply because of their most basic beliefs and convictions. To see why, take the not-so-hypothetical example of a nonprofit drug treatment organization that might be eligible for a government fee-for-service or voucher arrangement. What is masked by the simplistic distinction between "religious" and "nonreligious" (or "faith-based" and "non–faith-based") drug treatment organizations is that those that labor under the nonreligious or secular label hold highly contentious views about the nature of human beings, no less than those that are labeled "religious." How they implicitly or explicitly think about the "big issues" will profoundly influence their methodology. You might have a drug treatment program that is Freudian in methodology. Another might be modeled on a behaviorist approach. Another might be radically feminist or influenced by your favorite French post-modern philosopher. Justice dictates that all are and should be eligible to compete for public funds.

But what about a drug treatment organization that is theistic in its orientation, philosophy, and methodology? According to the separationists, the theistic approach must be treated differently from that of the Freudians, behaviorists, feminists, and French philosophers. In fact, the separationist insists that theistic organizations may not receive funding *even if* they can be shown to be more effective than the others in treating drug addicts, because their particular responses to the big questions are religious or faith-based, while the others purportedly are not. According to the separationists, when it comes to funding, the Establishment Clause requires the government to discriminate against those organizations *because* they are theistic.

But in truth, the answers to the big questions given by nontheists are no less faith-based that those given by theists. The choice is thus not really between faith-based and non-faith-based approaches to drug treatment, homelessness, job training, and other social problems, but among a variety of perspectives and methodologies. All of those perspectives are faith-based when it comes to the really big questions that orient, direct, and motivate their organizations: What is the nature of human beings? What is their place in the world? What is the ultimate solution to human pathologies? For that reason, it is simply unjust for the government to favor nontheistic over theistic providers of literacy and job training, drug treatment and counseling, care for the homeless, juvenile crime prevention programs, and so forth. To the extent that charitable choice legislation and the new White House Office of Faith-Based and Community Initiatives seek to remedy that injustice, they should be applauded and supported.

><del>—⊖—</del>◄

Even Church–State Separationists
Care about Serving the Poor

JULIE A. SEGAL

Everyone agrees that religious organizations play an important role in efforts to solve society's ills. In fact, even strict church-state separationists believe that government may cooperate with faith-based organizations in providing many social service programs. The disagreement over government funding of religious organizations is not about *whether* faith-based groups may form partnerships with government but about *how* those partnerships are structured. Among all the proposals for government collaboration with religious organizations in George Kelling's and John DiIulio's chapters, as well as the proposals that make up President George W. Bush's Faith-Based Initiative, charitable choice is the only one that fails upon closer inspection.

Although, at first glance, charitable choice appears benign, it violates the constitutional requirement of church-state separation by inadequately protecting social service beneficiaries from proselytization; by allowing discrimination on the basis of religion in hiring for positions funded with taxpayer dollars; and by leading churches and other houses of worship down the primrose path without alerting them to all the possible pitfalls associated with government funding. Further, while purporting simply to expand the good work of many faith-based social service programs, charitable choice will cause great damage to religious liberty—a price that some may not agree is worth the benefit. While many religious organizations may provide beneficial services in their communities, that does not negate the requirement that collaboration between those groups and government withstand legal and ethical scrutiny. The U.S. Constitution is not an obstacle to effective public policy or a pesky detail, and serving the poor and protecting religious freedom are not mutually exclusive. Because charitable choice has eclipsed the myriad appropriate ways in which religious groups can form partnerships with government to serve those in need, it is necessary to discuss the law and to elucidate the pitfalls.

The separation of church and state is one of the least understood and most maligned concepts in current political discourse. Created by the Establishment Clause and the Free Exercise Clause of the First Amendment, the separation of church and state simultaneously prohibits the government from advancing religion and protects religious organizations from government intrusion. Government funding of religious organizations therefore must be carefully examined. When the government funds faith-based social service programs, taxpayers will rightfully demand an accounting of how the money is spent, possibly compromising the autonomy of religious organizations and hindering religious programs by regulating them. Financial support also is problematic because few things could advance a religious mission more than paying for it. As a result, all nine justices of the current Supreme Court have consistently held that "special Establishment Clause dangers" exist when money is given directly to religious organizations.[1]

Many religious organizations provided government-funded social services long before charitable choice legislation was passed. For years, those organizations—among them Catholic Charities, Lutheran Services in America, and United Jewish Communities—have received billions of dollars from governments to provide faith-based social services, but without conveying a religious message and with other appropriate constitutional safeguards in place. Charitable choice obviously is not intended to apply to those programs.

Instead, charitable choice purports to end the so-called discrimination against religious organizations by permitting them to receive government money for their social service programs while allowing them to proselytize social service beneficiaries with private funds. It also allows them to discriminate on the basis of religion in hiring employees who are paid with taxpayer money. For some reason, charitable choice proponents claim that it merely "levels the playing field" by treating religious and secular organizations equally with respect to their ability to obtain government grants and contracts for social service programs. That is not so.

First, there is not pervasive discrimination against religious groups in government programs. As mentioned, religious organizations receive billions of taxpayer dollars to feed the hungry, care for the aging, house the homeless, and teach job skills to the unemployed. Second, charitable choice proponents want equal treatment only with respect to funding, not program implementation. Charitable choice does not require religious organizations to play by the same rules as all other social service providers. No other government contractor would be granted the privilege of discriminating on the basis of religion in hiring employees who are paid with tax funds.

It is important to note that, although religious organizations are permitted to discriminate on the basis of religion in hiring employees paid with private funds, charitable choice extends that concession, allowing them to discriminate in hiring employees who work on or who are paid through public grants and contracts. Accordingly, charitable choice allows religious organizations to exclude nonbelievers from government-funded positions and thereby to advance their religious doctrine with taxpayer money. This aspect of charitable choice is unconstitutional and amounts to federally funded employment discrimination.

Furthermore, in the context of employment, the term *religion* includes adherence to religious tenets and teachings. For example, if a church receives a government grant to provide welfare services on behalf of the government and it requires its employees to adhere to a religious tenet requiring sexual abstinence before marriage, it could fire an unmarried female social worker if she were to become pregnant and thereby violate that religious tenet.[2] Although religious organizations should retain that right in private employment, such discrimination should not be permitted with taxpayer dollars.

Finally, charitable choice threatens our country's religious liberty and jeopardizes the autonomy of religious programs. Religious organizations may feel compelled to compete for political favor and lobby for scarce government appropriations. Churches and other houses of worship also may be reluctant to continue their traditional and important role as critic of government conduct out of fear of losing a government contract. Furthermore, despite its goals, government money will lead to government regulation of faith-based organizations—a threat that has led many would-be supporters, such as Pat Robertson and Marvin Olasky, to question the wisdom of government grants to churches.

In addition to charitable choice, the new White House Office of Faith-Based and Community Initiatives is cause for concern. Although no federal agency has a prohibition against contracting with religious organizations, President Bush has ordered an audit of five federal agencies' rules and regulations to determine whether they "discriminate" against faith-based organizations. Regrettably, what the president considers a discriminatory barrier to entry may be another person's neutral, generally applicable safeguard. Only time will tell whether religious organizations will be granted an exemption from the rules and regulations that apply to all other government contractors.

Although there are no empirical or social science data on the effectiveness of faith-based social service programs, many observers, including strict church-state separationists, believe that religious organizations provide some of the best social services available. But enhancing those organizations' resources is a goal that can be achieved without charitable choice. The chapter entitled "In Good Faith: A Dialogue on Government Funding of Faith-Based Social Services," with an introduction by Melissa Rogers, aptly details the ways all of us—government, religious and community organizations, and the for-profit sector—can serve the poor together. If we direct our energies to increasing private funding, we could serve those in need with the Constitution's blessing.

NOTES

1. *Mitchell* v. *Helms*, 530 U.S. 793 (2000).

2. See *Boyd* v. *Harding Academy of Memphis, Inc.*, 88 F.3d 410 (6th Cir. 1996).

PART THREE

THE ROLE OF FAITH-BASED
ORGANIZATIONS IN

Community Development

CHAPTER SEVEN

Community Development
and Religious Institutions

JEREMY NOWAK

Over the past thirty years many of the poorest communities in American cities have become headquarters for nongovernmental organizations dedicated to neighborhood revitalization. At the center of that effort are community development corporations (CDCs): private, largely nonprofit, citizen-led organizations that use public and private resources to support programs to maintain and develop real estate, social services, and business.[1] The growth of CDCs has been accompanied by that of other service, civic, and finance organizations pursuing related goals. Together, these organizations constitute the field of community development.

While many community development organizations are the direct offspring of government-funded community action programs and philanthropic demonstration projects, they also are heirs to a rich tradition of community-based efforts that include immigrant mutual-aid associations, settlement houses, congregational outreach programs, cooperative business enterprises, and union-related programs.

This chapter focuses primarily on the work of community development corporations as a whole, not simply on that of faith-based institutions. Yet in many cases religious congregations are crucial catalysts, allowing CDCs to organize, win public support and financial backing, and develop roots in the community.

The role of faith-based organizations in building CDCs often falls outside the raucous debate on public funding of faith-based social service programs—partly because their role has, on the whole, not been controversial and partly because the congregations often serve as organizing and vouching forces for their community rather than themselves. It would be a great mistake to interpret the relative lack of controversy over the role of religious institutions in community development as an indication that their role is unimportant. Quite the opposite is true: their role is noncontroversial because so many of the key actors see it as essential.

Like all institutions that serve public purposes, community development organizations have complex histories. Their existence is the result of more than grassroots initiatives, although that is the view commonly held by the press. Instead, they are the product of the interaction of social activism and social isolation. Their existence says as much about what public policy and private markets do not do as it does about development mediated by civic groups.

Scratch the surface and you discover the activism generated by the1960s' war on poverty legislation, the role of national philanthropic organizations in funding antipoverty programs, ethnic identity politics, and community organizing efforts.[2] Look more deeply and you discover the institutional vacuum created by the reduction in federal support for cities, the transformation of settlement patterns in U.S. metropolitan regions, the persistence of a high degree of racial segregation, and a private sector that is less involved in local politics and civic affairs than before.

Community-based revitalization efforts in U.S. cities arrive as both symptom and cure, reflections of a historical renegotiation of power, capacity, and role. They assert the power of local institutions to act as a catalyst for social change, while also serving as an implicit reminder of the limited public investment in low-income populations and the economic gap between poor and mainstream America. Community development corporations emerge in the space left to them by changing market patterns and public policy. They can be defined, in part, by three characteristics. First, they are *local* institutions, in a society in which commitment to maintaining local identity is less important. A sense of local rootedness looms large in the CDC movement. Most urban CDCs define their territory of operation in terms of relatively small areas, through the affective ties of neighborhood or the administrative logic of service districts. In many instances, race and social class play an important role in defining place or locality. Strictly speaking, CDC interventions do not begin with the logic of markets or the logic of a poverty reduction strategy, but rather with the logic of communities, reinforced as it is through social and spatial boundaries.

Second, CDCs have excelled largely in the areas of residential real estate development and provision of place-based social services. While the earliest CDCs placed a heavy emphasis on job training and economic development, many of those efforts failed. There are important exceptions to that rule, and some important innovations in those areas are taking place today. The role of CDCs as drivers of affordable housing production from the late 1970s onward was heightened by public policy and the limits of private market incentives. They became housing and service providers to a constituency that suffered from lack of housing, for a product that had limited market profitability, and for projects that required access to multiple sources of public and private investment.

Third, despite their nongovernmental status and their entrepreneurial quality, most CDCs maintain a significant dependence on public or private subsidy, provided principally by government and private philanthropy. While they certainly are more market-driven than most public agencies and more entrepreneurial than traditional social service institutions, most CDCs require substantial subsidy to sustain operations. That need follows from the nonmarket role that they play, the high transaction costs of their services and products, and an organizational culture defined by a deep sense of civic responsibility and public purpose.

Community development corporations evolved from a variety of institutional contexts and experiences. If you search for the historical roots of the local neighborhood development organization in any city in the United States you will find links with schools, civic groups, block associations, business groups, unions, political organizations, and corporations. You also will find the persistent presence of religious institutions at almost every turn.

While often it is unrecognized or understated, the role of religious institutions in facilitating community development is fundamental. Religious institutions always have functioned as the most significant source of community development organizations and projects, serving as *institutional incubator, organizer, investor*, and *civic leader*. That is particularly true in the African American community, in which historically the role of the congregation in public life has been central.

Acting as incubator is among the more common functions of urban religious congregations. As one of the primary centers of civic life, churches, either alone or in coalition with other institutions, have launched a significant percentage of development organizations and projects in cities. That is as true today as it was when the late Reverend Leon Sullivan created one of the first CDCs in the country through Zion Baptist Church in North Philadelphia in the early 1960s. The structure of congregation-based development organizations varies widely—some are held tightly within the leadership and organizational culture of the congregation, some spin off into a more independent identity. But no matter what the nature of the ongoing connection, the historical relationship exists.

In addition to their role as incubator of CDCs, religious congregations throughout the country have been at the forefront of neighborhood organizing efforts from Los Angeles to Baltimore, creating a public space for citizen education and advocacy. Many of their efforts have been associated with national networks such as the Industrial Areas Foundation. Here it is important to recognize that congregations, operating as they do within an institutional framework that conveys a sense of permanence and discipline, often serve as the most important place within low-income communities for building secular public relationships. Congregations become a locus of citizen participation and interaction, which leads to longer-term civic change.

The faith-based community also has been among the most active investors in community development. Many of the earliest investors in community development financial institutions came from Catholic religious orders and several mainline Protestant denominations. In many instances it has been neighborhood congregations themselves that have taken the lead in making direct equity investments in their own projects or in incubating credit unions and microenterprises. More than most institutions, religious institutions have been able to bring not only organized members to the task of neighborhood renewal, but organized money and leadership as well.

Finally, the enormous social structure that religious institutions represent through their involvement in a variety of social welfare agencies and private sector relationships has been one of the principal sources of leadership for community development organizations. The presence of that leadership can be felt from the smallest homeless shelter to national efforts such as Habitat for Humanity. Even among the most secular community development institutions it is common to find leaders who are rooted in the ministry or financial and civic support that comes from local and regional religious bodies.

GROWTH AND ACCOMPLISHMENTS

Reports on CDCs during the past decade note their prominence in the production of affordable housing, their increasing numbers (2,500 to 3,500, depending on how they are defined), their more limited success in commercial development, their reentry into work-force development activity, and the breadth of their political support.[3]

CDC involvement in urban housing has produced some remarkable successes, in many instances priming the pump for non-CDC market involvement. At least four CDC strategies have influenced public and private sector investment in housing. First, community development organizations and development finance intermediaries not only have been responsible for the production of tens of thousands of new, low-income rental housing units during the past two decades but also have quietly championed a style of property management that incorporates delivery of social services.

Second, community development organizations have demonstrated the existence of a market for the sale of newly constructed low- and moderate-income units in a number of cities. East Brooklyn Congregations, for example, has constructed more than 3,000 townhouses in one of New York City's poorest neighborhoods, drawing almost 50 percent of its buyers from local public housing projects. Market values in the area have risen dramatically.

Third, working with banks, public agencies, and private sector institutions such as Fannie Mae, community development groups and many of the nation's best community development financial institutions (for example, Center for Community Self-Help in North Carolina) have helped lower the barriers to homeownership for low-income buyers through mortgage counseling programs, savings and downpayment support, and specialized lending programs.

Fourth, largely through the leadership of organizations such as Neighborhood Housing Services, community development organizations have instituted programs to combat the deterioration of relatively strong neighborhoods before they deteriorate further. Such projects have shown real success in both cities and inner-ring suburbs.

In the area of commercial real estate development, CDCs in cities such as Oakland, Denver, Kansas City, and Cleveland have been among the first investors in and developers of new inner-city shopping centers. They usually have performed best when functioning as the bridge institution (as planners, investors, managers, and builders) that makes it possible for private investors and commercial operators to enter an area.

In the nonretail end of commercial real estate, a few community development groups have successfully managed business incubators and light-industrial properties. Such organizations are led by people with industry-specific skills. WireNet in Cleveland is one of the most interesting examples of a community-based nonprofit with the business-related expertise necessary to add value to geographically clustered enterprises.

Commercial real estate linked to social service provision is an increasingly important product for community development. Spurred, in part, by changes in the health care system, school reform, and demand for daycare, community development groups have become builders and sometimes managers of clinics, schools, and child-care centers. Of the first half-dozen charter schools that the Reinvestment Fund in Philadelphia financed, for example, three were sponsored and built by community development organizations.

A number of community-based institutions play significant roles in workforce development. The major successes come from organizations that have specialized job skills training capacity and industry knowledge, such as Project Strive in New York City, Quest in San Antonio, Focus: HOPE in Detroit, or CET in San Jose, California.[4] None of those organizations would view itself as a CDC, although all have historical roots in some form of community-based service delivery and some of them have CDCs as partners. While few development organizations play a direct role in job training, hundreds offer job recruitment services and postplacement counseling, functioning as intermediaries between residents and employers.

In some urban neighborhoods the success of CDC housing developments and other services and relationships has achieved a significant scale, helping middle-class housing take root. In Newark, New Jersey's Central Ward, for example, the New Community Corporation has built several thousand units of housing as well as participated in the rehabilitation and management of commercial space, daycare centers, and business incubators. Today New Community is a major engine of economic development in the city. In the Bronx, CDC housing and services have been highlighted by the national media as one of the factors behind the physical revitalization of one of America's best-known symbols of decline.

The endurance of the CDC movement is aided by its ability to capture support across ideological lines. Liberal Democrats view community development through the lens of social equity while conservative Democrats and Republicans view it through the lens of volunteerism and self-help. The nongovernment, grassroots character of CDCs makes them ideologically malleable.

As community development organizations become part of the social structure of urban communities, they become integrated into the local political structure. In some instances they have become an important source of political leadership, with mayors, aldermen, and legislators from low-income neighborhoods coming through their ranks. As they become integrated into the culture of wards and political parties, they also become objects of political competition and patronage. Strong community development organizations learn to navigate turbulent political waters with their development capacity and programs intact.

Today a national community development movement has emerged through the activities of individual CDCs as well as trade associations, banking and philanthropic supporters, training programs, research institutes, and financial intermediaries. That movement has had an impact on public policy. Its lobbying efforts have been effective in maintaining some affordable housing subsidies, supporting bank reinvestment legislation, and shaping aspects of legislation regarding public housing reform, federal empowerment zones, and community development financial institutions. In many states, CDCs have created a broad range of state-sponsored development programs.

Community development financial institutions (CDFIs) have played an increasingly important role, during the past ten years in particular. The establishment of the Community Development Financial Institutions Fund within the U.S. Treasury Department in 1994 gave a name and national credibility to the financial services niche in the community development field.

CDFIs flourished and became particularly active and numerous in the 1980s and 1990s. Some were established to provide direct financing and technical assistance to CDCs, others to finance a broader base of low-income neighborhood institutions and borrowers: retail, service, and manufacturing businesses; household consumers; private developers; nonprofit facilities managers; and others. Unlike most urban CDCs, community development financial institutions are usually structured as intermediaries for multiple neighborhoods throughout a city, region, or state.

Rooted in both the early CDC movement as well as the social investment movement of the 1980s and 1990s, today's network of CDFIs includes regulated development banks, credit unions that serve low-income areas, unregulated loan funds that finance housing projects and businesses, microfinance funds that concentrate on small-scale entrepreneurs, and community development venture funds that provide growth capital to businesses unable to obtain equity from conventional lenders. Collectively they manage somewhere in the neighborhood of $5 billion, and they have demonstrated a strong portfolio management and lending record.[5]

The capital management role of CDFIs and their ability to establish regional and national relationships with public and private sector institutions allows them to build specialized capital access and real estate or business development networks among private capital sources, the public sector, and neighborhood-based institutions and borrowers. Citywide housing partnerships have done so in a dozen cities or more by combining public subsidy and bank capital into one-stop housing production systems for developers of affordable housing. National intermediaries such as Local Initiatives Support Corporation (LISC) and the Enterprise Foundation have done so on a national level by being syndicators of the low-income housing tax credit. And scores of other capital-led community development programs have been instituted by CDFIs such as the Illinois Facilities Fund, the Low-Income Housing Fund, and Boston Community Capital.

ASSESSMENT AND CRITIQUE

The community development field underwent an internal and external reassessment throughout the 1990s. From the perspective of community development practitioners and supporters, that reassessment revolved largely around the issue of the relevance, or impact, of CDCs. The relatively small scale of community development efforts stood in stark contrast to the extent of inner-city decline. Moreover, in an age of rapidly changing institutions and economic relationships, CDCs appeared to be removed from the mainstream. While some in the field were beginning to achieve some scale in real estate development, practitioners and supporters began to confront four challenges to long-term viability and legitimacy: the challenge of scale and public visibility, the challenge of comprehensive service delivery, the challenge of social capital, and the challenge of inner-city economic growth.

First, examples of significant impact by the best CDCs are not as numerous as most practitioners and supporters would like, particularly in areas not related to housing. There are too many examples of institutional marginality—small-scale organizations with limited track records searching for limited public subsidy. One promising route toward greater scale and visibility involves developing partnerships with some of the core institutions with which community development groups have some common interests—hospitals, universities, cultural institutions, and others.

Second, to balance physical development with human development, increased attention is now being paid to forming multiorganizational alliances to deliver a range of social services, from family counseling to job training. This approach has been linked, in part, to the self-sufficiency demands of welfare reform legislation.

Third, as high levels of unemployment, substance abuse, and crime continue to affect the quality of neighborhoods, the importance of building stronger social capital has become a more prominent issue. Community development groups are finding it increasingly important to identify ways to strengthen social networks through everything from block clubs to citizen crime patrols.

Fourth, aware of the inherent limitations of providing housing and human services, most large CDCs continue to identify ways to stimulate economic development in their neighborhoods, usually through involvement in work-force development and commercial real estate development. For most CDCs, however, undertaking a more substantial role in stimulating general business and minority enterprises remains relatively elusive.

The dialogue within the community development field about capacity and direction was further influenced by new thinking in the areas of regional development and market-oriented social policy. Both are firmly rooted in a sober assessment of the competitive disadvantages of many urban environments given the rapid rate of suburbanization and the accompanying loss of urban middle-class residents and jobs that has left impoverished minorities concentrated in the central cities.

While it was apparent to many observers in the 1960s and 1970s, the significance to cities, and inner-city neighborhoods in particular, of the geography of segregation by socioeconomic class became politically and economically stronger in the 1980s and 1990s. Regional approaches to inner-city decline and poverty are associated with the work of Myron Orfield and David Rusk,[6] as well as with the literature of housing programs and transportation-related development projects. Regional development arguments have several common characteristics. They assert that the dominant characteristics of regional growth are concentrated poverty and suburban sprawl; high levels of central city poverty, which drives away middle-class users, isolates low-income residents, and creates pressure on cities (and later inner-ring suburbs) to either raise taxes or reduce services; sprawl-like development that is caused not only by market and life-style choices but by public policies that provide subsidy and incentives for new infrastructure, outer-ring transportation, and single-family, large-lot housing; a continual process of outer-ring suburbanization that represents income or subsidy transfers from older central cities and inner-ring suburbs to newly developing areas; and an impaired capacity to address regional growth and urban poverty issues that results from the fragmented administration of metropolitan regions by multiple jurisdictions.

The regional perspective places the problems of inner-city neighborhoods in a more systemic framework than is found in most analyses of neighborhood development. Urban decline and renewal is viewed as a product of the self-reinforcing dynamics of multiple policy and market decisions, and the renewal of inner cities is seen to depend on the renegotiation of their structural disadvantages within the regional system. If those disadvantages are not redressed, current social and spatial processes will continue, increasing and concentrating poverty in the inner city, repelling middle-income residents, limiting the potential of public investment in older cities and towns, and transferring subsidy to new development in outlying areas.

Regional systems can help turn the tide by redirecting public incentives for development back to cities and towns through everything from growth boundaries to targeted subsidy allocation; creating more tax equity through regional or statewide systems of distribution that balance the playing field when it comes to paying for public goods and services; providing both incentives and requirements for deconcentrating affordable housing, distributing it throughout the regional area; and making better use of transportation subsidies to support the growth of central cities and multiple-income, multifunctional town-like developments.

Orfield and Rusk challenge traditional notions of community development in favor of metropolitan policy interventions that would spur neighborhood revitalization. In *Metropolitics*, Orfield views traditional approaches to community development as an inadequate response to a growth logic that cannot be changed through interventions at the neighborhood level. His six-part strategy—fair housing, tax-base sharing, reinvestment, land planning and growth management, welfare reform and public works, and transportation reform—requires metropolitanwide reforms to shift growth back to the urban core.

In *Cities without Suburbs* and *Inside Game, Outside Game,* David Rusk provides a similar analysis of regional growth and a similar critique of community development. While much of Rusk's work deals with the comparative impact of urban-suburban political connections on income and racial segregation, he undertakes a direct review of thirty-four of the best CDCs in the country. While he recognizes the quality of their work, judged by the reduction of poverty in their neighborhoods over time, nevertheless they appear lacking.[7] While improvements can be observed in several areas, most CDC target neighborhoods follow the same general trajectory of urban decline exhibited in non-CDC areas. The analysis is not an indictment of CDC activity per se; it demonstrates instead the overwhelming tide of market forces, policy decisions, and demographic changes against which an *inside game* is powerless.

Like Orfield, Rusk favors an approach that works simultaneously on the issues of urban reform and investment while also pursuing tax-base sharing, containment of sprawl, and the scattering of affordable housing throughout a region. The potential of the regional coalition politics that Rusk and Orfield propose is being tested throughout the nation through alliances of urban equity advocates, suburban environmental activists, and business interests concerned with economic competitiveness.[8]

The work of both Orfield and Rusk has much in common with the housing opportunity movement, a tradition of fair housing legislation and litigation as well as affordable housing policies and programs that promote opening suburban and other middle-income neighborhoods to affordable housing in an effort to increase racial and economic integration.[9] In contrast to community development, which has concentrated on rebuilding low-income and affordable housing in the inner city, the housing opportunity movement concentrates on increasing low-income individuals' choice of housing in order to link them to social networks and institutions that promote mainstream integration. Like community development practitioners, housing opportunity advocates note the differential access of low-income people to public goods (schools, jobs) and they argue for equity. They simply seek a different solution to the problem.

Research on the Gautreaux housing program in Chicago, the best-known and oldest of the housing opportunity programs, gives some cause for optimism about the effects of moving low-income residents to the suburbs, where better schools and public amenities can have a significant impact on everything from school performance to employment.[10] Information on housing opportunity replication programs across the country sponsored by the U.S. Department of Housing and Urban Development paints a more uneven picture of the potential scale, management, and acceptance of such efforts. At the same time, many new smart growth, inclusive zoning, and tax-base sharing efforts in states as diverse as Minnesota, Maryland, California, Oregon, and New Jersey include suburban affordable housing programs. It will be important to pay attention to the results of those efforts over time.

The housing opportunity movement has been reinforced by a number of efforts that use transportation planning and investment as a way to promote urban development and connect low-income people with regional job opportunities.[11] Demonstration projects sponsored by the federal and state governments have been accompanied by countless others—sponsored by chambers of commerce, local transportation authorities, business office parks, and welfare-reform programs—to promote ride sharing, new bus routes, and workplace shuttle services.

While the regional approach to development has gathered momentum, public policymakers increasingly have focused on the role of economic markets and private sector investment in revitalizing low-income communities. Michael Porter's work on the market positioning of inner-city economies played a significant role in this regard, given the importance of his classic study on national competitive advantages.[12] Porter's analysis of the inner city asserts the need to encourage inner-city revival through the logic of self-interested, profit-making business investors and entrepreneurs rather than the logic of social programs and social investment. In addition, it asserts the need for government and civic groups to concentrate on lowering the barriers to entry and cost of operations for new businesses, not through direct subsidy but through investment in infrastructure, work-force development, and business-friendly regulatory policies. It also asserts the need to concentrate on the competitive advantages of inner cities, particularly their willing labor force and proximity to regional economic growth clusters, geographically bound groups of similar firms that have a variety of horizontal and vertical links, including common infrastructure and work-force needs.

The Porter analysis was criticized by some community development activists and academics for being too dismissive of the history and role of community-based institutions in urban economic development. Others welcomed the attention it focused on the inner city as an asset whose market potential has been unrealized. Like that of the regional development analysts, Porter's work looks at systemic links between regional growth and urban decline—but not in order to intervene with equity-oriented social policies. Porter views the links in terms of economic opportunity: urban places and people, although they are strategically located, suffer from underinvestment; investors have a ready-made work force and network of firms and industries to build on; regional growth is the substance of inner-city growth possibilities, not a cause of urban decline. The challenge is to use the same economic principles in the inner city as in other areas, to build value through existing regional growth clusters, not to reorganize growth through policy interventions.

While Porter's work achieved some notoriety for its more market-focused approach to inner-city social problems, it was only one of many factors that have moved urban policy and some aspects of community development in that direction. At least three trends have played an important role in promoting market-oriented policy. First, the combined effects of a strong economy and welfare reform have caused policymakers and private investors to emphasize work-force development—both job training and mechanisms for connecting workers to the labor market.

Second, both policymakers and private investors have increased their attention to market-based strategies. There has been a significant, bipartisan shift in national public policies designed to assist cities since the push in the mid-1980s for enterprise and empowerment zones. For example, the most recent anti-poverty package, the New Markets Initiative, includes tax credits and regulatory changes that reflect a market orientation.[13] That shift in public emphasis had its correlate in private philanthropy. Before the 1980s major philanthropic organizations rarely directed their attention beyond traditional concerns such as education, health care, environmental issues, and the like. While that focus prevails, a new willingness to use philanthropic resources to support economic growth efforts has emerged. The Ford Foundation, Annie E. Casey Foundation, and Mott Foundation, for example, no longer think about their grants only in terms of social services; they also consider their wealth-building potential.

Third, the 1980s and 1990s witnessed the emergence of a new breed of entrepreneurial mayors who had to be more fiscally disciplined, friendlier to small business investment, and more willing to pursue market-oriented approaches to service delivery than their predecessors. New York City's Rudolph Giuliani, Richard Daley of Chicago, Philadelphia's Ed Rendell, Stephen Goldsmith of Indianapolis, John Norquist of Milwaukee, and others differ in many ways, but all became mayors at a time when residents, investors, and consumers were dissatisfied with public goods and services and were leaving.[14] Their political success—and the success of their cities—required a new package of public goods.

THE REPOSITIONING OF COMMUNITY DEVELOPMENT AND THE IMPORTANCE OF FAITH-BASED SOCIAL NETWORKS

Changes in metropolitan social structure and the market orientation of urban policymakers reflect fundamental changes: the frictionless nature of capital flows, the use of new telecommunications technologies in the workplace and home, the difficulty public institutions have in accommodating rapid change, the increasing dominance of market exchange in new areas of civic life, and the geographical disconnection between areas of poverty and of growth.

The increasing absence of institutional mechanisms for connecting low-income people with economic opportunities provides the community development field with a framework that can make it more economically relevant. In an era when the public sector has lost some of its capacity to keep up with change and when private sector institutions exhibit less loyalty to any one place, CDCs can play the intermediary. Just as the settlement houses of a century ago viewed themselves as midwives delivering new urban citizens, community development institutions can assume a similar role.

To do so requires changes in how CDCs are organized and how they operate, and it is more than a matter of adding a new product or function within the existing organization. It requires making changes in the relationships and positioning of organizations that are not too dissimilar from the changes that have occurred in the private sector in recent years. Community development organizations must move from narrowly local, single-organization program building to maintaining a market-oriented network of relationships that allows them to exert influence across a broader social geography. Many of the strongest and most agile community development organizations already have begun to make those shifts in structure and strategy. There are three aspects to their change in positioning.

First, it involves the need to expand the geography of influence of urban-based CDCs through institutional expansion, organizational consolidation, and the formation of strategic alliances between neighborhood and regional institutions. Overreliance on small-scale, neighborhood-based civic infrastructure limits CDCs' capacity to participate in and influence an ever-evolving market. The organization of regional and community development financial institutions and the formation of alliances between local and regional institutions create opportunities for CDCs to engage in the civic and market arenas across a regional trade area.

That is not to say that small-scale neighborhood civic groups have no important role to play; they do, within both low- and middle-income neighborhoods, in community organizing and planning. And locally oriented CDCs will continue to play an important role in residential and commercial development and in delivery of social services. Rebuilding urban areas requires the catalytic leadership that community development corporations sometimes are able to offer; moreover, the strength of regional connections relies on the knowledge and credibility of people and institutions at the local level.

But community development as a field cannot be overly defined by the aggregation of small parts; it needs to do business within the broader civic and economic market. That means that neighborhood development institutions must collaborate in substantive ways across the region. It also means that new regional institutions are needed—some with specialized development and investment capacity and others that are able to organize citizens or provide policy support.

Second, a repositioned CDC must organize its mission and activities as much as possible around the core issues of poverty—the need to increase low wages and employment rates and the need to build housing values, quality public services, and savings for low-income households. Place-based human service activities must be viewed as tools to support the core mission, which is to alleviate poverty; accomplishing that mission requires, in part, facilitating connections between low-income people and opportunities. That includes building affordable housing across the widest possible geographic area, providing the most convenient and high-quality child care, and making investments in transportation that facilitate access to jobs and in work-force training that lead to career growth and better wages. Such links and investments facilitate connections among neighborhoods, residents, employers, and a variety of public and private institutions and services.

The third attribute follows directly from a broadened geographical sphere of influence, a focus on poverty alleviation, and an organizational structure able to influence the environment by managing a variety of relationships and products. It is critical in the twenty-first century for the community development field to engage in a broader range of public policy issues. The traditional policy concerns of the field have been limited to subsidies and regulations that support the real estate activities of CDCs, such as the low-income housing tax credit or the Community Reinvestment Act. They are, of course, important. But they represent a very narrow response to the universe of policy that relates to poverty: employment opportunity, fair housing, child care, transportation, local tax policy, and building and investment incentives.

There is new opportunity today for CDCs to broaden their policy horizons. On one hand, the emergence of suburban antisprawl sentiment creates an opening for regional partnerships to promote reinvestment in cities and towns. At the same time, if labor markets remain tight, CDCs can forge a connection between a business community that promotes regional competitiveness and an urban constituency working to alleviate poverty. The so-called three E's of regional policy—economy, equity, and environment—form a natural field of new relationships and allies.

How does broadening the concept of community development and the agenda of community development organizations relate to religious institutions?

Just as religious institutions have been critical in forming community development organizations, they are in many ways even more critical to organizing regional civic networks that link low-income households with economic opportunities. More than any other nongovernment institution in the United States, religious institutions cross boundaries of race, class, and geography. And they are critical hubs of networks that can be deployed for broader purposes than serving their own congregations. Moreover, religious institutions often have a structure that includes both local (congregational) and regional (judicatory) bodies. They are accustomed to thinking about and planning within a framework of institutional diversity and place-based distinctions.

The judicatories (administrative bodies similar to a diocese), congregations, social networks, and para-church organizations of faith-based institutions are indispensable participants in any effort to build regional consensus on how, given the nature of regional growth, to give low-income people and places the best possible advantages. If the neighborhood organizing efforts that animated much of community development thirty and forty years ago—and still do—could make effective use of religious institutions as one foundation of neighborhood stability and civic care, a new regional community development strategy can do so today.

At the Reinvestment Fund in Philadelphia, religious community investors have played a fundamental role. They represent not only a source of capital but a source of social and institutional networks as well, with connections to colleges, hospitals, boardrooms, and political offices. A Catholic religious order may be the parent corporation of a group of urban hospitals with connections to insurance companies and business trade groups. The investment committee of a suburban church may be composed of some of the most important corporate leaders in the city. An inner-city church may have historical links to suburban voters. The challenge is to use those relationships to forge a connection between faith and everyday institutional interests. That requires a commitment that is more complex than volunteering to do weekend duty at an affordable housing site in the inner city, although that certainly is helpful and admirable. It involves claiming the alleviation of poverty—and community development—as a civic as well as religious value and employing religious institutions and their networks to help create and influence policies made in a new regional public sphere.

NOTES

1. This section draws on concepts and ideas from my experience in the field, as well as a variety of books, articles, and evaluation reports. References include the Ford Foundation, *Corrective Capitalism* (New York: 1989); Avis Vidal, *Rebuilding Communities: A National Study of Urban Community Development Corporations* (New York: Community Development Research Center, New School for Social Research, 1992); and Robert Halpern, *Rebuilding the Inner City* (New York: Colombia University Press, 1995).

2. For a good background on organizing see Sanford Horwitt, *Let Them Call Me Rebel* (New York: Knopf Press, 1989).

3. The problem of obtaining good numbers is fundamentally a problem of definition. The higher-end numbers tend to include a broader range of nonprofit institutions than some would use.

4. See the study by Bennett Harrison, Marcus Weiss, and Jon Gant, *Building Bridges* (New York: Ford Foundation, 1994).

5. Early work on CDFIs includes Richard Taub, *Community Capitalism* (Boston: Harvard Business Press, 1988) and Julian Parzen and Michael Hall Kieschnick (Philadelphia: Temple University Press, 1992). Currently the best data on the CDFI field are published by the National Community Capital Association in Philadelphia.

6. Myron Orfield, *Metropolitics* (Brookings, 1997); David Rusk, *Cities without Suburbs* (Washington: Woodrow Wilson Center Press, 1993); and David Rusk, *Inside Game, Outside Game* (Brookings, 1999).

7. Rusk, *Inside Game*, pp. 17–61.

8. Bruce Katz's Center on Urban and Metropolitan Policy at Brookings has done much to stimulate public debate on these issues.

9. A review of the issues can be found in Alexander Polikoff, ed., *Housing Mobility: Promise or Illusion?* (Washington: The Urban Institute, 1995).

10. See James Rosenbaum, "Expanding the Geography of Opportunity by Expanding Residential Choice: Lessons from the Gautreaux Program," *Housing Policy Debate*, vol. 6, no.1 (1995).

11. See Mark Alan Hughes, "A Mobility Strategy for Improving Opportunity," *Housing Policy Debate*, vol. 6, no.1 (1995).

12. Michael E. Porter, "The Competitive Advantages of the Inner City," *Harvard Business Review*, vol. 73 (1995).

13. See Roy Green, ed., *Enterprise Zones* (Newbury Park, Calif.: Sage Press, 1991) and Tamar Jacoby and Fred Siegel, "Growing the Inner City," *New Republic*, August 23, 1999.

14. A quick summary of many of the new governance ideas from these mayors can be found in Center for Civic Innovation, *The Entrepreneurial City: A How-To Handbook for Urban Innovators* (New York: Manhattan Institute, 1999).

CHAPTER EIGHT

Many Are Called, but Few Are Chosen: Faith-Based Organizations and Community Development

AVIS C. VIDAL

The interest generated by President George W. Bush's initiatives to encourage greater participation of faith-based organizations in government-financed social action programs relates primarily to the role of religious organizations in the direct delivery of social services. From one perspective, that is understandable: those initiatives build on the foundation laid by the charitable choice provisions of the 1996 welfare reform law and highlight activities in which religious organizations are believed—albeit without real evidence—to have been successful. But from another perspective, that focus is anomalous. It ignores numerous highly visible examples of investments in more fundamental neighborhood change by congregations determined to make a lasting difference in their communities—investments in new and rebuilt housing, improved retail facilities, new child-care centers, and other durable community improvements.

It is true that congregational commitments to community development are as poorly documented and understood as congregational participation in the delivery of human services. Indeed, they are among the least well researched aspects of the community development field. This field, brought to maturity by the community development corporation (CDC) movement, understands community development to be "asset building that improves the quality of life among

The author thanks the Office of Policy Development and Research in the U.S. Department of Housing and Urban Development (HUD) for its support of the research on which this chapter is based. The views expressed and any errors are her own and should not be attributed either to HUD or to the Urban Institute or its trustees.

residents of low- to moderate-income communities."[1] In that context, community development centers on housing and community economic development (both real estate development and business development) but also includes efforts, including job-training programs, to build human capital. In short, community development helps communities and their members to get ahead, not simply to get by.[2]

This chapter seeks to remedy the gap in public understanding by presenting a review, primarily an analytical literature review, of the current state of knowledge about the role of congregations in community development. Critical empirical analysis on community development is scarce; most works focus only on congregations' work in human services. There are no analyses of the outcomes of congregational activities, no assessments of the factors influencing the scale or quality of outcomes, and no comparisons of similar activities conducted by secular and faith-based organizations. For that reason, I interviewed twenty-seven leading practitioners and researchers in the field of community development to supplement the literature review.

CONGREGATIONAL ENGAGEMENT IN SOCIAL SERVICES AND COMMUNITY DEVELOPMENT

Mark Chaves finds in his National Congregations Study that 57 percent of congregations engage in some kind of service activity.[3] Those activities vary enormously, but most of them fall under the broad umbrella of health and human services. Youth programs, marriage and family counseling, and food services are the most typical human services; visitation and other assistance to sick individuals are the most common health-related services.[4]

As Chaves reports in his chapter in this volume, the community development activities of congregations are much more limited, and they are heavily concentrated in housing. While 18 percent of congregations support some type of housing or shelter activity, only 1 percent engage in employment activities.

Even those modest numbers overstate direct congregational participation in community development, because most congregations support development only indirectly. The most common form of congregational support for housing is providing volunteers for Habitat for Humanity, an ecumenical Christian housing ministry that produces primarily new single-family homes, many built with some sweat equity from the purchasing family. Congregations are a major source of volunteers, but most Habitat affiliates build a relatively small number of homes each year.[5]

Nevertheless, some faith-based organizations have been active housing developers. They have sponsored more Section 202 projects (which provide federally subsidized housing for the elderly) than any other type of organization, and a survey of all Section 202 projects in service in 1988 found that 49.7 percent of them had religious sponsors. Those projects included an estimated total of 161,000 housing units.[6] Anecdotal evidence indicates that many sponsors were congregations, but denominational organizations and their affiliates, particularly Catholic Charities and the Jewish Federations, have been active providers as well.

Faith-based organizations also were important participants in the Section 236 program, which provided subsidized housing for families. Here, the history is less positive. Congregational sponsors experienced high default rates in the Section 236 program, and nonprofit sponsors had higher default rates than for-profit ones.[7] No hard data are available about how faith-based groups performed compared with other nonprofit sponsors, but one HUD evaluation surveyed "several troubled nonprofit projects" and found that "church groups often looked upon the projects they sponsored as a form of charity, kept rents artificially low, and were willing to overlook rent delinquencies."[8] No information is available about the participation of faith-based sponsors in the more recent project-based Section 8 program, nor about their current use of low-income housing tax credits.

Congregational support for community economic development programs—most of which comes from African American churches—is much less common than support for housing. The best-known examples of commercial real estate development projects sponsored by faith-based CDCs include a strip mall anchored by a Pathmark supermarket in central Newark, New Jersey, developed by New Community Corporation; a similar development by Abyssinian Development Corporation in Harlem; and a smaller-scale retail development done by Allen African Methodist Episcopal Church in Jamaica, Queens, on the block that includes its school.

New business development, widely known as one of the most difficult and risky components of community development, is quite rare. One example is Greater Christ Temple Church in Meridian, Mississippi, which pulled together 35 members, 96 percent of whom were on welfare, to pool their food stamps in order to purchase groceries wholesale. That initial self-help activity (often known in faith communities as mutual aid) ultimately led participants to build a supermarket and subsequently led to the formation of several other nonprofit corporations.

Congregational support for community development financial institutions (CDFIs) appears to be more common than support for other types of community economic development.[9] Those institutions include microloan and other loan funds, but credit unions appear to be more common—perhaps the most common form of support for community development other than housing.[10] For example, Concord Baptist Church in Brooklyn follows a tradition in the African American church of serving community residents in areas in which society at large has failed to serve them. After eight members of the congregation were refused credit by conventional banks, the church established Concord Federal Credit Union (CFCU), a separately incorporated nonprofit organization accountable to the church through its 14-member board of directors. They manage the credit union with the help of a part-time paid manager. According to Pamela Ann Toussaint in *Signs of Hope in the City*, "CFCU offers a number of services, from payroll deductions to auto loans, and boasts almost 1,000 members and just under $3 million in assets."[11]

Some CDFIs benefit from social investments by denominational and related organizations in addition to the credit union deposits made by congregants, and they also receive funds from secular sources such as foundations. Like CDCs and other community-based organizations that have been spun off by congregations, some receive in-kind support from the sponsoring congregation, such as free office space. Some CDFIs are tied into familiar community development trade associations and membership groups, such as the National Federation of Community Development Credit Unions, but many are not, so their numbers are almost certainly underestimated. Much less common than support for credit unions is support for microloan funds like the one managed by First African Methodist Episcopal Church (FAME) in Los Angeles. After the violence in South Central Los Angeles that followed the announcement of the verdict in the Rodney King case, FAME's Reverend Cecil Murray became a prominent spokesperson for the African American community in South Central and played an important role in coalition building and social reconciliation efforts. When rebuilding began, FAME competed for and received a $1 million grant from the Walt Disney Company that led to establishment of a microloan program that supplies low-interest loans of $2,000 to $20,000 to minority entrepreneurs in the area.[12]

THE MOST ACTIVE TYPES OF CONGREGATIONS

According to Chaves's chapter, six factors appear to influence the likelihood that a congregation will engage in some type of social ministry: size, income, racial composition, need in the congregation's neighborhood, theological and political orientation, and leadership. Specifically, congregations that are large, wealthy, African American, located in high-poverty neighborhoods, liberal, and led by clergy who support community service tend to be more heavily engaged in social service activities.[13] It appears that the same broad features also are associated with participation in community development activities. However, qualitative evidence suggests that some kinds of congregations, including African American churches and Catholic churches, may find community development more consistent with their beliefs and outlook than others.

There was widespread agreement among those interviewed that involvement in community life comes most naturally to black churches, a legacy of the history of racial discrimination and segregation in the United States and the historic responsiveness of black churches to the exclusionary practices of mainstream secular institutions. The church was a vehicle through which African Americans organized alternative institutions, such as fraternities and sororities, burial societies, insurance companies, and banks. Until relatively recently, racial segregation ensured that the church's focus remained on the local community. The black church historically has been the only strong community institution controlled by the black community. Black churches are overwhelmingly congregation centered, a focus that gives them great flexibility in choosing the activities they wish to pursue. But it also means that generally they do not have access to the denominational resources available to Roman Catholic and some mainstream Protestant congregations.

The mainstream denominations vary greatly in how they view and relate to the community, and their service orientation affects the ease with which they move into community development and the technical assistance they require. The Roman Catholic church is most commonly cited as having a strong, clear orientation toward serving the local neighborhood. Roman Catholic parishes are defined geographically, and traditionally Catholics have been expected to attend the church closest to their residence. When parishioners move, they normally join a parish near their new home. If the composition of a neighborhood changes, the parish's mandate is to serve the new population. Such an orientation, combined with Roman Catholic teachings on social justice, lends itself philosophically to participation in community development.

In contrast, some denominations consider the members of the church to be the community. These churches seek to play an important role in the lives of their members, and while they may be drawn to social ministry to help the poor—caring "for the least of these"—historically they have had no institutional impetus to engage in, or assume responsibility for, the surrounding neighborhood. Moving into community development would require many such congregations to develop a new rationale to encompass this form of ministry, and it would affect the way they work. They would, for example, have to be willing and able to participate with nonmembers in setting a neighborhood development agenda and in speaking on the community's behalf when seeking funds or taking a stand on local policy issues.

The Need to Adopt Different Approaches

The way congregations support community development differs considerably from the approach that most of them use to deliver health-related and other social services. Whereas a substantial majority of community development activities sponsored by congregations are undertaken in collaboration with others, only the most intensive social service activities are conducted that way and only if suitable partners are available. Reliance on collaborative activity is a response to the technical and financial demands of community development, which make it difficult for congregations to engage in it effectively on their own. Direct congregational participation in development—especially real estate development—

Table 8-1. *Percentage of Congregations Engaged in Activity by Program Type*[a]

Activity	All congregations	All programs	Program run within congregation	Program separately incorporated	Participates in, supports, or is affiliated with programs in other organizations or in denomination
Human services					
Visitation or support for sick and shut-ins	84.7	116.1	72.5	3.7	23.8
Youth programs	72.6	101.8	44.4	8.9	47.2
Marriage counseling	70.5	89.3	68.5	5.4	26.1
Family counseling	61.8	78.8	57.4	6.0	36.7
Meal services/food kitchens	50.1	59.6	26.0	8.6	65.4
Community development					
Homeless housing/shelter programs	38.7	43.6	9.9	6.9	83.3
Affordable housing development or programs	19.7	22.5	13.8	12.9	73.3
Senior housing programs	19.2	20.8	3.4	10.6	86.1
Community programs, including economic development, job training, etc.	20.2	24.0	16.7	11.3	72.1

a. Number of congregations = 257,648. Congregations could give multiple responses.

Source: Author's calculations based on figures in Virginia A. Hodgkinson and others, *From Belief to Commitment* (Independent Sector, 1993).

is relatively rare. It also is legally and financially unwise, since it can leave the project sponsor and its assets at risk if the development falls into legal or financial difficulty.

Rather than run programs themselves, most congregations collaborate on community development by donating money or supplying volunteers for programs run by denominations. However, congregations may participate directly in community development in three ways: directly sponsoring a community development corporation; joining a coalition that forms a CDC (or similar entity); or participating in a joint venture with an experienced developer.

The most common way for congregations to enter community development on their own is to establish and spin off an affiliated nonprofit organization—typically a CDC. The Abyssinian Development Corporation (ADC), established by Abyssinian Baptist Church in Central Harlem, is a prominent example. During its early years, the church provided ADC with significant in-kind support, including rent-free office space, free telephone and telephone answering service, access to photocopy and fax machines, help from church volunteers, and financial management services provided by the church's financial manager. ADC's first project was a twenty-five-unit transitional housing development that included on-site services for formerly homeless families. ADC since has developed more than 400 units of housing and a variety of economic development projects.[14] Another widely publicized example is Allen African Methodist Episcopal (AME) Church in Jamaica, pastored by Reverend Floyd Flake. The development corporation started by the church began its work by developing a \$13 million, 300-unit senior citizens center—one of the largest faith-based elderly housing developments ever constructed—with funding from the Section 8 and Section 202 programs.[15] As in the ADC example, housing production marked the beginning of a steady stream of community development activity.

Although congregations commonly act alone in establishing CDCs, they sometimes take joint action. A prominent example is New Community Corporation (NCC) in Newark's Central Ward, by far the largest faith-based CDC. It has developed more than 3,300 units of permanent housing for both families and seniors, plus transitional units for formerly homeless families. It also has sponsored economic development projects, and it provides a variety of social services through affiliates. Although associated in the public's mind with St. Rose of Lima Church, where NCC's leader, Monsignor William Linder, is a priest, NCC's true origin lies in a coalition of urban and suburban churches formed in response to the Newark riots in 1968.[16]

The Nehemiah Project mounted by East Brooklyn Churches (EBC) is a coalition of congregations brought together after several years of discussion and exploration assisted by the Industrial Areas Foundation (IAF). The partnership was formed in 1981 to recreate livable neighborhoods in devastated parts of East Brooklyn by providing opportunities for homeownership. The Nehemiah Project built two- and three-bedroom rowhouses that it sold to families with average annual incomes of $15,000 to $25,000 for less than the actual cost of construction; by 1996 the partnership had built and sold 2,300 single-family rowhouse units.[17] Other well-known examples with a similar sponsorship structure include South Bronx Churches Nehemiah Homes and Harlem Churches for Community Improvement (HCCI), which spurred the redevelopment of Bradhurst, a forty-block neighborhood in upper-central Harlem.

A less familiar example is the Resurrection Project (TRP) in the Pilsen and Little Village neighborhoods of Chicago. It began with the collaboration of six Catholic parishes that later affiliated with the IAF and grew within about five years into a nationally acclaimed CDC involved in housing production; in homeownership, child-care, and community safety programs; and in promotion of minority enterprises.[18] Because Roman Catholic churches commonly have stayed in urban neighborhoods rather than following their parishioners to the suburbs and because the Catholic Campaign for Human Development has provided modest but steady financial support for IAF, TRP could be another model with real promise.

The nation now has approximately 3,600 community-based development organizations. Of those, about 500 (14 percent) report that they consider their organization to be faith-based.[19] My unpublished preliminary analysis indicates that as a group, faith-based CDCs (excluding groups whose only development work is done through Habitat for Humanity) have developed about 109,000 housing units. On average, the faith-based groups are younger and smaller than their secular counterparts, appear to have significantly smaller full-time staffs, and are more than twice as likely to have annual operating budgets of less than $500,000. They also are much less likely to be involved in development activities such as job training and placement than in housing development, commercial/industrial real estate development, or business enterprise development. However, nationally well-known examples, such as New Community Corporation and Abyssinian Development Corporation, make it clear that some do a great deal.

A third, less common approach is for a congregation to partner with a well-established community developer. Religious Institutions as Partners in Community-Based Development, a demonstration program launched by the Lilly Endowment in 1989, employed that approach. The program invited congregations to form partnerships with experienced community development groups and to propose an initial development project. It funded twenty-eight competitively chosen partnerships, the majority of which were in urban areas and served low-income communities of people of color. Although such partnerships appear to be infrequent outside the context of the Lilly initiative, they are instructive.

An evaluation of that initiative found that most partnerships accomplished all or most of what they set out to achieve.[20] At the end of the project period, 900 units of various types of housing had been built, rehabilitated, or repaired or were under construction; another 400 units were in the planning or design phase. In addition, eight businesses were started or strengthened; eleven new revolving loan funds with nearly $6 million in assets were established; and there was a total increase of $500,000 in the funds held by seven faith-based credit unions. The evaluation also found evidence that "bringing religious institutions and community development groups together opens up the possibility for building bridges across racial and class lines."

Those positive results no doubt rest on the important fact that many of the partnerships included very strong community development organizations. The congregations learned a great deal about community development, including which aspects fit—or did not fit—well with their organizational culture. They did not, however, shoulder the full burden and responsibility of development on their own. Their experience thus represents only one possible strategy for entering the field. Although they had strong partners and expressed great satisfaction with their accomplishments, the congregations' participants reported:

> The cautious or balky behavior of financiers and government officials was "frustrating"; the required technical knowledge of design, construction, finance, marketing, and property management was sometimes "overwhelming"; the persistence and attention to detail was "tedious"; and the tendency of secular partners to value religious partners' financial or property contributions more than their spiritual and interpersonal contributions was "irritating."

WHAT CONGREGATIONS CAN BRING TO COMMUNITY DEVELOPMENT

Community development that has a meaningful impact on the community is difficult to accomplish because it depends on conducting a set of specialized and complex activites over a considerable period of time. Successful CDCs secure resources from multiple sources, plan effectively, exercise strong and stable management and governance, and ensure community representation on their boards.

Given the difficulty of effective community development, affiliation with a congregation offers community developers advantages and disadvantages. As

Jeremy Nowak argues, "The most effective church-affiliated developers are able to maximize the advantages and minimize the disadvantages."[21] Nowak lists four possible advantages of congregational engagement in community development: The congregation can serve as an incubator and organizer. It can provide volunteers. It can provide access to financial resources. And it can engender public trust. Each of those advantages is countered by potential disadvantages and risks. Communities might perceive development activities as church rather than neighborhood initiatives. Church leaders and staff may lack the time and skills to undertake community development activities consistently and effectively. Religious values may conflict with the demands of the marketplace, especially since community development is unique among the charitable activities of most congregations. And there is always the risk that funds for secular community development services and funds for religious activities may be commingled. (See also Nowak's chapter in this volume.)

Those factors suggest that entering community development without partners is likely to be attractive to only a small fraction of congregations. Those congregations, however, could make significant contributions to community development.

CONGREGATIONS ARE NOT THE WHOLE STORY

Although this chapter has focused on the activities of congregations, the universe of faith-based organizations is substantially larger and more diverse. It includes national denominations; their social service arms, such as Catholic Charities and Lutheran Social Services; networks of related organizations, such as the YMCA and the YWCA; associations of clergy or other religious leaders; and a wide variety of nonprofit organizations and social service organizations that have a religious origin or basis.

Those groups have received even less research attention than congregations, but they are clearly significant forces in community development. A number of large denominational service organizations develop housing, including Catholic Charities, Lutheran Social Services, the Salvation Army, the Jewish Federations (United Jewish Communities), and B'nai B'rith. They also get involved in other ways—from social investing to start-up assistance and emergency financing for individual CDCs. Examples include providing a CDC with seed capital or in-kind contributions; donating staff time; and assisting affordable housing developments that get into financial trouble.

Many more denominational organizations, religious orders, pension funds, hospitals, and other religious institutions are engaged in social investing than are engaged in developing housing. The Interfaith Center for Corporate Responsibility (ICCR), an affiliate of the National Council of Churches, oversees more than $1 billion in social investments on behalf of 270 such investors. Of that amount, between $5 and $6 million dollars is invested in community economic development. Typical investments are deposits in minority banks, credit unions, various types of loan funds, and cooperative businesses. ICCR participants also make similar investments through a multitude of local and regional social investment vehicles. In addition, pension funds of various denominations and religious orders participating in ICCR have approximately $300 million invested in low-income housing.[22]

In short, congregations are the most familiar component of the faith-based universe, but they work in a rich institutional context. Denominational organizations, religious orders, and others control significant financial, technical, and, in some cases, political resources that they can bring to bear, either as independent actors or in support of congregational efforts. In some faiths they play a powerful role in encouraging and shaping the choice and conduct of the congregational ministry.

CONCLUSION: COMPASSION OR SOCIAL JUSTICE?

There is still much to learn about what it takes for congregations to succeed at community development and what their advantages and disadvantages are compared with those of secular agents. But we do know some things. It appears that only a small fraction of congregations currently are well positioned to become independent community development agents in communities where development is needed. An equally small proportion are able to attract the necessary financial and technical resources. The strongest candidates are those that are located in poor neighborhoods and have large congregations but are not themselves poor. Many of those are African American churches.

Enough good examples exist to make it clear that well-positioned congregations can make significant contributions to community development. To succeed, they need a professionally staffed, independent, nonprofit development organization, which can be supported by one or more congregations. They need a long time horizon. They also need to be committed to staying in the community. And they need to understand that development is a demanding, time-consuming process.

Capitalizing on the potential of congregations requires investing in the organizational capacity of both congregations and newly incorporated development organizations. They need technical assistance—above all to decide whether they want to become involved in community development in the first place. They need to understand their comparative advantages and capitalize on them.

Many also need specialized technical assistance to work through the issues involved in establishing a new nonprofit corporation. A better understanding of what has enabled existing faith-based CDCs to emerge and grow—and what distinctive problems they have faced—should inform that effort.

Finally, there are many other ways for a wide variety of congregations—including those in middle-income communities—to contribute to community development. They could adopt sound social investment practices in managing their bank deposits and other assets. They could provide mentors to participants in job-training programs and provide financial assistance to emerging faith-based CDCs in low-income neighborhoods. They could collaborate with others to create a supportive climate for local development of affordable housing. Coalitions of congregations are potentially significant allies for community developers in building local and regional coalitions to promote supportive local, state, national, and corporate policies.[23] Most important, all congregations could contribute by working to create a political climate that promotes social justice, rather than charity, as a national priority.

NOTES

1. Ronald F. Ferguson and William T. Dickens, eds., *Urban Problems and Community Development* (Brookings, 1999), p. 5.

2. This distinction is adapted from Xavier De Souza Briggs, "Brown Kids in White Suburbs: Housing Mobility and the Many Faces of Social Capital," *Housing Policy Debate*, vol. 9 (1998), p. 178.

3. Mark Chaves, *Congregations' Social Service Activities*, Charting Civil Society, no. 6 (Washington: The Urban Institute, December 1999).

4. Virginia A. Hodgkinson and others, *From Belief to Commitment: The Community Service Activities and Finances of Religious Congregations in the United States* (Independent Sector, 1993).

5. Applied Real Estate Analysis, *Making Homeownership a Reality: Survey of Habitat for Humanity, Inc. Homeowners and Affiliates* (U.S. Department of Housing and Urban Development, 1998).

6. Select Committee on Aging, Subcommittee on Housing and Consumer Interests of the House of Representatives, *The 1988 National Survey of Section 202 Housing for the Elderly and Handicapped* (Government Printing Office, 1989).

7. Comptroller General of the United States, *Section 236 Rental Housing: An Evaluation with Lessons for the Future* (U.S. General Accounting Office, 1978); Charles Calhoun and Christopher Walker, *Loan Performance of Management Cooperatives* (Washington: The Urban Institute, 1994).

8. Comptroller General, *Section 236 Rental Housing.*

9. The term CDFIs is used generically here, referring to all such organizations, not just those officially designated as CDFIs under federal legislation.

10. Jeremy Nowak and others, *Religious Institutions and Community Renewal* (Philadelphia: Delaware Valley Community Reinvestment Fund, 1989).

11. Pamela Ann Toussaint, "Concord Baptist Church: Taking Care of Business in Bed-Stuy," in Robert D.Carle and Louis A. Decaro, eds., *Signs of Hope in the City: Ministries of Community Renewal* (Valley Forge, Penn.: Judson Press, 1997).

12. Lloyd Gite, "The New Agenda of the Black Church: Economic Development for Black America," *Black Enterprise*, December 1993.

13. Mark Chaves and William Tsitos, "Congregations and Social Services: What They Do, How They Do It, and with Whom," paper presented at the annual meeting of the Association for Research on Nonprofit Organizations and Voluntary Action, December 2000.

14. Avis Vidal, "Abyssinian Development Corporation," in *Sustained Excellence Awards: Profiles of the Awardees* (Washington: Fannie Mae Foundation, 1998).

15. Louis A. Decaro Jr., "Bethel Gospel Assembly: Ministry to Harlem and Beyond," in Carle and Decaro, eds., *Signs of Hope in the City*, pp. 70–81.

16. Xavier De Souza Briggs and Elizabeth J. Mueller with Mercer L. Sullivan, *From Neighborhood to Community: Evidence on the Social Effects of Community Development* (New York: Community Development Research Center, New School for Social Research, 1997).

17. June Manning Thomas and Reynard N. Blake, "Faith-Based Community Development and African American Neighborhoods," in W. Dennis Keating, Norman Krumholz, and Phillip Star, eds., *Revitalizing Urban Neighborhoods* (Lawrence: University of Kansas Press, 1996), p. 131–43.

18. Avis Vidal, "The Resurrection Project," in *Sustained Excellence Awards*.

19. National Congress for Community Economic Development, *Coming of Age: Trends and Achievements of Community-Based Development Organizations* (Washington: 1999).

20. David Scheie and others, *Better Together: Religious Institutions as Partners in Community-Based Development*. Final Evaluation Report on the Lilly Endowment Program (Minneapolis, Minn.: Rainbow Research, Inc., 1991).

21. Nowak and others, *Religious Institutions and Community Renewal*, vol. I, p. 56.

22. Interview with Timothy Smith, executive director of Interfaith Center on Corporate Responsibility, June 7, 1999.

23. Michael W. Foley and John D. McCarthy as reported in Foley and others, "Social Capital, Religious Institutions, and Poor Communities"; Scheie and others, *Better Together*; Nowak and others, *Religious Institutions and Community Renewal*.

>━━◯━━<

Faith-Based Community Partnerships: Toward Justice and Empowerment

JOSEPH R. HACALA

Much recent discussion surrounding partnerships between the federal government and the faith-based community to implement social service and community development programs has treated such partnerships as a creative and radical new initiative of the current administration. While President George W. Bush's new White House Office of Faith-Based and Community Initiatives has focused renewed attention on them, these partnerships have a long and rich history. Indeed, through the years, faith-based groups as various as Habitat for Humanity International, Lutheran Services in America, the Catholic Campaign for Human Development, and B'nai B'rith have engaged in community organizing and community development strategies that have produced housing, created jobs and, most important, provided hope for millions. A recent study by the National Congress for Community Economic Development, for example, reported that in its survey of 3,000 community development groups, at least 15 percent were faith-based.

The U.S. Department of Housing and Urban Development's Center for Community and Interfaith Partnerships, which I directed for four years, has been deeply involved in partnerships between government and faith-based organizations. Initiated in 1997 by Secretary Andrew Cuomo, and building on earlier efforts by Secretary Henry Cisneros, HUD's Center for Community and Interfaith Partnerships grew out of Cuomo's experience in providing housing for the poor and homeless in the New York City area. The mission of the innovative center was "to focus, integrate, and intensify HUD's involvement with faith- and community-based organizations in an effort to maximize the use and impact of mutual resources in building community."

The center's objectives were to listen to community and faith-based groups, educate them about HUD and its resources, coordinate activities with them, and build new partnerships at the national level. The center's activities and successes

This essay is a revised version of an article that appeared in *America* magazine. Reprinted with permission.

were grounded in a multifaceted approach that involved building awareness, providing outreach and education services, and publicizing successful efforts and models. By responding to requests from faith-based groups, troubleshooting, promoting new and better partnerships, facilitating participation of community and faith-based groups in HUD initiatives, and shaping policy, among other efforts, the center worked to empower neighborhoods across the United States.

HUD administered nearly $1 billion in assistance to community and faith-based organizations in fiscal year 2000; made 230 grants to faith-based organizations specifically to provide homeless services and a similar number of grants to groups to serve individuals with HIV/AIDS; provided nearly 40 percent of the funds for Section 202 senior citizen housing programs; and set aside 40 percent of new technical assistance grant funds for previously unfunded faith-based and nonprofit groups. In addition, the center sponsored eight regional faith-based conferences that engaged some 4,000 churches or individuals; a resource guide highlighting best practices and sources of funds; and several nationwide educational satellite broadcasts.

It is against this long-standing backdrop of vibrant and varied activity that President Bush proposes his "new initiative," which, in fact, includes expanded cooperation with faith-based groups. The administration's objectives to "enlist, enable, empower, and expand the work of faith-based and other community organizations" are largely in the form of "social service initiatives" and, as such, are not entirely new, but they are important.

I find encouragement in some particular features of Bush's White House Office of Faith-Based and Community Initiatives: tax breaks to assist communities, perhaps along the model of the recent bipartisan New Markets legislation of the Clinton administration, whose goal is to empower communities left behind in the new economy; the embrace by the new administration of the Corporation for National Service, which could engage a significant force of deeply committed participants in faith-based community development efforts; and the extension of opportunities to form working relationships with the federal government. These should build on HUD's positive community and faith-based model, the Center for Community and Interfaith Initiatives, and lead to new initiatives in the Departments of Education, Health and Human Services, Justice, and Labor.

However, a variety of cautions and potential pitfalls have surfaced that need further investigation. As many have noted, there is a need to consider the legal tradition, history, and realities of the separation of church and state. And it is necessary to monitor religious proselytizing in the context of providing assistance to the needy and to adhere to local and state employment and discrimination practices. We must also avoid mere expansion of charitable choice, whose success in the implementation of the 1996 welfare reform initiatives has been mixed. Furthermore, it is imperative that this effort not promote charity at the expense of justice by underfunding real structural needs. When we merely provide more water for soup or additional cots for church basements, *we are only attempting to alleviate symptomatic problems while ignoring the cycles of disadvantage and persistent needs* for affordable housing and jobs for the unemployed and underemployed. One can question the effectiveness of the new White House proposals in view of the Bush administration's early budget cuts, which included the elimination of a rural housing program and a reduction in technical assistance funds for those faith-based groups most in need. Early efforts of the new administration's faith-based proposals have been further hindered by challenges and criticism from both far-right and religious conservatives and the threat of excessive legal challenges from the left.

My hope is that the Bush administration's plan will become substantive by building on a variety of ongoing and successful efforts, including the positive recent experience of HUD's Center for Community and Interfaith Initiatives. I believe this serves as a good model for meeting our nation's serious social needs. But the ultimate solution to poverty for the poor of Appalachia, the Mississippi Delta, the border colonias, Indian reservations, and rural and inner-city areas necessarily involves a combination of methods that *directly engage and empower the poor; provide increased and adequate government funding for housing, food programs, and social problems at all levels; and promote many kinds of collaborative partnerships between faith-based, community, and government entities.* Those partnerships should include and build on past models of collaboration between government and congregations that involved direct funding of religiously related nonprofit organizations with tax-exempt status.

As our nation continues to meet the challenges and opportunities of the new century under new political leadership, the issue of building stronger, more sustaining communities remains central to our future. The role of community and faith-based organizations in this process is particularly relevant in light of the history, success, and moral credibility of these groups. At this threshold in our history, recent experience has renewed hope that faith-based community participation may continue to lead neighborhoods and communities toward much-needed social change and authentic empowerment. If the Office of Faith-Based Initiatives, with its renewed public consciousness, also leads to a commitment of additional resources to fight domestic poverty, there will be cause for celebration, especially among the poor.

>--⊖--<

Comparative Advantages of Faith-Based Organizations in Community Development

WILLIAM T. DICKENS

Avis Vidal has looked at the contribution of faith-based organizations to community development as it typically is practiced; Jeremy Nowak has suggested a much more ambitious agenda. Rather than ask what FBOs can contribute to the current practice of community development, I would like to ask what they can do to contribute under a more expansive model: asset building that promotes the welfare of community residents. That model, for which Ron Ferguson and I have argued, considers social and organizational capital as well as physical capital as assets, so that organizing a tenant association or lobbying local businesses to provide more jobs for neighborhood residents is as much community development as refurbishing an apartment building.

As I see it, faith-based organizations have four unique advantages: they have particular experience, expertise, and legitimacy in dealing with issues of individual identity and human needs; they can engage highly and specially motivated people in their activities; they can claim to speak for the interests of the disadvantaged in public disputes more credibly than can most secular political leaders; and many have longer institutional histories and more stability than secular community-based organizations.

Building housing, the most common community development activity, draws on at most one of those four advantages. Houses cannot occupy the moral high ground, bricks do not care about the motivation of the bricklayer, and apartment buildings do not require ministry. Even the management of housing may not be the forte of religious groups, if as Vidal suggests, solid business practices are more important than compassion in the success of that activity.

The list of advantages indicates that faith-based organizations wishing to contribute to community development would be most effective at community organizing and delivering social services—particularly the treatment of substance abuse. Certainly churches have been active in both types of activities. However, as Vidal documents, a very large part of what congregations have done is to build and manage housing. Some of their biggest success stories involve those activities. Why is that?

I can think of three explanations for why churches engaged in community development would fail to fully employ their comparative advantages. First, the

CDC model of housing development is well known; a congregation that wants to aid a community has examples to follow, and institutional support is available for the CDC approach. There also are successful examples of faith-based community organizing and service programs, but they are fewer in number and they are not supported by as large and effective an institutional network. But saying that congregations adopt the CDC model because it is a common, well-supported approach just explains the success of the CDC model as a product of its own success. We have to look deeper for a prime mover.

Perhaps the explanation is that whatever the community development potential of faith-based oganizations, their allocation of effort is determined by the demands of the communities they wish to serve. In some sense, housing is where demand is greatest. Of all the needs of disadvantaged communities, housing is the biggest one for which there is an acknowledged gap between need and what is supplied by existing programs. Everyone who qualifies for food stamps can receive them; only a small fraction of people who qualify for public housing assistance receive it. Further, if a neighborhood is physically run down, the obvious and most direct way to address the problem is to refurbish or rebuild the buildings that constitute the neighborhood. Thus faith-based organizations are drawn into filling a need because other systems have failed or have proven inadequate.

Finally, it may be their disadvantages and not the advantages of faith-based groups that lead them to become involved in housing development. Faith-based groups can organize enthusiastic volunteers, but they seldom are sufficiently skilled to deliver specialized social services. However, they can help build or refurbish housing. That is how Habitat for Humanity works.

But when inner-city congregations get into the housing business it is not primarily to employ volunteer labor in construction. As Vidal has described, the people from the congregation end up doing the work of a housing developer: securing land, securing funding, securing financing, and negotiating with contractors, subcontractors, city authorities, and other development organizations. Volunteers sometimes go away feeling that their unique contribution—their faith—is not appreciated by those with whom they work.

That last consideration, more than anything else, convinces me that the energy of faith-based groups could be more effectively used if their housing activities were deemphasized and other sorts of activities expanded. If these organizations can become adept at building housing, then they can become adept at working to expand job opportunities, providing individual counseling, developing recreational activities, and helping prevent crime. Such activities are likely to be much more rewarding to church workers than negotiating with bankers.

What can government do to help congregations find their niche in community development? First, it can do more to remove the burden of providing housing from the private nonprofit sector. To date, I have seen no evidence to suggest that this sector has any advantage over the for-profit sector in building or managing housing; on the contrary, there is evidence that the for-profit sector is better at it. There are two primary impediments that keep the private sector from filling the housing needs of distressed communities: residents' low incomes and zoning and building regulations that make it difficult to provide housing that people with low incomes can afford. Simply setting building standards is not enough. If we truly believe that no U.S. resident should have to live in housing that is below a certain standard, then we need to ensure that everyone has the resources to afford housing of that standard; otherwise, government should lower standards enough that the private sector can provide affordable housing. In an era of trillion-dollar tax cuts, clearly the resources to fill the need are there, if we have the will.

What else can government do to promote the participation of faith-based organizations in community organizing and service delivery? The development of a substantial infrastructure of national and regional organizations that help local CDCs by providing information and access to resources has been essential to the success of the CDC movement. Government organizations could foster the development of such an infrastructure to support a wider range of activities by faith-based organizations, in part by funding research to determine what models and methods would be successful.

President Bush has initiated a major effort to promote the work of faith-based charitable organizations by establishing government organizations to promote their interests, eliminating federal barriers to their work, and promoting private giving. I suspect that good things will come of this initiative in several areas, but I fear that it will do little to promote the more effective deployment of the resources of faith-based organization in community development.

It will be good to have federal offices in high places that are charged with tapping faith-based resources and acting as ombudsmen for faith-based oganizations. But I see only one way in which congregational development activities are seriously constrained by federal regulation, and that is not discussed in the Bush proposal. Nearly all the problems created by the constitutional requirements for separation of church and state can be dealt with by having churches work through secular nonprofit spin-offs. Such organizations are restricted from proselytizing, but that is not a problem in most social service work. In the few cases in which it may be (for example, drug treatment, pregnancy prevention, and crisis counseling programs), direct government funding would likely be judged unconstitutional because it would have the effect of promoting specific religious beliefs. However, the government can provide vouchers to individuals so that those who want to can participate in faith-based programs.

As Vidal makes clear, the financial contributions of faith-based organizations to community development are dwarfed by government and foundation contributions. The effects of a small change in government funding for development activities would be vastly greater than any effect of changes of the sort that President Bush has proposed to promote more giving.

But again, charitable giving to faith-based community service organizations is a minor issue compared with the two major things that government could do to support faith-based community development: removing the burden of supplying low-income housing from the private nonprofit sector and facilitating the work of that sector in doing things that it can do better than the for-profit sector.

Eyes on the Prize

JIM WALLIS

As faith-based organizations become more deeply involved in partnerships with government, the fundamental question that must be raised is that of our vocation. Are we service providers or prophetic interrogators? And, if we are both, how do the two relate?

Those in power usually prefer that faith communities run service programs than raise our prophetic voice for social justice. Government will invite faith-based organizations into program partnerships because many faith-based programs work very well, but it will not so easily invite the same organizations to act as advocates. As the Bush administration proposes new partnerships with faith-based organizations, the most important issue is safeguarding our prophetic integrity. Our mission is to overcome poverty, not simply to service it, so we must constantly ask why so many people remain poor in the midst of amazing prosperity.

Practically speaking, that means evaluating all the administration's policies by how well they reduce poverty and challenging those that do not. We must continue working for a health care policy that includes the 10 million children who have no coverage. We must act as advocates for poor working families that need a living wage and affordable housing. When the debate on reauthorizing welfare reform begins, we must make sure that there is funding for the critical supports needed to help families move out of poverty's deadly cycle. We must challenge excessive tax cuts and misguided budget priorities that benefit the wealthy and leave few resources to invest in effective antipoverty strategies.

For many community development organizations—even for the model projects that are working best—the most significant issue is lack of resources. How can government help to mobilize new multisector partnerships and allocate its resources in the most effective, strategic way? The idea of new partnerships suggests that we can link problem-solving ability at the lower levels with resources at the higher levels. We need not only to recognize the work of both community groups and faith-based organizations but also to provide them the resources to do what needs to be done. Government must determine what already is working and then figure out how to apply those solutions on a broader scale.

We know that grassroots organizations cannot, and should not, be expected to provide a safety net for the entire society. The government still is responsible for handling fundamental issues such as Medicaid for poor kids, health care for the uninsured, education, and housing policy. We cannot allow government to abdicate its responsibilities, leaving hopelessly underfunded churches and charities to fight poverty on the cheap by forcing them to make bricks without straw. In all policy discussions, our voice must be heard.

And I would suggest that the larger issue involves more than questions of policy. Sometimes the policy choices that we need are not on the table. When what we need most is not even being discussed, it is not a lobbying issue, because there is no justice to lobby for. A deeper prophetic agenda then emerges, about how we can change society's sensibilities and the way we think about poor and homeless people. How do we think of our poorest children? Are all of them ours or just some of them? If we do not raise the fundamental religious and moral questions, then the right policy questions do not enter the conversation either.

Now that the administration is talking about new partnerships, we should seize the moment as a prophetic opportunity. If faith-based organizations and the government are to become partners, we must make clear that our role is not simply to make the government more efficient but also to make U.S. society more just. It is not simply to clean up the mess created by bad social policy or to assume what are legitimate responsibilities of the government, but to raise a morally prophetic voice for new policies. With all the attention on faith-based organizations, now may be the best time to speak the language of both love and justice. While doing our works of love in neighborhoods across the country, we can and must also make the demands of justice known to those in power.

We must not allow ourselves to be sidetracked into intellectual debates that leave our poorest children behind. We should keep our eyes on the prize, as the civil rights anthem says, and focus our energies on the most effective models for overcoming the poverty that imprisons our youngest and most vulnerable citizens. And we must ensure that those models have sufficient resources to do the work they do best in overcoming poverty.

>─·─⊖─·─<

Redefining the Mission of Faith-Based Organizations in Community Development

PIETRO NIVOLA

What is the purpose of community development? Should community development organizations redefine their missions? Jeremy Nowak's central point is that community development needs to move beyond its parochial focus on the provision and management of affordable housing to what he calls a broadened geography, one that includes not only the issue of access to housing but also of economic development and a better interface with emerging labor markets. I think his delineation of the challenges that face community development corporations is very much on target.

In my opinion (and I think it is also his), the continuing concentration and isolation of an urban underclass in U.S. cities and the relentless dispersion of everyone and everything else to sprawling suburbs is a problem. And I think we all agree that CDCs can make some difference—no one really knows how much—in relieving the concentration of poverty at the urban core and thereby persuading economically viable households and businesses to reinvest in cities.

But how? Nowak's point is that what is needed are regionally oriented housing, job placement, and networking strategies. Back in the 1960s that approach was called ghetto dispersal—not a pretty designation. What are my criticisms of his analysis? My only quibble is that I think Nowak may be too optimistic about the ability of CDCs to pull off the rather formidable paradigm shift that is implicit in his recommendation, which is to switch from a place-based orientation to become organizations with a wider geographic reach and a regional, market-oriented mission. That switch is difficult probably because, at the end of a day, most faith-based organizations have a vested interest in limiting their activities to the community.

FBOs, it seems to me, are intrinsically uninterested in acting as passport agencies, issuing exit visas to their members and clients. That would seem to be particularly true if they are congregations or parishes. To put it another way, there is an inherent contradiction, or at least a tension, between implementing programs that facilitate access of the inner-city poor to jobs and residences in regional markets and, on the other hand, undertaking community development, with its emphasis on improving existing inner-city neighborhoods. One approach says "We want you to stay put"; the other says "We want you to join the millions of other Americans who move every year." CDCs naturally are inclined to prefer the stay-put approach rather than the mobility-enhancement approach because mobility implies eventually disbanding one's membership, one's constituency. Regrettably, the place-based focus, which is trying to arrest the decline of inner-city neighborhoods without changing their demographics, may well prove futile.

For the most part, Avis Vidal's chapter conforms with my assessment: there is not much hard or measurable evidence that the CDCs that Vidal examines have had a large, visible impact in helping their members get ahead, as opposed to simply running in place, so to speak.

That is beginning to change; many of these organizations are beginning to develop asset-creation strategies. The chapter stresses that faith-based CDCs do, in fact, bring some unique assets to the game that they are trying to play. They bring, for example, a natural base of members. Members—better still, volunteers—are needed to get things done. A membership base is a significant plus.

Faith-based organizations also enjoy greater public confidence in their credentials. Put another way, they reputedly hold the moral high ground: they have moral authority to do their work, since churches generally are perceived as legitimate institutions, as distinct from fly-by-night operations that might abscond with funds. That is very important.

The chapter also notes, however, that the organizations carry their share of liabilities. They often have little sense of how to operate as entrepreneurs in the urban marketplace. They often have a cultural preference for performing acts of charity, as opposed to devising self-help strategies for the indigent, and so on.

To the list of liabilities, I would add at least two more. One is fairly obvious. Although I think it is true that faith-based institutions enjoy a good deal of public trust, that trust has its limits. A substantial part of the public does worry about church-state separation issues, especially when public funds are involved. The second concern, as mentioned, is that some of these organizations may not really want their members to get ahead if getting ahead means leaving the community. Helping one's members get out, after all, implies losing them.

Now, there are major differences among faith-based institutions. My guess is that the Catholic Church, for example, might play a distinctive role in disadvantaged communities. Because the church has a global reach, perhaps Catholic organizations may be in the habit of thinking beyond parochial confines more than are some other kinds of faith-based groups.

We have to ask a fundamental question: What do we want so-called community development to *do*? Do we want it to enhance the mobility of the nation's urban have-nots or to invoke in them and other community residents a greater sense of place, which sometimes means less rather than more mobility?

My own view is that national urban policy must make it a priority to raise the living standards of the urban poor, to make it easier for them to obtain employment, housing, and essential services—particularly better schools—anywhere in the metropolitan region. That cannot be accomplished by force-feeding or socially engineering inner-city revitalization projects that propose to keep the poor where they are.

Faith in Harlem: Community Development and the Black Church

DARREN WALKER

I have the privilege of living and working in an extraordinary place called Harlem and having a connection to a church—the Abyssinian Baptist Church—that has a rich history and tradition of activism on behalf of people of African descent. The Abyssinian Development Corporation (ADC) is an outgrowth of the ministry of the church, founded by Reverend Dr. Calvin O. Butts III and a group of local residents who were appalled by the conditions that existed in Harlem in the 1980s.

We proudly trumpet the many accomplishments of our organization: more than 2,000 children and families served annually through our programs in child care, education, human services, and civic engagement; more than 1,000 units of affordable housing; 300,000 square feet of commercial construction. Those achievements have not come easily, and we know that were it not for the institutional strength of the Abyssinian Baptist Church, our success would be more modest and muted. Yet while we have so much to be proud of and to share with others, we are a bit uneasy about just where we are going. It is most regrettable that we find ourselves caught in the current quagmire of hysteria and hyperbole around the role of faith-based organizations in ameliorating poverty, reducing teenage pregnancy, and building neighborhoods.

THE BLACK CHURCH TRADITION

It is our faith that inspires us to do our work; it is our belief that people and neighborhoods can be transformed. But especially now, we must be mindful of the fact that black churches were engaged in faith-based community development long before the term was popularized by highly credentialed urban planners and foundation executives. In fact, microenterprise lending, building housing, operating schools, running food pantries, and community organizing were staple activities of churches—especially black churches—since the nineteenth century. So it is only an extension of our historical role that brings us to this critical juncture. Much has been gained and much could be lost if we do not proceed adroitly as we consider the prospects under the current faith-based framework. We are grateful that President Bush affirms and exalts the contributions that black churches and other religious institutions have made to our society. However, that attention, coupled with the mistaken belief on the part of many congregations (especially small black churches), that money soon will begin falling from the sky into church coffers, compels me to offer some unsolicited rules of engagement to those who are considering embarking on community development in the name of faith.

Rule One: Always protect the integrity and independence of the church. Unfortunately, some have simply thrown any pretense of church-state separation out the window in pursuit of government grants. As some congregations have found out the hard way, when a church accepts direct grants from government, it places itself under the direct *supervision* of government. In some parts of the world, that is not unusual. In the United States, however, the last time a government placed organized religion under its supervision, a revolution was fought, thousands of people lost their lives, and a constitution establishing the strict separation of church and state was adopted.

Rule Two: Can you say transparency? No entity—government or private—currently requires religious institutions in this country to operate with transparency. That is true of the black church, which is characterized by a detached management style, with governance and power limited to a core group of church leaders. However, running a 501(c)(3) nonprofit organization, which any church with a marginally competent lawyer will be advised to do in order to separate its worship and social services, requires a complete change in disclosure and accountability. Church leaders running a CDC must be prepared to submit the organization's financial statements to public scrutiny and review. Contracting, salaries, procurement policies, and personnel standards become part of the public domain, easily accessed on the Internet and subject to misinterpretation and legal action if administration is not based on sound principles and practices and taken seriously.

Rule Three: The founding church is not the primary constituency of a faith-based CDC—the general community is the primary constituency. Service must be provided without preference or discrimination. Recently, a local church asked whether we would help it secure nominally priced, city-owned land and a housing subsidy that it wanted to use for a housing development exclusively for church members. The church's leaders were offended when we declined. But the city of New York's housing agency would not have supported such an action, and any attempt to circumvent agency policy would have required us to break laws designed to ensure fairness and nondiscrimination in publicly funded programs.

Rule Four: Most of the time, especially in the beginning stages of organizational growth, community development is a money-losing proposal. The church therefore needs deep enough pockets to withstand the drain on its financial resources. In addition, it must be willing to accept the undeniable fact that church staff will spend an increasing amount of their time working with consultants, researchers, evaluators, bankers, brokers, and a whole host of other nonchurch folks. Although it can be argued that such work is an extension of the ministry, it does put pressure on staff capacity, hindering the progress of other church-related objectives. Finally, those government contracts that appear so enticing often are performance based: the church does not collect a fee until specific outcomes are achieved—for example, a client obtains employment *and* spends six months on the job. Therefore, the church must finance a government-sponsored job-training program for six months. If the final objective is not met, the church could end up paying to train folks for the government and getting no financial compensation in return.

The debate over faith-based development has been framed in a way that creates a phony dichotomy between good and bad choices. Proponents of President Bush's faith-based initiative say that it should be obvious that religious institutions are better positioned than secular ones to deliver social services and a host of other programs and that not to accept that as fact minimizes the historic significance of faith in this country. The most regrettable aspect of the debate is that it has distracted us from public discourse about a much more fundamental question: Is it defensible in times of relative peace and prosperity to invest so little in housing the poor and feeding the hungry? The pie isn't getting any larger—we have just shifted our focus to the less important question of who gets to pass the pieces around the table.

>—◦—<

Housing Needs and Housing Resources: A Mismatch

CUSHING DOLBEARE

The resources that churches and others have to address housing are tiny in comparison to the need. The stark fact is that of all households, half of renters and one-quarter of owners—a total of 35.6 million households—have a significant housing problem. They pay more than they can afford for housing, they occupy dilapidated units, or they live in overcrowded conditions. Some 15.9 million of those households pay more than half of their income for housing or live in severely substandard units, and 5.3 million, those with the so-called worst case housing needs, live in unsubsidized very low-income rental properties. The others are very low-income owners (5.4 million), renters who live in subsidized housing but still pay more than half of their income for rent (1.9 million), or unsubsidized renters with incomes above 50 percent of median income (0.9 million).

Since 1937, the federal government has had a variety of programs and approaches to provide housing for low-income people and has added, bit by bit over most of those years, to the stock of federally assisted low-income housing. But the number of assisted households peaked at 5 million in the mid-1990s and has been dropping ever since.

In 1949, Congress adopted a national goal of ensuring "a decent home and suitable living environment for every American family." In 1968, Congress authorized construction or rehabilitation of 6 million low-income units—600,000 a year for ten years. If all of those units had become available and if Congress had continued to provide housing assistance at that level, 20 million subsidized units would have been ready for occupancy—more than enough, if properly located, to house all low-income households with critical housing needs.

Just before leaving office, the Ford administration submitted a proposed budget for fiscal year 1978 to Congress that would have provided 500,000 additional low-income housing units, including 100,000 for-sale units. If that level of production had been achieved and maintained, about 14 million families would now be living in federally assisted low-income housing.

Since 1981, when extremely low-income housing production programs were terminated except to replace some demolished public housing, the United States has not had a program capable of providing affordable housing for extremely low-income families. The low-income housing tax credit and mortgage revenue bond programs, both of which have substantial roles in expanding the stock of affordable rental housing, require additional subsidies—including ongoing operating subsidies—to provide affordable units for those households. Yet federal spending for maintaining and expanding low-income housing assistance has dropped by two-thirds since 1976, the last full year of the Ford administration.

Because resources are inadequate under current law, two major dilemmas have emerged that have to be addressed in order to serve people with incomes below 30 percent of the median income, many of whom are working households. First, CDCs, whether faith-based or not, face the dilemma of whom to serve. How do they meet the urgent needs of extremely low-income people, who constitute more than 60 percent of all households with severe housing problems, when the resources provided—public and private—are so inadequate? Many CDCs choose to assist families that have somewhat higher incomes and thus require less subsidy. As a result, they are able to provide more housing but they serve few extremely low-income people. Instead, they serve families with incomes of 50 or 60 percent of the median—families with genuine, but less critical, housing problems.

The second dilemma is the relationship between church-based CDCs' provision of housing and other social services and churches' advocacy for justice. Since 1980, a majority of the members of Congress have not represented districts where poverty is a significant problem. We will not be able to meet the nation's most critical housing needs until we solve the political problem of how to get voters in more affluent congressional districts to approve the necessary federal expenditures. In 1999, the gap between 30 percent of household income and housing costs capped at the relevant fair-market rent (which determines the amount of housing assistance for those lucky enough to receive it) was $67 billion. Neither the private sector nor state and local governments have the resources to close a gap of that magnitude, even if they make it a major priority. Also in 1999, the federal government spent a total of $29 billion for low-income housing assistance. In contrast, the cost to the federal treasury of homeowner deductions from federal income tax was $100 billion, with more than 95 percent of those benefits going to households in the top 40 percent of the income distribution. If an equal amount had been spent on addressing the housing needs of the bottom 60 percent, there would be no major housing problems.

Churches and church-based organizations are uniquely situated to overcome the economic gap between the inner city and rural areas and the more affluent suburbs. Most church members live in suburban areas, as does most of the rest of the U.S. population. It is critical that churches and church-based organizations not get so wrapped up in daily operations that they fail to address the all-important question of how to translate their faith and their experiences into advocacy of effective public policies. Members of Congress, including those who do not represent districts where poverty is a burning problem, must be made to feel a responsibility for solving the problems of poverty and for providing the resources essential to the undertaking.

Faith as the Foundation for the New Community Corporation

WILLIAM J. LINDER

It was the winter of 1963, and I was a newly ordained priest just a few months into my first assignment at a parish in Newark, New Jersey. I had been asked to take food to an impoverished mother and child who were living in a decrepit building in the Central Ward. The unheated apartment was freezing. In that stark unit, I found a baby deathly ill with pneumonia, lying motionless in a crib that had been covered with wire mesh to protect the child from rats.

When I returned two days later with more food, the mother told me that her child had died. I was stunned but also frustrated, for although I had brought them food, I could provide neither medical help nor a warm home. I had cared, but I had failed in the face of larger societal problems such as the racial hatred and class distinctions that left the city's low-income communities at a severe disadvantage. I was devastated by my inability to give the family the help it needed. Despite my goodwill, I was powerless to overcome the larger forces of evil on my own.

The discovery of my own limitations gave birth to the concept of the New Community Corporation—a community development corporation that would bring together and empower the very people in need of assistance. Together, with adequate support and training, they would work to overcome the inequities that faced them all. The death of that baby nearly forty years ago thus served as a catalyst in my life, compelling me to reflect on the essential elements of the community development model and eventually to put them into action after continuing inequities resulted in the riots of 1967.

New Community Corporation (NCC) serves low-income areas by developing and implementing a neighborhood development agenda that reflects local values—for example, by keeping money within the neighborhood rather than pushing out existing residents. Its first business venture was the conversion of a 120-year-old church into an office building housing NCC's offices, restaurants, shops, a banquet center, and an atrium that doubles as visual and performing arts venue. The building attracted members of the nearby university, medical center, and business community to come to enjoy and subsequently invest in the immediate neighborhood. Other business ventures include establishing a major supermarket that makes affordable food available while showing a profit; building a components plant that brought manufacturing jobs to the city; and providing affordable homes for more than 7,000 existing and new residents in safe and secure neighborhoods. NCC's coordinated ventures provide local residents quality job training, including training in new technologies; daycare; health care; charter schools and adult education programs; transportation services; community arts and recreation programs; and other much-needed services. Today, NCC is the nation's largest community development corporation, with a network of programs and services that affect more than 50,000 people every day, either through tangible improvements in their daily life or through a spirit of mutual understanding and respect that values the dignity and capacities of *all* people and especially those with low incomes.

NCC credits its successes to various factors, including strong leadership, personal strength, financial and strategic skills, and political acumen, but its mission and wide-ranging activities are rooted primarily in faith: a historically based and persevering faith on the part of its constituent population and a prophetic and challenging faith on the part of its agents for change. Without its religious center, NCC would not exist.

At least three interrelated and indispensable dimensions of religion are at work in the community development process: religion as a source of community, vision, and empowerment. As a source of community, religion answers the question "Who are we?" NCC's answer is that we are God's people. We find our identity not merely in our separate selves, but in the fact that we belong to one another and to God. As a source of vision, religion answers the question "Where are we going?" NCC's answer is that we are on a prophetic journey in a direction that God's design has revealed. As a source of empowerment, religion answers the question "How is God's design to be fulfilled?" NCC believes that the way to reach our goals is to struggle for justice and reconciliation in ways that strengthen and call upon those who most need God's love and His gifts. Our organizational mission and strategy thus combines all three elements and articulates the centrality of religion to our work: "To help residents of inner cities improve the quality of their lives so that they reflect their God-given dignity and personal achievements."

After more than thirty years of effort, it is fair to say that NCC belongs in and to Newark. Our mission is an indispensable, long-term strategy to bringing about the transformation that must take place in the inner city if justice is to be served.

Charitable choice legislation begins a new era in the community development movement, with a new set of problems. One major challenge is political identification: we must always identify with the poor, using our power and money to work for the betterment of the poor and not for our own glory. We must find new and creative ways to make the powerful listen. We also must juxtapose our desire for social justice with the concrete reality of our individual situation: if a church is not ready—if it does not have adequate resources or is not prepared to make a commitment to working with others—it should not attempt to take on what then will be an unbearable burden. Finally, though partnerships between congregations and the government offer several new opportunities, we must begin to exploit the possibilities of partnerships of congregations and private businesses. Although the New Community Corporation identified the need for a supermarket in a nearby neighborhood, no major chain would open a store there. So we raised $2.5 million and then negotiated a deal with Pathmark: we now receive two-thirds of the profits from what has become one of the most profitable stores in the Pathmark chain.

In entering this new era, we must recognize that ours is a project for the long term. Short-term solutions do not work. When we founded New Community, we asked board members to make a twenty-year commitment, believing that it would take that long to see results. Some of those board members have been with us now for thirty-two years. When performance determines funding, we must be careful not to judge too soon. Results in the world of community development take time, but CDCs like the New Community Corporation are committed for the long haul.

PART FOUR

THE ROLE OF FAITH-BASED ORGANIZATIONS IN

Education

CHAPTER NINE

Partnerships of Schools and Faith-Based Organizations

MAVIS G. SANDERS

Educational practitioners, policymakers, parents, and other key stakeholders in the current school reform environment are discussing, planning, and implementing school-community partnerships to improve schools and educational opportunities for students. Because of the influential role that faith-based organizations play in family and community life, they are seen as natural participants in those partnerships. The interest in a larger role for faith-based organizations in schools is becoming stronger as the public school population grows in its diversity and needs.

Statistics show that currently one in five children enrolled in U.S. public schools is poor and that about 40 percent of U.S. public school students come from racial and ethnic minority groups.[1] Many of those students are immigrants or members of immigrant families whose first language is not English.[2] An estimated 6 million children in U.S. public schools have learning disabilities that require special educational approaches.[3] To educate those and all students effectively, public schools require greater human and material resources. Community organizations, including faith-based organizations, possess such resources.

This chapter discusses the role of faith-based organizations in school-community partnerships, which are defined as the connections between schools and individuals, organizations, and businesses in the community that are forged to promote, directly or indirectly, students' social, emotional, physical, and intellectual development. Within this definition, community is not constrained by the geographic boundaries of neighborhoods but refers more to the social interactions that may occur within or transcend local boundaries.[4]

Faith-based organizations are defined as self-identified religious groups or institutions from a wide variety of traditions that include but are not limited to various Christian, Jewish, Islamic, Buddhist, and Hindu groups. This definition is not meant to ignore the existence or importance of other faith-based organizations, but simply to narrow the focus on what is a very broad topic. Discussion also is limited to community partnerships with state-funded public schools.

I first draw on the theoretical literature on school-community partnerships to describe their importance in school reform. Then I review literature on the role of faith-based organizations in youth development and on the effect of youth involvement in religious organizations on school outcomes. Next I discuss the role of faith-based organizations in school-community partnerships and the factors that influence the development of effective partnerships. In conclusion, I explore the limitations of these partnerships, contending that the nation's children, families, and communities are best served through both separate and collaborative practices among faith-based organizations and schools.

THE ROLE OF COMMUNITY PARTNERSHIPS IN SCHOOL REFORM

The family and the school traditionally have been viewed as the institutions that have the greatest effect on the development of children. The community, however, has received increasing attention for its role in socializing youth and ensuring students' success in a variety of societal domains. Epstein's theory of overlapping spheres of influence, for example, identifies schools, families, and communities as major forces in the socialization and education of children.[5] A central principle of the theory is that certain goals, such as student academic success, are of interest to each of those institutions and are best achieved through their cooperative action and support.

Similarly, Heath and McLaughlin argue that community involvement is important because "the problems of educational achievement and academic success demand resources beyond the scope of the school and of most families."[6] They identified changing family demographics, demands of the workplace, and growing diversity among students as some of the reasons that schools and families alone cannot provide sufficient resources to ensure that all children receive the experiences and support they need to succeed in the larger society.

Describing the importance of community involvement in educational reform, Shore focused on the mounting responsibilities placed on schools by a nation whose student population is increasingly at risk. She states: "Too many schools and school systems are failing to carry out their basic educational mission. Many of them—both in urban and rural settings—are overwhelmed by the social and emotional needs of children who are growing up in poverty."[7] She contends that schools need additional resources to successfully educate all students and that those resources, both human and material, can be found in students' communities. Waddock agrees. She explains that good schools are part of a system of interactive forces, individuals, institutions, goals, and expectations that are inextricably linked together.[8]

School-community partnerships take a variety of forms, the most common being partnerships with businesses, which can differ significantly in content and scope. Others involve universities and educational institutions; government and military agencies; health care organizations; national service and volunteer organizations; senior citizen organizations; cultural and recreational institutions; other community-based organizations; community volunteers; and faith-based organizations.[9]

Partnerships also focus on a variety of activities, which may be student centered; family centered; school centered; or community centered. Student-centered activities include those that provide direct services or goods to students—for example, mentoring, tutoring, contextual learning, and job-shadowing programs—as well as awards, incentives, and scholarships. Family-centered activities are those whose primary focus is on parents or the entire family; they include parenting workshops, GED and other adult education classes, family counseling, and family fun and learning programs. School-centered activities are those that benefit the school as a whole, such as beautification projects or the donation of school equipment and materials, or activities that benefit the faculty, such as staff development opportunities and classroom assistance. Community-centered activities focus primarily on the community and its citizens through, for example, charitable outreach programs, art and science exhibits, and community revitalization and beautification projects.[10]

Research suggests that partnership activities can lead to measurable outcomes for students and schools. Mentoring programs have been found to have a significant positive effect on students' grades, school attendance, and exposure to career opportunities.[11] School-community collaborations that focus on academic subjects have been shown to enhance teachers' and parents' as well as students' attitudes toward those subjects.[12] Documented benefits of initiatives among schools, health providers, and social service agencies to integrate services include behavioral and academic gains for students who received intensive services.[13] Research also has shown improved student attendance, immunization rates, and conduct at schools providing coordinated services.[14] Nettles reported positive effects on students' grades and attendance of school-community collaborations that had an instructional component.[15] Finally, partnerships with businesses and other community organizations have provided schools with needed equipment, materials, and technical assistance and support for student instruction.[16] School-community partnerships, then, can be an important element in programs to reform and improve schools.

The Role of Faith-Based Organizations in Education and Youth Development

Faith-based organizations often are effective partners in school-community collaborations because of their long history of involvement in the social and educational development of children and youth. For example, during the colonial period in U.S. history, religious or sectarian schools were the order of the day. According to Bryk, Lee, and Holland, "education was viewed as a fundamentally moral enterprise, and Protestants and Catholics alike sought to ground the education of their children in their particular beliefs."[17] Religious organizations also became involved in the education of youth in order to effect social change. Before the Civil War, members of the Quaker religion were instrumental not only in the abolitionist movement, but also in providing educational opportunities to African American youth when other religious denominations had little interest in doing so.[18] After the Civil War, both black and white churches played an important role in establishing schools for previously enslaved African American youth.[19] Moreover, during the mass immigration of the early nineteenth century, the Catholic Church played a significant role in educating and facilitating the assimilation of children from diverse European ethnic groups.[20]

After 1830, publicly funded common schools became increasingly secularized. By that time, most states had included in their constitutions clauses that prevented any kind of state-supported religious activity, thereby officially adopting the First Amendment principle of separation of church and state. The involvement of religious institutions in public schools continued to decline throughout the second half of the nineteenth century and into the beginning of the twentieth century as states passed compulsory school attendance laws that required students of various religious backgrounds to attend public educational institutions together.[21]

Religious institutions in the twentieth century, however, continued to be involved in the educational development of youth outside the public schools. For example, in a study of 216 churches, Billingsley and Caldwell found that 11 percent sponsored formal educational programs for children and older youth, including college preparatory and support programs as well as preschool programs, after-school academic programs, and full-scale elementary and secondary schools. A number of the churches also provided college scholarships.[22]

Faith-based organizations also have played a more subtle role in the educational development and socialization of youth. The intergenerational membership of such institutions has provided children and youth opportunities to develop warm, nurturing, and supportive relationships with caring adults.[23] Within those relationships, young people acquire social capital—information, attitudinal and behavioral norms, and skills that can improve their chances for success in societal institutions such as schools.[24]

The involvement of faith-based organizations in the socialization and development of youth has yielded measurable educational outcomes. In their seminal work, Argyle and Beit-Hallahmi reported that formal church membership and regular church attendance were positively related to educational attainment. About a decade later, Hansen and Ginsburg found that there was a link between religious values and success in school. They found that religious values affected school outcomes both directly and indirectly through out-of-school behavior. The effect of religious values as a whole was consistently greater than the effect of socioeconomic status in predicting both level of school performance and change in student performance.[25]

The relationship between student involvement in faith-based organizations and school success is particularly significant among African Americans.[26] Adding religious involvement to measures of socioeconomic status increased the variance explained in black children's IQ scores from 14 percent to 16 percent.[27] Brown and Gary also found that religious socialization was positively related to both educational achievement and attainment among African Americans under the age of forty-six.[28]

In a study designed to explain these documented effects, Freeman found that participation in church events and activities affected allocation of time out of school, school attendance, employment, and frequency of socially deviant activity—variables that were found to affect the achievement of inner-city African American male adolescents. More recently, my colleague and I found that religious involvement indirectly affected the achievement of African American adolescents through its direct effect on their academic self-concept. During interviews, students indicated that the church provided them the opportunity to engage—in a supportive environment—in a number of activities that required skills that also were required in school, such as public speaking and reading and analyzing texts.[29]

Such findings are not limited to African American youth. In a study of educational success among Chicanos, Galindo and Escamilla found that the church "was not just about spiritual matters, but also served as a support system to do well in school."[30] The study also found that church events designed to promote literacy—for example, reading and discussing biblical stories—had a positive impact on students' language skills and academic success.

Thus, in both their traditional and contemporary roles, faith-based organizations have provided educational opportunities and support to children and youth. Nevertheless, in our changing times—when the demands of the work-place have created greater stress on the family, neighborhoods and communities have become less cohesive, and schools have become increasingly overbur-dened—the need has increased for schools and faith-based organizations to pro-vide a more comprehensive and coordinated system of support to promote students' success in school. Greater collaboration between faith-based organi-zations and public schools can provide the human and material resources needed to make a difference in the quality of schooling and in the academic and social assistance provided to children and young people.

ROLE OF FAITH-BASED ORGANIZATIONS IN SCHOOL-COMMUNITY PARTNERSHIPS

The relationship between U.S. public schools and faith-based organizations has not been without conflict. Both groups have engaged in heated legal and philo-sophical battles over issues such as school prayer and other forms of religious ex-pression, school vouchers, the place of creationism in the teaching of science, government funding, and the role of religious values in public schooling. With the growth of Christian fundamentalism, many of those conflicts have intensi-fied over the last decade. Christian fundamentalist organizations such as the Christian Coalition and Citizens for Excellence in Education (CEE) have risen in national prominence and have been active in shaping the content and out-come of educational debates and reform efforts.[31]

In 1994, for example, the CEE waged a campaign in Pennsylvania to stop a statewide educational reform that would have required students to master fifty-five academic and nonacademic goals in ten subjects before they could graduate from high school. The CEE disputed the nonacademic goals dealing with per-sonal living, family values, and racial and cultural diversity and harmony. Other Christian fundamentalist groups have sought to influence public education re-form, especially around issues of sex education, gay rights, and school prayer, through membership and activism on public school boards. Still others have es-tablished private schools, often as an expression of their discontent with the sec-ular teachings of public schools.[32]

In contrast to this rising tide of conflict and divisiveness has been an equally prominent movement toward collaboration, coordination, and cooperation.[33] The spirit of this movement is reflected in a guide jointly published by the American Jewish Congress, the Christian Legal Society, and the First Amend-ment Center at Vanderbilt University and endorsed by national educational and faith-based groups. The introduction to the guide states: "By working together in ways that are permissible under the First Amendment, as interpreted by the

U.S. Supreme Court, schools and religious communities can do much to enhance the mission of public education."[34] Since the mid-1990s, various attempts have been made to clarify the appropriate, or constitutionally permissible, relationship between religious organizations and schools.[35] Those guidelines have helped many educational, religious, and other community leaders craft a role for faith-based organizations in public education that both upholds the establishment clause of the First Amendment and allows religious organizations to fulfill their service mission.

Although constitutionally prohibited from proselytizing, recruiting, or imposing religious views and doctrines on students, faith-based organizations, as social institutions, can participate in public school reform in a variety of ways.[36] They can partner with public schools and school districts in efforts to improve educational environments, processes, and outcomes.

For example, religious leaders can play an important role in educational reform and improvement in the United States by promoting greater understanding of and dialogue on educational issues among their congregants. Dryfoos contends that "church leaders definitely have 'bully pulpits' from which they are in a position to influence the thinking of their parishioners and congregants. They can help people understand the importance of assisting all children to overcome social, economic, racial, and other gender barriers to success."[37]

Faith-based organizations also can influence educational reform by working directly with schools to provide educational information to families. For example, many schools conduct workshops to promote families' understanding of the educational and socioemotional needs of their children at different stages of development. Family attendance at such workshops, however, often is low. Faith-based organizations and schools can create partnerships to ensure broader dissemination of the information provided at school workshops. The information can be summarized for families before, during, or after worship services, or videotapes of parenting workshops can be shown and discussed before or after services. Through such efforts, faith-based organizations and schools could provide larger numbers of parents and caretakers with valuable information on how to help their children become more successful in and out of school.

Faith-based organizations can affect students and public schools in other ways—for example, by providing college scholarships or recognizing the accomplishments of students, teachers, and school volunteers through award programs. Members of faith-based organizations also can act as volunteers in schools. Possible activities include phoning or visiting the homes of chronically absent students, participating on school improvement teams or committees, assisting with before- and after-school tutoring or enrichment activities, and volunteering labor and materials to renovate the school interior or exterior.

Faith-based organizations also can "adopt" schools or classrooms, providing supplies to students or books, computer software, science equipment, and other supplies to teachers.

In addition, faith-based organizations can contribute to educational reform by promoting their members' political awareness of legislation and policies that affect schools. They can do so by holding public forums in which school officials, state legislators, and school board members discuss their position and actions in regard to educational improvement. Faith-based organizations also can be "good neighbors" to schools by providing free space for school events and activities or simply by advertising and encouraging community participation in school meetings and events.

These partnership possibilities focus on secular educational goals and maintain religious neutrality, thereby complying with the establishment clause of the First Amendment of the U.S. Constitution. As further illustrated in the examples that follow, adherence to the principle of separation of church and state does not minimize the impact that such partnerships can have on educational reform and improvement.

EXAMPLES OF PARTNERSHIPS OF SCHOOLS AND FAITH-BASED ORGANIZATIONS

There is no "one size fits all" formula for school-community partnerships; the resources and objectives of the partners must guide the development of such collaborations. Descriptions of eight partnerships of schools and faith-based organizations are given below. The descriptions are not intended to be representative or exhaustive but simply to show the range of partnerships that currently exist in the United States.[38]

Alexandria, Virginia. The faith-based community and public elementary schools in Alexandria work together to tutor children in reading. A congregation-based coordinator recruits volunteer tutors and assists with scheduling; a school-based coordinator acts as the point of contact at the school. Classroom teachers identify children who need tutoring and assist coordinators with scheduling sessions. Tutoring materials and training for tutors is provided by the public schools. Tutors and students meet for three thirty-minute sessions per week.

Phoenix, Arizona. A coalition of faith-based communities and education associations in Phoenix uses America Goes Back to School, an initiative to encourage family and community involvement in schools, as a focal point each year to honor both current and retired teachers for their work on behalf of children and youth. Each participating religious community honors the teachers at its worship service; award certificates are presented later during a ceremony held at a central location.

Chicago, Illinois. The Chicago Public Schools Interfaith Community Partnership, a multicultural group of religious leaders, assists local schools in addressing issues such as student discipline, truancy and low attendance rates, school safety, and student and staff attitudes and interactions. The partnership provides crisis intervention services and workshops for parents, undertakes curriculum development in the area of character and values, and sponsors radio and television interviews with public school staff to promote Chicago public school initiatives.

Washington, D.C. Shiloh Baptist Church in Washington, D.C., established a learning center to teach critical thinking and problem-solving skills to children in grades four through eight by using a math-, science-, and computer-based curriculum. The center, which is staffed by both paid employees and volunteers, is open after school and during the evening. During the daytime, the center is used to teach adults job skills in a welfare-to-work program. The church also has established a reading tutorial program for children attending Seaton Elementary School and a program called the Male and Female Youth Enhancement Project. The project is designed to encourage healthy life-styles in African American youth between the ages of eight and fifteen by providing them with positive role models and educational and social activities.

The National Council of Churches. Each year, the National Council of Churches disseminates materials related to public education to its member denominations and congregations. The materials highlight education initiatives of the Partnership for Family Involvement in Education, urge local churches to participate in national educational projects such as the America Reads Challenge and America Goes Back to School, and list published resources available to local communities of faith.

Jackson, Tennessee. Ten churches in Jackson have designed a tutoring program in cooperation with the local school system to serve children residing in public housing. Three nights a week, church buses provide transportation to church facilities where 250 volunteers work with 350 children, helping them in reading and math. Volunteers from the tutoring program also raise funds to purchase school supplies and then operate a "store" where students can get school supplies.

The National Council of Jewish Women (NCJW) Center for the Child. The NCJW Center for the Child conducted the Parents as School Partners campaign, which included focus groups with parents, teachers, and principals to hear what parent involvement means to them and what they need to make school-parent partnerships work; surveys of school district superintendents regarding parent involvement policies and programs; a critical review of the research on parent involvement; and a compilation of material on promising school-based programs for enhancing parent involvement. They included the results of their efforts in a kit and disseminated the kits to school districts, teachers, parents, and advocates of parent involvement across the country.

Baltimore, Maryland. The Child First Authority (CFA) in Baltimore is a communitywide after-school program that seeks to improve the quality of life in low-income communities. The CFA, which is funded by the local government and coordinated by Baltimoreans United in Leadership Development (BUILD), established after-school programs in ten schools during its first year of operation. The schools become hubs of activity in which parents, staff, administrators, students, and church members work together to promote student achievement and socioemotional well-being.[39]

Promoting the Success of School Partnerships with Faith-Based Organizations

Because school-community partnerships are still in the emergent stage, comprehensive research on processes and outcomes of specific partnerships is relatively limited. However, available studies and descriptions suggest that at least three factors influence the effectiveness of school-community partnerships in general and partnerships between schools and faith-based organizations in particular. Those factors are a shared vision, clearly defined roles and responsibilities, and open communication.

Shared Vision

Research suggests that in order for successful partnerships to develop, participants must have a common vision.[40] When a shared vision exists, partnerships are more likely to develop in a manner that is satisfactory to all parties and to meet their stated goals. The need for a common vision is especially important in partnerships between schools and faith-based organizations because of the constitutional restrictions with which these organizations must comply.

For partnerships between public schools and faith-based organizations to thrive, participants on both sides must understand and accept the following principles:

—Under the First Amendment, public schools must be neutral concerning religion in all of their activities.

—Students have the right to engage in religious activities as long as they do not interfere with the rights of others, and they have the right not to engage in those activities.

—Cooperative programs between religious institutions and public schools are permissible only if participation in programs is not limited to religious groups and if students' grades, class ranking, or participation in any school program is not affected by their decision to participate or not participate in a cooperative program with a religious institution.

—Student participation in any cooperative program is not conditioned on membership in any religious group, acceptance or rejection of any religious belief, or participation (or refusal to participate) in any religious activity.[41]

Mutual understanding and acceptance of those principles helps to ensure that all stakeholders' rights are protected, especially those of the students for whom school-community partnerships are designed.

Clearly Defined Roles and Responsibilities

The literature on school-community partnerships also emphasizes the importance of clearly defined roles and responsibilities in successful collaborations.[42] All partners should understand what they are expected to contribute; without clearly defined expectations, misunderstandings can ensue that jeopardize the partnership's effectiveness. The need for clearly defined roles and responsibilities is not limited to but may be more pronounced in partnerships between faith-based organizations and public schools.

For example, in any community partnership in which privately owned facilities are used, it is critical to clarify the roles and responsibilities of individual parties regarding the preparation, use, maintenance, and supervision of the facilities. However, special arrangements may be required when schools use sanctuaries, playgrounds, libraries, or other facilities owned by religious groups, such as the removal of religious symbols or messages.[43] Successful partnerships between public schools and faith-based organizations must be aware of such requirements and determine who will be responsible for meeting them.

Open Communication

Open communication—the process through which shared visions are created and roles and responsibilities are articulated—is the foundation for any successful partnership.[44] It also is critical to carrying out other collaborative processes, including shared decisionmaking, conflict management, and reflection and evaluation.

Open communication also allows educational leaders and other community partners to express any concerns they may have about the motives and intentions of volunteers from religious organizations. According to one such volunteer, school officials often are afraid that volunteers from faith-based organizations seek involvement in public schools in order to proselytize. She commented that several public schools rejected overtures that her group made to volunteer time and resources to students because of their fears of blurring the separation of church and state.[45] If such concerns are to be dealt with effectively and fairly, open communication among all partners is necessary.

The success of partnerships between school and faith-based organizations rests on careful planning and implementation. In addition, all parties must have a common vision informed by a shared understanding of the principle of separation of church and state, and roles and responsibilities, especially as they relate to the use of religious facilities, must be clearly defined. Finally, educational and religious leaders must facilitate and engage in open communication to ensure that the perspectives, ideas, and concerns of all collaborative partners are heard and addressed.

CONCLUSION

Partnerships between public schools and faith-based organizations have tremendous potential to improve educational opportunities and outcomes for all students. However, as religious leaders work to identify common ground with public educators, they also must consider areas where their goals for children and youth are distinct and should remain distinct. In her theory of overlapping spheres of influence, Epstein argues that some goals for children and youth are best achieved through the collaborative efforts of adults in their families, schools, and communities.[46] The theory, however, also acknowledges the separate responsibilities to youth of each of these spheres.

Faith-based organizations, then, must identify when collaboration with public schools best meets their educational goals for youth and when strategies that do not include public schools would be more appropriate. For example, knowledge of religious tenets and texts contributes to the moral and intellectual development of youth. However, transmission of that knowledge by members of faith-based organizations may not be permissible or desirable in after-school or summer programs implemented in partnership with public schools. Religious organizations, however, can independently sponsor programs to provide children and youth with spiritual and moral instruction. Thus a major challenge for faith-based organizations committed to collaborating with public schools is to determine how to allocate time and resources in order to act both collaboratively and independently.

The nation is sure to face new and continuing challenges in extending equal educational opportunities to all children, irrespective of race, socioeconomic status, and linguistic background. Schools alone cannot adequately address all those challenges—families and communities also have an important role to play. Thoughtful collaboration among all parties is vital to ensure that schools are able to meet their fundamental obligation to provide all students with the tools necessary to be self-determining and productive citizens.

NOTES

1. National Center for Educational Statistics (NCES), *Digest of Education Statistics: 1999* (U.S. Department of Education, 1999).

2. Children's Defense Fund, "Comprehensive Immigrant Outreach through Building Community Partnerships," *Sign Them Up: A Quarterly Newsletter on the Children's Health Insurance Program*, Fall 2000.

3. NCES, *Digest of Education Statistics: 1999*.

4. S. M. Nettles, "Community Involvement and Disadvanaged Students: A Review," *Review of Educational Research*, vol. 61, no. 3 (1991), p. 380.

5. J. Epstein, "Toward a Theory of Family-School Connections: Teacher Practices and Parent Involvement," in K. Hurrelmann, F. Kaufmann, and F. Losel, eds., *Social Intervention: Potential and Constraints* (New York: DeGruyter, 1987), pp. 121–36.

6. S. B. Heath and M. W. McLaughlin, "A Child Resource Policy: Moving beyond Dependence on School and Family," *Phi Delta Kappan*, vol. 68 (April 1987), p. 579.

7. R. Shore, *Moving the Ladder: Toward a New Community Vision* (Aspen, Colo.: Aspen Institute, 1994), p. 2.

8. S. A. Waddock, *Not by Schools Alone: Sharing Responsibility for America's Education Reform* (Westport, Conn.: Praeger, 1995).

9. See C. Ascher, Urban School-Community Alliances (New York: ERIC Clearinghouse on Urban Education, 1988); M. Sanders, "A Study of the Role of 'Community' in Comprehensive School, Family, and Community Partnership Programs," *Elementary School Journal* (forthcoming).

10. Sanders, "A Study of the Role of 'Community.'"

11. J. M. McPartland and S. M. Nettles, "Using Community Adults as Advocates or Mentors for At-Risk Middle School Students: A Two-Year Evaluation of Project RAISE," *American Journal of Education*, vol. 99 (1991), pp. 568–86; S. Yonezawa, T. Thornton, and S. Stringfield, *Dunbar-Hopkins Health Partnership Phase II Evaluation: Preliminary Report—Year One* (Baltimore: Center for Social Organization of Schools, 1998).

12. B. A. Beyerbach and others, "A School/Business/University Partnership for Professional Development," *School Community Journal*, vol. 6, no. 1 (1996), pp. 101–12.

13. L. Newman, "School-Agency-Community Partnerships: What Is the Early Impact on Students' School Performance?" paper presented at the annual meeting of the American Educational Research Association (AERA), San Francisco, April 1995; M. Wagner, "What Is the Evidence of Effectiveness of School-Linked Services?" *The Evaluation Exchange: Emerging Strategies in Evaluating Child and Family Services*, vol. 1, no. 2 (1995), pp. 1–2.

14. C. Amato, "Freedom Elementary School and Its Community: An Approach to School-Linked Service Integration," *Remedial and Special Education*, vol. 17, no. 5 (1996), pp. 303–09.

15. S. M. Nettles, "Community Contributions to School Outcomes of African-American Students," *Education and Urban Society*, vol. 24, no. 1 (1991), pp. 132–47.

16. T. Longoria Jr., "School Politics in Houston: The Impact of Business Involvement," in C. Stone, ed., *Changing Urban Education* (University Press of Kansas, 1998), pp. 184–98; T. Mickelson, "International Business Machinations: A Case Study of Corporate Involvement in Local Educational Reform," *Teachers College Record*, vol. 100, no. 3 (1999), pp. 476–512; M. G. Sanders and A. Harvey, "Developing Comprehensive Programs of School, Family, and Community Partnerships: The Community Perspective," paper presented at the annual meeting of the AERA, New Orleans, April 2000.

17. A. Bryk, V. Lee, and P. Holland, *Catholic Schools and the Common Good* (Harvard University Press, 1993), p. 18.

18. W. Jordan, *White over Black: American Attitudes toward the Negro, 1550–1812* (Penguin Books, 1968).

19. A. Billingsley, *Climbing Jacob's Ladder: The Enduring Legacy of African-American Families* (Simon and Schuster, 1992).

20. Bryk, Lee, and Holland, *Catholic Schools.*

21. R. Pounds and J. Bryner, *The School in American Society* (Macmillan, 1967).

22. A. Billingsley and C. Caldwell, "The Church, the Family, and the School in the African American Community," *Journal of Negro Education*, vol. 60, no. 2 (1991), 427–40.

23. C. E. Lincoln and L. H. Mamiya, *The Black Church in the African American Experience* (Duke University Press, 1990).

24. J. Coleman, "Families and Schools," *Educational Researcher*, vol. 16, no. 6 (1987), pp. 32–38.

25. M. Argyle and B. Beit-Hallahmi, *The Social Psychology of Religion* (Boston: Routledge and Kegan Paul, 1975); S. L. Hansen and A. L. Ginsburg, "Gaining Ground: Values and High School Success," *American Educational Research Journal*, vol. 25 (1988), 334–65.

26. Nettles, "Community Contributions to School Outcomes of African-American Students"; V. Lapoint, "Accepting Community Responsibility for African American Youth Education and Socialization," *Journal of Negro Education*, vol. 61, no. 4 (1992), 451–54.

27. F. S. Blau, *Black Children/White Children: Competence, Socialization, and Social Structure* (Free Press, 1981).

28. D. Brown and L. Gary, "Religious Socialization and Educational Attainment among African Americans: An Empirical Assessment," *Journal of Negro Education*, vol. 60, no. 3 (1991), pp.411–26.

29. R. B. Freeman, "Who Escapes? The Relation of Church-Going and Other Background Factors to the Socio-Economic Performance of Black Male Youths from Inner-City Tracts," in R. B. Freeman and H. J. Holzer, eds., *The Black Youth Employment Crisis* (University of Chicago Press, 1986); M. Sanders, "The Effects of School, Family, and Community Support on the Academic Achievement of African-American Adolescents," *Urban Education*, vol. 33, no. 3, pp. 384–409; M. Sanders and J. Herting, "Gender and the Effects of School, Family, and Church Support on the Academic Achievement of African-American Urban Adolescents," in M. Sanders, ed., *Schooling, Students Placed at Risk: Research, Policy, and Practice in the Education of Poor and Minority Adolescents* (Mahwah, N.J.: Lawrence Erlbaum, 2000).

30. R. Galindo and K. Escamilla, "A Biographical Perspective on Chicano Educational Success," *Urban Review*, vol. 27, no. 1 (1995), p. 11.

31. W. Smith, "Religious Diversity in the Schools: Christian Fundamentalism, Educational Reform, and the Schools," paper presented at the Management Institute, Hilton Head, S.C., February 1994.

32. Smith, "Religious Diversity in the Schools"; G. Michel, "Religious Diversity in the Schools—The Overview," paper presented at the Management Institute, Hilton Head, S.C., February 1994.

33. Waddock, *Not by Schools Alone*; J. Epstein, "School/Family/Community Partnerships: Caring for the Children We Share," *Phi Delta Kappan*, vol. 79, no. 9 (1995), pp. 701–12.

34. *Public Schools and Religious Communities: A First Amendment Guide* (Annandale, Va.: American Jewish Congress, Christian Legal Society, and the First Amendment Center, Vanderbilt University, 1999), p. 1.

35. Partnership for Family Involvement in Education, *Faith Communities Joining with Local Communities to Support Children's Learning: Good Ideas* (U.S. Department of Education, 1999); American Jewish Congress and others, *Public Schools and Religious Communities.*

36. Partnership for Family Involvement in Education, *Faith Communities Joining with Local Communities*; D. Shirley, *Community Organizing for Urban School Reform* (University of Texas Press, 1997); Waddock, *Not by Schools Alone.*

37. J. Dryfoos, *Safe Passage: Making It through Adolescence in a Risky Society* (New York: Oxford University Press, 1998).

38. Unless otherwise indicated, the partnership examples described are taken from Partnership for Family Involvement in Education, *Faith Communities Joining with Local Communities.*

39. O. Fashola, *The Child First Authority After-School Program,* Report 38 (Baltimore: Center for Research on the Education of Students Placed at Risk, 1999).

40. B. Hopkins and F. Wendel, *Creating School-Community-Business Partnerships* (Bloomington, Ind.: Phi Delta Kappan Educational Foundation, 1997); M. Walsh, D. Andersson, and M. Smyer, "A School-Community-University Partnership," in T. Chibucos and R. Lerner, eds., *Serving Children and Families through Community-University Partnerships: Success Stories* (Norwell, Mass.: Kluwer Academic, 1999), pp. 183–90.

41. American Jewish Congress and others, *Public Schools and Religious Communities.*

42. Epstein, "School/Family/Community Partnerships"; J. L. Epstein and others, *School, Family, Community Partnerships: Your Handbook for Action* (Thousand Oaks, Calif.: Corwin, 1997).

43. American Jewish Congress and others, *Public Schools and Religious Communities.*

44. B. Gray, *Collaborating: Finding Common Ground for Multiparty Systems* (San Francisco: Jossy-Bass, 1991); C. Nasworthy and M. Rood, *Bridging the Gap between Business and Education; Reconciling Expectations for Student Achievement* (Washington: Office of Educational Reseach and Improvement, 1990).

45. Sanders and Harvey, "Developing Comprehensive Programs of School, Family, and Community Partnerships."

46. Epstein, "School/Family/Community Partnerships."

CHAPTER TEN

Faith-Based Organizations and Public Education Reform

DENNIS SHIRLEY

If you like paradoxes, you'll love the ones you'll find in an analysis of church-state relations in the United States. This country generally upholds the strictest separation of church and state among western democracies, with the possible exception of France. Yet it is here in the United States that citizens are most religious, in terms of their expressed beliefs, and most observant, in terms of their participation in religious institutions. Research consistently documents the socially beneficial effects of religious belief and practice, particularly for children, but strategies derived from those findings are handicapped because of the manner in which the First Amendment has been interpreted to erect a "wall" between church and state. Research indicates that some programs that have a clear evangelical mission and are run by community members (such as Teen Challenge) result in more positive outcomes than secular programs run by experts. And in spite of the Supreme Court's consistent rulings on "no aid to religion" since 1947 in *Everson* v. *Board of Education*, one recent survey found that 63 percent of religiously affiliated nonprofits receive more than 20 percent of their budgets from public funds.[1]

What is different about President Bush's new undertaking? The Bush administration has offered much more financial backing for faith-based initiatives than did the Clinton administration; further, by creating the White House Office of Faith-Based and Community Initiatives within the first fortnight of his term in his office, Bush sent a clear signal that the office forms an important part of his social policy. Can the federal government enhance the valuable resources that religious institutions have to offer schools and communities while minimizing possible negative consequences? How might we go about designing policies to enable faith-based organizations to play a powerful role in addressing social problems without trampling on the rights of religious minorities, atheists, or agnostics?

My focus in this chapter is on faith-based organizations and public schools. The U.S. Department of Education is one of five cabinet agencies that will have a center for faith-based and community initiatives. In the president's public statement defining the mandate of the Office of Faith-Based and Community Initiatives, the brief reference to the public schools is enigmatic. According to the text, "the Center in the Department of Education will be concerned with the agency's social programs, such as after-school programs and efforts to link public schools with community partners, including neighborhood faith-based groups. It will not work on K–12 or higher education policy as such." Yet as is clear to all parties, increasing department of education collaboration with and funding for faith-based groups will have policy ramifications. One of the major challenges for the new office will be to clarify those ramifications, including the likelihood of litigation on issues pertaining to the separation of church and state.[2]

I will comment briefly on the actual wording of the establishment clause of the First Amendment, note some historical realities pertaining to American public education, and suggest some reasons that faith-based groups should be given real opportunities to work with public schools. To ground the discussion in the real world, I turn to two examples of collaborations that demonstrate the capacity of churches to improve public schools. With those cases in mind, I then articulate some caveats pertaining to such collaborations.

My conclusion is one of cautious optimism. One must recognize from the very outset that there *are* dangers in collaboration between public schools and faith-based organizations. Concerns about proselytizing or coercion are legitimate and must be heard. However, it is my impression that there is a capacious middle way that has worked well in the past and can continue to serve us well in the future. Religious institutions have received resources in the past to provide social services—for example, through Head Start and after-school programs in urban churches—and there is no compelling reason why such efforts should not be continued and expanded when they reach populations in need and contribute to the public good. As much as possible, however, resources should not be provided directly to religious institutions but should be channeled through schools and affiliated nonprofit organizations that have a history of working successfully with government agencies and achieving desirable social outcomes.

THE FIRST AMENDMENT AND THE
HISTORY OF AMERICAN EDUCATION

A primary value of the study of history is that it awakens one to the relativity of contemporary attitudes by revealing widely varying assumptions from previous eras. If one looks at the wording of the First Amendment to the Constitution, one discovers an important demarcation: "*Congress* shall make no law respecting an establishment of religion, or prohibiting the free exercise thereof. . . ." The emphasis is my own, and it is intended to highlight a critical and often overlooked feature of the amendment. The wording was chosen to delimit the role of the *federal* government in establishing a national religion. There was universal agreement at the time that individual states could establish their own state religions if they so elected, and only Virginia and Rhode Island declined to do so at the time of the founding of the republic.[3]

One should note that the Constitution articulates no role for the federal government in education. Responsibilities for educating citizens are specified in each state constitution. It was not until 1947 that the Supreme Court determined that the establishment clause applied not only to the federal government but also to state and local governments, thereby broadening the First Amendment.[4]

A brief review of the history of American education reveals a tremendous interplay between religious groups and the schools. All of the first schools in British North America had religious origins, whether they were founded in Puritan Massachusetts, Quaker Pennsylvania, Catholic Maryland, or Anglican Virginia. New York City's earliest public schools were funded through a mix of public and private revenues and run by Protestant church groups. In a recent essay in the *History of Education Quarterly*, Siobhan Moroney contrasts twentieth-century historians' celebration of the separation of church and state in American educational history with a close reading of numerous primary documents from the late eighteenth and early nineteenth century. She found that modern historians have distorted the past by emphasizing the innovation entailed in Jefferson and Madison's articulations of a separation between church and state and neglecting the many statements in the popular press throughout the early republic that held religious education in the schools to be an integral part of a proper upbringing.[5]

The United States has, of course, undergone multiple revolutions since the framing of the Constitution and since the public schools were established. The nation is in many ways far more complex today, and there should be little doubt that Jefferson's language about "a wall of separation between Church and State" has often helped to protect the rights of religious minorities, agnostics, and atheists. Nonetheless, given current assumptions, it is important to recall that the separation of church and state is not an absolute value but a relative one that has undergone many revisions throughout U.S. history and that might experience further revision in the current context.[6]

President Bush's recent policy initiative made no reference to public support of private schools, and opposition to his proposed legislation concerning vouchers appears to have defeated that part of his platform. We are left, then, with a fairly simple truth: Americans like public schools, and they want their public schools to be as good as they can make them. Hence, the focus of discussions of faith-based organizations working with schools should be exactly where the President has placed it: on public schools.[7]

Are there ways out of these conundrums—strategies that can be used to engage faith-based organizations in improving public schools and promoting desired student outcomes while respecting the First Amendment? I submit that there are—that there is a balanced, middle-ground approach to improving public education through collaboration with faith-based organizations.

ORGANIZING FAITH-BASED GROUPS TO IMPROVE PUBLIC SCHOOLS

There is an extensive base of research on family and community partnerships that promote high levels of student achievement, especially in schools and neighborhoods that lack adequate resources.[8] The research on faith-based organizations' participation in efforts to improve public schools, however, is meager. We know that there are broad-based coalitions of churches, synagogues, and mosques throughout the country, such as the Chicago Public Schools Interfaith Community Partnership, the Ten Point Coalition in Boston, and the Interdenominational Ministerial Alliance in St. Petersburg, Florida, that have come together to establish innovative after-school, literacy, and youth-mentoring programs. We do not know whether there is a "faith factor" that makes the above-named initiatives any more successful than more orthodox strategies of school improvement, which might focus on the professional development of teachers or collaborations with the business community.

We do know that collaboration in and of itself is no magic bullet. Collaborations often break down because of rigidity on the part of one or more participants, differences of temperament among community leaders, and unclear goals. We have little reason to believe that collaborations of faith-based organizations and schools escape those problems, any more than collaborations with business partners or parent groups.

There is, nevertheless, evidence that congregations can be powerful allies with schools in the struggle to create a safe environment for urban youth and to provide them with a high-quality education. I would like to turn to my own research, which has followed a number of schools in low-income communities in Texas over the last decade, to present two case studies of schools that have worked productively with faith-based organizations allied with the Industrial Areas Foundation (IAF) to improve academic achievement in low-income communities serving children of color. These case studies are intended to whet the appetite of readers who suspect that much *could* be done to develop powerful collaborations between religious institutions and schools, but who have few real-world examples to verify that hunch.

It is important to note that the IAF construes itself primarily as a *political* organization that works to mobilize a broad base of stakeholders. Each IAF organization relies primarily on dues paid by congregations to support community organizers, staff, and overhead. Since the 1970s, the IAF has focused on organizing congregations, as the names of its individual groups suggest: the El Paso Interreligious Sponsoring Organization, Valley Interfaith, Dallas Area Interfaith, and so forth. The IAF consists of organizers, who are paid staff, and leaders, who are drawn from congregations and other IAF-affiliated institutions, such as unions or schools, and are not paid.[9]

The first case study concerns Morningside Middle School in Fort Worth, Texas. In the mid-1980s, Morningside was in a state of crisis. The principal of the school had his jaw broken in a playground scuffle, and when he resigned and a new principal came in, her office was firebombed on the first day of classes. Morningside ranked twentieth of the twenty middle schools in Fort Worth on the state standardized test of achievement in 1985.

The new principal, Odessa Ravin, recognized that she would have to do something dramatic if she was going to turn Morningside around. On her own initiative she began a campaign in the African American churches of South Fort Worth, introducing herself to congregations on Sunday mornings and stating frankly that she was frightened of her new responsibility and needed help. At the same time, the local IAF group, the Allied Communities of Tarrant (ACT), was exploring the possibility of improving an urban school. When ACT organizers and leaders heard about Ravin's outreach efforts, a partnership seemed imminent. One of ACT's primary leaders, Reverend Nehemiah Davis of Mount Pisgah Missionary Baptist Church, recalled that "not only did Mrs. Ravin have a very positive attitude toward parental involvement, but she had already been out visiting churches in the community and beating on our doors, *asking* us to get involved. I don't know anyone else who was such a pathbreaker in this area as she was."

Reverend Davis, Ravin, ACT organizers Mignonne Konecny and Perry Perkins, and clergy and lay leaders from ACT congregations such as the First

Missionary Baptist Church and the Community Baptist Church then began making home visits to the parents of all of the students in Morningside Middle School. During the visits, ACT leaders and organizers urged parents to attend upcoming school assemblies to discuss ways in which they could engage with the middle school. "People were incensed by the firebombing, and they wanted to react," Reverend C. M. Singleton of First Missionary Baptist recalled. ACT was careful not to dictate the terms of engagement, however. "We told our leaders not to attempt to answer the parents' questions," Reverend Davis said, "but just to keep them talking. We wanted them to answer their own questions."

The home visits and subsequent assemblies gradually transformed Morningside from a school with no ties to the community to a fulcrum of parental engagement. Many parents had never understood their children's actual course of study or how their children were assessed. ACT leaders held sessions to teach parents about the structure of the school and to advise them of ways that they could reinforce school activities at home. Parents contributed by volunteering to provide extra attention to children with special needs and to read aloud to small groups in the library, and they shared their concerns at staff development workshops. "Just being able to talk to a teacher, when they had never done that before, meant a lot to the parents," Reverend Singleton recalled, "and it meant even more when the teachers made an effort to reach out to talk with them." Teresa Chaney, who had taught at Morningside for nine years, was amazed at the transformation. "Parental involvement was almost nonexistent before," she said. "I've seen more parents this year than in all the years I've taught."

ACT and Morningside Middle School received the first major indication that home visits, training sessions, and parental engagement were paying off in December 1988. At that time Ravin, Reverend Davis, Reverend Singleton, and all of the parents and teachers who had been involved in shaping the new school climate learned that the middle school had moved from last place to third among Fort Worth's twenty middle schools on the state standardized achievement test. The percentage of students who passed the reading, writing, and math sections of the test had climbed from 34 to 71 percent from 1986 to 1988. Previously, 50 percent of the students were failing one subject; in 1988 only 6 percent were in that category.

A similar story can be told of Sam Houston Elementary School in McAllen, Texas, in the early 1990s. Like Morningside, Sam Houston served a low-income community; also like Morningside, the school suffered from low test scores on state standardized tests. Unlike Morningside, Sam Houston served predominantly Mexican American rather than African American students, and the town was close to the border with Mexico, which made it a natural point of entry for immigrants crossing the Rio Grande. Whereas black Baptist churches

predominated in South Fort Worth, most McAllen residents attended the one
large Catholic Church, Saint Joseph the Worker, on the south side of town.

If the transformation of Morningside Middle School began with Odessa
Ravin's unprecedented outreach to faith-based organizations in Fort Worth, the
revitalization of Sam Houston can truly be said to have been sparked by the leaders at Saint Joseph the Worker. Father Bart Flaat assumed leadership of Saint
Joseph's in 1991 after working closely with an IAF group in San Antonio, Communities Organized for Public Services (COPS), and learning about congregation-based community organizing strategies. At that time Saint Joseph's was
considered a "sleeping member" of the IAF group in the lower border region,
Valley Interfaith. Yet Father Bart sensed a hunger for change among many individuals with whom he had his first contacts in the parish, and he began a series of meetings in the homes of parishioners in the barrios of La Paloma,
Hermosa, Balboa, Alta Linda, and Los Encinos. "Basically, I asked them to tell
me two things," Father Bart said, "first their stories, and second, their dreams. I
wanted to know what they hoped for and what they dreamed for. And once they
had told me that, I had a pretty good agenda."

The parishioners of Saint Joseph's wanted a lively religious community that
enriched their Catholicism, so Father Bart began to establish *comunidades de
base*, or base communities, throughout his parish where they could engage in
Bible study, relating scripture to their own lives. In addition to having religious
yearnings, parishioners wanted improved public schools.

Through his previous work with the IAF, Father Bart knew of several successful efforts to turn around struggling schools in Texas. After Morningside's
transformation in the 1980s, IAF organizations throughout Texas had begun to
nurture collaborations with schools. By 1992 twenty-one schools throughout
the state were ready to form a network of "Alliance schools" with the Texas Education Agency (TEA) and the IAF's community organizations. The Alliance
schools received a limited amount of funding directly from the TEA to promote
parent participation in the schools, and they also received waivers of a number
of mandates that stifled innovation.[10]

Father Bart was intrigued with the development of the Alliance schools. He
and Sister Maria Sanchez began to meet with all school principals in south
McAllen and all school board members to identify schools that could join the
new network. When the Texas IAF organized a large statewide conference for
prospective Alliance schools in Houston in January 1994, representatives of six
of the eight public schools in south McAllen attended.

One of the principals in south McAllen was Connie Maheshwari. Married
to an Indian immigrant, Maheshwari is the daughter of Carmen Anaya, one of
the most powerful leaders in Valley Interfaith and a major force in bringing in-

frastucture improvements to unincorporated rural communities called *colonias* in the 1980s. Maheshwari was the principal of Sam Houston, and she instantly saw the Alliance school network as an opportunity for her school.

Unlike at Morningside, however, some of the teachers at Sam Houston expressed reluctance to work with the Texas IAF. Morningside teachers had been so traumatized by the school's low test scores, the chaos in the hallways, and the firebombing of the principal's office that they were desperate for help from any quarter to regain control of the school. While Sam Houston had low test scores and a fatal shoot-out between a youth and the police in South McAllen in the summer of 1993 had frightened families throughout the barrios, they were not sure that Valley Interfaith would help them solve their problems. Part of the teachers' hesitation was caused by fear of losing their professional autonomy. "Teachers are afraid that Valley Interfaith is going to come in and tell them what to do," Maheshwari said. "This is a real fear." Some teachers worried also about the religious dimension of Valley Interfaith, while others were anxious about its political nature.

It took Maheshwari several months to persuade her faculty that the Alliance school concept represented a calculated risk; the upside was that it could benefit their students by improving the relationship between the home and the school. Sam Houston became the first Alliance school in McAllen in April 1994. Valley Interfaith organizers then began working closely with faculty and parents to develop leadership in the community. Mentored by Sister Pearl Ceasar and Estela Sosa-Garza of Valley Interfaith, teachers and staff at Sam Houston began learning the nuts and bolts of organizing in the summer and fall of 1994. They learned how to conduct "one-on-ones"—an IAF term for individual meetings that quickly but respectfully identify individuals' major political issues. They learned how to do "power analyses" of the community in order to understand issues of accountability and control. Finally, they learned how to conduct "research actions" with public officials to identify latent resources, such as money or human resources, that could be used to attack the problems that confronted their community.

Throughout the fall and winter of 1994 Valley Interfaith organizers, Sam Houston teachers, and community residents conducted scores of house meetings in the neighborhood surrounding Sam Houston. A host of issues was brought to the table. Parents complained about poor lighting and lack of supervision in the numerous back alleys that students took to and from school. Others worried about abandoned houses close to Sam Houston where teenagers met to sell and use drugs. Many parents, especially single mothers, were concerned because they had to work full time and had no way to supervise their children in the late afternoon. Other parents were worried simply about the abundance of trash—old tires, broken glass, rain-soaked mattresses—that littered the streets and alleys around the school and seemed to escape the attention of city sanitation workers. Teachers who attended the house meetings and parents who were active in the school shared their concerns about the crumbling physical infrastructure of the school and the persistent presence of rats in the classrooms and cafeteria, and they expressed their hope for a new building.

Working closely with Valley Interfaith, Sam Houston teachers and parents established task forces to research and address each of the issues presented. Valley Interfaith organizers suggested that parents might be able to acquire the funds needed for an after-school program from McAllen's Department of Parks and Recreation. They helped parents to understand that it was important to initiate a relationship with the police and to work together to target high-crime areas if they wanted greater security in the neighborhood. The organizers also helped parents and teachers to comprehend that they could develop the political clout necessary to redirect city and school revenues to improve their school and community in each area of concern.

The momentum that was being generated by all of the "one-on-ones," house meetings, and task-force undertakings began to build to a peak in January 1995, when the community worked with Valley Interfaith to prepare a large public assembly—which participants called the Kids' Action Assembly—to create a climate of greater community accountability for the children. Sosa-Garza worked closely with parents and teachers as they engaged in role-playing to rehearse the statements they wanted to make and the questions they wished to address to public officials. According to IAF community organizing traditions, even if public officials have agreed to work with the community, those agreements must be made public. Large gatherings such as the Kids' Action Assembly demonstrate to the community the progress that it has made through months of political organizing, and they also demonstrate the leadership abilities that community residents have developed.

Parents, teachers, and Valley Interfaith organizers invited numerous public officials to come to the assembly, which was scheduled for February 1995, to commit themselves to improving educational conditions. Officials such as the chief of police, the director of the department of parks and recreation, the city manager, city commissioners, the superintendent of schools, and school board members were informed in advance of the nature of the assembly and the kinds of questions that they would be asked. When the evening of the Kids' Action Assembly finally arrived, more than 300 parents from the school attended—a theretofore unprecedented gathering of the community on behalf of its children. Entertainment was provided by the McAllen High School mariachi band, creating a festive atmosphere in the school cafeteria. Then Raquel Guzman, a teacher, gave the introduction in English, and David Gomez, a parent, repeated it in Spanish. Public officials heard parent leaders such as Delia Villarreal, Christina Fuentes, and David Gomez, as well as teachers such as Leticia Casas, Raquel Guzman, and Mary Vela describe the problems in the neighborhood. Speaking in both Spanish and English, the parents and teachers committed themselves to working together and to demanding accountability from their civic leaders.

The Kids' Action Assembly played a pivotal role in the history of Sam Houston Elementary School. For the first time, members of the community saw a host of leaders made up of their friends and neighbors seeking a new relationship with public officials and getting results. As a consequence of the meeting, the city department of parks and recreation agreed to fund an after-school program, which enrolled more than 200 children in its first year. A police substation was opened closer to the school, and additional officers were assigned to patrol the area. City commissioners made sure that the trash in the alleys near the school was cleaned up, and additional lighting was installed. And to make sure that the community developed its own capacity to improve its children's education, parents at Sam Houston signed a "parent contract" in which they agreed to ask their children over dinner about their day in school and to insist that homework be done punctually.

Valley Interfaith's efforts in Sam Houston paid off in the spring of 1998, when the South McAllen community learned that students' academic achievement on the state's standardized test was so high that the school would be rated "exemplary"—the highest designation the state school system conferred. In the following years, Sam Houston teachers and parents worked together to develop an innovative curriculum, to engage students in a "mini-society" program to learn everyday citizenship skills, and to focus on academic achievement. As with Morningside Middle School, the collaboration with the IAF paid off handsomely, and it led to an increase in the number of Alliance schools in the Rio Grande Valley in ensuing years.

PROMISES

One promising facet of collaboration between faith-based organizations and public schools relates to the use of religious assets in poor communities, which orthodox school improvement strategies entirely exclude. Poor people in urban neighborhoods tend not to view schools as community resources. Everything from the warning signs on the front doors to the sign-in sheets at the front desk tells parents that the school's relationship with the community is ambivalent. Consider the very different relationship of a religious institution in a poor community, which must earn the community's trust if it is to survive. It should not be surprising that the Bush initiative generally has been received more favorably by low-income Americans than their more affluent counterparts or that African Americans and Hispanics have been more responsive than whites.[11]

The second promising facet is that religious institutions offer a concentration of people who do not have to be recruited individually, who already have some cohesion based on their faith and its rituals. When schools go about recruiting parents to assist in their child's learning, the almost-universal strategy tends to be restricted to using students as conveyors of messages. Students bring home slips of paper inviting parents to PTA meetings, school dinners, sports events, and cultural activities. Yet the message of the importance of parental participation is much more powerful when it is reinforced by religious leaders. Individuals such as Reverend Davis in Forth Wort and Father Flaat in McAllen became community organizers as well as preachers of the gospel.

A third promising facet of partnerships of faith-based organizations and public schools is the element of faith itself. Disagreeable as it may be to many secular Americans, the notion of civic engagement as a good in its own right lacks meaning for many Americans who are looking for deeper beliefs to guide their lives and imbue them with them moral purpose. When Morningside religious leaders established the practice of praising during church services students whose school work had improved, or when Father Bart established base communities that reflected on the challenges in McAllen's barrios in light of Christian ethics, individuals were able to transcend purely political motivations to tap the deeper wellsprings of faith, which in turn served as a catalyst for civic engagement.

Perils

The most common peril facing collaborations of faith-based organizations and schools involves trepidation that laity or clergy will use the occasion to proselytize. In the cases elaborated above, that problem did not surface. The clergy and laity who worked in Morningside and Sam Houston respected the civic mission of the public schools and were more concerned with helping the schools to succeed than they were with evangelical activities. Alliance schools draw on the social capital of a community to improve learning; although clergy and laity may be driven by their faith to work in schools, that faith becomes channeled into educational activities that do not have an overt religious content, easily avoiding the courts' concern with government funding of pervasively sectarian organizations.

Having said that, I also should say that I have observed departures from that general respect for avoiding any religious references in working with public schools. For example, I was a presenter at an Alliance school conference held in Houston in February 2000. In a remarkable acknowledgment of the contribution of the Alliance schools to public education, the district had turned over an entire day of obligatory professional development for teachers to the Metropolitan Organization, the IAF group in Houston. The day's activities began with a prayer by a minister who concluded with the statement "in Jesus' name we pray." No one protested. If a teacher had protested—objecting either to the specifically Christian nature of the prayer or prayer itself as part of teachers' professional development activities—then the district would have had to acknowledge the legitimacy of the teacher's objections. At issue here is the specifically Christian nature of the prayer, along with the fact that attendance was mandatory—public school teachers could opt out only with a loss of pay. One should keep in mind also that Texas is a "right to work"—that is, largely nonunionized—state, so that dissident teachers do not have the same protections as teachers in northern cities with strong union contracts.

A second kind of peril relates to teachers' concerns at Sam Houston that their professional autonomy could be compromised through collaboration with a faith-based group like Valley Interfaith. I observed little of that effect during my field studies in Alliance schools. However, there were some noteworthy cases. In one middle school, after an assistant principal urged teachers to support Valley Interfaith's agenda during a team meeting, the teachers later expressed resentment. "This really isn't part of our job," one seasoned teacher complained. Members of faith-based organizations and their allies will need to be sensitive to teachers' concerns if they are to convince them that they are not subtly undermining their professional autonomy.

A third peril relates to goal displacement, in the sense of losing focus on the issues that relate directly to children's learning. The civic activism involved in meeting with city council members, attending school board meetings, and gaining media publicity can be thrilling for parents and teachers who had felt excluded from the political process before. Yet teachers and parents have to make sure that those activities are kept in balance with the daily challenges of teaching children to read, do mathematical problems accurately, and learn critical thinking skills. Without a constant return to the core activities of their profession, teachers can be viewed by their colleagues as having a wavering commitment to the central tasks of their educational mission.

Faith-based organizations have their own concerns about working in schools. One sad outcome of the Morningside story is that once the school had turned around and achieved public recognition, Allied Communities of Tarrant was edged to the margins. The principal placed more emphasis on orthodox strategies of teacher professional development than on community engagement, and

ACT leaders and organizers began withdrawing from the school. Some of the clergy and laity who had been most engaged in the transformation of Morningside felt that their work was completed and were ready to pass leadership of the school to the principal and teachers, but others felt that they had earned a right to continue to shape Morningside's culture, and they were disappointed as their influence waned. When I last visited Morningside in 1999, the new principal and her colleagues in ACT said that the school's collaboration with faith-based institutions had collapsed and would need to be revived again, almost from scratch. Clearly if schools would like to collaborate with faith-based institutions, they will need to commit to long-term relationships rather than call on churches only when they are most desperate for short-term assistance.

I regret that I am not in a better position to comment on one prevalent fear: many religious leaders worry that collaboration with public schools and other government agencies may undermine their autonomy. That is part of the grand "civil society" debate, with some (such as Theda Skocpol) arguing that government traditionally has worked well with voluntary associations and others (such as Melissa Rogers) suggesting that collaboration between faith-based organizations and government is "the wrong way to do right" because it will "diminish religion's prophetic witness, which sometimes includes the obligation to criticize those in power."[12]

Perhaps one way to circumvent the problem would be to channel government resources not to faith-based organizations, but to public schools and nonprofit organizations that maintain partnerships with faith-based organizations.

CONCLUSION

Religious institutions have tremendous potential to help improve public schools, and I greet the growing interest in exploring that potential with enthusiasm. I write this as a thoroughly secular person who was convinced through my research on Alliance schools that faith-based institutions provide a remarkable resource not only for school and community improvement, but also for moral uplift and inspiration. There must be real guidance and reflection about these matters so that the collaborative efforts made possible by the White House Office of Faith-Based and Community Initiatives will not be misdirected.

What is needed? First of all, it is time to establish a kind of national clearinghouse to help schools and congregations determine optimal ways to work together as well as identify potentially destructive kinds of relationships to be avoided. The First Amendment Center at Vanderbilt University provides an important public service by producing clear guidelines to help teachers understand how they can teach about religion in school while respecting the diversity of religious traditions. A similar center could be established to help public schools and congregations identify the best ways to work together to support student learning.

To establish guidelines, practitioners need examples to help them understand the possibilities for fruitful collaborations with schools. Hence a research base should be established to document the kind of work that is now going on between faith-based institutions and schools. The information should be expressed in a reader-friendly format that avoids social science jargon and resonates with teachers, parents, congregations, and clergy. Most of the work is local, and little is documented. Here is a field of inquiry that is relatively open and that should be supported through grants from philanthropic organizations and government agencies.

There is an extensive literature relating to school and community partnerships that can be drawn on in conducting this research. Collaborations break down or fail to reach their potential for a multitude of reasons. Teachers' preservice professional training typically neglects the theme of community collaboration. While administrators usually have some academic preparation in this area, it almost always excludes the kinds of relationships that can be forged with religious institutions. Clergy and congregations, for their part, are likely to be mystified by the bureaucratic mandates imposed on schools, which do so much to shape the schools' culture. Hence, technical assistance on a wide variety of levels is called for.[13]

My own preference is to fund faith-based and community initiatives as much as possible through entities like public schools and nonprofit organizations that have a history of working with government agencies and are not faith-based organizations themselves. Not only does that circumvent litigation, which can easily cripple innovative social policies, it also ensures that faith-based and community initiatives remain connected to the schools. Finally, it also should reassure those clergy and congregations that are eager to contribute additional resources to their communities but also want to maintain a mediated rather than a direct relationship with the federal government.

NOTES

1. Barry A. Kosmin and Seymour P. Lachman, *One Nation Under God: Religion in Contemporary American Society* (New York: Harmony, 1993), p. 280; Norman Garmezy, "Stressors of Childhood," in Norman Garmezy and Micahel Rutter, eds., *Stress, Coping, and Development in Children* (New York: McGraw-Hill, 1983), pp. 43–84; Charles L. Glenn, *The Ambiguous Embrace: Government and Faith-Based Schools and Social Agencies* (Princeton University Press, 2000); Stephen Monsma, *When Sacred and Secular Mix* (Lanham, Md.: Rowman and Littlefield, 1996), p. 68.

2. George W. Bush, "Rallying the Armies of Compassion" (www.whitehouse.org [February 2001]). The four other agencies to have a Center for Faith-Based and Community

Initiatives are the Department of Health and Human Services, the Department of Housing and Urban Development, the Department of Labor, and the Department of Justice.

3. James W. Fraser, *Between Church and State: Religion and Public Education in a Multicultural America* (New York: St. Martin's Griffin, 1999), pp. 9–13.

4. Ibid., p. 143.

5. Siobhan Moroney, "Birth of a Canon: The Historiography of Early Republican Educational Thought," *History of Education Quarterly*, vol. 39, no. 4 (Winter 1999), pp. 476–91; Diane Ravitch, *The Great School Wars: New York City, 1805–1973* (New York: Basic, 1974); Carl F. Kaestle, *Pillars of the Republic: Common Schools and American Society, 1780–1860* (New York: Hill and Wang, 1983), pp. 182–217.

6. Fraser, *Between Church and State*, p. 20.

7. One recent survey asked respondents "Which one of these two plans would you prefer—involving and strengthening the existing public schools or providing vouchers for parents to use in selecting and paying for private and/or church-related schools?" 75 percent of the respondents preferred to improve the public schools, and 22 percent preferred the provision of vouchers. See Lowell C. Rose and Alec M. Gallup, "The 32nd Annual Phi Delta Kappa/Gallup Poll of the Public's Attitudes toward the Public Schools," www.pdkintl.org/kappan/kpoll0009.html (September 2000), p. 6.

8. Partnership for Family Involvement in Education, "Faith Communities Joining with Local Communities to Support Children's Learning: Good Ideas." (U.S. Department of Education, 2000).

9. For fuller treatment of the Texas IAF and its politics of education, see Dennis Shirley, *Community Organizing for Urban School Reform* (University of Texas Press, 1997) and *Organizing the Valley: Community Empowerment and School Reform in South Texas* (University of Texas Press, 2001).

10. On the origins of the Alliance Schools see Shirley, *Community Organizing*, pp. 200–20.

11. Pew Research Center for the People and the Press, "2001 Religion and Public Life Survey," http:www.people-press.org. The Pew survey contains a host of intriguing data on public response to the Bush initiative; regrettably, it did not include reference to the potential relationship between Bush's initiative and public school reform. According to the Pew survey, "fully 81 percent of blacks and Hispanics support the proposal, compared to 68 percent of whites."

12. Theda Skocpol, *Protecting Soldiers and Mothers: The Political Origins of Social Policy in the United States* (Harvard University Press, 1992) and "Don't Blame Big Government: America's Voluntary Groups Thrive in a National Network," in E.J. Dionne Jr., ed., *Community Works: The Revival of Civil Society in America* (Brookings, 1998), pp. 37–43; Melissa Rogers, "The Wrong Way to Do Right: A Challenge to Charitable Choice," in E.J. Dionne Jr. and John J. DiIulio Jr., eds., *What's God Got to Do with the American Experiment?* (Brookings, 2000), pp. 138–45.

13. One survey revealed that only 15 percent of teacher education programs dedicate even part of one course to community involvement and only 4 percent devote an entire course to the subject. Another survey revealed that of the more than eight hundred skills, competencies, and objectives measured in state teacher certification tests, less than 2 percent had anything to do with influences on education outside of the classroom. See Gordon E. Greenwood and Catherine W. Hickman, "Research and Practice in Parent Involvement: Implications for Teacher Education," *Elementary School Journal*, vol. 91, no. 3 (1991), pp. 279–88; Nancy Feyl Chavkin, *Teacher/Parent Partnerships: Guidelines and Strategies to Train Elementary School Teachers for Parent Involvement* (Austin, Tex.: Southwest Educational Development Laboratory, 1987).

CHAPTER ELEVEN

Faith Communities and Public Education: The View from the Superintendent's Office

DAVID HORNBECK

I enter this discussion as one who has been a professional educator for more than twenty-five years, although my degrees are in law and theology, not education. My observations in this chapter grew not out of research but out of my six years as superintendent of the School District of Philadelphia from 1994 to 2000. A typical large urban school district, the Philadelphia district has more than 200,000 students, 80 percent of whom are minorities. Eighty percent also are eligible for free or reduced-price lunches. When we established baseline performance data in 1996, 40.6 percent of the students could read at the basic level or above on the ninth edition of the Stanford Achievement Test; by 2000 that number had grown to 52.3 percent, an increase of nearly 29 percent in four years. Forty-eight percent of the students entering the ninth grade in 1992 were graduated on time in 1996; in 2000, that rate had improved to 56 percent of the students entering the ninth grade in 1996. Faith communities were part of the effort that led to that dramatic growth.

The Philadelphia school district is critically and chronically underresourced, and the situation gets worse every year. About $2,000 less is spent on each Philadelphia student than is spent on average on each student in the sixty-one surrounding school districts.[1] Those sixty-one districts constitute the primary market within which Philadelphia competes for teachers and principals. The

The author wishes to acknowledge the generous support of his work by the Otto Haas Charitable Trust Number Two and the Pew Charitable Trusts. The opinions expressed in this chapter are those of the author and do not necessarily reflect the views of either trust.

paucity of resources, both financial and human, results in daily struggles throughout the district to educate the children in its charge.

The home of the typical Philadelphia student is less stable than the norm. A substantial proportion of the students are from financially struggling single-parent homes. The average education level of the parents, many of whom had poor educational experiences as children, is low. Violence, fear, abuse, and death are realities in the communities where many, if not most, of Philadelphia's children live. Safety and security—physical, economic, and emotional—are problematic for many students. The facts of daily existence in urban, poor America—young people planning their funerals, not their futures; the absence of a social safety net; no place to go after school—characterize the lives of a large number of public school students in Philadelphia.

During my tenure we considered those realities to be challenges that we needed to help the students overcome, not insurmountable barriers. As we struggled with the state of Pennsylvania's historic unwillingness to provide adequately for its poorest students, we turned to our communities of faith for help on two fronts that correspond to important religious traditions: the pastoral/service tradition and the prophetic tradition.

PASTORAL SERVICE TRADITION

In Matthew 25:35 and following, Jesus, drawing on the prophet Isaiah,[2] admonishes us to feed the hungry, give drink to the thirsty, welcome the stranger, and clothe the naked—that is, to provide everyone with the essentials of daily living. It is not a stretch to imagine a litany of commandments today that includes the admonition to ensure that every child has the skills and knowledge to get a good job, graduate from a four-year college, and practice the art of good citizenship. Today, those goals are essential to living effectively as an adult. Helping the "least of these" children to attain those goals is rooted in the great faith traditions. The first partnership between public schools and faith communities that I examine demonstrates how faith communities render service to schools.

Project 10,000, one of our early initiatives, was implemented to recruit 10,000 new school volunteers within five years; as it happened, we recruited 15,000 in less than three years. That extraordinary success arose from a very ordinary tactic: we simply asked people whether they would help us, and they did. We provided new volunteers with a modest amount of training to give them confidence that they were up to the task. In addition, we tried to greet them when they arrived at the school the first time and to offer them a meaningful task, sending the signal that they were valued. Each year, we found ways to thank them.

Faith communities were a central recruiting ground for Project 10,000. Of course, many congregations had taken the initiative long before Project 10,000 to partner with the schools; we simply built on that history. Congregants tutored, provided after-school programs, created and staffed computer labs in churches, monitored hallways and lunchrooms, and performed various administrative tasks in the school office. Our imagination proved to be the only limitation.

One interesting example of successful collaboration was the Safety Corridors program. As in most urban settings, a school in Philadelphia, while facing potential disruption and even violence during the school day, remains one of the safest places for a young person. However, the same cannot always be said of the route to and from school. Students are subjected to harassment, violence, shakedowns, theft of clothes and lunches, and other fearful experiences. To reduce such encounters, we established Safety Corridors en route to nearly sixty schools, partnering largely with churches. Parishioners were given orange vests and walkie-talkies, and they were posted on street corners along a corridor leading to the school. Parents were responsible for getting their young children to the corridor from the side streets. The parishioners then took over and kept a protective eye on the students as they continued their journey. That was done in the morning on the way to school and again on the way home at the end of the day.

Another wonderful example of a school-congregation partnership is the Reading Buddies program of the First Presbyterian Church in downtown Philadelphia, which works with Presbyterian Homes to match primary classrooms with senior citizen residences. Eight schools and eight residences are involved. Students travel to the senior residences weekly to work with their Reading Buddy, who helps them develop their language skills. The First United Methodist Church of Germantown is unusual in that it works with high-school students, providing an after-school program for ninth graders to help the young people make a successful transition to high school. It continues with academic assistance and other support in the upper grades.

The Philadelphia school district found these partnerships very useful. In 1997, I directed each of the district's more than 260 principals to establish at least one partnership with a faith institution located in the school's immediate neighborhood.

Another opportunity for a pastoral/service partnership arose when the school district imposed a new service-learning requirement for promotion and graduation. While we placed high value on the role of public education in preparing students for productive work and successful postsecondary education, we also believed that public schools have a duty to prepare students for effective citizenship. In 1998 the board of education raised the standards for promotion and graduation in the academic disciplines and at the same time enacted a service-learning requirement for promotion from grades 4 and 8 and for graduation from high school. During the 2000–2001 school year, about 35,000 students will participate in service learning as the capacity of the system to support the requirement is tested. When the requirement is fully implemented, 70,000 students per year will engage in service learning.

Since service is a tradition among faith communities, the question arose of whether students could receive credit for service performed within their congregation or whether such service would cross the constitutional line between church and state. We thought that it was clearly acceptable if the service was sponsored by a church, synagogue, or mosque and was unrelated to religious practice. The more difficult question was posed by activities such as serving as a junior teacher in a vacation Bible school, where part of the activity was directly religious. The district's general counsel concluded that the First Amendment prohibited a service-learning project with religious content. Since then, the district has abided by that interpretation.

In retrospect, I am not certain that we made the right decision. It can be argued that it is acceptable for a student to perform a service that includes religious content if the project meets three criteria: the choice of the activity is entirely voluntary; the student has membership in, or prior significant involvement with, the congregation (to avoid, for example, a teacher or fellow students suggesting service in their congregation as a subtle form of proselytization); and the service occurs in a context wholly separate from fellow students who are nonreligious or of another faith and might feel pressure, discomfort, or embarrassment.

One also might ask whether the practice would give religious students an unfair advantage by creating more opportunities for service than would be available to nonreligious students. That is possible, though unlikely. Service opportunities are determined by many factors, including a student's special interests, family contacts, available transportation, and individual initiative. A student's connection to a congregation is one of many parts of the student's life. If we prohibit service in congregations, it may put religious students at a disadvantage by withdrawing opportunities in a place that constitutes the central nonschool interest in their lives.

In order to illustrate the breadth of possibilities, I want to mention a few other ways that our schools integrated faith and faith communities into their mission. During my tenure as superintendent, we began to treat religious institutions as community institutions, allowing them to use school facilities outside of school hours; to recognize the significant way that participation in faith communities shapes students' behavior;[3] and to acknowledge the Muslim student population by excusing their absence on Islamic holidays and providing an appropriate place in school where they could perform their daily prayers.

The Prophetic Role

Both the Old and New Testaments are filled with admonitions—from the prophets in the former and from Jesus and the disciples in the latter—to beware of service to false gods. Indeed, God destroys virtually his entire creation in the flood because he is unhappy with human behavior, while prophets such as Jeremiah and Isaiah berate the children of Israel for not following the instructions of the Lord. In the New Testament, Jesus commands that we feed the hungry, house the homeless, heal the sick, and free the prisoners. We are warned of false prophets and of the principalities and powers that lurk among us doing evil.

Children and the poor are central themes of the Scriptures, which make clear that it is the duty of the faithful to nurture, serve, and protect children and the poor. Whether we look to the Beatitudes, where the last are declared first, or to Jesus' observation that it would be better for anyone harming a child "if a great millstone were fastened around your neck and you were drowned in the depth of the sea,"[4] those who believe are instructed "to do justice, and to love kindness, and to walk humbly with your God."[5]

My purpose is not to offer a scriptural exegesis but to emphasize that the Judeo-Christian tradition leaves no doubt about our responsibility to children and poor people or about our duty to act morally and to seek justice. We can predict the correlation of the following variables with unwavering accuracy: academic performance and income level; dropout rates and race; truancy rates and primary language; employment rate of high school graduates and disability; and college completion and incarceration rates and the zip codes of children when they were in elementary school. How can communities of faithful respond?

The question for faith communities is whether the dramatic disparities brought to light by those correlations reflect God's will or political choices. If faith communities decide that the disparities are God's will, then they probably should do little more than pray for understanding. If, however, they decide that the conditions under which our children are educated are fundamentally the consequence of political choices, not God's will, then they are called to prophetic action.

What must faith communities do? To paraphrase the late Rabbi Abraham Heschel, philosopher, theologian, and a member of the faculty of the Jewish Theological Seminary for many years: to speak about God and not protest gross unfairness to our children is blasphemous! Faith communities are called to speak and act courageously in response to the historic mistreatment of children in public education. Fighting for public education that is adequate and equitable should be the next great civil rights battle in our nation.

The prophetic voice of faith communities is needed because those people in positions of power and influence who make the decisions about public education policy attained their positions, at least in part, by accommodating the status quo. They are not likely, at their own initiative, to exercise their power in ways that will radically change the status quo. The large majority of elected officials dance, as the saying goes, "with them that brung them." Since ordinary people in general and poor people in particular did not finance their campaigns and do not wield much power, school districts with significant concentrations of poor children will exercise little influence at the traditional tables where the pie of opportunity is divided up.

The anti-child/anti–poor child policies of the commonwealth of Pennsylvania are bipartisan. While the present governor and legislature have been significantly less friendly to public education than any others during the last thirty-five years, the basic policies were created and sustained by both Republicans and Democrats. Something much more fundamental must be changed than either the party or the incumbents, although it may be necessary to change them as well.[6]

In the PBS documentary *A Force More Powerful*, which describes the most successful nonviolent movements of the twentieth century, Mahatma Gandhi is reported to have said that Great Britain did not dominate India by virtue of greater armed power—Great Britain dominated India because the people of India gave Great Britain permission to do so. When that permission was withdrawn, Great Britain withdrew. And so it is in Pennsylvania. We have given those who determine education policy permission to impose unjust conditions on our children. Sometimes that permission has been explicitly given; more often, however, it has arisen from the deafening silence of the vast majority of people. When polled, the people support fairness, including equity of funding.[7] But they have not found a way to speak powerfully to their leaders about issues of justice and fairness in public education. Faith communities are called to provide that prophetic leadership, to create the opportunity for their congregants to send a different message to Harrisburg.

But why faith communities? First, prophetic leadership is central to their mission, as I have described above. Second, as a factual matter, most, if not all, successful movements have had significant faith community leadership: the abolitionist movement; the fight to enact child labor laws; the civil rights movement; and the protests surrounding the Vietnam war come to mind. The second point is true because in the most difficult moments of every campaign against injustice, when the perpetrators seem to be winning again, faith sustains hope and reinforces commitment to moral values. Political, educational, legal, and economic concerns bring many allies to the cause, but too often their commitment flags. Often, they are too easily bought for the price of their narrower interest. In contrast, if a political, educational, legal, or economic concern is coupled with faith or moral standards, their price is less easily negotiated.

While I was superintendent, there were two collaborations of the school district and communities of faith that fit within the prophetic role. The first was the creation of the Alliance Organizing Project (AOP), a coalition of advocacy groups, many of which are related to faith institutions. We raised more than $3 million for the AOP with virtually no strings attached. Their organizing philosophy parallels that of the Industrial Areas Foundation. The AOP worked with parents to identify the issues that concerned them most and helped them develop the skills, knowledge, and other tools they needed to act as advocates. They worked with principals and other leaders, including me, and confronted us, when necessary, with demands for changes in school practices that they felt were required.

Many principals and other members of my staff were angered or mystified by my support of the AOP, because its members often were confrontational. It was difficult for many district leaders to understand that a real partnership with parents and faith institutions, which they professed to want, could develop only if the community was in a position to add value to the partnership. That is not possible when one partner in a collaborative effort is utterly subordinate to the other.

The second example of the school district's collaboration with faith communities in their prophetic role arose when the district asked the Black Clergy of Philadelphia and Vicinity to join a school district–initiated federal civil rights lawsuit as a co-plaintiff.[8] We alleged that under Title VI the commonwealth racially discriminates against poor, African American children because of the impact of its system of funding public education. For example, in districts where a majority of the students are poor and minority, for every 1 percent increase in the proportion of the minority population the district received $52.88 less in state aid per pupil per year. The lawsuit is presently in the federal district court.

Neither of these initiatives nor any other advocacy effort, with or without faith communities, has resulted in a fundamental change in the system. Advocacy has tended to consist of a few busloads of people from Philadelphia, with a scattering of people from other places, going to Harrisburg once a year. We listen to a few speeches and hold up a few placards; a small number of friendly legislators come out to press the flesh. Then we all go away for another year. The legislators have become very adept at enduring what little annoyance these annual treks cause, knowing that it will be short lived and that they will not have to respond. Between the annual treks, there are intermittent letter or postcard campaigns and other initiatives that also have failed to alter the basic structure of the system.

Conditions have gotten steadily worse over the years. In 1974–75, the commonwealth paid 55 percent of the state's educational costs. Today, it pays less than 35 percent. Expenditures per pupil across the state range from a low of $4,396 to a high of more than $13,500. The average expenditure on each student in the 100 highest-spending districts (20 percent of the total) in 1997–98 was $9,386. More than one-half of the state's 501 school districts had at least $2,000 less to spend per pupil than the wealthy districts. That amounts to at least $50,000 less for each classroom of 25 pupils in those districts.

Between 1994 and 2000, the achievement and graduation rates in Philadelphia improved dramatically, while the financial situation worsened from year to year. In 1998, we made it clear that we could improve performance for a few years by harder, smarter work without increased financial assistance, but that by 2000, significant additional resources would be necessary to maintain and increase the annual growth in student achievement. It is impossible for huge concentrations of disadvantaged children to reach the same level of achievement as their more wealthy counterparts with 25 percent fewer resources.

When we then faced a projected cumulative deficit of as much as $200 million for school year 2000–01, we were reduced to two choices: We could cut programs and make a bargain with the state to bail us out or fight the injustice that the commonwealth imposed on our children and all poor children across the state. For a variety of reasons, the new mayor and board of education chose the former route. The "deal" even included the suspension of the civil rights lawsuit. They bought a year's continued "normal" operation of the district, and the governor bought peace during the Republican National Convention and the ensuing general election for president. Unable to live with that strategy, I was effectively forced out as superintendent at the end of my sixth year in August 2000.

Frustrated by the absence of the will and courage in political and corporate communities to support the children despite what they and their teachers and administrators had accomplished, I spent several months probing the depth of appetite for a serious campaign by the citizens of the state on behalf of all children. There was considerable interest, particularly among leaders in the faith community.

A new activist advocacy campaign, Good Schools Pennsylvania: Every Kid Counts, is taking shape. As of May 2001, we had designed six strategies that will result in a dramatically different public education system in Pennsylvania, one that has adequate funds, equitably distributed. The overriding theme of all the strategies is to send a new message to state leaders in Harrisburg, making clear the commitment of ordinary people to a quality public education for all the children of the commonwealth. The prophetic voice of faith communities is central to the effort. The six strategies are as follows:

—Establish 1,000 groups of ten people (10,000 total) who meet monthly and engage in a variety of advocacy activities, including writing letters to elected officials and newspaper editors, appearing on talk shows, and speaking to groups. Faith community congregants and parents are the primary sources of the 10,000 participants.

—Organize networks of college students to act as advocates for quality public education for all students. The first cadre of college students was drawn from seven Pennsylvania colleges through their chaplains or evangelical organizations. After they were trained, their first activity was to engage fellow students in making nearly 400 calls one Wednesday to targeted legislators, urging them to support public education. With two full-time campus organizers on board, this network will be expanded dramatically over the months ahead. Campus faith communities will continue to play a central role, but we also will look to other student organizations that provide service, have aspiring teachers as members, or indicate interest in social justice issues.

—Organize networks of high school students to act as advocates for quality public education for all students. Our initial outreach will be through the Internet; in the beginning we will focus on editors and writers on hundreds of high school newspapers and students involved in their local faith community youth groups. We believe that if high school students know the facts about the disparities in opportunity they will raise serious questions and engage in creative activism to change the system.

—Hold rallies in different parts of the state to give all those involved the opportunity to see how many fellow citizens are concerned about the issues. We foresee these rallies as a cross between a pep rally and a revival.

—Witness through monthly interfaith vigils. Ten faith leaders, including several bishops and other heads of communion, went to Harrisburg in June 2001 and stood in silent vigil, framing fair opportunity in public education as a moral issue. Twenty went in July. Our plan is to double the number of faith-based participants each month for several months, thereby increasing the number to thousands of witnesses. On the same day each month, we will have a three-person interfaith vigil in front of a number of strategically chosen legislative offices in communities throughout the state.

—Make public education the number-one issue in the 2002 elections. A new governor will be elected, as will a new legislature. The primaries of both parties will be hotly contested, providing the opportunity to challenge the several candidates to compete with one another in demonstrating their commitment to quality education for all children and adequate, equitably distributed funds for public education.

To date, we have raised nearly $5 million, hired nine of fourteen full-time staff members, and established the first of what will be seven offices throughout the state. We have pledges of more than 550 of the 1,000 groups of ten (more than 360 of those pledges come from faith institutions). Five heads of communion have signed on to help with the groups of ten and to participate in the vigils.

The early support suggests that there is broad-based concern about the quality and fairness of public education that cuts across party, income, racial, and geographic lines. There is initial evidence that the silence of decades is rooted in the absence of a vehicle that allows people to raise their voices in witness and protest in a manner that gives them some hope for success. The hard work of sustaining the effort is just beginning across Pennsylvania, a state with almost no experience with large grassroots movements; more people living in rural communities than in any other state in America; the second-largest number of senior citizens; and much distrust between its large rural areas and its sizable urban centers.

But Pennsylvania also is said to be the most "churched" state in the union. We have 1.8 million children, a significant majority of whom go to schools victimized by the unjust system we have created. Nearly all of the parents and grandparents of those children want them to have the very best that is available. Others who enjoy the advantages the present system offers nevertheless recognize that they and their children also are victims of an unfair education system. Many of them are prepared to help.

The most important chapters of this story of collaboration between faith communities and public education will be written in the months ahead, but the prologue is promising. The epilogue will depend largely on the depth, breadth, and strength of the prophetic voices and actions of those who profess faith in a just God as revealed in the Scriptures of Jews and Christians, in the Koran, and in the holy books of other faiths.

NOTES

1. The import of that gap is particularly dramatic when it is translated into $60,000 for each class of thirty students, of which there are about 7,000 in Philadelphia.

2. New Revised Standard Version, Isaiah 58:7

3. There is not a principal or teacher who would not acknowledge the behavior-changing impact of serious involvement of students in the faith community. When I preached on weekends, as I often did, I always raised the issue of the faith community's responsibility to give direction to its young people, to teach right from wrong. In addition to provoking better behavior generally, one unusual example was the respect accorded young women who converted to Islam by young men when they began to wear clothes reflecting their new faith.

4. Matthew 18:6, New Revised Standard Version.

5. Micah 6:8, New Revised Standard Version.

6. In addition to my years as superintendent, since 1966 I have observed Pennsylvania's treatment of its children from several vantage points, including the positions of community education organizer and the commonwealth's executive deputy secretary of education.

7. For example, the annual poll of the Greater Philadelphia First Committee, an organization of Philadelphia's largest businesses, has supported this conclusion each year for at least the last five years.

8. Two previous equity/adequacy lawsuits much like ones decided by state courts in about three dozen others states had been dismissed by the Pennsylvania Supreme Court on the basis that they raised political questions and thus belonged in the legislature, not the court. The state judiciary thus placed itself beyond the reach of children in the some 275 school districts in rural, suburban, and urban Pennsylvania on whose behalf those suits were brought.

Mobilizing Communities to Improve Public Schools

ERNESTO CORTES JR.

My experiences working with the Industrial Areas Foundation (IAF) and the Alliance schools in Texas demonstrate how faith-based institutions can organize to improve public institutions. One of the troublesome things about the debate on participation of faith-based organizations in public programs is that the government and churches, synagogues, and mosques often are cast as enemies or competitors. In fact, the successful working of public institutions depends on the successful working of civil society, including religious institutions.

The vision of the Alliance schools is to increase the capacity of kids to achieve a high level of learning by developing rigorous standards of inquiry and accountability in public education. But we also think that public education has a larger role: the responsibility to teach all of us what it means to be an American and what it means to be involved in civic culture. I happen to believe that public schools are public institutions. And by "public," I do not necessarily mean "governmental." Public schools ought to be institutions that are the public expression of our commitment to the full development and education of our children.

The IAF has accomplished a great deal in its efforts to improve education. We developed a model of collaboration that creates powerful constituencies committed to school reform, a model that takes into account the role of parents, teachers, and principals in the schools and that of religious institutions, teacher organizations, unions, and other groups in the community. That model turned around Zavala Elementary, the worst-performing elementary school in Austin, Texas. At Zavala, if a kid in the fifth grade was performing at the second-grade level, he would get an "A" because his teachers felt that he was doing the best he could. When Al Melton, a new principal at Zavala, discovered that fact and had the temerity to tell parents the truth, there was what our British friends would call a "slaying match" that polarized the school. Melton turned to IAF because he was not sure where else he could turn. We put together the remnants of the faculty and community at Zavala, and as a result of the collaborative relationship that developed between parents and teachers, Zavala went from being last to being a blue-ribbon school. Since then, the Zavala model has spread to other parts of Texas, so that now there are about 120 Alliance schools collaborating for reform.

The collaborative vision at the core of the Alliance model comes from my own experience growing up in San Antonio, where there were 250 adults who felt responsible for me. Going to school in the morning was like going through Checkpoint Charlie: at every street corner I was interrogated by adults about what I was doing, where I was going, what was I going to do when I got there—all kinds of questions. The explicit understanding was that those 250 adults felt that they had the right to intrude in my life because they felt responsible for me. I compare that experience to what I now see in Los Angeles. Instead of 250 adults organized against every kid, you have communities in which fifty or sixty kids are organized against every adult. That adults also are isolated from one another and not connected to communal institutions does not bode well for public education.

What does this have to do with President Bush's faith-based initiatives? Maybe nothing, maybe everything. The kind of work that the IAF does with congregations does not depend on the kinds of government funding arrangements at stake in the current debate. But the Alliance schools are a clear example of how people of faith can draw from the deep reservoir of inspiration, understanding, and meaning that their faith tradition gives them and translate that tradition into understandable and meaningful public policy. Their actions have to be evaluated not on the basis of their individual faith traditions, but on the basis of the common faith that we all share—our civic culture. John Courtney Murray said it best: "We can operate out of the traditions of the Gospel, but we have the responsibility to translate those traditions and those ideas into understandable public conversations, dialogue, and actions."

Congregations can plug into the IAF model of organizing in several ways. First, they can help build the ties that the IAF believes are crucial to sustaining democracy. I have come to the conclusion that whether my wife and I go to church matters less than whether the parents of the kids that my kid hangs out with go to church—that is, whether a dense network of relationships exists that reinforces coherent values in which kids can find meaning and significance. But not all churches have dense networks; some have very sparse networks, and some have no networks at all. In those cases, the question is not how to use the church's networks to promote involvement in public education but how to enable the church to create the networks necessary to promote involvement. For example, most of the parents at Zavala were within the parish's boundaries, but they had a very weak, attenuated relationship with that particular congregation. We pointed out to the pastor that those parents were his parishioners, or potential parishioners. Once pastors recognize that they can build their congregation by becoming engaged, they begin to collaborate.

Second, congregations represent a pool of possible leaders. We teach congregations to identify, develop, train, and mentor leaders who can then relate to the public school. At the same time, we work inside the school to get parents, teachers, principals, and other potential leaders connected to the community. The school draws on the vision and values of a democratic culture in galvanizing the congregation, and the congregation draws on the vision and values of Judaism, Christianity, Islam, or whatever other tradition in agitating for the improvement of the school. The IAF organizations working with the Alliance schools are not faith-based institutions. They are political organizations that are involved in public policy and whose members draw deep inspiration and meaning from their faith traditions. We see our position as playing an engaged and prophetic role that comforts the afflicted and afflicts the comfortable in this business of building the system of public education needed to sustain a democratic society.

>━━◦━━<

Creating Partnerships of Schools and Faith-Based Organizations that Uphold the First Amendment

CHARLES C. HAYNES

Partnerships of public schools and religious communities are proliferating across the nation. From character education classes on the Eastern Shore of Maryland to after-school programs in Southern California, religious groups are working closely with public school teachers and administrators.

If the First Amendment Center's work in hundreds of school districts is any indication, many of those cooperative arrangements are fully constitutional. We can point to a considerable number of schools whose administrators are careful to engage religious communities in ways that are permitted under the First Amendment as interpreted by the U.S. Supreme Court. As Mavis Sanders and Dennis Shirley both point out, partnerships of this kind can greatly enhance the mission of public education.

There also are plenty of bad stories in school districts where the First Amendment is either misunderstood or ignored. We see clergy allowed on campus to proselytize during the school day, school officials who use their position to promote activities at their own church, and other clear violations of current law. At the same time, we are aware of places where school boards and administrators largely ignore religious communities or, worse yet, are actively hostile toward them. Those are the districts with no guidelines or policies, run by administrators who are unclear about what is and is not constitutional.

The widespread confusion about the ground rules for cooperation led to publication of the guidelines discussed by Sanders.[1] The lead drafters were Marc Stern of the American Jewish Congress and Steve McFarland, then of the Christian Legal Society. Twelve other religious and educational organizations—including the Baptist Joint Committee on Public Affairs, the National School Boards Association, the U.S. Catholic Conference, and the Council on Islamic Education—endorsed the document. We crafted, for the first time, the closest thing we could to a constitutional "safe harbor" for schools entering into cooperative arrangements with religious groups.

Not everybody was pleased with the effort. Some separationist groups are concerned that disseminating guidelines, no matter how carefully drafted, risks opening the door to activities that violate the establishment clause of the First Amendment. But I would argue that the greater risk is to ignore the problem, leaving school districts confused and conflicted about how to engage religious communities. Partnerships are here to stay. They were strongly encouraged by the Clinton administration, and they will be even more of a priority under President Bush's faith-based initiative. True, guidelines will not end the abuses. But it is far better to have them than to leave school districts scrambling to figure things out for themselves.

The push for more partnerships between schools and faith groups comes at a time when the nation is rethinking the role of religion in public education. We now have agreement among most educational and religious groups on most of the religious liberty issues that have long divided us. We agree on legal guidelines for many of the religious liberty rights of students, including the right to pray, to express religious views, to distribute religious literature, and to form religious clubs in secondary schools. And we agree on the importance of including study about religion in the curriculum.[2]

Far too many districts still ignore those agreements and continue to violate the First Amendment by either promoting or ignoring religion. But the emergence over the past decade of a shared vision of religious liberty in public schools has begun to change the school culture in many places. When we proactively address the role of religious liberty and religion in the school and the curriculum, we take seriously the worldviews—the deepest commitments—of millions of parents and students. That is the best foundation for creating partnerships that involve religious communities in the mission of public schools while upholding the First Amendment.

What is new under the faith-based initiatives proposed by President Bush—and what is not addressed in our current First Amendment guidelines—is the question of funding. All of the partnerships discussed by Sanders and Shirley are cooperative arrangements that are constitutional under current law. Many are "school-affiliated" programs that may use the facilities of religious institutions but are careful not to afford an actual opportunity for proselytizing of any school children by clergy, school employees, or adult volunteers during the program.

But what happens if—as the current administration proposes—religious groups become eligible to receive direct grants from the government to offer after-school programs? The president has indicated that he does not intend for tax dollars to be used to aid religion. But he also says that he does not want to force religious groups to eliminate the religious character of their programs, which is the dimension that the president believes makes their programs successful.

It remains to be seen whether that paradox will be addressed and if so, how. But it is safe to say that if the president's plan passes Congress, faith-based after-school programs receiving federal grants are likely to have religious content. Whether or not that arrangement violates the Establishment Clause will depend on what (if any) safeguards are in place to ensure that tax money is not used to promote religion. Even with safeguards and guidelines, the question undoubtedly will be the subject of much litigation.

Where does that leave public schools? At the very least, we will need to revisit the guidelines and work out the extent to which public school officials may cooperate with after-school programs that are faith based. Ironically, the partnerships between government and faith groups created by direct grants to religious organizations may discourage partnerships with public schools. School officials will find it difficult, if not impossible, to cooperate with after-school and other programs that are religious in nature. However the funding issue is resolved in the courts, school officials cannot be in the business of promoting religion through cooperative programs or partnerships with religious communities.

None of these uncertainties, however, should keep public schools and religious communities from reaching out to one another within the current guidelines. Public schools and faith communities may have different missions, but each is committed to the well-being of children. The key is for both parties to follow constitutional principles and guidelines that are intended to protect the conscience of all students and parents in the public schools. With the First Amendment as the civic framework, schools and religious communities can and should work together for the common good.

NOTES

1. *Public Schools and Religious Communities: A First Amendment Guide* (Nashville, Tenn.: American Jewish Congress, Christian Legal Society, and the First Amendment Center, 1999).

2. See, for example, *A Teacher's Guide to Religion in the Public Schools* (Nashville, Tenn.: First Amendment Center, 1999), which was endorsed by twenty-one religious and educational organizations.

Balancing Principles and Implementation: Muslim Responses to Charitable Choice

ABDULWAHAB ALKEBSI

In an impetuous effort to legislate the protection of Americans from terrorism, President Clinton signed the Anti-Terrorism and Effective Death Penalty Act of 1996, which overran the constitutional right to due process of law by giving the government broad discretion to use classified evidence in deportation proceedings without giving the accused the right to view the evidence and prepare an adequate defense. The debate among the Muslim community is whether President Bush's attempts to involve religious institutions in the provision of social services will cross that constitutional threshold again.

In a recent survey conducted by the American Muslim Council, three-quarters of the respondents showed support for the faith-based initiative in principle, although they remained concerned over details surrounding its implementation. Some leaders are fearful that in our rush to empower religious institutions to participate in publicly funded social service programs, we would be legislating away the same institutions' guarantee of independence in the First Amendment.

Will charitable choice expose religious institutions to government regulation, including compliance reviews, audits, and perhaps even the subordination of religious principles to government policies and objectives? Will these institutions lose their discretion in hiring practices and be forced to adhere to labor laws that so far they have been exempt from?

On the other hand, skeptics are fearful that in our attempt to protect the independence of religious institutions, Congress will continue to exempt them from Title VII of the Civil Rights Act, thus clearing the way for them to discriminate against prospective employees and recipients of social services on the basis of race or other factors. In the myriad of issues emerging around charitable choice, that one in particular presents an interesting dichotomy. We find ourselves between the anvil of the First Amendment and the hammer of Title VII of the Civil Rights Act. A wrong move in one direction could place the advances that we have gained in civil rights in peril, while an erroneous move in the opposite direction could run afoul of the Establishment Clause of the First Amendment.

The magnitude of the challenges presented by these issues should not be underestimated. Advocates must acknowledge that they are legitimate concerns that need to be seriously addressed. A laissez-faire approach will not work. Discussing difficult issues and devising solutions at this stage—before it is too late—is of paramount importance. This is an initiative that is attempting to gain traction, and either one of these two issues has the potential to slam the brakes on it altogether.

In short, the dialogue among Muslim leaders is not about supporting the initiative. Virtually all of those surveyed stated that religion is an effective source of better personal and community values, and 76 percent felt strongly that the faith-based community could be effective in helping the government address homelessness, job training for welfare recipients, and prevention and treatment of drug addiction. The dialogue is about the need for a concerted effort to clarify the issues and details. In any case, one of the many challenges facing the Bush administration is the need to seek innovative ways to alleviate the concerns of both sides. That would allow the administration to bridge the gap between promising initiative and sustainable practice. In order to meet such challenges, we need to establish a context for productive dialogue that can lead to viable approaches and action.

>———○———<

What Public Schools Might Learn from the Catholic School Experience

ROBERT MUCCIGROSSO

C. L. Glenn asserts that the major role that faith-based organizations can play in the improvement of private schools is that of an external force that demonstrates through its positive outcomes the superiority of nonpublic schools.[1] I suggest that there is another, less adversarial way to look at how the nonpublic school can contribute to public school improvement. Cast in the role of competitors, "publics" and "privates," often faith based, engage in little in the way of information sharing. There are few open avenues of communication, for instance, between public schools and Catholic schools, two of the largest educational establishments in the United States.

Public schools can learn much from the accumulated experiences, successes, and failures of private secular and faith-based schools, including Catholic schools like the ones I have served as principal.

Perhaps the most critical lesson to emerge from the Catholic school experience is the importance of ensuring a degree of *administrative autonomy* for the administration and teaching staff of individual schools. Simply put, private school principals serve their schools in much the same way that superintendents typically serve a public school district. Budget and personnel recruitment, training, and retention decisions are made at the individual school level. Each school, with accountability to school boards and central offices that function as monitors, is free to respond as it deems fit to curricular and instructional pressures in a manner that is sensitive to its perceptions of the needs of its students. Teachers are afforded great latitude in developing their own strategies and resources in response to the pedagogical challenges they meet. Central offices and school boards generally play the role of guarantor of quality results rather than operational decisionmaker.

The flip side of that issue is *tenure for principals*. Teacher tenure at the elementary and secondary levels is undergoing a dramatic review, and in the next decades the concept of tenure will be radically reconstructed. The lesson of Catholic schools, which typically extend some form of tenure to teachers, is that tenure has no place with respect to administrators. Give principals authority, reward those who succeed, and hold those who fail accountable.

Catholic schools often are constrained by budgetary factors from responding to every curricular innovation that presents itself. Other times, that resistance is born of deeply held convictions about the nature of the educational process. Whatever the source, *sticking to the curricular knitting* has served Catholic schools well. The back-and-forth of the reading wars, the old math/new math/newer math debates, the emergence and disappearance of language labs, and the recent geometric rate of growth in what we call special education all reflect pressures and influences that eventually become distractions from what private school educators have been compelled to recognize as the heart of the matter: allowing skillful, dedicated, and motivated adults to share their experience and knowledge with willing learners in a supportive, structured, and nurturing environment.

The nation's Catholic schools, for example, cannot afford to offer classes in English as a second language. Yet Catholic secondary schools often serve immigrant populations. If Catholic education plays an important cultural role in their native lands, first-generation immigrant families often send their youngsters, with little or no competence in English, to Catholic high schools. After a period of adjustment and with the help of teachers and peers, immigrant children often become competent students without the benefit of specially tailored programs.

As discussed in Bryk and Holland's *Catholic Schools and the Common Good*, one aspect of the success of Catholic schools has been the *preservation of a core curriculum* that students of all ability levels are required to complete.[2] That characteristic has emerged, in the case of Catholic schools, from deeply held religious convictions about the worth of each and every individual and finds its secular expression in a characteristic shared by successful schools of all sorts: the maintenance and communication of high expectations for all students. Catholic secondary school students pursue more demanding academic course work for longer periods of time than do public secondary school students.

The misguided notion that Catholic schools are bastions of exclusivity that indiscriminately toss aside students who fail to measure up flies in the face of the educational and formational mission of Catholic schools, which is based on the gospel's teaching of the value of each and every individual. A recent survey conducted by the National Catholic Education Association documents the openness and inclusivity of the admissions policies of the great majority of U.S. Catholic secondary schools. Let us learn from two of the central tenets of Catholic schools in *sustaining institutional integrity*: first, education is not something that can be *done to* anyone—the primary responsibility for learning resides with the learner; and second, the recalcitrance or outright ill will of one member of the learning community cannot be accepted at the cost of diminishing learning opportunities for the many.

The identity, integrity, and worth of the institution needs nurturing, and the learner needs to be kept cognizant of and sensitive to the privilege of being part of the learning community. Decisions to separate the individual from the community of willing learners need not be permanent, and alternative means of access need to be developed and preserved. But educational institutions, in order to succeed, need to be respected and cherished; full participation in them must again be conceived of as something to be earned, rather than taken for granted.

These aspects of at least one faith-based organization's educational program identify some content for a dialogue in which religiously affiliated schools would be viewed not as an "exit strategy" from inadequate public schools but rather as a powerful tool for public school improvement.

NOTES

1. Charles L. Glenn, Jr., *The Myth of the Common School* (University of Massachusetts Press, 1988).

2. Anthony S. Bryk, Valerie E. Lee, and Peter B. Holland, *Catholic Schools and the Common Good* (Harvard University Press, 1993).

PART FIVE

THE ROLE OF FAITH-BASED
ORGANIZATIONS IN

Child Care

CHAPTER TWELVE

The Child-Care Landscape

JOAN LOMBARDI

The increase in the number of women in the work force is one of the most significant social changes of our times. In the 1940s, fewer than one in five women with children under eighteen worked outside the home, compared with seven in ten women today.[1] Over the years, child care also has changed. Services have become more diverse as more families rely on nonfamilial care while parents are working. Today, child care consists of early care and education for children from birth until they enter school, and after-school services are offered from kindergarten through early adolescence. As indicated in this section, faith-based institutions have played a role in child-care and after-school programs for children of all ages.

According to the latest data from the U.S. Census Bureau, in 1995 there were 19.3 million children under the age of five; three-fourths of those children (14.4 million), were in care on a regular basis during a typical week. That includes care for children of parents who are employed or in school (11 million) and children with nonemployed parents (3.4 million). Young children are in care for an average of 28 hours a week; however, children of working parents are in care for an average of 35 hours a week. About half of the children are cared for by nonrelatives, with 30 percent of those children in center-based care.[2] The diverse delivery system is particularly important given the variation in the schedules of working families.

Again according the Census Bureau, in 1995 there were 38.2 million children five to fourteen years old. The parents of the vast majority of those children (24.7 million) were in school or employed. While many children are in school while their parents are working, care for school-age children during nonschool hours may be provided by relatives, family child-care providers, and center-based programs. A significant number of children, however, are without adult supervision during the nonschool hours. Despite growth in services in recent years, there continues to be a lack of school-age programs, particularly in low-income communities.

Families face the child-care trilemma of trying to find affordable, high-quality, and available child care. The number of hours children spend in care provides an important opportunity to promote education and to support parenting. Yet, there is a continued struggle to keep fees affordable while ensuring the quality of services. Faith-based institutions have played a role in each of these issues.

Over the years, churches and synagogues have been a critical source of facility support for programs and an important source of support for families. If you ask any child-care providers about their experiences, they probably have had some faith-based experience somewhere. It is possible to argue that in the child-care arena, at least, the discussion is less about religious content than about the availability of space. Religious institutions often have the only spaces available, especially for low-income families.

But we need more than free space to operate a good child-care system. In the United States, in contrast to many other countries, the system is paid for primarily by parents. Many leaders in the faith community have been strong advocates for increasing public investments in child care, which is particularly important since child care can take a serious bite out of the budget of low-income working families. Poor families who pay for child care spend 35 percent of their income on it; nonpoor families, on the other hand, spend 7 percent. The largest source of federal support for child care is the Child Care and Development Block Grant, under which the majority of funds are distributed in the form of vouchers (or certificates) that allow parents to choose from a range of options, including faith-based programs. Funding for child care has increased over the past decade, yet the U.S. Department of Health and Human Services reported that in 1999 we were serving only a little more than one in ten families eligible for assistance.[3]

While the history of the involvement of faith-based institutions in child care provides much promise, many challenges remain. The quality of care continues to be a concern, regardless of affiliation. It is very difficult to run a quality program solely on vouchers, particularly when reimbursement rates are so low. We need more direct assistance to programs; the full cost of care cannot be borne by sponsoring organizations alone. Faith-based and non–faith-based organizations alike face severe shortages of support to continue their services for working families. Faith-based institutions may bring in new volunteers, and that would be helpful, but when we are really struggling to staff child-care programs, we cannot pretend that volunteers can make up the difference or take the place of qualified staff.

The issues around after-school programs are even dicier, because public schools are a bigger part of the picture than they are in early care. The core of the debate here is over who should provide services: public schools or community-based groups, including faith-based organizations. I have always felt that there should be partnerships; it should not be an either/or thing. Inevitably, the issue will be joined—there is a new sense of urgency about providing more and better after-school programs. Here again, we cannot get away from the question of cost. There is a peril in thinking that private after-school programs will miraculously meet the demand for after-school services. It still takes money to do that.

Finally, in upcoming years the demand for child care will continue to grow. The United States needs a significant increase in public resources to support high-quality programs that meet the needs of working families and promote the education and overall well-being of children. Viewing faith-based groups simply as service providers ignores the vital role that the faith community plays in advocacy, including advocacy for better care and more public funding. We certainly would not want to lose that voice.

NOTES

1. Committee on Ways and Means, U.S. House of Representatives, *2000 Green Book* (Government Printing Office, 2000), p. 573, table 9-1.

2. Kristin Smith, *Who's Minding the Kids? Child Care Arrangements,* Current Population Reports, P70-70 (U.S. Census Bureau, 2000).

3. U.S. Department of Health and Human Services, "New Statistics Show Only Small Percentage of Eligible Families Receive Child Care," press release, December 6, 2000.

CHAPTER THIRTEEN

A Survey of Congregation–Based Child Care in the United States

MARY M. BOGLE

The provision of child care in sacred places is not a minor phenomenon, nor is it a new one. As a group, churches and synagogues may be the largest of the providers of center-based child care in the United States, including for-profit and secular nonprofit providers, employers, and public schools. In fact, the roots of faith-based child care are so deep that it is possible to ascribe religious motivations to the first daycare program offered in the United States. Even the history of church-state partnerships in providing early childhood education services can be traced back more than thirty years.

This chapter briefly reviews the history of congregation-based child care. It explores congregations' pragmatic and theological purposes for providing care and examines the child-care "trilemma" of availability, affordability, and quality as it relates to congregation-based care. Key church-state issues such as licensing and government funding also are reviewed. The chapter concludes by probing the impact of growing institutional responses from denominations and cross-faith partnerships.

The information is based on an analytic literature review that includes relevant study data where available and in-depth interviews with more than thirty informants. It is important to note that the only source of detailed descriptions of the nation's congregation-based child care is the study *When Churches Mind the Children: A Study of Day Care in Local Parishes* (referred to hence as the NCC study), which collected and analyzed data from member denominations of the National Council of Churches almost twenty years ago. Because of the impor-

The author gratefully acknowledges the support and insights of Joan Lombardi in the development of this chapter.

tance of congregation-based child care to the overall field, the NCC study should be updated and its sample expanded to include providers representing the full range of faiths, denominations, and geographic locations as well as children from various income, ethnic, and racial groups.

The term *congregation-based* child care is used to describe weekday early childhood programs provided in houses of worship. The term does not include, nor does this chapter address, religious organizations whose primary mission is to provide services (for example, Catholic Charities and Jewish Community Centers). Where more specificity is appropriate or necessary, terms like *church-based* to denote Christian institutions and *synagogue-based* to denote Jewish institutions and so on are used.

The term *congregation-operated* child care is used to refer to programs that are directly or indirectly operated by congregations, which relate to the child care provided through their facilities in three ways: direct operation, in which the congregation exercises full financial and programmatic control over the child-care center; indirect operation, in which the congregation incorporates the child-care center as a separate nonprofit but remains closely involved in its operation by seating representatives on the board of directors; and independent operation, in which the congregation rents out space to an independent entity such as a secular nonprofit.

THE HISTORY OF CONGREGATION-BASED CHILD CARE

The religious motivations of a group of Quaker women appear to have been the driving force behind the earliest known child-care facility in the United States, although it was not based in their meeting hall. It took the form of a nursery founded in 1798 as part of the Philadelphia House of Industry, which sought to counteract the breakup of families by offering poor women a way to support themselves and keep their children with them. Social justice was likely the "mission theology" that motivated the founders.[1]

Evidence of congregation-based child care emerges during the Progressive Era, when congregations began to respond to the tide of immigration from Europe by sponsoring day nurseries for immigrant children in settlement and neighborhood houses. For those new to the country, churches and synagogues were a natural place to turn for family support.[2]

It was in the post–World War II era that congregations came of age in their capacity to provide child care. That surge in capacity was not driven by theological or social imperatives but by a postwar boom in building educational wings on churches. Although the new stock of child-friendly physical plants was built to provide Sunday school space for the children of the baby boom, church stewards began to view child care as a natural use of space that was empty during the week.[3]

As the NCC study points out, church-based child care also can be understood as a modern-day grassroots phenomenon. During the 1970s and 1980s, many houses of worship responded to the need for child care that arose when large numbers of women began to leave full-time child rearing for the paid labor market.[4] And in response to that growing ministry, the National Council of Churches established the Child Day Care Project, publishing its landmark study in 1983.[5]

Today, the phenomenon of congregation-based child care has entered a new phase—one characterized by a wide and growing variety of responses from denominational home offices, cross-faith partnerships, and vendors and membership associations that serve the educational component of the religious community. Until the NCC study, "no national church agency even recorded the names or numbers of parishes operating child day care centers."[6] Since the publication of the study's findings in 1983, and perhaps in part because of them, that is no longer the case. The response of the central offices of specific faiths is a critically important component in the growing institutional response to congregation-based child care. This chapter concludes with a discussion of those responses and the potential implications for congregation-based child care and the field at large.

WHY CONGREGATIONS PROVIDE
EARLY CHILD CARE AND EDUCATION

On a practical level, the availability of suitable classroom space and child-sized furnishings continues to be the primary reason that congregations provide child care. In addition, the geographic placement of synagogues and churches at the heart of their communities as well as their tax-exempt status makes them natural venues.[7] Also, it is important to note that many congregations lease classroom space for child care to generate revenue or to offset mortgage costs on their buildings.[8]

Beyond merely practical concerns, congregations often point to theological reasons for providing early childhood services. Among Christian denominations, the most commonly cited theological imperative for providing *high-quality* child care is found in the promises that some make to children at their baptism. For example, in its policy statement on child care, the United Methodist Church expresses its commitment in this way: "Our service of Infant Baptism in The United Methodist Church recognizes the sacredness of each person from birth and our responsibility to nurture each child in faith. . . . Through the particular

ministry of child care, we extend the nurturing ministry of the church and proclaim justice to children, families, and communities. . . . The church has important responsibilities in initiating, encouraging and participating in the highest
quality of child care for children and families, not only in the local community,
but nationwide."[9]

Although no formal written statements could be located, Jewish sources
whom I consulted, including a rabbi with the conservative movement, identified deep theological underpinnings for both the outreach and "in reach" expressions of child care within Judaism. Child care that reaches beyond the
Jewish community is grounded in the Jewish ideal of Tikkun Olam, which says
that when God created the world it remained incomplete and that the Jewish
people are partners in assisting God to "fix the world." The dominant theological motivation behind synagogue-based child care, however, is found in the
heavy emphasis that the Hebrew Bible places on transmitting the tenets of the
Jewish faith to succeeding generations.[10] Thus, as a recent report by the Jewish
Council for Public Affairs states, "while hundreds of synagogues throughout the
Untied States are engaged in vital social action endeavors . . . most of that work
is being carried out in a pervasively sectarian context."[11]

It is possible to break the mission theology of most congregation-based care
into component parts. Although the following motivations are borrowed largely
from the NCC study,[12] they have been adapted to reflect purposes described by
both Jewish and Christian sources. Five purposes apply to both synagogue- and
church-based child care. *Pastoral care* is a form of ministry that views child care
as a service to families within the congregation. *Community service* is a form of
ministry that views congregations as having a responsibility to their neighbors,
whether or not they are members of the congregation. *Education* is a form of
ministry in which religious instruction is viewed as an integral program component. Although not raised in the NCC study, a closely related purpose is *en-
culturation*, the process of instilling the norms and beliefs of a cultural or faith
group. Finally, *social justice* is a form of ministry that defines child care as an expression of the faith community's outreach to particular populations, such as
low-income families or children with special needs.

Though common to church-based child care, two other purposes do not apply to synagogue-based child care.[13] One is *stewardship*, which is a form of ministry that views the effective use of physical resources as a trust placed in the
congregation's hands by God. Weekday use of educational facilities is an expression of good stewardship. The second is *evangelism*, which sees child care as
a way to proclaim one's faith and recruit new members to the faith community.

Although synagogue-based programs generally welcome children from outside their congregations and from other faiths, Jewish sources indicated that

education/enculturation is the foremost reason for the provision of weekday services for children in synagogues.[14] Among church-based programs, the NCC study found that twenty years ago, the prevalent impetus for the provision of church-based care was community service.[15]

CONGREGATION-BASED CHILD CARE
AND THE CHILD-CARE "TRILEMMA"

Although congregations' physical assets and theological motivations for providing child care may set them apart, they as well as nonsectarian providers face the child-care "trilemma" of availability, affordability, and quality.

Availability

Throughout the country, demand for child care is outstripping supply. Families of all income levels, from California to Washington, D.C., often remain on waiting lists for up to twelve months or longer.[16] According to the 1997 National Survey of America's Families (NSAF), 32 percent of children nationwide under the age of five whose mothers are employed are placed in child-care centers.[17] Other forms of care include care provided in the home of a private provider, nanny or babysitting services, and care by a relative.

Even the most conservative studies suggest that the availability crisis would be much more severe without congregation-based child care. Back in the early 1980s, the NCC study estimated that church-based programs as a group are the largest provider of center-based child care in the nation.[18] A more recent survey conducted by the trade journal *Child Care Information Exchange* (*CCIE*) estimated that one of every six child-care centers in the United States is housed in a religious facility.[19]

Child care and after-school care are provided by a significant percentage of congregations across the country. According to *From Belief to Commitment: The Community Service Activities and Finances of Religious Congregations in the United States*, a survey of the nation's Buddhist, Catholic, Jewish, Mormon, Muslim, and Protestant congregations, 24.2 percent of congregations provide daycare for very young children and 18.2 percent provide after-school programs.[20] There is some evidence that the availability of center-based child care is expanding more rapidly within congregations than throughout the field in general. The *CCIE* survey estimates that the number of child-care centers operated in religious facilities increased by more than 26 percent from 1997 to 1999, compared with 19 percent for the field overall.[21]

What role inner-city congregations play in the availability of care for low-income urban children is an important question, but one for which little specific data are available. That it may be substantial and deserving of further examination is indicated by a recent study of 100 older religious properties in six cities. According to Diane Cohen and Robert Jaeger in *Sacred Places at Risk*, "at the turn of the century, many urban congregations adopted a 'social gospel' that welcomed poor and immigrant people that had nowhere else to turn. To support that agenda, they hired the era's best architects to design ambitious, imposing facilities, some with gymnasia, theaters, bowling alleys, and meeting rooms adjacent to the main sanctuary. Now, contending with flight, blight, and other adversities, these same inner-city congregations have adapted their properties once again to address their communities' changing needs."[22] Foremost among those adaptations, say the authors, is the provision of services for children, including child care.

It is important also to understand the role that churches may play in making services available to low-income rural children. A primary reason for the establishment of the innovative Church Child Care Initiative of the North Carolina Rural Economic Development Center—the mission of which is to increase the number of church-based child-care centers available to rural children—was the discovery that often churches are the only facilities in rural areas that are appropriate for children and meet building safety codes.[23]

Affordability

A 1998 Census Bureau analysis demonstrated that, regardless of income level, child care is the third-largest expense after housing and food for families with children ages three to five.[24] Even after most parents have been stretched to the limits of their capacity to pay the price of the service, costs remain. Hidden subsidies typically are provided through the low wages offered to caregivers and noncash contributions provided by nonprofits. According to the NCC study, churches may be especially generous in that regard: they provided three-quarters of the centers surveyed with space and utilities free of charge or at below-market value.[25]

According to the *Cost, Quality, and Outcomes Study*, an analysis of center-based child care published in 1995, the fees that church-based providers charge parents are substantially lower than those found in other child-care sectors. The study also found that a higher percentage of total revenue came from parent fees for congregation-based providers than from other types of providers.[26] Both data from the NCC study and the more recent *Cost, Quality, and Outcomes Study* confirm that the use of public subsidies to support slots for low-income children is lower among congregation-based child-care providers than other nonprofit providers.

Quality

The quality of child care is vexingly low throughout the nation. The *Cost, Quality, and Outcomes Study*, which collected data on centers in four states (California, Colorado, Connecticut, and North Carolina),[27] found that the quality of care in most centers is "poor to mediocre" and that "only one in seven centers provides a level of quality that promotes healthy development."[28]

As for congregation-based care, the study's findings indicate that, in North Carolina, "the state with the most lax regulations," child-care centers in the for-profit sector scored lower on indexes of quality (for example, staff-to-child ratio, teacher education) than the nonprofit sector. The study found that in the other states the quality of care in the two sectors was comparably "mediocre." However, when both the for-profit and nonprofit sectors were broken into subsectors, "church-affiliated" centers across the four states were statistically similar to for-profits in scoring lower on indexes of quality than the other nonprofit subsectors. The for-profit subsectors were defined as independent, local chain, and national chain. The three types for nonprofit centers were church-affiliated centers, some operated by churches and some not; public centers operated by municipalities, school districts, or colleges and universities; and independent centers, which include all other nonprofit centers.

The principal investigators concluded that "the nonprofit sector [has] important differences among subsectors, mainly because the performance of church-affiliated centers differed considerably from other nonprofits. Compared with the other two nonprofit sectors, church-affiliated centers had lower staff-to-child ratios, lower levels of trained and educated teachers, a smaller percentage of assistants with at least a CDA, less educated administrators, lower staff wages, and lower labor cost and total expended cost per child hour. More importantly, they had lower overall quality."[29]

In a recent study that used the *Cost, Quality, and Child Outcomes* data set to probe more deeply into differences in quality among child-care centers, John Morris and Suzanne Helburn pin findings of lower quality more specifically on church-operated child care: "Church-operated and community agency–operated centers provided quality levels similar to for-profit centers but significantly lower than the other nonprofit sectors. [Independently-operated] church-affiliated centers provided higher-quality services than the [church-operated and for-profit] subsectors."[30]

Helburn and Morris indicate that findings of lower quality in church-operated care may be linked to the lower fees those centers typically charge: "Church-operated centers, however, may be serving a somewhat different clientele of families with somewhat lower incomes seeking lower-cost services because church-operated centers charged lower fees than most other subsectors."[31]

The isolation of church-based providers from the mainstream early childhood community also seems to be a strong explanatory factor.[32] As Deborah Hampton, director of the Ecumenical Child Care Network, indicates, church-operated centers must answer to their individual congregations and denominations first and then, in the time remaining, network and resource with the larger early childhood community. As anyone who has worked in child care knows, time is a precious and all-too-scarce commodity. The mission of the Ecumenical Child Care Network (ECCN), which began in 1984 in response to the NCC study findings, is to address the isolation experienced by congregation-based child-care providers through publications, technical assistance, special recognition of quality programs, and other program support services, such as an annual conference.[33]

Another frequently cited explanation for why church-operated care may be of lower quality is that the centers often are poorly administered. The skills it takes to run a church are different from those required to manage a high-quality early childhood program. For that reason, cross-faith partnerships like ECCN encourage church-operated providers to incorporate separately from the houses of worship in which they are located; in other words, to adopt the indirect operation model.

CONGREGATION-OPERATED CHILD CARE AND THE GOVERNMENT

Just as the phenomenon of congregation-based child care is not new, neither are the issues it raises concerning church-state relations. The following is a brief overview of the two biggest challenges for congregation-operated programs: licensing and the use of public funds.

Licensing

Most states require congregation-operated child-care programs to meet the same licensing standards applied to secular providers. Although numerous court cases have confirmed the constitutional right of states to regulate congregation-operated services, the U.S. Supreme Court also has held that, consistent with the establishment clause of the First Amendment of the U.S. Constitution, states may exempt congregation-operated facilities from regulatory oversight if they so choose.[34]

Today, about fourteen states exempt or partially exempt child care provided by a religious institution from licensing requirements. Generally, however, states that offer exempt status still require congregation-operated facilities to register with the regulatory agency and certify that they meet minimum health and safety standards. Besides not applying many standards that go beyond health and safety issues to congregation-operated programs, the primary difference between the licensure and registration methods of regulation is the breadth of state monitoring and enforcement. Under the licensure method, the state plays an active role in monitoring and enforcement; under the registration method, the state plays a much more passive role.

For example, in North Carolina religiously sponsored centers that choose not to be licensed must meet minimum standards regarding health, safety, child/staff ratio, and group size. The same child-care centers generally are exempt from standards concerning staff qualifications, training, and the use of developmentally appropriate activities and play materials. Following written certification and a visit from a state inspector, programs that choose not to be licensed receive a notice of compliance from the state department of health and human services.

The issue of corporal punishment is a particular source of church-state tension, especially for some conservative Christian congregations, and it illustrates the delicate balance of church-state relations in child care. North Carolina law specifically allows congregation-operated centers to use corporal punishment if the facility files a notice with the state stipulating that it "is part of the religious training of its program" and issues a written statement of its discipline policy to parents.

Again, however, the courts often are the final arbiters of disputes over such matters. In 1987, the United States District Court of California denied the petition of North Valley Baptist Church to have its preschool exempted from the state ban on corporal punishment in child-care facilities on the grounds that compliance would not burden the exercise of the plaintiff's religious beliefs. The court noted that while the plaintiff's beliefs permitted spanking, they did not require spanking.[35]

Several states, such as Texas, require religiously sponsored child-care centers to be fully licensed or to employ an independent accrediting body to verify their ongoing compliance with all licensing regulations. Currently, the Texas Association of Christian Child Care Agencies, an independent Baptist organization, is the only agency on the list approved to verify compliance by the Texas Department of Protective and Regulatory Services. An application from the Council on Accreditation, a national secular organization, is pending. A host of public policy and other issues raised by alternative accreditation merit further study, including the following: What are the implications for parent understanding of minimum standards in a state that allows multiple agencies to "quasi-regulate" child-care facilities? Are there variations among states in the rigor applied to assessing the expertise and legitimacy of an alternative accreditation agency? How do liability concerns affect the willingness of a private agency to undertake a traditionally public function? What are the implications of allowing one religious organization to monitor the compliance of another?

Most of the faith-based sources I consulted believed that congregation-operated child-care programs should be licensed just as any other provider. And, in fact, armed with data that the majority of church-based providers have no problem with licensing their child-care facilities, the NCC circulates a policy statement that says that licensing is an appropriate responsibility of the state and that it need not interfere with the free exercise of religion. The statement encourages churches to neither seek nor accept exemption from licensing standards.[36]

There is, however, hardly unanimity on this issue among Christian leaders. In response to a complicated debate over the state's authority to regulate any nonprofit child-care provider, the Pennsylvania Catholic Conference (PCC) recently drafted a bill to clarify and ensure the exempt status of congregation-operated child-care providers in that state. As to PCC's reasoning, executive director Robert J. O'Hara Jr. says: "It's the same rationale for why we don't want the department of education coming into our schools. We see this as part of the teaching mission of the church. That means that it's a religious mission, and we don't ask the government for permission to perform our religious mission. People choose to put their children in religious child-care facilities because they expect to have their child taught particular values—that's why they chose a Jewish facility, or a Catholic facility, or Presbyterian, or whatever. They chose a religious child-care facility because it is an extension of the religious teaching of the church. That is different than some of our Catholic Charities facilities, where we offer adoption services or a food bank. In those particular instances, there might be cause for licensing and we might accept that, but that's not the teaching mission of the church."

O'Hara states that his organization does not oppose Pennsylvania's "legitimate, yet limited, supervisory powers" over matters concerning child health and safety in religious child-care facilities but that it does object to any attempts to regulate staffing, curriculum, and general management. He adds: "Our concerns in this regard are not unwarranted; past [state] regulations required, among other things, that child-care programs provide 'appropriate' materials for 'affective development,' which was defined as acquiring proper behavior related to 'attitudes' and 'values.' Were such regulations imposed on religious facilities, government would be authorized to determine whether children in religious programs are obtaining 'appropriate' values and attitudes. If the materials used to instill values and attitudes in children were not deemed 'appropriate' by government, the facility could lose its license and be prevented from operating."

Ultimately, as William Gormley points out in *Everybody's Children: Child Care as a Public Problem*, it is important to move beyond the legal issues to examine the consequences for children. He and a number of other child-care policy experts believe that licensing exemptions play a role in pushing the quality of church-based care lower.[37] The bottom line is that any further study of congregation-based care needs to look carefully at this subsector in relation to the finding of the *Cost, Quality, and Outcomes Study* that states with more demanding licensing standards have fewer poor-quality centers.[38]

Public Funding

Historically, when "pervasively sectarian" institutions have been viewed as serving the public good, they have been permitted to use public funds in achieving the secular goals of their ministries. Although few pieces of legislation set guidelines on church-state relations before the 1990s, the nation's courts generally have held that religious organizations may receive government contracts and grants as long as they refrain from using them for sectarian activities.

And indeed, congregation-based early childhood programs have been supported by taxpayer dollars for at least thirty years. For example, since its establishment in the 1960s, the Head Start program has partnered with congregation-based providers, particularly those housed in predominantly African American churches. And in the 1980s, Title XX block grant funds were made widely available to congregation-based child-care programs.

Following Title XX, the next watershed in federal funding for child care was the Child Care and Development Block Grant (CCDBG), which was included in the Omnibus Budget Reconciliation Act, signed by President George H. W. Bush in 1990. The act represents the first significant legislative effort to define church-state roles in the provision of a social-service program.[39]

In so doing, the legislation was careful to distinguish between certificates or vouchers, which are viewed as aid to the parents, and grants or contracts, which are considered assistance to the provider or organization. Typically, under the certificate system, parents take their voucher directly to the provider, who may or may not be congregation based. The provider fills out the appropriate paperwork, which then is returned by the parents to a state representative. On submission of periodic timesheets verifying provision of care to the parents' child, the provider is reimbursed at the rate allowed by the state. The CCDBG legislation and a subsequent regulation issued in 1992 do not view the state as providing assistance to the child-care provider; the assistance is to the parent, who in turn uses it to exercise an independent choice.

The CCDBG was reauthorized under the Personal Responsibility and Work Opportunity Reconciliation Act of 1996. Although the 1996 version of the act consolidated separate child-care funding streams, including the certificates, into a single fund, no major changes were made to the language on sectarian providers. Table 13-1 sketches the major church-state issues that generally affect sectarian providers and how they are handled for contractors and certificates under both the 1992 and 1996 versions of the CCDBG law and regulations. There have been no court cases alleging violations or asserting constitutional issues with regard to sectarian providers who receive certificates through the CCDBG since its passage in 1990.

Although child-care certificates are widely available to congregation-operated programs as a result of the CCDBG, there are no quantitative data on how many such programs actually access public funding to serve low-income children. Many sources I consulted claim, however, that two factors drive the use of CCDBG funding among sectarian providers: awareness of the parent of the availability of certificates for use for a broad range of options, including congregation-operated care, and the willingness of congregation-operated providers to accept government aid.

Regulations issued in 1998 place greater emphasis on the responsibility of state lead agencies to make parents aware of all their child-care options, including the use of certificates for access to the "full range of providers," a term that encompasses congregation-based providers. There are those who claim, however, that states are generally ineffective in carrying out consumer education because the regulations do not specify how the lead agency is to ensure compliance by its regional or local agents. That represents yet another question for future studies to examine more closely.[40]

Table 13-1. *Sectarian Issues in the CCDBG Legislation*

Issue	*Grant/Contracts*	*Certificates*
Display of religious symbols	Not referenced	Not referenced
Religious instruction	Prohibited	Not prohibited
Employment discrimination based on		
Religious beliefs	Prohibited	Not prohibited
Adherence to religious tenets	Not prohibited	Not prohibited
Discrimination in admission of		
children based on religious beliefs	Prohibited	Not prohibited
Capital improvements	Sectarian and nonsectarian providers may apply for capital improvement funds (with a general bar on construction) if their state chooses to make them available. However, sectarian providers may engage in minor remodeling only to meet health and safety requirements.	

Gaining a clear picture of the willingness of congregations to accept child-care vouchers is equally difficult. Data collected before the advent of CCDBG funding indicate that church-run centers were less likely than secular nonprofits to provide care to subsidized children.[41] The 1995 *Cost, Quality, and Outcomes Study* supported that finding. However, the potentially growing impact of the certificate system, combined with the unknown effect of large increases in funding for child-care subsidies since 1996, underscores the need for new research on congregation-operated child care and the use of public funds.

Although no hard data are available, a number of my sources suggest that resistance to the use of federal funds for child care is most prevalent among congregations of particularly conservative denominations such as the Southern Baptist Convention. The fear generally expressed by conservative evangelicals is that any government money inevitably entails government intrusion into religious activities, curriculums, and hiring practices.

However, an important and largely unanswered question is whether the likelihood that a particular congregation will accept government funding has as much to do with its conservative theology as its history of social progressivism. In his 1998 National Congregations Study, University of Arizona sociologist Mark Chaves found that most of this country's 300,000 congregations engaged in some form of social service but that only 3 percent used public funds to do so. However, 28 percent of predominantly Caucasian congregations and 65 percent of predominantly African American congregations said that they would be interested in applying for federal funds. In addition, Chaves finds that Catholic and liberal/moderate Protestant denominations were significantly more likely to apply for government funds.[42]

Emmet Carson, in his essay "Patterns of Giving in Black Churches," provides a possible explanation for the phenomenon uncovered by Chaves: "American history is filled with examples of how blacks developed the capabilities of their churches to respond to racism and segregation. Black ministers not only gave their parishioners spiritual and material solace for their present conditions; they also instilled them with hope and engaged them in charitable and other activities so that the black church became a catalyst for the very societal changes that the ministers prayed for in their sermons."[43]

In a discussion of his findings, Chaves adds: "There is already a lower barrier—both culturally and institutionally—between church and state in African American religion than in other religious communities in the United States (Patillo-McCoy 1998)."[44] Several of my sources believe that there is greater use of public funds for child care among congregations representing predominantly African American denominations like the National Baptists, a theologically conservative faith, and the African Methodist Episcopal Church.

Institutional Response to Congregation-Based Child Care

In the NCC study, the authors conclude that "the church is a major provider of child care in this nation. As such, it is a major factor—however unintentional—in any national debate about child care. . . . Our evidence suggests that child care in churches requires more intentionality on the part of national church agencies if the quantity and quality of care offered is to continue and increase."[45] Almost twenty years later, it is clear that many faiths and denominations have taken up that implicit challenge. While the absence of consistent study data makes firm claims about expansion in the quantity of care impossible to make, it is evident that an institutional response to care is influencing the purposes of congregation-based care and may well be having an impact on the quality. The denominational response may also be increasing the number of programs that are directly operated by congregations. Back in the early 1980s, the NCC study found that 53 percent of all centers in churches were operated by the congregation.[46] Neugebauer says that, based on the results of the more recent *CCIE* survey, "in recent years, the trend has been to shift even more dramatically in this direction."[47] (See table 13-2.)

What is most evident is that the purposes of education/enculturation and evangelism (for Christian churches) are rising with the tide of institutional interest. Again, comparing the NCC study data with his own data, Neugebauer states: "In the 1983 National Council of Churches' study, only 13 percent of church-housed centers surveyed listed spiritual development as one of the primary goals of their program. Traditional early childhood goals of fostering 'love and worth,' 'sharing and cooperation,' and 'positive self-image' were the most common program goals cited (Lindner, 1983). This pattern appears to be changing. In a recent survey of the nation's twenty largest denominations, while traditional early childhood goals were still cited most frequently as denominational goals, spiritual development was identified as an increasingly important secondary goal."[48]

Because of the impact of isolation on the quality of congregation-operated centers, the most important institutional responses may be those that come from the headquarters of the various faith traditions. Several brief glimpses at how various national offices are responding to the needs of very young children in their facilities follow.

The Evangelical Lutheran Church in America (ELCA) offers the most highly developed support for early childhood programs within its community of all the denominations profiled. The ELCA promotes religious instruction and high-quality practice in collaboration with the Evangelical Lutheran Education

Table 13-2. *Religious Organizations Housing Early Childhood Facilities in the United States*

Organization	Members	Congregations	Centers
Roman Catholic Church	61,208,000	22,728	5,002[a]
Southern Baptist Convention	15,692,000	40,565	4,100[b]
United Methodist Church	8,495,000	36,361	—
Presbyterian Church (USA)	3,637,000	11,328	1,900[b]
Evangelical Lutheran Church in America	5,181,000	10,936	2,100[b]
Lutheran Church-Missouri Synod	2,601,000	6,099	2,184[b]
Episcopal Church (USA)	2,537,000	7,415	923[b]
Assemblies of God	2,468,000	11,884	888[b]
Jewish Organizations	5,981,000	3,416	951[a]
American Baptist Churches (USA)	1,503,000	5,807	750[b]
Disciples of Christ (Christian Church)	910,000	3,840	480[c]

Sources: Data on numbers of members and churches come from *The Yearbook of American & Canadian Churches 1999*. The estimates on the number of centers were arrived at as indicated in the footnotes.

a. Data supplied by the Wilson Marketing Group, Inc.

b. Count or estimate supplied by national office of the organization.

c. Count of centers reported in *When Churches Mind the Children* and increased by 30 percent to account for growth over past nineteen years.

Table reprinted with permission from *Child Care Information Exchange*, P.O. Box 3249, Redmond, Washington 98037.

Association (ELEA), which offers workshops and conferences, a quarterly newsletter, and geographic networking meetings and leadership retreats to its member early childhood education centers. ELEA recently added a three-phase certification process for early childhood programs that incorporates a self-study process, initiated by the ELCA department of schools, to assist congregations in reviewing and evaluating the relationship of the congregation and the early childhood program; formal certification from the ELEA, which begins with a program of self-study on high standards of quality and culminates in a visit from an ELEA certification team; and accreditation by the National Association for the Education of Young Children. In addition, Augsburg Fortress Publishers, along with the ELCA department of schools and the ELEA, is adapting a Lutheran Church of Australia faith-based curriculum for use among Lutheran and other churches in the United States. Known as Graceways, the curriculum includes an early childhood module and is advertised as providing "a framework for [programs] to develop their own sequence of content and learning . . . to suit [their] own needs" and as offering "a resource to enable and encourage Christian teachers to model and witness their own Christian commitment without manipulating students or coercing a similar commitment from them." Finally, the ELCA department of schools offers formal assistance to congregations wishing to open early childhood education programs.

The Roman Catholic Church is the most difficult to access on a national level of all the faith traditions profiled. Although the U.S. Conference of Bishops collects data on preschools operated within parochial schools, more detailed information on the full range of this faith's child-care and early childhood activities must be searched for diocese by diocese. Data from the *National Congregations* study and hard-to-substantiate comments from Catholic sources whom I consulted suggest several questions for further study: Given the Catholic Church's history and teaching on social action, would the social justice purpose in providing child care be particularly pronounced for this faith? Are Catholic churches playing a significant role in providing child care for Latino immigrants?

The Southern Baptist Convention (SBC) has the longest history of providing an institutional response to early childhood issues within its congregations. Because the tradition places a premium on congregational autonomy and independence, each church is considered an independent governing body. However, the SBC historically has provided technical assistance and group cohesion to its member congregations through nine "boards." The Sunday School Board, which was renamed Lifeway Christian Resources in the mid-1990s, is responsible for providing networking services, technical assistance, and curricular materials to the weekday early childhood programs of Southern Baptist churches. Today, Lifeway curricular materials may be the most widely distributed of all the religious early childhood teaching aids. The Lifeway mailing list includes 5,000 church-based directors of centers that span far beyond the congregations of the SBC. In addition to the curriculum, Lifeway holds an annual conference attended by 850 church-based early childhood professionals. All of the early childhood activities of Lifeway are oriented around eight competency areas: God, Jesus, the Bible, church, family, natural world, others, and self. However, the SBC has no official statement of policy or theology on the child care provided within its churches.

The Union of American Hebrew Congregations (UAHC), the central body of Reform Judaism, serves approximately 875 affiliated synagogues.[49] The UAHC supports its approximately 300 preschool programs, most of which are part-day programs, through its early childhood coordinator, a position that was established in 1999. Martha Katz, the current early childhood coordinator, says that her services include phone consultation with center directors on issues like start-up and program content; a semiannual newsletter that features articles on topics such as how to teach Jewish values to children of different ages; an annual networking conference for directors; and consultation with the UAHC publication and music departments on the development of printed materials and musical resources for children that feature Jewish content and themes. In the future, Katz hopes to provide more in-synagogue consultations and workshops.

Katz notes an important distinction between Jewish and Christian congregations on the issue of sharing space with a congregation. Within Judaism, school-age children of the congregation generally attend Hebrew school several times a week, not just on Saturday or Sunday. Thus, programs for preschool children operate on a part-day basis to accommodate synagogues' after-school education programs.

A final example is the United Methodist Church (UMC). All of the children's ministries within the UMC are provided guidance through the denomination's General Board of Discipleship (GBOD). The mission of GBOD, according to Mary Alice Gran, the director of children's ministries, is "to resource leaders in congregations as they work to make disciples of Jesus Christ." Gran's office provides support to leaders in UMC congregations for all children's ministries, including those that take place on Sunday morning, in the evening, after school, and on weekdays. GBOD activities fall into four categories: resource development, events, research, and networking. Although the UMC has not developed a specifically Methodist curriculum for its programs, it refers providers to Cokesbury Press, which produces a quarterly set of lesson plans for Christian preschool weekday ministries. Gran herself has produced a book, *The First Three Years: A Guide for Ministry with Infants, Toddlers, and Two-Year-Olds*, as part of the array of written materials she produces each year. The UMC policy statement on child care grounds the denomination's concern with quality firmly in the theology of infant baptism. The statement goes on to say: "Each congregation of The United Methodist Church that houses or supports any child-care program must intentionally assess its understanding of discipleship as it relates to this program. Child care is a valid expression of the Christian faith. However, too often, programs in local churches exist without much thought to intentional ministry. Concerns often focus on budgeting and facility use instead of viewing the programs as ministry. When this happens, misunderstandings arise between the child-care program and the congregation, and missed opportunities occur for witnessing and mirroring the Christian faith." With regard to licensing, the statement echoes NCC's guidance by saying: "The regulations of basic health and safety conditions in a building/program that serves children are the appropriate responsibility of the state and do not interfere with the free exercise of religion."[50]

These profiles confirm the *Child Care Information Exchange* survey finding that religious institutions may be focusing more on the purposes of evangelism and education in providing child care. In addition, they make clear that national faith offices are taking a greater interest in promoting quality as a theological concern—a welcome trend indeed. According to Deborah Hampton and others, congregation-based caregivers in need of support in dealing with the issues they face tend to call on their faith institutions first. Any further study of congregation-based child care needs to explore the implications for children now that those institutions are answering their call.

NOTES

1. Sonya Michel, *Children's Interest, Mother's Rights: The Shaping of America's Child Care Policy* (Yale University Press, 1999), p. 20.

2. Ibid., p. 53.

3. Eileen W. Lindner, Mary C. Mattis, and June R. Rogers, *When Churches Mind the Children: A Study of Day Care in Local Parishes* (New York: National Council of Churches of Christ in the U.S.A., 1983), p. 17.

4. Ibid., p. 22.

5. Ibid., p. 9.

6. Ibid., p. 7.

7. Ibid., p. 17

8. Ibid., pp. 18–19.

9. www.gbod.org/children/articles/childcarepolicy.html [December 18, 2000].

10. Interviews with Ruth Feldman, director of early childhood services, Jewish Community Centers Association of America (February 14, 2001); Rabbi Mayer Waxman, director of synagogue services, the Union of Orthodox Jewish Congregations of America (February 7, 2001); and Martha Katz, early childhood coordinator, Union of American Hebrew Congregations (February 23, 2001).

11. Guila S. Franklin, Rebecca Wind, and Laura Furmanski, *Pursuing* Tikkun Olam*: A Survey of Jewish Involvement in Family Development and Neighborhood Transformation Initiatives in Selected Sites throughout the United States* (New York: Jewish Council for Public Affairs,1998), p. 7.

12. Lindner and others, *When Churches Mind the Children*, pp. 20–21.

13. Interview with Martha Katz.

14. Interviews with Ruth Feldman, Rabbi Mayer Waxman, and Martha Katz.

15. Lindner and others, *When Churches Mind the Children*, p. 26.

16. *Opening a New Window on Day Care* (New York: National Council of Jewish Women, 1999), p. 6.

17. Jeffrey Capizzano, Gina Adams, and Freya Sonenstein, "Child Care Arrangements for Children under Five: Variation across States," in *New Federalism, National Survey of America's Families*, Series B, no. B-7, March 2000 (Washington: Urban Institute, 2000), p. 2.

18. Lindner and others, *When Churches Mind the Children*, p. 12.

19. Roger Neugebauer, "Religious Organizations Taking Proactive Role in Child Care," *Child Care Information Exchange*, May 2000, p. 19.

20. Virginia A. Hodgkinson and Murray S. Weitzman, *From Belief to Commitment: The Community Service Activities and Finances of Religious Congregations in the United States* (Washington: Independent Sector, 1993), p. 31.

21. Neugebauer, "Religious Organizations Taking Proactive Role," p. 29.

22. Diane Cohen and Robert A. Jaeger, *Sacred Places at Risk* (Philadelphia: Partners for Sacred Places, 1998), pp. 7–8.

23. Interview with Diana Jones Wilson, director workforce development, North Carolina Rural Economic Development Center (February 7, 2001).

24. *Opening a New Window on Day Care,* p. 7.

25. Lindner and others, *When Churches Mind the Children,* p. 74.

26. Cost, Quality, and Child Outcomes Study Team, *Cost, Quality, and Child Outcomes in Child Care Centers,* 2d ed. (University of Colorado at Denver, April, 1995), p. 61.

27. The principal investigators in *Cost, Quality, and Child Outcomes in Child Care Centers* note that "in the research design, we deliberately designed an intensive on-site study of centers in four fairly representative states with varying licensing standards and demographic and economic characteristics. Taken together, our results give a national overview. Individually, the results for given states are representative of other states with similar characteristics" (p. 1).

28. Ibid.

29. Ibid., pp. 60–61.

30. John R. Morris and Suzanne W. Helburn, "Child Care Center Quality Differences: The Role of Profit Status, Client Preferences, and Trust," *Nonprofit and Voluntary Sector Quarterly,* vol. 29, no. 3 (September 2000), p. 387.

31. Ibid.

32. Lindner and others, *When Churches Mind the Children,* p. 102.

33. www.eccn.org [December 14, 2000].

34. William T. Gormley Jr., *Everybody's Children: Child Care as a Public Problem* (Brookings Institution, 1995), p. 143.

35. *North Valley Baptist Church* v. *Linda McMahon* [in her capacity as director of the California State Department of Social Services], No. Civ. S-84-0767 RAR (1987).

36. *Policy Statement on Child Day Care,* adopted by the Governing Board of the National Council of Churches, November 7, 1984.

37. Gormley, *Everybody's Children,* p. 144.

38. *Cost, Quality, and Child Outcomes in Child Care Centers,* p. 1.

39. Elizabeth Samuels, "The Art of Line Drawing: The Establishment Clause and Public Aid to Religiously Affiliated Child Care," *Indiana Law Journal,* vol. 69 (Winter 1993), p. 42.

40. William J. Tobin, *Let the Children Come to Me: A Handbook for Faith-Based Early Childhood Centers/Programs Regarding the Federal Child Care and Development Block Grant* (Falls Church, Va.: William J. Tobin and Associates, 2000), pp. 12–13.

41. Gormley, *Everybody's Children,* p. 144.

42. Mark Chaves, "Religious Congregations and Welfare Reform: Who Will Take Advantage of Charitable Choice?" *American Sociological Review,* vol. 64 (1999), pp. 839–41.

43. Emmett D. Carson, *Faith and Philanthropy in America* (Washington: Independent Sector, 1990), pp. 234–35.

44. Chaves, "Religious Congregations and Welfare Reform," p. 843.

45. Lindner and others, *When Churches Mind the Children,* p. 101.

46. Ibid., pp. 14–15.

47. Neugebauer, "Religious Organizations Taking Proactive Role," p. 20.

48. Ibid.

49. Eileen W. Lindner, ed., *Yearbook of American and Canadian Churches 2000, Religious Pluralism in the New Millennium* (New York: National Council of Churches of Christ in the U.S.A., 2000), p. 22.

50. www.gbod.org/children/articles/childcarepolicy.html [December 18, 2000].

CHAPTER FOURTEEN

Promises and Perils: Faith-Based Involvement in After-School Programs

FRED DAVIE, SUZANNE LE MENESTREL, and RICHARD MURPHY

When we were approached to write this chapter, we were pleased to be able to address such a high-profile issue as the involvement of faith-based organizations in child-care and after-school programs. However, as we began to discuss the issue, we kept returning to two questions: "Why is something that has been going on for so long being viewed by so many people as a brand-new idea?" and "What are the real cost implications of leveling the playing field to include faith-based organizations?"

Faith-based organizations have had a long and rich tradition of providing social services and child care to children, youth, and their families in the United States, longer than government funds have been available at any level—federal, state, or local. From the settlement houses of the 1800s to modern-day Catholic Charities USA, "the largest private network of social service organizations in the United States," faith-based organizations have played an important role.

Fred Davie would like to thank Susan Beresford, president of the Ford Foundation, and Melvin Oliver, vice president for asset-building and community development at the Ford Foundation, for supporting his work on this chapter. Suzanne Le Menestrel and Richard Murphy would like to express their appreciation to the staff of the Center for Youth Development and Policy Research at the Academy for Educational Development, particularly Emmett Gill, Elizabeth Partoyan, and Alexia Zdral, for their useful comments on earlier drafts of this chapter.

Government financial support of faith-based organizations' operations is not a new phenomenon. For instance, Catholic Charities USA reported that in 1999 it received 62 percent of its income from local, state, and federal government grants.[1] What is currently at the heart of the debate is how the separation of church and state will be ensured and whether faith-based organizations have the capacity to provide additional high-quality services.

What makes this issue seem new are the actions of former President Clinton and, even more, of President Bush. Four major actions have been taken in the last five years:

—*1996.* The first charitable choice provision was included in the Personal Responsibility and Work Opportunity Reconciliation Act of 1996 during the Clinton administration. Charitable choice was defined as a "legislative effort to expand the universe of religious organizations that can participate in publicly funded social services programs."[2]

—*1998.* The second charitable choice provision, a modified version of the one included in the 1996 welfare reform legislation, was included in the Community Services Block Grant Program of the Human Services Reauthorization Act of 1998.

—*1999 to the present.* Bush's use of the bully pulpit as governor, presidential candidate, and president to expand the role of faith-based organizations in delivering social services.[3]

—*January 29, 2001.* Establishment of the White House Office of Faith-Based and Community Initiatives to increase charitable giving; level the playing field for community-based groups; and find effective models of public-private partnership.

In this chapter, we discuss the promises and perils of faith-based organizations' involvement in child-care and after-school programs. "Faith-based organization" refers to any organization that is affiliated with a religion or spiritual movement, whether traditional mainline faiths—Christian, Jewish, Muslim—or the growing minority religious groups in this country, such as Buddhists, Hindus, Wiccans, and others.

We describe current demographic and other "realities" of child care in the United States today and how those realities affect the supply of and demand for child-care and after-school programs as well as the programs' quality. We also consider how those realities affect providers' ability to deliver quality services.

We then turn to some of the promises or benefits of faith-based organizations' involvement in the provision of child-care and after-school programs as well as the perils, or potential dangers, of their involvement. Finally, we examine the implications for children, youth, families, service providers, faith-based organizations, and the community at large.

REALITIES OF CHILD CARE IN THE UNITED STATES

First, child-care use is increasing. There were approximately 21 million infants, toddlers, and preschool children under the age of six in the United States in 1995, and more than 12.9 million of them were in child care. Forty-five percent of children under age one were in child care on a regular basis.[4] Nearly two-thirds of school-age children and youth live with a single employed parent or two parents who are both employed.[5] Parents are working more. One study found that the typical married-couple family worked more than six weeks more in 1996 than in 1989 because of a variety of factors, such as increased employment of women, employers' increased expectations, reduction in the number of unionized workers, and falling wages.[6]

Second, many school-age children are spending some time at home alone. A recent study of families with working mothers indicates that 10 percent of six- to nine-year-old children are left alone or with a brother or sister younger than age thirteen on a regular basis each week and that 35 percent of ten- to twelve-year-old children regularly spend time in self-care or with a sibling younger than age thirteen.[7] However, surveys are not the best way to capture information on self-care because of the "social desirability" factor, or parents' propensity to report what they believe researchers would like to hear.[8] Estimates from recent time-diary data from the 1997 Panel Study of Income Dynamics indicate that 4 million (14 percent) of five- to twelve-year-old children spent some time at home alone after school.[9]

Third, there are concerns about the safety and well-being of children and youth who spend time unsupervised after school. The hours between 3:00 p.m. and 6:00 p.m. on school days are peak hours for violent juvenile crime. In addition, youth are most likely to become victims of violent crime, be in or cause a car crash, and engage in other high-risk behaviors, such as substance use and unprotected sexual intercourse, during those hours.[10] Spending time in self-care also affects children's social and academic competence. For instance, one study of sixth graders found that those who had spent more time in self-care during first and third grade were less socially competent and received lower academic grades than children who had spent less time on their own. That association is even more evident among children from low-income families.[11]

A fourth important reality is the affordability and availability of high-quality child care. A recent survey of local child-care resource and referral agencies conducted by the Children's Defense Fund found that the average annual cost of care for a four-year-old living in an urban area was more than the average annual cost of public college tuition in all but one state. The average cost of school-age care in an urban area can be as high as $3,500 per year.[12] Consequently, low-income families often are faced with placing their children in lower-cost, lower-quality care.

Many communities confront often severe shortages of openings in child-care and after-school programs because of a variety of factors, such as the strong economy, the increasing number of mothers in the work force, and the influx of children of former welfare recipients who are now holding jobs. For example, in the three cities (Boston, Chicago, and Seattle) that are taking part in the Making the Most of Out-of-School Time (MOST) Initiative, there are full-time after-school program slots for only between 9 percent and 35 percent of the school-age population.[13] In addition, child-care workers are leaving for better-paying jobs elsewhere, causing many centers to freeze enrollment or close their doors altogether.

One of the fastest-growing federally supported programs for after-school care is the U.S. Department of Education–funded 21st Century Community Learning Centers, which targets rural and inner-city public schools. Most of the programs in rural and urban elementary schools currently are operating at capacity or expanding to meet the demand for care.[14] In addition, in the 2000 competition for 21st Century Community Learning Centers grants, 2,252 communities sought assistance to establish or expand after-school programs, but the U.S. Department of Education had enough funding to provide only 310 grants. The Center for Youth Development and Policy Research estimates that available funding for the 2000 21st Century Community Learning Centers program covered only about 2 percent of the school-age population (ages five to seventeen) in the United States. In sum, in both urban and rural areas, there is a documented, extreme need for after-school programming in schools, especially for low-income families.[15]

REALITIES FOR CHILD-CARE AND AFTER-SCHOOL PROGRAMS

Early childhood programs are faced with turnover rates ranging from 36 percent for center directors to a high of 59 percent for teacher assistants.[16] Average annual salaries for teachers range from $13,125 to $18,988 for full-time employment, and average salaries for assistants are about $6 to $7 per hour.[17] After-school programs have similar problems with staff turnover and low salaries, compounded by the part-time nature of most of the available positions. In addition, rapid expansion of after-school programs and the introduction of new players, such as cultural institutions, religious organizations, and libraries, have led to increased competition for qualified staff.[18]

While both child-care programs and the emerging after-school programs share many of the same challenges, after-school programs are just beginning to establish program standards, curriculums, and staff training and credentialing requirements. As the field expands, all providers should be aware of the unrealistic expectations being attached to after-school care. Both private and public funders of after-school programs are expecting their funding to have a positive effect on academic performance and problem behavior. While there is some evidence of such short-term outcomes, there are too many other variables in young people's lives to expect after-school care to solve all their problems.

THE PROMISES

Involving faith-based organizations in providing child-care and after-school services has some promising aspects, among them increased public support for after-school programs and involvement of religion in daily life, access of faith-based organizations to pools of volunteers, and potential benefits in the socialization of young people.

Increased Public Support and Need for More Providers

Recent polls indicate that there is strong public support for after-school programs. For instance, 92 percent of registered voters polled in the 2000 Mott/JCPenney Nationwide Survey on Afterschool Programs said that children and youth should have some type of organized activity or place to go after school every day. That support cut across partisan lines. In addition, seven of ten voters believed that it is difficult for parents to find after-school programs.[19] In another recent poll conducted for Fight Crime: Invest in Kids, 67 percent of adults said that providing access to after-school programs is a higher priority than a tax cut.[20]

There also is strong support for increased involvement of religion in daily life. In a recent national survey of Americans, 70 percent of those surveyed said that they want religion's influence on American society to grow. Sixty-three percent of the respondents were in favor of giving religious groups and churches government money to fund programs aimed at helping the poor.[21] Thus strong public support may make it easier for faith-based organizations to adopt the role of provider of child-care and after-school programs.

Close Community Connections

Child-care and after-school programs sponsored by faith-based organizations have the potential to address many community needs. In 1997 most of the 353,000 religious congregations in the United States were located in residential neighborhoods within metropolitan areas.[22] Parents might be more comfortable having their children attend programs in their own neighborhoods rather than transporting them across town. Program staff and volunteers are likely to be members of the faith-based organization offering the program and to come from the same communities as the children who attend.

After-school programs often face difficulties obtaining adequate space in school buildings, and they have to compete with school personnel for use of school supplies, utilities, and custodial staff. Physical space limitations affect the type of programming, program size, and children's behavior.[23] Many faith-based organizations have large physical spaces, such as recreation halls, gyms, or outdoor areas that go unused, particularly during after-school hours, and they also may have access to vans or other modes of transportation.

Pools of Volunteers

Faith-based organizations traditionally rely on volunteers to carry out many of their programs. For example, in 1998, Catholic Charities USA reported the participation of nearly 300,000 volunteers (and only 52,000 paid staff) in the administration of its social service programs.[24] A recent study conducted by Independent Sector found that nine of ten religious congregations used volunteers. Fifty-seven percent of total volunteer time in those congregations was devoted to religious worship and education; 15 percent to education; 9 percent to health; and 8 percent to human services and welfare.[25]

In a 1997 study of 113 historic urban congregations that reported providing 449 programs, 338 of the programs used volunteers, for an average of 148 hours each of volunteer time per month. The estimated monthly value of volunteer time for the entire sample was $577,751.[26] Given the shortage of qualified staff in general in the child-care field, faith-based organizations may be well situated to staff programs from already existing pools of volunteers.

Benefits to Child and Youth Development

Youth development can be defined as the "ongoing growth process in which all youth are engaged in attempting to (1) meet their basic personal and social needs to be safe, feel cared for, be valued, be useful, and be spiritually grounded; and (2) to build skills and competencies that allow them to function and contribute in their daily lives."[27] How youth meet those needs depends, in part, on the quality and availability of people, places, and possibilities.

The youth development field has identified a series of psychosocial and competency outcomes that "reflect the goals that adults have for youth and youth have for themselves."[28] Spirituality is one psychosocial outcome that faith-based organizations may have a considerable role in developing. There are within most faith traditions universal values that transcend dogma and doctrine; for example, there is the ethic of love, especially love and respect for oneself and one's neighbors. Coupled with that ethic is the notion of love for those in need, a love that manifests itself in service. A second value, hope, engenders the courage to believe that no matter how dire the circumstance, one should persevere to overcome it; that no matter how bleak things are today, they can always be better tomorrow. Many individuals of faith believe that love and hope are the best inoculation against hate and nihilism, two realities that sometimes characterize the lives of young people from both the barrios and the "burbs."

Additional important psychosocial outcomes include a sense of closeness/ affiliation and belonging.[29] Those outcomes may also be referred to as a sense of "connectedness," feeling close to and cared for by someone, which research has demonstrated to be an important protective factor for youth.[30] In addition to being connected with parents, youth also may benefit from being connected to a community of adults outside their immediate environment, such as those found in faith-based organizations. For example, "resilient" youth, those who display competence in the face of adversity, are more likely to seek support from nonparental adults, especially teachers, ministers, and neighbors.[31]

Another benefit of participation in child-care or after-school programs sponsored by faith-based organizations may be an increased appreciation for human diversity and tolerance of others with different religious backgrounds. Given the scarcity of available child-care and after-school slots, parents may need to place their children in programs sponsored by religious organizations that are different from their own, with corresponding opportunities for children and youth to learn about and appreciate other faith traditions.

Increasing the Pool of Informed Advocates

Leaders in faith-based organizations are strong advocates for programs for children and youth. For example, the Children's Defense Fund has a Children's Sabbath program that involves mobilizing tens of thousand of churches to support issues related to children and youth. On the Children's Sabbath, religious congregations hold worship services, religious education programs, and other congregational activities that focus on supporting long-term commitments to children and families. Another example of faith-based organizations' involvement in advocacy can be found in North Carolina. In early 2001, the Piedmont Interfaith Council of Greensboro hand-delivered a letter signed by interfaith leaders to the Guilford County commissioner demanding the release of funds for the public school budget. The funds were released the next day.

Examples such as those abound, proof of the potential for gathering a substantial pool of informed advocates for the cause of children and youth. Involving community-connected providers in the world of child care and after-school care will provide them with firsthand knowledge of the weak and underfunded infrastructure that exists for developing the community's youngest citizens. Those new providers could become an important voice for improving the quality and quantity of child-care and after-school programs.

THE PERILS

Involvement of faith-based organizations in child-care and after-school programs also entails some potential perils, among them inadequate programs, poorly trained volunteers, and sectarianism.

Program Quality

One of the first potential perils of increased involvement of faith-based organizations in the provision of child-care and after-school programs is their ability to operate quality programs. There is scant empirical evidence at present to demonstrate that private sector service delivery is any more or less effective than public service delivery.[32] Congregations themselves often fail to evaluate the quality of their programs because of lack of expertise, resources, or interest.[33] More important factors may be whether an organization can ensure clear accountability for results, clear public objectives, and clear contracts for services.[34]

Many organizations that traditionally have been involved in providing social services, youth programs, or child care are small and do not have the staff capacity to comply with government regulations. Ironically, the primary factor preventing most organizations from meeting government regulations is government's insufficient funding of quality services. In addition, a recent Charles Stewart Mott Foundation/JCPenney poll of registered voters found that only 7 percent of respondents wanted to see after-school programs take place at churches or temples, whereas 50 percent said that they would like to see daily after-school programs take place in public schools.[35] While it is not certain why the respondents expressed that preference, it suggests that public schools are recognized as providers of after-school programs. Another challenge for congregations that focus on serving high-risk youth is that they often become fragmented and stretched to the limits of their capacity to provide the necessary services. Competing demands for limited resources may lead to weakening of the congregation's service delivery infrastructure and burnout among its leaders.[36]

Results from the National Congregations Study, a nationally representative sample of congregations, indicate that congregations are more likely to be involved in activities that address immediate, short-term needs for food, clothing, and shelter than programs that require a sustained long-term commitment.[37] In addition, only 12 percent of the congregations in the study reported that they ran one of the most common types of programs (food, housing, and homeless services) by themselves. Furthermore, only 12 percent of the congregations that reported some sort of social service provision had a staff person who devoted at least 25 percent of his or her time to social service projects.[38] Those results raise the question of whether the majority of faith-based organizations have the capacity and expertise to run high-quality, larger-scale child-care and after-school programs.

It also is uncertain whether the White House Office of Faith-Based and Community Initiatives will loosen government regulations for faith-based organizations that receive federal funding. President Bush has said that the new office will "clear away the bureaucratic barriers in several important agencies that make private groups hesitate to work with government."[39] He also noted in his education plan that "before- and after-school learning opportunities will be expanded by granting states and school districts freedom to award grants to faith-based and community-based organizations."[40]

John DiIulio, the first director of the Office of Faith-Based and Community Initiatives, remarked in a speech delivered at the conference of the National Association of Evangelicals in March 2001 that the "conversion-centered program that cannot separate out and privately fund its inherently religious activities can still receive government support, but only via individual vouchers."[41] Those vouchers would be given to clients who then could choose from a variety of programs. How the system of awarding grants to some organizations and vouchers to others will be implemented has yet to be determined. At any rate, it has not been specified whether faith-based and other community organizations will face less stringent government regulations, such as those for meeting certain licensing standards and ensuring fiscal accountability.

Finding, Training, and Maintaining a Pool of Volunteers

While many faith-based organizations rely on volunteers to carry out their programs, it is uncertain whether they will have the resources to develop a well-trained and committed staff of volunteers if they expand their programs to provide child-care and after-school services. Data from the National Congregations Study point to the fact that the number of volunteers that congregations can mobilize actually is very small. Of the 80 percent of congregations involved in social service activities, the average congregation mobilized only ten volunteers in 1998.[42] In the Independent Sector study of religious congregations, "personnel issues" was named one of the three most common challenges over the next five years. Specifically, congregations were concerned with staff burnout, training volunteers as opposed to paid staff to carry out the congregation's programs, and being able to retain a large pool of volunteers.[43]

Moreover, recruiting, training, and managing volunteers is costly. In its evaluation of the Big Brothers Big Sisters program, the research firm Public/Private Ventures determined that it cost approximately $1,000 to train a volunteer, develop a match between a child and a volunteer, and supervise a volunteer.[44] In addition, many nonprofit organizations have discovered that it is time-consuming to develop the set of skills required to manage volunteers. Whether most faith-based organizations can devote sufficient resources to recruit, develop, and retain a trained volunteer pool remains to be seen. As a final note, it should be remembered that the child-care and after-school programs are having difficulty finding staff even when they can pay a salary, albeit a low one.

Disadvantages for Child and Youth Development

While youth involvement in programs sponsored by faith-based organizations has many advantages, several potential risks or perils also exist. First, there is a danger in engaging faith-based institutions in values development because they often confound values and doctrine. Doctrines can be judgmental, condemning behaviors without any regard for the political, economic, and social conditions that generate the behaviors. Doctrine often establishes who is saved and who is damned, setting up people outside a particular faith as "other" or "deviant" and thus deserving of their poor status, discrimination, imprisonment, and so forth.[45] Many young people may consider such a doctrinal approach irrelevant in their lives and too rigid to be of any use to them and so turn away from faith-based organizations, as many already have done.

In addition, developmental theorist Erik Erikson noted that during adolescence, young people are faced with a crisis of identity versus role. During that period, a young person is faced with developing a sense of self in relation to others and to his or her own internal thoughts.[46] Thus youth are attempting to establish their own identities, separating from their parents or caregivers. Consequently, they may reject involvement in any type of organization that they identify with their parents or caregivers.

In any partnership of faith-based organizations and government, faith-based organizations should be encouraged by government to teach the importance of acceptance of diversity, rooted in the ethic of love and consistent with contemporary notions of community building. Government must discourage, indeed disallow, the teaching of doctrine and dogma because it violates the Constitution and is extremely inappropriate for when services are supported with public resources. There also is the danger that faith-based organizations may create "provincial worlds" that greatly reduce children's and youths' exposure to the religious, ethnic, and cultural diversity found in the outside world. That exposure is more important than ever to develop the skills and competencies needed to negotiate in an increasingly diverse society.

Faith-Based Organizations as Court Prophets

One of the biggest perils to confront religious institutions that align too closely with government is the loss of their independence and thus their ability to hold government accountable. The United States has had no shortage of religious leaders who provide justification for questionable government policies. Yet we have come to expect our religious leaders and institutions to challenge government when government transgresses the rights of people who live on the margins—the poor, the disenfranchised, racial minorities, and others. The concept of religious leader as a critical or prophetic voice to government is older than the republic itself. The first voices to decry slavery in this country came from the faith community, including Reverend Henry Ward Beecher, a Presbyterian minister and the brother of Harriet Beecher Stowe, who said that "liberty is the soul's right to breathe."[47] The Quakers and the Methodists were some of the earliest religious communities to stand against the institution of slavery. Methodism, for example, has "typically been concerned with ministry to the poor and disadvantaged, expressing its faith in compassion for the human condition."[48]

Among African Americans, resistance to racial discrimination and other forms of social injustice was born in the church. The prophetic voice best known to contemporary Americans is Martin Luther King Jr., but many others preceded him. From the religious leaders who held secret meetings in the bush arbors (known as hush harbors) of the antebellum South to Dr. King's predecessor, Vernon Johns, of the Dexter Avenue Baptist Church in Birmingham, there is a rich tradition of religious leaders challenging government-sanctioned and -supported injustice.

An example of the tradition of prophetic religious leaders speaking to those in power comes directly from the Hebrew scriptures. Isaiah, Amos, Jeremiah, and Micah all inveighed against royal excesses and religious practices that had gone awry. Amos cried, "Instead let justice flow on like a river and righteousness like a never-failing torrent."[49] Micah stated, "The Lord has told you mortals what is good, and what it is that the Lord requires of you: only to act justly, to love loyalty, to walk humbly with your God."[50] Isaiah and Jeremiah accused those in power of forgetting the widow and trampling the poor and the orphaned under foot.[51] Out of this tradition came some of this country's most dynamic prophetic religious voices, men and women who did not depend on the resources of "Caesar" and thus were free to hold "Caesar" accountable.

Nevertheless, there were religious leaders who became much too dependent on the state, and instead of speaking truth to the powerful, they began to say what the powerful wanted them to say. Those leaders often were called court prophets, for they served in the king's court and spoke in support of the king's position or remained silent for fear of falling out of favor. Johannes Lindblom states that "one of the main professional tasks of these cultic [court] prophets was to announce [a message] in the interest of the royal house and of official policy, to encourage the people, and by the power of their prophetic words influence the course of events in a favorable direction [for the king]."[52]

Religious leaders who become too dependent on government will be compelled to speak favorably of the government or risk delay or defunding of their publicly supported projects or programs. An example is provided by the experience of Reverend Calvin O. Butts and the Abyssinian Community Development Corporation (ADC) in New York City, which receives government money and needs public approval for most of its development projects. When Reverend Butts became a vocal critic of Mayor Rudolph Giuliani's policies and actions, several of ADC's projects were delayed, and, in one case, the mayor sought to completely arrest the development of the ADC-sponsored Pathmark Shopping Center, at that time Harlem's first major economic development project in thirty years.

In considering the role of faith-based organizations in child-care and after-school programs, especially programs supported by public dollars, there is a critical need to keep in mind the peril of undermining the power of religious leaders to speak a prophetic word to power on behalf of the young people they serve. Distance must be maintained between government and the sacred place. An intermediary, either a separate organization or a separately incorporated nonprofit affiliate, would help to ensure at least some independence for the religious institution and its leaders.

Maintaining the Focus on Faith-Based Work

Many faith-based organizations are wary of applying for public funds because of the strings attached, including a perceived threat of government control of their programs, increased accountability for positive results, and more red tape.[53] Data from the National Congregations Study indicate that theologically and politically conservative congregations are significantly less likely to express a willingness to apply for public funds, regardless of denominational affiliation and other background characteristics.[54] That finding suggests that those congregations may fear government intrusion and control. Finally, there is the reality of managing time and dual responsibilities. Being both a spiritual and educational leader may be too demanding for many leaders of congregations.

Separation of Church and State

Many questions have arisen about the constitutionality of the charitable choice provisions as well as the intent of the White House Office of Faith-Based and Community Initiatives. The First Amendment to the U.S. Constitution establishes that "Congress shall make no law respecting an establishment of religion or prohibiting the free exercise thereof."However, we defer an in-depth consideration of this complex issue to the legal scholars who currently are involved in the debate.

IMPLICATIONS

Implications for families. If faith-based organizations were to become increasingly involved in providing child-care and after-school programs under the auspices of the White House Office of Faith-Based and Community Initiatives, families, especially low-income families, may have increased options, particularly in their own neighborhoods. However, parents and caregivers might also be faced with increased "homework" when selecting a program, such as ascertaining whether a program is licensed by the city, county, or state; whether it meets quality standards established by organizations such as the National Association for the Education of Young Children and the National School-Age Care Alliance; and whether the staff (volunteers and paid staff) are well-trained and experienced. The stability of the program (that is, whether the program will exist in another year or two) and the staff, especially for those programs that rely on volunteers, also are significant considerations.

Moreover, parents and caregivers may need to know whether a program is secular or incorporates a particular religious philosophy. If a program focuses on a religious ideology that is different from their own, parents and caregivers need to decide whether they are comfortable with having their children spend a considerable amount of time exposed to teachings that may or may not be compatible with their own religious beliefs. In any case, it is important to educate parents and caregivers about their options, and they must know how to determine whether a particular program will meet their children's needs.

Implications for service providers. Removing regulatory barriers could be beneficial for old and new providers, with or without a faith-based connection. However, many practitioners would argue that the field of child care and after-school care needs additional regulation in the form of uniformly adopted standards that translate into quality programming. Likewise, they could easily say that the biggest barrier to providing quality services is the fact that the government does not fund programs on a real-cost basis to allow for hiring qualified staff who are paid a living wage. Both President Bush and John DiIulio have used the phrase "level the playing field" to allow new providers onto the field. Making the playing field suitable for children and the adults who work with them is equally important, if not more urgent.

The issues that are being raised have profound implications. First, will government now fund programs at the real cost of service delivery? Second, will government eliminate or modify some standards that could lessen program quality? Those are big questions, but the White House office must tackle them.

Implications for faith-based organizations. The foregoing information describes a fairly complex, if not complicated, situation for faith-based organizations. For example, many of the country's leaders now are presenting faith-based organizations' involvement in social service delivery as if it were a new phenomenon. It is not. Second, for faith-based organizations to do their work well and truly meet the needs of children and youth, they need to be fully funded. Third, full funding requires faith-based organizations to be able to manage both the increase in funding and expanded service provision. Failure to focus on enhancing their capacity guarantees the failure of effective program delivery. Finally, faith-based organizations must be partners with government, not a substitute for government, in meeting the needs of children and youth.

CONCLUSION

The short- and long-term implications of involving faith-based organizations in child-care and after-school programs are multiple, complex, and often contradictory. For example, running cost-effective child-care programs often means not paying caregivers a living wage. The cynical side of human nature says that the establishment of the White House office and the attendant rhetoric constitute the ultimate political spin and that many good and sincere faith-based organizations are being set up to fail. The more optimistic side wants the new emphasis on the spirit of community to make a measurable difference. Did not President Bush himself have a positive transformation through a faith-based connection?

Imagine that in the year 2003 President Bush were to visit a "Reverend Michaels," who ministers to a small congregation in north Philadelphia, to find out what impact receiving government money has had on the reverend's programs. Reverend Michaels received two grants—one to reduce juvenile delinquency, the other to run an after-school program. The reverend operated both initiatives with great success. Juvenile crime was reduced in her catchment area, and in the first year of her after-school program, thirty children were doing better in school.

By year two, the reverend's catchment area no longer qualifies for funding for the delinquency prevention program and the youth in the after-school program hit a learning plateau. The reverend visits their schools and discovers wretched physical conditions, few books, and teachers who are not certified to teach in their subject areas. In addition, the youth that were in the juvenile delinquency prevention program no longer have their outreach worker, and two young people in the group cannot live at home. Moreover, the city cannot restore the local park, open the library on weekends, or maintain a Saturday bus route. Armed with this information, Reverend Michaels prepares to give a sermon in a suburban church in Chestnut Hill, a wealthy neighboring suburb.

The Chestnut Hill congregation is horrified by what they hear, and they are moved to action. One Chestnut Hill congregation member does a sophisticated fiscal analysis comparing his and the reverend's resources. Youth in Chestnut Hill receive about twice as many government resources (for example, funds for education, parks, street maintenance) as the reverend's youth. Chestnut Hill engages in a successful statewide campaign to increase resources to Reverend Michaels's community so her youth have economic equality with Chestnut Hill . . . and everyone grows and prospers developmentally and spiritually ever after.

That scenario may be apocryphal, but it does dramatize some of the realities the nation needs to address if we want better outcomes for all of our youth. But better outcomes will elude us until we figure out how much money we need to develop each child in the United States and ensure that that amount is made available. A small church with or without limited government resources cannot make up for years of neglect of education and community infrastructure. It is dangerous to imply that poor communities can turn around their youth and families if government provides a limited amount of money directly to faith-based organizations. We have been trying to do this for years, and we have some wonderful anecdotes and some true success stories. What we have not done is the math to determine what it would take to support the models that we have seen work in a ten-block radius and then expand that scale to include all children and youth in a community. The challenge for President Bush and like-minded leaders is this: Are you willing to do the math?

NOTES

1. Catholic Charities USA, "Our Story in Stats" (http://www.catholiccharitiesusa.org/who/stats.html [February 2001]).

2. David Ackerman, "Charitable Choice: Background and Selected Legal Issues." CRS Report for Congress (Congressional Research Service, Library of Congress, September 2000).

3. The C-SPAN congressional glossary explains the term *bully pulpit* as follows: "This term stems from President Theodore Roosevelt's reference to the White House as a 'bully pulpit,' meaning a terrific platform from which to persuasively advocate an agenda."

4. National Child Care Information Center, "Child Care for Young Children: Demographics," *Child Care Bulletin*, no. 17 (September/October 1997).

5. U.S. Bureau of the Census, March 1998 Current Population Survey, P20-514, table 6, 1998 (http://www.census.gov/population/www/socdemo/ms-la.html).

6. Jared Bernstein, Edie Rasell, John Schmitt, and Robert E. Scott, "Tax Cuts No Cure for Middle Class Economic Woes" (Washington: Economic Policy Institute, 1999).

7. Jeffrey Capizzano, Kathryn Tout, and Gina Adams, "Child Care Patterns of School-Age Children with Employed Mothers," Occasional Paper 41 (Washington: The Urban Institute, September 2000).

8. See for example Sandra Hofferth, "Family Reading to Young Children: Social Desirability and Cultural Biases in Reporting," paper presented at Workshop on Measurement of and Research on Time Use, Committee on National Statistics (Washington: National Research Council, May 1999).

9. Sandra Hofferth, Zita Jankuniene, and Peter Brandon, "Self-Care among School-Age Children," paper presented at the biennial meeting of the Society for Research on Adolescence, Minneapolis, 2000.

10. Sanford Newman, James Alan Fox, Edward A. Flynn, and William Christeson, *America's After-School Choice: The Prime Time for Juvenile Crime, or Youth Enrichment and Achievement* (Washington: Fight Crime: Invest in Kids, 2000).

11. Gregory S. Pettit and others, "Patterns of After-School Care in Middle Childhood: Risk Factors and Developmental Outcomes," *Merrill-Palmer Quarterly*, vol. 43 (1997), 515–38.

12. Karen Schulman, *The High Cost of Child Care Puts Quality Care out of Reach for Many Families* (Washington: Children's Defense Fund, 2000).

13. Robert Halpern, "After-School Programs for Low-Income Children: Promises and Challenges," *Future of Children*, vol. 9, no. 2 (Los Altos, Calif.: David and Lucile Packard Foundation, 1999).

14. Mark Dynarski, principal investigator of the National Longitudinal Study of the 21st Century Community Learning Centers Program, Mathematica Policy Research, personal communication, June 2000.

15. *Future of Children*, vol. 9, no. 2.

16. Marcy Whitebook, Laura Sakai, and Carollee Howes, "NAEYC Accreditation as a Strategy for Improving Child Care Quality: An Assessment," Final Report (Washington: National Center for the Early Childhood Work Force, 1997).

17. Deborah Lowe Vandell and Barbara Wolfe, *Child Care Quality: Does It Matter and Does It Need to Be Improved?* (Office of the Assistant Secretary for Planning and Evaluation, U.S. Department of Health and Human Services, May 2000).

18. Joyce Shortt, *Spotlight on MOST: Building a Stable High-Quality After-School Work Force* (Wellesley, Mass.: National Institute on Out-of-School Time, 2001).

19. The Afterschool Alliance, *Afterschool Alert Poll Report No. 3* (Washington: June 2000).

20. "More Than Two-Thirds of Public Say Boosting Investments in Kids Is Higher Priority Than Tax Cut" (http://www.fightcrime.org/pressdocs/taxcutrelease.html [February, 2001]).

21. Steve Farkas and others, *For Goodness' Sake: Why So Many Want Religion to Play a Greater Role in American Life* (New York: Public Agenda, 2001).

22. Susan K. E. Saxon-Harrold and others, *America's Religious Congregations: Measuring Their Contribution to Society* (Washington: Independent Sector, November 2000).

23. Halpern, "After-School Programs for Low-Income Children."

24. Catholic Charities USA, "Our Story in Stats."

25. Saxon-Harrold and others, "America's Religious Congregations."

26. Ram Cnaan, "Our Hidden Safety Net: Social and Community Work by Urban American Religious Congregations," *Brookings Review* (Spring 1999), pp. 50–53.

27. Karen J. Pittman, Ray O'Brien, and Mary Kimball, *Youth Development and Resiliency Research: Making Connections to Substance Abuse Prevention* (Washington: Center for Youth Development and Policy Research/Academy for Educational Development, 1993), p. 8.

28. Ibid., p. 9.

29. Ibid.

30. Robert W. Blum and Peggy Mann Rinehart, *Reducing the Risk: Connections That Make a Difference in the Lives of Youth* (University of Minnesota, Division of General Pediatrics and Adolescent Health, 1997); Bonnie Benard, *Fostering Resiliency in Kids: Protective Factors in the Family, School, and Community* (San Francisco: Far West Laboratory for Educational Research and Development and the Western Regional Center for Drug-Free Schools and Communities, 1991).

31. Emmy Werner and Ruth S. Smith, *Vulnerable but Invincible: A Study of Resilient Children* (New York: McGraw-Hill, 1982).

32. Harold Dean Trulear, *Faith-Based Institutions and High-Risk Youth* (Philadelphia: Public/Private Ventures, Spring 2000); Demetra Smith Nightingale and Nancy Pindus, *Privatization of Public Social Services: A Background Paper* (Washington: Urban Institute, October 1997).

33. Trulear, *Faith-Based Institutions and High-Risk Youth*; Saxon-Harrold and others, *America's Religious Congregations*.

34. Nightingale and Pindus, *Privatization of Public Social Services*.

35. The Afterschool Alliance, *Afterschool Alert Poll Report No. 3*.

36. Trulear, *Faith-Based Institutions and High-Risk Youth*.

37. Mark Chaves, "Congregations' Social Service Activities," *Charting Civil Society*, no. 6 (Washington: Center on Nonprofits and Philanthropy, Urban Institute, December 1999).

38. Ibid.

39. "Bush Establishes White House Office of Faith-Based and Community Initiatives," *White House Bulletin*, January 29, 2001.

40. George W. Bush, "No Child Left Behind," The White House, January 22, 2001, p. 21.

41. John J. DiIulio Jr., "Compassion 'In Truth and Action': How Sacred and Secular Places Serve Civic Purposes, and What Washington Should—and Should Not—Do to Help," speech delivered before the National Association of Evangelicals, Dallas, Texas, March 7, 2001, p. 26.

42. Chaves, "Congregations' Social Service Activities."

43. Saxon-Harrold and others, *America's Religious Congregations: Measuring Their Contribution to Society*.

44. Joseph P. Tierney, Jean Baldwin Grossman, and Nancy L. Resch, *Making a Difference: An Impact Study of Big Brothers/Big Sisters* (Philadelphia: Public/Private Ventures, 1995).

45. Richard Snyder, *The Protestant Ethic and the Spirit of Punishment* (Grand Rapids, Mich.: Eerdmans Publishing Company, 2001), p. 12.

46. Erik H. Erikson, *Identity: Youth and Crisis* (New York: Norton, 1968).

47. Henry Ward Beecher, *Proverbs from Plymouth Pulpit: Selected from the Writings and Sayings of Henry Ward Beecher, by William Drysdale. Revised in Part by Mr. Beecher, and Under Revision by Him at the Time of His Death* (New York: D. Appleton and Company, 1887).

48. Frank S. Mead, *Handbook of Denominations in the United States*, 10th ed., revised by Samuel S. Hill (Nashville: Abingdon Press, 1995), p. 194.

49. M. Jack Suggs, Katharine Doob Sakenfeld, and James R. Mueller, *The Oxford Study Bible: Revised English Bible with the Apocrypha* (Oxford University Press, 1992), Amos 5:24.

50. Ibid., Micah 6:8.

51. Ibid., Isaiah 1:17, 23; Jeremiah 7:6, 22:3.

52. Johannes Lindblom, *Prophecy in Ancient Israel* (Philadelphia: Fortress Press, 1962), p. 215.

53. Mark Chaves, "Religious Congregations and Welfare Reform: Who Will Take Advantage of 'Charitable Choice'?" Working Papers Series, Nonprofit Sector Research Fund (Washington: Aspen Institute, 1998).

54. Chaves, "Congregations' Social Service Activities."

CHAPTER FIFTEEN

Sacred Places? Not Quite.
Civic Purposes? Almost.

EILEEN W. LINDNER

Some of you may remember *The Children's Cause*, by Gilbert Steiner, published by the Brookings Institution at a time when some other similar institutions failed to consider children's issues a serious matter. It records, among other things, the development, advocacy, passage, and ultimate veto of the 1971 omnibus child-care bill. You may remember that President Nixon vetoed it, saying that it was "the broadest plan yet advanced for the Sovietization of American children." I say that not to ridicule or belittle, but to note how far we have come in our understanding of the role of child care in rearing children in this society. Thirty years ago the debate, heated and ideological, still raged. Today, while there is still some debate, the vast majority of parents see child care as a tool to use in their own good parenting.

I am a pastor who happened to take up the issue of child care, not a child advocate who happened to take up the ministry. I want to be straightforward about that because I think that it conditions how I see things. It was as a pastor that I undertook the study of church-housed child care twenty years ago. The results were reported in *When Churches Mind the Children*,[1] and are, of course, central to Mary Bogle's findings.

Twenty years ago we had a hunch that the church was playing a role in child care; we came to find out that we were the McDonald's of the industry. Our share of the market for child care and McDonald's share of the market for hamburgers were roughly analogous. In 1980, for every child in our sample attending church school on Sunday, there were nine children at the church on Monday morning. That is especially important when we recall that the sample consisted of 120,000 congregations, making ours the largest study of child care in the

United States. We hope to undertake a twentieth-anniversary study to see what has changed in the intervening years.

Mary Bogle's chapter does a fine job of summarizing the findings of our study of church-housed child care. In addition to discovering the primacy of church as a provider, we learned that several broadly held assumptions about church-housed care were not borne out by empirical evidence. Very few congregations limit child-care provision to their own members and virtually none fail to make some form of financial contribution to the child-care centers they house. Often that is done by the contribution of in-kind services or through a reduction in costs of utilities, custodial services, and the like. Generally speaking, child care does not serve as a membership outreach or evangelical program. In the aggregate, churches provide a staggering array of child-care services within church-owned properties.

In a final introductory comment I want to say that I have adapted the book's title, *Sacred Places, Civic Purposes*, to explore the hypothesis "Sacred Places? Not Quite. Civic Purposes? Almost."

First, the issue of sanctity. The churches and congregations that provide space for child care generally do not use their most sacred space for that activity. It does not take place in the nave or the sanctuary—that is, in the worship space. There would be many more issues to consider if that were the space that was used. Such space often is laden with religious artifacts and symbols and reverentially maintained, and by custom it is a place of specialized behaviors. Child care is more commonly offered in educational rooms and all-purpose facilities. So it is important to understand that the space is not quite "sacred." It is, for example, the educational wing that was built and mortgaged along with the sacred space, often space in the basement underneath the sanctuary. The congregants do not feel about that space quite the way they feel about what is truly a sacred worship space. That may seem like hair splitting, but I don't think it is. Few congregations that have only worship space offer child-care services. It is important to note here that I am not making a legal distinction. The whole of the church property is exempt from taxation. Sacred activities, such as prayer, counseling, hymn singing, and so forth do take place in such spaces. Yet I believe that in the present discussion of faith-based initiatives subtle differences will be very important. The precise location—classroom or altar—makes a difference to the provider of the service and perhaps to the recipient.

Now, as for the civic nature of the purposes. I think that we have almost phrased this correctly, but many congregants might disagree, because the question of motivation is important. In the Christian tradition we would say, with regard to child care, for example, that we allow our buildings to be used in that capacity so that children might live the lives for which they were created. Now, I'm not sure that that would meet the test of a civic purpose. It really is a theologically informed call to a mission and ministry of faithfulness. What is true of child care may prove to be true of many social services offered by religious organizations. Pastors and congregations perceive and talk about the services they offer as "ministries and missions." They are more apt to ask "Is it faithful for us to provide this service?" than to ask "Should we provide this social service to the community?" Both religious and secular parties need to take special care in describing and discussing these issues, making allowances for different perspectives and vocabulary. When we look at these things from inside the religious community they do not quite square with how we look at them from a secular perspective.

It therefore matters what questions we ask and how we ask them. If we ask, "Can churches provide child care?" the answer is yes. In fact, they will continue to provide more child care than any single institution in this land. "Should they, and under what terms?" Those are different questions, and they are the questions that are really before us.

What have we learned about child care that may be instructive as we look at the broader range of faith-based initiatives? Church-housed child care grew up in direct response to local needs all across the United States. Not one single denomination suggested to its congregations that they provide child care. Not one single national parent church organization suggested it, nor did any ecumenical agency. Perhaps more significant is that no financial incentives or technical assistance was offered to local churches. The fact that child care is so prevalent in churches is evidence that congregations are highly responsive to local needs.

In contrast, we have worked hard to get churches to respond to Habitat for Humanity and other initiatives, such as Crop Walks, in which participants walk on behalf of the hungry. No one asked for local congregations to start child-care programs. As it says in the Book of Judges, "There was no king in the land, and everyone did what was right in their own eyes." In the eyes of many, many congregations during the 1960s and 1970s, it was right to provide some weekday child program. Following World War II, as you may know, the church either suffered or profited from what has been called "the edifice complex." It was a time of the highest religious affiliation rate in American history; as a result, church infrastructure was significantly developed at mid-century.

In order to enhance the quality of life in new communities, builders during that time left the corner lots open so that churches and banks could use the space to build. Initially most child-care programs were "mother's morning out" programs that offered women a place to leave their children for a few hours. The fittings and furnishings of the buildings were just right, and the space was available during the week. Over time the programs evolved into three-day nursery schools, often run on a co-op basis. It was a very common pattern throughout the 1950s and into the 1960s. The baby boomers, the largest age cohort ever to reach parenthood, were enrolled there in nursery school. The initiative was authentically local, and its evolution was by and large responsive to community need and interest.

The degree to which pastors were unaware of these services is startling. Most of the programs evolved under the leadership of laywomen and did not involve the pastors, in contrast to today's faith-based efforts. We wrote to all those pastors to ask whether they had child care or daycare, writing almost half a page to describe what it might look like. We asked them to specify whether they had infant care, toddler care, or preschool care. As returns began to come in, it began to look as if we had more infant care available than there were infants in America. To sort out our findings we made some follow-up calls. A typical exchange follows:

"Good morning, Reverend. I'm from the National Council of Churches. You responded that you have a child-care program."

"Yes, we do. It's Noah's Ark Preschool. We're very, very proud of it."

"Fine, Reverend. Just a few simple questions. How old are the children in your program? Is it an infant program, or a toddler program, or a preschool program?"

"They're little."

"Yes, Reverend. How little are they?" [Pause] "Do they talk?"

"Kind of."

And so it went. We would talk some more. Sometimes the pastor would say things like, "Well, I'd go down and ask them how old they are, but they're on a field trip to a zoo today." Well, we know that infants don't take field trips to the zoo!

I am not saying this to poke fun at male pastors, but to say that the church in its ecclesiastical and theological manifestation had almost nothing to do with the rise of child care in its midst. That ought to be the first lesson here—not only for child care but for drug counseling or any other services that we might consider. If there is not an authentic need in the community the program will not succeed. If there is an authentic need, the program in some rudimentary form already exists.

We learned that the quality of child-care programs varies not only by socioeconomic class but also by the sponsoring denomination. Churches that run their own child-care programs rather than allow their space to be used by other providers are a distinct subset, and they tend to be more conservative, both theologically and socially. Other churches are more apt to use a Maria Montessori or Head Start–based curriculum than a church-based curriculum. In the case of child care, churches tend to offer programs that are consistent with the social class of their members and with community standards rather than with their denominational identity. For example, in terms of curriculum, class size, and program characteristics, a child-care program in a Methodist or Episcopal church in a conservative upper-middle-class community is more apt to resemble other child-care programs in the community than it is to resemble Methodist or Episcopal child-care centers nationwide.

When it comes to issues of quality and standards there often has been great confusion about church-housed programs. While some church programs are of poorer quality than secular programs, generalizations have to be avoided. Most mainline Protestant churches have a national policy requiring church-housed programs in their congregations to comply voluntarily with state regulations even in states that exempt church-based programs from compliance. Other denominations and independent churches often actively advocate exemption from licensing standards for church-housed programs.

The licensing issue illustrates the complex interaction of theology, ideology, and practical considerations in church-based social service provision. Some well-meaning attempts to improve church-housed child care by insisting that churches meet licensing standards were misdirected at the very churches that complied voluntarily while ignoring those that used the religious exemption to avoid costly features such as appropriate group size. We do not want churches to slip away from adhering to quality standards because they are exempt from licensing standards. It is a very difficult problem.

That brings me to another point that I think is terribly significant. It is very important to underscore that the faith community brings three things to any social undertaking; in ascending order, they are as follows: First, they bring their material resources, that is, the physical plan. Religious organizations have parking spaces and cribs, small tables, and other furnishings and fittings needed, for example, for a child-care program. Sometimes they are not so nice, but quality has to be measured not by some absolute, unrealistic standard, but in relation to what is available in the community.

Second, religious organizations bring human resources, sometimes in the person of volunteers. The third thing that they bring is moral authority. That moral authority is a terribly underestimated but highly significant characteristic of religiously sponsored programs. Sometimes moral authority is consciously and intentionally exercised by the sponsoring organization; other times it is simply bestowed by the fact of religious sponsorship and its impact on the outcome of programs is little recognized or studied.

We conducted research so that we would have a basis for saying to churches that it is unethical—nay, immoral—to use their church status to exempt themselves from health and safety regulations that were established to safeguard all children, including those in their care. Churches that seek exemption to offer substandard care generally are outside the universe that we sampled here. That, in turn, tells us whom we ought to be talking to in the religious world. We do not have to say the same things to all the different churches and religious organizations. That suggests that those who wish to see churches provide more publicly funded social services will need a sophisticated understanding of religious communities and how they differ from one another.

Now, on the matter of church-state relations. Child care has a lot to offer all of us by way of instruction in the nature of church-state relations. For example, the organizational life of the church is altered by the provision of services to those outside the congregation. Why have there not been more lawsuits? There are two realities that we need to recognize. When Aunt Hester walks out of the church on Sunday morning, slips on ice, breaks her hip, and ruins her new dress, she praises the Lord because she lived through it. She does not sue the church.

People who bring their children to the child-care center may not have such devotion. And one of the realities that churches are going to have to grapple with is the issue of ascending liability. Nobody has ever successfully sued a local child-care center. They could succeed, of course, but the net worth of a child-care center would be too low for any financial incentive to exist. Let's talk instead about liability ascending to the Episcopal Church in America. Now, there are some pretty deep pockets! So one of the questions is whether in the era before us child-care centers will be welcome in church facilities. Will they be too expensive? Will they raise new questions about the need for churches to indemnify themselves?

Just as a cautionary note, in recent discussions we have been speaking as though a separate 501(c)(3) organization is a magic tonic. It isn't. It is a good first step. When the pastor's, priest's, or rabbi's study becomes a social services administration office, it may not matter. Faith groups need to know that they will have to alter more than their legal status to comply with the law. That is just one example of how providing a service can ultimately change the character of a religious organization.

In light of these issues, what is the future of church-housed child care itself? Church-housed child care does not exist in a vacuum. Indeed, it exists as a feature in the highly dynamic, ever-changing religious landscape of the American people. You all have heard the statistic that there are more Muslims than Episcopalians in America.[2] That is an indication of what I mean by change.

In March 2001, a Hartford Seminary study found that just over half of all congregations in the United States now have fewer than 100 adults participating in their worship services. Those small congregations still have the educational wing that was there when they had 800 people at worship on Sunday. They still have the space, but they lack other characteristics that they need to offer and manage social programs. In many congregations there also are notable differences that we have not begun to explore, such as socioeconomic status, racial factors, and geographical location. Again, just about half of all churches today are in towns or in suburbs, not in inner-city communities.

I am not qualified to speak for the Jewish community or the Muslim community, but I think that I can speak for child care. Church-based child care is a local response to need at the door. There is a danger in allowing each congregation to respond in any way it wishes to that need. I think there is a distinct possibility that two hermetically sealed strains of church-housed child care may emerge in the United States: one that incorporates child care as a part of its witness and ministry, in faith formation and faith development; and one that offers it as part of its mission identity, unrelated to faith training. The struggle for those of us who care about the whole field of child care will be to understand how the issues of quality, availability, and affordability can be addressed within that two-part picture.

It also is likely that before- and after-school programs will continue to burgeon, as they have since the time of this study. All over the country, congregations, sometimes at the behest of their local school boards and sometimes at the behest of parents, have initiated various after-school programs.

Historic black churches recently developed an extraordinary number of after-school programs in tutoring that are well worth our attention. For so many in the black community, the public school has been a place and an instrument of failure. The church has been a very different place. In the black churches and in nearly every quarter, after-school programs are more numerous.

Another factor in the provision of faith-based services is that available property is often in inverse proportion to need. To use the New York area as an example, a church in affluent Larchmont in Westchester County is likely to have a lot of parking spaces and excellent furnishings, finishings, and so forth. However, there probably are few people looking for entry-level keyboarding skills there. And those who need drug rehabilitation check into some place like a spa in Hilton Head.

Now, the Temple of El Redentor on 167th Street in Manhattan is a storefront church. Its members and friends have need of such programs, but they have very little space. So before we get too excited about the threat of faith-based initiatives breaking down the wall of separation between church and state that we have so long cherished, we ought to remember the inverse proportion of facilities to population in need and scale back our estimate of what is possible.

Continuing with church-state relations, I remember the days in early childhood education when we used to make sure that the churches removed the pictures of Jesus to preserve the secular nature of the services they offered. Every Monday morning those pictures would be put away in a drawer, and every Friday afternoon they would be hung up again so that they were there for Sunday school. We never seemed to bother with the $3.2 million dollar steeple with the crucifix on top that stayed in place all week long. Children are short, and they are young, but they are not stupid! They probably cannot tell you the difference between blood theories and substitutional theories of atonement, but when they see a steeple, they know they are in a church. Hiding the 69-cent picture of Jesus is not what ensures children's religious freedom. It is what is expected, even demanded, of them by adults that determines whether or not their right to religious freedom is honored. And we cannot regulate that with a few ill-conceived rules.

I want to say one final word. Church-housed child care has been a wonderful laboratory for research into and development of child care in America. When we did the National Council of Churches study, we were hampered in some ways that we would not be now, given the advances in computer science. At the time of the study, we sorted the responses into infant care, child care, preschool, and the like. Then we had a box that was labeled "other." In that leftover box, we found magnificent programs. One was in a church in Cherry Valley, Colorado. When we asked them what kind of child care they offered, they said that they had everything, from birth to age 16. When we asked them about their hours of operation, they said that they were open from 5:00 a.m. to 7:00 p.m.—and then they noted, "for four months a year." It turned out that for those four months, women of the church arise at 4:00 a.m. and go out to the fields to pick up the children of the migrant workers who are in town because the crop is ready to be picked. They take the children to the church, where they provide child care, some tutoring, a family meal in the evening, and the like. That is completely off our radar, but it is a great program. Of course, it is operated with private, not public, funds.

There was another place in Florida, across the street from a children's hospital, where a group of senior citizens provide respite care for children with terminal illnesses. They wrote on their form, "We, like the children, are near life's end. Their predicament is not nearly as frightening to us as it is to their parents." They provide child care on a drop-in basis from 10:00 a.m. to 3:00 p.m., three days a week. Parents do not have to say why they need the time off: it may be to fill out insurance forms, to go home to cry, to deal with their other children, to go get their hair done, or to pretend that the whole horrible dream is not happening. We don't know. But because the church is the church, it wants to respond. If those children also are poor, we want them to be fed. And if the church is too poor to feed them, we want a program like Women, Infants, and Children to be available. Those are not programs with religious content, unless kindness and courtesy are considered religious content. So, you can see that sacred places and civic purposes are not as easily distinguished as some have suggested. The venerable example of church-housed child care can offer us much wise counsel as we seek to find our way.

NOTES

1. All data from the National Council of Churches study are reported in Eileen W. Lindner and others, *When Churches Mind the Children: A Study of Day Care in Local Parishes* (National Council of Churches of Christ in the U.S.A., 1983).

2. All church membership data are drawn from the annual *Yearbook of American and Canadian Churches* (Nashville, Tenn.: Abingdon Press, 2001).

Ensuring Quality and Accountability in Faith-Based Child Care

FLOYD FLAKE

After twenty-five years of experience in religion, politics, and a variety of social services, I have reached the conclusion it is possible for faith-based institutions to deliver almost any community or social service. Certainly that is true for day-care. The issue becomes one of delivering daycare without requiring parents to make a faith statement or any statement whatever about their religious beliefs. Religious content of the program should be kept to a minimum, but it should not be a disqualifier.

I have discovered that parents are not looking for religious- or non–religious-based daycare, but quality daycare. If it happens to be religious based and they do not subscribe to that particular religion, it is irrelevant, as long as the child receives a quality daycare education.

Allen Christian School opened on March 1, 2001, offering two kinds of day-care: a private, church-sponsored program with a tuition of $3,800 and a government-funded Head Start program. The programs are operated under separate corporations, and a clear distinction is maintained between the church program and the Head Start program in terms of financial accountability.

If a child cannot be accommodated in the limited spaces in our funded program or any of the other funded programs in the community, parents find the means to pay for our private daycare center. Our church-sponsored daycare center's phenomenal growth is evidence of that: on opening day, people were lined around the corner and we had a waiting list of more than 150 people after filling our spots. The religious devotional programming clearly was not of primary concern to those parents.

What was essential was that the school has a good reputation and that once a child is enrolled, he or she has nearly automatic acceptance into our first-through eighth-grade program. We rarely reject a child who has been inculcated in the system—not the religion, but the system. Parents realize that their child is better able to survive by enrolling in our daycare center because the foundation of the multilayered educational pyramid is sound daycare.

Although I am a supporter of faith-based initiatives and of charitable choice, I have some concerns. I remember the precariousness of the Model Cities era, and I do not want to see a replay of the mistakes that led to the destruction of that program. The process was much too open. People came into the business to provide funding, but once the funds were lost, people who were benefiting from services suddenly were left without them. We do not want to get children, especially, involved in programs that will not survive.

There are three important principles for setting up faith-based daycare. First, there must be some way to analyze capacity. Not every group that wants to deliver daycare services has the pedagogical, academic, or material wherewithal to do so. Not being able to do a qualitative analysis to determine whether providers actually have the capability and capacity to properly run a daycare center ultimately results in failure. There still must be a request for proposals (RFP) process to ensure that capacity can be determined ahead of time.

Second, it is imperative to have a firewall in place once the program is established. Generally, a firewall is maintained by having a congregation's service arm incorporate separately as a 501(c)(3) corporation that speaks specifically to its needs. I have eleven corporations, in part because I run a $29 million operation and I am trying to protect the interests of all components. My child-care component is a totally separate corporation. If the daycare center is involved in a lawsuit because a child got hurt, I do not want the lawsuit to affect the church. So, my liability constraints required that I set up the 501(c)(3). I would argue that, if we are serious about making these programs work, partnerships, which would allow us to serve more children, make sense. However, firewalls must be in place.

Third, I know of too many churches that do not have adequate accounting or bookkeeping procedures. If you commingle federal, state, and city dollars with church dollars, you are headed for disaster. The number of churches that are in operation but remain unincorporated amazes me. I am afraid that those unincorporated entities will see charitable choice as an opportunity to expand, by way of daycare or another program, without recognizing the importance of getting their books straight. If they do not understand accounting principles and refuse to hire professional help, they can open themselves up to some very serious problems.

I would summarize my position this way: I strongly support faith-based child-care initiatives and I strongly support charitable choice, but with a cautionary note: *we have to do this in a way that ensures accountability and quality programs.* We must set standards that do not reflect negatively on the overall principle of involving faith-based institutions in daycare and guarantee that whatever has been promised in response to an RFP is in fact delivered to our children.

><del>—⊖—</del>◄

Harnessing the Potential of Partnerships without Violating Cherished Values

LISBETH B. SCHORR

Two urgent social problems are central to the discussion of child care in this volume: many more families need good, affordable, out-of-home child care than are now able to obtain it, and many disadvantaged children are arriving at school with the odds already stacked against them because their early needs were neglected. The research and experience of the last few decades can illuminate strategies that could involve faith-based organizations in addressing these problems without violating constitutional or other cherished values.

The data make clear that the nation could not do without church-based child care, in large part because churches offer conveniently located, usually safe, and often inexpensive physical space. The country's dependence on faith-based child care also is related to the many motivations that faith-based organizations have for engaging in child care in the first place. They range from the Jewish mandate to contribute to "repairing the world" to the evangelical view of child care as a way to recruit new members to a particular faith. They also include service to members of the congregation or the neighborhood; the desire to instill the traits, norms, values, and beliefs of a particular culture or faith; the determination to promote pride and hope among marginalized ethnic and racial groups; and the pursuit of social justice by serving low-income or immigrant families and special-needs children.

While some of those motivations make liberals nervous, it is important to note that they are more than incidental to achieving valued social purposes. Motivations to serve, to instill values, and to promote social justice all are potentially powerful promoters of quality services. Many efforts to intervene systematically to improve child and family outcomes are more effective when those making the effort *believe* in what they are doing and when they are *driven by a mission* that transcends the self—characteristics that are sharply at odds with an impersonal, bureaucratic model of service delivery. That means that we have to find ways of promoting urgently needed quality standards in the child-care field without imposing regulations that make it harder to do the job right.

Dorothy Stoneman, founder of YouthBuild, a marvelous youth development and training program, says that YouthBuild encourages staff to bond with trainees by responding to their needs in a way that goes well beyond their job descriptions. Staff give trainees their home telephone numbers and are on call twenty-four hours a day. If youngsters have a personal emergency, such as a death or illness in the family, staff accompany them to funerals and hospitals. Stoneman says, "When staff simply do what they are paid to do, trainees remain agnostic or negative concerning whether the staff really care . . . and can be trusted not to betray or to abandon them." Almost every successful human service program I have studied points in some way to the importance of going above and beyond the call of duty if staff are to help participants learn to trust. An obvious show of caring is an important signal to parents and youth that this experience will be different.

Professionals, managers, and agencies seeking to redefine professionalism to ensure quality standards while supporting more personal interaction do not simply go with whatever feels right. Rather, they function within the boundaries of well-developed standards and theories of effective practice while pushing the constraints imposed by job descriptions and bureaucracies.

That is why I believe that we have to contend not only with the church-state problem, but also with the tension between bureaucracy and effectiveness. When churches or other organizations that pride themselves on their flexibility and responsiveness worry that their effectiveness will be undermined once they become subject to government rules and regulations, theirs is a realistic fear. The landscape is littered with social programs that were highly successful as pilots but that were demolished, or at the very least diluted into ineffectiveness, as soon as they scaled up. The need for child care is so urgent and so widespread that we have to make sure, on one hand, that every source of care that meets quality standards and protects constitutional, individual, and civil rights is enlisted. On the other, we have to make sure that mainstream funding does not bring with it inappropriate, self-defeating regulations that undermine the very attributes that made a pilot program effective.

The Bush administration is shining a spotlight on the government rules, regulations, funding patterns, and accountability requirements that can interfere with the effective operation of promising faith-based initiatives. I join E. J. Dionne Jr. in his hope that "these faith-based efforts might become a small oasis of nonpartisan possibility." But I would like to see that oasis enlarged. I am hopeful that the new interest in flexible programming also will encourage the search for ways to make government more supportive of all community-based initiatives—faith-based and others—that produce results because they are mission driven, relationship oriented, and responsive to local needs . . . and because their staffs believe in what they are doing.

My plea, then, is that we pay attention not just to the church-state problem, but also to the bureaucracy-effectiveness issue. We must figure out how to harness those aspects of bureaucracy that are essential to promoting both quality and accountability (as the military has done so successfully in the child-care field) while shedding those aspects that undermine our best efforts.

If we want to see models that have worked in a ten-block radius enlarged in scale to serve all the community's children, we have to face up to the funding implications. We have to stop thinking that we can get the same results when the inputs are diminished because we are determined to do it on the cheap. We also must face up to the equally formidable barriers raised by the rules that govern how money is spent, who is eligible, what the service mix is, who determines compliance, and how results are measured.

Let us commit new energy and resources to figuring out how programs operating with public funds can promote the values of love, respect, and service (which, as many authors in this book point out, can transcend dogma and doctrine) while protecting participants from being coerced into conversion.

Let us commit new energy and resources to figuring out how to ensure that program providers can hire people who share the program's convictions about the possibilities of human redemption and how to prevent them from hiring people on the basis of sectarian convictions or affiliation.

Let us commit new energy and resources to figuring out how to monitor and evaluate programs that are truly community based, that change every day in response to changing circumstances, and that operate with a significant number of what social scientists call "unobservables."

In my work in a variety of successful social programs, I repeatedly have seen evidence that being part of a movement that transcends the individual's material needs contributes to success—whether the movement springs from religious, political, ethnic, or ideological roots. Paul Light, director of governmental studies at the Brookings Institution, has written that one cannot underestimate the importance of faith as a core value that makes it possible to persevere in the face of stress, uncertainty, and disappointment. That faith, he found in his study of effective organizations, may be "rooted in formal religion, culture, one's vision of a just society, or simply confidence in human capacity." I would like to think that together we can find ways to permit all organizations operating on principles that rise above the forces of the marketplace to become a solid and significant part of the effort to alleviate our most urgent social problems.

>——⊖——<

Church–Based Child Care in Rural Areas

DIANA JONES WILSON

Although the need for child care is great in rural areas, the supply is scarce. Child care is less available in rural than in urban areas, and even when it does exist, rural parents are less able to afford it. Public dollars are failing to reach many poor rural families that are eligible for child-care subsidies, yet working mothers make significant contributions to their families' income and to the rural economy.

The North Carolina Rural Economic Development Center established the Church Child Care Initiative in 1993. Its goal was to increase the number of church-based child-care programs available to rural children, with special emphasis on helping children from poor families that were eligible for but not currently receiving help from Head Start and other public programs.

The Rural Economic Development Center looked to the one entity that existed in most communities—the church. Through a policy forum and a series of meetings and workshops, we began to understand the issues and myths that prevented the church from engaging in subsidized child care. During the early 1990s in North Carolina, where eighty-five of the state's 100 counties are considered rural, counties were returning subsidies because they had no child-care centers in which to use them. A significant number of families, however, needed child care. The establishment of the Child Care Loan Guarantee Fund by the state legislature as a pilot program for distressed counties addressed some of the capital requirements for rural child-care programs, including faith-based programs. We initiated efforts to equip churches to offer licensed programs capable of addressing the issues of child-care quality and affordability.

Discussions regarding quality care often reference the *Cost, Quality, and Child Outcomes in Child Care Centers* study released in 1995. A secondary analysis indicates there are two categories of churches involved in child care: those that operate child-care programs as a mission and those that operate them as a source of income. Richard Clifford, a researcher at the University of North Carolina–Chapel Hill and coauthor of the study, recently stated, "It looks like there are some churches that operate child care as a mission, and they tend to be pretty high quality. Other churches operate child care as a business to increase church revenue; they do not seem as concerned about quality."[1]

The Church Child Care Initiative joins organizations such as the Ecumenical Child Care Network at the national level to encourage faith-based child-care programs to operate as separate 501(c)(3) nonprofit corporations. The nonprofit designation gives rural faith-based programs the option of tapping the community for expertise that might not otherwise be available to a small rural congregation, increasing the likelihood of quality programs, sound program management, and fiscal accountability.

Policymakers and funders should not make the mistake of pitting child-care programs in rural areas against those in the inner cities when they decide how to allocate funds. The need for child care exists in both places. However, rural children and providers may have "extra-special" needs because of the limited resources available for and within rural communities. And when engaging the faith community in child care, you cannot craft one set of policies for one denomination and another set for another denomination—or exclude any groups, whether formal denominations or faith-based groups that are not affiliated with a formal denomination. The needs of children transcend that kind of categorizing of care as rural or urban, denominational or nondenominational.

How do you get denominations and independent churches to understand that they have a calling to deal with the needs of "the least of these"? You demystify child care. You help churches understand quality; you introduce them to child-care licensing experts as "partners," as a resource to help them provide quality programs. You take a program that might be extremely complex and technical and break it down as we have in the guidebook *A Child at the Door*. This guidebook helps churches understand how to embrace child care—how to prepare a sound needs assessment and business plan and how to deal with licensing, sanitation, and health issues in the planning process. Introducing regulatory issues and personnel at the beginning establishes a resource base and builds partnerships, thereby enabling churches to avoid costly mistakes.

The Church Child Care Initiative also provides consultants to facilitate planning sessions. How do you equip churches so that planning takes place, so that the congregation has a sense of ownership in the program, so that there is a partnership? The resources of the church must be recognized so that the advantages of providing faith-based child care are recognized and facilities that can offer services to children are no longer empty.

The initiative has worked to provide those services. We have built partnerships along the way. When we talk to members of the state general assembly about resources, we do not say that we want to take child-care funds from the fifteen urban counties to give them to our eighty-five rural counties. We ask how we can come together to deal with the needs of all the children. We say let us find more dollars for the urban areas if there is a greater need; however, let us also provide adequate resources to meet the rural child-care crisis. We believe that a thoughtful discussion of the church's ministry to children among policymakers and leaders of the faith community can prove to be a turning point—one that will open eyes, challenge complacency, and stimulate personal as well as collective action.

NOTE

1. Personal telephone conversation, spring 2001.

>——⊝——<

The Child-Care Trilemma and Faith-Based Care

JUDITH C. APPELBAUM

The "trilemma" of child care summarized in Mary Bogle's chapter—the challenge of addressing availability, affordability, and quality without sacrificing any of those goals in the service of the others—is well known. In an era when more than 70 percent of American women with children are in the paid labor force, the demand for child care is at an all-time high. But for many, high-quality care is too expensive or just not available.

There is no mystery about how to tackle these problems effectively. Several European countries have done it. Closer to home, the U.S. military's transformation of the military child-care system into a model for the nation demonstrates that a comprehensive system of affordable, high-quality child care is attainable if the necessary steps are taken—such as improving caregiver training and compensation to increase professionalism and reduce turnover, implementing and enforcing comprehensive standards, and subsidizing the cost so that all families have access to good care.[1]

In the civilian realm, the Child Care and Development Block Grant (CCDBG), enacted in 1990, addresses at least part of the child-care trilemma by providing funds to the states for child-care subsidies for low- and moderate-income families. A critically needed program, the CCDBG remains severely underfunded; the U.S. Department of Health and Human Services estimates that currently CCDBG subsidies reach only 12 percent of eligible families.

There is little doubt that faith-based organizations make an important contribution to meeting the need for child care. Sectarian child care expands the array of options for parents, although to the extent that it entails the inculcation of religious teachings, it cannot be a serious option for families that do not share those beliefs. And sectarian care may offer affordable care for some families, especially to the extent that faith-based providers take advantage of public subsidies, as the CCDBG allows them to do when the funds flow through certificates (vouchers) to the parents, rather than through direct state grants to or contracts with providers.

Some quality concerns do arise, however. Bogle indicates that the quality of child care in at least some faith-based settings tends to be lower than in other settings. That is undoubtedly related to the fact that in many states, religious child care is exempt from the licensing requirements and regulations that apply generally to child care—notwithstanding strong evidence that vigorous enforcement of strong standards, as in the military system, is essential to ensuring high-quality care.

Another problem is that quality cannot be addressed effectively through a voucher-based system, which is the only way that public funds are permitted to flow to sectarian care under the CCDBG. Quality improvements are possible only through investments in the system's infrastructure, for example, by allocating funds to help states with licensing and enforcement or to help individual programs meet higher standards. Vouchers that enable individual families to defray the cost of care will never lead to systemic reforms.

Moreover, when public dollars flow to sectarian institutions, the church-state issues do not evaporate just because support is provided through vouchers. When the CCDBG was passed, some supporters were uncomfortable with the voucher approach for that reason and some legal scholars expressed doubts about its constitutionality. Others cited precedents suggesting that the Constitution permits public support for sectarian institutions when the individual recipient of assistance makes an independent choice about where to spend the money, as is the case with vouchers. The constitutionality of vouchers for religious child care under the CCDBG has not been tested in the courts.

Legal issues aside, those with misgivings about the appropriateness of spending public funds directly on sectarian activities could raise the same concerns about support provided through vouchers. Whether spent directly or provided through vouchers, public funds can end up paying for materials or services with religious content, such as an overtly religious curriculum. The chapter by Fred Davie and his colleagues suggests one of the benefits of faith-based child care is that within most faith traditions there are universal values (like respect for oneself and one's neighbors) that transcend dogma and doctrine. But there is no guarantee that those values, or only those values, are transmitted by every sectarian program—as opposed to, for example, promoting the subordination of women or antipathy to other religions or to racial minorities. Indeed, the fact that a child-care program is sectarian is neither necessary nor sufficient to ensure that the positive values identified by Davie and others will be inculcated in the children.

Finally, concerns about employment discrimination also arise when public funds are used to support sectarian programs that hire and fire employees on the basis of religion or religious tenets (which CCDBG allows when the funds flow through vouchers) or programs that in effect discriminate on the basis of sex by, for example, refusing to employ unmarried mothers—but not unmarried fathers—because of a religious objection to the women's conduct.

The CCDBG has become a cornerstone of federal child-care policy and indeed should be significantly expanded. However, the balancing act that it embodies, which aims to maximize parental choice while avoiding direct public funding of sectarian activities, is not perfect. More extensive analysis should be done before a similar approach is considered for areas beyond the complicated and unique world of child care.

NOTE

1. See National Women's Law Center, *Be All That We Can Be: Lessons from the Military for Improving Our Nation's Child Care System* (Washington: 2000), available at www.nwlc.org.

PART SIX

Should Government Help Faith-Based Charity?

CHAPTER SIXTEEN

Compassion in Truth and Action: What Washington Can Not Do to Help

JOHN J. DiIULIO JR.

In "Rallying the Armies of Compassion," the blueprint for the White House Office on Faith-Based and Community Initiatives, President George W. Bush states:

> Government cannot be replaced by charities, but it can and should welcome them as partners. We must heed the growing consensus across America that successful government social programs work in fruitful partnership with community-serving and faith-based organizations—whether run by Methodists, Muslims, Mormons, or good people of no faith at all.[1]

The consensus cited by the president runs wide and deep. Americans of every socioeconomic status and demographic description have faith in faith-based and community approaches to solving social problems.

Solid survey data compiled over several decades by George Gallup Jr. and associates indicate that most citizens—including 86 percent of blacks and 60 percent of whites in 1995—believe that religion can help "answer all or most of today's problems." The same week that the president signed my office into being, the Pew Charitable Trusts released a national poll showing that most Americans believe that "local churches, synagogues, or mosques," together with "organizations such as the Salvation Army, Goodwill Industries, and Habitat for Humanity," are top problem-solving organizations in their communities. Americans appreciate our community helpers and healers, and so should our government.

This chapter was adapted from a speech delivered before the National Association of Evangelicals, Dallas, Texas, March 7, 2001.

Metaphorically speaking, community-serving faith-based organizations are the army ants of civil society, daily leveraging ten times their human and financial weight in social good. Or, as I have elsewhere described them, they are the paramedics of urban civil society, saving lives and restoring health, answering emergencies with miracles.

But, make no mistake: while faith-based organizations can supplement and strengthen public social service programs, they can by no means substitute for government support. To dramatize the point, just consider that even if all 353,000 religious congregations in America doubled their annual budgets and devoted them entirely to the cause and even if the cost of government social welfare programs was magically cut by one-fifth, the congregations would barely cover a year's worth of Washington's spending on those programs and never even come close to covering total program costs.

COMPASSIONATE CONSERVATISM FOR CHURCH-STATE SEPARATION

President Bush has been steadfast in articulating a caring, common-sense vision of compassionate conservatism, one that enlists government effort but resists government growth. His vision comprehends both the strengths and limits of faith-based and community initiatives. It calls on the rest of us to help those who help the "least of these" by giving them more of our own time and more of our own money.

Compassionate conservatism warmly welcomes people of faith back into the public square while respecting and upholding, without fail, our constitutional traditions governing church, state, and civic pluralism. It fosters model public-private partnerships so that community-based organizations, religious and non-religious, can work together and across racial, denominational, urban-suburban, and other divides to achieve civic results.

And it challenges Washington to work overtime and in a bipartisan fashion to ensure that tax-supported social programs and the nonprofit organizations that help to administer those programs are performance managed, performance measured, and open to competition from qualified community-serving organizations, large or small, new or old, sacred or secular.

WHY AN OFFICE OF FAITH-BASED AND COMMUNITY INITIATIVES?

The White House Office of Faith-Based and Community Initiatives aims to do several interrelated things.

First, we aim to boost charitable giving, of both human and financial resources. The first financial boosts are in the president's budget plan, which

among other things would permit the 80 million taxpayers who do not itemize deductions—70 percent of all taxpayers—to deduct charitable contributions. The human boosts are embodied in the president's use of the bully pulpit
to affirm the value of volunteers and in the hopes of Stephen Goldsmith, former mayor of Indianapolis, for retooling AmeriCorps in ways that put col-
lege-educated, public-spirited young adults at the disposal of the small
faith-based and community organizations that need them. (AmeriCorps already has people in urban community-serving ministries and such, but we aim
to refine and enlarge their participation on behalf of needy children, youth,
and families.)

Second, we are authorized to form centers and conduct program audits in
five Cabinet agencies—Justice, Labor, Education, Health and Human Services,
and Housing and Urban Development. That is easily the most crucial but least
well understood part of our mission. It is about paving the path to civic results
through greater government solicitude for faith-based and community organizations—the real civic rationale for charitable choice.

In sum, since the end of World War II, virtually every domestic program that
Washington has funded in whole or in part has been administered not by federal civil servants alone (there are about 2 million of those today, roughly the
same number as in 1960), but by federal workers in conjunction with state and
local government employees, for-profit firms, and nonprofit organizations.

Certain nonprofit organizations, both religious and secular, have long been
funded in whole or in part through this federal "government-by-proxy" system.
Some, no doubt, deserve their privileged positions in that system because they
have produced measurable civic results. Others, however, are in simply because
they are in. Despite a far-reaching 1993 federal law requiring federal agencies
to do performance-managed, performance-measured grant making, you still can
count on your fingers and toes the number of government-by-proxy programs
that have really put nonprofit providers to the test.

If many nonprofits in the government-by-proxy network have never had any
meaningful performance evaluation; if their claims of greater capacity are based
mainly on their bigger staffs; and if their public pose as providers of "up close
and personal" services to the citizens whom they serve are belied by the fact
that they have more personnel in the suites than on the streets, then—purely
in the interest of helping those in need while generating a better return on the
public's investment in social programs—why should the leaders of qualified
community and faith-based organizations, local groups that really do serve the
poor and have been doing so for years, not be able, if they so choose, to seek
partial government funding on the same basis as any other nongovernment
provider of social services?

WHAT IS CHARITABLE CHOICE FOR?

Community and faith-based groups *should* be able to seek government funding, and that is why President Bush has directed my office to help level the federal funding playing field to "encourage and support the work of charities and faith-based and community groups," including small ones "that offer help and love one person at a time."

> These groups are working in every neighborhood in America, to fight homelessness and addiction and domestic violence, to provide a hot meal or a mentor or a safe haven for our children. Government should welcome these groups to apply for funds, not discriminate against them.[2]

That is also precisely what charitable choice is about. What, exactly, is charitable choice, how does it "welcome" faith-based organizations to the federal government-by-proxy fold, and what, if any, real church-state or other problems does it pose? Let me highlight some of the main points.

In brief, President Clinton signed charitable choice into law on August 22, 1996; thus it has been on the books for five years now. It was a largely bipartisan and by-consensus provision in the otherwise uproarious debate over the 1996 federal welfare law (the Personal Responsibility and Work Opportunity Reconciliation Act of 1996). Essentially, it covered temporary assistance to needy families and welfare-to-work funding. Another charitable choice provision passed in 1998 (part of the Community Services Block Grant), and yet another, reaching some faith-based drug treatment programs, passed in two separate bills last year. Five years ago, charitable choice was a little-noticed landmark. Today, it is a much-noticed, mainstream, landmark.

Under charitable choice legislation, both religious and secular community-serving organizations can seek federal support on the same basis as any other nongovernment for-profit or not-for-profit provider of services. Sacred places that serve civic purposes can seek federal (or federal-state) funding without having to divest themselves of their religious iconography.

As Stephen Monsma has documented, for decades the sacred and secular have mixed in the administration of hundreds of taxpayer-supported programs. By some estimates, for example, one-third or more of all daycare programs in low-income urban neighborhoods with high concentrations of welfare-to-work recipients are provided by faith-based organizations.[3]

However, as Monsma shows, all too many other laws and regulations do not clearly authorize such involvement. Charitable choice gives community-serving religious nonprofits and government officials specific guidelines that legitimate and guide the participation of faith-based organizations in federally funded programs.

To wit, faith-based providers that receive any public money cannot discriminate against beneficiaries on the basis of race, color, gender, age, national origin, disability, or religion. Regarding religion, charitable choice reinforces federal antidiscrimination laws by explicitly prohibiting participating faith-based organizations from denying service to anyone "on the basis of religion, a religious belief, or refusal to actively participate in a religious practice."

Moreover, government must provide beneficiaries with religious objections to receiving services from a faith-based organization with an equivalent secular alternative, without placing an undue burden on the beneficiary (no ridiculously long drives and such). And, according to the statutes, if government fails to provide ample and equivalent secular alternatives, if its actions have the effect of "diminishing the religious freedom of beneficiaries of assistance," then beneficiaries may enforce their rights against the government in a private cause of action for injunctive relief.

In addition, federal law has long required an independent audit by a certified public accountant of any group, religious or secular, that receives more than $300,000 a year in government funds. Charitable choice flatly prohibits federal funds from being used "for sectarian worship, instruction, or proselytization." In the case of faith-based groups, charitable choice favors segregated accounts—so do I—and only the walled-off government accounts used for public purposes may be audited.

Despite these hefty and wholesome protections, critics variously charge charitable choice with seven supposedly deadly sins. To alliterate, let's call them "huge leaks, horrible louts, hiring loopholes, and hijacked faith," plus "bogus alternatives, bloated agencies, and beltway business-as-usual."

Huge leaks? Some critics of charitable choice assert that, even when religious organizations form 501(c)(3) entities, there is no effective way to segregate fiscal accounts. Money, they remind us, is fungible, and tax dollars will leak between Bible studies and soup kitchens.

Well, money is fungible in the entire government-by-proxy network. Anyone who has ever worked in or studied secular nonprofits that get government grants knows that funds sometimes leak between projects. But government has adequate ways to detect and minimize that leakage, and there is nothing about religious or secular community-based organizations that places them beyond the reach of personnel, procurement, and other relevant protocols.

Horrible louts? Others wrongly suppose that disagreeable, even hate-mongering, individuals and organizations that call themselves religious somehow will suddenly become eligible for federal funding under charitable choice. For starters, what the Constitution requires of government is equal treatment, neither favoring nor disfavoring groups because they are religious. The federal government will not distribute funds on a religious basis. Funds must go to nongovernment providers, religious or secular, that meet all relevant anti-discrimination laws, procurement procedures, and performance protocols.

Second, before charitable choice, any organization that could fill out a grant application and afford the postage to send it in could apply for federal support. Some religious or quasi-religious groups that many citizens find offensive did so, and some got contracts for particular services. With and since charitable choice, the law still applies. But by making it easier for all qualified community-based organizations to become part of Washington's government-by-proxy network, charitable choice will, if anything, increase competition, raise performance standards, and thereby make it less likely than before that groups more interested in advocacy than in service will obtain grants.

Third, currently there are many federally funded secular nonprofits that represent ideological (as opposed to theological) worldviews that are offensive to many Americans (for example, the American Civil Liberties Union and Planned Parenthood). In some cases, their approach to service delivery is rather plainly anchored more in their ideology than in any empirical evidence about what works or in any independent confirmation of the efficacy of their program.

Still, the Constitution gives taxpayers no right to insist that government decisions, including procurement decisions, not offend their sense of morality. Evenhanded performance standards, not illegal, a priori blacklists, have been and continue to be the best constitutional method for keeping horrible louts, religious or secular, out of the game.

Hiring loopholes? Under section 702, Title VII, of the Civil Rights Act of 1964, religious organizations are permitted to discriminate in employment decisions on the basis of religion. Charitable choice preserves that thirty-seven-year-old right. Should receiving public money require religious organizations to hire people who are not co-religionists and who may be actively opposed to their beliefs, benevolent traditions, and service goals? As Jeffrey Rosen pointed out in an essay in the *New Republic*:

> Without the ability to discriminate on the basis of religion in hiring and firing staff, religious organizations lose the right to define their organizational mission enjoyed by secular organizations that receive public funds. ... Planned Parenthood may refuse to hire those who don't share its views about abortion; equal treatment requires that churches, mosques, and synagogues have the same right to discriminate. The Supreme Court accepted this reasoning in 1988, when it upheld religious nonprofits' exemption from the federal law prohibiting religious discrimination. And by extending this exemption to religious groups that receive government funds, the charitable-choice law is careful to insist that these groups can discriminate in the hiring of staff but not in the treatment of beneficiaries.[4]

Critics who contend that Title VII furnishes religious organizations with a special hiring loophole are simply wrong, unless by "hiring loophole" they mean "equal treatment." To accept ideological reasons for employment discrimination as legitimate while rejecting theological ones out of hand is to arbitrarily, unfairly, and—or so I believe the courts will find—unconstitutionally relegate the civil rights of religious individuals in the public square to a limbo of lesser moral, intellectual, and civic significance. Besides, all government-funded nonprofit organizations ought to be judged by whether they follow all relevant laws and achieve measurable, positive civic results.

Furthermore, the Title VII controversy is so heated because critics assume that the extent to which community-serving ministries engage in religion-based employment discrimination is so vast. Especially in urban America, that is not a safe assumption. For starters, remember that we are talking mainly about volunteer organizations. "Employment," save for the minister and an assistant pastor or two, often is a moot issue, and any organization with fifteen or fewer paid employees can take religion into account in hiring without having to invoke the exemption. The vast majority of urban community-serving ministries and faith-based organizations have far fewer than fifteen paid employees; most have only one or two.

Next, while no reliable data are yet available, my last six years studying the ways and means of urban community-serving ministries all across the country tell me that typically theirs is an all-hands-on-deck world in which people of all faiths—and of no faith—are "employed," as volunteers or paid staff, as long as they will enter the prisons, change the bedpans, counsel the probated juvenile, tutor the inner-city child, and so on.

Finally, among other "areas of agreement concerning government funding of religious organizations to provide social services," the American Jewish Committee's *In Good Faith* document, which also appears in this volume, correctly advises:

> The Supreme Court has not addressed whether a religious organization retains the liberty to make employment decisions on the basis of religion in the case of employees who work in programs or activities funded (in whole or in part) by, or paid with, government money. [W]e agree that religious organizations retain their ability to use religious criteria in employment for those positions in nongovernmental programs that are wholly privately funded, regardless of whether other programs or activities of the organization receive government funds.[5]

That is right, and it is important. We will defend the right of religious organizations to take religion into account in making employment decisions. When and if the Court rules, we naturally will follow its decision and reasoning both in letter and in spirit. Even if the Court ruled that a church-based program that receives public funds thereby loses its Title VII exemption, it would not follow that in all "non-governmental programs that are wholly privately funded" the parent church itself would, too. And neither, of course, would the long-standing tax-exempt status of religious organizations be affected.

Hijacked faith? Some religious leaders, especially of conservative evangelical Christian communities of faith, have worried out loud that religious bodies that receive government support will, over time, become dependent on Caesar's coin. In turn, they fear, partnerships of government and faith-based organizations will enervate the spiritual nature of the participating churches and stifle their prophetic voices. Even if public support is strictly applied to specific social service programs, they fear, the resulting secularizing influence will put churches on the super-slippery slope to losing the "faith" in "faith-based." And, despite the fact that charitable choice protects participating religious organizations from having to divest themselves of their religious symbols and such, it does, as they correctly note, require them to meet all relevant federal antidiscrimination and other laws, to ensure that program funds are not spent for religious worship, and so on.

Such concerns are entirely understandable, and for many faith communities they should be the deciding factor. Charitable choice ought to be open to all qualified community-serving groups, but not all groups ought to participate. Faith leaders, organizations, and communities that perceive the slope as slippery and secularizing simply ought to opt out.

But, in all fairness, let's remember that the types of public-private partnerships that America's faith communities form are as diverse as their theological understandings. In particular, compared with predominantly ex-urban white evangelical churches, urban African American and Latino communities of faith have traditions and histories that make them generally more dedicated to the mission of serving the community and generally more confident about engaging public and secular partners in achieving that mission without compromising their spiritual or religious identity. To be sure, there also are many urban clergy who want nothing whatsoever to do with government. But the "hijacked faith" fears expressed by some are less pointed and less prevalent in metropolitan America. Finally, the concern that nonprofit organizations can grow overly dependent on government funds must be taken seriously, but no more seriously for religious than for secular ones. While there are no well-researched rules for avoiding that fate, it seems clear that once any organization, religious or secular, receives more than one-quarter to one-half of its funding from any single source, it risks its independence and ability to remain faithful to its core values and original missions. Among other reasons, that is why, as I will explain, performance-based contracting should be short term and why, with respect to the so-called Compassion Capital Fund proposed by President Bush, the federal contribution would constitute no more than one-quarter of the total funds of any model public-private community-serving program, religious or secular.

Bogus alternatives? As discussed, charitable choice requires government to provide beneficiaries of services with an equivalent secular alternative to faith-based programs. Still, some worry that even with the best intentions and most stringent administration, the government will not be able to honor that guarantee.

Providing an alternative in rural areas might be quite a challenge. So far, though, as a Center for Public Justice study last year by Amy Sherman shows, officials are doing just fine.[6] In the nine states she investigated, there were only two instances in which a person needing help requested a secular alternative to the faith-based provider, and officials immediately provided that alternative. Since in the past officials typically contracted with secular programs, charitable choice most likely will increase the options available in rural and urban areas rather than diminish them. In any case, charitable choice requires government officials to find a way to provide that secular alternative. We will hold to that requirement.

Bloated agencies? I have heard reports and read magazine articles asserting that my office would have more than 100 employees, mostly new hires, and require an explosion in state and local government employment to monitor and manage the billions of dollars that will come coursing through the Department of Education alone. Not so.

The office opened on February 20, 2001. The core office staff, me included, is composed of nine people, including support staff. The five Cabinet centers, when fully operational, will have a total of fewer than forty workers (they now have only five), many of them assigned career public servants, not new hires. The five audits will recommend changes in regulations that discriminate against qualified community-based providers, religious and secular. Those recommendations could be accepted or rejected. If accepted, they could in due course result in changes that affect the granting of billions of dollars. The White House office does not disburse grants itself, but rather works to help ensure that federal programs are as accessible, open, and hospitable to faith-based groups as they are to others.

Beltway business-as-usual? Some have asserted or insinuated that, because charitable choice provisions have passed four times and despite the problems that we ourselves have identified with its implementation to date, our "real endgame" is simply to ram another set of charitable choice laws through Congress, claim political credit, pacify interested constituencies, and, win or lose, be able to say that we made good on President Bush's campaign promises.

Anyone who believes that does not understand how close to the president's heart faith-based and community initiatives are. That is why we are taking a deliberative approach, first conducting our audits, studying competing ideas, and assessing other perspectives and looking forward to forging model public-private partnerships later. That is why we are following our principles, correcting misconceptions, and reaching out widely.

COMPASSION CAPITAL: SEEDING PUBLIC-PRIVATE PROGRAMS

In addition to increasing charitable giving, leveling the federal funding playing field, and improving government-by-proxy programs through performance-based grant making and charitable choice, our fourth goal is to seed or expand selected model public-private programs that involve community-based organizations in meeting civic needs.

Washington must look for such models beyond the beltway. It must look to mayors and local leaders like Philadelphia's Mayor John F. Street, who beat the president to the punch by establishing his own Office of Faith-Based and Voluntary Action in city hall last year. On New Year's Day of 2001, Mayor Street, joined by four-score of local clergy, visited inmates in the city's prisons.

The Compassion Capital Fund proposed by the president would provide federal matching funds to model public-private initiatives that harness the strengths of community-based organizations, religious and secular, and hold promise of being able to address unmet civic needs on a citywide or national scale. While we are still discussing the framework of the fund (there are several federal precedents worth examining), my hope and expectation is that it will be structured and administered so as to implement the president's idea of devolution: "Resources are to be devolved, not just to the States, but to the neighborhood healers who need them most."[7]

Ideally, beyond any seeding phase, fund support would never constitute more than twenty-five cents of any fully operational, at-scale program dollar, with the rest coming from local government, private, corporate, or philanthropic support. Where possible and appropriate, secular nonprofits could serve as lead agencies.

POSTSCRIPT: *ENLIGHTENED STATESMEN V. FACTIONS*

The foregoing essay was adapted from the much longer text of a speech that I gave in March 2001. In the half-year between then and September 2001:

—The U.S House of Representatives passed the Community Solutions Act, which is broadly consistent with the principles and goals of President Bush's plan to encourage faith-based and community initiatives.

—The five Cabinet centers completed their first annual departmentwide performance audits, documenting various barriers to the full and fair participation of qualified grassroots groups in federal social service delivery programs. The White House Office of Faith-Based and Community Initiatives summarized the main findings of the audits in an aptly entitled report, *Unlevel Playing Field,* which was released at a Brookings Institution public forum.

—Former mayor of Indianapolis Stephen Goldsmith, board chairman of the Corporation for National Service (CNS), worked with me in identifying ways to increase technical assistance for community-serving, volunteer-based organizations, both sacred and secular. CNS and the White House Office planned a joint task force.

—Hundreds of independent sector leaders, religious and secular, representing virtually every race, ethnic group, religion, and region, endorsed the president's call for more public-private partnerships to benefit the needy and neglected, as did organizations such as the U.S. Conference of Mayors.

—The faith initiatives debate raged among the policy elite, in the press, and in Washington, D.C., but awareness of and support for providing more public help to sacred places serving civic purposes exploded in communities from coast to coast. One indicator: Our early town meetings on the issue in cities across the country drew crowds of a few hundred, but by July, during my last town meeting at a church in Brooklyn, New York, nearly 3,000 folks came—early on a Saturday morning.

—Sticking with the 180-day plan that brought me to the White House in January—and with the legislative, administrative, and outreach missions that President Bush had asked me to initiate all duly launched or accomplished—I announced in August that I would be returning home to Philadelphia once a new director was in place.

A week after the House bill passed in July, I joined the president and my good friends U.S. Senator Joseph Lieberman, Democrat of Connecticut, and U.S. Senator Rick Santorum, Republican of Pennsylvania, in the Oval Office to discuss the next steps. Shortly thereafter, Senator Santorum announced that, as far as he was concerned, the charitable choice (or, as he prefers, "beneficiary choice") provisions of any Senate bill should neither add to nor subtract from the existing body of civil rights and, to the extent possible, ought to mirror kindred provisions enacted previously, with bipartisan majorities, under President Clinton. Likewise, earlier in July, Senator Lieberman, speaking at a Democratic Leadership Council meeting, exhorted his fellow Democrats to express whatever differences they may have with specific provisions of the House bill—or with the president's broader vision—but to do so in a manner that caused no one to suppose that Democrats are somehow uniformly and reflexively hostile to fellow citizens who (as the Senator has so eloquently phrased it) "serve God with gladness" by serving their own communities' disadvantaged children, youth, and families.

Numerous Democratic leaders, including former United Nations Ambassador and mayor of Atlanta Andrew Young and Philadelphia Mayor John Street, have strongly echoed Senator Lieberman's intraparty counsel. As the senator told *USA Today* in early September, "It won't be easy, but I do think that we can come together and find common ground."

In President Bush and Senator Lieberman, we are blessed to have genuinely public-spirited leaders who truly care about increasing support—public and private, human and financial—for community-serving organizations, both religious and secular, that truly do the Lord's work among the least, the last, and the lost of our society. The president has consistently stressed that while "government cannot be replaced by charities, it must welcome them as partners, not resent them as rivals." The senator has consistently argued that government at all levels should become more open to addressing social problems by partnering with faith-based and community organizations.

Thus, much common ground already exists; but, as Founding Father and chief author of the Constitution James Madison himself might advise, in this case whether it can be built on must depend largely on the extent to which our most "enlightened statesmen" can overcome the "factions" that beset their respective parties.

In Federalist Paper Number Ten, Madison defines a "faction" as any group of citizens, whether it encompasses a vast majority or a tiny minority, that attempts to advance its ideas or interests at the expense of other citizens' rights and well-being and that does so in ways that conflict with "the permanent and aggregate interests of the community," or the greater "public good." The "causes of faction" are "sown" into human nature, and the most fertile soil for factions include "a zeal for different opinions concerning religion." Wise and public-spirited leaders, Madison says, must "adjust these clashing interests and render them all subservient to the public good."

The issue of the role of sacred places in serving public purposes presently is beset by at least two species of minority factions that, for lack of better appellations, may be termed *orthodox secularists* and *orthodox sectarians.*

Many individuals and organizations have legitimate concerns about the implications of both existing and proposed charitable choice laws for Americans' constitutional rights, civil rights, and civil liberties. They are to be distinguished from orthodox secularists, mostly on the political left, who—while often paying lip service to the good works done by faith-based organizations and the right of religious people to enter the public square, *as religious people,* and participate fully in civic life—insist that government foster or fund religious activities and programs only if they are nominally religious or thoroughly secularized.

Likewise, many individuals and organizations have legitimate concerns about keeping the "faith" in "faith-based," including many Christian conservatives who have venerable theological reasons for avoiding any other than incidental contact with government. They are to be distinguished from orthodox sectarians who, far from insisting on strict church-state separation, insist that public social welfare service delivery funds be used for expressly religious purposes, including worship services and proselytization, who further insist that the programs they favor are far more efficacious than less pervasively sectarian and strictly secular alternatives, and who dismiss any constitutional, empirical, or other arguments to the contrary as antireligious.

The minority factions are magnets for other factious individuals and groups that threaten to turn the healthy debate over how best to support sacred places in advancing civic purposes into a bloody battleground over other issues—supporting or opposing homosexual rights and state and local laws governing the same; supporting or opposing delivery of social welfare programs funded in whole or in part by the federal government, the vast majority of which now are statutorily administered through direct grants and indirect disbursement arrangements including vouchers; and so on.

Each minority faction, it seems, issues weekly or monthly political ultimatums. The best way for our enlightened statesmen—and the rest of us—to respond is with corresponding invitations to search for common ground in accordance with what President Bush himself has repeatedly referred to as his own guiding principles on the issue: evenhandedness, neutrality, nondiscrimination, a desire for better civic results, and a respect for pluralism.

Take, for example, Title VII and the question of faith-based organizations' right to take religion into account in hiring. In principle, President Bush, Senator Lieberman, most other leaders, and most Americans agree that that right ought to be upheld, but they may differ on how to balance it against competing rights and liberties when public funds are involved. Those differences, however, except at the factious extremes, do not appear to be so broad as to prevent bipartisan cooperation in the public interest. *In Good Faith*, a document developed by the American Jewish Committee and included in this volume, as well as statements prepared by the constitutional and legal beagles in the White House Office of Faith-Based and Community Initiatives and available upon request are roadmaps for resolving reasonable Title VII differences. I think the actual differences can be measured in inches, not miles, and accommodated along the lines advocated by Senator Santorum.

Or, take the issue of how literally thousands of government social welfare programs are presently administered. In principle, President Bush, Senator Lieberman, most other leaders, and most Americans want them to be administered through whatever legally appropriate fiscal or other arrangements result in the most cost-effective results. Most of those programs now work through direct grants, some work through both direct grants and vouchers, and a small fraction work through vouchers only. Overall, nobody seems truly satisfied with the results, but policy decisions about whether to change a given program's disbursement procedures or other administrative features ought not to be the basis of all-purpose ideological or nebulous sentiments for or against "big government." Fortunately, except at the factious extremes, everyone seems inclined to make administrative reform decisions consistent with reasonable case-by-case, program-by-program assessment of how such changes might result in better performance. I have no doubt that, if such reforms are pursued, relatively more programs, but by no means most or all programs, would feature indirect disbursement procedures, or vouchers.

As I said in the conclusion to my March speech, to me, the essential Christian social teaching is that there are no "strangers," only brothers and sisters whom we have yet to meet, greet, get to know, and come to love. As the Bible says in I John 18, "Little children, let us love, not in word or speech, but in truth and action."[8] If our enlightened statesmen focus on poor children and others in need, then the mischief wrought by factions will cease to bedevil the bipartisan push to enlist our national government more squarely in the support of America's diverse community helpers and healers.

NOTES

1. George W. Bush, "Rallying the Armies of Compassion," January 29, 2001.

2. Quotation from George W. Bush's speech to Congress, February 28, 2001.

3. Stephen Monsma, *When Sacred and Secular Mix* (Lanham, Md.: Rowman and Littlefield, 1996).

4. Jeffrey Rosen, "Religious Rights: Why the Catholic Church Shouldn't Have to Hire Gays," *New Republic*, February 26, 2001.

5. "In Good Faith: A Dialogue on Government Funding of Faith-Based Social Services," a statement arising from discussions convened by the American Jewish Committee and the Feinstein Center for American Jewish History at Temple University (2001).

6. Amy Sherman, *The Growing Impact of Charitable Choice* (Annapolis, Md.: Center for Public Justice).

7. Bush, "Rallying the Armies of Compassion."

8. John 3:18, New Revised Standard Version.

CHAPTER SEVENTEEN

Testing the Assumptions: Who Provides Social Services?

MARK CHAVES

The establishment of the White House Office of Faith-Based and Community Initiatives by the Bush administration is part of a larger initiative to expand the role of religious organizations in the U.S. social welfare system. Beyond enacting and enforcing charitable choice legislation of the sort that began with section 104 of the Personal Responsibility and Work Opportunity Reconciliation Act of 1996, that initiative seeks to fight poverty by encouraging religious organizations—including those that have never engaged in social services in a serious way—to start, expand, and seek public support for social service activities.

This chapter assesses the soundness of several assumptions behind the initiative by discussing empirical evidence about the provision of social services by congregations. Religious congregations—members of churches, synagogues, mosques, temples, and so forth—constitute only a subset of the faith-based organizations involved in social services, and in most respects they are far less important actors than are faith-based social service agencies like the Salvation Army and Catholic Charities. Still, congregations are the core religious groups in American society, and advocates of faith-based social services often point to congregation-based programs as models. Furthermore, congregations are the prototypical "pervasively sectarian" organization; their inclusion in large numbers in our publicly supported social welfare system would constitute a qualitative change in church-state relations regarding social services. It is therefore appropriate to examine the provision of social services by congregations in the context of charitable choice initiatives.

This chapter addresses several specific questions: What social services do congregations typically offer? Do congregations provide social services in distinctive ways? Which types of congregations provide more social services? To what extent are congregations inclined to take advantage of funding available under charitable choice? With whom do congregations collaborate? Does collaboration affect their activities? The answers to those questions are sometimes surprising. They dispel certain assumptions about congregations and their provision of social services and provide a more realistic view of congregations' current and potential role in our social welfare system.[1]

WHAT SOCIAL SERVICES DO CONGREGATIONS PROVIDE?

Charitable choice advocates sometimes argue that congregations already are an important component of the U.S. social welfare system, giving the impression that the vast majority actively and intensively engage in social service delivery. The truth is somewhat different. Although virtually all congregations engage in what might be considered social service activities and although a majority— 57 percent—support provision of some type of more or less formal social service, community development, or neighborhood organizing projects, the intensity of congregational involvement varies widely. For example, congregations may donate money to a community food bank, supply volunteers for Meals on Wheels, organize a food drive every Thanksgiving, or operate an independent food pantry or soup kitchen. They may supply volunteers to do occasional home repairs for the needy, assist first-time homebuyers with congregational funds, participate in neighborhood redevelopment efforts, or build affordable housing for senior citizens. They may donate money to a neighborhood shelter, provide volunteers to prepare dinner at a shelter on a rotating basis with other congregations, or actually provide shelter for homeless women and children in the congregation's facilities.

One measure of the depth of congregational involvement in those activities is the percentage having a staff person who devotes at least 25 percent of his or her time to social service projects. *Only 6 percent of all congregations and only 12 percent of those reporting some degree of social service involvement have such a staff person.* Other measures also are informative. The median dollar amount spent by congregations in direct support of social service programs is approximately $1,200, or 3 percent of the median congregation's total budget. In the median congregation with some sort of involvement in social service activities, only ten individuals are involved in those activities as volunteers. The basic picture is clear: although most congregations participate in some sort of social service activity, only a small minority actively and intensively engage in such activity.

Congregations also favor certain types of projects. Housing, clothing, and, especially, food projects are more common than programs dealing with health, education, domestic violence, tutoring/mentoring, substance abuse, or job training. Fewer than 10 percent of congregations have programs in any of the latter areas. By comparison, 11 percent have clothing projects, 18 percent have housing/shelter projects, and 33 percent have food projects. Eight percent of congregations report providing services to homeless people.

In other words, *congregations are much more likely to engage in activities that address the immediate needs of individuals for food, clothing, and shelter than to engage in projects or programs that require sustained involvement to meet longer-term goals.* Programs that appear to involve only short-term or fleeting contact with clients are far more common (36 percent of congregations) than programs that involve more intensive, long-term, or sustained face-to-face interaction (10 percent of congregations).

Those results contradict the widely held assumption that religious organizations provide social services in a distinctively holistic or personal way. There is indeed substantial congregational involvement in social services, but not of the sort usually envisioned. Congregational social service provision is much more commonly characterized by attention to short-term emergency needs, especially for food, clothing, and shelter, than by more personal and intensive interaction or by holistic attention to cross-cutting problems. That pattern is found in *every* extant survey of congregations that provide social services.[2]

How Do Congregations Provide Social Services?

Beyond the tendency to focus on short-term, emergency needs, congregations tend to structure their social service involvement in a distinctive way. When they do more than donate money, canned goods, or old clothes, they are most apt to organize small groups of volunteers to perform relatively well-defined tasks on a periodic basis: fifteen people spending several weekends renovating a house; five people cooking dinner at a homeless shelter one night a week; ten young people spending two weeks in the summer painting a school in a poor community; and so on. When congregations do provide social services, virtually all—90 percent—do so with volunteers from the congregation. At the same time, the total number of volunteers provided by the typical congregation is rather small. As mentioned above, in the median congregation that engaged in some level of social service activity, only ten congregants volunteered to participate in those activities. In 80 percent of the congregations, fewer than thirty volunteers participated. In light of that, it probably is no accident that congregational involvement in social services is highest in areas in which organizations such as

homeless shelters or Habitat for Humanity have emerged to exploit congregations' capacity to mobilize relatively small numbers of volunteers to carry out
well-defined and delimited tasks.

   Research thus points to a more modest—and realistic—vision for congregational involvement in social services than is sometimes trumpeted. That more
realistic vision does not deny that some congregations engage in important antipoverty projects and programs—those are the congregations that have received
the most media attention in recent years—nor does it trivialize the contribution
that they make to the U.S. social welfare system. If only 1 percent of congregations deliver social services in an intensive way, that still represents about 3,000
congregations across the nation. Nevertheless, it is important to recognize that
they are the exception rather than the rule. Understanding that congregations
that are deeply engaged in providing social services are very uncommon—and
likely to remain so—does not minimize their contributions, but it should caution all parties against making sweeping claims about the capacities of idealized
congregations. A more realistic assessment would recognize that, on one hand,
only a very small percentage of congregations is likely to play an active role under a new welfare regime and, on the other, that most congregations' social service activity is now and will continue to be limited to organizing small groups
of people to perform specific tasks on a periodic basis.

WHICH CONGREGATIONS PROVIDE MORE SOCIAL SERVICES?

Although the percentage of congregations that are deeply engaged in social service activity is rather low, some congregations participate intensively. Which
congregations are most active? Four patterns emerge. The first is unsurprising
but important: larger congregations do more than smaller congregations. Although only about 1 percent of congregations have more than 900 regularly participating adults, the largest 1 percent account for about one-quarter of all the
money spent directly by congregations on social service activities. Only about
10 percent of congregations have 250 or more regular participants, but that 10
percent accounts for more than half of all the money that congregations spend
on social service activities. *Clearly, the minority of large congregations provide the
bulk of social services carried out by congregations.*

   The second pattern is less obvious. On one hand, congregations located in
poor neighborhoods tend to engage in more social service activity than those located in nonpoor neighborhoods. On the other hand, congregations with more
middle-class members engage in more social service activity than those with
more poor members, *and that is true even of congregations in poor neighborhoods.*
Taken together, those two findings imply that congregations located in poor

neighborhoods but composed of less poor or more middle-class people engage in the most social service and community activity. That pattern suggests that a congregation's own resources are crucially important in generating social service activity. Congregations located in poor neighborhoods, but without the internal resources that come with middle-class constituents, do not engage in as much social service activity as congregations with more of those resources.

The third pattern suggests that religious tradition matters. Congregations associated with mainline Protestant denominations provide more social services than conservative Protestant congregations, and Catholic congregations are neither more nor less active than conservative Protestant congregations. Beyond denomination, self-described theologically liberal congregations provide more social services than self-described conservative congregations. That pattern is consistent with previous research that shows that theologically more liberal individuals and congregations are, in a variety of ways, more connected to their surrounding communities than are more evangelical or conservative individuals and congregations.[3]

The fourth pattern indicates that race also matters. Although African American congregations do not, in general, provide more social services than white congregations, African American congregations are more likely to be engaged in certain key types of social services, such as education, mentoring, substance abuse, and job training or employment assistance programs.

Beyond the intrinsic importance of identifying the most active congregations, these findings take on special significance when combined with data on which congregations are inclined to take advantage of new opportunities for public funding and government collaboration that might emerge from current initiatives.

WHO WILL TAKE ADVANTAGE OF CHARITABLE CHOICE?

The current involvement of congregations in social service delivery is only part of the story. We also might ask about congregations' interest in expanding their participation by taking advantage of funding opportunities presented by charitable choice legislation. Whatever social services they currently provide and whatever their current level of collaboration with secular and government agencies, are religious congregations inclined to take advantage of new funding opportunities?

The National Congregations Study collected data from congregations through sixty-minute interviews with a key informant (a minister, priest, rabbi, or other leader) from each congregation. Informants were asked whether they thought that their congregation would apply for government money to support

its human services programs. Fifteen percent of congregations had a congregational policy against taking government money; 36 percent, however, indicated
interest in applying for government support.

That should not be taken to mean that more than one-third of U.S. congregations are likely to apply for government grants and contracts in the coming
years. That a member of the clergy expressed interest in moving in that direction is not at all the same thing as willingness among members of the congregation. Other research shows that clergy tend to be more supportive of such a
move than parishioners. That number probably should be interpreted as a maximum—an estimate of the percentage of U.S. congregations that *might* apply for
government funds if given the opportunity. Since only about 3 percent of congregations currently receive government money for social service projects, even
a small increase—say, 5 percentage points—in the proportion of congregations
receiving public funds could represent a major increase in the participation of
religious congregations in the U.S. social welfare system and a major change in
church-state relations. The overall level of expressed willingness to seek government support indicates that potential exists for increasing the numbers of
government-congregation partnerships in social service delivery. There is a market for charitable choice.

Whatever the absolute level of interest among congregations, which subsets
of congregations are likely to take advantage of the opportunities presented by
charitable choice? The basic patterns are similar to those described above regarding which congregations provide more social services; once again, size, religious tradition, and race are the key factors. Again, it is not surprising that large
congregations are considerably more likely to express interest in seeking government funds. The most interesting findings, however, demonstrate the enduring power of both race and ideology in determining the engagement of U.S.
congregations in state and society.

A congregation's ethnic composition is by far the most powerful predictor of
willingness to apply for government funds. Informants from 64 percent of predominantly African American congregations expressed a willingness to apply
for government funds compared with only 28 percent from predominantly white
congregations. Controlling other congregational features, predominantly black
congregations are *five times* more likely than other congregations to seek public
support.

The importance of this finding is enhanced when it is viewed in the context
of two other facts about African American congregations. First, there already is
a lower wall—both culturally and institutionally—between church and state in
African American than in other religious communities in the United States.
Second, clergy in predominantly black churches enjoy greater power than their

counterparts in predominantly white churches to initiate and implement congregational programs of their own choosing. Both of those features increase the likelihood that clergy-reported interest in seeking government funding will translate into concrete action. In light of that, if charitable choice initiatives successfully redirect public monies to religious congregations, African African congregations are likely to be substantially overrepresented among those who take advantage of those initiatives.

Catholic and liberal/moderate Protestant congregations are significantly more likely to apply for government funds to support social service activities than are conservative/evangelical congregations. Forty-one percent of congregations in liberal/moderate Protestant denominations said that they would be willing to apply for government funds compared with 40 percent of Catholic congregations and only 28 percent of congregations in conservative/evangelical denominations. Furthermore, when informants were asked to classify their congregations as liberal leaning, conservative leaning, or middle-of-the-road, congregations identified as theologically and politically conservative were significantly less likely to express willingness to apply for government funds, and that was true even after controlling for denominational affiliation and other characteristics. Although denominational affiliation remained salient, liberal/conservative ideology cross-cut denominational lines in important ways, and that divide mattered when it came to expressed willingness to pursue charitable choice opportunities.

Combining the results reported in this section with those in the previous section yields an important conclusion: the assumption that charitable choice initiatives are likely to involve *new* sorts of religious congregations in providing publicly funded social services—those that have not been involved before—is questionable. Larger congregations, African American congregations, and Catholic and liberal/moderate Protestant congregations are more likely to apply for funds, and those are exactly the congregations that already are most likely to be more deeply involved in social services.

WITH WHOM DO CONGREGATIONS COLLABORATE AND WHAT ARE THE CONSEQUENCES?

Congregations provide social services primarily in collaboration with other organizations. Eighty-four percent of congregations that provide social services have at least one collaborator on at least one program. Seventy-two percent of all programs are operated in collaboration with others. Although other congregations are the single most common type of collaborator, congregations are as likely to collaborate with some sort of secular organization (59 percent of congregations) as with some sort of religious organization (58 percent of congregations).

Although only 3 percent of congregations currently receive government financial support for their social service activity, about one-fifth of those with programs collaborate in some fashion with a government agency. Clearly, when congregations offer social services it is mainly in collaboration with others, including secular and government agencies in nontrivial numbers.

Congregations are not equally likely to collaborate. Large, mainline Protestant, theologically liberal congregations with more college graduates are significantly more likely than others to collaborate on social services. Interestingly, although there is no race difference in the likelihood of collaborating in general, predominantly African American congregations are significantly more likely than white congregations to collaborate with *secular* organizations.

When congregations collaborate with secular, especially government agencies, are they less likely to engage in the longer-term, more holistic or transformational kinds of social services some claim to be their special purview? The answer is no. Looking first at individual programs, congregational social service programs involving secular collaborators of any sort are slightly *more* likely (10 percent versus 7 percent) than programs involving nonsecular collaborators to be personal and long-term, and they are significantly *less* likely (25 percent versus 35 percent) to be fleeting and superficial. Programs involving government collaborators are significantly *less* likely to be fleeting and superficial (21 percent versus 32 percent). The pattern is similar for congregations as a whole: with many other variables controlled, congregations with secular collaborators are significantly *more* likely to be engaged in longer-term, personal, face-to-face kinds of social service activities than are congregations without such collaborators. Congregations with government collaborators are no less likely than congregations without government collaborators to participate in or support such programs. None of the differences is large, and these results alone do not indicate that secular collaborations actually encourage more holistic kinds of social services. Still, they clearly do not support the notion that such collaborations are likely to discourage holistic social services.

Thus, research on provision of social services by congregations contradicts yet another common assumption about charitable choice initiatives: that a distinctively holistic or personal approach to social services is potentially threatened by collaboration with secular, and especially government, agencies. That assumption is sometimes used to justify calls for allowing religious organizations, when collaborating with government, to operate under looser accountability and monitoring standards than those imposed on secular social service organizations. But there is no evidence that collaborating with government agencies makes congregations less likely to engage in the more personal and longer-term social service activities that some think are more likely to occur within a religious organization that guards its autonomy. If the call for loosening the regulatory environment in which religious organizations deliver social services is based on the assumption that a stricter environment threatens their holistic approach to social services, that call is on shaky empirical ground. In the main, congregations do not employ a holistic approach to social services, and the minority that do are not discouraged from doing so by government collaborations, including financial collaborations.

CONCLUSION

We are in a moment of enthusiasm about the role that religious organizations may be able to play in our social welfare system, a moment also of considerable interest in expanding that role and creating new kinds of partnerships between government and religious organizations. This chapter has tried to present a realistic, pragmatic, and clear-headed assessment of the possibilities—and limits—of religious congregations' current and likely future role. Research indicates that congregations do indeed engage in a wide range of social services and that many congregations already collaborate with secular and government-funded groups in providing those services. But only a tiny minority of congregations engage in social services in more than a superficial way, and the congregations that are most likely to take advantage of charitable choice initiatives and the activities of the White House Office of Faith-Based and Community Initiatives are those that already are most actively involved in social services: large, African American, Catholic, and liberal/moderate Protestant congregations in poor neighborhoods. From that perspective, it is difficult to see how charitable choice initiatives might succeed in involving new sorts of congregations in social services, publicly funded or not.

Perhaps most important, some of the results described in this chapter speak to one of the fundamental ambiguities within the charitable choice movement: is the goal of this initiative, including the White House Office of Faith-Based and Community Initiatives, to remove discrimination against religious organizations in public funding or is it to actively prefer religious organizations? The activities sponsored and encouraged by charitable choice initiatives sometimes go well beyond rooting out discrimination, as when state or federal agencies favor religious organizations in competition for funding—perhaps even setting aside public funds for which only religious organizations are eligible to apply—or when religious organizations are allowed to operate in a looser regulatory environment than secular organizations while delivering the same services. Even if that sort of preference for faith-based over secular social service agencies were to pass constitutional muster, it can be justified on pragmatic grounds only by assuming that the social services provided by religious organizations are distinctive and ultimately more effective than those provided by secular organizations. But there is little reason to think that congregations—or, for that matter, other types of religious organizations—deliver social services that are distinctively holistic, more focused on individuals' long-term needs, or generally more effective than those provided by secular organizations. Even if the charitable choice movement succeeds in institutionalizing a preference for religious organizations in awarding public funds—either by favoring religious organizations in funding competitions or by allowing them to operate under laxer standards and regulations—there is little reason to believe that doing so will advance the battle against poverty in our society.

NOTES

1. This chapter uses data from the National Congregations Study (NCS), a 1998 survey of a nationally representative sample of 1,236 religious congregations. For more information about the National Congregations Study methodology, see Mark Chaves and others, "The National Congregations Study: Background, Methods, and Selected Results," *Journal for the Scientific Study of Religion*, vol. 38 (1999), pp. 458–76. This chapter is a condensed version of two articles: Mark Chaves, "Religious Congregations and Welfare Reform: Who Will Take Advantage of Charitable Choice?" *American Sociological Review*, vol. 64 (1999), pp. 836–46, and Mark Chaves and William Tsitsos, "Congregations and Social Services: What They Do, How They Do It, and with Whom," *Nonprofit and Voluntary Sector Quarterly*, vol. 30 (2001, forthcoming). Readers interested in more detail should consult those articles.

2. See, for example, Ram A. Cnaan, *Social and Community Involvement of Religious Congregations Housed in Historic Religious Properties: Findings from a Six-City Study* (Philadelphia: University of Pennsylvania School of Social Work, 1997), and *Keeping Faith in the City: How 401 Urban Religious Congregations Serve Their Neediest Neighbors* (Philadelphia: Center for Research on Religion and Urban Civil Society, 2000); Tobi J. Printz, *Faith-Based Service Providers in the Nation's Capital: Can They Do More?* Charting Civil Society, no. 2 (Washington, D.C.: The Urban Institute, 1998); Nancy T. Ammerman, *Doing Good in American Communities—Congregations and Service Organizations Working Together: A Research Report from the Organizing Religious Work Project* (Hartford, Conn.: Hartford Seminary, 2001a); Lester M. Salamon and Fred Teitelbaum, "Religious Congregations as Social Service Agencies: How Extensive Are They?" *Foundation News* (September/October 1984); Carol Silverman, "Faith-Based Communities and Welfare Reform," in *Can We Make Welfare Reform Work? California Religious Community Capacity Study* (Sacramento: California Council of Churches, 2000), pp. 66–84; Melissa Stone, "Scope and Scale: An Assessment of Human Service Delivery by Congregations in Minnesota," paper presented at the annual meeting of the Association for Research on Nonprofit Organizations and Voluntary Action, New Orleans, 2000; Robert J. Wineburg, "Local Human Services Provision by Religious Congregations: A Community Analysis," *Nonprofit and Voluntary Sector Quarterly*, vol. 21 (1992), pp. 107–17.

3. Concerning individuals, see Robert Wuthnow, "Mobilizing Civic Engagement," in Theda Skocpol and Morris Fiorina, eds., *Civic Engagment in American Democracy* (Brookings, 1999), pp. 331–63. Concerning congregations, see Chaves and others, "Religious Variations in Public Presence: Evidence from the National Congregations Study," forthcoming in Robert Wuthnow and John H. Evans, eds., *Quietly Influential: The Public Role of Mainline Protestantism* (University of California Press, 2001), and Nancy Ammerman, "Connecting Mainline Protestant Churches with Public Life, " also forthcoming in Wuthnow and Evans, eds., *Quietly Influential.*

CHAPTER EIGHTEEN

Appropriate and Inappropriate Use of Religion

DAVID SAPERSTEIN

Religious individuals and organizations have the constitutional right to practice their religion however they please. If a religious organization wants to create a religious political party, there is no constitutional bar to doing so, although it would likely lose its tax exemption. If a presidential candidate wants to do nothing but proselytize, she or he may do so, although much of the electorate will be alienated. The 2000 presidential campaign dramatized the need to draw a line between "appropriate" and "inappropriate" religious rhetoric and activity in U.S. political life. The terms "appropriate" and "inappropriate" are used intentionally rather than "legal" or "not legal." In the United States, we have a right to do a lot of things—including things that may be, in the views of others, wrong or inappropriate. And religious and political groups and leaders (including candidates for office) may well do things that are within their rights—and even within the short-term interests of a political campaign—but that are bad for religion, bad for America, or bad for democracy. So what, then, are appropriate uses of religion in political life? Let me suggest three.

First, discussion of religion can help explain who candidates and political leaders are and what they are about. Profiles of George W. Bush, Al Gore, or Joseph Lieberman (we learned less about Dick Cheney's religious beliefs in the 2000 campaign) would be neither accurate nor complete if they did not describe the candidate's religious beliefs and the role that religion plays in his life. And since Americans knew comparatively little about Orthodox Jews and Orthodox Judaism before Senator Lieberman's selection as Vice President Gore's running mate, it was legitimate to seek more explanations than usual.

Second, candidates for election not only can but should express their views on policy issues concerning religion. Such views need to be part of the public debate. The American people have a right to know where candidates stand on crucial proposals that arise at the intersection of religion and public policy. Present proposals include religious freedom legislation; constitutional amendments to weaken the establishment clause of the First Amendment; and legislation on school prayer, scientific creationism, the posting of the Ten Commandments, protection of the religious rights of American workers on their jobs, and charitable choice.

Third, the American people have a right to know how candidates' religious beliefs and values will inform their views on a whole range of issues beyond what are broadly seen as "religious issues," such as school prayer and charitable choice. In that respect, while the Anti-Defamation League's (ADL's) public letter to Senator Lieberman complaining of his frequent use of religious rhetoric on the campaign trail raised vital concerns and sensitized the public and the candidates to the dangers of misusing religious rhetoric, the ADL was woefully off base in its subsequent assertion that it is inappropriate for candidates to suggest that their religious beliefs shape or inform their public policy perspectives and that religion "belongs in the church, in the synagogue, in the home and in the heart; it doesn't belong on a political campaign, and certainly not in politics or government."

Almost every member of Congress and public figure with whom I have worked in my twenty-seven years in Washington has been influenced by his or her religious beliefs. Religion has a long tradition of inspiring American political values, and much of Senator Lieberman's language resonated with the rhetoric of the Declaration of Independence, Abraham Lincoln, and Martin Luther King Jr. While using religion to establish the moral context for their views, those leaders went on to explain their policies in terms that were open political debate and that included all Americans, regardless of faith. Thus, the Declaration of Independence roots our rights in our Creator, but the Constitution, in formally setting forth our rights, does not mention God. King presented his views in nonsectarian, inclusive religious language to prick the conscience of the nation and to establish a moral context for the powerful public policy arguments he would then make—arguments made in secular language that all people could relate to.

Politicians and candidates have asserted in recent years that God's "pervasive preference for the poor" should animate our welfare policy; that respect for God's creation should deepen our concern for endangered species; and that religious "just war theory" can provide moral insight into U.S. policies in the Gulf War or Kosovo conflict. To suggest that such assertions are by virtue of their religious nature inappropriate is to foist on political discourse an artificial straightjacket that has no place in American history or law. It morally weakens much of the vital debate our nation needs. Lieberman was well within the bounds of propriety in stating that the Fifth Commandment to "Honor your father and your mother" strengthened his resolve to ensure prescription drug benefits for the elderly. Not only do our candidates and leaders have a *right* to talk about their faith, they have a *responsibility* to explain how their religious views shape their political agenda. Such use of religious language in the public forum can serve to goad the conscience of the nation.

What uses of religious rhetoric are not appropriate? Let me again suggest three guidelines. First, it is inappropriate to suggest that one should support or oppose a policy on the basis of religious belief exclusively. Policies justified by belief alone cannot be tested in the free marketplace of ideas, and they must be tested if democracy is to work and if meaningful public policy debate is to flourish. Had Lieberman dropped his strong policy justification for prescription drug benefits to argue that we should adopt such a policy only because the Ten Commandments enjoins us to, he would have stepped over the line and greatly weakened the case for a policy he supports.

Second, it is never appropriate for candidates, explicitly or implicitly, to suggest that there is a religious test for holding office. While Article VI of the Constitution expressly prohibits only the government from creating such tests, the spirit of that prohibition should extend to political statements and policies. Article VI, together with the First Amendment's religion clauses, led to one of America's greatest contributions to political thought: that one's status as a citizen does not depend on one's religious beliefs or practices. That concept has provided more rights, freedoms, and opportunities to religious minorities in the United States than are available in any other nation. That concept made it possible for Joseph Lieberman to be nominated for vice president.

The religious test also arises when candidates suggest that their religious beliefs or practices qualify them for office or that others' beliefs or practices disqualify them. That occurs not only when someone like Pat Robertson asserts it directly, as he did when he said, "The Constitution of the United States is a marvelous document for self-government by Christian people. But the minute you turn the document into the hands of non-Christian people and atheist people, they can use it to destroy the very foundation of our society"[1]—and as he did when he said, ten years later, "When I said during my presidential bid that I would only bring Christians and Jews into the government . . . the media challenged me . . . 'How dare you maintain that those who believe the Judeo-Christian values are better qualified to govern America than Hindus and Muslims?' [they asked]. My simple answer is, 'Yes, they are.'"[2] It also happens when candidates put forward their religious beliefs so persistently that those beliefs become a political tool that implies that such beliefs are an inherent qualification for office. For example, if a candidate asserts that he or she is a born-again

Christian in an interview, it helps the electorate to understand the candidate; making that assertion at a prayer breakfast is likewise appropriate. In contrast, repeatedly inserting that identifier in every political speech or debate suggests that the candidate is saying to the public, "Vote for me because my belief in Jesus as savior makes me better qualified for office than someone who believes otherwise." In the 2000 presidential election, many candidates who ran in the primary and general elections either crossed or came perilously close to crossing that line.

Finally, candidates should minimize their use of divisive and exclusive language. While some religious language is far less sectarian and divisive than other language, all religious speech excludes some people. As a general principle, Americans should not be made to feel like outsiders because of their political leaders' rhetoric. (That is the key idea behind Supreme Court Justice Sandra Day O'Connor's "endorsement test," now widely used to determine whether the government has acted in a manner that violates the establishment clause.)

Is there a double standard in tolerating Senator Lieberman's religious rhetoric while condemning the use of religious rhetoric by some conservative Christians during the campaign? No, there is a consistent standard, and it applies to remarks rather than to individuals. Inclusive, aspirational, historically resonant comments like Bush's "our nation is chosen by God and commissioned by history to be a model to the world of justice" or Lieberman's "our equality . . . was an endowment of our creator" contrast starkly with the sectarian and divisive tone of Bush's suggestion that he could not explain how Jesus had affected his political views if listeners had not themselves been changed by Jesus and Bush's declaration of "Jesus Day" in the state of Texas. Exclusivity also was the major problem with Franklin Graham's Christological invocation and benediction at President Bush's inauguration. He absolutely had the "right" to give that invocation, and the president had a right to ask him to give it. But it made many Americans feel like outsiders.

On a political level, the president needs to confront the problem of exclusivity, because the concern about rhetoric is not just about the language used. It is, at its core, about the policies the language represents and justifies. Depending on how a candidate's political agenda is perceived, the same religious rhetoric may sound different. From the mouth of a candidate who is identified with religious tolerance, explicitly religious language is less likely to be seen as code for religious intolerance. From a candidate who is perceived as being religiously exclusive or intolerant, the same language might well be fairly seen as offensive. Not just the words themselves, but what the words are seen to represent, define public reaction.

Thus those who contend that separation of church and state is essential to ensuring freedom of religion did not hear in Lieberman's rhetoric an abandonment of that principle or a justification for changing or violating the Constitution. But in the rhetoric of the religious right, separationists hear an agenda that would change the Constitution, impose organized school prayer on children, and mandate teaching biblical creationism. Likewise, when Lieberman borrowed one of the religious right's favorite phrases—"the Constitution guarantees freedom for religion, not freedom from religion"—not only was he factually wrong, his words legitimized the religious right's legislative agenda, which smacks of exclusivity.

As long as religious rhetoric is aimed at inspiring the conscience of the nation, is inclusive, is not transformed into a political tool, and is not aimed at justifying an agenda that would alter the constitutional protections that make the United States the most religiously free and vibrant democratic country in the world, we should celebrate and not fear its presence in our political process.

THE DEBATE OVER CHARITABLE CHOICE

How does the foregoing discussion apply to charitable choice? First, opposing voices in the debate are equally committed to a robust role for religion in American public life and in providing social services. They differ profoundly on how to achieve that goal and on what is best for religion.

Currently, two types of social service programs are offered by the religious community. The first type is operated by religiously affiliated entities created by religious communities to act on their theological obligation to help the poor and needy, often more professionally and effectively than any individual church could do. Such programs do not proselytize, engage in worship, or promote religious education, nor do they discriminate in whom they serve or hire. These programs represent a constitutional way for government and faith-based organizations to work together, and they receive enormous amounts of government assistance. The second type is offered by churches, synagogues, and mosques—that is, "pervasively sectarian" institutions—and they engage in religious worship, proselytization, and education. They can discriminate in whom they hire and serve as long as they are not funded with government money.

Members of the Bush administration deserve credit for offering some revolutionary and visionary new ways for government and faith-based organizations, even pervasively sectarian institutions, to strengthen their partnership. The major issue is whether the government should directly fund pervasively sectarian entities to provide social service programs of the second type.

Is direct funding bad for religion? First, direct funding can exert a secular influence on religious organizations because government money comes tied to government rules, regulations, restrictions, audits, monitoring, and interference. The specter of government intrusion in the bookkeeping and daily operation of religious institutions frightens some people who care about religion. But equally alarming is the reverse: having the federal government fund religious organizations with tax dollars and not monitor those organizations. We know that the inherent religious mission and culture of many pervasively sectarian institutions will exert significant pressure on those churches that receive government funding to discriminate, to proselytize, and to fulfill their complete religious mandate. There is documented evidence of that pattern in churches that received funding under earlier charitable choice provisions. The only way to counterbalance that pressure and ensure that government regulations are met is through extensive government monitoring, which threatens religious autonomy.

Second, dependence on government money weakens religious organizations in several ways. An obvious consequence is that reliance on government funding obviates the need for individuals to support their own churches, synagogues, and mosques. But it also results in the weakening of distinctive legal protections that religious organizations enjoy. Take the debate over whether programs taking government money should be allowed to discriminate in hiring. There is a constitutional right and policy need for religious groups to select people to run their programs who share their religious identity and beliefs. But there are serious concerns over whether government-funded programs should be allowed to discriminate. One way to avoid the problem is to deny government funding to those programs. Another way is to deny a program a religious exemption if it receives significant amounts of government money. That, however, would force religious institutions to sacrifice their unique constitutional and legal status for the privilege of lining up at the public trough to fight with one another over scarce federal dollars. As tempting as having government funding to assist in meeting the church budget may be, it is an enormous price to pay for very little in return. Further, when churches voluntarily give up such exemptions and protections in one set of circumstances, it gives political weight to the arguments of those who seek to strip them of such exemptions in all circumstances.

Third, charitable choice will do little to help and will undoubtedly harm the recipients of social services. Not only will charitable choice divert money from successful programs to pervasively sectarian programs (some of which may be great successes but many of which may, at least at first, struggle to meet their goals), the religious rights of recipients will be compromised as they are forced to turn to programs with religious content to receive government-supported services. Those pitfalls are magnified by the government's refusal to increase existing funds. The money will necessarily be taken out of strong, successful faith-based entities such as Catholic Charities, Lutheran Social Services, and Jewish Federations and distributed among the approximately 350,000 churches, synagogues, and mosques in the United States that may decide to seek government funding. If one-tenth of those eligible apply, there will be 35,000 pervasively sectarian institutions competing with each other for limited government grants. That kind of competition will undermine the fabric of religious tolerance that has served our nation so well and dilute, if not altogether eradicate, funding for long-standing, effective, religiously affiliated social service programs.

Finally, the fungibility argument has been central to the Supreme Court's refusal to uphold direct government funding of pervasively sectarian institutions. Charitable choice proponents insist that as long as funding flows only to the secular components of programs run by pervasively sectarian institutions, no harm will be done. But they have to be honest about that. Even in a pervasively sectarian institution where government funds support only secular social services, every dollar in the church budget freed up by government funding is going to be used for religious activities. That is problematic. If a church literacy program receives government money to run the program and to help rehabilitate the classroom and that classroom is used on Sunday for religious instruction, the government has helped to fund the underlying religious nature of the institution. Thomas Jefferson said it well when addressing a taxing scheme over 200 years ago: "[T]o compel a man to furnish contributions of money for the propagation of opinions which he disbelieves is sinful and tyrannical."[3]

President Bush must recognize in the charitable choice debate a far-reaching test of his intention to unify and heal the nation. He faces a choice. If he rallies the nation around the substantial parts of his faith-based initiative on which almost everyone agrees he can forge a new, constitutionally permissible partnership between the faith community and government. If he insists on including a major funding program aimed at supporting houses of worship in their social service efforts, he will draw the nation into a painful, divisive, sectarian dispute that will mar his legacy. Reverend Jerry Falwell's attack on Islam and the attack by Reverend Eugene Rivers, who runs wonderful inner-city programs, on conservative evangelicals as racist is just a foretaste of what might be before us. Thousands of local churches, synagogues, and mosques competing for limited government funds in coming years will only exacerbate such rancor.

There are many simple, constitutional ways to achieve our common goals: using the tax system to encourage more charitable giving; providing technical assistance and staff training for all programs; sharing best practices; researching possible program improvements; diminishing or eliminating fees for all small organizations, including religious organizations, to establish separate 501(c)(3) corporations. With mutual respect and some hard work, we can ensure religious liberty, protect our Constitution and our religious institutions, maintain religion's vital role in the public square, and promote the excellent work that our religious institutions do in carrying out their prophetic mission to help those in need.

NOTES

1. Pat Robertson, *Washington Post,* March 23, 1981.
2. Pat Robertson, *The New World Order* (Dallas, Tex.: Word Publishing, 1991).
3. Excerpts from Jefferson's *Virginia Statute for Religious Freedom,* 1786.

CHAPTER NINETEEN

In Good Faith:
Government Funding
of Faith-Based Social Services

A Statement Arising from Discussions Convened by the
American Jewish Committee and the Feinstein Center
for American Jewish History at Temple University

The project that became In Good Faith *began in what may be seen as the dawn of
the national discussion on government funding of faith-based social service programs.
The project took shape in the wake of the enactment of the first charitable choice provision, which was part of the 1996 welfare reform legislation.*

*While the group drafted the document, charitable choice provisions were added to
several more federal laws and both presidential candidates called for extending them
to cover new streams of federal social service funding. Since the release of the document,
President Bush has unveiled a spate of new policy proposals through his Office of Faith-
Based and Community Initiatives, and his agenda has come under close scrutiny and
triggered heated debate. A bill has been introduced in the House of Representatives to
cover a number of new sources of federal social service funds under charitable choice
legislation while a bill introduced in the Senate would create new tax incentives for
charitable giving without extending charitable choice provisions. Many more voices
have joined the dialogue, and the political winds have shifted in sometimes surprising directions.*

*None of us could have predicted the ways in which the dialogue on this subject has
evolved. Nonetheless,* In Good Faith *continues to set forth the relevant issues and helps
to clarify the contours of an often-confusing debate on the principle of separation of
church and state. Those of us who were involved in the project continue to work on*

these issues in various ways. In Good Faith *surely does not represent the end of the dialogue, but it may fairly represent the beginning.*

Melissa Rogers

The debate over the 1996 welfare reform legislation turned national attention to a question of critical and enduring importance—what is the best way for our nation to assist those in need? This question has triggered many wide-ranging discussions about the role of the federal and state governments in social services, the most effective way to move people from welfare to work, and how better to coordinate government services with the business sector, nonprofit organizations, and community groups. Another issue about which welfare reform has generated debate is financial collaboration between government and faith communities to serve the needy. This issue has sparked great interest and also strong concern. It is this question that is the focus here.

The conversation regarding cooperative efforts between government and religious organizations occurs at a time when there is great enthusiasm for the contribution of faith communities to social well-being, and a sense that some on the Supreme Court of the United States are moving toward a narrower interpretation of the Establishment Clause of the First Amendment. This conversation also occurs, however, in the context of concern that some forms of collaboration between religious organizations and the government could seriously undermine the religious freedom of social service beneficiaries, religious providers, and taxpayers generally.

This document originated in two discussions: a project to seek common ground concerning government funding of faith-based groups to provide social services, organized by The American Jewish Committee and the Feinstein Center for American Jewish History at Temple University and underwritten by The Pew Charitable Trusts;[1] and monthly meetings of persons who in 1998 were participants at a conference on welfare reform and faith-based organizations organized by the J. M. Dawson Institute of Church-State Studies at Baylor University. The two groups merged in the fall of 1999 to work on this document in a process that has included a series of consultations with experts and practitioners with a range of views.

The group formed in an effort to provide guidance to those involved in the policy process. We hope also to provide illumination to others interested in government's relations with religious organizations and the shifting structure of the social safety net. While each participating organization has formulated its own policy statement, we recognized the unique value of forming a representative panel of the various points of view on these issues. By engaging in sustained conversation we worked to identify areas both of agreement and disagreement regarding collaboration between the government and religious organizations. This document is the fruit of that labor.

INTRODUCTION

The shape and scope of government collaboration with faith-based organizations[2] has been undergoing a historic transformation. The legislative focal point for this attention has been "charitable choice." "Charitable choice" is a term of art that refers to a specific legislative proposal first enacted by Congress in the 1996 federal welfare reform law. Although the concept is often used loosely to refer to government funding of faith-based social service programs in general, in fact it refers more particularly to the new statutory conditions under which states may enter into funding relationships with religious organizations that provide social services[3] using federal or state funds that originated with enactment of the TANF[4] Program in 1996. Other legislative initiatives also popularly referred to as "charitable choice" have since been introduced in Congress and the states, and some have been enacted.[5] These apply variations of the TANF language to other program areas, such as drug rehabilitation or housing.

The new idea represented by "charitable choice" is not the involvement of faith communities in the social service arena, as many religious organizations have a history of involvement in such services. Nor is government funding of religious social service providers in itself an innovation, as many organizations with a religious affiliation have long received government funds[6] to carry out their work. Before "charitable choice," governments at all levels awarded grants and contracts to religiously affiliated organizations. There are no uniform statutory provisions regarding the participation of religious providers, and there was and remains controversy over whether an organization could be a pervasively religious entity[7] (such as a house of worship) and receive government money to provide social services.

"Charitable choice" alters previous practice through new federal statutory language that specifically addresses the participation of religious providers. "Charitable choice" permits all faith-based organizations to compete for government social service funding, regardless of their religious nature. Thus "charitable choice" significantly broadens the scope and extent of government financial collaboration with faith-based organizations. This change is welcome to some but highly problematic to others. The legal, philosophical, and ethical dimensions of the change have generated substantial controversy.

People who care deeply both about religious liberty and about the provision of effective social services disagree about the constitutionality and advisability of "charitable choice." Some believe that "charitable choice" is a long overdue correction to the discriminatory exclusion of some religious providers on the basis of an unconstitutional judgment about their religious character, and that the changes benefit society by expanding the capacity of faith communities to address social problems. Others believe that by allowing government funds to flow to pervasively religious entities like houses of worship, or to religiously affiliated programs without appropriate safeguards, "charitable choice" unconstitutionally and unwisely opens the door to government advancement of religion, excessive government entanglement with religion, government support of religious discrimination, and a general weakening of religious autonomy.

Our dialogue has been undergirded by the following common core values:

—Concern for human needs, particularly those of the economically and socially disadvantaged, and for the social health of the nation.

—Affirmation that promoting the well-being of the nation is a responsibility jointly of the private sector, faith communities, nonprofit organizations, and government, and that religious organizations cannot replace government's role in upholding the social safety net.

—Preservation of religious liberty under the Constitution of the United States.

—Identification of common ground while bringing clarity and civil discourse to bear on areas of significant disagreement.

—Recognition that the support by businesses, philanthropies, and other non-governmental organizations of the good work done in society by religious organizations is valuable, and, of course, constitutional.

Within this broad framework, this document discusses specific areas of agreement regarding government collaboration with faith-based social service programs. The discussion bears on relationships structured by "charitable choice," but it is not limited to this concept and it is not an attempt to interpret any statute. The document also outlines areas of substantive disagreement on matters of constitutional interpretation and policy implementation related to collaboration.

We hope that this document will produce several benefits for policymaking and policy implementation. First, we hope that those who design and implement policies will be guided by the significant points of agreement we have forged as a way to promote healthy cooperation between government and religious organizations in the social service realm. Second, we hope that the document will provide a clear statement about where the agreements and disagreements lie in a complex area of the law as an aid for readers to develop their own informed conclusions. Third, we hope that the document will obviate the need for decision makers to collect from different sources the various positions on this matter. While we continue to differ about what is constitutional and advisable on some points, all of us believe that religious organizations and the government can work together in productive ways to bring about the greater good of society.

This topic will continue to be at the forefront of policy debates. Those engaged in the debate should acknowledge that no one side is the sole protector of the poor or of religious liberty. The most fruitful public debate will result when all acknowledge our shared stake in both the general welfare of our nation and the flourishing of religious freedom.[8]

AGREEMENT CONCERNING GOVERNMENT NONFINANCIAL COOPERATION WITH RELIGIOUS ORGANIZATIONS

Regardless of one's position on the constitutionality and advisability of "charitable choice," certainly government may, in many ways, include religious organizations among the community organizations with which it cooperates. Legitimate nonfinancial support includes:

—Providing information to the public and to persons in need about the availability of programs offered by religious and other community organizations.

—Providing access to education and training opportunities for program staff and volunteers of religious and other community organizations.

—Inviting faith community representatives to join community wide program task forces.

—Calling attention to the successful work of religious as well as secular providers.

—Providing letters of recommendation for faith-based and other community organizations that can help them raise funds from other sources.

—Advising social service beneficiaries of mentoring, support, and advocacy resources available from community organizations, including religious nonprofit agencies or houses of worship.

—Listing houses of worship and religious nonprofit agencies among the organizations that may provide community service placements to welfare recipients.

—Making information about the community, such as census tract data, directories of service providers, or needs assessments, available to help community service providers, including religious organizations, do planning, networking, and grassroots organizing.

—Encouraging charitable contributions through appropriate tax relief.

In addition, last year's enactment of the Religious Land Use and Institutionalized Persons Act (Public Law No. 106-274 [2000]) prevents zoning and other land use authorities from discriminating against or unnecessarily burdening the religious practices of houses of worship and other religious institutions, including their ability to provide social ministries.

Areas of Agreement Concerning Government Funding of Religious Organizations to Provide Social Services

Our shared values lead us to agree on the following important considerations, even as there remain strong differences among us as to the constitutionality and advisability of "charitable choice" (see Section IV):

1. Government funding for social services provided by religiously affiliated entities. Organizations that are affiliated with a house of worship or other religious body but are separate institutions performing secular functions should continue to be permitted to receive government money to fund their secular work.

2. Availability of a secular alternative. Beneficiaries have a right to a secular alternative if they do not wish to receive services from a religious organization. When government contracts with or awards grants to religious organizations for services, it must have a mechanism in place to provide a readily accessible secular service of equal value should any beneficiary require it. When the service is provided via a voucher mechanism, government should seek to include at least one secular alternative. If that is not possible, then government must have a mechanism in place to supply a readily accessible, equal value secular service in some other way.

3. Notice to prospective and current beneficiaries. Government must inform prospective and current beneficiaries about the religious nature of any participating programs and providers and of their right to receive equivalent services from a secular provider if they want.

4. Nondiscrimination in the provision of government-funded social services. Religious providers of government-funded social services should not discriminate against beneficiaries on the basis of religion or religious belief, either in admitting them into a program or in providing the government-funded services.

5. Ability of beneficiaries to opt out of religious activities. Whenever social service programs are funded by government, or participation in such programs is mandated by government, beneficiaries have the right not to participate in religious activities. Beneficiaries should be able to exercise this right within a program that has a religious component or dimension by declining active and passive participation in religious activities.

We disagree about the threshold question of whether government should fund programs where religious exercise is an integral element of the program. Notwithstanding the underlying objection of some of us to any government funding of these programs at all, if such programs do receive government funds, beneficiaries should be given notice of the religious and integral nature of the program, their right to choose between such a program and programs which do not require religious participation (including secular programs), and their option to leave the integral program at any time. If government does fund an integral program, then a beneficiary's religious liberty should be protected by ensuring choice between readily accessible programs of equal value, rather than through the right to opt out of the religious activities in a particular program.

6. *Prohibition on use of government grant or contract funds for religious activities.* The Supreme Court has held that organizations may not constitutionally use government grant or contract funds for religious activities. In federal statutes, this proscription is commonly expressed as a requirement not to use government funds for worship, religious instruction, or proselytizing. It is difficult, if not impossible, to define these concepts. In most situations, determining whether particular activities fall into these categories will depend on the facts and circumstances of each case. Some situations will present difficult questions.

Teaching values or beliefs as religious tenets constitutes religious instruction or proselytizing. An example would be urging a beneficiary to accept Jesus Christ or some other religious faith as the only way to move from welfare into employment. Discussing with a beneficiary commonly held values such as abiding by the law and being honest does not automatically represent religious instruction or proselytizing, although most, if not all, religions also teach these values. Worship includes such acts as offering prayers and reading scripture, but observing a neutral moment of silence does not constitute worship.

7. *Privately funded religious activities.* A provider that receives government contract or grant money may offer religious activities as well as the government-funded services as long as the religious activities are privately funded, purely voluntary, and clearly separate from the activities funded by government. For example, a religious provider that offers government-funded welfare-to-work counseling may post notices about support groups that engage in prayer and Bible study as long as the support groups are privately funded, participation in them is voluntary, and it is clear that the groups are separate from the welfare-to-work counseling. A provider that offers government-funded services may leave religious literature on tables in waiting rooms if the religious literature is paid for with private funds and it is clear that acceptance of the materials is voluntary and not a part of the government-funded program.

8. *Employment decisions on the basis of religion.* Federal law does not prohibit religious organizations from taking religious beliefs and practices into account in making decisions about hiring, promotion, termination, and other conditions of employment. The Supreme Court has not addressed whether a religious organization retains the liberty to make employment decisions on the basis of religion in the case of employees who work in programs or activities funded (in

whole or in part) by, or paid with, government money. Although the law is not settled in this area of government-funded positions, we agree that religious organizations retain their ability to use religious criteria in employment for those positions in nongovernmental programs that are wholly privately funded, regardless of whether other programs or activities of the organization receive government funds.

9. Display of religious art and use of a religious name. A religious provider receiving government funds is permitted to display religious art, icons, symbols, and scripture under certain conditions. Religious providers should not be required to eliminate religious references from their names (e.g., government should not require a St. Vincent de Paul Center to be renamed the Mr. Vincent de Paul Center). In constitutional rulings, the presence of religious art, icons, symbols, and scripture within a private organization offering social services has not, by itself, disqualified an entity from receiving government funds. However, the presence of such art, icons, and symbols has been considered by the Supreme Court in the overall determination of whether an entity is constitutionally permitted to accept government funding.[9]

10. Fiscal accountability. The federal government has the right to audit the funds it disburses. If a religious organization does not segregate the government contract and grant funds it receives, all of its accounts could be subject to an audit. Segregating the government money will decrease a religious organization's risk that all of its funds will be examined in a government audit.

11. Creation of a separately incorporated organization. Government is not precluded from requiring a pervasively religious organization to create a separate organization to provide government-funded services.[10] Even if government does not require such a separate organization, houses of worship and other pervasively religious organizations may wish to (and, some of us believe, should) create one. A separate organization facilitates keeping separate accounts to limit audits and helps to shield them from certain federal requirements that otherwise are triggered by the receipt of federal funds (see paragraph 12 below). Separate incorporation can also afford protection for the religious organization against liabilities incurred by the separate corporation.

12. Civil rights regulation of social service providers receiving government funds. Receipt of federal funds triggers the application of a number of federal civil rights statutes. These laws prohibit discrimination on the basis of race, color, national origin, sex, age, disability, and visual impairment.[11] Religious organizations that receive federal funds are subject to these laws. Religious organizations should consult legal counsel regarding the requirements of these laws and other regulations that may apply, including other federal, state, and local laws and ordinances.

CONFLICTING PERSPECTIVES ON GOVERNMENT FUNDING OF RELIGIOUS ORGANIZATIONS TO PROVIDE SOCIAL SERVICES

Notwithstanding the broad areas of agreement noted above concerning government funding of religious social-service organizations, the groups involved in this discussion remain deeply divided about "charitable choice." Some are strong supporters of "charitable choice"; others are equally strong opponents of this change in law and policy. The disagreements involve political philosophy, interpretation of current law, beliefs about the best way to protect and support the work of religious institutions, and pragmatic concerns. The contrasting positions are briefly sketched below both to illuminate the importance of the concerns raised on the two sides and to highlight the importance of the agreements we have reached after extensive discussion.

In Favor of "Charitable Choice"

"Charitable choice" is an innovative and carefully crafted means to expand government financial collaboration with religious organizations to meet critical social needs, while protecting beneficiaries, providers, the public trust, and constitutional values.

The past approach was, roughly, for government to permit funds only to religiously affiliated organizations providing secular services in a secular setting. "Pervasively religious" organizations, which displayed an integral religious character, were excluded. "Charitable choice" instead permits religious and secular organizations alike to participate as government-funded social service providers. "Charitable choice" enables government to fulfill its constitutional obligation not to establish religion and its constitutional duty to protect the religious liberty of beneficiaries without imposing illegitimate secularizing requirements on religious social service providers.

"Charitable choice" is constitutional. The U. S. Supreme Court, which has never wholly excluded "pervasively religious" organizations from government funding, has turned away from the strict separationist concept that undergirds opposition to "charitable choice." Recently, the Court did not use the "pervasively religious" criterion as the determining factor in deciding whether a religious organization may receive government funded services.[12] Even before this decision the Court had upheld direct governmental cash reimbursements for secular services performed by institutions that had been considered pervasively religious.[13]

"Charitable choice" ends government discrimination in the treatment of religious providers. The new standard is government neutrality. Government may now select from among all providers, based only on their ability to supply the needed

social services. "Charitable choice" does not guarantee funds to religious organizations; it creates a level playing field, removing the past bias against religious providers whose faith visibly shapes the organization's staff, character, and service delivery. This is not government endorsement of religion, but rather the end of the presumption that government should endorse only secular prescriptions for poverty and need.

"Charitable choice" protects the religious character of faith-based providers without establishing religion. It safeguards their autonomy by protecting their religious character if they accept government funds. They may maintain a religious environment and continue to select staff of like beliefs as long as they provide the assistance that government seeks and do not spend direct government funds on inherently religious activities. They may accept vouchers to aid beneficiaries who seek faith-based help. Providers are accountable for how they spend government funds, but without excessive government entanglement. They may limit government audits by establishing a separate account for government funds; government may require them to establish a separate organization for the government-funded services. When government buys services, it is not aiding the religious organization, but rather obtaining needed social services.

"Charitable choice" protects the religious liberty of beneficiaries. Beneficiaries may not be denied help on account of their religion nor be forced to participate in inherently religious activities to obtain help. Government must ensure that a secular alternative is available. These are specific requirements of "charitable choice" as enacted in the 1996 federal welfare law and they are crucial to guard against religious coercion. Early experience shows that beneficiaries have not had to bend to someone else's faith in order to receive help, but rather have enjoyed an expanded range of services and providers.[14]

"Charitable choice," prudently implemented, enhances social provision. Religious organizations are not required to contract with government nor to stop seeking donations and voluntary support. They should evaluate carefully the new funding opportunities, being mindful of the risk of dependency on government funds, the paperwork and regulatory burden, and the temptation to mute criticism of government or to adapt their mission to whatever government will fund. They should reject government money if accepting it will compromise their convictions or undermine their effectiveness. Government officials, for their part, should welcome the opportunity to select whichever provider offers the most effective help and the chance to offer a greater diversity of services. They must ensure that their rules effectively protect both the religious character of providers and the religious liberty of beneficiaries.

"Charitable choice" serves the needy. Government's desire for effective social services often coincides with faith-based organizations' ability to serve the poor

with excellence and respect. There is no need to choose between the First Amendment and the expanded involvement of faith-based providers. "Charitable choice" is a constructive alternative to an inequitable strategy which sought to protect beneficiaries and prevent religious establishment but at the price of excluding many religious providers. It is constitutionally sound, socially valuable, and pragmatically wise that such organizations are now permitted to use government funds, as other providers do, to provide the services government desires and that hurting families, individuals, and communities need.

Opposed to "Charitable Choice"

"Charitable choice" undermines governmental neutrality toward religion and promotes government funded discrimination. It also jeopardizes beneficiaries' rights to religious liberty, and threatens the autonomy and vitality of religion and religious liberty.

"Charitable choice" undermines governmental neutrality toward religion. "Charitable choice" is designed to allow houses of worship and other organizations that integrate religion into their social services to receive funds generated through taxation. When the government funds these institutions, it inevitably results in governmental funding and advancing religion itself, which is unconstitutional. Every member of the current Supreme Court has expressed concern about government funds flowing directly to pervasively religious organizations.[15]

Governmental advancement of religion is not just some abstract legal problem. It creates resentment when taxpayers are forced to support religions they reject. Legal and ethical claims are triggered when taxpayers are denied tax-funded employee positions because they aren't the "right" religion or don't hold the "right" religious beliefs. Furthermore, by requiring elected leaders to pick and choose among competing religions to award a limited number of social service grants and contracts, "charitable choice" creates an opportunity for using religion as a political tool and heightens religious divisions.

"Charitable choice" promotes government-funded discrimination. "Charitable choice" expressly allows religious organizations that receive government funds for their services to discriminate on the basis of religion in their employment practices. We believe that this results in government-funded discrimination and violates the Establishment Clause by using taxpayer money to advance a particular religious viewpoint. While churches and religious agencies retain the ability to make employment decisions on the basis of religion for privately funded positions, that right should not extend to those who provide the services that are funded by the government.

"Charitable choice" jeopardizes beneficiaries' rights to religious liberty. By making it possible to integrate tax-funded secular services with religious ones, "charitable

choice" practically invites the use of social service beneficiaries as a captive audience for proselytizing and other religious activities. Although "charitable choice" ostensibly requires access to alternative providers and a limited right to opt-out from religious activities, it will be very difficult for some beneficiaries to exercise these rights. Our concern is not with religious activities themselves, of course, but with governmental coercion in religious matters.

"Charitable choice" threatens the autonomy and vitality of religion and religious liberty. It is the government's obligation to demand accountability for its funds. When government funds flow to houses of worship and other pervasively religious groups, this obligation will invite excessive and unconstitutional entanglement between the institutions of church and state. If a house of worship accepts government money, for example, the regulation that attaches to the government money could bind the entire church, the church's books could be audited, and "charitable choice" lawsuits could jeopardize the church's assets.

Furthermore, we are concerned about religion's dependency on government funds and the effect that this will have on religion's willingness to serve as a prophetic critic of government. We also fear that, as many policymakers come to view religion as simply a cog in the vast engine of social reform, religion will be distorted, distracted, and demeaned. Religion in America is vibrant because it is fully owned and operated by believers, rather than by any governmental bureaucracy.

"Charitable choice" is part of several laws; therefore, we offer the following general recommendations to religious organizations:

—Houses of worship and other pervasively religious organizations (those that cannot or do not wish to clearly separate any privately funded religious activities from secular activities and refrain from discrimination on the basis of religion in hiring with government funds) should refrain from seeking government funds. Houses of worship and other pervasively religious institutions should remain self-supporting to protect taxpayers' consciences, governmental neutrality, and religious vitality. These organizations may cooperate with the government in nonfinancial ways (see areas of agreement) and seek funding from various private sources, including charitable foundations and corporate sponsorships.

—If houses of worship or other pervasively religious organizations would like to create separate organizations to receive tax funds, they must ensure that the secular services that are offered are clearly distinct from any privately funded religious activities, that tax money is not used for religious activities, including discrimination on the basis of religion in hiring, and that any participation in religious activities by beneficiaries is purely voluntary. These organizations must be prepared to be subject to the same general regulations that apply to any other recipient of government funds. Many organizations already operate in this fashion and we strongly recommend that other religious organizations create such religious affiliates.

Because government officials are charged not only with implementing "charitable choice," but also with upholding the Constitution, we urge them to seek guidance from an attorney because "charitable choice" conflicts in many respects with the Constitution.

APPENDIX: NON-GOVERNMENT COMMUNITY SUPPORT FOR FAITH-BASED ORGANIZATIONS

Regardless of one's position on the constitutionality and advisability of "charitable choice," partnerships and sources of funding in the private sector are available to religious organizations that desire to serve members and neighbors in need.

Funding possibilities include special appeals within houses of worship or denominations, grants from charitable foundations, and corporate giving alliances. Partnerships with various other sectors in the community could include

—Partnerships with banks to create non-profit housing programs.

—Partnerships with businesses in job training and placement programs.

—Partnerships with private hospitals in staffing and supplying congregation-based health clinics.

—Partnerships with community organizations in adult education, literacy, ESL, childcare and youth violence intervention programs.

—Partnerships with national social service coordinating organizations (such as Catholic Charities or United Jewish Communities) that facilitate local community work.

Signatories

The undersigned are a diverse group of religious, charitable, civil rights, and educational organizations. Each recognizes and respects the historical and contemporaneous importance of the role that religious freedom, as embodied in the Free Exercise and Establishment Clauses of the First Amendment, has played and will continue to play in the life of this country. Each also recognizes that government and the private sector, including religious organizations, have legitimate, distinct, and important responsibilities in addressing societal needs. Organizations that share these core assumptions may nevertheless have differing interpretations of the United States Constitution, particularly as applied to the question of government funding for the social work of religious organizations. The legislative provisions known as "charitable choice," which represent a particular approach to the participation of religious organizations in the delivery of government-funded social services, have focused attention on this controversial area. Some of the organizations listed below supported the "charitable choice" provision; some opposed it and some took no position. While not every organization listed below agrees with every statement in this document, it is their hope that the document will provide useful insights for government officials, social service providers, and beneficiaries in this complex and sensitive area.

Signatories

American Baptist Churches USA; American Jewish Committee; Baptist Joint Committee; The Becket Fund; Call to Renewal; Catholic Charities USA; The Center for Public Justice; Columbus School of Law, Catholic University of America; Evangelicals for Social Action; Feinstein Center for American Jewish History, Temple University; First Amendment Center, The Freedom Forum World Center; Friends Committee on National Legislation (Quaker); General Board of Church and Society, The United Methodist Church; Islamic Supreme Council of America; National Association of Evangelicals; National Council of Churches of Christ in the USA; The Salvation Army; Sikh Mediawatch and Resource Task Force (SMART); Soka Gakkai International–USA Buddhist Association; United States Catholic Conference

Draftees

Professor Marshall Breger, *Columbus School of Law, Catholic University of America;* Stanley Carlson-Thies, *Director of Social Policy Studies, The Center for Public Justice;* Professor Robert A. Destro, *Acting Dean, Columbus School of Law, Catholic University of America;* Richard T. Foltin, *Legislative Director and Counsel, American Jewish Committee;* Dr. Murray Friedman, *Director of the Philadelphia Chapter of the American Jewish Committee and Director of the Feinstein Center for American Jewish History, Temple University;* Nancy Isserman, *Associate Director, Feinstein Center for American Jewish History, Temple University;* John A. Liekweg, *Associate General Counsel, United States Catholic Conference;* Forest D. Montgomery, *Counsel, NAE Office for Governmental Affairs, National Association of Evangelicals;* Melissa Rogers, *former General Counsel, Baptist Joint Committee;* Duane Shank, *Issue and Policy Advisor, Call to Renewal;* Julie Segal, *former Legislative Counsel, Americans United for Separation of Church and State;* Jeffrey Sinensky, *Director of Domestic Policy and General Counsel, American Jewish Committee;* Dr. Stephen Steinlight, *Senior Fellow and Director of Publications, American Jewish Committee;* Heidi Unruh, *Policy Analyst, Evangelicals for Social Action.*

NOTES

1. The opinions expressed herein do not necessarily reflect the views of The Pew Charitable Trusts.

2. The terms "faith-based organization" or "religious organization" are used here as umbrella terms encompassing any organization that is motivated by faith, affiliated with a faith tradition, or that incorporates religion in its activities in any way. The term applies, therefore, to a range of organizational forms including houses of worship as well as separately incorporated nonprofits.

3. For the purposes of this document, the phrase "social services" includes services such as job training, counseling, child care, and job search assistance, but does not include elementary and secondary education.

4. TANF is Temporary Assistance for Needy Families, the program that in 1996 replaced the long-standing Aid to Families with Dependent Children (AFDC) welfare program.

5. The "charitable choice" provision applies to the following government funds (as of December 31, 2000): the Temporary Assistance to Needy Families (TANF) funds provided in the Personal Responsibility and Work Opportunity Reconciliation Act (Public Law 104-193 [1996]); the Community Services Block Grant funds provided in the Community Opportunities, Accountability, and Training and Educational Services Act (Community Services Block Grant Act, Public Law 105-285 [1998]); the Children's Health Act of 2000 (Public Law 106-310 [2000]); and the New Markets Venture Capital Program Act (Public Law 106-554 [2000]).

6. Government funds means any funds received by government by taxation or any other means.

7. The phrase "pervasively sectarian" has been used by the Supreme Court in some of its decisions. Some have criticized the term "sectarian" as being pejorative and reflecting bias. See the plurality opinion in *Mitchell* v. *Helms*, 530 U.S. 793 (2000). Because the term "sectarian" is controversial, this document will use the phrase "pervasively religious" in place of "pervasively sectarian." The concept of religious pervasiveness is discussed in the "Conflicting Perspectives" section, below.

8. This document does not constitute legal advice, nor does it create any attorney-client professional relationship. A knowledgeable attorney should be consulted for specific advice about religious organizations and government funding.

9. The Supreme Court has in some cases used the presence of religious symbols as one of the indicators of whether an organization is, in the Court's words, "pervasively sectarian." This concept of "pervasively sectarian" and its validity are discussed in the "Conflicting Perspectives" section below.

10. In cases where separate organizations are created, we disagree about whether they have to be secular. Some of us believe the Constitution requires that a separate organization cannot be pervasively religious if it is to receive government funds. Others of us believe that the Constitution does not permit government to require such a separate organization to have a particular religious or secular character.

11. 20 U.S.C. Section 1681 et seq. (1990), 29 U.S.C. Section 794 (1985), 42 U.S.C. Section 2000d et seq. (1994), 42 U.S.C. Section 6101 et seq. (1995).

12. *Mitchell* v. *Helms*, 530 U.S. 793 (2000).

13. *Committee for Public Ed. And Religious Liberty* v. *Regan*, 444 U.S. 646 (1980).

14. A. Sherman, "The Growing Impact of Charitable Choice," Center for Public Justice, (March 2000).

15. In *Mitchell* v. *Helms*, 530 U.S. 793 (2000) (upholding a program of government-funded loans of computers to religious schools), a four-justice plurality of the Court observed: "Of course, we have seen 'special Establishment Clause dangers' [cite omitted], when money is given to religious schools or entities directly rather than . . . indirectly [cites omitted]. But direct payments of money are not at issue in this case. . . ." 530 U.S. at ___ (Thomas, J., for the Court). The views expressed by the five concurring and dissenting justices were even firmer on the Establishment Clause concerns that are presented when taxpayers' funds flow to religious institutions. As Justice O'Connor has noted, "our concern with direct monetary aid is based on more than just [concern about] diversion [of tax-funded aid to religious use]. In fact, the most important reason for according special treatment to direct money grants is that this form of aid falls precariously close to the original object of the Establishment Clause's prohibition." 530 U.S. at ___ (O'Connor, J.) (concurring).

CHAPTER TWENTY

The Breaking Points:
When Consensus Becomes Conflict

MELISSA ROGERS

Americans are engaged in a vigorous and multifaceted debate on government funding of the provision of social services by religious groups. There is significant agreement and also strong disagreement in this area, and some of the differences represent multiple and competing visions of religious freedom.

Even people with vastly different perspectives on the appropriate relationship between church and state can agree on certain methods of cooperation between the government and religious social service providers. They can agree, for example, that the government may create certain tax incentives, such as the one that would allow taxpayers who do not itemize to take a deduction for charitable giving. Similarly, there is strong agreement that the government may call upon corporations and foundations to give more to those in need. President Bush has noted, "[c]urrently, six of the ten largest corporate givers in America explicitly rule out or restrict donations to faith-based groups." Even those who vehemently disagree about some church-state issues agree that those restrictions are unnecessary and in many cases unwise. Virtually everyone agrees that the institutions of religion and government may share information, serve on task forces together, and work in nonfinancial cooperation.

Increasing government-supported technical assistance to nongovernmental organizations, including religious ones, is another important yet largely unheralded point of agreement. The government may offer workshops to help nongovernment social service providers learn how to apply for grants and contracts and educate them about the substantive opportunities and obligations created by various laws and regulations.

Government funds may be used and the government itself may train volunteers gathered by and from houses of worship and other community groups for service in tax-funded social service programs. The government also may assist in the formation of new nonprofit organizations. Although some providers may choose not to take advantage of those opportunities, there does not appear to be opposition to offering that kind of assistance.

There is even some agreement relating to the most difficult and important questions in the debate. How religious may a group or program be and remain eligible to receive government funding to provide social services? There is widespread agreement that religious providers may retain their religious name and receive tax funds to provide secular services that stem from religious motivation. Despite President Bush's complaint that "[s]ome critics [of charitable choice] object to the idea of government funding going to any group motivated by faith," the right of groups to provide services because they feel a religious motivation to do so is not a matter of serious debate. Many also agree that a religious provider should not be required to clear its buildings of all religious symbols in order to be eligible to receive tax money.

Nonetheless, there is serious debate on how the religious activities and character of a social service provider coexist with the tax-funded aid or program. The debate is squarely raised by the charitable choice provision that President Bush wishes to expand. As *In Good Faith* notes, charitable choice "is a term of art that refers to a specific legislative proposal first enacted by Congress in the 1996 federal welfare reform law." It refers specifically "to the new statutory conditions under which states may enter into funding relationships with religious organizations that provide social services" and "permits all faith-based organizations to compete for government social service funding, regardless of their religious nature." One of the premises of charitable choice, therefore, is the notion that it is unfair and discriminatory to label certain religious organizations "too religious" to compete for tax funds. The Bush administration is pursuing an expansion of the charitable choice concept through legislation as well as through revision of existing regulations regarding certain social service providers.

The charitable choice provision of the 1996 welfare reform law states that a religious organization may receive government money for its provision of social services while retaining "control over the definition, development, practice, and expression of its religious beliefs." It also states that no grant or contract money may be spent on "sectarian worship, instruction, or proselytization" and that no beneficiary may be discriminated against on the basis of religion.

Although many agree that the charitable choice safeguards against government establishment of religion are necessary, they disagree over whether they are sufficient. Some believe that ensuring that tax money is not used to buy Bibles or force conversion is important but that it leaves significant issues open regarding the coexistence of tax aid and privately funded religious activity.

More specifically, those critics worry that tax money will flow to churches and other institutions that weave religious activities and emphases into tax-funded ones, creating captive audiences for religious outreach and indoctrination and resulting in government establishment of and excessive entanglement with religion.

The Bush administration has proposed further safeguards to address some of those dangers. With respect to government grants and contracts, the administration has suggested that any privately funded "sectarian worship, instruction, or proselytization" activities should be separate from government-funded activities and voluntarily attended by beneficiaries. Critics are skeptical that such safeguards could or would be adequately implemented and are resolute in their belief that other constitutional dangers remain.

Meanwhile, the last thing some conservatives want is more regulation of religious providers who participate in the faith-based initiative. Indeed, a vocal band of conservatives believe that its safeguards regarding religious activities are unnecessary and unacceptable. The problem with charitable choice, according to those critics, is that it does not go far enough toward allowing any religious group to receive government money free of rules and restrictions.

Michael Horowitz and Marvin Olasky have jointly called for certain modifications of charitable choice. They argue that "[g]overnment officials with the power to award or withhold discretionary grants should be unconditionally barred from directly or indirectly influencing or dictating the form or frequency of prayers offered by or required of participants in faith-based grant programs, and they should never be permitted to exercise any authority over the religious content of such programs."

Indeed, such concerns have led some conservatives to urge that any government faith-based initiative be conducted entirely through tax incentives or individual social service vouchers; their belief is that doing so greatly diminishes the risk of government regulation. As mentioned earlier, most parties can find some common ground on certain tax incentives, like the deduction for nonitemizers. Vouchers, however, are controversial for a number of reasons, some of which are related to church-state concerns.

Charitable choice vouchers are not subject to any restrictions on expenditures for "sectarian worship, instruction and proselytization." Further, some proposals would not provide a beneficiary with the right to opt out of religious activities if the beneficiary uses a voucher. For those reasons, vouchers provide multiple points for debate. On one side are those who believe that vouchers are on firm constitutional ground, pointing to the Supreme Court's recognition that individual choice may function as a sort of "circuit breaker" in the link between government and religion in particular cases. On the other side are those who question whether truly voluntary choices can be made in certain situations and who emphasize other Supreme Court cases in which the Court seems to have laid the groundwork to reject vouchers. It is important to note that the Supreme Court has recently agreed to decide whether it is constitutional to include religious schools in a tax-supported voucher program. The decision in the case will be closely scrutinized for its impact on the debate over religious organizations and tax-funded social services.

Another crucial question in the debate concerns the regulation of religious providers that receive tax funds. The Bush administration has released an "audit" of five federal agencies for "barriers" to the participation of faith-based and community organizations. Some limited agreement may emerge on the topic of regulatory reform. All can agree, for example, that because constitutional principles do not vary from program to program or agency to agency, regulations—to the extent that they express constitutional principles—should not either. All will also agree that there should be no religious set-asides—in other words, no money should be reserved for use only by religious social service providers. And, if the church-state debate is put to the side, there may be more significant agreement about regulatory reform efforts aimed broadly at nongovernment social service providers.

But some of the items that the administration identifies as unnecessary "barriers" to the participation of religious social service providers are what others consider crucial constitutional protections or necessary requirements of public policy. The administration, for example, counts as a barrier regulatory prohibitions on hiring on the basis of religion with regard to tax-funded employee positions within religious groups. There is strong agreement that religious groups have the right to hire on the basis of religion for positions that are wholly privately funded, but fierce debate about whether that right does or should exist in hiring for tax-funded positions.

Those who count that type of regulation as a barrier believe that robust religious autonomy need not and should not be diminished when a religious organization receives tax funds. Successful results are an important form of accountability to the taxpayer, they say, and such results can best be produced when the organization's members are united by shared religious belief. Furthermore, they point to a Supreme Court decision that upholds the statutory right of religious organizations to hire on the basis of religion.

Critics of the idea acknowledge that the Supreme Court has upheld that right as a general matter in a case that did not involve tax funds, but they stress that the Court has not addressed the issue of whether a religious organization may hire on a religious basis for tax-funded positions. They argue that an organization offends basic notions of taxpayer accountability when it makes religious distinctions in employee positions supported by tax funds. These critics believe that when such conflicts arise between the right to religious autonomy and the obligation of accountability for tax funds, the organization should either refuse to accept the funds or give way to the government.

A host of related regulatory issues may come into sharper focus as new religious providers, including houses of worship, enter the tax-funded social service delivery system. While charitable choice promises religious providers that they can maintain their independence from government, including "control over the definition, development, practice, and expression of [their] religious beliefs," the receipt of tax funds will create new accountability obligations for first-time participants in the "government-by-proxy" system. Novel issues will arise regarding the strength of the right to religious autonomy when tax funds are involved.

The government's obligation to protect beneficiaries' rights to religious liberty when tax money flows to religious social service providers is another key area of discussion. There is widespread agreement that an alternative should be available for anyone who wants one and that beneficiaries should not be turned away from tax-funded programs because they are not of the "right" religion. Many on different sides of the debate also agree that some work must be done to ensure that theoretical rights in that area translate into practical ones.

But differences emerge here as well. There is disagreement over whether the alternative must be a clearly secular one or one that is "unobjectionable to the individual on religious grounds." And, while all oppose barring beneficiaries from tax-funded programs on the basis of their religious beliefs, some argue that funding certain religious programs without adequate safeguards will effectively result in discriminating against some beneficiaries in that way.

One of the most fundamental disagreements is over the issue of whether a beneficiary should have a choice only *among* providers or whether that choice should be married with a choice *within* particular tax-funded, faith-based programs about whether to participate in religious activities. Some believe that there is no need to provide a right to opt out of religious activities in a faith-based program if there is an adequate alternative program. Others insist that opt-outs are critical in all cases, in part because there will be many times, they argue, when the beneficiary will not know about or have easy access to a secular alternative that is of equal value. Still others find opt-outs necessary when the tax-supported program is conducted through grants and contracts, but not when participants pay with vouchers.

Philosophical divisions on these issues also are reflected on the Supreme Court. The Court is deeply divided, for example, over the meaning of government neutrality toward religion on funding questions. A plurality of the justices define this neutrality as requiring that the government aid itself must be secular and offered in an evenhanded way to religious and nonreligious bodies alike. The plurality argues that the government is decidedly not neutral toward religion when it gives any consideration to whether the potential recipient institution is pervasively religious in nature. On the other side of the debate are three justices who argue that, while evenhandedness in the distribution of aid has been an important factor in particular cases, neutrality also describes the obligation of the government to occupy the middle ground between governmental encouragement and discouragement of religion. These justices claim that this middle ground is lost if there can be no consideration of the pervasively religious character of the recipient institution or if the government cannot apply the safeguards necessary to ensure that the aid will not be used to advance religion. The justices between these two camps find the plurality's neutrality factors to be significant and agree that there should be no presumption that aid to certain religious institutions will inevitably result in governmental aid for religion. But these justices argue that the plurality's factors cannot be assigned singular importance because they ignore such issues as whether aid was direct or indirect and whether it has been diverted to advance a religious mission.

There are many ways in which the government and religious social service providers may cooperate that do not implicate these fundamental divisions. When proposals touch on these fundamental issues, however, we will continue to witness the clash of multiple visions of religious freedom.

CHAPTER TWENTY-ONE

Holy Waters:
Plunging into the Sea
of Faith-Based Initiatives

PETER STEINFELS

Is there anyone who has not, as child or adult, stood fascinated on a beach, trying to predict which of the ceaseless, crisscrossing ranks of foam-specked waves would prove the largest? Which swells, converging or coming quickly on one another, would break modestly and quietly flow back? Which would rear up and, with a huge splash, dash farthest up the sand?

Why are we so easily transfixed by that seaside drama? Surely one reason is the tension it creates between fear and delight. We never entirely shed that instinctive wariness, the tremor that braces us, on all but the calmest days, to dodge back from the oncoming surf. We never lose the small, secret dread that this breaker will be the monster that sucks everything out to sea. But then there is a counterimpulse, the sheer exuberance in being part of the pounding, rhythmic wash, the anticipation of new patterns drawn in the sand, new bits of sparkling shells and well-worn shining pebbles left behind.

It now is evident that the current debate over government support for faith-based initiatives is just such a big breaker, one that could be seen building, wave by wave, from a long way off—and one that for me, but obviously not for everyone, has produced far more delight than anxiety.

Everyone recognizes that one swelling force contributing to the current debate was the political resurgence in the late 1970s of conservative Christianity—the "religious right," to use the useful shorthand for the most outspoken and militant sector of a larger, more diffuse movement. Reactions to that resurgence, pro and con, fed a national discussion about the role of religion in public life, a discussion already stimulated by periodic civil libertarian challenges to government-sponsored displays of Christmas trees and other religious symbols, by conservative attempts to restore or defend religious activities in public school settings, and most seriously by the question of whether opposition to the 1973 legalization of abortion by the Supreme Court in *Roe* v. *Wade* constituted an illegitimate intrusion of religious belief in political life. That discussion added new phrases to our political vocabulary: "naked public square" and "culture of disbelief" joined older imagery like "wall of separation."

Meanwhile, another movement had been growing since the 1960s, one of dissatisfaction with large-scale government agencies and programs of all kinds, from highway building to urban renewal, from public housing and welfare to big-city school systems, from institutions for the mentally disabled to the Army Corps of Engineers. Initially, many of the critiques came from the "new left" of civil rights and antipoverty activists. Then, as affirmative action programs and environmental controls complicated business operations, traditional antigovernment and pro-market advocates began to inspire a new array of policy proposals. The left talked grass roots and community control; the right talked entrepreneurship and privatization. Both revived Toquevillian notions of intermediate associations.

Two other currents reinforced the wave. American conservatives have always emphasized moral discipline as essential to social cohesion—even while they promoted a market economy that, as Daniel Bell noted in *The Cultural Contradictions of Capitalism*, has had few equals in undermining established patterns of living. By contrast, many liberals viewed that moral emphasis, often associated with traditional religion, as one of the tools by which the powerful maintained an unjust status quo: pie in the sky when you die, but caffeine, clean living, and hard work to keep you productive in the meantime. The suggestion that social policy should address matters of personal character or living habits among those in need was quickly labeled "blaming the victim." By the late 1970s, however, political backlash from the countercultural outbreaks of the preceding decade had forced liberals, if only for self-protective reasons, to acknowledge that social policy could not ignore issues of character, conduct, and moral norms. By the 1990s, a good number were maintaining without embarrassment that liberalism's emphasis on economic improvement had to operate in tandem with attention to personal responsibility and personal transformation.

Not unrelated to that shift in liberalism were developments among the African American leadership. Once at the center of national soul-searching and consequent political upheaval, black leaders increasingly appeared to be running in place. Their by-now familiar concerns were accepted as predictable components of interest-group politics; their consistent demands for expanded federal programs were registered or ignored as confidence in those programs rose or fell. Black politics often seemed distant, except rhetorically, from the most obvious needs of the black community and the persistent disparities between black and white. The compelling identification of the civil rights movement with ordinary people struggling mightily to retain or regain their dignity in oppressive circumstances seemed attenuated. The story is a complicated one of generational transition, of economic change, and, to borrow from Max Weber, of inevitably routinized charisma, and the end is by no means clear. In the meantime, however, new energy has flowed from what was always the wellspring of African American leadership, the church. If momentum was stalled at the national level, it would pick up again in the neighborhood and on the street corner. If faith-based initiatives have resonated far beyond the church basements, it is because of their link with the most morally significant movement in American politics of the last century.

Each one of these forces—the reentry of conservative Christians into active citizenship, the intense discussion of religion's legitimate place in political discourse and civic life, the criticism of entrenched bureaucracies by advocates of entrepreneurship and of community, the "re-moralization" of social policy, the religious reincarnation of the black drive for dignity and equality—strikes me as essentially healthy. Not that I do not find problematic aspects—of the religious right's emergence, for example, and the free marketeers' enthusiasm for privatization. Others may have different worries. Nonetheless, much of what is freshest and best in American politics has converged in the debate about faith-based initiatives, and almost no matter how the debate turns out, I rather expect to be happy that it has taken place.

If nothing else, the debate has allowed religion to "get some respect." It may sound strange to suggest, in one of the world's most publicly religious nations, where no presidential speech ends without mention of God, that religion is in any way wanting for respect. Yet for all the public professions of faith and overt or covert appeals to religious voters, when it comes to designing social policy, religion and religious institutions ordinarily have been bracketed. The reason is not antireligious sentiment (I will get to that in a moment), but the deeply bred conviction that faith is essentially personal and private, no more to be hauled into conscious policymaking than to be recorded in the census. At one level, most people have probably assumed that religious beliefs and affiliation might have a great deal to do with work habits and family stability, without knowing precisely what. At another level, that very big hunch was not considered pertinent to policymaking or to policy-oriented research, any more than, one suspects, the current administration considered religion and faith-based initiatives something to be factored into its energy policy.

So while many religious leaders may be feeling satisfied at the very public acknowledgment of faith's social role inherent in charitable choice proposals, their satisfaction reveals a measure of religion's new weakness as well as its continuing strength. After all, there was a time when no one required statistical proof of faith's efficacy in shaping lives. That was taken for granted, so much so as normally to escape notice. Fish aren't aware of water until it begins to drain away. Nonetheless, even a somewhat diminished and contested religious presence in American life remains enormously powerful, and recognizing that fact simply enlarges our political elite's grasp of reality.

But the debate about government and faith-based initiatives also has given us a new, and I think helpful, way of approaching a long-standing American quandary recently rendered ever more complicated. How does a society so dramatically diverse—and so committed to the rights of the venturesome, freewheeling individual—maintain the minimal degree of moral consensus any society needs to survive? Two centuries ago, the United States effectively invented religious pluralism in spite of the general belief that such an arrangement could end only in religious, moral, and social chaos. That didn't happen. Instead, religion flourished as in few comparable societies; morality and social norms, rooted in religion, held firm. The truth, however, is that for much of that time, religious diversity in the United States was only a fraction of what it has become today. Throughout the nineteenth century, a broad evangelical Christianity was established culturally if not politically, and despite some surface squabbling and at least one major conflict—Prohibition—it managed to graft Roman Catholics and Jews into what became, up through the middle of the twentieth century, a successor "Judeo-Christian" establishment, quite similar in its moral and cultural function. Only recently have we had to imagine getting along without any such establishment. Only recently have we had to contemplate the meaning not only of true religious pluralism but also of moral pluralism. Does our generally positive experience with the government's religious neutrality now extend logically to a kind of moral neutrality on the part of official institutions that increasingly touch all aspects of our lives, from genetic experimentation to child care and education, from economic security to health care and treatment for terminal illnesses? Would such a position really be neutral or constitute itself a morality of a particular sort, although probably packaged in the superficially amoral quantitative language of polls, markets, cost-benefit analysis, or utilitarianism? And if we back away from such a questionable neutrality, do we inevitably stumble back into the tangle of religious traditions from which the vast majority of citizens draw their moral sense?

All this may seem quite distant from the concrete, very human concerns about teenage pregnancy, child care, public schooling, addiction, crime control, housing, and employment addressed by contributors to this volume. "Oh no," I can hear them saying. "We never wanted to get into questions so grand and theoretical as those." But it is precisely because they have not begun with grand, theoretical questions but with very concrete, human realities, on the street and in the neighborhood, that the proposals about faith-based initiatives have injected a new creativity into the thinking on larger problem of juggling government, religion, religion-linked morality, diversity, and pluralism. Maybe small experiments will be the stepping-stones to a new social wisdom.

Here, however, I must add my disappointments with the current debate to my enthusiasm for it. It has been disappointing to hear the debate often cast in alarmist terms that detect First Amendment conflicts even before the varying specifics of different faith-based initiatives can be set out. There is no denying potential First Amendment problems. But the speed and emotion with which they have sometimes been evoked suggests to me a desire to cut off discussion at the earliest stage possible. I admit that my attitude is shaped by the conviction that the vast majority of Americans, including those who support faith-based initiatives, are deeply committed to separation of church and state; in my view, we run no great risk if the public is allowed time and tranquillity to assess the legitimately contending ways that this fundamental Constitutional principle can be applied to ambiguous cases.

It also has been disappointing to encounter the occasional antireligious response that is truly visceral, fortified with a store of stereotypes, historical images, and worst-case scenarios defying rational explanation. Similarly disappointing is the way in which "horrible possibilities" have been paraded in this debate—will tax money go into the coffers of the Nation of Islam, Scientologists, witches' covens, goddess worshipers? The prospect of money going to, say, a Wiccan group, since it cannot absolutely be ruled out, is supposed to shock us into opposition to the proposal. There is nothing wrong, indeed there is everything right, with following out the logical implications, however unlikely, of a policy proposal. But such appeals to our supposedly common sense of the "unthinkable" are just too reminiscent of past evocations of other once-marginal groups like Catholics, Jews, Mormons, Jehovah's Witnesses, and Pentecostals. And, when all is said and done, the possibilities being paraded today might be no more horrible than those paraded in the past. In that respect, my final disappointment has been the sudden loss of interest by Pat Robertson and some other conservative Christian leaders in government assistance to faith-based programs when they realized that faiths that they did not approve of would be treated as equals of their own. There is a first lesson here about religious pluralism that apparently they have not learned.

There is one other aspect of the debate that I might find disappointing, were my disappointment not drowned by my sheer puzzlement: the weight given to the two most recurrent objections to government support for faith-based initiatives.

The first common objection is to the possibility that such support would fund religious proselytizing. The second common objection is to the possibility that such support would (indeed, as presently conceived, quite likely would) permit discriminatory hiring by faith-based organizations that require employees to affirm certain beliefs or adhere to certain moral codes. What puzzles me is that the second of these two issues has been given a weight in recent debates at least equal to, if not greater than, that of the first. After all, the first objection—proselytizing people with government funds—touches on the very heart of the First Amendment prohibition of any official establishment of religion. The second objection—religious discrimination in staffing—is a much more recent concern and much less thoroughly founded.

Let me explain. From early in our constitutional history, the power to tax has been recognized as the power to destroy, and the recognition of that power underlies one of the arguments for exempting religious bodies from taxation. The power to determine whom an association or organization employs can also be the power to destroy. That is why, while we have laws barring employment discrimination of various kinds, those barriers against discrimination have to stop short of insisting that enterprises employ people who are unable or unwilling to carry on the enterprise's core activity. Restaurants do not have to hire as chefs people who cannot cook or as waiters people who cannot serve. Hospitals do not have to hire unqualified physicians or nurses who are not devoted to health care.

How should competing protections for hiring organizations and potential hires apply to religious groups? Religious organizations should not be required to hire people, at least in key positions or in significant numbers, if hiring them risks altering the nature of the organization as reflected in its beliefs and practices. Southern Baptist congregations can "discriminate" by ordaining only Southern Baptists. Catholic schools can "discriminate," if they wish, by hiring only Catholics as principals. That principle is reflected in the many exceptions for religious organization found in antidiscrimination statutes, although there remain complicated and unresolved cases in this area. (If the director of an Orthodox Jewish school converts to Pentecostalism, no one doubts the school's right to dismiss him—but what about the school janitor or an athletic coach?) Without such exemptions, prohibitions against religious discrimination could very well work to undermine the capacity of religious organizations to maintain their core identity. The courts have recognized that the power to determine employment would be the power to destroy.

But what happens when a religious body offers services eligible for government funding, such as many of the secular social services mentioned in this volume? One workable model for minimizing the problem of religious discrimination in those cases has been to offer the services through nonprofit organizations that are affiliated with the religious body or its tradition but also organizationally distinct from the worshipping (and possibly proselytizing) community. Leading organizations of that sort that receive government funds include many religiously affiliated hospitals, universities, relief organizations, and social service agencies such as Catholic Charities and Lutheran World Service. They can, and do, hire staff on strictly professional grounds without regard to religious requirements—at least to an extent that has diminished, without entirely eliminating, questions of discrimination.

Critics of expanded government involvement with faith-based organizations have pointed to decades of cooperation with such "secular" affiliates and asked, "If it ain't broke, why fix it?" Certainly, no one would claim that those impressive organizations are "broke." Yet questions have been justly raised about their capacity to make full use of the resources of their own religious traditions in delivering social services and ultimately about their long-term viability. Have they really resolved the dilemma inherent in reducing or removing religious staffing requirements while maintaining a strong religious identity and a strong link to their religious communities? More than one observer, including some within those organizations themselves, have worried that they have been steadily moving away from their religious roots toward becoming generic and thoroughly professionalized human services agencies. Is that bad? At the very least, it means a reduced ability to draw on the energy and resources of religious volunteers. At the most, it threatens the organizations' very raison d'être.

Why should we pretend that we have worked out a good model for cooperation between government and faith-based groups ("It ain't broke") if working with government funds means that Catholics operating Catholic Charities must accept a high risk that the "Catholic" in the title will become meaningless and that, over time, the organization will mirror the Red Cross, the public housing authority, or the state welfare bureau? Why should the Catholic Church run, support, or maybe merely lend its name to an essentially secular or pseudo-state agency? The relationship between a religious group's convictions and its social service agencies and their activities must at some point be maintained by personnel who share those convictions.

Who or what, on the other hand, would be threatened if faith-based organizations that are receiving government funds employed religious criteria in hiring more directly than generally occurs with such nonprofit affiliates? Some professional social workers, perhaps. Gays and lesbians who are struggling to bring themselves under the umbrella of anti-discrimination sentiment and who are aware of religious strictures on homosexuality, perhaps. Maybe anyone who feels that any justification whatsoever for discrimination in hiring, *even* religious discrimination for religious organizations, undermines the general principle of nondiscrimination and eventually harms racial minorities, women, the elderly, the handicapped, and so on. I do not find it puzzling that concern over discrimination against those groups might obscure what to me are weighty considerations in the other direction (that is, concern for protecting the fundamental character or mission of the religious organizations that are making the hires). I do find it puzzling, frankly, that so much of the public goes along with it and apparently shares little of my sense that, when it comes to hiring by religious groups, the objection to discrimination on religious grounds is not only less founded in our Constitutional tradition than the objection to proselytizing but actually runs athwart the First Amendment rights of religious bodies.

The sentiment that no one should be barred from employment without good cause is a sound one, but when it comes to defining "good cause," it almost seems that religion is especially suspect. I do not think that the general public considers hiring on the grounds of a potential employee's "fit" with the hiring organization to be objectionable per se. Other forms of values-related discrimination in hiring appear to be accepted. Suppose that a Planned Parenthood clinic receiving public funds chose not to hire an antiabortion accountant, or a community housing program for low-income elderly people rejected an applicant who opposes government subsidies in general (or doesn't like seniors), or a subsidized arts group refused to consider someone who thinks the arts are a waste of time and money. Whatever the legal status of such decisions, the public would find such "discrimination" understandable, even if the person's performance of the particular job in question was not affected by his or her views. Religious groups, however, appear to be held to a different standard: just as long as a job candidate can do the daily tasks of the position competently, a Southern Baptist group, for example, has no business refusing to hire someone who thinks that the Southern Baptist Convention's approach to the Bible is preposterous and a Catholic group has no business refusing to hire someone who considers the papacy a nefarious institution.

According to a poll taken in March 2001 by the Pew Forum on Religion and Public Life along with the Pew Research Center for the People & the Press, more Americans (78 percent) are troubled by allowing government-funded faith-based groups "to only hire people who share their religious beliefs" than are concerned about proselytizing (60 percent). The question was tweaked for an independent sample that was asked simply whether such groups "should be allowed to hire people on the basis of their religious beliefs." Although the word "only" was dropped in this version and the vaguer "on the basis of their religious beliefs" substituted for "share," 69 percent still said no. That sample also answered yet a third variation, asking whether "religious organizations using government funds to provide social services" should be allowed to hire only people "who share their moral values." Although "moral values" is a broader notion than "religious beliefs," again the respondents overwhelmingly (62 percent) said no.

On this point, then, people of my outlook have a lot of persuading to do. The entire discussion of faith-based initiatives makes little sense, except as a short-run policy fix, if the faith communities mounting such initiatives cannot maintain strong, vibrant identities. There is good evidence that religious groups without distinctive beliefs and practices, preaching nothing but a generic Golden Rule religiosity, cannot mobilize the energies and resources needed even to pass on their faith, let alone address the kind of human problems described in this volume or create and reinforce the civic bonds that any society requires. Most religious charities were founded and are still run on the basis of very distinctive beliefs and practices, very strong group loyalties, and the convictions inculcated by each group's history rather than on the basis of abstract, universal principles or general good will. There is also good evidence, although it is by no means conclusive, that many religious groups are using up that stock of "religious capital"—analogous to the "social capital" that Robert Putnam argues is being depleted[1]—and that it is not being renewed.

The challenge of maintaining religious communities with distinctive and compelling identities will not be met by any program to bolster faith-based initiatives with government aid. The challenge goes well beyond anything that government can or should do. Yet the awareness stirred by the contemporary debate, however it turns out, may help. Already it has turned bright lights on programs and congregations that are brashly uninterested in disguising their religious commitment with a veneer of professional neutrality. And if the debate ends by affirming sharp limits on government involvement with faith-based organizations, it may encourage involvement of private foundations, corporate donors, and individual philanthropists.

The breaker rising up before us may be an imposing one, but not, I am convinced, a destructive one. To those who feel panic, who view the current debate only as menace, who may even be tempted to call the lifeguard to clear the beach, my response is twofold. Relax. Plunge in.

NOTE

1. Robert Putnam, *Bowling Alone* (Simon & Schuster, 2000).

Contributors

ABDULWAHAB ALKEBSI is the executive director of the Islamic Institute. Previously he served as deputy director of the American Muslim Council, executive director of the American Muslim Association for Democracy, and director of international affairs at the Islamic Institute.

JUDITH C. APPELBAUM is vice president and director of employment opportunities at the National Women's Law Center, a nonprofit organization in Washington, D.C. She is an attorney specializing in employment-related issues such as sex discrimination in the workplace and child-care policy.

MARY M. BOGLE serves as a private consultant on early childhood development, youth development, and nonprofit management. Before that she was executive director of Grantmakers for Children, Youth & Families; program specialist for the Head Start Bureau; and a member of the Early Head Start design team. She is co-author of *The Statement of the Advisory Committee on Services for Families with Infants and Toddlers*.

THE REVEREND DR. JOHN BUEHRENS served as president of the Unitarian Universalist Association of Congregations from 1993 to 2001. He is a leader in interfaith cooperation and theological education who helped draft the "Religious Declaration on Sexual Morality, Justice, and Healing."

MARK CHAVES is an associate professor in the Sociology Department of the University of Arizona and principal investigator of the National Congregations Study. His research focuses on the interaction between religion and formal organizations.

MING HSU CHEN, a Paul and Daisy Soros Fellow at New York University Law School, served as a research assistant at the Brookings Institution and as a research fellow at the Pew Forum on Religion and Public Life, where she focused on American politics, civil society, and faith and public life.

ERNESTO CORTES JR. is the executive director of the Southwest Region of the Industrial Areas Foundation (IAF). He founded a network of twelve IAF organizations in Texas and additional IAF projects in Arizona, New Mexico, Louisiana, Nebraska, and the United Kingdom.

FRED DAVIE is vice president for faith-based programs at Public/Private Ventures and an ordained minister in the Presbyterian Church. Previously, he served with the New York City Mission Society, the Brooklyn Ecumenical Cooperatives, and the Presbytery. He also was a program officer in the Community and Resource Development program at the Ford Foundation; Charles H. Revson Fellow at Columbia University; chief of staff to the deputy mayor for community and public affairs in New York City; and deputy borough president of Manhattan.

WILLIAM T. DICKENS is a senior fellow at the Brookings Institution specializing in economics, poverty, trade, income support, labor markets, unemployment, and monetary policy.

JOHN J. DIIULIO JR. is a professor of politics, religion, and civil society and professor of political science at the University of Pennsylvania and nonresident senior fellow at the Brookings Insitution. During his leave from Penn in academic year 2000-2001, he served as assistant to the president of the United States and as the first director of the White House Office of Faith-Based and Community Initiatives. He also serves as senior fellow at the Manhattan Insitute, where he founded the Jeremiah Project, and as board member and senior counsel at Public/Private Ventures.

E. J. DIONNE JR. is a senior fellow at the Brookings Institution, where he focuses on American politics, civil society, and faith and public life. He is a columnist with the *Washington Post* and co-chair, with Jean Bethke Elshtain, of the Pew Forum on Religion and Public Life. He is the author of *Why Americans Hate Politics* and *They Only Look Dead*. He is editor or co-editor of several Brookings volumes: *Community Works*; *What's God Got to Do with the American Experiment?* with John DiIulio; and *Bush* v. *Gore*, with William Kristol.

CUSHING DOLBEARE is the founder and chair emeritus of the National Low Income Housing Corporation. She currently is a freelance housing policy consultant and a member of the Millennial Housing Commission.

PATRICK F. FAGAN is the William H.G. FitzGerald Fellow in family and culture issues at the Heritage Foundation. His work documents the relationship between marriage and family and national trends, such as teen pregnancy.

THE REVEREND FLOYD FLAKE is a senior fellow at the Manhattan Institute; senior pastor of the Allen African Methodist Episcopal Church; and the president of Edison Charter Schools. From 1986-1997, Reverend Flake served as a representative in the U.S. Congress.

WILLIAM A. GALSTON is a professor at the Maryland School of Public Affairs and director of the Institute for Philosophy and Public Policy. He is a member of the board of the National Campaign to Prevent Teen Pregnancy and serves as chair of the campaign's task force on religion and public values.

JOSEPH R. HACALA is rector of the Jesuit Community and special assistant to the president at Wheeling Jesuit University. From 1997-2001 he served as special assistant to Secretary Andrew Cuomo and director of the Center for Community and Interfaith Partnerships at the U.S. Department of Housing and Urban Development (HUD). Formerly he was the executive director of the Catholic Campaign for Human Development at the United States Catholic Conference.

DEBRA W. HAFFNER is the codirector of the Religious Institute for Sexual Morality, Justice, and Healing and the former president and CEO of the Sexuality Information and Education Council of the United States. She is the author of four books, including the award-winning *From Diapers to Dating: A Parent's Guide to Raising Sexually Healthy Children.*

CHARLES C. HAYNES is senior scholar at the Freedom Forum First Amendment Center in Arlington, Virginia. He is best known for helping schools and communities throughout the United State find common ground on First Amendment issues.

DAVID HORNBECK serves as chairman of the board of directors for both the Children's Defense Fund and the Public Education Network, and he was Philadelphia's superintendent of schools from 1994 through August 2000. He has served as state superintendent of schools in Maryland, executive deputy secretary of education and deputy counsel to the governor in Pennsylvania, and executive director of the Philadelphia Tutorial Project.

GEORGE L. KELLING is a professor at the School of Criminal Justice, Rutgers University; a research fellow at the Kennedy School of Government, Harvard University; and a senior fellow at the Manhattan Institute.

JOYCE A. LADNER is a senior fellow at the Brookings Institution. She specializes in disadvantaged women and children, governance of urban public institutions, race/ethnic relations, and social welfare policy. She is the author most recently of *The New Urban Leaders.*

SUZANNE LE MENESTREL, a developmental psychologist, is a senior program officer in the Center for Youth Development and Policy Research at the Academy for Educational Development, where she directs a project that identifies and disseminates information on promising after-school program practices.

MONSIGNOR WILLIAM J. LINDER developed New Community Corporation (NCC) after the civil disturbances in Newark, New Jersey, in 1967. NCC became the largest community development organization in the United States.

THE REVEREND DR. EILEEN W. LINDNER is the deputy general secretary for research and planning in the Office of the General Secretary of the National Council of Churches of Christ in the USA and editor of the *Yearbook of American and Canadian Churches*. Before that she served as director of the Child Advocacy Office and director of the Child and Family Justice Project; she also was an adviser to the Children's Defense Fund and a member of the board of directors of Stand for Children.

JOAN LOMBARDI is the director of the Children's Project. She served as the deputy assistant secretary for children and families in the U.S. Department of Health and Human Services and as the first associate commissioner of the Child Care Bureau. She is co-author of *Right from the Start* and *Caring Communities*.

SISTER MARY ROSE MCGEADY is a clinical psychologist and president of Covenant House, which maintains international shelters and rehabilitation centers for teenage runaways and homeless children. She is a board member of the National Campaign to Prevent Teen Pregnancy.

ROBERT MUCCIGROSSO has served as the principal of two Catholic high schools and as the associate superintendent for schools in his native Diocese of Brooklyn. Most recently, he served as principal of Nazareth Regional High School in New York..

RICHARD MURPHY is a vice president at the Academy for Educational Development (AED) and the director of the Center for Youth Development and Policy Research. Before joining AED, Murphy served as commissioner of New York City's Department of Youth Services and was the founder and director of the Rheedlen Centers for Children and Families.

PIETRO NIVOLA is a senior fellow at the Brookings Institution. His research focuses on energy policy, federalism, regulatory politics, trade policy, and urban policy.

JEREMY NOWAK is the president of the Reinvestment Fund, a development finance institution that specializes in inner-city real estate and business lending.

KEITH PAVLISCHEK is a fellow at the Center for Public Justice and director of the *Civitas* Program in Faith and Public Affairs.

EUGENE F. RIVERS III is pastor of the Azusa Christian Community, a Pentecostal church affiliated with the Church of God in Christ. He is founder of the National Ten Point Leadership Foundation, president of the Ella J. Baker House, and general secretary of the Pan African Charismatic Evangelical Congress.

MELISSA ROGERS is executive director of the Pew Forum on Religion and Public Life, a project supported by the Pew Charitable Trusts that serves as a clearinghouse for information on issues relating to religion and public affairs. Rogers is a lawyer who has been active in the discussion of government funding and religious social service providers since 1996.

MAVIS G. SANDERS holds a joint appointment as research scientist at the Center for Research on the Education of Students Placed at Risk (CRESPAR) and assistant professor in the graduate division of education at Johns Hopkins University. Her research and teaching interests include school reform, parent and community involvement in education, and African American student achievement.

RABBI DAVID SAPERSTEIN is director of the Religious Action Center of Reform Judaism. A First Amendment lawyer, he teaches church-state law at Georgetown University Law Center.

ISABEL SAWHILL is a senior fellow at Brookings and the codirector of the Welfare Reform and Beyond Initiative. She also is the president of the National Campaign to Prevent Teen Pregnancy.

LISBETH B. SCHORR is director of the Project on Effective Interventions at Harvard University and co-chair of the Aspen Institute's Roundtable on Comprehensive Community Initiatives. Her work focuses on identifying policies and practices that improve outcomes for disadvantaged children, families, and neighborhoods.

JULIE A. SEGAL is an adjunct professor of government at the American University. As the former legislative counsel of Americans United for Separation of Church and State, she led the national coalition against charitable choice legislation.

DENNIS SHIRLEY is associate dean in the Lynch School of Education at Boston College. He has written several books on the role of faith-based groups in improving public schools, including *Community Organizing for Urban School Reform* and *Valley Interfaith and School Reform: Organizing for Power in South Texas.*

He is the director of the Massachusetts Coalition for Teacher Quality and Student Achievement.

PETER STEINFELS was the senior religion correspondent at the *New York Times* from 1988 to 1998 and continues to write a biweekly column for the paper on religion and ethics. He is a codirector of American Catholics in the Public Square, a project funded by the Pew Charitable Trusts.

THE REVEREND CARLTON W. VEAZEY, president of the Religious Coalition for Reproductive Choice since 1997, is founder of the coalition's Black Church Initiative and a national leader on progressive religious issues. Reverend Veazey is pastor of Fellowship Baptist Church in Washington, D.C., and a former chair of the Theological Commission of the National Baptist Convention. He also was a member of the Washington, D.C., City Council from 1970-73.

AVIS C. VIDAL is principal research associate in the Metropolitan Housing and Communities policy center at the Urban Institute. Her research focuses on community development and building community capacity.

DARREN WALKER is chief operating officer of the Abyssinian Development Corporation, a faith-based community development corporation in Harlem. He is a member of the boards of the National Low-Income Housing Coalition, National Housing Institute, and Association for Neighborhood Housing and Development, Inc.

JIM WALLIS is editor of *Sojourners*, convener of Call to Renewal, and author of *Faith Works: Lessons from the Life of an Activist Preacher* and *The Soul of Politics: Beyond 'Religious Right' and Secular Left*.

DIANA JONES WILSON is senior director for work force development for the North Carolina Rural Economic Development Center. She directs the Communities of Faith Initiative and the Church Child Care Initiative. She has served as a member of the N.C. Child Care Commission for the last seven years.

CHRISTOPHER WINSHIP is a professor of sociology at Harvard University. For the past seven years he has been working with and studying the Ten Point Coalition.

Index

Sacred places, civic
purposes : should government
help faith-based charity?